BY FRANK FREIDEL

Franklin D. Roosevelt: *The Apprenticeship*

Franklin D. Roosevelt: *The Ordeal*

Franklin D. Roosevelt: *The Triumph*

Franklin D. Roosevelt
The Apprenticeship

Franklin D. Roosevelt
The Apprenticeship

by

FRANKLIN FREIDEL

With Illustrations

Little, Brown and Company · *Boston*

LIBRARY OF CONGRESS CATALOG CARD NO. 52-5521

FOURTH PRINTING

The author wishes to thank Duell, Sloan & Pearce, Inc., for permission to quote from *F. D. R.: His Personal Letters,* Vols. I and II, copyright 1947, 1948, by Elliott Roosevelt; and Appleton-Century-Crofts, Inc., for permission to quote from *Gracious Lady: The Life of Sara Delano Roosevelt,* copyright 1935, by Rita Halle Kleeman.

Publi
in Canada by McClelland and Stewart Limited

PRINTED IN THE UNITED STATES OF AMERICA

For my father and mother,
Frank Burt *and* Edith Macy Freidel

Contents

List of Illustrations

Franklin D. Roosevelt

The Apprenticeship

CHAPTER I

The Roosevelts and the Delanos

> We want gentlemen to represent us . . . Frankness, and largeness and simplicity, and a fine fervor for the right, are virtues that some must preserve, and where can we look for them if not from the Roosevelts and the Delanos?
>
> — FRANKLIN K. LANE, *August, 1920.*[1]

THE new Assistant Secretary of the Navy bore the most magic name in American politics; it seemed almost sacrilege for any politician other than Theodore Roosevelt to carry it, and the more so when the bearer was a Democrat. Consequently, the audience in San Diego that evening in 1914 was curious about him. As he began to speak, they could read in his handsome, youthful face little of the rugged pugnacity of the Colonel, but his quick smile and candor of manner hinted a similar dynamism. And in the course of his talk, he told them an anecdote which revealed much about himself.

When he was a small boy, Franklin D. Roosevelt declared, his father introduced him to President Grover Cleveland. The President was sad and worn, and rather dolefully expressed to the lad the wish that he would never have the misfortune to grow up and become President. Some years later, Roosevelt continued, he heard someone ask another President how he enjoyed being Chief Executive. Flashing his teeth in the "Teddy" grimace, Franklin reported the reply, "Ripping, simply ripping!"[2] As he gleefully related the story, he left little doubt which view he took of the Presidency, and it was easy for sycophants and shrewd observers alike to whisper that here was another Roosevelt with his eye on the White House.

If this was Franklin Roosevelt's goal, his parents, like President Cleveland, had never wished it for him. When, after the 1932 election, someone asked his mother if during his childhood she had ever thought Franklin might become President, Sara Delano Roosevelt retorted: "Never, oh never! That was the last thing I should ever have imagined for him, or that he should be in public life of any sort." Rather, "the highest ideal I could hold up before our boy" was that he should "grow up to be like his father, straight and honorable, just and kind, an upstanding American." [3]

From the day of Franklin's birth his parents concentrated upon rearing him to that same secure and sane position in life which they and their parents had always known. Inherent in this gentlemanly position were both acceptance of community responsibilities and abstention from too active participation in politics. One might lend moral support, or participate in dignified local affairs, but most certainly one should not risk the sweat and mud of the hustings.

The fall before Franklin was born, James Roosevelt in keeping with this pattern accepted re-election as a Hyde Park School trustee. But within the year, as Sara noted, he "went to Hudson to a Democratic Convention to *prevent* their nominating him" for Congress.[4] In the same election that returned James Roosevelt to the school board, Theodore Roosevelt, who was a younger brother of Sara's close friend "Bammie," brought upon himself the disapproval of his circle by winning election to the New York State Assembly. The engine of his success was the Jake Hess Republican Club, an aggregation of coarse men who met above a saloon. If the route to the White House were so sordid, Sara would certainly want to guide her boy in other directions. Nevertheless, in later years nothing was more powerful than that same Theodore in luring Franklin along a remarkably similar road.

One of the most singular things about both these two Roosevelts who so badly frightened the defenders of the *status quo* was the parallel both in their careers and their backgrounds. They were two of the few Presidents since John Quincy Adams who were brought up in the aristocratic way of life.

James Roosevelt devoted much time and thought to the upbringing of his boy, yet in the popular image he occupies a shadowy, grandfatherly role beside the more lustrous Sara Delano Roosevelt. In part this was inevitable, since he died when Franklin was eighteen, while she lived to see her son enter his third term in the White House. Throughout the New Deal era, her coming and going was as minutely reported as that of a Queen Mother. As the years passed and the jut of the son's jaw more and more nearly coincided with that of the mother, the President physically at least seemed more a Delano than a Roosevelt.*

* Professional writers helped Sara Delano Roosevelt tell the story of her upbringing of Franklin, and an old friend who had access to her diaries skillfully

Actually questions of resemblance were academic, since the male members of both clans bore a strong similarity to each other in many of the characteristics reflected in Franklin. They headed wealthy merchant families whose prosperity led to landownership and social distinction. Both fortunes had a salty tang to them. Much of James Roosevelt's money came through his mother from the seafaring Aspinwalls, while most of Grandfather Warren Delano's originated in shipping. Franklin inherited from these forebears not only their love of the sea but also their willingness to take heavy risks for the sake of large gain. These gains went into coal lands and railroad securities from which came the income for comfortable living and careful philanthropy. Franklin was running according to form when he took daring gambles in the business world of the speculative 1920's, then placed most of his capital in the Warm Springs Foundation. James was a plunger in business, Franklin in politics.

Both James Roosevelt and Warren Delano settled down into semi-retirement on the banks of the Hudson where they devoted themselves with patriarchal care to the cultivation of their estates, families, and friendships. Evenings and a day or two a week, they attended to business affairs in New York City. Church, charities, and civic duties each received their allotted time. Basically (except for a heavy emphasis upon politics) this was also the pattern of life Franklin D. Roosevelt followed in the 1920's during his eight mature years as a private citizen.

It is somewhat ironical that pride of family was of consequence to this, one of the most democratic of Presidents, and that he ascribed his democracy to Roosevelt tradition. His mother could recite pedigrees from a repertoire that seemed to include half the aristocracy of Europe and all that of the Hudson River Valley. At least a dozen lines of Mayflower descent converged in Franklin, and Sara could name every one of them. There were times when she thoroughly irritated her daughter-in-law with her genealogical talk.[5]

Franklin, who had effortlessly acquired the knowledge from his mother, could as a matter of course plunge into similar recitations – but not as though they were matters of any importance. On the surface his interest seemed that of the antiquarian and collector. One of the main bodies of knowledge he mastered at Harvard – if one were to

wrote her biography. In marked contrast, the only attention James Roosevelt received was a brief chapter in Schriftgiesser's account of the Roosevelt family, and a belated sketch in a biographical dictionary.

judge only by his letters to his mother – was genealogy. He unearthed several Puritan Pomeroys to add to the family records, and wrote an essay on the most famous of his forebears, the rebellious Anne Hutchinson. In 1901, when he was writing a history thesis on the "Roosevelts in New Amsterdam," he asked his mother [6] to copy for him "all the extracts in our old Dutch Bible." *

Roosevelt enjoyed as his birthright the self-assurance as well as the sense of responsibility that came from membership in a well-rooted aristocracy. He suffered nothing like the introspective feeling of Henry Adams and his brothers that they were overshadowed by the brilliant achievements of their ancestors. Though he possessed the greatest vote-getting name of the twentieth century, that name did not acquire its magic until he had reached manhood, and his cousin Theodore was President. In 1901 when Franklin wrote his thesis, it already meant much to him to be a Roosevelt:

> Some of the famous Dutch families in New York have today nothing left but their name – they are few in numbers, they lack progressiveness and a true democratic spirit. One reason, – perhaps the chief – of the virility of the Roosevelts is this very democratic spirit. They have never felt that because they were born in a good position they could put their hands in their pockets and succeed. They have felt, rather, that . . . there was no excuse for them if they did not do their duty by the community, and it is because this idea was instilled into them from their birth that they have in nearly every case proved good citizens.[7]

This, basically, was Roosevelt's attitude throughout his adulthood. In 1935 when someone inquired if the Roosevelts were originally Jewish, he replied: "In the dim distant past they may have been Jews or Catholics or Protestants – what I am more interested in is whether they were good citizens and believers in God – I hope they were both." [8]

What manner of men were these Roosevelts whose history he traced with offhand intellectual curiosity, whose exploits he recounted frequently in his presidential small talk?

Claes Martenzen van Rosenvelt, the first of the line in the New World, arrived at New Amsterdam in the seventeenth century. He and his son Nicholas were the only ancestors Franklin shared with

* This is the Bible upon which Roosevelt four times took his oath of office as President of the United States.

Theodore Roosevelt. Third in line was Jacobus, whose Bible had come down in the family, and it was his son Isaac, born in 1726, who first attained distinction for the Roosevelt name. Starting with this Isaac the line assumed a pattern: Isaac, James, Isaac, James – and then, Franklin.

The original Isaac was a successful merchant. The sugar refinery behind his Wall Street home in time became so lucrative that it formed the foundation of the Roosevelt fortune. To have prospered so, Isaac must have run it with a certain disregard for the British Molasses Act of 1733 and the Sugar Act of 1764. Parliament passed these laws to channel all trade to the British West Indies, and sugar merchants who obeyed them made scanty profits. This goes far to explain why – when most other New York merchants, unaffected by the sugar acts, ultimately became Tories – Isaac sided in with the minority of patriots.* He was one of a handful of well-to-do merchants who tried to lend stability and direction to the turbulent laboring men who made up the rank and file of the Sons of Liberty.[10]

After the Battle of Lexington, a *de facto* government took over New York State. Isaac was active in it – he helped draft the state's first constitution, sat in its first senate, and supervised issuing paper money. He was a Federalist, and to the pride of his presidential descendant, voted for the ratification of the Federal Constitution. But Isaac was a figure of lesser importance; when Mrs. Roosevelt died, President George Washington decided it would be beneath his dignity to attend the funeral.[11]

Isaac's son Jacobus (or James) married Maria Eliza Walton, daughter of his father's Tory friend, Abram. Although Jacobus dabbled in Federalist politics (he was a member of the New York State Assembly in 1796–1797) his main interests were sugar refining and banking. With the proceeds of these, he maintained a stately town house near Washington Square, and a rocky farm between what is now 110th and 125th Streets in Harlem. There he bred horses and edged

* In the neutrality period of 1939 when Ernest K. Lindley wrote a column quite correctly enumerating FDR's close connections with the British and French, FDR sought to refute him by citing his pride in Isaac's tradition: "If he would look into the question of 'family ties,' he would realize that the Roosevelt family, in the West Indian sugar business was compelled to contend many years against the British and French interests in those Islands – and that is what made them revolutionists rather than tories in 1776." FDR was adding the French as sheer embellishment here, since doubtless Isaac made his largest profits from illegal trade with them.[9]

toward the life of a country gentleman. Later he emulated his maternal relatives, the Hoffmans, who owned a larger estate on the Hudson River in Ulster County. He sold his Harlem farm,* bought land on the Hudson near Poughkeepsie, and began to set the pattern that later Roosevelts were to follow.[12]

Upon the death of this first James Roosevelt, obituaries referred to him as a "gentleman of the old school" – a phrase used to describe each succeeding Roosevelt until the advent of Franklin. James's son, the second Isaac, acquired a medical degree but never practiced; neither did he take the slightest interest in business or politics. Instead, he devoted his time to botany, the history of medicine, and the breeding of cattle and trotting horses. His legacy and the wealth of his wife's Aspinwall family made possible this comfortable, quiet existence.[13]

Franklin's father, the next James in line (born in 1828), enlivened the family saga with an extraordinary interlude in Europe between his graduation from Union College and matriculation at Harvard Law School.† This vacation coincided with the Revolution of 1848 and James spent part of it fighting for the unification of Italy in Garibaldi's legions.[14] Franklin Roosevelt once described the episode:

> He became close friends with a mendicant priest – spoke only Latin with him – and the two of them proceeded on a walking tour in Italy. They came to Naples and found the city besieged by Garibaldi's army. They both enlisted in this army, wore a red shirt for a month or so, and tiring of it, as there seemed to be little action, went to Garibaldi's tent and asked if they could receive their discharge. Garibaldi thanked the old priest and my father and the walking tour was resumed by them.[15]

James Roosevelt soon outgrew Byronic adventuring. The picture that has emerged in the biographies of his wife and son is almost entirely that of the country squire, glimpsed at Hyde Park, at Campobello Island, and on leisurely jaunts through Europe. Squire Roosevelt with his muttonchop whiskers and benign visage is remembered

* Part of the Harlem farm, which in time was worth millions, was purchased by John Jacob Astor, whose enormous family fortune came largely from holding on to Manhattan real estate through the many decades when those less foresighted sold out.

† James Roosevelt received an A.B. from Union College in 1847, and an LL.B. from Harvard Law School in 1851. In the latter year he was admitted to the New York Bar and began practice with Benjamin Douglas Silliman, a prominent Whig attorney.

sitting at a desk in the Hudson River State Hospital, in which he took a philanthropic interest, signing checks and discoursing elegantly the while.

The talk was not about his estate or trotting horses, but rather the types and qualities of coal involved in his current negotiations.[16] The Victorian reticence that masked these money-making activities obscured an important counterpart to the squire: the vigorous financier ambitious to maneuver consolidations and create monopolies in the dawning era of big business.

Had James Roosevelt been born a decade or two earlier, he would quite possibly have adventured in the China trade, as did so many of his mother's kin and his own business associates. But the 1850's, which marked his coming to maturity, were less the golden years of the clipper ships than the era of the shift to steam power on sea and land. Britain could build steamships more cheaply than the United States, and gradually the Union Jack began to replace the Stars and Stripes upon the seas. Men of vision did not invest on a basis of sentiment or nostalgia. There might be more romance in clippers and carriages; there was profit in railroads and the coal to power them.

Such a man was James Roosevelt, whose enterprises illustrated both the shift of capital from sail to steam and the growing tendency toward consolidation and monopoly in the latter half of the nineteenth century. Within his Hyde Park world, an idyllic sphere of gracious living where nothing dissonant could intrude, he pursued the leisurely avocations proper to a gentleman; but from it he went forth regularly into a business world of rapid tempo and almost cataclysmic change. The mushrooming of innumerable small enterprises led to ruthless competition which destroyed profits. After the Civil War men of foresight began to promote combinations or even holding companies through which to gain control over markets. These monopolies could eliminate undesirable competition, and in its absence raise prices to levels that would bring in large returns. The work of James Roosevelt and those more successful than he, led directly to that of Franklin D. Roosevelt and the New Dealers. The father built monopolies; the son coined the epithet "economic royalist."

Through William Henry Aspinwall, his uncle, James Roosevelt took part in building the largest bituminous coal combination in the United States, the Consolidation Coal Company. By the time Roosevelt became a director in 1868, the company had already moved from sixth to first place among shippers of Cumberland coal, and it soon controlled about five-sixths of the coal deposits in the area. But its expected profits did not materialize. Too much coal was pouring into the market from other areas. Then came the Panic of 1873; the demand for coal contracted sharply, miners grumbled over layoffs, and railroadmen struck against wage cuts. The Consolidation Company lost heavily, and in 1875 the stockholders voted Aspinwall, Roosevelt and their coterie out of control. The Baltimore and Ohio Railroad, which took advantage of the company's distress to buy a controlling interest, later made large profits out of it.[17]

The depression beginning in 1873 thwarted James Roosevelt in a still more ambitious bid for power – an attempt to gain monopoly control of the railroads of the Southeast. He took a leading part in an enterprise that used one of the newest weapons in the arsenal of big business, the holding company technique. Immediately after the Civil War the Pennsylvania Railroad began pouring money into construction of a line from Baltimore to Washington, designed to compete with the Baltimore and Ohio for the Southern traffic. To guarantee success the suave and imaginative senior vice-president of the Pennsylvania, Thomas A. Scott, tried in 1871 to create a railroad monopoly south of the Potomac through a holding company, the Southern Railway Security Company. James Roosevelt was elected president of it the following year. Through this company the Pennsylvania Railroad and a group of New York investors began flooding millions of dollars into Southern railroad stocks in order to secure a network extending from Washington south into Georgia and west into Tennessee. They gained their immediate objective and brought extensive holdings under Pennsylvania Railroad control. As in the case of Consolidation Coal, they won the battle but lost the campaign. Southern poverty, the high taxes imposed by Reconstruction governments, and the depression robbed the venture of profit. Several of the lines lost heavily and only one earned more than 3 per cent. Within a few years the Southern Railway Security Company was forced out of existence.

For Scott and the Pennsylvania Railroad the gamble was successful since they blocked the Baltimore and Ohio ambitions. The losses were relatively light compared with the gains from controlling two Southern lines during the next few years. For Roosevelt and his New York associates, the speculation was an unmitigated disaster. Another near miss kept James Roosevelt outside the select circle of financial giants.[18]

The third major venture was the dramatic project to dig an inter-oceanic canal across Nicaragua in competition with de Lesseps' French company which was excavating in Panama. James Roosevelt was prominently associated with a group of capitalists who formed the Maritime Canal Company of Nicaragua. In the winter of 1887, which Roosevelt spent in Washington, the associates obtained concessions from Nicaragua, and two years later lobbied an act of incorporation through Congress which Roosevelt's friend, President Cleveland, promptly signed. Roosevelt became chairman of the executive committee of the new company.

Considering the enormous scope of their project, the Maritime Canal Company functioned with remarkably small capital – only six million dollars. With this, it was able between 1889 and 1892 to engage in limited preliminary construction. The scheme, which was popular in the United States, could probably have obtained the many additional millions to dig the canal, either from private investors or from Congress, except for the outbreak of another paralyzing depression in 1893. When efforts to obtain funds from abroad also failed, construction came to a halt.

Beginning in 1894, a small group in Congress led by John T. Morgan of Alabama repeatedly proposed that the government subsidize or buy out the Maritime Company. American opinion so strongly favored a Nicaraguan route that Morgan's proposals seemed on the verge of success when prosperity returned at the end of the '90s. Franklin D. Roosevelt, then at Groton, followed the canal affair with close personal interest. When Groton students debated the Nicaragua Canal bill in February, 1897, he took advantage of the occasion to make a two-minute oration – probably his first speech.[19] Two years later he wrote his parents, "I forgot to tell you how pleased I was about the Canal Bill passing the Senate, and I wonder whether you think it will pass the House? . . . I hope there won't be much opposition now." [20] Unfortunately, there was. Although it had passed the Senate with only six dissenting votes, the House replaced it with a bill merely calling for an investigating commission. At about the same time a rival group of American promoters obtained new concessions from the President of Nicaragua which voided those of the Maritime Canal Company. These promoters also failed and ultimately it was the United States Government, not private interests, that built a canal – an achievement which led another Roosevelt to assert, "I took Panama." [21]

These visionary ventures were peripheral to the financial success of James Roosevelt. The main thread of his business career involved no such spectacular efforts or failures.* His primary interest over many years was the Delaware and Hudson Canal Company, another concern in which the Aspinwalls were involved. In May, 1875, he was elected to the board of managers, and in 1894 became vice-president. Franklin D. Roosevelt once reminisced [23] to an old friend of his father's, "I remember very well the days when he was Vice President of the good old D & H and going with him to the Cortland Street offices. He was, as you know, also President of the Champlain Transportation Company and the Lake George Steamboat Company, and I used to go with him on inspection trips on the boats and over the D & H lines." †

Anthracite coal was the prime earner of the 10 per cent D & H dividends. Together with several other lines it owned or controlled 96.29 per cent of the mines; acting jointly they enjoyed most of the advantages of a monopoly. During the coal strike of 1902, the companies stood firmly together.[26] On that occasion the operators of railroads and mines ran headlong into an even more powerful operator of a new sort, the President of the United States. Franklin, probably influenced more by his Harvard classmates and professors than by his anthracite background, was for once highly displeased with his idol, Theodore Roosevelt.

> In spite of his success in settling the trouble, I think that the President [made] a serious mistake in interfering – politically, at least. His tendency to make the executive power stronger than the Houses of Congress is bound to be a bad thing, especially when a man of weaker personality succeeds him in office.[27]

When Cornelius Vanderbilt, third of his line to rule the New York Central, died he left an estate estimated at $72,500,000.[28] That of James Roosevelt was $300,000. Yet the two men sat on the same Delaware and Hudson board, and the Roosevelts as well as the Vanderbilts enjoyed high status in New York society. James Roosevelt may have engaged in speculative ventures more in the spirit of a tremendous

* In 1884 Roosevelt for a year assumed the presidency of the Louisville, New Albany and Chicago (Monon) Railroad.[22]

† James Roosevelt also had mining interests and owned a business block at West Superior, Wisconsin, not far from Duluth. On several occasions he journeyed out there in his private railroad car to inspect his holdings, and at least once took Franklin along.[24] Leisurely jaunts like these set a pattern for one of Roosevelt's favorite means of relaxation when he was President of the United States – to set off on a transcontinental trip in a private railway car, rarely going faster than thirty-five miles an hour.[25]

poker game than with any real hope of building a towering fortune. His serious purpose, in which he never failed, was to earn enough to maintain a dignified and pleasant way of life. This attitude toward business must have seemed entirely normal to Sara Delano, his young second wife, for it was part of the tradition in which she grew up.

Sara's father Warren Delano, while he was still a young man, made a comfortable sum in the China trade. His tales of sailing ships seem to have made considerably more impression upon Franklin than the lore of coal and railroad securities. Delano retired with his fortune to a country gentleman's life on an estate, "Algonac," near Newburgh on the Hudson. When the depression of 1857 menaced his investments, he returned to Hong Kong and recouped his losses through the opium trade, which flourished at the time because of the large needs of Civil War hospitals.* Before the war ended, Delano was back in the United States, his money so securely invested in coal and other mineral properties that he could again devote a minimum of his time to business and the rest to his family and estate.[32]

Warren Delano's legacy to his daughter was about a million dollars, three times the estate of James Roosevelt. Both sums, while puny compared with the wealth of the Vanderbilts and Astors, were enormous in an era when the average income of factory workers was below five hundred dollars a year. They did not allow excesses like gold dinner sets and baroque rooms imported tile by tile from Italy, but they enabled their possessors to live in the fairly unostentatious luxury and

* FDR loved to expatiate upon the family interest in the China trade. It may have influenced his conduct at times, and was always a good subject for conversation. When Raymond Moley tried to steer him away from the Stimson Doctrine in 1933, he immediately remarked that of course he would accept it and pursue a strong policy in the Far East, because of the Delano ties with China.[29] In 1939, he cited the early American trade rivalry with the British in China as evidence (in this case quite feeble) that he was not pro-British by family tradition.[30] But the most effective use of it was as a discourse to turn off embarrassing questions. When General "Vinegar Joe" Stilwell sought instructions at Cairo on how to meet a sharp and unexpected change in China policy, Roosevelt, according to the exasperated Stilwell, replied in part:

> Well, now, we've been friends with China for a gre-e-e-at many years. I ascribe a part of this good feeling to the missionaries. You know, *I* have a China history. My grandfather went out there, to Swatow and Canton, in 1829, and even went up to Hankow. He did what was every American's ambition in those days, – he made a million dollars; and when he came back, he put it into western railroads. And in 8 years he lost every dollar. (Ha! Ha! Ha!) Then in 1856 he went out again, & *stayed there all through the Civil War*, and made another million. This time he put it into coal mines, and they didn't pay a dividend till 2 years after he died. Ha! Ha! Ha! [31]

graciousness shared and admired by their circle. A glance through the Hyde Park home reveals that their way of life was the ultimate in a kind of spacious old-fashioned comfort comprehensible to an ordinary middle-class observer, and not in the Renaissance museum style of the multimillionaires. Their status depended more on impeccable ancestry than on extravagant elegance. Even Ward McAllister, Mrs. Astor's social postilion, he who helped coin the term "four hundred," much though he might prefer the free-spending "smart set," could not snub these Knickerbockers. They came of unsnubbable stock.[33]

Both the Roosevelt and Delano families belonged to this solid Knickerbocker mainstay of New York society, this shadowy world glimpsed in the novels of Henry James and Edith Wharton.[34]

They enjoyed a security so fundamental, so stable, so permanent that they need feel no envy over the meteoric rise of the multimillionaires. Likewise, they could feel little anxiety over the misery of the jobless and hungry, save to do their Christian duty towards assisting these unfortunates. The older attitude of stewardship on the part of those to whom God had entrusted riches had come down through the New England Puritan lines, to blend with the concept of noble responsibility long cherished by the landholding aristocrats of the Hudson River Valley. These families, like others of the same mold throughout seaboard America, had acquired the attitudes as well as the acres that distinguished the English country gentleman.

This was particularly true along the middle reaches of the Hudson in the nineteenth century. Just as the town name Stoutenburg[35] had long since given way to Hyde Park, so in less obvious ways little of the patroon tradition remained. In the Hyde Park township a quarter of the land – the desirable quarter along the river – had come into the hands of thirteen of the gentry. Their estates averaged nearly five hundred acres.[36] James Roosevelt's in particular would have fitted well into the landscape of southern England. Its walls and lanes divided fields where Alderney and Jersey cattle grazed, and its spacious home commanded a sweeping view of the Hudson. Among these serene meadows and groves, along these rural bluffs the master moved commandingly and at ease in his role of country squire. In this aspect his son Franklin best knew him and eventually came to emulate him.

In 1853 when he was twenty-five, James Roosevelt had married Rebecca Howland, whose family had been partners in shipping with his uncle. Their only child, born the following year, was James Roosevelt Roosevelt, his middle name a New York Dutch circumlocution for "junior." "Rosy" Roosevelt was a fascinating example of what his half brother Franklin might well have been had he followed the family pattern. Rosy was normal, Franklin the political sport. Rosy was graduated with honors from Columbia in 1877, studied law, and married Helen Astor, eldest daughter of Mrs. William Astor, who was *the* Mrs. Astor. When Ward McAllister finally published his list of the "four hundred" in 1892, inevitably Rosy's name was there. He devoted himself vigorously to society and sport – hunting, fishing, boating and horses. The only thing he ever wrote for publication was an article for *Harper's Weekly* on the rapid improvement in the breeding of American carriage horses due to the beneficent effect of horse shows and public coaching in New York City.[37]

Though Rosy Roosevelt performed faithfully as a trustee of the Astor estate and a director of a New Jersey railroad, as early as the 1890's he was by profession a retired capitalist. A generous contributor to charities, he was for forty years an active trustee of the Cathedral of St. John the Divine. He also gave lavishly to Cleveland's campaign funds and received socially acceptable political rewards. In 1886 he went to Vienna as first secretary of the American legation, and in 1893 to London in the same capacity.* His adventures in politics and diplomacy were limited to these episodes; they were his proper and expected service to his country and no more.†

Rosy, twenty-eight years older than his half brother, took an almost fatherly interest in Franklin. Although he could not agree with Franklin's progressive politics, he liked him none the less for it. His Vandyke beard may have hidden a face much like his young kinsman's. A similar generosity and geniality characterized them both, but their enthusiasms coincided at only a few points, such as fishing and the Cathedral of St. John the Divine.

James Roosevelt had been four years a widower when, in the spring of 1880, he met Sara Delano at the home of Bammie Roosevelt. He

* His wife died shortly before he went to London, and Anna ("Bammie") Roosevelt, Theodore's sister, who had been a devoted friend of the Hyde Park branch of the family, ran his household for him. While there she became engaged to the naval attaché at the embassy, Sheffield Cowles.

† FDR liked to tell an exciting story about his brother's role in the Venezuela crisis of 1895. When Ambassador Thomas F. Bayard received a highly belligerent note from Secretary of State Richard Olney for delivery to the British Foreign Minister, he exclaimed that it meant war, and refused to deliver it until Rosy Roosevelt strongly insisted that he do so. However, Bayard's biographer, Professor Charles Tansill, has pointed out that the episode could not possibly have taken place.[38]

was fifty-two, exactly twice her age, but his warm courtliness almost immediately fascinated her. Within a few months they were married, over her father's protest, and she moved from the Delano house on the west bank of the Hudson to the Roosevelt estate on the east bank.

"I have been an unusually fortunate woman," Sara Delano Roosevelt once wrote to her son. "First I had the love and protection of your grandfather, then of your father; and in my old age you have made possible for me the interesting life that I am now leading." [39]

Sara Delano, who in time became such a dominant mother, was herself the product of a dominant father. She was born into a pleasantly patriarchal family, September 21, 1854, the seventh of eleven children. Her father, without in the least assuming the manner of a tyrant, managed the household as he did his business affairs, with a firm and competent hand. Toward his sweet and submissive wife he assumed an attitude of loving protection which the children were quick to emulate. Sara grew up adoring her mother but worshiping and respecting her father.[40] Delano effectively guarded his children from knowledge of the acute business and political troubles which shook the nation and affected him personally during the depression that preceded the breakup of the Federal Union. Despite the turmoil without, he trained them in a happy routine which filled but did not crowd their childhood days: lessons, reading aloud to their mother, sewing, and suitable household duties such as gathering and arranging flowers, outdoor sports, social calls, and unbroken church attendance.[41]

The orderly unhurried pattern of their lives was so firmly fixed that it continued without pause when the hard times forced Warren Delano first to sell his fashionable town house on Lafayette Place near the Hones and Astors, and then in the fall of 1859 to leave for Hong Kong to re-engage in business. He thoughtfully left the family at spacious Algonac in the care, not only of their mother, but also of their Uncle Ned and Aunt Sara Delano, who now took over his role of making decisions and providing necessary discipline. It was Uncle Ned and Aunt Sara who insisted that the children walk and sit with erect posture, speak clearly but not too loudly, and wash and dress properly before joining the family for dessert.[42]

The Civil War intruded dimly on this routine, a shadowy brawling in the outside world. The girls were expected to sew for the war effort, and after long and painful effort Sara sent off an unbleached muslin shirt for a soldier, complete with fine seams and buttonholes, marked "Made by a little girl seven years old." [43] In 1862, three years after Warren Delano had left for China, he sent for his family. In spite of danger from the *Alabama* and other Confederate commerce raiders, the June to October voyage on the square-rigger *Surprise* * was a sojourn as serene as the life at Algonac. Nevertheless it impressed numerous memories indelibly upon Sallie – the rest of her life she could sing several of the sailors' chanteys – and provided her with a fund of reminiscences of the sailing age of which her son never tired.[45]

Similarly, the new life in Hong Kong, with its round of lessons and placid social life, was much like the old life in New York. Occasionally exciting days at the races, where they sat in the stand of Messrs. Russell and Company, made a break in the even tenor of existence, but China itself impinged hardly at all upon the developing child. Their associates were almost entirely British. Little that was Chinese intruded upon them, and Warren Delano did not even allow his children to learn the language since he preferred they should not understand the servants' chatter.[46] The Delanos carried their way of life around them like a transparent but impenetrable envelope wherever they went.

After two years, Delano sent his older children, including Sallie, back home for schooling. Shortly the rest of the family followed. In the ensuing years, Sallie circulated gaily between New York and New England, America and Europe. She wholeheartedly enjoyed a winter of study in Dresden, but was perhaps most impressed by her glimpses in Paris of the Empress Eugénie and other royalty.[47]

By the time Sallie reached young womanhood she might herself have been of royal line. The third of a quintet of beautiful sisters, all slim, tall and of an aristocratic manner that marked them as gentlewomen, she could have modeled even in her forties as one of Charles Dana Gibson's haughtier beauties. At eighteen she obtained her father's permission to attend balls in New York City.[48]

At Algonac, while the drawing room buzzed decorously evening after evening with Sallie's suitors, Warren Delano worked watchfully in the library close by. There was "an avalanche of young men in the evening," he would often note, and sometimes his added comments did not indicate pleasure. When a large basket of flowers arrived for Sallie one day from an especially ardent admirer, her father remarked to her, "I suppose that these are from the red-headed trial. Remember that I don't care for that at all." Sallie promptly dismissed the unfortunate from her court.[49]

* FDR years later bought a model of the *Surprise*, and kept a small oil painting of it on the wall of his study at Hyde Park.[44]

The belle was twenty-six before she met James Roosevelt. He had been for some years a business associate of her father, who liked and admired him. Indeed it was James Roosevelt who caused her father to admit that a Democrat might indeed be a gentleman. As Roosevelt began to call with increasing frequence at Algonac, Warren Delano easily assumed it was primarily to see Sallie's friend, Bammie, who was visiting them at the time. When, however, it became apparent that Roosevelt was courting his own daughter, he raised objections. James Roosevelt was much too old for his Sallie. She listened respectfully as ever; many times he had condemned her suitors and each time she had bowed to his wishes. But the tilt of her chin was not without meaning. Now, for the first time, she brushed aside his protests, and when, a few weeks later, James Roosevelt wrote formally to ask permission to propose to Sallie, Warren Delano gave his consent.[50]

The wedding was held early in October, 1880, at Algonac. Late in the afternoon the couple left by carriage for Hyde Park, twenty miles away. There, on James Roosevelt's estate, "Springwood," they immediately adopted a routine not unlike that which the bride had known at Algonac. After breakfast each day they strolled about the farm and inspected the greenhouse and stable. At ten, Sara properly attired in derby and habit went riding with her husband through the woods, and after lunch they went rowing on the Hudson. At teatime they received calls from their neighbors and later dined with each of them in turn. Sundays they went to church. Early that November they sailed for an extensive tour of Europe which lasted until the following September. Thus they established a pattern which they maintained during the twenty years of their married life: placid existence at Hyde Park broken by frequent vacation interludes.[51]

For Sara Roosevelt these were serenely happy years. She turned upon her husband the same strong-minded singleness of devotion, the same faith in his infallibility, which she had lavished upon her father. He reciprocated with the loving guardianship to which she had always been accustomed. "James too devoted to me,"[52] she confided ecstatically in her diary when she fell ill at Granada on her honeymoon. Then, upon her return, "James was wonderful in the way he did it all and we have had such happy days all along. . . . He has been untiring and thoughtful of everything."[53] This protective kindness never dulled or altered, and Sara responded to it with a full measure of affection. "James keeps busy," she recorded after their return from Europe. "He goes to town at least once a week and has school meetings, etc. I always go to the train with him and go for him again so he is not so long away from me."[54]

Sara Roosevelt was alert and attentive as she accompanied James on the rounds of the estate and listened to him direct its husbandry, but she never interfered. Her own tasks were clear: the managing of the household servants, the organization and supervision of a sewing class at the Hyde Park School, and the sending of food, clothing, or flowers to the poor or ill. All these offices she performed with grace and efficiency. In her husband's realm as manager of the farm and head of the family she remained a lieutenant, seconding his wishes and seldom questioning his judgment. When he asked her not to see the dearest friend of her girlhood, who had divorced and remarried under circumstances that seemed scandalous to Victorian eyes, she lamented, "It is not easy to make up my mind!" but ended by submitting to his request.[55] She was herself a strong and vital personality; nevertheless her world rested upon an unquestioning acceptance of the dominant role of the stronger males around her. Unlike some powerful women of a later era, she found no place in her life for weak men she could command and manage.

CHAPTER II

Boyhood

> We wrote to ask Warren if he would object to our naming our baby Warren Delano Roosevelt, & he writes that he could not bear it. . . . We are disappointed & so is Papa, but of course there is nothing to say, so we shall name him for Uncle Frank.
>
> — SARA DELANO ROOSEVELT, *March 19, 1882.*[1]

ON Monday, January 30, 1882, James Roosevelt recorded in his wife's diary, "At quarter to nine my Sallie had a splendid large baby boy. He weighs 10 lbs., without clothes." [2]

From the first, the baby gave his parents much joy and little trouble. He was healthy and happy, and was "at the very outset plump, pink and nice." [3] Within a few weeks they hired a nurse, Ellen, or "Mamie," who remained with the family for nine years.[4] But Sara, although she belonged to a class that took for granted the services of a nurse, believed that "every mother ought to learn to care for her own baby, whether she can afford to delegate the task to someone else or not," and so she did. She enjoyed bathing and dressing her son, and for almost a year she breast-fed him. Shortly he began to accompany his parents on rides; when he was two months old they took him for some weeks' stay in New York City and Coney Island. Still he had no name, and for many months after he *did* have a name his mother continued to refer to him as "Baby."

Sara wished to name Baby after her father, Warren Delano. Since he was the second boy, this would have been in keeping with Roosevelt family custom. But out of deference to her brother, whose son of the same name had just died, she called him Franklin after her father's brother.

Franklin Delano Roosevelt was christened March 20, 1882, at St. James Episcopal Church in Hyde Park.* Sara chose as his godparents

* James Roosevelt broke the traditional "James-Isaac" cycle among oldest sons by calling his older son James Roosevelt Roosevelt. His own younger brother was

her brother-in-law, William Howard Forbes, and her friends Eleanor Blodgett and Elliott Roosevelt. Elliott Roosevelt, seven years younger than Sara, was the brother of Bammie and Theodore Roosevelt. Sara had known him since he was a lad in knickerbockers, and she and James had become very friendly with him on their honeymoon trip to Europe.[5] Before the end of the year following Franklin's birth, Elliott married Anna Hall, whom he met at a house party at Algonac; their daughter was Eleanor Roosevelt.[6]

As the months passed, Sara jotted happily in her diary every step of the baby's development. She had acquired the diary-keeping habit from her parents, and now turned it to account in preserving a record of her son's activities. For more than twenty years she mentioned him in thousands of entries. Not content with this, she wrapped his socks, shoes, shirts and dresses as he outgrew them in carefully labeled bundles, as though sure they would be of significance to posterity.*

No item was too trivial for Sara's enthusiastic pen. "Baby Franklin . . . crows and laughs all the time," she wrote. Again, "Baby went to his first party yesterday . . . wanted to dance and I could hardly hold him." On November 11, 1882: "Baby tries to imitate Budgy [the dog] and the cats, and manages to say a semblance of Papa and Mama." December 23: "Trimmed a tree for Baby." January 8, 1883, when they were packing to go to New York: "Baby takes quite an interest in our packing and stands up against the trunks." May 17: "Baby walked quite alone. He is quite proud of his new accomplishment."[7]

In the summer of 1882 Franklin's parents took him with them to visit relatives at Fairhaven, Massachusetts. The following summer, as for many years to come, they vacationed with him at Campobello, a small Canadian island on the Bay of Fundy, across the harbor from Eastport, Maine. There the Roosevelts were so delighted with the cool, invigorating sea air and the congenial social life that they bought four acres of land and built a summer home.[8]

Franklin went to Europe for the first time when he was three, and on the return journey his memories began. Their ship, the *Germanic*, ran into extremely heavy seas on Easter morning, two days out from Liverpool. The waves damaged the ship, knocked the captain un-

---

named after his maternal grandfather, John Aspinwall – as was Franklin's fourth son. Franklin named his first three sons consecutively after his father, his father-in-law, and himself.

* They now lie in glass cases in the Franklin D. Roosevelt Library.

conscious, and smashed a bulkhead over the Roosevelt cabin, through which water poured down into their quarters. As the flood rose higher and higher on the floor, Sara was sure the vessel was sinking. She met the emergency by wrapping her fur coat about her son, who sat on the berth enjoying the excitement. "Poor little boy," she said to her husband. "If he must go down he is going down warm." Franklin had no worries until he noticed his favorite toy floating down in the water. Afterwards he recalled not the near catastrophe but himself crying "Mama, Mama, save my jumping jack!" [9] The vessel returned to England for repairs. This voyage, though fortunately not the mishap, was also the beginning of a custom. During most of his boyhood, Franklin lived abroad a few months of each year.

Until Franklin was fourteen, he spent most of his time with his parents. His life, like theirs, soon flowed along a well-ordered routine. He rose at seven, breakfasted at eight, and had lessons for two or three hours in the morning. From noon until lunchtime at one, he was allowed to play, then returned to his lessons until four. After that he had a second period of recreation.[10]

James Roosevelt entrusted the training and disciplining of Franklin to Sara. Knowing that her husband would never countermand her orders [11] she took her maternal duties seriously and focused upon this lone child all the intense maternal energy that her own parents had diffused among a brood of eleven. But she continued to be a devoted companion to her husband. Frequently she left Franklin behind when she and James went to the opera or parties in New York City, or journeyed on lengthy railroad inspection trips. The year Franklin was four, she left him at Algonac for three months * while they toured Mexico and California.[12] As a result, Franklin was not as overmothered as he might have been. A good bit of the time he was under the immediate care of his nurse "Mamie" and of a Scottish girl, Elespie, whom he called "Tiddle." Both of them shared the adoration his mother felt, but not her strictness. In their eyes he could do no wrong.

As a small boy Franklin also passed a great deal of time with his father, who, far from treating him with Jovian sternness, was an understanding guide and playmate.[13] From the time Franklin was in dresses he frequently accompanied his father on the rounds of the estate. James Roosevelt took him sledding for the first time when he was not yet

* They left Franklin, for consolation, a fine hobbyhorse which he called "Mexico."

two, and by the time he was six his mother was regularly recording, "James took Franklin out ice-boating. . . . James coasted with Franklin yesterday and the day before. . . . Franklin tobogganing with James." [14] Later, when the weather turned warm, his father took him fishing for minnows.[15]

It was from his father that Franklin absorbed considerable knowledge of the land and its management. His early interest in care of the trees led years later to his own extensive forestry. The dairy cattle and a remaining pair of fine trotting horses fascinated him, and he shared his father's pride in the memory of Gloster, a champion trotter which James Roosevelt had sold some years before Franklin's birth to Senator Leland Stanford, founder of Stanford University. Later Gloster was killed in a train wreck, but his tail, strangely enough, was presented to Franklin D. Roosevelt over fifty years later, and ultimately it adorned a wardrobe in a corner of the President's bedroom in the White House.[16]

The Roosevelts, teaching through example and admonition, wished to make Franklin honest, fair, considerate, and a good sport. He was such a tractable boy that his rare breaches of conduct were memorable occasions. His mother never forgot the time when he played a steeplechase game with her and sulked because he did not win. She picked up the toys and informed him she would not play with him again until he could learn to lose like a gentleman.[17] Yet it may indicate considerable indulgence on her part that in relating this many years later, she added, "I dare say I was thought a rather hard disciplinarian at the time." [18]

Sara Roosevelt enforced at Hyde Park the rules on personal neatness that she herself had obeyed as a child at Algonac.[19] James Roosevelt "believed in keeping Franklin's mind on nice things, on a high level; yet he did it in such a way that Franklin never realized that he was following any bent but his own." Sara once explained, "We never subjected the boy to a lot of unnecessary don'ts, and while certain rules established for his well being had to be rigidly observed, we never were strict merely for the sake of being strict. In fact, we took a secret pride in the fact that Franklin instinctively never seemed to require that kind of handling." [20] What was apparently instinctive in Franklin was a desire to please and an inborn intuition of what means would attain that end.

In sum, the record indicates a sheltered rather than an overly stern upbringing. Few of the worries of American life of the '80s and '90s intruded beyond the gates of Hyde Park, since Sara believed in the principle followed in her own upbringing: "older members of a family carefully kept away from the children all traces of sadness or trouble or the news of anything alarming." [21] Her concept of teaching him responsibility and self-reliance was to insist that in return for the gift of a Welsh pony and a setter, pets which few children were lucky enough to enjoy, he must personally care for them. This was a terrible task, the mature Roosevelt once commented.[22] By and large, from his mother Franklin could obtain "anything within reason," as she herself granted, and from the adoring servants, anything at all.[23]

But Franklin's gilded role had its drawbacks: through his early years he had to put up with the dresses and shoulder-length blond curls then customary among small boys. When he shed these finally at the age of five, his mother shifted him into the almost equal indignity of kilts made out of Murray plaid, which she regarded as "very becoming." [24] He was nearly eight before he was able to persuade her to take him to Swears and Wells in London and buy him some sailor suits to replace them.[25] He was eight and a half when he wrote, "Mama left this morning and I am going to take my bath alone." Though the solitary bath soon fitted into accepted routine, he never grew old enough to go out on a wet day without his mother reminding him to put on his rubbers.[26]

Not every child would have accepted such a patterned existence, but Franklin seldom rebelled. At Campobello the summer he was nine, he suddenly demanded the right to do as he pleased. His parents listened, considered, and freed him from his schedule, except for meals, for a single day. He appeared about the same in the evening, and the next day returned to his regular round without argument. His mother and father prided themselves upon the fact that they never questioned him about what he did with his hours of freedom.[27]

More often Franklin's distaste for one or another aspect of his scheduled round of activities would take the form of mild circumventions. Although he was unquestionably religious, there were times when he balked at the unfailing regularity of Sunday morning church attendance. On a cold and windy February day when he was ten he fortuitously came down with an almost undetectable ailment, which would have been more impressive had he not laughingly announced its imminence the day before.[28] By the time he was twelve this illness struck so regularly that Sara once commented "Franklin has what his dear Popsy calls a Sunday headache." [29] Similarly the allegation that his hand hurt "just a little" or that he had "*un petit bobo*," a little cut, on

Photo by Vail Bros., Poughkeepsie, N. Y.

FDR in his "Murray" Scotch suit, February, 1888

J R & S D R at St Blasien, Baden Aug 25 1896
Taken by F W R

a finger frequently interfered with distasteful piano * and drawing lessons.[31]

In marked contrast, when Franklin was really hurt he suffered in stoic silence, so as to avoid alarming or upsetting his parents. Once when he was in his teens, a heavy steel bar fell and gashed his forehead while he was traveling in their private railway car. He had his mother tape the wound, then spent most of the day on the car platform, wearing his cap in an attempt to conceal the accident from his father. At Campobello, when he was hit in the mouth by a stick which broke off one tooth and chipped another,† he tried to prevent his mother from discovering his trouble, though the pain was excruciating.[32] Having always received consideration from his parents, he assumed naturally that they in return were equally entitled to it.

Like many another only child, Franklin spent most of his time in the company of adults and, as a small boy, impressed people as being rather serious and precocious. Even around the servants he was acutely shy. "No one knew better than I," Sara recollected, "what a time Franklin had in hiding the self-consciousness he felt when he spoke to any one other than the members of the immediate family." In the kitchen, even the offer of a cookie could not lure him out from behind his mother's skirts.[33]

Still, he did not entirely lack the companionship of a normal childhood. He was describing the experiences of innumerable generations of seven-year-olds when he wrote concerning the games at a party: "Saterday we had a lovely time. Nuts and May was one, London Brige, and some others." And again, "We are going to see Barnoms Circus and it is going to march through the streets and we are going to see it."[34] Franklin played almost daily with Archie and Edmund Rogers, whose father, one of Rockefeller's lieutenants, lived next door. Cousin Warren Robbins came sometimes, and once his godfather's daughter, Eleanor Roosevelt, spent a happy afternoon riding around the floor on his back.[35] On these occasions Franklin habitually assumed the initiative and ordered his playmates around. Once when Sara

* By means of passive resistance of this sort, FDR managed to avoid learning much about piano playing (although he did get a piano for his rooms at Harvard). When he was President, he wrote his former governess, "The only thing you failed in teaching me was the art of playing the piano."[30]

† A peg tooth filled the gap. When FDR was President, it had to be screwed into place before each Fireside Chat, and on at least one occasion, when it was missing at the last minute, caused considerable scurrying among the White House staff.

reprimanded him for this, he replied, "Mummie, if I didn't give the orders, nothing would happen!" [36]

Gay and high spirited, Franklin was, according to his own account, also mischievous at times.[37] At ten he had reached the entirely normal stage of considering himself a devastating wit: "I am flourishing & have only fallen 3 times from the top story window," he wrote his mother. "With bales of love to everybody Your devoted baby NILKNARF." [38] He was a boy of remarkable vitality who gave the impression that he was glowing with good health. Perhaps because he played only within a small circle of children, he postponed some of the common diseases.[39] Nevertheless, in childhood as in manhood, his magnificent physique and conspicuous vigor distracted attention from the fact that intermittently he was plagued with his full share of ailments. One of these was serious. When he was seven he was ill for several months with typhoid fever, contracted probably when he took swimming lessons in the Hudson River.[40] Usually the sicknesses were no more than chicken pox, a bad attack of hives, or severe colds and fever,[41] but they came frequently.[42]

Few boys could boast of a happier childhood than Roosevelt. The nearest he came to the untrammeled world of Huck Finn was to shake hands with Mark Twain,[43] but he was familiar with many of the joys of country life. He hunted, fished, played in a tree house high in a hemlock, and with his friend Edmund Rogers built a raft which promptly sank upon launching. He dug snow tunnels in the winter, and floundered in the drifts of the blizzard of '88. When he was old enough, he sailed a splendid iceboat of his own on the Hudson. The Rogers neighbors usually won the iceboating championship cup, but one winter when Franklin was at Groton he shared the family triumph of his uncle, John Aspinwall Roosevelt, whose *Icicle* defeated Archibald Rogers's *Jack Frost.*[44]

Added to these rather typical experiences were others which only a limited few could know. He not only hunted like other boys, but learned early, and on his own initiative, to follow when the grownups rode to the hounds. One morning, just as the Roosevelts, Rogerses, and others of a hunt club reached the end of the chase, Franklin came galloping up behind them on his pony Debby.[45] He was a sturdy rider. The summer he was eight he rode with his father from Hyde Park to the Delano estate, Algonac, a distance of over twenty miles.[46]

Franklin was ten when his lifelong interest in birds began. On his eleventh birthday he received a collecting gun. Within a few weeks his mother recorded, "Franklin went out at 7.45 with his gun and shot his first crow." [47] At first he tried to fix the skins of the birds himself. As this turned out to be a distasteful process and the results amateurish, he began patronizing a taxidermist. During the next few years he built up a large collection in which both he and his parents took great pride. Ultimately his mother placed the cabinets of birds in the entrance hall of the house where visitors would see them as soon as they came in the door.

During the visits to Europe, Franklin often went on bird walks with a family friend, a Liberal Member of Parliament, Cecil G. S. Foljambe.* When Foljambe invited the Roosevelts to visit at his Nottinghamshire home where he kept an excellent collection, the elder Roosevelts were unable to accept, but to their surprise their shy son volunteered a willingness to go without them. "I'd go anywhere alone to see those birds," he explained.[48]

Occasionally the Roosevelts took Franklin to exhibits and lectures at the Museum of Natural History in New York City. On the basis of some of these lectures, Franklin wrote an essay on birds which so delighted his Grandfather Delano that the patriarch gave him a life membership in the museum. Later in London this was useful. Franklin and his tutor Arthur Dumper went one afternoon to the South Kensington Museum to see the bird collections there, only to be told they could not obtain admission without special cards, as the Prince of Wales was presiding over ceremonies there that afternoon. Franklin gave his tutor the Museum of Natural History membership certificate; Dumper displayed it to the guard, and the big gates promptly opened.[49]

The interest in bird observation and collection continued into the Groton years. † Even in his final term there, he was far more excited about birds than about girls. "I had a most delightful experience yesterday," he informed his mother, and went on to describe how he had been privileged to visit, in Cambridge, Massachusetts, the private museum of William Brewster, president of the American Ornithologists' Union, who owned "the *finest private collection of American birds in the world!*" [51]

* In 1893 he was elevated to the peerage as the fourth Baron Hawkesbury; subsequently he became Earl of Liverpool.

† Bird watching was a lifelong hobby. Occasionally while FDR was President he would rout out guests at Hyde Park before dawn and take them into the woods to identify bird songs. "He always said he was shortsighted when he passed people on the streets and didn't recognize his friends," Eleanor Roosevelt once commented, "but he could always point to a bird and tell me what it was." [50]

While birds were Roosevelt's love, sailing was his passion. "Papa is going to buy a cutter that will go by naphtha and we are going to sail in it at Campobello and here," wrote Franklin when he was nine. That summer, James Roosevelt acquired a fifty-one foot sailing yacht, the *Half Moon*, first of several craft of that name.[52] Franklin was so fascinated he could hardly be lured ashore; photographs show him at the helm in choppy weather, his head scarcely coming above the wheel. Among his compositions that autumn was one on navigation: "the art of conducting a ship or vessel upon the sea from one port to another in the most comodious way posibel." [53]

As soon as Franklin grew old enough he began to take the *Half Moon* out with his mother as a passenger, and would sail for hours while she read to him.[54] The summer he was sixteen marked his coming of age as a sailor. His parents let him have a twenty-one foot knockabout of his very own, the *New Moon*.[55] Apparently Franklin paid in part for the boat with money of his own. This craft bore Franklin and his friends up and down the countless inlets and coves of the Bay of Fundy, summer after summer, granting him a freedom of space and movement that must have seemed a priceless gift after the measured routine of early boyhood and the discipline of Groton. He gained an amazing knowledge of tides and currents in those dangerous waters. While digging for Captain Kidd's buried treasure on Grand Manan Island, he enjoyed the momentary thrill of turning up a plank upon which W. K. had been carved by some hoaxer.[56]

The sea held a rare fascination for him. From his parents and grandparents and his nurse Mamie he heard tales of the old China trade, clipper ships, and whaling. These experiences inspired the most graphic reminiscences of his childhood:

> Forty years ago a little boy sat on the old string piece of his grandfather's stone wharf at Fairhaven. Close by lay a whaleship, out in the stream another rode at anchor, and over on the New Bedford shore near the old winding wooden bridge a dozen tall spars overtopped the granite warehouses. Even then he knew that these great ships were but the survivors of a mightier age, that in some way they were no longer the focal point of the busy community, that the cotton mills with their tall stacks had superseded the whaling industry.
>
> He knew, though, of the stories of the older days. In the library of his grandfather's homestead, bound volumes of the pictorial reviews of the '50's' showed woodcuts of the Whaling Fleet—

ships by the score, sailing for the South Atlantic, for the Indian Ocean, for the North Pacific. On the wall was a lithograph of the Stone Fleet – mile after mile of vessels headed South to be sunk at the mouth of a Confederate harbor.

He was brought up on the stories of how the Florida, the Shenandoah, the Sumter and the Alabama drove the whaleships off the seas – or burned them.

Up in the attic in one of the old trunks were the old log books, canvas bound, the official reports to the owners from the whaling masters of the first half of the century. Stencilled whales in the margin, the speaking of other ships, the total of the catch, the visits to Fayal, to the Falklands, to Unalaska, the accountings to the owners, the lay of the crew – here was the tale.

Years later, with a budding historical sense I revisited the old trunk.[57] Here in one of the early logs is listed as mate the name of a man who became in later years a pioneer railroad builder of the West. Here in another, the names of families now associated with mill holdings. Here in a bundle of accounts, the beginnings of American participation in the old China Trade – there a letter telling of the laying of the keel of a tea-clipper. . . .

Less than fifty years marked the rise and decline of the whaling industry, and comparatively few men were engaged in it. . . . Yet its influence on the growth of America was out of all proportion to its size.[58]

Of all these memories, the ones relating to naval warfare in the days of sailing vessels were the most exciting. He recalled how in the '80s two gentlemen "came to New York to visit the Roosevelt family. Because those two brave and distinguished officers had fought in the Navy of the Confederacy, there were some Roosevelts who still regarded them as 'Pirates.' "[59]

Naturally, Roosevelt dreamed of Annapolis and a naval career. "I've always liked the navy," he remarked shortly after he became Assistant Secretary of the Navy. "In fact I only missed by a week going to Annapolis. I would have done so, only my parents objected."[60] The Roosevelt clan was landbound; insisting that he must prepare himself to take over his father's business interests, they directed him toward Groton, Harvard, and law school. His parents had given him the sea and taken it back again, and he had to content himself with his summer sailing in Maine and New Brunswick waters.[61]

The formal education of Roosevelt, while it deprived him of the salutary give-and-take of the public schools, saved him also from inept or mediocre teaching. His quick mind was never held back in order to allow slower students time to catch up. While public school children of his age were barely mastering their three R's in English, he was learning them simultaneously in French and German. Before he was six he knew his letters well enough that, with the aid of someone to spell for him, he could write his mother: "we coasted! yesterday nothing dangerous yet, look out for tomorrow!! your boy. F." [62]

On October 22, 1888, his formal education began with an arrangement for him to go up the road to study two hours a day with the Rogers children under supervision of their governess, Fräulein Reinhardt. Shortly he was able to write his mother in German script, "I will show you, that I can already write in German. But I shall try always to improve it, so that you will be really pleased." [63]

From 1891 to 1893 he studied under Mlle. Jeanne Sandoz from Switzerland, who worked diligently to teach him in both English and French. As she confessed to him years later, Mlle. Sandoz always "experienced a certain timidity with respect to your mama," but nevertheless she had a strong and active mind. While her primary purpose was to drill him in English and French, it was no doubt her teaching that injected some slight social consciousness into his compositions.* When he was nine he wrote concerning Egypt, "The working people had nothing. . . . The kings made them work so hard and gave them so little that by wingo! they nearly starved and by jinks! they had hardly any clothes so they died in quadrillions." [65] Franklin's high spirits often broke through his laborious penmanship, and sometimes honesty compelled him to interject that this or that was "a big wapper." [66] When unguided, his spelling at times displayed a charming originality.[67]

During the two years that Mlle. Sandoz tutored him, Roosevelt did acquire a sound grounding in French, something which made him rare among American political leaders. "I have often thought that it was

* The bent of mind of FDR's governess is shown by what she wrote him in January, 1933:

> The ignorance of the masses, the collective selfishness of nationalists, the cupidity and violence of the masters of money, the spiritual weakness and poverty of the men in power led the world to the tragedy of 1914. The churches and the men in power must now put the cause of humanity above everything and must not rest until the spirit of the gospel is diffused throughout the external world, – that of business, of national and international politics.[64]

you, more than anyone else, who laid the foundation for my education," he wrote her shortly after he became President. "The lessons in French which I began at that time have stood me in good stead during all these years." Again he wrote her that "it has been the greatest possible help to me to be able to speak French – not only during the days when I was in France and Belgium, but also here in Washington where I meet so many foreigners and Diplomatists who cannot speak English." [68] As late as 1944, on the occasion of the transfer of a destroyer to France, he spoke publicly in French.[69] His vocabulary may have become weak, but his accent remained fair.

The German governess had gone into a sanitarium after leaving Hyde Park; Mlle. Sandoz left to be married. In adulthood, Roosevelt liked to remark that he had driven one governess to insanity and the other to matrimony.[70]

Franklin read omnivorously, and here also his opportunities were above average. When he was small he had numerous beautifully printed European children's books, some of which contained mechanical cutouts. During his illnesses his mother read to him, not only the sentimental and moral children's tales of her youth, but also when he was only seven, *Little Men*, *Robinson Crusoe*, and for a second time, *Swiss Family Robinson*.[71] Soon he was foraging in his parents' sizeable library, especially for books on the sea, which as a rule were spiced with battle accounts. He particularly liked *The Boys of 1812* and *Sailor Boys of '61*, thrillers written by an Annapolis instructor, his father's cousin James Russell Soley. He read accounts of fighting on land too: Kipling's *Plain Tales from the Hills* and, when he was older, Parkman's *Montcalm and Wolfe*. Among magazines he preferred the *Scientific American*, which he was reading by the time he was nine. On occasion he would devour almost anything in print. One rainy day his mother found him reading his way through a dictionary.[72] He loved books, read them at top speed, and retained the gist of their contents with remarkable ease.*

Once when his mother became irritated with him because he was

* FDR's blithe approach to literature and uncanny speed of reading never ceased to confound those close to him. While he was in the White House, Eleanor Roosevelt tried to persuade him to read *Gone With the Wind*. In spite of his reluctance, she left the book by his bedside. The next morning Roosevelt informed his wife that he had read it. Incredulous, she quizzed him and found that while he might not have studied it word for word, he knew all the high points of the plot.[73]

playing with stamps on the floor while she read to him, he startled her by reciting back what she had been reading. "Why, I'd be ashamed if I couldn't do at least two things at once," he remarked.[74] He lacked that pale, indoor myopic look – no one could have described him as they did his remote cousin Theodore, as "a bookish lad." Certainly he was not of a particularly contemplative nature, and there is no evidence that he thought much about what he read, or was influenced a fraction as much by books as by what he heard and saw. Well before he reached manhood his approach to books, as to so many other things, became that of the collector rather than that of the scholar. Birds, stamps, naval prints, and souvenirs of all sorts appealed to him in much the same way, as objects to assemble, classify, and treasure.

Most children learn their geography from the pages of textbooks; Franklin learned his also from the rare and valuable stamp collection he inherited from his mother and from frequent touring of Europe and parts of the United States as far west as Wisconsin. His parents often took him with them on trips, and he became accustomed to meeting important personages. He was only five the winter the Roosevelts were in Washington going the social rounds with John Hay, William C. Whitney, and President Grover Cleveland. "Everyone is charming to us," Sara commented. "Even Franklin knows everybody." [75]

Franklin visited the White House for the gloomy interview with President Cleveland, but got a more glamorous glimpse of American politics at home in Hyde Park on election night, 1892, when Cleveland was re-elected. He saw his "first torchlight parade. . . . I was asleep, or supposedly asleep . . . and I was listening, and I didn't know what was the matter – a queer light outside the window, with people coming up on farm wagons – before the days of the automobile. It was Hyde Park – a large part of it – coming down here to have a Democratic celebration. And I got up and appeared down here in an old-fashioned nightgown of some kind, on this porch, and I wrapped up in an old Buffalo robe that came out of a wagon. And I had a perfectly grand evening." [76]

That same autumn, James Roosevelt, as New York State Commissioner to the Chicago World's Fair, went to Chicago to make advance arrangements. Franklin remembered: "When we stepped off the train at the Illinois Central station, we were met at the platform by a delightful old gentleman with one of those flowering bell-shaped coats, and a whip in his left hand, and a shiny, black-top hat on his head, and he stepped forward and . . . said to my father, 'How do you do, Cousin James?' Well, he was a Roosevelt too . . . the head of one of the livery stables of those days and was dressed accordingly." [77] The following summer, Franklin returned to the fair with his playmate Edmund Rogers, to be fascinated by the spectacle of Indians picking up pennies by lashing long whips.[78]

Intermingled with these typically American scenes were those of Europe. Along with his memory of President Cleveland, there was the glimpse in southern France of the exiled Emperor of Brazil, Dom Pedro II.[79] In time, London and Paris were as familiar to him as New York City. Year after year the family sailed on one of the White Star liners, usually the *Germanic* or *Teutonic*, and most often they spent several months at the springs at Bad Nauheim where James Roosevelt took the cure for his heart condition. Franklin enjoyed these voyages tremendously. "I am writing to you on the 'Teutonic,'" he noted grandly to a friend when he was nine. "She is the largest ship I ever saw. She is 582 feet long and 56 feet broad and 39 feet depth of hold. She has almost everything on board: there is a library, a barber shop, lots of baths, and lots of other things where you get quite lost. We are rolling so now I can hardly write. The waves are quite high. When one is sitting down one has to take care one does not slip off." [80]

When the Roosevelt family arrived at Bad Nauheim that summer, Franklin was sent to a small *Volksschule* for six weeks in order to improve his German. His mother thought it was "very amusing, but I doubt if he learns much." [81] Franklin was delighted with his first and only venture into elementary school life.[82] He was a year older and more mature than his classmates, but got along well with them.* "I go to the public school with a lot of little mickies," he wrote, "and we have German reading, German dictation, the history of Siegfried, and arithmetic . . . and I like it very much." [84] As it turned out, he learned a good deal in addition to the German language. This was the third year of the reign of William II, and the new Emperor had introduced new courses in map reading and military topography which so impressed Roosevelt that years later he was able to describe

* His German schoolmaster, Christian Bommersheim, in 1933 remembered FDR as a child in a blue sailor suit: "His parents brought little Franklin here for six months in 1891 and when they put him in my class he impressed me very quickly as an unusually bright young fellow. He had such an engaging manner, and he was always so polite, that he soon was one of the most popular children in the school." [83]

them in detail * as an example of German planning for aggression.[87]

The summer he was fourteen Roosevelt went on a bicycle tour with his tutor, Dumper. By this time he was so proficient in German that on several occasions when the two were arrested for minor violations of the law, he was able to argue them out of trouble. They picked cherries from trees alongside the road, made the mistake of taking their bicycles into a railway station, and worst of all, as they rode into Strasbourg at dusk they were arrested for "entering a fortified city of the Empire on, with, or in a wheeled vehicle after nightfall." [88]

Not even Franklin could talk his way out of a fine of five marks for running over a goose, and it must have hurt as they were making the tour on an allowance of four marks, or a dollar, a day. They lived upon black bread and cheese, and slept at small inns or peasants' cottages as they made their way from Bad Nauheim to Heidelberg, Baden-Baden, Strasbourg, Frankfurt, and Wiesbaden. But in spite of fines and difficulties, the pair handled their money so carefully that upon their arrival they still had a small amount left.[89]

When Franklin returned, his parents took him to Bayreuth for the music festival where they heard Wagner's operas, *Rheingold*, *Die Walküre*, *Siegfried* and *Götterdämmerung*. "Franklin really appreciated it far more than I thought he would," Sara wrote with gratification. "He was most attentive and rapt during the long acts and always sorry to leave, never for a moment bored or tired." [90]

All this took place in the summer of 1896, while in the United States a harsh depression and years of starvation prices for farmers were coming to climax in the uprising of the West against the East. While Roosevelt was pedaling through the Rhineland, William Jennings Bryan was campaigning for President on the silver issue. That autumn, Franklin returned and entered Groton. Even there, in one of the most exclusive and sophisticated schools in the country, he was ridiculed because he spoke English with something of a foreign accent.[91] It would have seemed preposterous to believe that this stripling, almost too high-toned for Groton, would in another generation become a new Bryan, a professed champion of the common man.

* FDR's reminiscences of Germany shifted focus with the times. In October, 1939, when he was trying to emphasize that his background was not pro-British and pro-French, he asserted, "As a matter of simple fact, I did not know Great Britain and France as a boy but I did know Germany. If anything, I looked upon the Germany that I knew with far more friendliness than I did on Great Britain or France." [85] But at a press conference on his way back from Yalta in 1945, he described how he had witnessed the rapid militarization of Germany.[86]

CHAPTER III

Groton

As long as I live, the influence of Dr. and Mrs. Peabody means and will mean more to me than that of any other people next to my father and mother.

— FDR, *June, 1934.*[1]

WITH heavy hearts the Roosevelts took Franklin to Groton School in September, 1896. After helping him unpack and settle, they returned to Hyde Park, sad in the knowledge that a momentous change had taken place. "It is hard to leave our darling boy," Sara lamented. "James and I both feel this parting very much."[2]

Going to school for the first time at the age of fourteen, this rather shy youth moved from one sort of rigid discipline to another: from the steady, gentle routine of the old life, to both the firm extraparental authority of the Headmaster, Endicott Peabody, and the much sterner tyranny that adolescent boys in the aggregate exercise over each other. Long skilled in conforming, Roosevelt adjusted to the standards of his new environment with eagerness if not ease. In time he became, not outstanding, but altogether typical, and to his death he bore the unmistakable stamp of a Groton man.

Groton School was young in years if not in ideas when Roosevelt entered. Many of its traditions had their roots in the Middle Ages, but the expanse of lawns where its Georgian buildings and timbered chapel now stood was a hillside pasture when Franklin was born. About that time, the James Lawrences of Groton gave the land to Peabody for his school. When James and Sara Roosevelt visited the Lawrences in 1883, Lawrence recommended that Franklin's name be registered, though he was but a year old and the school not yet open. Few schools began so auspiciously: the First Board of Trustees included two renowned clergymen, Phillips Brooks and William Lawrence (son of Amos the wealthy merchant), and J. Pierpont Morgan, whose family had been business associates of the Peabodys. During the early years, 90 per cent of the students came from social register families.

As a result, Groton acquired almost immediately a reputation for being the most exclusive of that small group of swank church schools which prepared boys for the Ivy League universities. Grotonians, by repute, could "gaze fixedly two inches over the head of a slight acquaintance while they carried on a conversation." [3] It was logical for a boy of Franklin's background to enter the school. His childhood playmate from next door, Edmund Rogers, entered at the same time, and his nephew Taddy (James Roosevelt Roosevelt, Jr.) was already in the form ahead.

Groton's reputation was scarcely of the sort to aid would-be politicians. When Josephus Daniels listed the major handicaps Roosevelt had to overcome in order to succeed politically, he put the Groton education second only to the patrician birth. Yet, paradoxically, Groton served more to encourage than to deter Roosevelt in his choice of a future career.

It was a novel and challenging world that the fourteen-year-old boy entered in the fall of 1896. He wrote of his new and rather circumscribed orbit, "The buildings are built on three sides of a square; the new building, where we eat, sleep, and study at night, on one side, the old building, now used as the study and recitations building on the other, and the gymnasium and fives court between. There are three football fields." [4] It did not occur to him to describe the six-by-ten cubicle in which he slept, which contained a bed, bureau, chair, small rug, and hooks on the wall for suits. He did not even comment on the cold showers before breakfast or the long black soapstone watering trough where he had to draw cold water into a tin basin in order to wash. Neither did he question the regulation that he must wear a stiff collar and patent leather dress shoes for supper and evening study hall. But in time-honored boarding-school fashion, he did complain again and again about the poor quality of the food, in spite of the fact that he rapidly gained weight on it. The first time he ate out, "The food tasted perfectly delicious after the school food. We have [had] sausages or sausage-croquettes for the last three days, but I have managed to keep perfectly well." [5]

The author of this program of enforced simple living was Rector Peabody. Around him revolved the school and most of its activities. His powerful six-foot frame was the most conspicuous and awe-inspiring sight on the campus, and his all-pervading influence was never far from Franklin from morning chapel to the final good-night handshake. In his letters home, Franklin did not write much about him any more than he did about the sun in the sky, but like the sun the Rector was always there, and the force of his precepts both direct and indirect could best be measured in the subsequent thoughts and actions of the man he helped mold.

During the New Deal years, when many of Roosevelt's classmates felt he had betrayed the old school, Peabody did not agree with them.* He firmly defended the President. He did so not as a gallant gesture toward an underdog nor with the undying loyalty toward a boy gone astray which led him to visit another prominent Grotonian, Richard Whitney, two weeks after he began serving a term in Sing Sing,[9] but with a sincere faith in Roosevelt's good intent.

Though much of what Roosevelt did as President must have startled and alarmed the Rector, more was in keeping with the basic principles which Peabody always exhorted the boys to follow. In 1932, the Rector frankly supported President Hoover as the abler man, but became so converted to Roosevelt's policies that he voted for Franklin in 1936, and again for a third term in 1940.[10] Roosevelt once reminded the Rector: [11] "More than forty years ago you said, in a sermon in the Old Chapel, something about not losing boyhood ideals in later life. Those were Groton ideals – taught by you – I try not to forget – and your words are still with me."†

These Groton ideals included the concept of service. Incessantly Peabody preached service to church, fellow man, and country. His own life was a model of the faith he preached. He came from several of New England's proudest families; his father was a wealthy financier

* During the New Deal, Peabody kept a portrait of President Roosevelt on the mantel in his study, and on several occasions warmly welcomed him when he returned to the campus. The thinly veiled hostility of graduates and undergraduates alike could not have added to Roosevelt's pleasure in these visits. When Peabody gave the school a holiday upon Roosevelt's election in 1932, the *Third Form Weekly* editorialized, "Whatever his reasons, every boy welcomes the day off." [6] Five or six years later, when Peabody was addressing a responsive audience of Groton alumni at the Union Club in New York, he paid tribute to Roosevelt, and was greeted with absolute silence.[7] When the President attended the fiftieth anniversary celebration at Groton in 1934, Frank Ashburn, historian of the school, noted, "For the Peabodys' sake even his bitterest opponents welcomed him, and he and Mrs. Roosevelt, for their part, showed the utmost consideration and self-effacement all through the weekend, subordinating themselves in all things to the Rector and the Madam." In warm contrast to the polite formality of the Grotonians, Mrs. Peabody on that occasion dashed up to the President, kissed him, and exclaimed, "Franklin, dear boy, I am *so* glad to see you!" [8]

† The admonition, whether or not Peabody had given it, made a strong impression upon FDR. In an extemporaneous address in 1933, he ascribed it to Bishop Phillips Brooks.[12]

who had served as a Morgan partner in England. Peabody was educated, therefore, in an English public school, Cheltenham, and later at Cambridge University. He came heavily under the influence of the Church of England, and of those aristocratic reformers, Tory in background and socialistic in leaning, who were preaching the gospel of service toward the less fortunate. Upon his return to New England, he rejected the counting house for the pulpit, and renounced his ancestral Unitarian creed for Episcopalianism.

Peabody's lodestar was that canon of the Church of England and professor at Cambridge, Charles Kingsley, who, although one of the founders of the Christian Socialist movement, had more interest in social reform than socialism and a closer affinity to Toryism than radicalism.[13]

Although at the outset Peabody spent a remarkable six months as minister in a Western mining town, Tombstone, Arizona, he subsequently centered his interests in New England, and for inspiration continued to draw upon old England. What he wished to do was to create in America a church school functioning along the lines of Thomas Arnold's Rugby, which could develop in boys from leading families that moral and physical vigor, and that sense of religious and civic responsibility which he summed up as "manly Christian character." [14]

One of the Rector's most acute observers concluded that his morals – and even his sense of humor – were to be found bound up in the volumes of *Punch* for the decade of the 1870's, the period of his English education.* At the same time, like others, this commentator found it difficult to equate the Rector's aristocratic bearing with his professed liberalism. Had this observer gone beyond *Punch* to Hansard's *Parliamentary Debates* for the same decade, there he would have found Peabody's liberalism: the liberalism of those financially secure Tories who were so far removed from the terrors of the balance sheet that they were ready even to take a "leap in the dark" and grant the franchise to laboring men, ready also to inaugurate a paternalistic program of welfare legislation to woo the workers to their party. The liberalism of Peabody was akin to that of Disraeli.

If England's battles were won on the playing fields of Eton, it was even more true that her government was run by those wearing the

* When the Roosevelts sent Franklin *Punch* and the *Spectator*, their son thanked them, and added, "They were most welcome to me . . . [though] hardly appreciated by others, as they are 'so English you know.' " [15]

proper old-school ties. There was no such parallel in America, where as late as 1936, *Fortune* pointed out that among the 67,000 graduates of the twelve best American private schools, there were only twenty-seven Senators, one Supreme Court justice, and one President. Of all these alumni, the only really towering political figure besides Roosevelt was Exeter's Daniel Webster.[16]

Peabody had tried to change this. "How distressing the political outlook seems to be! One looks almost in vain for men who are willing to serve their country," he lamented in 1894. "If some Groton boys do not enter political life and do something for our land it won't be because they have not been urged."[17] While most of the graduates were inevitably slated for careers in finance, business, and the professions, his words did catch fire among a handful. The *Fortune* survey recorded that of the thousand alumni of Groton, only ten listed "government" as their occupation; nevertheless these ten placed Groton proportionately far above the other schools. Along with its spate of bankers and brokers, Groton produced Bronson Cutting, Sumner Welles, Francis Biddle, Joseph C. Grew, Averell Harriman, and Dean Acheson. The Roosevelt type was rare among Groton graduates, but it was a species not a sport.[18]

In his chapel talks, Peabody time and again elaborated on the service theme. Occasionally he brought in his friend and kindred spirit, Theodore Roosevelt, who reiterated the same ideas in even more vigorous fashion. And he invited a steady succession of speakers who challenged the boys to go forth and right wrongs in a multitude of fields from heathen China to the slums of New York.

Peabody had more than the social gospel to impress upon his boys. He was a man of simple religion but profound and unquestioning faith. He had little patience for abstruse theological argument; he never introduced his boys to the skepticism of Renan; rather he had the overwhelming confidence that came with the conviction that he was living and acting in accord with Divine will.[19] It was the faith of a man of action, a spiritual athlete, rather than a contemplative scholar, and Roosevelt came to accept it as his own.[20]

All this worked its effect upon Franklin gradually and almost imperceptibly, day after day, term after term, for four impressionable years of his life, and there can be little doubt that the ferment continued to work in him during the years that followed.*

* Concerning her husband's religion, Eleanor Roosevelt said: "I think he felt that in great crises he was guided by a strength and wisdom higher than his own,

Peabody himself was not of course the sole influence at Groton. The Rector had assembled a singularly effective set of masters, who like him took seriously their task of molding adolescents into outstanding young men. Especially there were Sherrard Billings and William Amory Gardner, the two original masters who had helped Peabody found the school. Billings, a short, bewhiskered and exceedingly pious Episcopalian clergyman, referred to by the boys as "Mr. B." or "Beebs," made such an impression upon Franklin that the boy invited him to visit at Hyde Park over the Christmas holidays.[22] During his last two years at Groton, Roosevelt frequently accompanied Billings on preaching or charitable expeditions around the nearby countryside. Roosevelt was a willing disciple of Mr. B. in his pursuit of Christian humanitarianism.

Amory Gardner, "Uncle Billy Wag," was on the surface a beloved wealthy eccentric and a magnificent showman; beneath he was a brilliant progressive teacher. He had been reared by his aunt, the fabulous Boston art patroness Isabella Stewart Gardner, and sometimes she came to visit him at Groton. On one of these occasions Ellery Sedgwick, a few years Roosevelt's senior, entered the gymnasium in time to witness a most singular spectacle: Mrs. Gardner running at full tilt, with John Singer Sargent in gay pursuit.[23] While Roosevelt never stumbled upon any such entertaining sights he did, like the rest of the boys, visit Gardner's "Pleasure Dome" to drink "google" – a very sweet lemonade which came in two colors and one flavor. Gardner punned, joked, threw in anecdotal asides, and somehow in the process taught much Greek to the boys. "I can learn better & quicker with him than anyone else," Roosevelt wrote to his parents, referring to Gardner's Greek.[24] Perhaps this was true of his showmanship also.

The Groton curriculum was highly classical, loaded with Latin and Greek, heavy with French, German and English. Sacred studies, and a smattering of science and social studies, made up the rest. Aside from allusions in the social studies, and *Hiawatha* in a lower form,

---

for his religious faith, though simple, was unwavering and direct. . . . I always felt that my husband's religion had something to do with his confidence in himself. As I have said, it was a very simple religion. He believed in God and in His guidance. He felt that human beings were given tasks to perform and for those tasks the ability and strength to put them through. He could pray for help and guidance and have faith in his own judgment as a result. The church services which he always insisted on holding on Inauguration Day, anniversaries and whenever a great crisis impended, were the expression of his religious faith."[21] And whenever possible, the President obtained Peabody to conduct these services.

there was nothing on the United States in the entire program. In spite of Gardner, Franklin had trouble with Greek and was only fair in English. He maintained his relatively high average through consistently high grades in French and German, which he had studied so long and so thoroughly under his tutors and during his European sojourns. His course in political economy was scarcely preparation for New Deal economics. He wrote in his notebooks, for example: "Gold is stable, silver is unstable, therefore gold is the only suitable standard of value." However, there was a twentieth century note in this: "Trade Unions . . . can resist unjust exactions by the employers by means of strikes. A strike is like a war, costly and cruel, and it would seem that boards of arbitration are the rational way of settling differences between Capital and Labor." [25]

Intellectual brilliance could be something less than an asset for a young Grotonian, since it might lead to the conspicuousness which at all costs must be avoided. Roosevelt trod cautiously and nervously at first, skirting between the Scylla of the Rector's Jovian wrath and the Charybdis of barbaric disciplining by fellow students. Peabody was formidable beyond belief when in conference with wayward students. Young Averell Harriman once told his father, "You know he would be an awful bully if he weren't such a terrible Christian." [26] The path to his office was paved with black marks which masters and student prefects allotted for misconduct. An average high-spirited youth would normally accumulate three or four a week.[27] Individual ones brought work penalties, but a block of six (the maximum) led to a visit at the Rector's study. Any boy thus summoned underwent much soul-searching on the way: "After dinner today Mr. Peabody called the choir into his study and all expected a big talking to," Franklin once reported, "But he surprised and delighted us by saying that he had decided to let the choir go to Southboro' for the game next Saturday." [28]

Franklin seldom underwent nervous moments like this. At the end of the second week he could report to his parents, "I have not had any blackmarks or latenesses yet," and he went on to establish an exemplary record [29] both in conduct and punctuality.* He had reached nearly the end of his first academic year before it dawned upon him that this sort of thing was seriously damaging his reputation among the boys, and proceeded to mend his ways: "I have served off my first black-mark today, and I am very glad I got it, as I was thought

* FDR won the Punctuality Prize his second year.

to have no school-spirit before. Old Nutter Barbarossa gave it to me for talking in the schoolroom." [30] Thenceforth he took care to pepper his record discreetly with sufficient black marks to guarantee his "spirit," but apparently never in his Groton career did he make a forced appearance in the Rector's study.

With greater anxiety and equal success, Roosevelt managed to stay clear of the student-inflicted penalties: the boot box and pumping. Upper classmen who wished to discipline fresh new boys forced them to double up in the locker in which they kept their overshoes. Continued offences, or even – in the absence of specific missteps – a general feeling that the "tone" or "form" of an individual was bad and substandard, could lead to the very serious punishment of pumping. This was a somewhat gentler version of the "water cure" which American troops several years later found effective for extracting information from Filipinos.* In the Groton edition a boy was held face upward over the soapstone trough, and basins of water poured down his throat for eight or ten seconds until he had undergone the excruciating sensations of drowning. Here was a strong deterrent against bumptiousness and a powerful incentive to remain inconspicuous. With a politician's inborn social radar, Franklin succeeded magnificently in this. He not only avoided trouble, but soon came to regard those less inhibited than himself with lofty scorn: "The Biddle boy is quite crazy, fresh and stupid, he has been boot-boxed once and threatened to be pumped several times." [31] Nothing like that ever happened to Roosevelt.

The twin symbols of the pump and the boot box were more than enough to make young Franklin conform to the standards of decorum and social order which his classmates so savagely maintained. Without them, he would still have been deeply anxious to acquire that intangible and all-important factor in every Groton education, the proper "tone." So far as that meant gentlemanliness and good manners, the discipline was certainly all to the good – though it is inconceivable that Franklin was not already perfectly trained in these matters. So far as it meant getting along with others of the same age, the experience was new to him and he had much of importance to learn. Outwardly, at least, he quickly sloughed off his troublesome shyness, and mixed energetically with his classmates. Whatever his accent may have become after his nine trips to Europe, he quickly discarded

* The American troops learned the technique from the Spaniards, not the Grotties.

it in favor of the Groton broad "a" and inaudible "r" which henceforth marked his speech.*

Roosevelt suffered a disadvantage from the fact that, because his mother had not been able to bring herself to part with him, he was entering two years late. Out of the sixteen boys in his form, there was only one other newcomer. Though he soon came to be on good terms with the new boy and did slowly acquire many other acquaintances, he made only a few strong friends. There was not much fraternization among the forms, and within his own form the pattern of friendships had been set before he arrived. He so keenly sensed having always remained somewhat of an outsider that he insisted each of his own boys should enter the first form at about the age of twelve.[33]

None of the disciplining was overwhelmingly bad, and since Roosevelt always did to the utmost what was expected of him, his four years at Groton were by no means a failure. But in his small orbit he was accustomed to lead and to dominate, just as his parents did in theirs. In this he failed. He had no particular interest in scholarship, but socially that was unimportant – the incomparable Cutting brothers, Bronson and Bayard, were almost alone in winning Groton eminence by this means. What counted above all was athletics; little else mattered. Roosevelt unquestioningly accepted this criterion, tried valiantly, and inevitably failed because of his light build. When he entered he was only five foot three, and although by his final year (at eighteen) he had acquired his full height, he remained quite spindly.[34] Unfortunately prestige centered in football, baseball, and crew; tennis or golf in which he excelled were of no consequence. In his last year he became manager of the baseball team, a position which his mother thought was of great importance; Franklin knew better.[35]

In the fall of 1896, when Franklin first entered Groton, in a very immediate sense his world turned upside down. Suddenly he was no longer the main center of attention under the immediate eyes of two doting elders. The ties were still there – his mother wired him when he went a week without writing[36] – but they were stretched across the miles to Hyde Park, where his mother consoled herself by "dusting Franklin's birds," a responsibility she "dared not trust to any one else,"[37] and watching with loving tenderness over his aged father, who was gradually declining in health and vigor.

* However, most speech experts assert that FDR spoke not with a "Groton-Harvard" accent, but like most educated people of New York City and its vicinity.[32]

At times the boy must have been homesick, but he never mentioned it in his letters to his parents. "I am getting on finely both mentally and physically," he reported in his first letter home.[38] He joined the choir, in which he sang soprano. On one evening a week he went with other boys to play games in Mrs. Peabody's parlor, and on Sundays after supper he sometimes went there to sing hymns.[39]

Franklin plunged manfully into football, but since he was small and slight, had to play on the next to the poorest team: "Our 4th twenty-two play four times a week, and we have had some very desperate battles. My head is a little bunged up, but otherwise I am all right." [40] His subsequent letters throughout the four autumns at Groton contained an almost never-ending catalogue of injuries, fortunately all minor though often painful.[41] Whatever reservations Roosevelt might have about the game as a participant, as a spectator he thoroughly thrilled to it. Already that first November when Groton beat its traditional rival, he overflowed with excitement and exulted: "Hurrah, Hurrah, Hurrah

GROTON

46

St. Marks

0

I am hoarse, deaf, and ready to stand on my cocoanut!" [42]

Christmas season soon followed. The boys decorated the chapel with greens, sang, and feasted on turkey and cranberry sauce. One afternoon and evening before vacation began they listened while the Rector's father, Samuel Endicott Peabody, read Dickens's *Christmas Carol*. It was an annual custom. Two years later, Franklin wrote,[43] "It is more fascinating each year & I would not miss it for the world." *

Upon his return from vacation Franklin entered joyfully into the winter sports. Warm and gaudy in his new red turtle-neck sweater, he went skiing, sledding and tobogganing.[44] His dining table was crowded. Two new boys had been added to it, one of them Edwin Corning, and the other "a McCormick boy from Chicago," † and

* Roosevelt adopted this as a custom of his own, and every year read the *Christmas Carol* to his assembled family on Christmas eve.

† Corning became Lieutenant Governor of New York under Alfred E. Smith, and Robert R. McCormick, nicknamed "Rufus" by his classmates, publisher of the Chicago *Tribune*. McCormick never cared much for Groton.

Franklin chafed "to be moved up to a table, where I really belong."[45] As his wish was shortly granted, he could begin to exult over being no longer at that "kid table where I suffered three months."[46]

As the months passed, his self-assurance grew and his spirits lifted. At the same time, his intellectual horizon began to broaden. As a member of the Junior Debating Society, he participated in a debate on the question, "Resolved that the United States increase the navy." This was March, 1897, when jingoist spirit against Spain was already running high, so he undoubtedly considered himself in luck to be assigned the affirmative (the boys did not choose topics or sides). He wrote out a six-minute speech, and painstakingly memorized it. On the memorable evening he was "not at all nervous" and his speech "came out without a hitch." One of the opposing debaters blew up, and the result was a rout: out of thirty votes, the opposition received only three.[47]

The day of the debate was momentous for Franklin in another respect: he finally won in an athletic competition. This was the third form "high kick," a strenuous event involving such serious pain for the contestants that his victory indicated very well the Spartan extremes to which Roosevelt was willing to go in order to succeed at some sport. A pan was suspended from the ceiling of the gym and each boy kicked up at it as it was gradually raised. Franklin's winning kick was seven feet, three and a half inches – just two feet over his head. "At every kick I landed on my *neck* on the left side so the result is that the whole left side of my body is sore and my left arm is a little swollen!"[48]

With the coming of spring, not too far ahead glimmered the alluring vista of summer vacation. Franklin's parents had sailed for Bad Nauheim for the annual cure, and would not return until Groton was out. In their absence he accepted an invitation to spend the Fourth of July with Anna Roosevelt Cowles, and was greatly chagrined when his mother sent a long-distance veto. With rare rebelliousness he retorted, "I am very sorry to hear that you refused Cousin Bammie's invitation for the 4th and as you told me I *cd* make my own plans and as Helen [Roosevelt] writes me there is to be a large party & lots of fun on the 4th, I shall try to arrange it with Cousin B next Wednesday. Please don't make any more arrangements for my future happiness."[49] When Bammie and his niece Helen arrived a few days later, Franklin, contrary to his mother's instructions, promised to spend the Fourth with them.

Further complications developed when Theodore Roosevelt, the new Assistant Secretary of the Navy, arrived at Groton the next day. Already he was a highly glamorous figure, a mighty champion of the right who as New York Police Commissioner had downed the forces of evil and darkness: "After supper tonight Cousin Theodore gave us a splendid talk on his adventures when he was on the Police Board. He kept the whole room in an uproar for over an hour, by telling us killing stories about policemen and their doings in New York."[50] When Theodore also invited Franklin for the holiday, the lure was irresistible, and the lad compounded his insubordination by again accepting.*

A few days later, the term ended and grades must be faced. Franklin found he had failed one examination, Greek, and received a sad 65 in geometry; nevertheless his average was 7.86 out of a possible 10.00, and he stood fourth in a class of seventeen.[52]

Franklin, after spending most of the summer golfing and sailing at Campobello, returned to Groton in the fall considerably taller and heavier, weighing about 112 stripped.[53] Since he could no longer sing soprano, he dropped out of the choir.[54] Overflowing with the jaunty self-assurance appropriate to being one of the older boys, he approved wholeheartedly of the pumping system, and boasted to his parents of his black marks.[55] He took boxing lessons, but when he fought a two-round lightweight bout he came out second best with a bloody nose and a cut lip.[56] †

Gradually in the late winter and early spring, an air of excitement began to filter into Groton from the outside world. The newspapers blazoned startling headlines and exciting predictions of a war against Spain for the liberation of Cuba. There was also a good bit of talk about what America's new role should be as a world power – talk derived in considerable part from the writings of a suddenly popular naval officer, Alfred Thayer Mahan. For Christmas, 1897, Franklin received from his Uncle Fred and Aunt Annie Hitch a copy of the

* This did not end the controversy between FDR and his mother. On June 8, 1897, he wrote her: "I am going to Oyster Bay to stay with the Theodore Roosevelt's on Friday July 2nd & shall stay there all Monday." He added June 11: "I am sorry you didn't want me to go to Oyster Bay for the 4th but I had already accepted Cousin Theodore's invitation & I shall enjoy it very much. . . . I am so sorry you have refused Cousin Bammie's invitation and I wish you had let me make my own plans as you said. As it is, I have accepted Theodore's invitation and I hope you will not refuse that too."[51]

† "Did you ever box?" a reporter asked FDR in 1911. He replied, "Oh, yes, I was quite a boxer when I was interested in such matters."[57]

twelfth edition of Mahan's *Influence of Sea Power upon History*, and on January 30, 1898, they acknowledged his sixteenth birthday with a copy of Mahan's latest, *The Interest of America in Sea Power, Present and Future.*[58]

Mahan was already an important source of Roosevelt's ideas and arguments. That same January, Franklin cited him in a debate on "Resolved, that Hawaii be promptly annexed." Roosevelt argued from the negative: "We should for the first time in our history have a vulnerable point. . . . If we own the islands it means that we must protect them, and to do that we should have not only to fortify the Islands themselves but also maintain a much larger navy." Besides, Franklin pointed out, the United States already had all that it needed – a coaling station at Pearl Harbor and a favorable trade treaty – and the Hawaiian people obviously did not want annexation. "Why," he inquired, "can we not leave Hawaii alone, or else establish a sound Republic in which all Hawaiians shall be represented not a government such as they have at present, under the influence of Americans." [59]

Within six months, the United States annexed Hawaii amidst the general expansionist excitement accompanying the Spanish-American War. Less than a month after the Groton debate, the battleship *Maine* blew up and sank in Havana harbor. "We heard the news . . . & everyone is much excited," wrote Franklin. "If the accident turns out to have been done by the Spaniards, I think the whole school [will] take up arms and sail to Spain!" [60]

As the nation balanced on the edge of war early in April, Franklin's gravest concern seemed to be that the crisis might prevent his ailing father from taking his annual treatment at Bad Nauheim. He urged his parents to sail in spite of war rumors.[61] Agreeing reluctantly, his mother lamented in her diary, "Nothing but James' health would induce me to cross the ocean without Franklin." [62]

For a romantic sixteen-year-old, Franklin remained remarkably calm in his letters to his parents. "The Spanish situation seems to be unchanged, but I feel that every moment of delay is in the interests of peace, and that the President is doing all he can to prevent war," he wrote on April 8.[63] "Somehow I feel as if I would mind having the ocean between us much more than I did last year," he wrote his parents the day before they sailed, and added, "War seems pretty threatening now." [64] Restlessly he began confiding his feelings to a "letter-diary" in which he made daily entries, planning to mail it later in installments.

"War began today!" he recorded on April 22, ". . . and of course everyone is wildly excited." For the next few days, except for a casual mention of two cases of scarlet fever in the school, he jotted down little but the spectacular and sometimes false reports filling the newspapers: "Spain has sent a squadron of 50 to 60 ships against N. Y. and the coast." "The gunboat Nashville captured a Spanish merchantman off Cuba." And so forth.[65]

"We are all kept much excited over the war," he reiterated on April 24. He did not add that he and Lathrop Brown and another fourth-former had learned that the Navy was recruiting on Long Wharf in Boston, and that the three boys were scheming to slip away in the pieman's cart the following Sunday and enlist there.[66] Franklin was so dutiful a son, so troubled about his father's bad heart, that he might well have backed out when the moment came to run away. As it happened, the decision was taken away from him by the scarlet fever epidemic that he had all but ignored in his excitement over the war. On Wednesday he came down with a mild case, which shortly developed complications and brought his mother back from Europe to sit on a stepladder outside the infirmary window and read to him. As Franklin lay and listened, so wan and thin that someone referred to him as a *reconcentrado*, he was free to dream of the great deeds in which he might have shared if only he had not become ill.[67]

In the fall of 1898, he entered the fifth form. Now completely one of the older boys, he gloried in new perquisites: "You have no idea how nice it is to have a study, and do just as you like." [68] But the study was no ivory tower: politics was coming closer to home and he was sharing fervently his parents' interest in Theodore Roosevelt's campaign for the governorship of New York. James Roosevelt bolted his party to work in Hyde Park for his cousin. "We were all wild with delight when we heard of Teddy's election," Franklin exulted from Groton, "the whole dormitory went mad." In January, Franklin went with his parents to attend the inauguration in Albany.[69]

Other matters less earth shaking also held his attention: "I have been practising on the mandolin quite a good deal, and find that I did not do it right at Campobello at all. I did not understand the tremulo at all and it takes a good deal of practise to master it." [70] Christmas vacation was approaching and it was time to think of music and festivities; he had plans to make for dances and a house party at Hyde Park. For the first time, girls seemed to come within his sphere of interest, though in a rather negative fashion, since he feared he might end up with unsuitable dance partners.* In this exigency as in others he turned to his mother. "I wish you would think up some decent partner for me," he implored her, "so that I can get somebody early, and not get palmed off on some ice-cart." [72] Later, he "was in a quandary as to whom to ask . . . and not caring at all, I drew lots." [73] This indifference to girls in general did not hinder him from extending invitations to several special young people: "How about Teddy Robinson and Eleanor Roosevelt?" he inquired. "They would go well and help to fill out chinks." [74]

At this period Franklin was developing considerable interest in religious and charitable work. He had attended the Rector's confirmation lectures, been one of a class confirmed by Bishop Lawrence. Later he was elected to the Missionary Society which conducted church services in small rural localities nearby, managed a summer camp for underprivileged boys, and contributed to the maintenance of a club for them in Boston.[75]

He spent a good bit of his time golfing; in the summer of 1900 he served as Secretary-Treasurer of the Campobello Golf Club, and in succeeding years frequently won the tournaments there.[76] But his greatest interest in the summer of 1899, as before and later, was his twenty-one foot sailboat, the *New Moon;*† his love of the sea was undiminished. One of his Groton masters, George Marvin, recalls that he was already collecting old prints of sailing ships.[79]

In the fall of 1899, Franklin began his last and happiest year at Groton. He was a "full-fledged dormitory prefect," no great honor since about half the class were prefects before the year was out. Nevertheless, the position carried with it an excellent study and the duty (exhilarating, at first) of maintaining order over the smaller boys. "All is confusion and Babel; the new infants are like the sands of the sea," he proclaimed from his new heights. Again, "I must go up to see that the kids in my dormitory are behaving themselves." [80] He was successful, according to Marvin, in helping keep thirty-six boys in satisfactory order day and night. "He was a good prefect." [81]

* In his letters of the next several years, FDR more than once sprinkled derogatory labels in his mention of girls: "Brat," "Elephantine," and "awful pill." Elliott Roosevelt in editing the letters left the epithets but charitably deleted the names of their objects.[71]

† His father's larger yacht, the *Half Moon*, caught fire and sank while coming up the Hudson in October, 1898,[77] so in the summer of 1899, the *New Moon* was Franklin's only boat. The following summer, his father purchased a sixty-foot, eighteen-ton auxiliary schooner.[78]

One of the younger boys remembered how Franklin appeared when they met at the Hundred House for a midmorning snack and walked back to the schoolhouse together: "He was gray-eyed, cool, self-possessed, intelligent, and had the warmest, most friendly and understanding smile."[82] To boys in his own form, Franklin seemed more lively and less Olympian: "He developed an independent, cocky manner and at times became very argumentative and sarcastic. In an argument he always liked to take the side opposite to that maintained by those with whom he was talking. This irritated the other boys considerably."[83]

On his return from Easter vacation, Franklin visited an oculist, who told him that he must wear glasses in order not to become more near-sighted. He ordered a pince-nez and spectacles. "I'm writing in 'specks'!" he informed his parents. "It seems so strange."[84]

All that spring as baseball manager, he labored long, hard, and somewhat truculently, laying out and rolling the diamond, handling equipment, and accompanying the team on trips. He grumbled about this "thankless task," but when baseball duties conflicted with dental appointments (he was having his teeth straightened) he felt duty-bound to sacrifice the latter. "Now I don't want you to think that I am not just as anxious as you are to get the teeth straight," he explained to his parents, "but you do not realize what it means my being away on days of games. I should have either to give my work to the Ass. Manager, a V former or else *resign*. The first is impossible & I don't intend to do the second, as it would lose me not only the ribbon but the respect of the entire school."[85] His managerial responsibilities ended on a happier note late that May, with a 7–6 victory over St. Mark's. "All my work is over, & over successfully," he commented with relief, "& there has not been a single complaint."[86]

At the end of June, 1899, Franklin finished his studies at Groton. To his delight, he received the Latin Prize, a forty-volume set of Shakespeare, but with his pleasure was mixed a certain element of nostalgia: "'The strife is o'er, the battle won!' What a joyful yet sad day this has been. Never again will we hold recitations in the old School, and scarce a boy but wishes he were a 1st former again," he mused – sentimentally, but with excellent "tone."

On Franklin's final grade report the Rector inscribed the comment, "He has been a thoroughly faithful scholar & a most satisfactory member of this school throughout his course. I part with Franklin with reluctance."[87] Thirty-two years later, when Roosevelt was President-elect, Peabody added to the evaluation: [88] "There has been a good deal written about Franklin Roosevelt when he was a boy at Groton, more than I should have thought justified by the impression that he left at the school. He was a quiet, satisfactory boy of more than ordinary intelligence, taking a good position in his Form but not brilliant. Athletically he was rather too slight for success. We all liked him. So far as I know that is true of the masters and boys alike. I have always been fond of him." *

* In 1936, when a Grotonian questioned Roosevelt's sincerity, Peabody replied, "He was at Groton for four years, and so far as I can remember there was no suspicion of untruthfulness or insincerity during his entire course; nor did I hear of anything against his reputation at the University." [89]

CHAPTER IV

Harvard

> It is here that the first, and in many cases the final judgment will be made of the work of every individual. In the four years of undergraduate life . . . individual careers [can] be made much as they are in the outside world. . . . It is not so much brilliance as effort that is appreciated here – determination to accomplish something.
>
> – FDR, Harvard Crimson, *September 30, 1903*[1]

> Perhaps the most useful preparation I had in college for public service was . . . [on] the Harvard Crimson.
>
> – FDR, *March, 1929.*

ANY chronicle of Roosevelt at Harvard must inevitably bear much outward resemblance to *Stover at Yale*, with its hero ever striving onward and upward from one extracurricular triumph to another. But there was more than that to the four-year period, for Harvard contributed much to the development of a future great political leader. At Groton, Roosevelt learned to get along with his contemporaries; at Harvard he learned to lead them.

Many a successful American politician has received effective early training for his career while attending a university. It is an ironic fact that this comes less often from inspiring instruction or, as in European universities, from active participation in national politics, than from keen competition involving men and issues of a purely campus-wide significance. Intricate maneuvers to elect a student-body president may set the mold for the election years later of a governor or senator. Roosevelt's training fell easily into this typical American pattern.

The Harvard student body, like a binary stellar system, consisted of two worlds, each revolving around the other in its fixed orbit. Those who came from outer darkness – from the high schools of Philadelphia, Buffalo, and scores of outland communities – populated the larger and less scintillating of these worlds. These outsiders, William

James, the philosopher, pointed out, "seldom or never darken the doors of Pudding or the Porcellian; they hover in the background on days when the crimson color is most in evidence, but they nevertheless are intoxicated and exultant with the nourishment they find there." [2] It was they who stood in awe of Harvard's brilliant professors: in philosophy, not only James, but also Hugo Munsterberg, Josiah Royce, and George Santayana; in English, George Lyman Kittredge and George Pierce Baker; in history, Edward Channing and Albert Bushnell Hart, and so on through the departments – all under the leadership of the patriarchal president, Charles Eliot.[3]

Such luminous faculty minds made little impression upon most of the occupants of the smaller world in which Roosevelt automatically took his place. These young aristocrats were primarily responsible for Professor A. Lawrence Lowell's lament, "We fail to touch the imagination of the students. We awake little spontaneous enthusiasm for knowledge or thought. We arouse little ambition for intellectual power." [4] Yet these were the pace-setters, the ones who molded the popular image of Harvard.

Amidst the rapid expansion – seven new buildings were going up, and the student body had doubled in eleven years – the caste system remained untouched. The magnificent new Harvard Union was optimistically designed to bring together the two worlds of Harvard.[5] But student houses in the Yard seemed more and more uncomfortable in comparison with the sumptuous dormitories that private owners were building on nearby Mt. Auburn Street. Into these "Gold Coast" dwellings poured the well-to-do graduates of Groton and other private schools. The previous winter Roosevelt and his friend Lathrop Brown had engaged a suite of three rooms in Westmorly Court; his mother helped him furnish it in the elegant fashion so firmly prohibited at Groton. If Roosevelt were democratic at Harvard, it was by comparison with others of his social class. He continued to bear the indelible mark of Groton. He returned frequently to the school, and as soon as he arrived at Cambridge he began eating at a Groton table, "great fun & most informal." Evenings at Sanborn's billiard parlor on Massachusetts Avenue, he could find "most of the Groton, St. M[ark's], & St. Pauls & Pomfret fellows." [6]

Despite his social standing, Roosevelt took his studies seriously enough so that, while he won no honors, he was never in jeopardy. Since he had anticipated many of his courses at Groton he was able, under a new Harvard plan, to finish his requirements for the bachelor's degree in three years. Even in his freshman year he had considerable choice of electives, but under the competent supervision of his advisor, Archibald Cary Coolidge, he stayed clear of the notoriously easy courses so popular with athletes and clubmen. Electing the maximum number of courses possible, he undertook a program of a quality to earn from the *Harvard Alumni Bulletin* the comment: "Judged by football standards . . . [it] was anything but a snap."[7] It included the history of English literature under Kittredge, Baker, and Barrett Wendell; a survey of European history under Coolidge; French prose and poetry with C. H. C. Wright and Irving Babbitt; American government under A. Lawrence Lowell;[8] and year courses in Latin and geology.*

Each year Roosevelt demonstrated a phenomenal capacity for hard work by carrying a similar academic load without letting it interfere with a wide array of extracurricular and social activities. These took such a large proportion of his time that the surprising thing is not his failure to take honors, but his success in passing. There is one story about how he and most of his classmates one by one slipped down a fire escape to leave a nearsighted English-history professor, Silas M. MacVane, lecturing to an almost empty room.[10] Such conduct was a rare exception. Philip G. Carleton, who assisted in Professor Baker's course in "Forms of Public Address," remembers that Roosevelt "regularly attended the lectures and always appeared to give close attention and to take notes." Members of the class wrote long themes every two weeks. In the latter part of the course, they were in the form of hypothetical speeches. In Carleton's judgment, Roosevelt's were consistently good, but deficient in emotional appeal. When he conferred with Roosevelt, Carleton found him "always completely courteous . . . never jocose, and perhaps . . . a little austere. He accepted criticism without any contention." Roosevelt received C+ in the course.[11]

Starting a new school career on a level with the top newcomers, Roosevelt seemed from the first to make friends much more readily than at Groton. "Tomorrow," ran typical week-end plans, he was going with a friend "to spend Sunday at Newburyport where his place is & we are to shoot ducks. It is not the pleasure of going with him that induces me to go, but the chance to get some good duck shooting. . . . Gerry Chadwick may go with us. I was asked to go

* FDR received a midyear grade of B– in French, and C+ in geology, B in history, D+ in Latin.[9]

to Naushon for Sunday by Alex. Forbes who is in our class, but I should have had to take 3 cuts so thought it better not."[12]

Roosevelt sent home for a pipe he had inherited from an uncle – pipes were essential paraphernalia for college men – but since he was in training he did not use it. He doggedly tried out for every conceivable sport, but his lightness continued to plague him.* Although he was now a full six foot one and a half, he weighed only 146 pounds and was no heavier until after graduation.[14] For all his valiant efforts he failed to become an end on the freshman football squad, and shortly dropped down to a scrub team where, as at Groton, there was no opportunity for glory but plenty for minor mishaps. Following a familiar pattern, he reported home, "I have had most of the skin on my left hand kicked off in football, but it is not bad."[15] He did somewhat better in crew where through the fall of 1901 he stroked on one or another of the intramural teams.[16] Thereafter he did little or no rowing, but did keep in training sufficiently to row on an alumni crew against the Groton varsity in June, 1904. The Groton varsity won. He made the Freshman Glee Club, but his voice was not good enough for the varsity his sophomore year. What distinguished this experience from similar failure at Groton was that he now began to make up for his athletic deficiencies by winning an office almost every time there was an election. He became captain of his scrub football team – the only freshman captain among the eight teams; he was elected captain of the third crew of the Newell Boating Club, and secretary of the Freshman Glee Club.[17]

Above all, his success on the *Crimson* compensated for his athletic deficiencies.[18] At the start he was one of sixty-eight candidates, and by spring when most of the others had dropped out, he was working six hours a day on it.[19] There was one taboo – he might not interview President Eliot. An erroneous legend persists that Roosevelt, acting from ignorance, broke the rule by going to President Eliot and obtaining from him the biggest scoop of that autumn, a statement that he would vote for William McKinley and Theodore Roosevelt. Strangely, the source both of the yarn and its refutation was Franklin D. Roosevelt himself! †

* Lightness was not as serious a handicap then as in recent years. Of 143 candidates for the freshman team, only four weighed over 170; one of them weighed only 115. Roosevelt survived the first weeding down of the squad, but succumbed to the second.[13]

† In 1913, FDR told a reporter in elaborate detail how he had approached President Eliot:

It is quite authentic, though, that in his enthusiasm for Theodore Roosevelt, the future Democratic President joined the Harvard Republican Club and marched in a torchlight procession of over a thousand students. "We wore red caps & gowns," Franklin reported at the time, "& marched by classes into Boston & thro' all the principal streets, about 8 miles in all. The crowds to see it were huge all along the route & we were dead tired at the end."[21]

A few days later the Republicans won decisively. In the spring, shortly after he became Vice President, Theodore Roosevelt unwittingly gave Franklin an excellent story for the *Crimson.* Franklin once reminisced: "I telephoned to ask when I could see him. 'Don't come in,' he said, 'because I'll see you when I come out to lecture. I'm speaking for Professor Lowell, in Government One,' and he gave me the night and the hour. That was a beautiful piece of news and the neatest scoop in the world. But Government One only held about 500 and long before the time for the Vice President's lecture, there were about 2,000 persons gathered together who wanted to hear it. It was, well, it was embarrassing for Professor Lowell. I had every reason to know that he was disturbed quite a bit about that crowd."[22]

But it was good luck for Franklin, who had made the main spot in the *Crimson.* He had failed in the fall tryouts, but in June was elected one of five new editors.[23]

It was pleasant for Franklin to be connected with as exciting a figure as Theodore Roosevelt, even if newspapers did incorrectly describe him as a nephew in the "royal family." It was considerably less pleasant to be an actual uncle of Taddy Roosevelt, who in the

"Who are you?" he asked.

I told him, and without further preliminaries put my question.

"I came to ask you, Mr. President, whether you are going to vote for McKinley or Bryan?"

"Wh-a-at?"

Then I realized just what the situation was, and wished the floor might open and let me through to any kind of darkness that would hide me. Still, I had come for news, and I stood there while Dr. Eliot looked me through and through.

"What do you want to know for?" he asked finally.

"I want to get it for the Crimson," I said.

And so, Eliot, according to this version, told him.
But in 1931, FDR wrote:

In some way I was a number of years ago given credit for getting a scoop from President Eliot in regard to the way he was going to vote in the autumn of 1900. The real man who got that scoop was Albert W. DeRoode, now a lawyer in New York City, and he should have the credit and not I.[20]

fall of 1900 was receiving lurid attention in the yellow journals. For some time there had been indications of trouble ahead. The previous spring Franklin had repeatedly warned his parents in almost priggish fashion that Taddy was on probation at Harvard and reputedly had been skylarking in New York. "He may be off on a bat now for ought I know," Franklin declared. "Some measures should be taken to prevent his having his full allowance next year, as even this year he has had just *twice too* much." [24] But when Taddy came of age in August he began receiving an income of $40,000 a year. In the fall, his father found that he had contracted an unfortunate marriage in New York, and whisked him back to Hyde Park. The newspapers made the most of it.[25]

Franklin took Taddy's misadventures with an air of patient resignation. "It will be well for him," he suggested to his parents, "to go to parts unknown . . . and begin life anew." [26] Nevertheless, the scandal quite possibly hurt Franklin's social standing at Harvard; it might even explain his failure, despite his prominence in student activities, to win election to the most elite of the clubs, Porcellian. This failure was a serious blow. Eleanor Roosevelt thinks it even gave him an inferiority complex and led him to become more democratic than he otherwise would have been. It may well have developed in him a trace of humility and caused him to associate somewhat more widely with the rank and file of his classmates.*

Interwoven with this touch of melodramatic farce was real tragedy. For years Franklin's father, now seventy-two, had suffered from heart disease; since spring it had rapidly grown more serious. In the very letter in which Franklin relieved his feelings concerning Taddy, he expressed his distress over news of another heart attack and announced his readiness to come immediately at any time his presence was wanted.[28] In the weeks that followed, James Roosevelt gradually grew weaker. More than once his devoted wife sat up all night in order to give him "remedies at regular intervals." Several times Franklin

* A Harvard friend recalls, "Franklin was not a typical club man of his generation at College. He had more on his mind than sitting in the Club's front window, doing nothing and criticizing the passers-by. Thus his not 'making' the Porcellian meant only that he was free of any possible restraining influence of a lot of delightful people who thought that the world belonged to them, and who did not want to change anything in it. . . . Franklin had an inherited social position which nothing except his own actions could change. Any feeling of inferiority was that of a young man standing uncertainly before the awakening body politic of the United States." [27]

came home or to New York City to visit his father. Finally, on December 8, James Roosevelt died. Sara lamented, "I wonder how I lived when he left me." [29]

For twenty years Sara Roosevelt had divided her abundant energies and intense devotion between her husband and her son. Now, widowed at forty-six, she naturally concentrated everything upon Franklin. "I am grateful to have had Franklin here these first dreadful days," she recorded in her diary. "I try to keep busy, but it is all hard. . . . I had all F's birds out to dust and air." [30] Her efforts to "keep busy" led her among other things to take over the supervision of the estate and run it as she thought her husband would have wished.[31] With these executive duties and her household to direct she managed to struggle through the first winter alone at Hyde Park, but the following two winters she rented an apartment in Boston in order to be near her boy.[32] She wanted to be "near enough to the University to be on hand should he want me and far enough removed not to interfere with his college life." [33] Some week ends in 1902 and 1903 Franklin held gay parties in his mother's rooms; other week ends he left her completely to her own devices.[34]

Life at Harvard was too kaleidoscopic and fascinating for Franklin to stay melancholy for long over the loss of his father.

As a diversion the following summer, Franklin persuaded his mother to tour Europe with him, together with the recently bereaved widow and the daughter of their old friend Alfred Pell, and Franklin's classmate, Theodore Douglas Robinson.[35] As they cruised up the Norwegian coast to the North Cape, their ship anchored in a fjord beside the yacht of Kaiser Wilhelm II and they went aboard. Franklin returned with a souvenir he claimed to have filched from the Kaiser's desk, a lead pencil supposedly bearing the Imperial tooth marks.[36] Subsequently they visited Dresden, Munich, Geneva and Paris. It was at Paris that they heard the news that President McKinley had been shot, but was recovering. Twelve days later when they landed at New York, they learned that he had died; Cousin Theodore was now President of the United States.[37]

Franklin's sophomore year at Harvard was highly satisfactory.* He

* He took the famous "Ec.1," "Outlines of Economics," under Professor Abram Piatt Andrew; American History to 1783, under Edward Channing; Constitutional and Political History of the U. S. Since the Civil War, under the brilliant and liberal William Garrott Brown; English Parliamentary History, under MacVane; General Paleontology, under Nathaniel Southgate Shaler; English Composition, and Public Speaking.[38]

concluded his crew career by stroking the second Newell crew to a four-foot victory.[39] He gloried in his new eminence as one of the editors of the *Crimson*, and even represented the paper at the Yale bicentennial celebration – an occasion notable in retrospect because among the many notables, there sat on the same platform at the same time Theodore Roosevelt, Woodrow Wilson, and Franklin D. Roosevelt.[40] At Christmas he had a house party at Hyde Park, and sailed the new iceboat that his mother gave him.[41] Immediately after New Year's he went to Washington to attend Alice Roosevelt's debut at the White House. The dance was "Great fun, & something to be always remembered." [42] No sooner had he unpacked at Cambridge than new excitement began. "I am about to be slaughtered, but quite happy nevertheless," he wrote his mother; he was going to be hazed into the sophomore clubs, the Institute of 1770 and the D.K.E. or "Dickey." Later he added, "My back is a bit raw, but I am through the first ordeal O.K." Several days of "Agony" running for the Dickey followed, but Roosevelt apparently never doubted it was well worth while.[43] That winter he was also elected to the organization thereafter of most importance to him, Alpha Delta Phi – the Fly Club.[44]

The Fly Club placed Roosevelt on its library committee, and his junior year he became head librarian.[45] Enthusiastic over the work, he gave the library twenty-five dollars for the purchase of the works of St. Armand and Rousseau. During his junior year he was elected to the library committee of the new Harvard Union and in his senior year he also became librarian of the Hasty Pudding Club.[46] He became keenly interested in building these libraries and began spending some of his spare time in secondhand bookshops. A Mr. Chase, a "rare and delicious man" at N. J. Bartlett & Co., advised him on book purchasing, and soon he was buying numerous volumes not only for the libraries but for his personal collection also. As he put more and more of his spare funds into the purchase of Americana, he came to realize that the field was too broad and began concentrating upon his childhood love, the Navy. It was a specialty not yet cherished by very many collectors, and before long he was able to build up a notable library of books, pamphlets, articles and manuscripts.* He also began

* Roosevelt's naval collection, while outstanding, was never, as sometimes described, the finest in the country. He also collected quantities of books, manuscripts, and pictures on the Hudson River Valley, and had several other minor interests: children's books and miniature books. His love for the collections never diminished. He collected through his presidential years, and wrote his name or

a collection of naval prints which in time came to be worth many times the price he had paid for them.[47]

In the early months of 1902 Roosevelt was swept into a whirlpool of excitement over British mistreatment of the defeated Boers. One of his favorite professors, Abram Piatt Andrew,* wrote the *Crimson* denouncing the "unutterable criminality" of the British imprisonment of Boer women and children in concentration camps.[49] Despite warnings of caution, two prominent Boers were brought to Harvard and described the suffering in the camps. The following week, Roosevelt joined with two other students to establish a "Boer Relief Fund." In May, he cabled $336 to Capetown.[50]

Roosevelt received much approving publicity in the Boston newspapers.[51] His reaction on an earlier occasion to stories like this was that they "make me excessively 'tired.'"[52]

By June, 1903, Roosevelt had completed the requirements for a bachelor's degree, and he marched in cap and gown to Sanders Theater to receive his diploma. † But as he had been elected president (editor in chief) of the *Crimson,* he returned in the fall to take up his role as a prominent Harvard senior. His professors advised him to enter graduate school. "Great fight in my mind between it & Law School, but latter too much with outside duties," he noted in his diary.[54] It was good advice, since less time-consuming "outside duties" his previous three years had kept his academic average down to only slightly better than a "C." The wonder was that his social life had left him time or energy to attain that.

Although Roosevelt enrolled as a candidate for a master of arts degree, he had no serious intentions of trying to obtain it. He signed up for "four or five history and Economics courses which really in-

---

initials on the flyleaf of hundreds of books. He even brought back books with him from Yalta, a few months before his death.

* Andrew, a handsome and brilliant young professor, was one of the few faculty members who seemed to make an impression upon Roosevelt. Later he went into politics, was elected to Congress, and served as Assistant Secretary of the Treasury in the Taft Administration. Roosevelt took several economics courses from him, and in the spring of 1902 went riding with him, and spent a week end at his home in Gloucester.[48]

† His third year, Roosevelt took Baker's speech course; English Letter Writers, from Charles Townsend Copeland; Constitutional and Political History of the U. S., 1783–1865, under Channing; International Law, under Albin L. Richards; Administration of the Government of the United States, under Charles Sumner Hamlin; Tendencies of American Legislation, under Frederic Jesup Stimson; one "football course," Fine Arts of the Middle Ages and Renaissance, under Charles H. Moore; and General Introduction to Philosophy, under Josiah Royce.[53]

terest me," * but there is no indication that he allotted much time to them.[57] "The courses will do me lots of good, whether I get B or D in them," he blithely assured his mother, "and to do the former would make me work so hard that I could not do justice to my senior year." [58]

Franklin had no intention of wasting this important year on studies. As president of the *Crimson* during the first semester, he not only wrote all the editorials, but also assumed the mantle of student-body leadership. On his way to Europe on the *Celtic* the previous summer, he had reviewed the editorials of the year before, and laid his own plans. Shortly after his return to Harvard he declared, "Every spare moment has been taken up with the paper."

What this leadership was to be, Roosevelt demonstrated in his second editorial which challenged every freshman to take seriously the responsibilities which faced him at Harvard – "responsibility to the

* He enrolled in a course on recent currency legislation by Professor Andrew, and another on transportation by Professor William Zebina Ripley, an authority on railroads. In history, he took "The Development of the West" from visiting Professor Frederick Jackson Turner; History of Continental Europe, from Professor MacVane; History of Germany from the Reformation to the Close of the Thirty Years' War, and History of England during the Tudor and Stuart Periods, both from Professor Roger Bigelow Merriman. In English he took a course on Bacon from Professor Fred Norris Robinson.[55]

An eight-page essay on Alexander Hamilton that Roosevelt wrote about 1904 is a gauge of the knowledge and attitudes that he acquired in his Harvard classes in history and political science. It is full of hero worship, and points the contrast between his thinking as a student and as President. After sketching Hamilton's origin and role in the Revolution, Roosevelt declared:

> It was because of his insistence that in May, 1787, a convention met at Philadelphia to form a permanent union of the States. At this convention he brought Washington, Benjamin Franklin and others to agreement with his principle that the Government should consist of three branches: the President, Congress, and a Supreme Court.

Next, Roosevelt described Hamilton's success in obtaining the New York ratification of the Constitution (he did not mention the *Federalist*):

> This was the climax of the greatest moment in the life of Alexander Hamilton, now thirty one years old. And yet there were other moments.
>
> Washington, the first President under the Constitution, made Hamilton Secretary of the Treasury – the greatest of the Cabinet offices. As he had stabilized the problems of State so now he ordered the finances of the country and it was his impetus that removed for all time the risk of disintegration of the States.

Thus disposing of Hamilton as Secretary of the Treasury, Roosevelt concluded:

> The bullet of Burr brought his life of high moments to an end. But Hamilton had made his way in the world.[56]

University, to his class and to himself!" He explained, "The only way to fulfill this is to be always active. The opportunities are almost unlimited: There are athletics – a dozen kinds – and athletic managements, literary work on the University publications and the outside press, philanthropic and religious work, and the many other interests that are bound to exist." Indeed he mentioned every possible activity except studying.[59] He followed this up with an address to the freshmen, which he admitted, "scared me to death. . . . I drooled on journalism here & also on strenuousness etc." [60]

Thus Roosevelt set the keynote of his *Crimson* editorship. Both at the time and in retrospect, it meant a remarkable amount to him – so much so that after he entered public life, he occasionally told reporters he was an ex-newspaperman.*

It is understandable that those searching into Roosevelt's past have been led by his own emphasis upon his *Crimson* phase to hunt back through his editorials in search of precocious progressivism. They have found vigor aplenty, but little of interest to a public not steeped in Harvard and its environs. Roosevelt's policies varied little from those of other alert college editors of his generation. The *Harvard Alumni Bulletin* accurately evaluated his regime as being "at least mildly distinguished for the animation of his many editorials, and for certain college reforms which he engineered." [62] He did relatively little to improve the quality of the paper. Most notably, he persuaded professors to review campus magazines, and in one number of the *Crimson* published a pleasant essay on the *Lampoon* by the philosopher George Santayana. Despite such enlivening bits, the *Crimson* continued to bear more resemblance to a bulletin board than a newspaper, and Roosevelt's editorials were seldom better than unspectacular variations on well-worn themes.

It is possible that Roosevelt suffered from too close proximity to Lathrop Brown, his roommate and manager of the football team. Whether or not at Brown's instigation, he devoted an overwhelming number of his editorials to lashing the team. Even in an era when a preponderance of *Crimson* comment every fall dealt with football, Roosevelt's columns were outstanding for their abundance, ponderousness, and humorless spirit of do-or-die competitiveness. He repeatedly admonished the team because it played listlessly, and the students be-

* In Portland, Oregon, in 1914, for example, while posing willingly for a press photographer, FDR remarked that he had been a newspaperman himself in Boston ten or twelve years before, and had often lined folks up before the camera.[61]

cause they did not show more school spirit. After the Wesleyan game he complained that the "cheering was not what it should be," [63] and gave token of his concern by leading cheers himself even though he "felt like a D. . .F. . . waiving my arms & legs before several thousand amused spectators!" [64] The climax of his heckling was a column of vitriolic scorn upon the famous occasion when the Carlisle Indians duped Harvard Varsity by hiding the ball under a jersey and carrying it for a touchdown. He proclaimed that the undergraduates were "weary of a spirit that will not awake till the team is in a desperate crisis" when actually "all that is needed is a spirit in the team of aggressive, vigorous determination." [65]

The result of this editorial application of Cousin Theodore's strenuousness was a considerable furor – although Roosevelt asserted in his own defense that "at least half the college think it was quite called for." A third-year law student, Henry James II, called for a halt on "dealing out editorial sarcasms – practically personal in one paragraph – to amateur athletes." James protested that the *Crimson's* exhortations to build winning teams had been so lacking in a sense of proportion and were so contrary to the amateur spirit, that if they were heeded, "The season's training will be made a real nightmare for the players, and the cheering-practice by the rest of the University will become as important as the work of the squad. The fun of the game will be spoilt for all." [66]

Thereafter Roosevelt's football editorials were less tart, though no less numerous. After the end of the season, he turned his attention to other sports; early in January he solemnly paid tribute to the systematic training and hard work which had made possible the splendid intercollegiate triumphs of the Harvard chess team.[67]

Into the interstices of his journalistic sports temple he thrust various editorials on matters of interest in and around the Yard. On the day academic distinctions were awarded, he even gave a left-handed endorsement to scholarship. "Of late years . . . " he granted, "the prominence of the unacademic side has, perhaps, been unduly emphasized." [68]

With the approach of Senior Class Day elections, Roosevelt came out in favor of reforms begun a year or two earlier to democratize election procedures.[69] For a long time the elite clubs had produced and elected a slate without much competition. Roosevelt did not mention this at the time in so many words, but he did remind the men of '04 that "there is a higher duty than to vote for one's personal friends, and that is to secure for the whole class leaders who really deserve the positions." He admitted that the elections of the previous year "were fairly free from any combinations or 'electioneering,' but the size of the vote was far too small." *

The voting was perhaps too small in 1904 also. Roosevelt himself was one of six nominees for Class Marshal; the top three would win election. When results came in, he had run a close fourth. Only 332 out of 607 eligibles had voted; the distribution of votes for a first, second and third choice clearly indicated a "ticket," and Roosevelt was not on it.[71] Several days later, however, he was elected to the important position of Permanent Chairman of the Class Committee with an easy 168 votes out of 253.[72]

Toward the close of his term as *Crimson* president, Roosevelt suggested several small reforms.[73] Early in January, he endorsed a letter pleading for a board walk on a muddy path from the Union to Gore Hall,[74] and when the University physician warned students to wear overshoes to avoid tonsillitis, he cleverly hitched the warning onto his campaign by noting that the greatest opportunity for wet feet was along the poor paths, which "one might suppose in their present condition to be licensed highways to the Stillman Infirmary." [75] Roosevelt's greatest triumph came from an editorial outlining the need for greater fire protection in the dormitories.[76] A few days later, the Iroquois Theater fire in Chicago provided a ghastly illustration of what lack of adequate fire protection could mean. Yet when a correspondent compared the conservatism of the Corporation to the criminal negligence of the public officials in Chicago, Roosevelt recoiled from such a bald and ungentlemanly approach: "In its sarcasm the communication

* By the time Roosevelt ran for the Presidency in 1932, this admonition had grown into a full-scale myth that in his senior year he democratized class elections. He himself perhaps was not responsible for this, but he had the gift of bestowing a Midas touch upon his reminiscences; in the telling they turned to gold. Thus, only a decade after graduation he granted that there was much plutocracy in the Harvard of old:

> Years and years ago class officers there were not really nominated by classes. Certain clubs . . . put up a slate which invariably went through. . . . The class of 1904, to which I belonged, pulled the joists from under this "upper crust" and made the class elections a popular affair. They nominated at least two men for each office, and the best man won. This, I believe, was the first time this slate-making power had ever been wrested from the clubs. It was the beginning of a reform that has accomplished great things and is still reforming.
>
> Harvard is today really a Democratic institution. The boys there are actually leading the simple life in the "commons." [70]

on the provisions against fire in Yard buildings seems to us in rather bad taste." Nevertheless he reiterated in politer terms the need for more extinguishers, hydrants and ladders – and by May the Harvard Corporation was actually installing them.[77]

This was a notable achievement, and here he was at his best in providing a collegiate version of responsible journalism. This is the most that can be said for his *Crimson* writing. Probably it was the most he should have undertaken, but the self-limitation was not noticeably a matter of principle or public requirement. His personal letters of that period indicate that his own horizons, except for his Hudson River Valley habitat, ordinarily did not extend much beyond those of the *Crimson*. He did go home to cast his first ballot: "Hooray for the Dimocrats of Hoide Park!" [78] And he did have rare moments of wider awareness.

On the whole, however, he still accepted Harvard standards as unquestioningly as he had those of Groton; he still was saturated with a sort of provincialism that he came eventually to deplore. While he was an undergraduate, he was capable of mild jokes about "blue-blooded, blue-stockinged, bean-eating Boston," but not about the sacred rituals of Harvard. Twenty-four years later, from a far different perspective, he criticized his class for its lack of leadership, due "not to the lack of possible leaders, but to the enormous wet blanket which is offered to any individual or group which might seek to encourage leadership. Sometimes I wonder just a little if Harvard is not suffering from a slight infection of the same disease which is making industrial and business New England so sick at the present time." [79] Again he wrote in facetious retrospect: "Once upon a time when I was in Cambridge I had serious thoughts of marrying a Boston girl and settling down in the Back Bay to spend the rest of my days. Such was the influence of four years of that . . . kind of association I am complaining about. By the grace of God I took a trip at that time, meeting numbers of real Americans, i.e. those from the west and south. I was saved, but it was an awfully narrow escape." [80]

While at Harvard, Roosevelt displayed a talent for personal leadership in his relations with other workers on the *Crimson*. "Mac" and "Ed," the Scottish printers, also did other presswork besides the Harvard daily and consequently were usually short with editors who failed to make deadlines, but Roosevelt could always cajole them into opening their forms and remaking a page for a last-minute piece of news.[81] He managed the staff with such smoothness that his co-editor

W. Russell Bowie recalled, "in his geniality was a kind of frictionless command." [82]

At the wedding of one of his Fly Club brothers, Herbert Burgess, he took over without prearrangement at the receiving line, and introduced each of the club members in turn to the bride's mother. She "was much impressed by his *savoir faire*," said Burgess. "His charm and ease of manner were apparent in those early days." [83]

Frictionless command of the situation was exactly what Roosevelt needed most in the winter of 1903–1904. For there was a new and momentous development in his life. He had fallen in love with Eleanor Roosevelt, and proposed to her. Her acceptance confronted him with the delicate task of breaking the news to his mother, and selling her on the engagement. Obviously it would be a rude jolt to her, since she had been counting on the companionship of her son after he left Harvard, and when he told her at Fairhaven during Thanksgiving vacation, she did take it rather hard. "Franklin gave me quite a startling announcement," she confided to her diary.[84] Writing from Harvard upon his return, Franklin summoned all the diplomacy at his command to be at once consoling and adamant: "Dearest Mama – I know what pain I must have caused you and you know I wouldn't do it if I really could have helpd it . . . ! I know my own mind, have known it for a long time, and know that I could never think otherwise: Result: I am the happiest man just now in the world; likewise the luckiest – And for you, dear Mummy, you know that nothing can ever change what we have always been & always will be to each other – only now you have two children to love & to love you – and Eleanor as you know will always be a daughter to you in every true way – " [85]

Eventually, after trying procrastination and change-of-scene and other time-worn antidotes without success, Sara came to accept her new daughter-in-law on exactly that basis: another child for her to mother and manage. And Eleanor was a fine candidate for this position. She was exactly the sort of young woman Sara would have wished her son to marry, if she had wished him to marry. But she did not want him to marry anyone just yet. He should finish his training first. Her own father, she reminded him, had not married until he was thirty-three and had become "a man who had made a name and a place for himself, who had something to offer a woman." [86] Upon this major issue her dutiful son, who for years had striven to please her in every way possible, set his Delano chin and displayed a stubbornness superior even to hers. Behind him, he had Eleanor. She wrote her formidable future mother-in-law a tentative, wistful letter: "I know just how you feel & how hard it must be, but I do so want you to learn to love me a little. You must know that I will always try to do what you wish for I have grown to love you very dearly during the past summer." [87]

On many occasions during the years when he was growing up Franklin had met his godfather's daughter, Eleanor. Ties of distant relationship and common social set dictated these casual meetings. But if social background was common to his upbringing and hers, the resemblance ended there. Her childhood had been the antithesis of his – sad, and pervasively overshadowed by the illness of her warm-hearted, genial father to whom she has referred as "the one great love of my life as a child." [88] He drank heavily, and after Eleanor was five or six could not even live with the family most of the time. Eleanor's beautiful mother, a sternly religious woman, showed little understanding of her solemn-faced young daughter. She tore down the child's self-esteem by calling her "Granny" because she was so sober, and gave her a lasting impression of herself as homely and awkward. When Eleanor was dismissed in disgrace from a convent school for telling a small fib to gain attention, her mother treated her as though she were almost a criminal. This unhappy woman suffered frequently from splitting headaches. At such times Eleanor would sit by her side for hours massaging her forehead.

In all Eleanor's childhood world of somber giants, only her handsome, dashing sportsman father seemed to understand her. His own nickname was "Nell" (for Elliot) and he called her his "little Nell" or his "Golden Hair." While he was away, she built her dreams around him. Before Eleanor reached her tenth birthday, both her parents had died, and thereafter she was brought up by her Grandmother Hall. This grandmother, a petted and spoiled beauty of another day, had so indulged her own children after her husband's death that they had turned out badly. Now she reared her grandchildren with more sternness than intelligence; she always found it easier to say "no" than "yes." [89]

During these years Eleanor occasionally saw her distant cousin Franklin. Once, at a Christmas party – when she was a gangling adolescent, miserable in the long blond braids and knee-length little-girl skirt her grandmother still forced her to wear – Franklin came up to her and asked her to dance. She remembered the incident with echoes of the gratitude she felt at the time.[90]

When Eleanor was fifteen, her grandmother sent her to England to study with Mlle. Souvestre. The Frenchwoman was a great teacher and a warm personality; Eleanor adored her, and acquired from her liberal attitudes and beliefs. A far more self-confident and independent Eleanor returned permanently to New York at the age of eighteen. At the Hall country home in Tivoli, on the Hudson above Hyde Park, these newly established traits received severe test, and the measure of gaiety and spontaneity Eleanor had acquired in Europe was rapidly sapped away. This household had somewhat the decadent undertones of a Poe story. Aunt Pussie was still there – she who a summer or two earlier had bluntly labeled Eleanor an ugly duckling among the beautiful Hall women, a misfit who never could hope to have many suitors. Aunt Pussie, on the other hand, still had love affairs enough for several women; unfortunately each seemed to turn out badly and led to endless weeping and heartache. Urbane Uncle Vallie had become a habitual drinker who returned home for his more serious benders. Uncle Eddie was not much better. The resulting atmosphere, though it might have been appealing to a dramatist, was trying to a serious young woman. Only real intimates, to whom the situation could be explained, might be brought home to meals.[91] *

As a whole, the Hall uncles and aunts were a scintillating lot, people who dressed and talked brilliantly, played cards for stakes, and lived with a flair that was beyond their means. They imbued Eleanor with a sense of basic insecurity, against which she began to rebel. Soon she herself started to take responsibility, to become like a mother toward her younger brother, Hall Roosevelt. She and her grandmother entered him in Groton; thereafter she, and she alone, went up once a term to see him.[93]

Fortunately Eleanor was able to leave the turbulent Hall ménage and take up a different sort of life with her cousins in New York, Mr. and Mrs. Henry Parish, Jr. They were a kind, stable couple, conservative in their way of living. Mr. Parish taught her how to keep her personal accounts, and encouraged her as she made new and interesting friends. But she was not content merely to be in society. Already she was developing a keen awareness of the underprivileged and a desire to help improve their condition. For the Junior League,

* When FDR visited at Tivoli during his engagement, he reported, "Vallie has been exemplary – I seem to have a good effect on him." [92]

she taught a course in fancy dancing and calisthenics at the Rivington Street Settlement House in the slums, and for the Consumers' League she helped investigate the working conditions of department store girls and dress factory workers.[94]

Contrary to her own conception of herself, Eleanor Roosevelt was far from being an "ugly duckling"; she possessed a rare animated beauty and liveliness. Once in a tableau she fittingly represented a willow tree.[95] Franklin soon discovered this. In the spring of 1902, he came upon her on a train bound up the Hudson, and took her back to his car to talk to his mother. He was fascinated with her, and a succession of meetings followed. Eleanor began to appear frequently in the gay groups around Franklin at Hyde Park, New York, and Boston. His mother saw nothing significant about this – Franklin had long been devoted to his cousin "Moo," Muriel Delano Robbins, his niece Helen Roosevelt, and to Frances Pell and Mary Newbold. While at Harvard he had seen much of a beautiful Dedham girl, Dorothy Quincy. Sara easily dismissed Eleanor by classing her with these old and reliable comrades. When forced to the shocked realization that Franklin was in love with Eleanor, she reviewed the recent social events in a new light and reasoned that the announcement "probably surprised us only because he had never been in any sense a ladies' man. I don't believe I ever remember hearing him talk about girls or even a girl." *

Sara had no objection to Eleanor as a person, for it was in every sense an acceptable match. They had much to offer each other. Endicott Peabody sensed this when he congratulated Franklin upon his formal engagement: "I have always particularly liked Miss Roosevelt. She has been a devoted Sister – you a devoted Son. I can hardly imagine a better training in each case for a happy married life." [97] Eleanor could find in Franklin the personal attractiveness of her father, for he was in appearance a veritable beau ideal of the times.† But unlike her father, Franklin and his relatives had about them the sort of stability toward which she yearned. She went to a Delano party at Fairhaven at Thanksgiving, 1904, and felt they possessed "a sense of

* One of FDR's Harvard friends declares: "Franklin had no serious affair with any girl, which was remarkable in view of his exuberance. In the back of his mind there was always Eleanor as an ideal." [96]

† FDR was the male counterpart of the Gibson girl. Mark Sullivan has quoted: "Gibson also created a type of man, the square-shouldered, firm-jawed, clean-shaven, well-groomed, wholesome youth . . . and the American man, less self-consciously than the American girl, set himself to imitate the type." [98]

security which I never had known before."[99] Franklin, for his part, must have been strongly drawn to this shy, highly feminine girl who shared his interest in people and perhaps even surpassed him in the keenness and quickness of her perception. Besides, it detracted nothing from her glamor that she was a niece of his idol, Theodore Roosevelt.

When Franklin broke the news to his mother in the fall of 1903, Sara looked upon her son as too young and immature to marry – not entirely without cause, as Franklin was twenty-two and Eleanor nineteen. Determining that he should at least spend some time thinking it over, she did not prevent them from seeing each other, but allowed no immediate announcement of their engagement. In February she took Franklin off on a six weeks' cruise of the Caribbean so that he might have time to reflect without any distracting influences. He sailed, Sara noted with pity, "tired and blue."[100] Though either Sara or Eleanor might have been tempted to assess specific blame for this weariness, even aside from the struggle with his mother his life during his senior year was exhausting.* "I have been up every night till all hours," he admitted in mid-January, "but am doing a little studying, a little riding & a few party calls. It is dreadfully hard to be a student a society whirler a 'prominent & democratic fellow' & a fiancé all at the same time – but it [is] worth while."[101]

The trip was pleasant and relaxing. Lathrop Brown, Franklin's roommate, went along with them. They visited the Virgin Islands, Puerto Rico, Martinique, Barbados, Trinidad, Venezuela, Curaçao, Jamaica, and Cuba. Franklin gazed with great excitement at the rusting hulks of the Spanish fleet awash off Santiago, and climbed San Juan Hill, near which Theodore Roosevelt and his Roughriders had fought less than six years earlier. At Caracas he heard Caruso sing *Pagliacci* at a time when the great tenor was still unknown in the United States.[102] They went on to Havana, Nassau, Palm Beach, and Washington. They

* FDR's diary gives proof of his strenuous Harvard existence:

Wed., Jan. 13 [1904]. Sleep all a.m. Ride in p.m. Dine with other ushers before [Alice] Sohier dance. Supper D[orothy] Quincy & German M[inna] Lyman. Very good dance[.] Back at 5.30 a.m.

Thurs., Jan. 14 [1904]. To bed at 11 a.m. & sleep till 5 p.m.! Work on paper & meetings in evening.

Friday, Jan. 15 [1904]. To N. Y. on 1 o'clock w[ith] L[athrop] B[rown]. Find S[arah] D[elano] R[oosevelt] at apartment. E[leanor] comes to dine & go back at 10.30. I alone to the [Ogden?] Mills' dance[.] Very good time. Home at 4 a.m.

had dinner at the White House and afterwards the President sat rocking in the family sitting room and told them about Panama.

The trip was delightful – but if its purpose were to take Franklin's mind off Eleanor, it was a complete failure. Sara did not give up hope; at the capital she took Franklin to meet Joseph Choate, Ambassador to England, and tried to persuade Choate to take him to London as his secretary. Choate declined; he already had a secretary, and Franklin was too young. As it happened, Eleanor also was in Washington. While Sara visited Congress, and went to the Supreme Court to hear Justice J. M. Harlan deliver the Northern Securities decision, the first great victory for President Roosevelt's antitrust program, Franklin was spending almost all his time with Eleanor.[103]

Gracious in defeat – once defeat was obvious to her – Sara took Eleanor in as a beloved daughter. On the occasion of a house party that summer, she commented, "Always a pleasure to have the nieces and an added joy to have Eleanor now." [104] Taking literally Franklin's suggestion that she now had a daughter, she set out to absorb and dominate Eleanor as overwhelmingly as she had Franklin.

Commencement came almost as an anticlimax. Sara and Eleanor and several cousins attended. Franklin gave a tea for them, and the next day they watched him participate in the Class Day fun. When gifts were handed out, he received a policeman's uniform, and a few minutes later was called upon to arrest the baseball captain for stealing sundry bases.[105]

At the official ceremonies, Franklin sat on the platform in cap and gown as one of the class officers. Though Sara was inordinately proud of her son, she took his relative prominence for granted. "His father and I always expected a great deal of Franklin," she explained years later. "We thought he ought to take prizes, and we were pleased but not surprised when he did. After all he had many advantages that other boys did not have." [106]

After graduation Franklin went to Groton to participate in the gala celebration of the twentieth Prize Day, and it was there, rather than at the Harvard commencement, that he really listened and took note of the speaker's exhortation. President Theodore Roosevelt was the orator, and he summed up the attitude of Franklin's family when he told assembled students and alumni, "Much has been given you, therefore we have a right to expect much from you." [107]

Franklin D. Roosevelt was ready to accept that responsibility in full measure.

How well Harvard equipped him for the tasks this involved is not easy to say. Certainly there is little clear-cut proof that his courses gave a permanent mold to his thinking. For example, he particularly liked his classes in economics but subsequently had no difficulty in abandoning his classical training in the field. "I took economics courses in college for four years, and everything I was taught was wrong," he remarked in an extemporaneous speech in 1941. "The economics of the beginning of this century are completely out of date." [108] Again, his last semester, he signed up for a course on the history of the West under Frederick Jackson Turner, famous for his thesis that the frontier was the most significant factor in American history.[109] But an historian trying to trace back to this class Roosevelt's espousal of the "frontier safety valve" theory,* would have to reckon with the difficulty that during about the first six weeks of Turner's lectures, Roosevelt was in the Caribbean.

There is even less evidence that, although this was the age and locale of James, Roosevelt acquired any knowledge of pragmatism in the classroom. He registered for only a single philosophy course, one of Josiah Royce's, and "dropped that after three weeks." † Yet in later life he functioned with a realism and opportunism which many analysts have labeled "pragmatic." Whatever of this he acquired at Harvard came indirectly; it was the dominant spirit of the era and the place; it was in the air, and infectious. In this spirit, he occasionally expressed to his roommate, Lathrop Brown, his disgust because his courses did not bear more directly upon everyday realities. His program, he said, was "like an electric lamp that hasn't any wire. You need the lamp for light, but it's useless unless you can switch it on." [111]

And this was typical, for while Roosevelt learned much at Harvard,

* FDR declared September 23, 1932, "There is no safety valve in the form of a Western prairie to which those thrown out of work by the Eastern economic machines can go for a new start."

† In 1922 when as a member of the Board of Overseers of Harvard he was Chairman of the Committee on Philosophy and Psychology, FDR wryly commented, "Why I was ever made Chairman of this particular Committee an inscrutable Providence has not yet informed me."

When FDR in 1933 proposed putting unemployed young men to work in the national parks and forests, in a Civilian Conservation Corps, Raymond Moley remarked the similarity of the idea to that of William James in "The Moral Equivalent of War." Moley "asked F.D.R. whether he hadn't been influenced by the vague memory of his student days under James. He admitted there might be some connection, though he wasn't consciously aware of it. And then he went on, 'But look here! I think I'll go ahead with this – the way I did on beer.'" – meaning send the suggestion to Congress in a hurry.[110]

most of it seems to have come from his social and extracurricular activities, not his studies. The contrast between his Harvard career and Theodore Roosevelt's underscores this. Theodore was not yet twenty when he wrote *The Naval War of 1812;* at the same age Franklin was writing flamboyant editorials deploring lack of school spirit. By comparison, Franklin's intense preoccupation with the winning of class office and his incessant campaigning for better football teams seems juvenile. Certainly, Roosevelt's activities at Harvard were often of a sort scorned by serious students, but this was largely because it never occurred to him to be one of the scholars or to accept their standard of values. The pleasure gained from the sport of maneuvering and manipulation, and the status that came with political prize, held strongest appeal for him. Unwittingly, in these pursuits he took the first stride toward becoming an effective politician. If he did not, like Theodore, earn his Phi Beta Kappa key by academic endeavor, he did learn techniques that would one day raise him to such distinction that he could graciously accept an honorary one.

CHAPTER V

Beginnings

[The Democrats] have made a new and valuable discovery, Franklyn D. Roosevelt. . . . Mr. Roosevelt is a graduate of Harvard and this is his first jump into politics. Presumably his contribution to the campaign funds goes well above four figures – hence the value of his discovery. . . . Senator Schlosser, we imagine, will not be greatly disturbed by Mr. Roosevelt's candidacy.

—*Poughkeepsie* Eagle, *October 11, 1910.*

As Ellery Sedgwick shrewdly observed about his Harvard classmates who later became leaders, like transplanted trees or shrubs they outwardly stood dormant awhile. Though they put forth no fresh growth above the ground, their roots took hold and gripped the unfamiliar earth and thrust down new offshoots. Then, firmly settled, they shot up rapidly.[1]

The half decade after he graduated from Harvard was such a dormant phase for Roosevelt. During this time he demonstrated no particular promise of becoming anything more than a solidly successful lawyer, husband and parent, and a member of the New York social set. These were his quiet years during which he seemed to be finding himself – years that he climaxed with a sudden burst of political energy in the campaign of 1910. Careerwise, he spent them rather indifferently: the first three in law school, the next three serving a sort of apprenticeship as a law clerk. Personally they were momentous: he married and founded a family. And he climaxed them with his decision to go into politics.

In the fall of 1904, Roosevelt entered the Columbia University School of Law. The New York location meant that he could be near Eleanor Roosevelt until his marriage, and after it establish a home from which he would not have to move when he finished his course. His enthusiasm was more for the location than for the law school, although Columbia had one of the most distinguished law faculties in the country. Among the law school faculty and alumni, four were on the United States Supreme Court at one time; two became Chief Justices.[2] To some extent Franklin was already paralleling Theodore Roosevelt, who after Harvard entered Columbia Law School but found it dull. Certainly Franklin demonstrated no greater enthusiasm for his legal studies than for his Harvard classes, and he missed the exhilarating extracurricular activities. Eleanor predicted with remarkable insight, "He will not find himself altogether happy with the law he is studying at Columbia unless he is able to get a broad human contact through it." [3] This he did not seem to acquire. With the self-depreciation he had learned at Groton — and perhaps a grain of truth — he reported to Endicott Peabody at the end of November, "I am . . . trying to understand a little of the work and of course I am going to keep right on." [4]

His problem was more lack of interest than failure of understanding. He found little here that touched upon his growing absorption in human relationships. He was impatient with theory, and learned little he deemed practical about the everyday work of a lawyer.[5] Nor did he bother, at the one point possible, to tie in the program with his love of the sea; he did not elect the course in admiralty law. He had a strong liking for American history and government, but even in that field his law studies hardly inspired him, and understandably so.

Theodore Roosevelt during his single year at Columbia had flattered Professor John W. Burgess by his avid interest in the lectures on constitutional law (actually constitutional history). Franklin took the same course just before Burgess went on leave to fill the new Theodore Roosevelt Chair at the University of Berlin. He attended the course with fair regularity and kept a careful, clear set of notes. Burgess, an ardent nationalist, was one of the most famous teachers of his day, yet there was little or nothing in his lectures to stir or excite a would-be politician. For the first month, Burgess described colonial charters; by December he had reached the Constitutional Convention; thereafter, throughout the winter and spring, he embroidered upon such a detailed discussion of slavery that by the end of the course (or of Roosevelt's notes) in May, he was only up to the Fugitive Slave Act and the Dred Scott decision of the 1850's. If there were lectures on John Marshall's Supreme Court decisions, Roosevelt missed them. However well such disquisitions might prepare a future President to deal with problems of slavery, they did little to equip him to cope with the worst depression in American history.[6]

Nevertheless, this course probably interested Roosevelt more than any other that he took his first year. While he remained lukewarm towards the classroom, he failed to compensate by acquiring any close friends among his classmates, although several were destined to be leaders and distinguished lawyers. Notable among them was the football hero, "Wild Bill" Donovan, who became one of the most famous soldiers of the First World War, and head of the "cloak and dagger" Office of Strategic Services in the Second World War. A year ahead of Roosevelt was J. Reuben Clark, Ambassador to Mexico in the '20s. Two years behind was Stanley Reed, whom Roosevelt appointed to the Supreme Court in 1938. Reed, like Roosevelt, did not take his law degree.

While Roosevelt lacked real enthusiasm for his studies and classmates, he concentrated upon his courtship, marriage, and the diversions of New York society. All things considered, his academic record during the first year of law school could have been worse, and in the succeeding years he survived despite a fairly high mortality rate. His class numbered 106 at the beginning of the second year, and only 84 at the start of the third. During his first year he failed two courses but passed the others with "B." * He was a bit bewildered by this verdict: "It certainly shows the uncertainty of marks," he commented, "for I had expected much lower marks in some of the others and failures in one, and thought I had done as well on the two I failed as in those I passed with B." [9]

In the spring of his third year Roosevelt passed the New York Bar Examinations. Having achieved his main goal, he demonstrated his indifference towards law school by not bothering to complete his courses and so never received his LL.B. degree.[10] Biographical sketches frequently credited it to him anyway; in 1927 he returned the draft of

* Roosevelt failed "Contracts," taught by Professor Charles T. Terry, a brilliant exponent of the Socratic method, and "Pleading and Practice I," taught by Professor Henry S. Redfield. He sent at once for the texts, and in the fall took and passed make-up examinations.[7] His grades at the end of the second year were quite respectable:

Agency	C
Bailments	B
Equity Jurisprudence	B
Negotiable Paper	D
Pleading and Practice	C
Quasi-Contracts	B
Real and Personal Property	C+
Comparative Constitutional Law	P[?] [8]

one with the comment, "I wish you would change the LL.B. after my name to LL.D. of which I hold two!" [11] President Nicholas Murray Butler of Columbia once twitted Roosevelt on his failure to obtain the degree: "You will never be able to call yourself an intellectual until you come back to Columbia and pass your law exams." Roosevelt retorted with a laugh, "That just shows how unimportant the law really is." [12]

Roosevelt once declared, "You know you don't learn law at the best of our law schools. You learn how to think." [13] There is not much indication that he learned either at Columbia.

Although the law studies were dull, these years were nevertheless an exciting period for Roosevelt. In the fall of 1904, he purchased Eleanor's ring at Tiffany's "after much inspection & deliberation" [14] and they officially announced their engagement. This led to festivities and wedding preparations. There was the additional excitement of a presidential campaign in which Theodore Roosevelt was running against a conservative Democrat, Judge Alton B. Parker. Franklin cast his first ballot for President, and of course voted the Republican ticket. Theodore Roosevelt won by a landslide.*

The following March 4, Franklin and Eleanor were invited to Washington for the inaugural. They were very much part of the clan; they traveled down on the private car of cousin George Emlen Roosevelt, stayed with the President's sister, Mrs. W. Sheffield Cowles, and during the ceremonies sat on the Capitol steps just behind the President and his family. Later, after lunching at the White House, they watched the inaugural parade with proprietary satisfaction.[16]

This was only a preview of the greatest excitement for them. Less than two weeks later, on March 17, 1905, President Theodore Roosevelt came to New York to review the St. Patrick's Day parade and give away his niece in marriage. While it may have been libelous exaggeration to claim that Theodore Roosevelt wanted to be the bride at every wedding, he might as well have been the bride at this one. The date was set to meet his convenience, and over seventy-five policemen were assigned to guard the adjoining homes of Eleanor's cousin Susie Parish and Mrs. Parish's mother Mrs. E. Livingston Low, where the

* As President, FDR declared: "My father and grandfather were Democrats and I was born and brought up as a Democrat, but in 1904, when I cast my first vote for a President, I voted for the Republican candidate, Theodore Roosevelt, because I thought he was a better Democrat than the Democratic candidates . . . if I had to do it over again I would not alter that vote." [15]

wedding was to be held. The two houses – on East 76th Street between Fifth and Madison – had sliding doors separating them which could be thrown open to form a large area. Around these houses the police formed a cordon to try to keep crowds off the block. Although they delayed a few of the accredited guests until the ceremony was over, several hundred boys broke through and greeted the President's arrival with a deafening din.

As Theodore Roosevelt escorted the bride down a stairway from the second floor, one society reporter noted that she "was considerably taller than the head of the nation, suggesting to many present her beautiful mother. . . . She has much of that supple grace that characterized her." They reached the chancel of pink roses and palms where the Rector of Groton and his one-time pupil awaited them. Even there Uncle Theodore was not easily shoved out of the picture: When the Reverend Endicott Peabody asked "Who giveth this woman to be married to this man?" the President did not, as was customary, step forward to place the bride's hand in that of the groom, but remained in his place as he answered emphatically, "I do."[17]

After the ceremony was over, the President congratulated the bride and groom, and remarked that he was delighted they were keeping the Roosevelt name in the family.[18] Then he strode over into the library of the adjoining house where a collation was being served. Within a short time, Franklin and Eleanor Roosevelt found themselves deserted, and could do nothing but trail on after the crowd to listen to the stories of the "lion of the afternoon."[19]

The newlyweds spent their honeymoon week at Hyde Park and then returned to a small apartment in the Hotel Webster on West 45th Street, where they lived while Franklin finished the spring term at law school.[20] As soon as classes were over in June, they sailed on the *Oceanic* – alone – for a three months' grand tour of Europe. Franklin had already enjoyed the delightful experience of being "on his own" in Europe with a friend, but for Eleanor it was a new and ever delicious luxury to be able to come and go and do as she pleased. For both it was a halcyon summer, filled with memories of cathedrals and art galleries, moonlight gondola rides in Venice, magnificent vistas of the Alps, gay and delicious dinners at quaint restaurants and innumerable forays upon antique dealers, secondhand bookstores, and dress shops.*

* Franklin, who was planning to remodel the home at Hyde Park, quite seriously queried his mother as to whether she would like the interior of a Venetian Palazzo: "By the way the furniture and woodwork, also mosaic floors

They visited London, Paris, and the Rhineland as well as the Alps, and climaxed their journey with visits at magnificent estates in Scotland and England. Everywhere they saw only the quaint and picturesque, and although they often worried about prices, they lived luxuriously as they drifted dreamily through the picture postcard Europe of well-to-do tourists before the First World War.*

For Franklin it must have been more exhilarating than annoying to be identified often with Theodore Roosevelt. Though his social prestige had always been high, through his marriage to the President's niece it was now much higher; all doors were open to him, all deference shown him, though sometimes it cost him plenty. Brown's Hotel in London insisted upon ushering the young couple to the royal suite, "price $1,000 a day – a sitting room 40 ft. by 30 [ft.], a double bedroom, another ditto and a bath," Franklin facetiously informed his mother. "Our breath was so taken away that we couldn't even protest, and are now saying 'Damn the expense, Wot's the odds'!" [23] And a soothsayer in Paris, undoubtedly with more knowledge of American politics than clairvoyance predicted, Franklin reported, that he would "be President of the U. S. or the Equitable, I couldn't make out which!" [24] Near the close of the summer Franklin wrote, "Everyone is talking about Cousin Theodore saying that he is the most prominent figure of present day history, and adopting towards our country in general a most respectful and almost loving tone. What a change has come over English opinion in the last few years! Even the French were quite enthusiastic, but the German tone seemed to hide a certain animosity and jealousy as usual." [25]

Everywhere they found relatives or interesting people to add to their enjoyment, though at times the Roosevelts may not have been mature enough to take full advantage of their opportunities. While they were visiting their friends Robert and Isabella Selmes Ferguson at Novar in Scotland, the Fabian Socialists Sidney and Beatrice Webb came to lunch. "Franklin discussed the methods of learning at Harvard with the husband," wrote Eleanor, "while I discussed the servant problem with the wife!" [26]

---

of one of the old palaces can be got for about $60,000. If you care to have it cable me." [21]

* Already the world was turning rapidly. Eleanor Roosevelt commented after visiting the Lido at Venice, "I never saw anything like the bathing clothes the ladies wear. Their upper garment could not be called a skirt, it was hardly a frill! But Franklin says I must grow accustomed to it as France is worse!" [22]

Eleanor Roosevelt felt miserable upon the return voyage; she was normally susceptible to seasickness, but there was an added reason. Her first child was on its way. In the next ten years she had six children.* Even more than for Franklin, for Eleanor these were intellectually dormant years. She devoted herself almost entirely to her household.[27] Although she read extensively, she had few of the outside interests which so distinguished her in the 1920's and thereafter. During this stage, in which she became highly dependent upon her husband and mother-in-law, her intense desire to please them made her avoid controversial discussion and allow them to dominate her completely.[28]

She and Franklin divided financial responsibility. After he showed her how to set up account books, under his supervision she handled all household finances. Each contributed an equal share from personal income to provide six hundred dollars a month for running expenses – adequate in those years to maintain a house and servants in New York City, and a summer cottage next to Sara Roosevelt's on Campobello Island.[29]

Upon their return from Europe, they moved into a house at 125 East 36th Street, three blocks from Sara Roosevelt's home. Sara had already rented, redecorated and furnished it, and had even provided it with servants.[30] Franklin thriftily declined his mother's offer to equip the house with electricity rather than gas, on the grounds that they would live there only temporarily. They lived there two years while the elder Mrs. Roosevelt constructed two adjoining houses, one for herself and one for them, at 47 and 49 East 65th Street. Franklin discussed the project with his mother while it was underway, but throughout the procedure Eleanor sat back unconsulted. All was done for her and without her, down through details of furnishings, decorations and arrangements. A few weeks after the young couple moved in, her keen resentment broke through the self-imposed silence. She sat before the dressing table Sara had chosen for her and wept. "When my bewildered young husband asked me what on earth was the matter with me, I said I did not like to live in a house which was not in any way mine, one that I had done nothing about and which did not represent the way I wanted to live." [31]

This attitude baffled Franklin, but he did not let it bother him. Apparently he seldom pondered such matters. Once Eleanor tried to

* Anna Eleanor Roosevelt, born May 3, 1906; James, December 23, 1907; Franklin Delano, Jr., March 18, 1909 (died November 8, 1909); Elliott, September 23, 1910; Franklin Delano, Jr., August 17, 1914; John Aspinwall, March 13, 1916.

start a serious discussion of the religious training of their children: "He looked at me with his amused and quizzical smile, and said that he thought they had better go to church and learn what he had learned. It could do them no harm. Heatedly, I replied: 'But are you sure that you believe in everything you learned?' He answered, 'I really never thought about it. I think it is just as well not to think about things like that too much.' "[32]

Nor was Franklin particularly irritated over his mother's firm management, even when it occasionally conflicted with his own interests. Already interested in conservation and scientific farming, he proposed experimenting with the Hyde Park acres. Sara refused. They must continue to be used as James would have wished. So Franklin bought an adjoining plot of land and began his forestry experiments there.[33]

Franklin Roosevelt never discussed his marriage, but Eleanor has provided ample testimony that they did not talk over analytically what they expected of it and of each other. She expected much; so did Franklin, but he seemed to get what he wanted effortlessly, and apparently took for granted that now in addition to a doting mother, he should have a devoted wife and a growing number of adoring children. In return he gave his unquestioning affection, and until politics claimed him, much of his time. Yet that sensitivity of his which became razor-sharp in political affairs never seemed to extend to domestic matters.

For the first five years after he married, Roosevelt drifted toward the pattern of life of his father and friends. He enjoyed a pleasant but very limited coterie of the sort he had always known. Except for one summer at Seabright, New Jersey, he continued to vacation at Campobello and to spend much of his time there in golfing, hunting, fishing, and sailing on the *Half Moon*.

In keeping with his station in life, he assumed civic and community responsibilities. In 1909 he became a member of the Hudson-Fulton Celebration Commission, and supervised the setting up of Red Cross relief stations along the line of march of the parades.[34] At Hyde Park, where he often spent week ends, he became more and more engrossed in the local activities his father had carried on until his death. He joined the Eagle Engine Company and the Rescue Hook and Ladder Company of Hyde Park, and became a director of the First National Bank of Poughkeepsie.[35] He was initiated into a fraternal organization or two and elected vice-commodore of the Hudson River Ice Yacht Club.[36] Although there were Sundays when he went golfing while

Eleanor took the children to church, he served as vestryman of the St. James Episcopal Church.[37]

As his community activities flowed into channels set for him by his forebears, so did his career. In the fall of 1907 he began an apprenticeship which logically would have led him to develop into a corporation lawyer. He became a clerk in the distinguished and conservative firm of Carter, Ledyard, and Milburn, at 54 Wall Street, and announced the step with an exuberant handwritten mock-advertisement:

FRANKLIN D. ROOSEVELT

COUNSELLOR AT LAW
54 WALL STREET
NEW YORK

I beg to call your attention to my unexcelled facilities for carrying on every description of legal business. Unpaid bills a specialty. Briefs on the liquor question furnished free to ladies. Race suicides cheerfully prosecuted. Small dogs chloroformed without charge. Babies raised under advice of expert grandmother etc., etc.[38]

His arrangement with the firm was typical – no salary the first year; thereafter a salary, at the outset necessarily small.[39] His pleasure in thus getting his foothold in the law world must have been considerable, but it was an ironic start for him. No firm stood more adamantly athwart Theodore Roosevelt's assault on trusts, which was in full tilt during the fall of 1907. The partners were defense counsel in several of the most spectacular antitrust cases. John G. Milburn * was counsel for Standard Oil of New Jersey in the suit which resulted in its dissolution in 1911, and Lewis Cass Ledyard similarly served the American Tobacco Company. Both admirably served their clients by arranging to dissolve the corporations in a manner singularly painless to their interests, and with little increase in real competition or decrease in the prices consumers paid. Although Franklin idolized Theodore Roosevelt, none of this seemed to trouble him. Indeed, some time after his graduation from Harvard he sketched the opening of a novel in which a wealthy self-made Chicago businessman, presumably a sort of Silas Lapham, was to be the hero.

There was a slight nautical air to the firm that appealed to Roosevelt. Ledyard had succeeded his friend the elder J. P. Morgan as

* Milburn had been a clerk in Grover Cleveland's law office. It was in his home in Buffalo that President William McKinley died.

commodore of the New York Yacht Club. The firm had an expert on admiralty law, Edmund L. Baylies, and it was he who hired Roosevelt. In retrospect, Roosevelt regarded him as "my very dear friend and Counselor." He declared, "Of all the people in the office in 1907 I felt that I could go to Mr. Baylies with my troubles and that he had a genuinely, fatherly eye over me."[40] Baylies was president of the Seamen's Church Institute, for which he raised $1,250,000, and a member of the ultra-exclusive Knickerbocker Club. Roosevelt drifted into his orbit by becoming a director of the Institute, a member of both the New York Yacht Club and the Knickerbocker Club.

The contrast between the theoretical world of the classroom and the practical life in a law office was sharp, and Roosevelt many years later was critical of his law school training for not having better prepared him for the change:

> I went to a big law office in New York, and somebody the day after I got there said, "Go up and answer the calendar call in the Supreme Court tomorrow morning. We have such and such a case on."
>
> I had never been in a court of law in my life . . .
>
> Then the next day somebody gave me a deed of transfer of some land. He said, "Take it up to the County Clerk's office." I had never been in a county clerk's office. And there I was, theoretically a full-fledged lawyer.[41]

Highly adaptable, Roosevelt learned rapidly, but his three years with Carter, Ledyard and Milburn did not make him a defender of corporate power against the progressive onslaught. They did not even make him much of an expert on admiralty law. What the experience did prepare him for, more than anything else, was the give and take of shirt-sleeve politics. In addition to its major cases, the firm handled much minor litigation before the municipal courts, and Roosevelt was made managing clerk in charge of municipal cases. Time and again he went down to the courts to defend the American Express Company or another of his clients from some petty claim against them. Usually the atmosphere was less than genteel; sometimes the claimant's lawyer, working for a percentage, was less than scrupulous. For the first time Roosevelt came into continual direct contact with those who were neither of his own class nor servants of his class. And he liked it.

In one case he faced a Columbia Law School classmate, a man who had worked his way through law school and still lived in poverty. His opponent's client, a poor woman, was pressing a claim against a corporation without much evidence to support a high valuation of the loss. The lawyer, desperate for money (he had taken the case on a fifty-fifty basis), tried to get Roosevelt to settle for three hundred dollars, then a hundred and fifty. The actual damage was eighteen dollars. Roosevelt visited the lawyer's rooms on Hester Street to try to arrange a settlement. He was not there, but his mother blurted out the true facts of the case – and the poverty was obvious. Roosevelt scribbled out an offer to settle for thirty-five dollars, and left a personal check covering a loan of a hundred and fifty dollars.[42]

This work involved matching wits with opponents, an exercise Roosevelt heartily enjoyed. In addition to the small-claims business, he kept careful, clear and systematic entries in the logs of cases, and handled a certain amount of business for relatives.[43] But it was the human contacts he liked best, and it was to this aspect of his beginning career that he referred later. He advised boys preparing to become lawyers to gain social service experience. "That will help you in your court practice later on," he suggested. With some exaggeration he added, "When I was at Harvard, I got a social service job in Boston one summer. I learned enough about the poorer classes, the people who are having a desperately hard time making a living, so that I knew their language and their way of thinking. Later, that helped me a lot in my first law job when I was working for a firm of New York City lawyers and had to appear in two-by-four cases in the municipal courts." [44]

Understanding how the common man thought and talked helped even more when one entered politics.

Although the lively give-and-take of the municipal court held Roosevelt's interest, there was no future in it. There was a real future in the handling of the sort of corporate litigation which Roosevelt recorded in the firm's ledgers, but there was little excitement in it. During at least part of his term on Wall Street, Roosevelt must have succumbed to boredom. One story relates that as he was fidgeting aimlessly around the clerks' room one day, Ledyard came out and asked him for some specific information. Always anxious to please, Roosevelt replied dreamily, "Yes, yes," which as it happened was not at all an appropriate answer. Ledyard barked at him that he must be drunk and walked off in considerable irritation.[45]

Sometime during these years Roosevelt made his decision. He would build upon his municipal court work, not through going on to handle bigger and duller cases before higher courts, but by going into politics.

It was a decision only a few young men in his circumstances would have taken. He could have moved on into a life of ease and security almost effortlessly. He was no legal scholar, but his numerous high-placed business acquaintances and classmates would have sent many cases his way, and his personality would have guaranteed him success before the bar. Besides, this kind of life would have given him ample leisure for his other favored roles – Hudson River gentleman, yachtsman, philatelist, and naval historian. Like his Harvard classwork, he could have undertaken it with a minimum of effort while he devoted his strenuousness to activities beyond his career.

But the hobbies and social life – the adult counterpart of his college pursuits – were not enough. He enjoyed them, but he was not content with them. His father, in an age when the building of corporate empire had offered great prestige as well as substantial reward, had tried to become a master of capital, but had achieved greater success as a country squire. His elder brother, coming a generation later, like most of the moneyed gentry of his time, devoted himself almost entirely to being a sportsman. Franklin, in point of time a member of still another generation, had come of age in an era when neither business nor social triumphs longer carried such acclaim. The new age acclaimed success in building overseas empire, or in achieving humanitarian or political reform, and Roosevelt was swept along by the age. His income was adequate, so that he had little interest in making additional money, especially if the means of making it were dull. Once – at Harvard – he had sought social standing as a primary goal, but now he had achieved the ultimate in marrying President Roosevelt's niece. In these fields no real conquests could lie ahead, no means of achieving wide approbation, and yet he still was driven by a keen sense of competitiveness and restless ambition. His standards were those set for him by Peabody, and he chose the road the Rector indicated. He set off on the rugged mountain trail of the Roughrider, and left to brief holiday moments the pleasant country lane of the squire.

Beyond question the example of Theodore Roosevelt influenced Franklin in his decision to enter politics. On several occasions the young Roosevelts visited their Uncle Ted in Washington or at Oyster Bay. As early as New Year's Day, 1903, Franklin had written in his diary, "Dinner at White House & have talk with President." When Alice Roosevelt married Nicholas Longworth, Franklin went to the wedding.[46] On these occasions, he listened carefully to the advice of the President, who continued to stress his favorite theme – that young men of good background and education owed their country public service.[47] *

The greatest opportunities for service and status were at the top, and at least jokingly, Franklin Roosevelt aimed there. One of his fellow law clerks, Grenville Clark, remembered later a conversation that had taken place one day at the law office when the young clerks were sitting around at their desks in the large room they occupied together, discussing that favorite theme, their ambitions. When Roosevelt spoke up, recalled Clark, "I remember him saying with engaging frankness that he wasn't going to practise law forever, that he intended to run for office at the first opportunity, and that he wanted to be and thought he had a very real chance to be President.

"I remember that he described very accurately the steps which he thought could lead to this goal. They were: first, a seat in the State Assembly, then an appointment as Assistant Secretary of the Navy (an office held by Theodore Roosevelt early in his career), and finally the governorship of New York. 'Anyone who is governor of New York has a good chance to be President with any luck' are about his words that stick in my memory. . . . I do not recall that even then, in 1907, any of us deprecated his ambition or even smiled at it as we might perhaps have done. It seemed proper and sincere; and moreover, as he put it, entirely reasonable."[49]

If Roosevelt daydreamed aloud, so did countless other young law clerks. Only in the light of his subsequent career did Roosevelt's musings come to look less like smoke rings and more like a blueprint.†

The first step was simple enough. For a wealthy young man to enter

* FDR had a favorite anecdote about Theodore Roosevelt which he told countless times:

> Once upon a time when I was in the White House (as a visitor) T. R. was walking up and down the room in front of the fireplace one evening, thoroughly excited because some national reclamation measure of his had failed in Congress. He was heard to exclaim, "Oh, if I could only be President and Congress too for just ten minutes!" I remarked that I had heard him express that wish before and asked him what he would do. He replied, "I would pass an amendment to the Constitution requiring every candidate for the House or the Senate to file an affidavit that he had travelled in every state of the Union and had visited foreign countries at least once."[48]

† Another of his fellow clerks, Edwin De T. Bechtel, wrote him upon his election to the Presidency: "It thrills me to realize that your decision in 1910 as you sat at your old roll-top desk at 54 Wall Street and the political principles which you chose then and have always followed should have led to such a very marvelous goal."[50]

politics was by no means difficult, and the Democrats gave him an opportunity to do so in 1910. Despite his admiration for Theodore Roosevelt, he considered himself a Democrat, since his father had been one. No one was particularly surprised that the politicians offered him a nomination, for well-to-do gentlemen of the Hudson River Valley occasionally carried the Democratic banner in hopeless assaults on the rural Republican bastions. Only an occasional Democratic enclave like Poughkeepsie dotted the Republican hinterland of New York State. A few of the guardians of these strong points were progressive-minded, and restless in their vassalage to the Tammany machine of New York City. Most of them, a sort of modern political *condottieri*, were shrewd and not too ambitious for their own good. They made obeisance to the boss of Tammany, Charles Murphy; kept a firm grip on their bailiwicks; and in election years made cynical use of gentleman politicians for halfhearted sorties. Occasionally these gentlemanly amateurs appealed to enough independents to win; always they bore enough of the expenses so that limited party funds were not wasted in lost causes.

The finest knight in this political aristocracy, standard-bearer for a family equally well known to the readers of the society pages and the lurid Sunday supplements, was Lewis Stuyvesant Chanler. Chanler rose to the lieutenant-governorship in 1906, was Democratic candidate for governor in 1908, and after his defeat by Charles Evans Hughes contented himself with a seat in the state assembly.[51]

Early in 1910, the Democratic district attorney of Dutchess County, John E. Mack, took some papers to New York City for Roosevelt to sign. The talk turned to Dutchess County politics and Mack, expressing fears that Chanler was getting tired and might drop out, asked Roosevelt if he would be interested in entering the local lists on Democracy's side. Roosevelt was.[52] Subsequently he came to Poughkeepsie, and the Democrats took him to a picnic so that the party workers could size him up. "On that joyous occasion of clams and sauerkraut and real beer I made my first speech," Roosevelt once recalled jokingly, "and I have been apologizing for it ever since."[53] He made a pleasing impression upon all of the leaders except the county chairman, Edward E. Perkins, who was a loyal ally of Tammany. Perkins developed a strong and lasting antipathy, but although he preferred another candidate, granted that the committee should be able to pry Roosevelt loose from a serviceable wad of money.[54] Roosevelt commented in retrospect, "I guess several people thought that I would be a gold mine, but, unfortunately, the gold was not there."[55] However, Roosevelt, his mother, and friends did contribute over $2500 to the campaign.[56]

In their bargaining for campaign cash and the Roosevelt name, the lure the politicos held out was the possibility that Chanler might be willing to relinquish his seat in the assembly, in which case a considerable block of Poughkeepsie votes would assure it to the Democrats. Despite the confidence with which he had sketched his plans to the law clerks, Roosevelt hesitated before he took the plunge into politics. The party leaders told him it would add to his prestige and further rather than hinder his law career. Others expressed opposing sentiments. Ledyard was disturbed that a promising lawyer would allow himself to be sidetracked into the state legislature; Sara Delano Roosevelt* was not pleased at first.[58] Aside from these objections Franklin apparently felt a little nervous about running in the party opposite to that of Uncle Ted, who at the moment was deeply involved in New York State. If Theodore Roosevelt were to make one campaign wisecrack in Dutchess County about his kinsman, he could easily abort Franklin's career.

There is a charming but apocryphal tale that Franklin called up at Oyster Bay to announce his entry into politics. Theodore was delighted. Franklin added that he was running on the Democratic ticket – immediately Theodore sizzled the wire with his rage.[59] What actually happened was that in midsummer Franklin cautiously sounded out his powerful relative through Auntie Bye Cowles; Theodore Roosevelt replied to his sister, "Franklin ought to go into politics without the least regard as to where I speak or don't speak." He added that at that time he had no intention of speaking in Dutchess County, but of course could not tell about the future.† "He is a fine fellow," Theodore granted, but he wished Franklin had Republican views.[61]

In spite of misgivings, Franklin D. Roosevelt decided to run. He

* Sara Delano Roosevelt reminisced years later: "I was one of the few sympathizers Franklin had among his own people. Many of our friends said it was a shame for so fine a young man to associate himself with 'dirty' politicians. Some of them hoped he would be defeated and for his own sake learn his lesson. But by this time I knew Franklin's ideas and ideals in going into politics. I knew not only that I would always be proud of him, but I predicted the time when their ideas, too, would change."[57]

† On September 29, Theodore Roosevelt did speak in the county, before 40,000 people at the fair, and did Franklin the favor of not mentioning him.[60]

Photo by Pach, New York City

Eleanor Roosevelt in her wedding dress, in New York, March 17, 1905

Eleanor Roosevelt on her honeymoon, in Venice: "The last day" – FDR. Photo taken by FDR, July 7, 1905

took Chanler to lunch and tried to persuade him to abandon the assembly and run for the state senate. Chanler refused, since it was an almost hopeless task to run for the senate. Only one Democratic senator had been chosen from the district – which comprised the agricultural counties of Columbia, Dutchess, and Putnam – since the emergence of the Republicans as a national party in 1856.

Consequently the choice was between running for state senator – a better prize than assemblyman, but apparently unobtainable – and not running at all. By this time Roosevelt was so enthusiastic that although Mack told him he had no better than one chance in five of winning, he decided to make a try for it. Apparently it offered him little opportunity except to gain campaign experience, and to obtain a lien upon the party that he might later cash in for an assembly seat. Theodore Roosevelt once participated in a similarly futile race for mayor of New York.

As it turned out, this candidacy in rural New York was not nearly as unpromising as it appeared. It was not a lost cause at all. Probably the most important reason for this was something over which Roosevelt had no control whatever, the unusual circumstance of a rapidly widening rift in the Republican party all over the nation. This was sheer luck – the Roosevelt luck. Again and again in his political career, Roosevelt was blessed with phenomenal good fortune, so much so that one critic described him as no more than a pleasant person who won repeatedly by blind chance until finally he took the presidential sweepstakes. What invalidates this theory is the overwhelming evidence that he anticipated his luck with careful groundwork, and, when fortuitous opportunity came his way, capitalized upon it to the utmost.

It was significant that voters were restless in 1910, ready to jump party lines, and that Roosevelt was a magic name, but it is equally important that Franklin Roosevelt made the fullest possible use of both factors. His success was far more than chance. One way of gauging how much he added to the name and the luck is to compare his career with that of another amiable young man, also a bearer of the name, and likewise possessed of strong political ambitions, who in addition had the backing of the nationally dominant party. Theodore Roosevelt, Jr., who seemed to have every opportunity to become his father's successor, became Assistant Secretary of the Navy, and in the 1920's when the Republicans rode high, was their candidate for governor of New York. He did not win and little more was heard of him politically. He also had luck, but unlike Franklin did not succeed in cashing in on it.

In 1910, farmers and middle-class progressives within the Republican party were becoming more and more discontented with President William Howard Taft and the Old Guard. These, they felt, had wrecked Theodore Roosevelt's policies. A small group of Republican Insurgents in Congress, mainly from the farm belt of the Middle West, whittled down the near-dictatorial powers of Speaker Cannon, protested against the apparently anticonservationist policies of Taft and his Secretary of the Interior, and aroused the country against the Payne-Aldrich tariff. Republican farmers even in the East were angered over the tariff, which they felt kept high the prices of what they bought, and allowed prices of what they sold to drop low. Nowhere did the conflict between the two wings of the Republican party develop more spectacularly than in New York State, where Theodore Roosevelt, already straining for a comeback, clashed violently with the Republican boss, William Barnes, Jr. T.R. bested the Old Guard and dictated the nomination of Henry L. Stimson for governor; Barnes and his forces retaliated by stepping aside and doing little to prevent the election of a conservative Democrat, John A. Dix.[62]

From the perspective of Poughkeepsie in the summer of 1910, John E. Mack's pessimism seemed justified. It was hardly likely that rural voters would take much interest in this young man with his Wall Street business address, Groton accent, and upper-class garb. According to one story, he walked into a political conference three days before his nomination wearing riding boots and breeches. Perkins told him he would have to go home and put on some regular pants.[63] Several months after that Roosevelt created quite a stir by coming to a Tammany ball wearing cuff links, which were just coming into fashion.[64] This patrician appearance, combined with his background of wealth and position, laid Roosevelt open to the charge of being undemocratic, an accusation that his opponents in the Hudson River Valley used against him repeatedly. He always resented it keenly.*

* On September 12, 1928, FDR wrote out longhand a remarkable letter which he hoped "some fairly leading Republican" would sign and send to the press:

To the Editor, Eagle News, *Poughkeepsie, N. Y.*

Sir:

May I as a Republican express through your columns my protest against the manner and tone of several of your recent editorials on one of our Dutchess County neighbors, Mr. Franklin Roosevelt of Hyde Park. Many other Republicans have told me that while they may not agree with Mr.

On October 6, the Democratic leaders at a convention in Poughkeepsie formally nominated Roosevelt for state senator. He replied with a short, stereotyped speech which set the keynote for his campaign: "As you know, I accept this nomination with absolute independence. I am pledged to no man; I am influenced by no special interests, and so I shall remain." He added prophetically, "In the coming campaign, I need not tell you that I do not intend to sit still. We are going to have a very strenuous month." [66] At first no one took Roosevelt's candidacy at all seriously. The Republican papers predicted that the incumbent "will not be greatly disturbed"; the Democrats paid him polite, meaningless compliments, and even a Democratic editor admitted, "Mr. Roosevelt . . . is more of a stranger than either of the other nominees." [67]

Then things began to happen. With Theodore Roosevelt benevolently unconcerned about this minor candidacy in three upstate counties, Franklin began to campaign as Theodore would have done – "strenuously." He paid little attention to the safe Democratic majority in Poughkeepsie, and turned his abounding energies upon the farmers. He broke precedent spectacularly by hiring a red Maxwell touring car, decking it out with flags, and setting out with the perennial congressional candidate, Richard Connell, to tour every corner of the district. Calamity howlers predicted that they would frighten farmers' horses and thus lose more votes than they could possibly gain. But the car was a strategic asset as well as a gaudy advertisement in which they could roll along at about twenty-two miles an hour. Without it they could not possibly have covered the area in four weeks. Roosevelt remembered, "When we met a horse or a team – and that was about every half mile or so – we had to stop, not only the car, but the engine as well." [68] They made an asset of this by exchanging po-

---

Roosevelt's expressed views they resent what appears to be on your part a definite attack both on his good faith and his personality. . . .

Neither can I in the least understand any reference by you to 'high talk' or 'condescension' or 'indirection in political argument' on the part of Mr. Roosevelt. His many friends in both parties in the County have always thought him far more free than most people from any of these qualities. What he says is always simple and to the point, and he is the last person in the world to be called condescending. He is less like a snob than any one I know.

This kind of editorial attack is not only unjustified and unfair, but is not useful from the point of view of politics as it is resented by lots of Republicans.[65]

The *Eagle News* did not publish the letter.

litical banter with each teamster as he passed. They also talked to farmers husking corn, sitting around country stores, or lounging at crossroads, and even engaged in one of Connell's long-standing specialties, the passing out of campaign literature to school children who presumably might take it home to their parents. (Besides, Connell claimed that ultimately the children would grow up and vote for him.) After one of these forays upon school children, they discovered that they had unwittingly campaigned in Connecticut, which Roosevelt thought was a wonderful joke.[69]

Before the end of the campaign, Eleanor Roosevelt went to hear him make one of his speeches. She had not heard him give a political talk before, and was rather alarmed by his long pauses,[70] but the farmers did not seem to mind. "I know I am no orator but . . ." Roosevelt interjected one time, as he launched an attack upon corruptionists. "You don't have to be an orator, Roosevelt," someone in the audience yelled back. "Talk right along to us on those lines – that's what we like to hear."[71]

Talk he did, identifying himself with the popular Insurgents in Washington (although they were insurgent Republicans) and denouncing the state and local bosses, both Republican and Democratic. He played upon the rural-urban conflict – the farmer's suspicion of the city machine – and constantly hammered upon the good government which Democratic Mayor John K. Sague, a banker, had given Poughkeepsie, and District Attorney Mack, the county. Mack was a good one to tie to – he had become especially popular with the farmers through stopping an epidemic of pilfering and chicken stealing. "You can't tell the people that [Tammany Boss] Murphy controls the Democratic party here," Roosevelt emphasized, "or has any influence whatever with any of these men who have made these local reforms possible." Someone shouted, "That's common sense."[72]

On the other hand, Roosevelt maintained, the Republicans in power both nationally and locally, were failing to carry out the mandate of the people who had elected them. That was popular doctrine with the farmers, and time and again groups of them listened appreciatively while Roosevelt lambasted one of Theodore Roosevelt's most notable enemies in the state, Boss Barnes's lieutenant Lou Payne, of Chatham. It was Payne who when accused of "voting tombstones" replied that he only cast the ballots of the deceased as they would have voted if alive.[73] Payne and his henchmen had thwarted the Republican governor, Charles Evans Hughes; Roosevelt charged that his opponent,

State Senator John F. Schlosser, had aided them in blocking Hughes's reform measures. Someone asked Roosevelt if he, then, supported Hughes's policies. "You bet I do," Roosevelt retorted. "I think he's one of the best governors the State has ever had." The questioner shouted back, "That's what I'm glad to hear. I'm going [to] vote for you." [74]

In one attack upon his opponent Schlosser, Roosevelt foreshadowed his future rhetorical trademarks: "Whether it is that he has represented the Sage of Chatham by long distance 'phone, or whether it is that he has represented nobody at all except himself I don't know. But I do know that he hasn't represented me and I do know that he hasn't represented you." Roosevelt promised that, if elected, he would represent them personally, indeed that he would tour the district twice a year to consult their wishes.

The campaign rapidly turned into a popular battle against the senatorial henchman of Theodore Roosevelt's enemy, and that was sound sales appeal. Although the farmers would have to commit the heresy of voting the Democratic ticket if they cast their ballots for this Roosevelt, they could take comfort in the feeling that they were striking a blow for Teddy. Franklin seldom let them overlook the relationship, both blood and ideological. He frequently used the word "bully," then in wide usage but particularly identified with Theodore, and at times was even more direct. After being introduced at one meeting, he grinned and said, "I'm not Teddy." The audience laughed. He added, "A little shaver said to me the other day that he knew I wasn't Teddy – I asked him 'why' and he replied: 'Because you don't show your teeth.' " [75]

There was more truth to that statement than Franklin Roosevelt had meant to convey. During the campaign he was unfailingly vigorous, good-humored, and ingratiating. He aligned himself against absentee bossism; but he said little or nothing specific on any policy. "I am running," he would assert, "squarely on the issue of honesty & economy & efficiency in our State Senate, and I am on the right side of that issue." [76]

It was an effective campaign, which succeeded in winning over a number of Republican voters. One utilities man who had been president of the Village of Chatham for three successive terms, and a Republican for forty years, worked for Roosevelt in order to fight Payne.[77] The weather was favorable too. During the last days, rain fell in sheets, driving the farmers indoors so that, having no work to do, they came in considerable numbers to Democratic meetings.[78]

Republicans took note of these developments and became somewhat alarmed. Congressman Hamilton Fish * charged that Roosevelt was not a resident and was unknown in the district; Roosevelt supporters retorted that not only was he a bona fide resident, but that fully two thirds of the men he met on his campaign trips remembered his father. And, too late to be effective because of Roosevelt's emphatic stand in the campaign, the Republicans tried to tie him to Wall Street. Their accusations were logical enough at the time, but amusing in the light of his subsequent career:

> Franklyn D. Roosevelt represents just the opposite of what Theodore Roosevelt stands for. The News-Press reports him as managing clerk of the firm of Carter, Ledyard & Milburn of 54 Wall Street, New York City. It is well for the electors of this Senatorial District to bear in mind that this firm are the lawyers for some of the great trusts which are being prosecuted by President Taft's administration, such as the Standard Oil Co., and the Sugar Trust.[79]

On the eve of the election, Roosevelt spoke in Hyde Park. He had already acquired the trait of greeting his audience as "my friends." He reminded them, "You have known what my father stood for before me, you have known how close he was to the life of this town, and I do not need to tell you that it is my desire always to follow in his footsteps." [80]

The election day was rainy, and numbers of the farmers who habitually voted the Republican ticket stayed away from the polls. In Dutchess County alone there was a slump of 2300 in the total vote. Throughout the country there was, as the Poughkeepsie *Eagle* sadly proclaimed, a "Democratic avalanche," which gave to the party control of the House of Representatives, and governorships in a number of normally Republican states, including New Jersey, where the president of Princeton University, Woodrow Wilson, won election. The Dutchess County Democrats rode in on the avalanche. Roosevelt defeated Schlosser by a vote of 15,708 to 14,568, a plurality of 1140, while John A. Dix, the Democratic candidate for governor, carried the district by only 663 votes. In Dutchess County, both in the rural areas and Poughkeepsie, he ran well ahead of the Democratic ticket,

* This was the father of Roosevelt's sharp critic during the New Deal.

even in districts which he lost. He carried Hyde Park overwhelmingly, 406 to 258, while Dix squeaked by, 345 to 323.[81]

Where did he stand – this strenuous neophyte Roosevelt who did not show his teeth? Had observers been interested, they could have learned little about his political principles on the basis of his background and his campaign. In general he regarded himself as a progressive, but failed to demonstrate that he had very much idea of what a progressive really was. He was ready instantly to take issue against slurs upon Theodore Roosevelt's program when he overheard them at a tea dance,[82] but except for conservation, he probably did not understand much about the specific policies involved. He favored humanitarian welfare measures; one of his interests in New York City was a movement to obtain cheap, pure milk for children in the slums. He was at least aware that there was a labor movement, for his work to establish milk stations brought him into association with Samuel Gompers, the president of the American Federation of Labor.[83] In general he was "against trusts" for the simple pragmatic reason that it was good politics to be against trusts; nevertheless the builders and sustainers of the large corporations were his friends in Albany. After he went into the state senate, one of them wrote facetiously, "If a word of praise from the 'ticker crowd' will not hurt your political aspirations, I want to send you my heartiest congratulations." [84] Roosevelt replied: "All Wall Street is not bad, as a residence there of four years has shown me." [85]

Roosevelt's 1910 campaign was built around clean government and antibossism, the program of liberals within both parties a generation before. In New York this platform had elected Samuel J. Tilden and Grover Cleveland; it had been the ideal of his businessman father. Roosevelt had endorsed in general the more modern reform program of the Republican governor, Charles Evans Hughes, and specifically those proposals, such as the direct primary, aimed at cracking the power of the machine. Otherwise he stood for almost no specific proposals, not even, as legend has it, uniform apple barrels. That too came later.* If he had any strong feelings on Theodore Roosevelt's controversial

* In the 1912 campaign, Roosevelt's friend and colleague, Assemblyman Saunders of Columbia County, devised an apple barrel plank for the platform, which Louis Howe accepted as part of FDR's program. Many old-timers ascribed this to 1910, and gave it a significance far beyond its actual worth. FDR commented in a memorandum to Earl Looker about 1932, "not even mentioned in the 1910 campaign." [86]

proposals for government regulation of big business, he did not expound them to voters or reporters. These deficiencies were of no consequence but the adroitness he had demonstrated in the campaign was of real significance. In the months that followed he formulated a rather complete pattern of progressive thought, and intellectually as well as politically advanced at a remarkable pace. Roosevelt had reached the end of a period of relative dormancy.

CHAPTER VI

Roosevelt or the Tiger?

> Theodore Roosevelt, as a young man, merely took advantage of all opportunities to keep himself in the public eye, and to strengthen the impression that he was a fighter. A known fighter is always well on the road to being taken for a popular hero. Franklin D. Roosevelt is beginning his public career fully as auspiciously. . . . If none of the colonel's sons turn out to be fit objects for popular adoration may it not be possible that this rising star may continue the Roosevelt dynasty?
>
> —*Cleveland* Plain-Dealer, *January 23, 1911.*

HUNDREDS of Americans have unexpectedly won office through freakish turns of the ballot. Even a street cleaner was once accidentally elected to Congress. To gain election in some such fashion is common enough, but thereafter to earn favorable public notice and re-election is more unusual. Those Democrats elected to the New York State legislature in 1910 from traditionally Republican districts were almost certain to lose their seats as soon as the political climate returned to normal. Roosevelt could hardly expect to fare much better than the others. He would have a slight advantage at the start, since his name would lead to a flurry of initial publicity. He could be sure that newspapermen, always in search of lively material amid the dullness of Albany, would turn out feature articles comparing him to young Assemblyman Theodore Roosevelt of the 1880's. And so they did. But that was likely to be the end of it, since state legislators, even with districts solidly behind them and long seniority, were comparatively humble and inconspicuous minnows in the political pond. "A new senator at Albany," Louis Howe once wrote sardonically, "is of an importance somewhere between that of a janitor and a committee clerk."[1]

If Roosevelt wished to go further in politics, he must make a far more spectacular reputation in two years than the average secure state legislator ever achieved in two decades. The prospect of serving only one term freed him from normal home controls (since for him to behave circumspectly would be no guarantee of re-election). On the other hand, it gave him only a short time in which to carve his initials on the State of New York. He would not have been Roosevelt if he had not accepted the challenge.

At Albany he was welcomed by a ready-made circle of staid acquaintances, his father's old political friends from among the Cleveland Democrats. The two most important of these were Colonel William Gorham Rice, who had been secretary to Governor Cleveland, and the new governor, John A. Dix, a dull, unimaginative, and eminently respectable manufacturer. Had Roosevelt followed his father's example, he would have remained close to Dix, but he immediately strayed far from genteel moderation in politics in order to do battle like Theodore Roosevelt or Peabody of Groton * as a modern knight pledged to holy combat against the loathsome Tammany monster. Into this cause, the young aristocrat, well armored with self-righteousness, threw himself full tilt. What distinguished him from many other knights-errant before and since was that as he fought he learned, and learned with remarkable rapidity. His model was St. George, not Don Quixote.

Roosevelt arrived at Albany with his family in January, 1911. His first step was to rent a large three-story house at 248 State Street for four months at $400 per month; it "seems palatial after New York," he noted, "and it is a comfort to have only three stories instead of six." [3] This house proved a substantial asset – an immediate reflection of Roosevelt's ample funds. Unlike most of the members of the legislature he would not have to commute from his home to the sessions, and moreover, could use this spacious dwelling as headquarters for his political allies.

The most important business of the Democratic majority in the legislature would be to elect a successor to United States Senator Chauncey M. Depew, for New York had lagged behind more progressive states

* Sherrard Billings, his Groton mentor, congratulated him at the height of his struggle, "You are making a good fight, are setting the right sort of example for our boys to follow, and incidentally are having, I suspect, a first rate time." Roosevelt replied that he was "certainly having a very strenuous time." Although he had been in politics less than six months, he went on to comment, "As you probably know I have always felt that enough Groton boys did not take an interest in public affairs; in fact when one goes over the list of graduates it is surprising to me how very few of them have gone into it. This applies almost equally well to college men as a whole but it is the kind of help that we need in just such a situation as this." [2]

and did not yet have direct election of Senators. Indeed, before the election, the Democrats were not pledged to any candidate; seemingly the Democratic legislators at Albany had an open choice. Already Roosevelt was warily eyeing Tammany Boss Murphy's candidate, the traction and utilities magnate, William F. ("Blue-eyed Billy") Sheehan.

In the 1880's, Sheehan as a Buffalo politician was most notorious for his unsavory tactics and strong opposition to the emergent Grover Cleveland.[4] Later, he went to New York, and in time acquired a fortune and greater respectability. Like many men of wealth he aspired to a seat in the Senate – it was still occasionally called a "Millionaire's Club." In the fall of 1910, when the Republican bosses began to sabotage the progressives in their own party, and the upstate farmers to grumble against Taft and the Old Guard, Sheehan saw an upset in the making and shrewdly acquired a lien on the Democrats. He deftly distributed large sums of money in doubtful districts and even gave considerable support to Dix's campaign. While he provided no financial assistance to Roosevelt, he did offer to send the New York *World* through election day to any list of Republican or doubtful voters that Roosevelt might submit.[5]

Until after the election, few people seemed to realize that a Democratic victory carried with it the choice of a Senator. Various candidates then put their names forward, among them Edward M. Shepard of Brooklyn, counsel for the Pennsylvania Railroad, but long an advocate of clean government in New York City. His candidacy precipitated a struggle with Sheehan that was reminiscent of the battles within the New York Democratic party of the Cleveland era. Many of Cleveland's old adherents aligned themselves with Shepard against Sheehan; and heredity as well as inclination caused Roosevelt to join them.

By the time the legislature began to assemble, Murphy obviously was putting the quiet pressure of his organization behind Sheehan. Roosevelt was quite concerned. On January 1, he wrote in his diary: "Shepard is without question the most competent to fill the position, but the Tammany crowd seems unable to forgive him his occasional independence and Sheehan looks like their choice at this stage of the game. May the result prove that I am wrong! There is no question in my mind that the Democratic party is on trial, and having been given control of the government chiefly through up-State votes, cannot afford to surrender its control to the organization in New York City."[6]

The following day, at the inauguration of Governor Dix, Franklin

Roosevelt demonstrated his precocious ability as a scene-stealer. He brought to Albany a delegation from his district, headed up by a fife-and-drum corps. As the ceremonies began, he reported: "Bishop Doane, very old and feeble led with prayer, and to my horror was almost 'drowned out' by the discordant notes of what I easily recognized as my Hyde Park Fife and Drum Corps . . . in the street below.

"I hurried from the Capitol and when a block from home was met by the sight of a dense cheering mob in front of the house – It was the delegation from the Senatorial District – Four Hundred strong! The band and my Fife and Drum corps were working overtime, but all finally managed to get into the house, shaking hands as they passed into the Dining Room – I had provided only chicken salad, sandwiches, coffee, beer and cigars, but it seemed sufficient. . . .

"In the evening the Governor called me up on the telephone and asked us to go up to the Executive Mansion for a little informal dancing. Accordingly E[leanor] R[oosevelt] and I hurriedly dressed, drove up and had a very delightful evening. It was almost a family party, only the military aides, two or three Albany girls and ourselves being there." [7]

Governor Dix treated Roosevelt with easy friendliness, and Roosevelt responded in kind. First encounters led them to misgauge each other. "The governor is very calm and quiet," Roosevelt commented, "but his reserve power grows on me." Lulled by appearances, Dix encouraged Roosevelt in his ambitions. Tom Grady, the eloquent but alcoholic Tammany leader of the Democratic forces in the senate, was about to be deposed; the governor suggested that Roosevelt be elected president pro tempore in his place. Roosevelt was relieved when nothing came of the suggestion, for gossip indicated that Grady would "be a free lance and try to raise Hell generally." Already, on January 3, when the novice senator attended his first Democratic caucus to depose Grady, thoughts of insurgency were running through his head. "The decision to throw over Senator Grady . . . is splendid," he jotted in his diary. "His ability is unquestioned – not so his habits or his character. If the New York members had insisted on him, a split at the outset would have been probable. I for one would with difficulty have supported such a choice – and I would not have been alone in bolting the Caucus, though at the expense of harmony and possibly of my whole future." [8]

In place of Grady, Murphy directed the election of one of the most likely-looking young Tammany men, Robert F. Wagner, who was only thirty-three. Roosevelt predicted that he would be "fairly good": "He has good intentions; the only obstacle is the pressure of his own machine." [9] At the same time, Tammany elevated Alfred E. Smith, at thirty-seven already a veteran of seven terms, to be majority leader in the assembly. With these competent young men in positions of leadership, and with the governor cautious and vacillating, the boss apparently would have little to fear during the session. There were numerous anti-Tammany Democrats in the legislature, but without leadership they were no threat. Quite possibly that is the biggest reason why the city Tammanyites immediately felt animus against Roosevelt. He was an alien in their midst bearing a name they did not like and, still more important, he had the ambition and the money to provide leadership for malcontents.

On the first day of the session, the clerk rasped out, "Mr. Roosevelt," and the deposed Tom Grady, the only legislator there who had seen Theodore Roosevelt come to Albany, glowered through a sheaf of American Beauty roses on his desk at the youngster who had been proposed for his position.[10]

Within a fortnight, Franklin Roosevelt more than confirmed the fears of the bosses. He became increasingly incensed over the manner in which Murphy was preparing to thrust Sheehan down the legislators' throats. All Murphy needed was a simple majority of the Democrats. They would meet in caucus on January 16. There they could vote for any candidate they pleased, but once they had attended the caucus they were thereafter bound to vote for its choice in the legislature. Out of 200 legislators, 114 were Democrats; 101 could elect a Senator. If all 114 Democrats attended the caucus, they would be bound in the legislature to vote for the choice of a majority of the caucus. Thus Murphy could parlay as few as 58 caucus votes into the election of a United States Senator.

This outrageously undemocratic procedure galled Roosevelt, who decided that regardless of the caucus he would never vote for Sheehan. Yet he did not wish to break openly with the party. He asked Al Smith about procedure, and Smith told him with a candor which Roosevelt remembered and appreciated, that if he attended the caucus he would be bound to vote for its candidate, but if he stayed away he would remain free to vote for whomever he pleased. Smith could not have been alarmed at Roosevelt's intransigence, since the Democrats had so many votes to spare.[11]

Meanwhile a small group of assemblymen centering around Edmund

R. Terry of Brooklyn grew incensed at Murphy for holding up their patronage and committee appointments and putting pressure upon them through their county committee chairmen. They began to lay plans. Terry, a man with a mind of his own, calculated that if eighteen of them refused to attend the caucus and retained their freedom to vote against Sheehan, they could combine with the Republicans to block his election. This was on January 12. Before the evening was over, Terry had sufficient followers to inform Murphy's headquarters that a revolt was under way. He "did not want to be accused by the leaders of taking them by surprise." [12]

Word that a rebel block was organizing reached Roosevelt. On Monday, January 16, the day of the caucus, he joined the insurgents and together with a requisite number of assemblymen signed a manifesto that he would not enter the caucus – that he refused to be bound to vote for Sheehan.[13]

That evening the legislature met briefly, then adjourned so that the real business, in the caucus, could take place. Immediately the insurgents left the chambers – not for the caucus, but for their headquarters at a hotel. Roosevelt and Terry arrived first. "For ten long minutes that seemed like hours," Terry wrote later, "we assured each other that there was no doubt of the speedy arrival of the other eighteen." Finally the others appeared, and the defeat of the caucus was consummated. Informally electing Roosevelt chairman, they waited for Murphy's representatives to come and negotiate. Nobody came. This was the beginning of a two-and-a-half-month deadlock.[14]

The insurgents under the leadership of Roosevelt immediately became the focus of public interest.[15] The next day the Tammany forces went to work upon them to try to win them over before the joint session of the legislature cast ballots for Senator. Roosevelt and his associates stood firm; indeed they gained a recruit, and in the ensuing weeks, several more. "We have decided to stand to a man and to the end against William F. Sheehan," Roosevelt told a reporter.[16] He emphasized that they were not committed to any one man, but were "fighting against the boss rule system" as a matter of principle, and would keep on fighting, he said in a paraphrase of General Grant, even "if it takes all Summer." [17]

Murphy's men made one other effort to prevent a deadlock before the balloting began. "Big Tim" Sullivan of the East Side tried to persuade Boss Barnes and other Republican leaders to keep enough of their legislators away so that Sheehan could win. The Republicans refused to do this, but did agree to remain steadfast for the retiring senator, Chauncey M. Depew, long enough to give Murphy every opportunity to break down the opposition. "Senator Grady told me," Roosevelt testified subsequently, "that in his judgment the deadlock would continue for a long time." [18] Sheehan received the votes only of the Democrats who had attended the caucus, 91 out of a requisite 101, and for several weeks the balloting went on with little change.

As the deadlock continued, Roosevelt and the insurgents received increasing publicity throughout the nation. Progressives everywhere had long disliked the way in which the United States Senate was blocking a proposed constitutional amendment to provide for direct election of its members. The Illinois legislature that same winter chose a Senator under circumstances so scandalous that the Senate refused to seat him, and in New Jersey the new reform governor, Woodrow Wilson, was struggling to keep the legislature from electing Boss James Smith, Jr. Liberals linked Roosevelt's fight with Wilson's as part of a general movement to displace machine dictatorship with vigorous popular control. "I am delighted with your action," a prominent clergyman informed Roosevelt, "& told Woodrow Wilson today of how he & you are serving your country." [19] Roosevelt always had something – it might be trivial, but was usually interesting – to tell the reporters. He was shrewd enough again and again to tie in the fight with national issues: "When the time comes – and I, for one, am convinced it is not far distant – that New York State will have direct primaries and direct nomination of senators, then all such exhibitions as we have been treated to in Albany recently will be done away with." [20]

Papers hastily obtained photographs of Roosevelt – in one instance so hastily that it turned out to be a picture of someone else.[21] The *Herald* on January 19 published what was probably the first caricature, an unrecognizable drawing of a spindly young man. Reporters from New York City searched their thesauri for adjectives with which to describe how this younger Roosevelt, whose appearance was so dissimilar to Theodore's, at the same time bore a fundamental resemblance. He has "the strong natural insurgent tendencies of his family," commented the *Post*.[22] "His face is boyish," groped the *American* correspondent, "but those who remember Theodore Roosevelt when he was an Assemblyman say the Senator bears a striking likeness to the Colonel." [23] If one were to believe the *World*, he was almost an Ichabod Crane, "of spare figure and lean intellectual face, suggesting in appearance a student of divinity rather than a practical politician.

Gold bowed spectacles loop his long thin nose, and a frock coat drapes his figure." [24] A newspaperwoman, even though she overgauged his age by a year, did much better:

> He is thirty years old, but only when you are close enough to see the lines about his mouth that a strenuous fight may have made can one believe him even that age. Tall, with a well set up figure he is physically fit to command. His face is a bit long but the features are well modelled, the nose is Grecian in its contour, and there is the glow of country health in his cheeks. His light brown hair, closely cut and crisply curling at the top, is parted on the side over a high forehead.
>
> His eyes are deep set and gray, and he wears glasses. It is the chin, though, aggressive and somewhat prominent, that shows what a task the leaders in Albany have if they have thought of making this particular young man change his mind. His lips are firm and part often in a smile over even white teeth – the Roosevelt teeth.[25]

Roosevelt's one serious weakness was his lack of experience. Considering how new he was to politics, he performed admirably in meeting the maneuvers of his adroit opponents, but he leaned too heavily upon advisors outside the group, most of them clean-government Democrats who had favored Shepard, and several of them powerful figures on Wall Street. His association with the unpopular financiers made him vulnerable to Tammany attacks, and the most unassailable of his liberal advisors made conflicting suggestions that more often confused than clarified.[26]

This weakness was seldom outwardly apparent. From the outset, Roosevelt gave an impression of strength and vigor. He was the "head and shoulders" of the revolt, the New York *Sun* declared. "He bustles about at all hours of the day and night keeping his insurgent friends in line." [27] In fact, however, Roosevelt functioned more as the insurgents' presiding officer than as their policy maker, and usually followed rather than molded their will. Shortly after the end of the siege, Terry wrote, "Too much cannot be said of the untiring zeal and efforts of Senator Roosevelt to advance our cause. While not, in the ordinary sense of the term, leader, as everything that was done and every step taken came after a full and free discussion by all of us, nevertheless, we had to have some one to represent it. During the time when we were hounded and harassed, he was the shepherd of the flock, and his house was indeed during the early days a harbor of refuge nearly every evening." [28]

Roosevelt moved the headquarters of the insurgency to the library of his own home on State Street. There they met twice a day, at ten in the morning, when they marched to the Capitol in a group to vote, and again at five in the afternoon. They kept no secrets from each other, but there was usually not much for them to discuss. "There is very little business done at our councils of war," Roosevelt admitted. "We just sit around and swap stories like soldiers at the bivouac fire." [29] The bivouacs went on most of the day, and well into the night. They marked Eleanor Roosevelt's initiation into politics as well as her husband's. She spent her evenings with the insurgents, sometimes listening while Terry read her his poetry, and finally at a late hour bringing out crackers and cheese and beer as a hint to go home. Over the weeks, the hypersaturation of cigar smoke from the library gradually seeped into the nursery above, and the children had to be moved to the third floor. But the siege went on.[30]

For many of the legislators, the inconvenience was more serious. They normally came to Albany only for the Monday evening sessions, and perhaps a day or so more; receiving only $1500 in salary, they would soon suffer serious financial loss as well as disruption of plans if they had to stay in daily session. This applied to all the other legislators as well as the insurgents, and added to the burden of the rebels the knowledge that they were far from popular in the Capitol. Superficially, the opposition leaders were polite to them – Smith, Wagner, and Foley dined at the Roosevelt home – but beneath the surface politeness or even camaraderie, a vigorous struggle went on. Everyone in the group had to withstand loss of patronage and threats of political and personal reprisals. Sheehan hinted as much at the outset, when he talked privately to Roosevelt in a room at the Ten Eyck Hotel. There were no witnesses, but Roosevelt jotted down an account of the conference: "He said in substance: 'Having a majority of the Democratic Caucus which according to all precedence should elect me, this action against me is assassination[.] I will give up my law practice and devote my time to the vindication of my character, and I will go into the counties where these men live and show up their characters – the character in which they have accomplished this thing.' " [31]

Sheehan meant it too. All the insurgents came to feel the weight of his wrath. "What pressure has been brought to bear on the insurgents in order to get them to surrender?" Axel Warn of the New York *Times* asked Roosevelt. "Every conceivable form of pressure, that's all I can say – now," Roosevelt replied.* Terry added: "They said that the road of the transgressor is hard. The transgressor's path is pleasant compared to that of a legislator trying to do what he regards as his duty. His way is beset with temptations on every side." [33] One insurgent commented more bluntly, "I wish I had been in Halifax before I got into this mess." [34]

Before the end of January, Roosevelt was hinting that Wall Street financial interests were reaching out into the insurgents' home towns and were putting pressure upon local banks to foreclose mortgages on their property. "Some of us have means," he proclaimed, "and we intend to stand by the men who are voting for principle. We shall see to it that they are protected in the discharge of their public duty. They shall not suffer because they are faithful to the people." The Buffalo *Enquirer* went into raptures over this display of *noblesse oblige:* "How poor and mean by comparison are the egotistical 'donations' of a Carnegie or the Pharisaical 'philanthropy' of a Rockefeller! A man of wealth like Senator Roosevelt, who interposes his financial power to bulwark the interests of the state, to uphold civic righteousness, and to protect public men from all the evils of corrupt coercion, recalls an elder day of patriotism, when rich men were the defense and not the menace of the State." [35]

Again, the attack shifted to whispers that the insurgents were anti-Catholic and anti-Irish. "This is absolutely untrue!" retorted Roosevelt at the start of the fight. "We do not ask and we do not care from what stock a man may have sprung or what his religious beliefs may be. All we ask is that he be a fit man for United States Senator." [36] A few days later, the story went around that Roosevelt had on his desk circulars published by the viciously anti-Catholic American Protective Association. They came in the mail, Roosevelt explained, and he threw them into the wastebasket.[37] The charge became more serious when the aged Catholic bishop of Syracuse, the Rev. Patrick Ludden, publicly labeled the movement as a resurgence of "the old spirit of Knownothingism." He asserted that what the insurgency really

* FDR had been made chairman of the Forest, Fish, and Game Committee of the senate; his appointee as clerk, Morgan Hoyt, was discharged. Also, Roosevelt had just formed a law partnership with Langdon Marvin and Henry Hooker; the new firm lost one of its clients.[32]

meant was the often quoted, "You are an Irishman and that's agin you; you are a Catholic and that's agin you." [38]

"Gentlemen," Senator Roosevelt lamented when he met his colleagues the next morning, "this is a most uncalled for and most unfortunate incident. I fail to comprehend what would prompt the Bishop of Syracuse to make any such criticism." [39] He and several other insurgents pointed to the fact that three or four of their number were Irish; three were members of the Knights of Columbus. They even selected a Catholic candidate for the United States Senate, John D. Kernan, for whom they expressed a willingness to vote as a body.[40] Nevertheless, Roosevelt's political enemies were so successful in smearing him as an anti-Catholic that it took him years to rid himself completely of the label.*

Instead of meeting the Catholic issue directly, Roosevelt preferred to counterattack by charging that Sheehan was conniving with Thomas Fortune Ryan, a notorious Wall Street operator and a power behind the Democratic party. If the charge could be made to stick, it would bolster the insurgents, since their chief argument against Sheehan was that he was the tool of nefarious financial interests. However, Roosevelt's evidence was apparently no more than the flimsy bit of information that both Sheehan and Ryan attended 10 o'clock mass at St. Patrick's Cathedral in New York City on Sunday, January 22. They were not together.[41]

Sheehan counterattacked a few days later by trying to link Roosevelt with his illustrious Republican relative. Only a few days before Warn had asked him, "Are you an admirer of your uncle-in-law?" Roosevelt replied, "Why, who can help but admire him? . . . My uncle-in-law will come back all right, no matter what some people believe. It is only a question of time before people generally will appreciate what he has done in arousing the public conscience and in driving corruption out of politics." [42] This lent conviction to a detailed story which Sheehan's press agent handed out, supposedly repeating certain after-dinner remarks of ex-President Roosevelt. Theodore was pictured as chuckling over the Democratic impasse and boasting that Franklin was following his suggestions in the fight against the caucus:

* FDR could have almost heard the whistle of a shillelagh in the anonymous admonition from "a Bklyn Democrat," January 24, 1911: "Sheehan is a Irish man and that is why you don't wante him for Senator now you better look out for your slef [*sic*] if you dont we will get after you . . . we are Strong for Murphy and dont forget it. . . . Shepard is not like by the poor."

"We've split the Democrats in two." When Franklin Roosevelt was told of Sheehan's charge, he laughed and retorted, "That's absurd. Why I haven't seen my distinguished cousin since the first of the year. We've had absolutely no communication on this subject." [43] *

Sheehan's countercharge was a strategic error, since it was likely to strengthen Roosevelt among his normally Republican constituents; Sheehan's operations in Roosevelt's district fared no better. With justifiable optimism, Roosevelt asserted, "Our support is spontaneous, while the opposition against us has been in nine cases out of ten manufactured." When the irate Sheehan went to Poughkeepsie to try to build a fire under Roosevelt, Edward E. Perkins and a few of the leaders were sympathetic but discreet. They refused to hold a mass meeting in Sheehan's behalf, though they did give him a dinner. And they circulated a petition calling upon Roosevelt to heed the caucus.[45] When the petition came, Roosevelt with relief dismissed it as "certainly a fizzle." [46] It "contained but two hundred and sixty-five names, many of them in the same handwriting, instead of the twelve hundred claimed and it did not cause me much worry at any time." [47] The Democratic papers in Poughkeepsie, the *News-Press* and the *Enterprise*, ignored or opposed Roosevelt, while at the same time Edmund Platt's Republican *Eagle*, so condescending during the campaign, gave him a flattering surprise. "Of all the papers in the world," Roosevelt declared, it "has been my chief source of support." [48] Dutchess County party regulars had to be content with journalistic frowns and feeble petitions; they did not dare crack the whip at Roosevelt more forcibly for fear of alienating independents and anti-Tammany Democrats.

All this Sheehan-inspired opprobrium had the end result of strengthening Roosevelt among those normally suspicious of the Democrats. Thomas Newbold, whose estate was near the Roosevelts', wrote at the start of the fight, "I have seen a great many people yesterday & today & they are all most enthusiastic. . . . I am perfectly delighted & *very very* proud of you." [49] Professor James F. Baldwin, of Vassar College,

* This was not strictly accurate, for a letter had come from Sagamore Hill a week earlier:

DEAR FRANKLIN,

Just a line to say that we are all really proud of the way you have handled yourself. Good luck to you! Give my love to dear Eleanor.

Always yours

THEODORE ROOSEVELT [44]

expressed the approval "of most men who vote faithfully but do not otherwise take an aggressive part in politics." [50]

Meanwhile, day after day the deadlock continued. The Murphy men continued to label Roosevelt as a publicity-seeking "calf still wet behind the ears," [51] and vowed they would never accept terms from "college kids" – a rather strange label for a group the age of which averaged forty-two, and whose patriarch, Charles W. Cosad of Seneca, was a septuagenarian with a long white beard.[52] The regulars chanted:

> We'll stick to Sheehan, we'll stick to Sheehan
> Until the grass is turning green.

Nevertheless Murphy tried to open peace negotiations and on January 30, Roosevelt's twenty-ninth birthday, conferred with him for an hour. They issued no statement. Years later Roosevelt recounted what had happened:

> We talked about the weather for five or ten minutes. Then, with a delightful smile, Murphy said, "I know I can't make you change your mind unless you want to change it. Is there any chance of you and the other twenty men coming around to vote for Sheehan?"
>
> "No, Mr. Murphy," I replied. "The opposition is not against Sheehan personally. In the first place, we believe a great many of our Democratic constituents don't want him to be the United States Senator, and, in the second place, he is altogether too closely connected with the traction trust in New York City."
>
> Murphy said, "Yes. I am entirely convinced your opposition is a perfectly honest one. If at any time you change your minds, let me know." [53]

Murphy was supporting Sheehan only to fulfill a political obligation. If he did not press Roosevelt at the conference, it was because he was already convinced that Sheehan could not be elected and should be eliminated. Tell Sheehan to his face, he now urged Roosevelt, that you will never vote for him, and tell him why. Roosevelt agreed to do so. On February 2 he invited Sheehan to luncheon at his home on State Street. It was a nervous occasion. While Mrs. Roosevelt and Mrs. Sheehan groped for polite conversation their husbands talked for hours in another room. Roosevelt stood firm, though he regretted to find that Sheehan thought the insurgents were motivated by anti-Catholicism.[54] Afterwards Roosevelt told reporters, "Mr. Sheehan is delightful personally, but that is one thing, the senatorship fight is another.[55]

Sheehan remained doggedly in the contest, to the embarrassment of Murphy, who could not openly repudiate him. Quietly, however, Murphy broached to Roosevelt and thirteen or fourteen others the name of his real choice, his chief aide and son-in-law, Dan Cohalan.[56] None of the insurgents would accept Cohalan as a compromise candidate. Other names came up, and as Sheehan's hopes faded, the two factions negotiated more and more.

Even after Sheehan gave up at the end of February, Tammany suggested only names that the insurgents considered unsuitable. "The tail cannot wag the dog," Roosevelt had repeatedly conceded, but the insurgents were ready to make continued use of the veto power. Roosevelt was anxious to choose someone "conservative in regard to business interests and yet a man whose position can never be questioned by the radical element of society."[57] If he could not obtain a good candidate through Tammany, perhaps he could persuade the Republicans to join in voting for a conservative Democrat.[58] He proposed this scheme in mid-February to Boss Barnes, but the Republican leader retorted, "We can't do it now."[59]

Next, Roosevelt tried to work with the Republicans through an intermediary, Francis Lynde Stetson, a former law partner of Grover Cleveland. Stetson was a remarkably inappropriate person for supposedly antimonopolist insurgents to choose as an agent, since he was an attorney for both J. P. Morgan and Thomas Fortune Ryan, and had been midwife in bringing United States Steel into existence. Associated with Stetson were several like-minded Democratic lawyers, notably Montgomery Hare and Austen G. Fox.[60] They seemed to hope that the insurgency could lead to a permanent anti-Tammany organization within the party, and some of them thought that Roosevelt's group, holding a balance of power in the state legislature, should take an immediate conservative stand upon economic matters in which they had large interests. Fox, who subsequently distinguished himself by leading the legal fight against the confirmation of Louis D. Brandeis to the Supreme Court, urged them to use their power to block New York ratification of the pending income tax amendment to the Constitution. Hare, who was more realistic, sadly granted that this was politically impractical. As for Roosevelt, he was astute enough to jot on the letter outlining the proposal, "No ans[wer]." But the suggestion did indicate the nature of some of the support from New York City.[61] The presence of these lawyers, originally for Shepard, and now behind the insurgents, lent credence to the cynical view some observers had advanced from the outset that the struggle was no more than a *sub rosa* conflict between two sets of powerful financial interests.[62]

There is some indication that, while the insurgents as a group dealt with Stetson only upon one occasion, Roosevelt throughout March listened to his advice with rather startling results. After the announcement that the regular Democrats would hold a second "unbossed" caucus on March 27, Sheehan finally released those who had been voting for him, and a new crop of candidates appeared. Mayor William J. Gaynor of New York City came to Albany bearing the name of a friend of his, Samuel Untermeyer, who, though nominally a Tammanyite, could not possibly be suspected, like Sheehan, of being a tool of the financial interests. Untermeyer had organized and led the stockholders' fight against the New York Life Insurance Company and had repeatedly battled against Wall Street. His friends later claimed that Governor Dix broached his name to Roosevelt at a breakfast conference at the Executive Mansion, that Roosevelt was enthusiastic and expressed a willingness to vote for him. A few hours later Murphy arrived and also gave his approval. Subsequently, the story went, Roosevelt completely reversed himself and openly opposed Untermeyer. This effectively blocked Untermeyer's election.

Untermeyer, anxious to find out why the insurgents opposed him, called upon Stetson on Monday, March 27. Stetson admittedly told him that "were I to appear as his advocate, it would excite the surprise of personal friends who felt aggrieved by his attitude since 1902." According to Untermeyer's friends, Stetson added that Morgan and all the Wall Street and steel interests were against Untermeyer because of his fight to destroy the shipbuilding trust in 1904, his championship of the insurance stockholders, and his opposition to the Morgan interests.[63] If Roosevelt did indeed veto Untermeyer, as seems likely, he was functioning as a cat's-paw for J. P. Morgan! *

The negotiations of Stetson and the Republicans did frighten Tammany into action. On March 27, the Republican legislative leader assured Roosevelt that he would personally support a Democrat of high caliber, and he suggested several names. The immediate Tammany response was a caucus that same evening of the regular Democrats.

* Untermeyer claimed that in addition to Stetson the group behind the insurgents included Herbert Satterlee, Morgan's son-in-law; Charles A. Peabody, president of the Mutual Life Insurance Company; and George F. Baker of the First National Bank. Satterlee was a friend and admirer of Roosevelt's.

Although, as Murphy had promised, it was unbossed and the regulars deserted Sheehan to vote for some twenty-seven different candidates, the insurgents stayed away.[64]

Barnes, the Republican boss, played an interesting game; he ostensibly – but only ostensibly – offered to join with the insurgents in the election of a Senator. On March 28, he persuaded Depew to release the Republicans bound to him by caucus, and on March 30 he sent a manifesto to the Republican legislative leaders that they should join with the insurgents in supporting a conservative Democrat. At the same time, he raised objections to the name of everyone the insurgents suggested.[65] He was abetting rather than undercutting Murphy in the war of nerves.

The final blow fell quickly. On the night of Wednesday, March 29, the Capitol caught fire, and the legislative chambers were badly gutted. Thereafter the legislators met temporarily in the City Hall. Everyone was anxious to reach a quick solution, and the insurgents were losing their will to fight. John Godfrey Saxe, a Tammany man who had joined them late in the struggle, helped split their ranks by denouncing the plan to join with the Republicans in electing a Senator. He then moved back to Tammany and began to act as a go-between, to bring compromise proposals to the troubled band. Roosevelt admitted several weeks later that "between the conflagration in the Capitol and attempts to split us up, we came near going on the rocks several times." [66]

At this critical point, Roosevelt himself was the victim of a determined onslaught by his wily and experienced antagonists. He was, as the New York *Tribune* reported, "outwitted and outgeneralled." [67] Thursday's newspapers carried Murphy's charges that Stetson – the founder of the steel trust, Northern Securities, and the New York State power trust – was the evil genius behind the insurgents. At the same time, Untermeyer prepared a letter claiming that at Stetson's behest, the insurgents had refused to accept him as a compromise candidate. Gaynor sent Roosevelt a copy, with the threat that if there was not a settlement by Saturday he would make it public and thus torpedo the insurgent movement. When all this became public at the end of May, Roosevelt at first claimed that he had not received the letter until after the compromise, then admitted that it might have arrived sooner. "What I am absolutely positive of," Roosevelt emphasized, "is that the contents of the letter were not communicated to any of the insurgents and in no way affected the election of a senator." [68]

This undoubtedly was accurate, since by Thursday Roosevelt had lost control of the battle-weary insurgents,[69] and up to the close of the fight on Friday, was struggling to reassert his authority and persuade them to carry on. The last two days were filled with almost constant negotiation, and some of the insurgents were well disposed to bolt the State Street Roosevelt home for the Tammany lair. In this atmosphere Murphy was able to finesse a result which only the most optimistic could interpret as other than an outright Tammany triumph.

"Mr. Murphy," reported Roosevelt, "after finding it impossible to elect Cohalan or any of the particular friends of the interests suggested the name of Justice [Edward E.] McCall. This . . . we refused to consider." [70] The insurgents countered with a list of ten men, any of which they would accept. There was only one Tammany man on the list, James W. Gerard, and Murphy was afraid of him, so he countered by suggesting that they add an eleventh name which, he assured the insurgents, would be the Tammany choice, Justice Victor Dowling. The insurgents agreed. Cohalan, who was bitter over his own rejection by the insurgents, urged Murphy not to take anyone proposed by the minority. It would be bad for his dignity and leadership, and now that the game was going his way, he clearly need not allow the insurgents even the fictional triumph of submitting the name of the compromise candidate.[71]

The insurgents accepted Judge Dowling, but when they met at Roosevelt's home at nine Friday morning to go in a body to the caucus,[72] they learned to their dismay that Dowling had refused the nomination. Murphy had substituted the name of Justice James Aloysius O'Gorman, who was far more of an organization man than Sheehan ever had been. Indeed, O'Gorman was a former Grand Sachem of Tammany Hall. After his elevation to the bench though, he had kept out of politics and had made an excellent judicial record. Among the Irish he was highly popular, having served three terms as president of the Friendly Sons of St. Patrick. A short, stocky man of fifty-one with a reddish-brown pointed beard, he was an incisive speaker, a man of his word, and thoroughly independent. He would be a hard man for the insurgents to swallow, but a harder one for them to reject.

Two of the insurgents immediately went into the caucus; the remainder stayed at Roosevelt's home to debate the pros and cons of O'Gorman. At first they voted eighteen to six against accepting him, but, as the day wore on, they began to reconsider. They opposed O'Gorman primarily because he was a Tammany man; they knew nothing whatever about his political beliefs. They finally decided it would be unfair to hold these against him! O'Gorman wired that he was "thoroughly in accord with the principles enunciated in the platform of the last Democratic national and state conventions." That was sufficient for a majority of the exhausted insurgents.[73]

That same morning it became evident, according to Roosevelt, "that we could expect little help from the Republicans. It would have been practically an impossibility for us to have secured sufficient of the Republican votes to elect a man of our own choice." [74] Besides, they heard whispers that if they failed to accept O'Gorman, Barnes's minions were now ready to unite with Murphy's and vote Sheehan in. Only one thing deterred the rebels from yielding – the fear of reprisals after their surrender. They sent word to the caucus for assurances that they would not suffer, and Senator Wagner and Assemblyman Smith quickly appeared to promise a warm welcome back into the fold. Stetson and Hare sent word from New York that O'Gorman had promised that if elected he would intercede for them. That ended the struggle. A majority voted to accept the "compromise." Roosevelt and ten others would have liked to go on, but under the circumstances it was futile. They agreed to vote for O'Gorman in the legislature, but they stayed out of the caucus. Ten who attended the final conference, together with four others who did not even bother to attend it, went into the caucus, which quickly nominated O'Gorman.

Soon afterward, Roosevelt and the rump of the insurgents who had not attended the caucus filed into the Chamber amidst cheers and jeers. Before the Speaker could bring the session to order, someone started the victory song, "Tam-ma-nee . . . Tam-ma-nee," and almost half the members picked it up, shouting and screaming with joy, hugging each other, and paying no attention to the frantic banging of the gavel. Finally, when the Speaker restored order, the Republican minority leader arose to rub salt in Roosevelt's wounds. "God moves in a mysterious way his wonders to perform," he began, and went on tritely to compare the insurgents to the mountain that labors and brings forth a mouse. It was, said the New York *Tribune*, "like a dash of acid in the face to the insurgents." [75] Amidst mild hissing,[76] Roosevelt arose to rescue what dignity he could from the occasion. Against the cacophony of Tammany groans, he declared:

> Two months ago a number of Democrats felt that it was our duty to dissent from certain of our party associates in the matter

> of selecting a United States Senator. The party had been restored to power after seventeen years of Republican misrule. We have followed the dictates of our consciences and have done our duty as we saw it. I believe that as a result the Democratic party has taken an upward step. We are Democrats – not irregulars, but regulars. I take pleasure in casting my vote for the Hon. James A. O'Gorman.[77]

Editorial writers and correspondents were almost unanimous in agreeing that the brave battle of the insurgents had reached an ignominious end. Yet even the Republican *Tribune*, which cynically suggested that O'Gorman was probably no better than Sheehan, felt the episode should teach Murphy moderation. Oswald Garrison Villard's liberal *Post* saw material gains. The Tammany braves returned to New York City bearing scars as well as scalps, for while the deadlock had shown there was little opportunity to organize an upstate or city anti-Tammany machine, conversely it had demonstrated that Murphy could not run the state in as highhanded a fashion as he did the city. Upstate Democrats had learned that they could block Tammany without too much difficulty.[78]

Roosevelt hurried down to Poughkeepsie, and found to his pleasure that the great majority of people there, and at meetings in Pleasant Valley and Staatsburg, "seemed thoroughly pleased with the result of the breaking of the deadlock and they did not feel that the victory belonged at all to Murphy." [79] He unabashedly proclaimed an insurgent victory.[80]

Whether or not insurgency triumphed was of less significance than the undeniable fact that a new political luminary had made his appearance. In the course of the battle Roosevelt attracted some mention outside of the state; within it he became a well-known personage. Indeed, in the publicity and political stature he gained, he seemed the real beneficiary of the siege. Those American progressives who had learned his name associated him with the nationwide fight against bossism, and more particularly the struggle for direct election of Senators. He had functioned primarily as a conservative clean-government Democrat, but he had earned the label "Insurgent." This was particularly appealing to farmers, who had followed with approval the struggles of a group of Midwestern Republicans in Congress against the arbitrary powers of Speaker Joseph Cannon and the high Payne-Aldrich tariff. Progressives within the Republican party liked the words "Roosevelt" and "Insurgent." Franklin Roosevelt himself appreciated the value of the words, and he lost no time in espousing the full program that went with them. Thereafter no one could identify him with the Wall Street Cleveland Democrats, for he had moved far beyond the political world of James Roosevelt.

Progressives within both parties soon became hazy about the outcome of the struggle against Murphy. They forgot how unanimously newspaper correspondents had agreed that on the dismal Friday evening of March 31, 1911, the smile was on the face of the Tammany tiger. They did remember, though, that Sheehan had not been elected. Roosevelt began to say that he would have favored O'Gorman from the start,[81] and Murphy was in no position to deny this. Roosevelt began to say, further, that he had helped put an Irish Catholic in the Senate, and O'Gorman did not contradict him. With Murphy and O'Gorman silent and Roosevelt proclaiming a triumph, the general impression grew that indeed the insurgents had won. Eventually the smile passed completely from the tiger's face to Roosevelt's. In January, 1928, he reminded an old acquaintance:

> Do you remember the old Sheehan fight of 1911? *When the final Murphy surrender came* the flag of truce was brought to me by Assemblyman, Alfred E. Smith, Assemblyman, Jim Foley and State Senator, Bob Wagner. What a change has taken place all along the line! [82]

CHAPTER VII

Progressive State Senator

> From the ruins of the political machines we will reconstruct something more nearly conforming to a democratic conception of government.
>
> — FDR, *December, 1911.*[1]

IN the unpleasant aftermath of the insurgency, the Tammany Tiger still held mastery of the Democratic party in New York State. It was a snarling, peevish Tiger, in no mood to honor its pledges of amnesty to the surrendered rebels. No machine ever could afford to be magnanimous under the circumstances, since forgiveness would be likely to encourage further irregularity. Unpleasant things happened in ensuing months to several insurgents. One of them who was a country editor lost his official printing * and went bankrupt.[2] Roosevelt himself, less vulnerable financially, managed to maintain and even to increase his political strength by cultivating a remarkable reputation as a champion of clean government, conservation, and aid to the farmer – all attractive to progressives of both parties. With strong political logic, considering the make-up of his Hudson River constituency, he concentrated his attention upon rural Republicans rather than urban Democrats. In New York State as in the nation, progressivism was primarily the program of middle-class farmers, and business and professional men. As it approached flood tide in 1911 and 1912, no one could have been more typically progressive than Roosevelt.[3] This does not mean that he endeared himself to all the reformers he encountered.

One of them, Frances Perkins, a young woman who was lobbying for social legislation on behalf of the Consumers' League, was disappointed because Roosevelt seemed less interested in improving the wages, hours and working conditions of women than were some of

* Legal advertising by the local government – a customary form of patronage for newspapers.

the hard-bitten Tammany men like Big Tim Sullivan of the Bowery.[4] Not that Roosevelt was breaking faith with the agrarian progressivism of Dutchess County. Miss Perkins could not complain that he voted incorrectly on measures of interest to women workers but merely that his main effort and attention went elsewhere. Had it not, he would not have survived as a state senator; he was the sort of progressive his constituency wanted him to be.

Roosevelt's somewhat toplofty air, which is what annoyed Miss Perkins the most, came from his patrician background and his limited experience in politics. He still bore as a normal heritage from Groton a good bit of self-righteousness as he strode about the legislative chambers, serious and rather aloof. As yet, he showed little of that willingness to compromise or temporize which later became second nature to him. As Eleanor Roosevelt has pointed out, he was still shy during these first years in politics. Perhaps he was not entirely insincere when he declined an invitation to deliver an address with the comment, "I am an extremely bad speaker anyway." [5]

Tammany men soon discovered that the easiest way to undermine him was to caricature his patrician demeanor. Whether maliciously or not, a newspaper photographer caught a picture of him at the beginning of his legislative term wearing a top hat and pince-nez, his head tossed back with a disdainful, almost supercilious look on his face. It was the epitome of the stage dandy, the popular "Van Bibber" character of Richard Harding Davis's stories, and a rank libel upon the flesh-and-blood Roosevelt. During the insurgency, Senator Grady frequently arose and accused Roosevelt of stirring up trouble to get his picture in the paper; Roosevelt's response, one reporter wrote, was "a dry and mirthless smile of bitter recollection." [6] Yet this was the photograph of him that circulated for several years in the small papers of rural New York.* As late as May, 1913, when Roosevelt went to Sackets Harbor, New York, to speak, a newspaper reported: "Attired in a neat dark gray business suit and straw hat . . . Mr. Roosevelt presented a marked contrast to the stereotyped picture of him in the silk tie and costume which shows him . . . like an English duke. . . . For that reason the score or more of traveling men and others in the hotel lobby failed to recognize him as he sat reading his paper." When a friend's picture turned out badly, Roosevelt wrote in commiseration, "after a bad experience of my own, I can assure

* Part of the fault may have been Roosevelt's. In March, 1911, when the Springfield *Republican* asked for a picture, he confessed that he had none to send.[7]

you that you want to thank Heaven that the newspaper cut makes you look like a reasonable human being." [8]

"Awful arrogant fellow, that Roosevelt," Tim Sullivan commented once to Miss Perkins.[9] To Sullivan, he must have been a baffling figure. One night in the legislature, early in June, 1911, he asked to have an item of $381.54 (to repair a bridge over Wappinger's Creek in Dutchess County) thrown out of an appropriation bill. He knew of no need for the sum. Sullivan exclaimed, "Frank, you ought to have your head examined." [10] Certainly the Tammany men and Roosevelt did not speak the same language. Another night Roosevelt launched into an attack upon the Tammany men because they had not reported out a bill to appropriate $50,000 for forest fire protection. "As a result," he warned dramatically, "hundreds of thousands of dollars' worth of property is likely to go up in smoke at any time." Pointing to Senator Jim Frawley, he added, "and here . . . is one of the men responsible for this situation."

"Senator Roosevelt has gained his point," shouted the president pro tempore, Robert Wagner. "What he wants is a headline in the newspapers. Let us proceed to our business." [11]

A few days later, going into Democratic caucus to consider a particularly unsavory piece of Tammany legislation, Roosevelt announced before the vote was taken that he would not abide by the result. Frawley declared, "I move that the senator from the Twenty-sixth be excluded from the caucus." The chair appointed Frawley, who was an expert amateur boxer, as a committee of one to expel Roosevelt. Afterward, to an inquiring newspaperman, Roosevelt boasted of his boxing ability. Said Frawley, "Match me with him? Certainly! I'll meet him in a pulpit or a rat pit." [12]

On other occasions Roosevelt was studiously conciliatory toward Tammany. He voted to replace Republicans with Democrats in three $6000-a-year political jobs, explaining that he was not endorsing the spoils system as Tammany and Senator Grady indulged in it, but was seeking to undo "a worse wrong" which the Republicans had "committed for partisan advantage" when they controlled the legislature! "Senator Grady," he elaborated, "belongs to the old school of politics. It is a school which is not any longer popular with the people. Its day has departed. I, on the contrary, am of the new school of politics which is assuming control in both parties." Whatever his incomprehensible line of reasoning, the Tammany senators were delighted when he voted "Aye," and several of them shouted, "Good boy!" [13]

Gradually Roosevelt came to learn much of political value from his Tammany colleagues. He soon patterned his own conduct after their good fellowship and naturalness. He came to realize that they were more than what he had first taken them to be, more than just a band of corruptionists cynically out for graft and plunder. The older ones kept in touch with the common man in a way that amazed Roosevelt, with his sheltered upbringing. "Poor old Tim Sullivan never understood about modern politics," he remarked once in the White House, "but he was right about the human heart." [14] As for the younger Tammany men, he later came to believe that in 1911 they had given the state a surprise by backing much progressive legislation. "Mixed up with the usual run of wholly partisan measures were proposals for sound steps in social reform – factory laws, workmen's compensation, the protection of women and children in industry." * A Republican had commented to him at the time: Smith and the others "represent a new spirit in Tammany Hall, are organization followers, of course, but they seem to have discovered that there is something more important than ward picnics and balls." [15] These were the first intimations of a shift of basic significance in American politics. It was something rather different from the Progressive movement: workingmen's support of welfare legislation through the urban machines. One irony of it was that, when the state took over various welfare functions from the machines, their power waned. At the same time new voting configurations were in the making, and a generation later the greatest beneficiary of these was the New Deal.

Roosevelt's appreciation of this came much later. One incident indicates the limitations in his thinking during this period. Near the climax of the insurgency there came a tragic episode of considerably more significance in New York State legislative history than any senatorial contests – the Triangle shirtwaist factory fire. Late in the afternoon of March 25, 1911, flames swept the top three stories of a supposedly fireproof building on Washington Place in New York City. There was only one fire escape, which proved a deathtrap: more people were killed using it than were saved by it. Of the 148 who died, fifteen were men, and the rest young women between the ages of sixteen and thirty-five. "This calamity is just what I have been predicting," said the New York fire chief.[16] Hundreds of buildings and scores

* Frances Perkins recounts how Boss Murphy supported factory legislation after he came to realize how many votes Tammany had gained from the successful passage of a bill limiting women to 54 hours of work a week.

of factories were obviously as bad fire traps. Responding to public agitation, the legislature created a New York State Factory Investigating Commission. This commission, on which Smith and Wagner played leading roles, framed and passed a series of safety laws. Roosevelt in 1911 took no part in the work of the commission and in his copious correspondence did not even mention the Triangle fire.*

His attitudes toward organized labor were in part the product of his Harvard training, but they were thoroughly in keeping with the progressivism of his district. For many years he had disapproved the idea of giving labor the weapons with which to obtain its own concessions. He especially disliked the boycott, which had led to the notorious *Danbury Hatters'* and *Buck Stove* court decisions, both heavily penalizing the unions. When organized labor looked toward the Democratic party for redress, Roosevelt privately commented, "There is no question in my mind that we cannot permit legislation which will legalize the practice of boycotting."[18] He seemed to take for granted the use of force to suppress disturbances during strikes. At a time when many men refused to enlist in the National Guard because it was used against strikers, he endorsed a proposal to create a state police force which could maintain order and remove the stigma from the Guard.[19]

On the other hand, Roosevelt showed an almost equal willingness to foster paternalistic labor legislation as long as it did not run contrary to the interests of his constituents. In May, 1911, he accepted an honorary office in the New York branch of the Association for Labor Legislation, which numbered among its national officers Samuel Gompers, Jane Addams, Louis D. Brandeis, and Woodrow Wilson.[20] This did not mean he would push labor bills that farmers did not like, particularly those involving the harvesting or canning of crops. Although he received much prodding from unions and civic organizations he was noncommittal on bills to limit to 54 hours per week the work of boys from sixteen to twenty-one, and to regulate the work of children in canning sheds.[21] On the other hand, he sponsored a bill, more to the liking of churches than unions, to provide one day of rest in seven.[22]

* FDR did declare in March, 1911, that the two fields of social service work that he knew most about were that "being done in New York City for the seamen of all nationalities who enter that port and the work that has been done by the New York Milk Committee toward obtaining purer milk for the poor and lessening the infant mortality."[17]

Later, when the 54-hour bill manifestly became popular among all liberals, he became one of its prime supporters. It failed to pass the state senate by only a single vote and the senate was about to adjourn when its promoters persuaded another senator to give it his support. By that time, however, one of those who had previously voted for the bill – Tim Sullivan – was missing. As Louis Howe later told the story, Roosevelt, with his customary flair for the dramatic, refused to give up, and promised he would hold the senate floor until Sullivan could be found. He arose, said he wished to make a few remarks for the record on the bill, and – when it began to take some time to get Sullivan out of bed on the night boat for New York – switched over to a discussion of birds. The Republican leader, Brackett, protested that birds had nothing to do with the 54-hour bill. Roosevelt retorted that he was "trying to prove that Nature demands shorter hours," and went on talking until Sullivan appeared. The bill finally passed.[23]

It was in the same spirit that Roosevelt gave close attention to complaints from labor unions in his district. He investigated and tried vigorously to bring about improved safety conditions in hazardous Adirondack iron mines.[24] He also gave his steady backing to a workmen's compensation bill, and during the 1912 campaign offered to reintroduce it for the State Federation of Labor. The chairman of the Federation expressed his pleasure, and gave Roosevelt his endorsement. "Your support in behalf of all labor legislation has been that of an earnest representative of the people," he said, "and if our compensation bill is placed in your hands I have no fear of the result."[25]

In the spring of 1913 Roosevelt readily accepted the request of Abram I. Elkus, chief counsel of the Factory Investigating Commission, to speak at a legislative hearing on behalf of the entire thirty-two bills which the Commission proposed. Thus speedily had his education in the field of welfare and labor legislation progressed.[26]

Roosevelt's endorsement of Tammany-sponsored welfare legislation by no means indicated a willingness to swallow Tammany. For many years the Hall was hostile, and while this was a menace to Roosevelt, it was also one of his most important political stocks in trade. It strengthened him in his district, and throughout the state brought him the support of most reform or anti-Tammany factions in the party. Also, while the Democrats were not very successful in their running of the state during 1911 and 1912, Roosevelt's sporadic criticisms gave him an immunity from blame for the bad record.[27]

Roosevelt seldom missed an opportunity to bait the Tammany men in the senate, always in full view of the reporters. Before the Sheehan fight he had introduced a resolution favoring the direct election of Senators. On April 20 his resolution came up in the senate and since Democrats in their platform had favored the reform, they did not dare oppose it. After a five-hour debate it passed 28 to 15 and four days later passed the assembly.[28] It was only an expression of sentiment, but it heightened Roosevelt's prestige.

Immediately thereafter Roosevelt began an attack upon a Tammany-sponsored bill to reorganize the state highway commission. Governor Dix wished to create a single highway commissioner with full authority and responsibility, but weakly capitulated when Boss Murphy insisted upon divided authority, with appointive power vested in the state engineer, who was a Tammany man. Murphy's bill, said Dix, "seems to be the best that can be had." [29] Roosevelt hoped to rally the insurgents to a second fight, but much as some of them still admired him, they had had enough. It was impossible, he admitted, "to get a sufficient number to refuse to listen to the crack of the party whip." [30] So, for more than a month, Roosevelt alone among the Democrats in the senate fought against the bill. Again, as in his opposition to Sheehan, he spelled out for the benefit of the public the broad principles involved.

The bill was "a vicious measure" which would open the way to patronage, and he demonstrated exactly how, and named those behind it.[31] He elaborated its strange mixture of inconsistencies and errors in a confidential letter to the editor of the New York *Times* [32] and, vehemently mixing his metaphors, denounced it in the senate. It was, said Roosevelt, "ill-conceived in the beginning, re-hashed and amended from time to time by various hands and finally thrown like a bundle of kindling wood before this Senate in disgust . . . this horrible pudding which everybody has stirred and which has not even been put in the oven, must either be eaten in its indigestible state by the people of New York or must be thrown out of the window." It would throw increased maintenance and repair costs upon counties and towns, and would use a fifty-million-dollar bond issue for reconstruction rather than for the building of new roads for which it had been voted. In these and many additional details that he cited, it would be repugnant to his rural constituents. Beyond this there was the basic principle that good government meant responsible government, and this bill would result in just the contrary: "I should be the first to favor any measure looking to concentration of responsibility in one man who would be responsible to the governor, and through the governor to the people," Roosevelt asserted in the most accepted progressive fashion. "This, after all, is to my mind the best kind of democratic doctrine." [33]

Finally the measure went through the senate with just one vote to spare. The Democratic New York *Times* congratulated Roosevelt upon his courage; he was the only Democratic senator who voted against it. [34] *

Roosevelt had an even better issue in the direct primary bill, and he wisely concentrated his efforts upon it. It was so popular that both parties had included direct primary planks in their previous year's platforms, but neither party had any intention of enacting an effective law. Again he was running athwart Tammany. The bosses had not yet learned how easy it was to pervert a direct primary to their own ends, and fought against it with as dogged relentlessness as though it foredoomed their political existence. Roosevelt had no such illusion about its possible effectiveness. "Direct nominations," he explained to a constituent, "will not destroy the party organization, inasmuch as the organization will have the opportunity to place its own candidates before the people, but it will be possible for other candidates to be nominated by other members of the party." If, as seemed likely, few people bothered to vote in the primary, it would be little improvement, but direct primaries should arouse greater interest among the voters in the candidates. "If I am right in this," he concluded, "I believe it will be for the good of the whole Country as the whole theory of our Government is built upon the assumption that every citizen takes an active interest in his own government." [37]

Roosevelt delivered an address in April, 1911, in which he made a luminous analysis of the implications of the direct primary and its role in the American political party system. The object of a party, he said, should be to enunciate the principles of government for which it stood, and to provide candidates to carry them out. Inevitably each party would have leaders, but they should represent the will of the people, not dictate to them. The line between leaders and bosses was

* As a sign of the times, Roosevelt cautiously proposed that to aid motorists the Highway Act should require all vehicles to carry a light at night on all main roads. Further than this he did not dare go for fear of offending the farmers.[35] The following year he sponsored a bill bearing his name to require automobile tires to bear the date of manufacture. They were still so primitive that after two years they were virtually worthless.[36]

often thin. A boss was a leader able to force his wishes upon the party as a whole through his tight control over a small clique within it. Through patronage, he held the unquestioned loyalty of these faithful few. The boss therefore represented, not the party as a whole, but only that small segment always ready to attend caucuses and vote in primaries. In New York, Roosevelt estimated, only about 7 to 8 per cent of the members of the party belonged to the organization. In theory, the direct primary could break their control, but in practice, it could do so only if the electorate came to feel a personal responsibility to choose candidates. Just as in the town-meeting era, it was a public duty to participate in government. The bosses were in control simply through default on the part of the voters. "Professional politicians offered to run things for them, and they were so busy with new things they didn't even stop to answer 'All right.' They just let them." [38] Roosevelt's misgivings about popular inertia continued. A year later he again declared, "I do not believe with some people that the rule of pure democracy as opposed to representative government is going to accomplish the result." [39]

Although Roosevelt doubted the effectiveness of the direct primary, it was highly popular among the progressives of both parties; through giving it strong sponsorship he could gain additional strength. At the same time, since he had no doctrinaire faith in it as a cure-all, he was not disposed to insist upon an effective primary law or none. A good compromise could serve as the first step toward a better measure.[40] To this point, he seems to have reasoned it out. Additional advantage came to him through having his name linked with some sort of primary measure – even a very bad one. Public memory for details was short, and as in the Sheehan deadlock tended to give him credit for more than he achieved – not for a weak compromise, but a clear-cut progressive victory.

After some weeks of agitation, Roosevelt and his cohorts, who rejoined him for this battle, forced Tammany in mid-July to produce a direct primary bill. A worse bill would be difficult to visualize. This one would allow the organization to place a list of candidates at the top of the ballot and, for the sake of the illiterate, identify them with the party emblem. The measure was so bad that even Governor Dix awoke from his lethargy to send a message of denunciation to the legislature. Roosevelt then by his own account "raised a riot" in the senate by moving that the senate judiciary committee "report a bill conforming with the message. It upset the plans of the organization and precipitated a 3-hour angry debate."[41] Not unexpectedly, he lost in the senate, and was not able to force out a good bill, or even obtain action upon the bad one; the legislature recessed without acting.

In September the primary measure came up again and Roosevelt once more dominated the debate. After obtaining a few minor concessions, he voted for the bill, though two of his erstwhile followers refused to do so. It still allowed the organization to spend money upon its candidates and to identify them on the ballot with the party emblem. Roosevelt boasted, "One of the regular organization men in the Senate, told me when I said there had been a fair compromise that we had the whole apple, and that the strictly organization Senators got the core." A disgruntled follower, Saxe, retorted, "I don't want either the apple or the lemon after the heart is taken out of it."[42]

The following year, Roosevelt co-operated with progressives in the Republican party to work for a better primary law.[43]

Logically, Roosevelt's forthright endorsement of the direct primary should have led him to take an unequivocal position in favor of woman suffrage. Both meant more popular control over government. He undoubtedly favored it, but was already too astute a politician not to hedge a bit. Although his district embraced Vassar College, a stronghold of feminism, it was mostly a farm area where many a male voter still looked askance at the thought of giving women the ballot. From the faculty members of Vassar, both female and male, came a flurry of letters in favor of extending the suffrage; many women not associated with the college were equally militant. Roosevelt, not wishing to alienate the farm vote, took refuge in a formula which he then believed in, and often practiced: "I am trying to get the sentiment of Dutchess County . . . as much as possible," he informed a Poughkeepsie woman attorney in February 1911, "and I shall be guided very largely by the result."[44] At the end of May he was still undecided about his constituents. "I am not opposed to female suffrage," he explained, "but I think it is a very great question whether the people of the state as a whole want it or not." Therefore, the legislature should pass an act providing for a referendum on the question before it submitted to the voters an amendment to the state constitution.[45] This undoubtedly satisfied opponents of the reform; it only irritated the Dutchess County suffragettes.[46] Of the two pressures, theirs was the greater. The story later spread that Inez Milholland converted him while sitting on his desk in the state senate, but Eleanor Roosevelt says her husband had already decided two months earlier to support woman suffrage. In any event by the spring of 1912 he discarded circumventions and directly advocated a woman suffrage amendment.[47]

Roosevelt was on much safer ground when he fell in with a New York *Herald* campaign for an amendment to the United States Constitution to provide a national uniform divorce law. He promised to introduce a resolution in the legislature memorializing Congress on the subject. "As to objections that have been made that Congress might pass bad or absurd divorce regulations," he commented, "I feel assured that Congress will be able to frame a divorce law that will be generally satisfactory and one that will raise the standard of divorce regulations throughout the country. Certainly no conceivable law that would meet the approval of a majority in Congress could be one-tenth as bad as the present condition of our chaotic divorce laws." [48] No state senator, either Republican or Democratic, would dare raise objections to this proposal. The National Christian League for Promotion of Purity was delighted.[49] The only objection was a mild one on states'-rights grounds: Could not the same objective be better reached through uniform state laws? To this, Roosevelt replied, "Of course, as a Democrat I have always preferred [state legislation] as a matter of principle . . . rather than the giving of additional powers to the Federal Government," but he felt it would be extremely difficult to persuade "the more 'advanced' western states" to accept uniform restrictions.[50] The legislature unanimously adopted Roosevelt's resolution, and that ended the issue, and the publicity.[51]

Although Roosevelt could be ruthless in trampling upon lax divorce (adultery was the only legal grounds in New York State), he was more cautious in jousting with John Barleycorn. Through the device of local option, Prohibition was spreading rapidly throughout the United States; it was anathema to Tammany Democrats in New York City, but popular in rural areas and among Protestant churchgoers in cities. Local option seemed an entirely safe device for Roosevelt to support. He could point out to wet constituents that it did not mean that he himself was a dry, but merely that he was willing to let the people of an area decide for themselves. In his campaign in 1910 he endorsed the principle, and promised he would support its extension to cities of the third class (meaning Poughkeepsie), with the qualification that he would do so "only that it might be seen how . . .[it] would work out." [52]

As with the referendum on woman suffrage Roosevelt could use local option as a means of hedging on Prohibition by asserting his desire to allow the voters to decide for themselves. But it was so unpopular in the big cities that too close identification with it might make it impossible for Roosevelt at some future time to be elected governor. In January, 1913, he reluctantly introduced a city local option bill for the Anti-Saloon League. There was "very little chance of obtaining favorable action at this session," he warned, and "more results could be accomplished by taking up the matter of option in cities on the basis of wards or districts within the cities." [53] While he was in the senate, Roosevelt co-operated closely with the Commandant of West Point to dry up Highland Falls, the town nearest the Academy, and voted correctly, from the Anti-Saloon League viewpoint, on every liquor issue. The League even published a laudatory editorial about him in its magazine, *American Issue*.[54] The damage was done; he had weakened himself further in New York City. All through the Prohibition era, even down to 1932, the story persisted that whatever Roosevelt might say, at heart he was a "dry," and there was his state legislative record for proof.[55]

As long as Roosevelt's political horizons did not extend beyond the Hudson River Valley, he could gain votes by being strait-laced. Many people in his district looked askance at Tammany because it worked not only against Prohibition, but in favor of legalized horse racing, Sunday baseball,[56] and prize fighting. Roosevelt opposed all three. "While I am personally devoted to horses and to races," he wrote in 1911, "I have always felt that a sport cannot be a healthy one when its existence depends on gambling." [57] Although it was contrary to his nature and upbringing, it was sound politics to be a puritan at Albany.

Roosevelt and his reformer friends became a bit confused about clear-cut principles of good government during the next controversy, over a new city charter for New York. As in many states, every new municipal charter required special state legislation, and opened the way for much political haggling. In theory the progressives believed in ending this sore spot through municipal home rule, enactment of a standard state law which would allow municipalities to choose by referendum the form of government they wished without having to resort to the legislature. Roosevelt ran athwart the abuse in May, 1911, when he decided it was useless even to try to get through a commission-type charter for Poughkeepsie, because Tammany was quietly burying all such proposals in committee.[58]

Two years later, Roosevelt as an "opening wedge" introduced the standard bill approved by the Municipal Government Association.[59]

It would extend home rule to all cities except Buffalo and New York, which the reformers felt were separate problems. Although they disliked Tammany meddling in upstate charters, they were quite ready in reverse to insist upon serious modifications in the Tammany-sponsored charter for New York City.

By June, 1911, Roosevelt had already conferred about the charter with its most ardent advocate, Mayor Gaynor of New York. Gaynor wished among other things to replace the unwieldy school board with a small, paid body. Roosevelt thought that the nature of the New York City government would make it "a highly dangerous experiment."[60] Another provision, that women teachers should receive equal pay with men, brought to the charter the support of women teachers and feminists. Roosevelt regarded this as going too far, and cautiously hinted that it was "opposed . . . by a good many of the leading educators of the Country" and later would be dropped from the charter.[61] During the summer, Roosevelt's Harvard classmate, Albert de Roode, counsel of the Civil Service Reform Association, strongly urged Roosevelt to lead a powerful fight against the charter. Many strong organizations would be behind him, including the Reform Association, the City Club, the Citizens' Union, and the Allied Real Estate Interests. De Roode warned that the charter would be "very harmful to the progressive wing of the Democratic party"; it would cut down the independent Democratic vote in the city, and give Tammany additional power in the state conventions.[62]

Roosevelt returned from Campobello ready to make the charter a state issue.* Although reform sentiment was behind him, by this time he was too clever to assume an unequivocal attitude. Instead he stood ready to compromise if the mayor would give up his power of veto over public franchises, and would accept some state supervision of the municipal Civil Service Board. In the temporary absence of two Tammany senators, Roosevelt held enough votes to defeat the charter in the senate.[64] Mayor Gaynor sent an emissary to negotiate, and Roosevelt heard rumors that he would surrender. Instead, Tammany counterattacked by threatening in the reapportionment of congressional districts to reshuffle Dutchess County into an overwhelmingly

* As later, FDR had the happy knack of sloughing off the most involved political concerns during his vacations. During August while the fight over the charter was shaping up, he was sailing down the coast of Maine on the *Half Moon,* his hand "so stiff from handling ropes" that he could hardly hold a pen to write Eleanor, who remained behind at Campobello, "My health is *wonderful* and you won't know me."[63]

Republican district. If Roosevelt would listen to reason on the charter they would consider more favorable reapportionment. If he failed to do so, he would not only let down the Democratic congressman, "poor old Connell," but further alienate the regular Democratic politicians in Dutchess County. This latter was so serious a threat that while Tammany called the tune, Roosevelt danced and reformers winced. On September 29, he announced his support of the charter bill; the reapportionment committee simultaneously reported a favorable congressional district to include Dutchess County. Progressive constituents protested so loudly that, the following evening, Roosevelt reversed himself and came out against the Charter again; the reapportionment committee again made the congressional district normally Republican. To retrieve what little dignity he could, Roosevelt repeatedly stated that there was no connection between his vote on the charter and reapportionment.[65] Ultimately he lost both ways. The measures went through, his congressional district went Republican, and the new charter went into effect to weaken civil service and strengthen the ability of Tammany to plunder.[66]

In this disheartening fashion, the lengthy 1911 session of the legislature came to an end. No matter how skillful, clever, and popular Roosevelt had been, he was a Canute before the Tammany tide.

Altogether the 1911 session of the New York legislature had increased the New York City payroll by $350,000 [67] and in other ways had come uncomfortably close to proving the contention of the Republicans, that a state victory for the Democrats meant a state-wide domination by the New York City machine. Assemblymen were elected annually; and not surprisingly, upstate New York voters in the 1911 election shifted back toward Republican normalcy. Only four out of twenty-three insurgent assemblymen survived. One of them was Chanler who edged through in Dutchess County by a seven-vote margin. However, this did not signify a machine purge of the irregulars, for in New York City, Tammany won by uncomfortably narrow pluralities, and two years later lost to a Fusion reform slate. Rather it seemed to indicate a voter reaction against all Democrats.

Roosevelt chose to interpret the election as a progressive triumph rather than a Democratic defeat. He renewed his battle cry that the bosses must go, and told a Buffalo audience that while they could blame machine control of the legislature partly upon the bosses, the ultimate failure was theirs for not voting the bosses out of existence. "There is only one remedy," he asserted with a new boldness. "C. F.

Murphy and his kind must, like the noxious weed, be plucked out, root and branch. . . . The good work has begun. . . . Cassidy in Queens County went out on the toe of a boot last week. McCooey is hanging on by the skin of his teeth in Brooklyn. The Bronx has thrown off Murphy domination." Defective as it was, the new direct primary law would make it easier for the young man who thought politics a dirty business, for the busy man and the lazy man to complete the ouster. In terms that echoed Theodore Roosevelt, he egged them on. "For those of you who are fond of hunting, it is no longer necessary to go to the Canadian Rockies or the Jungles of Africa for sport; there is bigger game and better hunting right here in New York State. . . . The hunt is on, and the beasts of prey have begun to fall. The American citizen is again fighting for his freedom." [68]

Roosevelt was overestimating his success on the trail of big game in the jungles of New York politics. While he was engaged in hunting the Tiger, the Tiger was as actively stalking him. Patrick E. McCabe, clerk of the senate, sneered at the speech as "bristling with the silly conceits of a political prig," and savagely denounced Roosevelt:

> Disloyalty and party treachery is the political cult of a few snobs in our party who attain prominence through the exigencies of a turn-over in the politics of the State and who are simply political accidents. . . .
>
> Mr. Roosevelt admits that he is the best-informed man in the party in this State on obsolete and remote questions of government. I have heard him time and again quote or misquote . . . Solon. . . . He also gives several years of his life on the Continent conning the Governments of Europe. All this by contrast with my humble equipment . . . as my leadership here in Albany depends absolutely upon human sympathy, human interest, and human ties among those with whom I was born and bred. . . .
>
> I believe the vigorous men of the party are largely responsible for this embarrassing situation because they have humored and coddled too much the little fellows, fops and cads who come as near being political leaders as a green pea does a circus tent.
>
> Some leaders may stand for the impudence and arrogance of these political prudes, but I won't.[69]

From a later viewpoint, these early political maneuvers of Roosevelt's seem significant primarily for his rapid development of political techniques and his formulation of a progressive pattern of thought. Before the end of his first term in the state senate he had replaced the vague inclinations he aired in the 1910 campaign with fairly tangible ideas in a number of fields. On March 3, 1912, he undertook in a speech before the People's Forum at Troy, New York, to outline his basic philosophy. It was almost a unique effort and it is of particular interest because it sums up his thinking as a progressive before the First World War. Through his confused but earnest statement there ran hints of Theodore Roosevelt, Herbert Croly, Woodrow Wilson, and Harvard History 1, but in its adroit use of innocuous terms in place of obnoxious ones, it foreshadowed the mature Franklin D. Roosevelt.

In his talk, Roosevelt tried to explain the reasons for world-wide discontent among workingmen: "Competition has been shown to be useful up to a certain point, but co-operation, which is the thing that we must strive for today, begins where competition leaves off." He did not wish to call this co-operation "community interest," for that was a socialist term, nor "brotherhood of man," which was too idealistic. Instead, he termed it "struggle for liberty of the community rather than liberty of the individual," and said it was "what the founders of the republic were groping for."

As an example of a field where co-operation, or "liberty of the community," was essential, he cited conservation, which he was ready to extend not only to forests but also to food supplies. "If we can prophesy today that the State (or in other words the people as a whole) will shortly tell a man how many trees he must cut, then why can we not, without being radical, predict that the State will compel every farmer to till his land or raise beef, or horses? For after all if I own a farm of a hundred acres and let it lie waste and overgrown, I am just as much a destroyer of the liberty of the community, and by liberty, we mean happiness and prosperity, as is the strong man who stands idle on the corner, refusing to work."

The same principle applied to trusts. There, too, the public must insist upon "co-operation." "If we call the method regulation, people hold up their hands in horror and say 'Unamerican,' or 'dangerous,' but if we call the same identical process co-operation these same old fogies will cry out 'well done.'" Trusts run upon the theory of monopoly. Co-operation, he expounded, and here he drew upon Theodore Roosevelt's New Nationalism, "puts monopoly out of date." He added, "We now understand that the mere size of a trust is not of necessity its evil. The trust is evil because it monopolizes for a few and as long as this keeps up it will be necessary for a community to change its features. . . ."

"What we want today," Roosevelt emphasized, "is, not . . . laws aimed at this, that or the other business or class or system of government off hand in the hope that some target will be hit somewhere. . . . Every new star that people have hitched their wagon to for the past half century, whether it be anti-rebating, or anti-trusts, or new fashioned education, or conservation of our natural resources or State regulation of common carriers, or commission government . . . [each is a step] in the evolution of the new theory of the liberty of the community." [70]

CHAPTER VIII

The Roosevelt Wagon and the Wilson Star

Woodrow Wilson in his life gave mankind a new vision of pure democracy.

— FDR, *February, 1924.*[1]

DESPITE brave words and deeds, Roosevelt could hardly expect to free the Democratic party in New York from the grip of Tammany, which stood in the way of his political progress within the state. When he hitched his wagon to the rapidly rising star of Governor Woodrow Wilson of New Jersey, he found a means of getting around the obstacle of Tammany hostility. At the time, the optimistic Roosevelt probably was unaware of the predicament he was in. As a self-avowed progressive he was simply taking a logical step when he allied himself with the strongest liberal contender for the Democratic nomination for President. Anyhow, he was already growing restless in the close atmosphere of Albany, and would be glad for a chance to move upward to the freer air of Washington. Wilson provided that opportunity.

Before the end of 1911, Roosevelt, like many another progressive Democrat, went to New Jersey to talk with Wilson about the presidential nomination. As president of Princeton, Wilson had been such a militant conservative speaker and writer that J. P. Morgan's associate, Colonel George Harvey, dreamed of putting him forward as the Wall Street answer to Bryan. In 1910, as an opening move toward the White House, Colonel Harvey helped arrange his nomination for governor of New Jersey. As a candidate, however, Wilson espoused a progressive program, and as governor he transformed New Jersey from one of the most backward to one of the most progressive states.[2]

Roosevelt conversed with Wilson at Trenton, then rode on the train with him and his secretary, Joseph Tumulty, as far as Princeton. He assured Wilson that sentiment for him was increasing among both conservative and progressive Democrats in New York State. But when Wilson inquired how much support he might expect from the New

York delegation at the nominating convention, Roosevelt had to admit that while a third might favor him, they would be powerless to give him their ballots. They would function under the unit rule, which worked like the legislative caucus, and would have to vote as a block for the majority's choice, which meant Murphy's choice. Murphy disliked Wilson.[3]

Nevertheless, it was a meeting full of portents, for Franklin D. Roosevelt in a very real sense was to spend seven years in Professor Wilson's school of public administration. Those tracing the origins of New Deal ideas go back to two main fountainheads – Wilson's New Freedom and Theodore Roosevelt's New Nationalism. The ideology and techniques of both men left a deep impress upon Franklin D. Roosevelt. During the New Deal, on the basis of his own long political experience, he made a perceptive comparison of the two leaders:

> Theodore Roosevelt lacked Woodrow Wilson's appeal to the fundamental and failed to stir, as Wilson did, the truly profound moral and social convictions. Wilson, on the other hand, failed where Theodore Roosevelt succeeded in stirring people to enthusiasm over specific individual events, even though these specific events may have been superficial in comparison with the fundamentals."[4]

In other words, he felt that Wilson had a keener sense of the basic issues, Theodore Roosevelt the better timing in manipulation of public opinion.

Franklin Roosevelt's first meeting with Wilson brought forth no sudden outburst of warm personal friendship between the two men. Wilson had far too much reserve for that, though he was interested in this spectacular young man who was ready to try much in upstate New York. In their later relations, Wilson inspired more awe than love in Roosevelt, and stood in relation to him as to a sort of superschoolmaster, another Rector Peabody. When Roosevelt showed signs of being insubordinate, it was in the same spirit.

For the next few months, Roosevelt could not do much for Wilson nor achieve much in the legislature. The sessions began in January, 1912, and Roosevelt found them dreary. In the 1911 assembly, the Democrats had held a majority of 22; now the Republicans held a majority of 53 and could easily block the Democratic senate. Roosevelt gingerly worked with several of the progressive Republican assemblymen, most notably his friend and Harvard classmate, Theodore Douglas Robinson,* but had difficulty threading his way between the machine Democrats and old-guard Republicans. Whatever hope he might have once had for vigorous leadership from Governor Dix was long since gone. "As to seeing the Governor," he lamented, "there is no earthly object in doing so. I keep on going every few days but only because of local bills, etc. There is no other point to it." [5]

In one area, Roosevelt did continue to co-operate with Dix. The governor was still pressing for conservation legislation, and Roosevelt, as chairman of the Senate Forest, Fish and Game Committee, heartily seconded him. As a result he now assumed state leadership and gained significant experience in this critical field in which progressives and their successors were so keenly interested. In 1911, Roosevelt's opposition to Tammany had led him to oppose relaxation of the game laws. The clue to Tammany interest in this seemed to lie in a warning from the president of the New York State Fish, Game, and Forest League that "dealers in game and millinery supplies contributed substantially to the [city] Democratic organization . . . and have a right to expect legislation in their favor." [6] Despite Roosevelt's vehement opposition, the senate in March, 1911, passed a bill allowing spring duck shooting on Long Island,[7] but it was later defeated in the assembly.[8] Roosevelt prevented Tammany from weakening the law which prohibited the sale of plumage. These were years when, to the delight of milliners and the horror of Audubon societies, women gloried in large hats bedecked with bird feathers.[9]

In January, 1912, Roosevelt tried to develop a comprehensive conservation program. He wished to recodify and shorten the entire fish and game law, and enact water storage and timber preservation measures.[10] A number of persons with vested interests fought against one or another of the provisions of the new fish and game code, and it became law only after many weary weeks of debate and compromise. "I am slowly getting the taste of rotten fish and game out of my mouth," one of Roosevelt's allies in the assembly wryly commented. "That bill nearly put me out of business, physically, mentally, and morally. NEVER AGAIN." [11] Roosevelt concurred.[12]

Roosevelt failed in the other part of his enterprise, to try to pass a similar timber preservation code. He himself had long been interested

* FDR's family relationship with Teddy Robinson was complicated. Robinson was a nephew of Theodore Roosevelt, a first cousin of Eleanor, and the husband of Franklin's niece, Helen.

in scientific forestation of his own lands. That very spring, as in most other years, he planted thousands of trees at Hyde Park.[13] Gifford Pinchot, whose fiery advocacy of conservation had done much to arouse widespread progressive interest, whipped Roosevelt's interest to a high point by showing him a photograph of an abandoned Chinese city, surrounded by denuded mountains and ridges. A few days later, referring to the picture, Roosevelt warned, "This is what will happen in this very State if the individuals are allowed to do as they please with the natural resources to line their own pockets during their life."[14]

In keeping with Pinchot's advice, Roosevelt introduced a bill for the "Protection of Lands, Forests, and Public Parks." It contained the most drastic restrictions being advocated by the state conservation commission and the Camp Fire Club – including a clause to restrict the cutting of trees below a minimum size even on private timber lands. This stirred up the wrath of the lumber interests, who came to Albany in force to object to every feature of the bill.[15] "The same old fight is going on up here," Roosevelt noted indignantly, "between the people who see that the Adirondacks are being denuded of trees and water power and those, who in the early days, when grants of timber and water were given for a song, succeeded in getting for nothing what they would have to pay well for today. Nobody here has any desire to confiscate property and the bill before my Committee is a conservation measure, solely."[16] Nevertheless, Roosevelt could not convince even his own committee members that the restriction on timber cutting was constitutional. After "four or five stormy sessions," he reluctantly struck out the clause "because of fear that the whole bill, which was made to codify the existing laws, would fail because of this." However, he was certain that ultimately some similar statute would pass.[17]

Roosevelt's bill was too popular for Tammany legislators to oppose it openly. They voted for it in the senate and, after it passed, quietly co-operated with the Republican Speaker of the assembly to block it there. Al Smith, the minority leader of the assembly (who had yet to take a progressive view of conservation), supported a complicated bipartisan substitute measure which appeared to promote conservation but actually granted valuable concessions to private utility companies. The machine tried to push it through in a rush at the close of the session, but Roosevelt so loudly "raised the alarm" against this "frame-up . . . of the private power interests," that the senate did not dare pass it. He thereupon congratulated the people of the state upon their narrow escape from a piece of vicious legislation.[18] The victory was purely negative, for the machines had effectively killed his own conservation measure.

As a result of Tammany tactics of this sort, many of the upstate Democratic legislators again became restless during the last weeks of the legislative session and voted independently on several measures.[19] This was a mere rumbling rather than a new major eruption of revolt, and Roosevelt had no hope that he could mobilize it into a powerful stand at the state Democratic convention in April. Nevertheless, it was of some small importance since, through Governor Dix's default, he was the most likely heir to the support of a group of Cleveland and progressive Democrats who comprised the Democratic League.[20] These men had no love for the machine, and still inclined toward Woodrow Wilson.

Roosevelt's Republican friend Robinson introduced a presidential primary bill in the state assembly. Had it succeeded, upstate New York Democrats could have expressed their preference for Wilson. But it would have been still more of a boon to Theodore Roosevelt, who had "thrown his hat" into the Republican ring and in states with presidential primaries was rapidly winning delegates despite the strong opposition of the Old Guard.* Because the bill would have appeared an open gesture in favor of Theodore Roosevelt, Franklin decided not to introduce it in the senate.[22]

In the middle of March, Roosevelt was gloomy about Wilson's chances, and indeed about those of the Democrats in New York State. He did not anticipate a national breakup in the Republican party, and he recognized that the Democrats in the state had been weakened by the fight against Murphy. By this time, Colonel Harvey and his financier backers had split completely with Wilson. Roosevelt predicted that Tammany would force the New York delegates to obey the wishes of powerful anti-Wilson Wall Street forces, by voting for Governor Judson Harmon of Ohio first, Senator Oscar Underwood of Alabama second, and Speaker Champ Clark of Missouri third. He reasoned that Wilson offered the best hope of Democratic success, but probably would not get the nomination.[23]

The political tide continued to run against Wilson when the

* Concerning the primaries, Franklin Roosevelt commented at the beginning of June, "It is indeed a marvelous thing that [Colonel Roosevelt], acting with the support of untrained militia[,] has succeeded in overcoming the well organized opposition of the trained soldiers of the Republican party."[21]

Democratic state convention met in New York City on April 12. Roosevelt invited a number of upstate Democrats who were coming to New York City for the convention to attend a Wilson dinner at the Hotel Belmont the evening before. Out of twenty who responded, seventeen declined.[24] This symbolized how completely Murphy had control. The convention itself was short, smoothly oiled, and a complete Tammany triumph. Roosevelt's ally, John K. Sague, the mayor of Poughkeepsie, introduced one dissident resolution, and it was quickly voted down. Roosevelt himself was conspicuously silent; the only evidence that he was even present was a composite photograph in the New York *Herald*, which placed him next to one of the hated Wall Street Belmonts. Murphy obtained ninety uninstructed delegates, who would be bound by the unit rule to vote for whomever he might choose, and had the minor additional satisfaction of eliminating Roosevelt as either a delegate or alternate.[25]

Independent Democrats immediately began plans for an organization through which they could at least campaign for Wilson within the state. The day after the state convention, Roosevelt went on a vacation trip, but he left with Thomas Mott Osborne authorization to sign his name to a call for a Wilson conference.[26]

The junket to Panama must have been a welcome relief. Although Franklin Roosevelt would not further his Uncle Ted's drive for the Republican nomination, he did uncritically admire the vigorous fashion in which Theodore Roosevelt had started work on the Panama Canal. It was now in final stages of excavation, and Franklin reasoned that his brother-in-law Hall Roosevelt, who was planning to become an engineer, would benefit from a firsthand inspection.[27] Roosevelt, his brother-in-law, and a Republican friend from the state senate, J. Mayhew Wainwright, had a lively time sight-seeing in Jamaica, but it was the construction at Panama that impressed Roosevelt. "I saw the famous cut through the mountains," he recalled in 1938, "and from the top of it, the trains, great huge trains of dump cars, locomotives, steam shovels, looked like gnats." [28] It was not only the engineering feat, "this wonder of the world, greater than the Tower of Babel or the Pyramids," [29] which had him bursting with pride at the time, but the efficient way in which Americans were conquering the tropics. The city of Panama was "clean and fairly orderly – a very different Panama than under the French." [30] At the Corozal Y.M.C.A., he spent an evening with "a couple of hundred young Americans who are all making good and have to a man the same kind of spirit which is putting the Canal through ahead of time." [31] He had a "nice long talk" with Colonel George W. Goethals, who summed up Roosevelt's own emotions when he "said in his quiet way: 'We like to have Americans come down, because they all say it makes them better Americans.' " [32] Whatever Roosevelt's views on imperialism might have been when he was a debater at Groton, he now glowed with patriotic faith in American tropical enterprise.

Upon his return to New York in the middle of May, Roosevelt found a Wilson movement well under way. In New York City William F. McCombs, Wilson's principal manager, had collaborated with William Gibbs McAdoo and Senator James O'Gorman to build up an organization, and O'Gorman was defying Tammany with all the independence that Roosevelt had hoped for. In upstate New York, Osborne had created a similar but independent movement. Though Roosevelt felt the odds were very much against Wilson's nomination,[33] he was willing to take a public stand for him on the ground that "we may do some good and can certainly do no harm." [34] He accepted the chairmanship of the executive committee of the New York State Wilson Conference, which raised considerable funds, largely from Osborne,[35] and sent five or six young men to important cities throughout the state to hold meetings and establish Wilson clubs.[36] In addition, Roosevelt hired one of the most competent newspapermen in the state, a New York *Herald* reporter, Louis McHenry Howe, to spread publicity. Howe began turning out quantities of articles and letters, and sent Roosevelt some samples. "As masterpieces of the English language," Howe joked, "you better have them framed." [37]

Wilson's chief manager, the emaciated McCombs, was making a mighty effort, and nationally the political tide showed some signs of turning back toward Wilson. Even more surprising, it was running for the first time in a score of years toward the Democrats. This was because of a Republican split at their convention. The Old Guard completely dominated the proceedings, but when they renominated Taft, Theodore Roosevelt's followers seceded and prepared to organize the Progressive party and run a third ticket. As a result, whatever candidate the Democrats nominated at Baltimore was almost sure to win, and Franklin Roosevelt became more hopeful that it might be Wilson.[38] "Unless the Democrats nominate a strong Progressive," he commented, "[Theodore] Roosevelt will cut into the Democratic Progressive vote." [39]

There was little Franklin D. Roosevelt and his associates could do in New York except whip up public sentiment, and assure doubtful delegates from other states that Wilson was more likely than any other candidate to carry the state with its weighty block of electoral votes. Thus they might help pave the way for a Wilson stampede at the convention.[40]

The New York State Wilson Conference, under Roosevelt's leadership, provided a rather ineffective claque of one hundred and fifty men at Baltimore.[41] They opened headquarters across the street from the Wilson and Clark headquarters,[42] and issued a manifesto to the assembling delegates:

"New York has a large 'Progressive' vote. Unless you give us a candidate that will get this vote, we shall lose the State." No Democrats except Madison and Buchanan, they asserted, had ever been elected President without the electoral vote of New York; no Democrat could carry New York without the independent vote. Wilson alone could get both regular and progressive support in the state. In conclusion, they paraphrased one of the most widely known whiskey slogans of the era, "*NOMINATE WILSON – THAT'S ALL.*"[43]

For all their hullabaloo, Roosevelt and the Wilson Conference were drowned out in the general uproar of the convention; they did not attract as much attention as a delegation of Ivy League college boys who had come to yell for Wilson. Roosevelt himself was a little more successful than his followers in getting publicity. The day before the convention opened, some wag started the rumor that Roosevelt had arrived – everyone gawked at the thin young man, and turned away chagrined that it was not the Colonel.[44] Through the intercession of Senator O'Gorman, he obtained seats in the gallery for the Wilson Conference where they kept up a noise for Wilson.[45] Roosevelt himself held credentials from the sergeant at arms, countersigned by the Wilsonian national committeeman from Wisconsin, Joseph Davies, which admitted him without badge or ticket. He had a good seat in the gallery, but preferred to spend most of his time in the press stand with several New York friends.[46]

In March, Roosevelt had predicted that the contest would be wide open at the start.[47] This was a good guess. The balloting went on for several days, with Clark in the lead most of the time, and at first apparently close to victory. It took two thirds of the votes to obtain the nomination, and this was exceedingly difficult to achieve except with Southern support. Wilson was second, Harmon third, and Underwood fourth, clinging tenaciously to a block of Southern delegates.

There is an exciting story that at a crucial point in the convention on Saturday after Clark obtained a majority on a ballot, Roosevelt got wind of a plot to slip several hundred Baltimore ward heelers onto the convention floor that night to start a big demonstration and stampede the delegates into nominating Clark. Roosevelt, the tale goes, knowing that the doorkeepers would admit everyone wearing Clark buttons, lined up his New York following together with about a hundred Baltimore Wilson men, provided them all with Clark buttons, and rushed them into the Armory close behind the Clark men. Tremendous noise and confusion resulted; the Clark demonstration fizzled, and both groups were ultimately evicted. By implication, Wilson was thus saved.[48]

The story has at least a grain of truth, though its significance is small; too many delegations were standing firm to make likely a "stampede" for any candidate for several days. On Friday, the night of the nominating speeches, the Clark managers salted the galleries with 2500 toughs, hired to yell for an hour for Clark, and perhaps even bring about nomination by acclamation.* Their means of access past Tammany doorkeepers were narrow pasteboards bearing the words "Champ Clark" in red letters.[50] Some of these may have slipped into Roosevelt's hands. A half hour after the Clark demonstration ended, at eight minutes past two on the morning of June 28, a New Jersey judge came to the platform to nominate Wilson. Before he could even begin his speech, a demonstration burst forth. Murphy and his ninety New York delegates remained quietly in their seats, but down from the galleries and in through a side door came the members of Franklin Roosevelt's Wilson Conference, carrying banners proclaiming twenty upstate counties to be for Wilson. Their numbers were strangely swollen – there were even a half-dozen liveried messenger boys in their midst.[51] The demonstration lasted ten minutes longer than the one for Clark, but had scarcely any effect on the balloting which followed.

After a few ballots, Murphy swung the votes of New York from Harmon to Clark, although there was little real sentiment for Clark among Tammany men. A day or two earlier, Al Smith had walked up to a Clark picture. It bore the inscription, "Don't he look like a President?" and Smith wrote beneath, "No he do not." [52] When Murphy

* At the height of the demonstration, a Clark man got onto the platform, moved that Clark be nominated by acclamation, put the question, and declared it passed. Of course, no one paid any attention to him.[49]

switched to Clark, Bryan dramatically announced that as a consequence he was changing his vote to Wilson, but only for so long as Wilson did not have New York's votes. This started no Wilson landslide as has been frequently stated, but did forestall the Wilson managers from bargaining for the New York delegates.* Gradually through adroit negotiations with other bosses, they picked up votes until they achieved the nomination without Tammany aid, on the forty-sixth ballot.[55]

Roosevelt joyously wired Eleanor, who had become bored in Baltimore and gone to Campobello, "ALL MY PLANS VAGUE SPLENDID TRIUMPH." [56] It was a remarkable victory for Wilson, and in a very minor way for Roosevelt as well. Although his part in the convention was unimportant, he had stood forth as the Wilson leader for upstate New York. "I am especially pleased," wrote Montgomery Hare, an opponent of Tammany, "at the strong position it has placed you in." [57]

The question was how Roosevelt could make the most of it. The answer, on the part of members of both the Wilson Conference and the older Democratic League, was that the nomination of Wilson despite Tammany should be the signal for an all-out onslaught against Murphy. "Don't for Heaven's sake," Hare warned, "let Wilson or his managers make any agreement or agreements express or implied with Murphy or . . . treat him with other than formal courtesy. Tammany cannot refuse a *formal* support to the ticket and nothing under the sun could induce the ring to go any further. The independents will have to do the rest. It is a great chance for the Democratic League if T. M. O[sborne] will handle the matter skillfully and make a broad appeal to the old Cleveland Democrats – as well as the young progressives, for the munitions of war have got to come from the former." [58] This was gratuitous advice, for the Wilson Conference had drafted plans of action – undoubtedly to try to pressure the New York delegation – even before Wilson's nomination.[59]

In the final analysis what was to be done depended upon Wilson. Theodore Roosevelt was sure to pull sufficient votes from Taft so that

* There is inconclusive evidence that some of Roosevelt's conservative Democratic associates arranged a deal with Murphy to swing the delegation to Wilson after balloting a few times for Clark. The key figure was DeLancey Nicoll, a wealthy Wall Street lawyer, a "gold Democrat" in 1896, and a member of Tammany. During the 1912 convention, he spent much time in the press stand with Roosevelt.[53] Montgomery Hare wrote after the convention, "I do not quite understand what went amiss in the N. Y. delegation. . . . Nicoll . . . peremptorily changed the plan after Murphy had agreed to it Thursday night. However, it is much better as it worked out, is it not?" [54]

Wilson would carry New York regardless of Tammany. When Roosevelt went to Sea Girt, New Jersey, the day after the nomination to confer with Wilson, he threw the reporters off the trail by telling them that he had seen Kermit Roosevelt in New York City that morning, and that Kermit had admitted, "Pop's been praying for Clark."[60] Theodore Roosevelt's chagrin was beside the point. The question was whether the Democratic delegation from New York in the next Congress would be friendly to Wilson's legislative program. To work in this direction, Franklin Roosevelt (with at least the tacit consent of Wilson) immediately organized a militant pro-Wilson anti-Tammany faction, which bore close resemblance to earlier upstate Democratic coalitions.[61]

The Empire State Democracy, Roosevelt proclaimed at a preliminary meeting, was to be a permanent progressive organization. Its first goal, he declared, was to carry New York for Wilson; to do so it must prevent Murphy from meddling with the state ticket.[62] The movement quickly gained a following. The *World* and *Post* in New York City and a number of influential papers upstate backed it; two hundred Democrats attended a second meeting at the Hotel Astor on July 29. Osborne pointed out to them that Tammany was on the wane, that in the past six years the Democratic vote had fallen off 46,000 in New York City, while it had increased 32,000 above the Bronx. Roosevelt developed the theme:

> I think we represent the majority of the democrats in the State and Charles F. Murphy doesn't. We're not a small minority. We're a big majority, that's kicking for its rights. They refer to us as "irregular." We are the regulars. The system, Tammany, has prevented the democrats from having control in New York for sixteen years. The ring exists for the benefit of the ring and not for the benefit of the people. This is the year to go ahead and strike, and we've got the club. We hope we won't have to use it, but if we do have to we'll use it for the benefit of the democratic party.[63]

An emphatic dissenter on behalf of some close friends of Wilson had warned that an independent movement would injure his chances of carrying the state,[64] but this was unlikely since the national and state tickets were printed upon separate ballots. The Republican schism almost guaranteed that the Democrats not only would carry New York for Wilson, but pull along the unpopular Murphy-Dix state ticket too. The greatest possible menace to a Democratic state victory would be the introduction of a fourth state ticket. This was the club to which Roosevelt was referring, and the Empire State Democrats prepared to use it if Murphy insisted upon bossing the state Democratic convention. To split the Democratic party would mean certain defeat, Roosevelt had pointed out a month earlier.[65] While they could keep Tammany from winning, they could not win themselves. Consequently, the fourth ticket was a threat they hoped not to have to put into execution. However, they passed a resolution to set up the full machinery for it. Members in the counties were to choose delegates to meet immediately after the Democrats, to "take appropriate action upon the nominations for State officers made by the Democratic State Convention."[66]

Sadly enough, this was the climax, not the opening, of the movement. In mid-August, Osborne, the financial angel, ran out of funds, and in the critical period just before the state convention Roosevelt, the temporary chairman, contracted typhoid fever. The Empire State Democracy was of only small effect, and that largely attained from earlier momentum. Wilson conferred with Senator O'Gorman, then sternly voiced his concern that the New York convention make a free choice of a gubernatorial candidate of real stature. Combined with Roosevelt's moribund movement this was a serious enough threat to force Murphy into an adroit maneuver.[67] He announced that while he favored the renomination of Governor Dix, the convention would be entirely unbossed. Thus far he was following standard procedure. The difference was that he did not then push through an immediate renomination of Dix. His restraint tricked the Empire State Democrats into proclaiming that their conditions were met, that the convention was in truth unbossed. Few would have been so naïve as to think that Murphy, in dumping Dix, had left the 390 delegates out of a total of 450 free to vote as they pleased. Those "in the know" whispered that Murphy was the one who gave the word that led the convention to switch on the fourth ballot to a perennial aspirant for the governorship, "Plain Bill" Sulzer,[68] the Henry Clay of Tammany Hall. Sulzer, who had served many years in Congress, fancied himself a friend of the common man. He immediately asserted that he would "give the government back to the people." The Empire State Democracy endorsed him and announced it would put up its own candidates for the state assembly and senate only where the Democrats were unsuitable.[69]

Even had the more militant Roosevelt remained in good health and at the head of the movement, the result could not have been much different. Already in many small ways he had demonstrated that his irregularity extended only to matters within the party. He had no wish to participate in any third- or fourth-party movement, and remained firmly within the Democratic party within the state. As he had said at the end of July, he wanted to prove that he was "regular," and Tammany "irregular." Because of his illness he took no blame for the ignominious end of the movement, and once again he attracted applause from the independents for his progressive leadership.

While the Empire State Democracy was fizzling out, Roosevelt, from his bedroom in New York City faced the difficult task of trying to win re-election to the state senate without making an appearance in his district.

The previous spring, Roosevelt asserted privately on several occasions that he was not sure whether or not he wished to run for re-election to the state senate.[70] At that time, before the breakup of the Republicans, he faced certain defeat despite his personal popularity. Chanler's seven-vote margin of victory the previous November in the most Democratic section of the district was proof of that.

A few of Roosevelt's political admirers began to boost him for the governorship. He had become technically eligible when he had reached the age of thirty the previous January, but had nowhere near the requisite strength or stature. This was pleasant political moonshine, of no immediate significance, but important in building him to the point where he would be serious gubernatorial timber a few years hence. A few organization men were in favor of him, for the simple reason that he could obtain as many votes within New York City as any Tammany man (if Tammany willed it), and a large number of independent votes upstate that no organization candidate could capture.* If a close election had been in prospect, and if Murphy had felt

* The statement of an anonymous organization man is of significance because it indicates clearly why Tammany was ready ultimately to form an alliance with Roosevelt:

> I would rather an organization man were elected, but we can't win with an organization man. . . . Even in the city of New York, a large percentage, and a growing percentage at that, are talking independence, and against Tammany organization rule, and would prefer Roosevelt to an organization man.
>
> My reasons for favoring Mr. Roosevelt are as follows:
>
> First – He is a young man, who would go up and down the state capturing the great army of young men. . . .

that victory with Roosevelt was preferable to a Republican triumph, it is barely conceivable that he might have swallowed Roosevelt.[72]

In the early summer, the Bull Moose movement killed any vague chance that Roosevelt might capture the Democratic nomination for governor, since Tammany could win with any candidate who did not produce an upstate Democratic bolt. At the same time, it practically insured Roosevelt's re-election as state senator.

The main problem was to obtain renomination. Roosevelt outwardly was on good terms with Edward E. Perkins, chairman of the Dutchess County Democratic Committee, treasurer of the state committee, and ally of Tammany. He even asserted early in 1912 that he would heartily favor Perkins as head of the state committee – "the most able Chairman we could possibly have." [73] At the same time, he complained privately because he continued to receive far more favorable attention in the Republican Poughkeepsie *Eagle* than in the Perkins-controlled *Enterprise*. "People can read . . . [it] for weeks," he complained, "and not know that they have a . . . Senator representing them." [74]

At the end of July, when Roosevelt took a day-long trip to visit Democratic leaders throughout his district, he found that "Tammany and the 'interests' are really making an effort to prevent my renomination." They were charging him with discord because of his hand in organizing the Empire State Democracy, and were raking up the anti-Catholic implications of the Sheehan fight again. Nevertheless, he was so popular among the voters that the Republican *Eagle* came editorially to his rescue, and the machine politicians did not dare make an open fight against him. "Perkins has no spine," Roosevelt explained, "but he knows now that if he listens to orders from 14th St. [Tammany headquarters] he will have a perfectly delightful little fight on his hands that will not stop easily or quickly." [75]

Perkins must have been well aware of this, for on August 24, the Democratic committee unanimously renominated Roosevelt for the state senatorship.[76] A month later, when Roosevelt was about to begin

Second – The name of Roosevelt would mean at least 10,000 votes to the Democratic ticket.

Third – He is worth several millions of dollars, and could finance his own campaign, if necessary.

Fourth – He is independent and is known throughout the state as a man who will fight for what he believes to be right.

Therefore the writer advised Tammany to emulate the Republican machine, which in 1898 swallowed Theodore Roosevelt in order to avoid defeat.[71]

his active campaign, he contracted typhoid fever. Had he been well, a repetition of his personal appearances of two years before would have won him a comfortable plurality. Because he was ill, and only a few Democrats were willing to work for him, he seemed almost certain to lose the election by default. It was then, fortunately, that he thought of Howe.

Louis McHenry Howe was a strange little newspaperman who rather gloried in his unlovely personal appearance – someone once called him a "medieval gnome," and he happily picked up and repeated the appellation. A Hoosier by birth, he had grown up in Saratoga Springs when it was the gayest racing and watering place in the country. There was much talk there of the two great games, playing the horses and politics, and Howe as a young reporter became fascinated with both. He also loved a kindred amusement, amateur theatricals. At Saratoga, Howe observed much manipulation and himself became a master of the techniques of swaying public opinion. After a fair education at Yates Saratoga Institute, he took a trip abroad. His favorite author was Carlyle, and like him he came to believe in the hero in history. Theodore Roosevelt had once filled that role, but by 1912 Howe's ambition was scarcely to be realized by participating in the Bull Moose crusade. For him to achieve personal eminence in politics was impossible, for he was short, sharp-featured, with an almost marmoset-like visage, and he dressed with a contempt for fashion or neatness. He was brilliant in wit, and equally gifted in sarcasm and excoriation; his ability to make enemies came close to surpassing his capacity for making friends.

When he first met Franklin D. Roosevelt in the state legislature, Howe was Albany correspondent for the New York *Herald*, not a position of any great eminence or reward. Apparently his income from the paper was slight except when the legislature was in session, and he scurried from one free-lance side activity to another to round out his living. While he was by no means in poverty, he suffered from chronic financial difficulties. In sum, he was far from a success personally, yet consumed with aspirations which by himself he could never hope to achieve. In his thinking, it would be hard to label him either conservative or progressive. Rather he was somewhat comparable to a New Yorker of a much earlier generation who served another hero in history – Martin Van Buren, the "Little Magician" behind Andrew Jackson. While Howe alone could do little, linked with a dashing young man like Roosevelt, he might go far. Just when it occurred to him that with his bag of political tricks he could prestidigitate Roosevelt into the White House is impossible to know. Perhaps his tongue was only partly in his cheek when he facetiously addressed Roosevelt in the autumn of 1912 as "Beloved and Revered Future President." Certainly it was not long before Howe was deadly serious about this. To make Roosevelt President became the objective of his life.[77]

In the summer of 1912 the goal was much more limited. Howe had gambled on working for Osborne in the Wilson movement until the session of the state legislature began in January. Consequently, he declined a job covering the campaign for the *Herald*, and when Osborne failed to finance the Empire State Democracy, was left without work.[78] Sometime in the summer, he appealed to Roosevelt for aid. When Roosevelt became ill, he called in Howe to run his campaign. Except for several short periods, Howe worked steadily for Roosevelt from this time until his death in 1936.[79]

Howe was singularly unworldly about money matters. Roosevelt never tired of laughing over the way Howe during that first campaign added the amount of each check onto the stub instead of subtracting, and thus soon had a fine balance in his checkbook when he was overdrawn at the bank. Roosevelt himself still had a certain unworldliness in political matters which unfriendly Tammany critics labeled as haughtiness; Howe completed his orientation to practical politics.[80] With his long experience at political poker, Howe directed Roosevelt's tactics, argued long and heatedly against foolish moves, and generally added finesse to his game. It was a Damon and Pythias relationship, with each supplementing the other. Just twenty years after they formed their partnership they played for the highest stakes of all, and won.

The stakes in the fall of 1912 were only the state senatorship, but a setback would be difficult to overcome, and Howe entered the contest with a firm sense of long-range consequences. He did not have to fight entirely alone. Outside of the district, several powerful conservative Democrats were ready to demand of machine men under obligation to them that they help Roosevelt win (or at least not openly dump him). Colonel Rice thus conversed with Martin Glynn of Albany, the candidate for lieutenant governor. Glynn claimed not only that he himself was for Roosevelt, but that he had converted Murphy. This seems hardly likely, but at least machine opposition within the district remained under cover.[81]

With the aid of the state Democratic chairman, William Church Osborn, Howe concocted an issue – "a great farmer stunt" – of marked effect in the campaign. Osborn in his capacity as chairman of the market committee of the state food commission wrote Roosevelt that there was "a margin of over 50% between the producer and the consumer in this State," and outlined proposed legislation to protect farmers from abuses in their dealings with New York City commission produce merchants. Howe printed this and attached it to letters from Roosevelt which, while they simulated typing, were in fact multigraphed. These, addressed to individual farmers, inquired what they thought should be included in the bill, and requested them to discuss the proposals at their Grange meetings. Roosevelt (ghosted by Howe) pointed out that if he were re-elected he would be chairman of the senate agricultural committee, and was "being counted on to make the fight" for the passage of the bill. "The matter so directly affects the farmers and is so important as to be above partisan politics," he declared. "I trust you will help us in getting the right kind of a bill drawn without regard to political considerations. I am sorry that my severe illness has prevented my talking this over with those interested in farming in my district personally but hope you will write me what you think about it."

This direct, personal appeal, accompanied by a stamped, self-addressed envelope, was an illustration of Howe's peculiar genius. Again and again in the next two decades he repeated it with excellent results, until finally it gave way to an even more effective device, the radio "Fireside Chat."

Howe also sent personal letters from Roosevelt to the shad fishermen along the Hudson River, informing each one that the conservation commission had assured him it would rescind new, high license fees over which they were upset.[82] He even promised on Roosevelt's behalf that he would back legislation for standard apple barrels, so that farmers would not be cheated through having their apples measured in oversize barrels.* In addition to the farm program, Howe committed Roosevelt to support woman suffrage,[84] and other progressive measures. He prepared a statement of these in the form of a full-page newspaper advertisement, and sent a copy to Roosevelt prior to running it, so that Roosevelt could veto by telegraph any items of which he did not

* FDR stood by this campaign pledge, and introduced Senate Bill 934 which would provide standard-size barrels for pears and quinces. A bill on apple barrels was to follow. It failed to pass after Roosevelt left the senate.[83]

approve. "As I have pledged you in it," Howe wrote, "I thought you might like to know casually what kind of a mess I was getting you into." [85] Throughout the district, Howe spread an unprecedented number of eye-catching newspaper advertisements, which seemed to have a marked effect. He followed them up just before the election with another multigraphed personal letter from Roosevelt to 11,070 of his constituents. The Columbia County version read:

> I am just recovering from a six weeks attack of Typhoid Fever, which has prevented me from making a personal tour of Columbia County, which I had planned.
>
> I believe that a Candidate for the Legislature should make his position plain on all matters in which his people are interested and in spite of my illness, I have endeavored as far as possible, through the press, to explain my position upon certain Legislative matters affecting the district, such as the regulation of the commission business and the State development of water power, etc.

There followed an attack upon Roosevelt's opponent, Jacob Southard, a banker and president of a light and power company, for not visiting Columbia County during the campaign.[86]

Howe traveled extensively around the district, whipping up enthusiasm among the loyal, and trying to thwart skulduggery from both within and without the party. The Republicans in Putnam County tried to register men temporarily working on the New York City aqueduct.[87] Among the regular Democrats the word went around not to vote for Roosevelt, but friends like John E. Mack and William Church Osborn campaigned actively nevertheless, and brought Roosevelt considerable numbers of normally Republican votes.[88] George E. Schryver of Hyde Park wrote Roosevelt:

> Frank Cleary and others of the Democratic ring in Hyde Park seem to think that the crowd are not with you this fall, and your chances are not good for re-election, but I have talked quietly with a number of Republicans and think I can safely promise you 35 or 40 who did not vote for you before are willing to do so now on the good showing you made in Albany, against the Murphy ring.[89]

That, in a nutshell, was the way the election went. At the last minute the Republicans spread stories that Roosevelt's fight against Sheehan had been motivated by anti-Catholicism, and beyond doubt took away from him a considerable amount of the normal Democratic vote.* This could not have surprised Roosevelt. He had been so worried over persistent rumors that he was anti-Catholic that the previous St. Patrick's Day he had put in an appearance at a Catholic celebration at Matteawan even though it was his wedding anniversary.[91] If Roosevelt's war upon Tammany cost him normally Democratic votes, it gained him sufficient normally Republican ones to more than offset the loss. "I quite realize," he commented after the election, "that it is only because of the support of Republicans and Independents that I have succeeded twice in being elected in a district which is normally Republican." [92] Mack analyzed a number of ballots afterwards, and found quantities of Democrats who crossed the party line to vote against Roosevelt, and Republicans who crossed it to vote for him.[93] He gained a large segment of the Progressive vote; many of those who voted for Theodore Roosevelt for President at the same time voted for Franklin Roosevelt for state senator. George A. Vossler, his Progressive opponent, received only 2628 votes – fourteen hundred less than T. R.! Roosevelt received eight hundred votes more than the Democratic candidates for President and governor. Nevertheless, he won by a narrow plurality. He received 15,590 votes to 13,889 for Southard, or almost a thousand less than his opponents combined.[94]

"Congratulations upon your deserved and notable victory!" wrote a constituent. "When a bull-moose and a G.O.P. elephant are both outrun by a man sick-a-bed it would seem 'Manifest Destiny.'" [95] In this instance, Howe had given "Manifest Destiny" a vigorous shove. All Roosevelt's friends testified to the value of his efforts. "Howe did gallant work under very adverse circumstances," reported Osborn. "He was about as loyal and wholehearted as a man can be." And he had accomplished these wonders for a total cost of less than $2500; he himself received only $300 salary and $120.50 expenses.[96]

Roosevelt's victory under adverse circumstances was additional proof of his strong position of leadership among upstate Democrats. There was one hint that he might hope not to spend the next two years in Albany; he rented only a small apartment rather than a house.[97] Nevertheless, he plunged into an aggressive program when the legislative session began in January, 1913. This, whether or not he stayed in Al-

* After the election, Roosevelt snapped, "Any candidate who brings any question of religion into politics acts in a manner wholly unAmerican and unChristian, and is not fitted to be the holder of any office." [90]

FDR in his seat at the state senate, Albany

FDR inspecting an American battleship, *c.* 1915

bany, would demonstrate beyond dispute that the farmers had no stancher friend.

Since the Democrats had elected "Plain Bill" Sulzer governor, and controlled both houses of the legislature, they were again in a position to enact a positive program. Roosevelt introduced into the senate a set of five agricultural bills which he drafted in co-operation with the state Grange and one of the most famous American agricultural experts, Liberty Hyde Bailey, director of the New York State College of Agriculture at Cornell University.[98] These went even beyond Roosevelt's campaign promises, and established him within the state as the most vigorous champion of government aid to the farmer. The most important bill provided for regulation of the commission merchants through licensing and inspection. Another would facilitate formation of farmers' co-operative associations for both the purchasing of supplies and marketing of produce. A third would permit establishment of Agricultural Credit Banks to loan money at a low rate of interest for farm improvements. The fourth would create a Deputy Commissioner of Agriculture to take charge of co-operative work in the state, and the last would provide state aid to county Farm Bureaus.[99]

The Russell Sage Foundation expressed strong interest in the Agricultural Credit Banks, which were to function along credit union lines, and asked Roosevelt to amend his bill to include a similar plan for urban areas.[100] Roosevelt himself regarded the co-operative bill as "of the greatest importance," and pointed out that "Five or more persons could under it get together and save money on the purchasing of supplies as well as co-operate on the marketing of their produce."[101] Nevertheless, it was the commission merchant bill which attracted almost all the attention because of the angry and determined attacks upon it by the merchants' lobby.

At the end of January, the members of the Fruit and Produce Trade Association of New York and the New York branch of the National League of Commission Merchants held a meeting to organize against the bill. Ninety men or firms attended, and each contributed fifty dollars, or a total of $4500 for a campaign fund. With this they established a publicity committee which immediately began issuing highly colored manifestoes. They claimed that the price of the bonds the merchants would be forced to obtain would push them into bankruptcy, and that the inspection of damaged goods would cost merchants, farmers, and consumers millions of dollars a year.[102]

When Roosevelt presided over hearings on all of his bills, few farmers came. As Osborn pointed out, few could afford the railway fare to Albany.[103] On the other hand, the commission merchants sent a trainload of about 250 from New York City, under the leadership of a former Republican state senator, himself owner of a commission house. Oddly enough, in their testimony the merchants made little attack upon the basic philosophy of the bill. Only one Republican state senator, himself a fruitgrower, denounced the bill as "paternalism of the worst kind." [104] Instead the opponents emphasized, in exaggerated terms, the damage that would come from various technicalities in the bill. Most of these, Roosevelt promised, would be amended.

The farmers for their part presented serious grievances which they would have difficulty remedying even with state regulation of the merchants. Some of the merchants were dishonest and irresponsible; the legislation would at least purge these out of existence. Other merchants sometimes auctioned off quality vegetables as "damaged" to their own subsidiaries which then increased the prices. At best there was a drastic markup. Roosevelt later related how he himself had gone down to the New York docks about two-thirty one morning and traced a crate of spinach that had come up by boat from Norfolk, Virginia, as it passed from one agent to another on its way to an Italian grocer in the Bronx. The farmer received sixty cents for what cost the consumers at least $2.50.[105]

In order to obtain the legislation, Roosevelt demonstrated a readiness to compromise with the merchants by accepting amendments which would place less burden of proof on them, and reduce a bond required of them from $10,000 to $3,000 (an expense of only $17.50 a year).[106] At the same time, Howe, on the payroll of the New York State Markets League, sent out letters to local Grange leaders to build up state-wide sentiment for the bill.[107] The Grange, with a membership of 105,000 farmers, formed a lobby more powerful than that of the merchants,[108] who in the end had to capitulate. They negotiated a bill with some compromises but which provided for essential regulation. By this time Roosevelt was out of the state senate, and they took what slight consolation they could in seeing that his name was eliminated from the final measure.[109] But Roosevelt, even though in Washington, never let the farmers forget what he had done for them.

The first hint that Roosevelt might become a member of the new Administration came in the middle of January when he received a telegram from Joseph Tumulty, private secretary to Woodrow Wilson, asking him to come to Trenton for a conference.[110] He had a "very satisfactory talk" with Wilson about patronage matters, and suggested the names of several of his associates in the Empire State Democracy.[111]

Roosevelt must certainly have mentioned his own aspirations. There is one bit of evidence that he did so. A young Philadelphia lawyer, Michael Francis Doyle, who had been of service both to Bryan and Wilson, had received word through Bryan that Wilson was favorably disposed to appoint him Assistant Secretary of the Navy. Then, a month or six weeks before the inauguration (after Roosevelt's trip to Trenton), Bryan saw Doyle again, and informed him that while the President-elect was willing to make good on his promise, Senator Roosevelt had expressed a desire to go down to Washington, and had his eye on the position.* Bryan advised Doyle to withdraw, and Doyle did.[112] Eleanor Roosevelt's recollection is that in the weeks before the inauguration, her husband was hoping to go to Washington, but did not know whether or not he would be able to become Assistant Secretary of the Navy.[113]

What happened subsequently is better authenticated but not necessarily contradictory. About three days before the inauguration, Roosevelt went to Washington. William Gibbs McAdoo, the new Secretary of the Treasury, asked him if he would like to become Assistant Secretary of the Treasury or Collector of the Port of New York. Roosevelt expressed appreciation but did not accept, even though the collectorship would have provided him with an unparalleled opportunity to build an anti-Tammany machine.[114] On the morning of the inauguration, he encountered the new Secretary of the Navy, Josephus Daniels, in the lobby of the Willard Hotel. Roosevelt was in high spirits, enthusiastic about the new Administration, and congratulated Daniels upon his appointment. Daniels, as he frequently recalled, countered by inquiring of Roosevelt:

> "How would you like to come to Washington as Assistant Secretary of the Navy?" His face beamed with pleasure. He replied, "How would I like it? I'd like it bully well. It would please me better than anything in the world. I'd be glad to be connected with the new administration. All my life I have loved ships and have been a student of the Navy, and the assistant secretaryship is the one place, above all others, I would love to hold." [115]

* This would place FDR's lien on the assistant-secretaryship earlier than Wilson's invitation to Josephus Daniels to become Secretary of the Navy, which did not come until February 23.

Secretary Daniels, according to his account, asked President Wilson two days after the inauguration if he had anyone in mind for Assistant Secretary of the Navy, and when he received a negative reply, suggested Roosevelt:

> "How well do you know Mr. Roosevelt?" Wilson asked, "and how well is he equipped?"
>
> "I never met him until the Baltimore Convention," I replied, "but I was strongly drawn to him then and more so as I met him during the campaign when I was in New York. . . ." I expressed the conviction that he was one of our kind of liberal.
>
> "Very well," he said, "send the nomination over." [116]

Senator O'Gorman readily assented and Daniels out of courtesy also queried Elihu Root, the Republican Senator. Root was agreeable but warned Daniels: "Whenever a Roosevelt rides, he wishes to ride in front." On March 11, President Wilson sent Roosevelt's nomination to the Senate.[117]

Roosevelt took a few days to wind up his affairs as state senator while confirmation of his appointment pended before the United States Senate. Agricultural and reform leaders were dismayed at the sudden loss of their champion in the legislature. "It's a trick of the enemies of your progressive ideas," one rural Republican protested. "I beg of you to stay with old New York State. We need you." [118] Seth Low, the aged New York City reformer, confessed, "I am concerned for the farmers of the State of New York, at your disappearance from the Senate of the State at this juncture." [119] But William Church Osborn granted that Roosevelt would find life in Washington most interesting, and "a great relief after the somewhat squalid pressure of Albany." [120]

CHAPTER IX

At T.R.'s Desk

I was very much pleased that you were appointed. . . . It is interesting to see that you are in another place which I myself once held. I am sure you will enjoy yourself to the full as Assistant Secretary of the Navy, and that you will do capital work.

— THEODORE ROOSEVELT TO FDR, *March 13, 1913.*

"I AM baptized, confirmed, sworn in, vaccinated — and somewhat at sea!" the new Assistant Secretary of the Navy wrote his mother after his first afternoon in office. For over an hour he had signed papers on faith; he would "have to work like a turbine to master this job." But, he assured her, he would do so "even if it takes all summer."[1]

Roosevelt was only a few weeks past his thirty-first birthday when he took his oath of office on March 17, 1913. The youngest of a long line of Assistant Secretaries, he was twenty years junior to Secretary Josephus Daniels, and only half the age of many of the admirals with whom he transacted business.* It was an important position for so young a man to fill, one in which during the ensuing seven years he gained invaluable administrative experience as he gradually changed into a mature public figure. At the outset he demonstrated traits often the attributes of youth — adaptability and zest for action. These he never lost.

* FDR was the most youthful of fifteen Assistant Secretaries who served between 1890 and 1936. While he was thirty-one upon taking office, the average age was slightly under forty-eight. He also served the longest of any of the group — seven years and five months.[2]

His youth was in some respects a handicap. Senator Hale of the Naval Affairs Committee remarked in 1946 that he was regarded just as a boy — a nice boy.[3] Just before the inauguration in 1913 when FDR and his wife were guests at a Washington dinner, the wife of a naval officer chided him with mock severity for making some cynical remark: "Naughty, naughty," she said. "Little boys just out of college should not say such things." A few weeks later upon meeting the new Assistant Secretary of the Navy she was shocked to find that he was the "little boy." He, of course, thought it very funny.[4]

There was always the possibility that this position would lead rapidly to bigger things, since it was one of the few subordinate offices in Washington which attracted much attention. Most cabinet underlings received little more publicity than state senators, but not so the Assistant Secretary of the Navy. Theodore Roosevelt was responsible for this. Only fifteen years earlier, at the very desk which was now Franklin's, Theodore had planned the capture of Manila Bay, and four years later he was President. The parallel thus far between the two Roosevelts was suggestive of what was to come, and newspapers and well-wishers made the most of it. "Battleship man – or mad! – though you be I am truly glad of your appointment to Washington," wrote Villard. "May it lead straight onward for you as it did for T.R. – but *not* by means of that barbarism known as war." [5]

Roosevelt quietly encouraged this sort of speculation. He was not deliberately cultivating parallels when he moved into the "Little White House" where Theodore had stayed while waiting for McKinley's widow to move out of the Executive Mansion. It was only logical for him to rent the home of his mother's dear friend "Bammie," his wife's aunt, Anna Roosevelt Cowles. But he certainly made the most of the comparison two days after he took office when Secretary Daniels went away for a short while. This left him Acting Secretary of the Navy. Under comparable circumstances Theodore had sent orders to Commodore Dewey to attack Manila in the event of a war with Spain. Franklin D. Roosevelt made no bold moves, but he did remind reporters with a grin, "There's a Roosevelt on the job today. . . . You remember what happened the last time a Roosevelt occupied a similar position?" [6] Not long afterwards, he speculated in a public address upon what he would do in case of war. Since he was a navy man, he said, he would prefer serving on shipboard, but "I suppose that I must . . . follow in the steps of T.R. and form a regiment of rough riders." [7]

In one respect, Roosevelt would have no easy time if he aspired to follow the example of his illustrious predecessor. Secretary Daniels was neither easy-going nor weak-willed; he took to heart the advice of the outgoing Secretary, who had said, tapping his desk, "Power lies here." [8] Under the benign but quite firm administration of Daniels, any insubordination would have to be petty and surreptitious, not of the grand manner involved in ordering a fleet to Manila. Daniels's dress and demeanor, his warm smile and disarming modesty belied his granite stubbornness and wholehearted devotion to a just cause. It was probably his unassuming simplicity which was most misleading, for while he acted as though he were no more than a rural Southern editor, in his evaluations of men and measures he was remarkably shrewd.

The background and interests of Daniels better fitted him to head the Navy Department than critics later inferred. He had accepted the appointment, the *Army and Navy Journal* reported approvingly, because of his keen personal interest in the Navy.[9] His father had been a shipwright and left him a chest of tools; a brother-in-law, Ensign Worth Bagley, was an outstanding athlete at Annapolis and later died heroically in the Spanish-American War. Daniels had written his biography. Another brother-in-law, David Worth Bagley, ultimately became a vice-admiral.[10]

As chief clerk in the Interior Department during the Cleveland Administration, Daniels had acquired a thorough knowledge of government functioning, and as one of the leading editors in the South, had developed strong political sense and an extensive following. The fact that before he gave his allegiance to Wilson he had been one of the most ardent supporters of William Jennings Bryan caused many conservative naval officers to scoff at him, for to them Bryan stood for crackpot reform, pacifism, and Prohibition. And to be sure, pacifism and Prohibition were two of Daniels's leading ideals. It was a great deal more relevant that he saw the need for extensive progressive reform within the Navy Department and worked courageously to try to bring it about. When he did so, outraged officers and lovers of the old Navy traditions heaped epithets upon him as a mollycoddler of enlisted men. They especially raged because he dried up the officers' wine mess, although they had said little or nothing when the enlisted men had lost their liquor some years earlier. Quite typical of the ridicule he underwent were some verses the *Army and Navy Register* quoted: *

When I was a lad I pondered some
On the horrible effects of the Demon Rum;
I scorned to dally with the dread highball,
And I never saw a bottle of champagne at all.
I kept away from guzzling men —
Till now I am the ruler of the U.S.N.

With remarkable agility, Roosevelt was able to side-step all such jibes. It was typically his good fortune to be on the Pacific Coast when

* These were probably among the earliest writings of a naval officer's son, Thorne Smith.

the liquor order appeared: he could disclaim all knowledge, since Daniels had not consulted him upon it in advance.[12] *

In his impatience and ambition, Roosevelt was likely to misjudge Daniels. He had some grounds for aspiring to be the real power in the Navy Department, for since 1901 most of the Secretaries had been nonentities. President Theodore Roosevelt, wishing to be his own Secretary, had staffed the office with a succession of ineffective mediocrities; President Taft put in a strong man, but one who was absent from Washington much of the time. Consequently, Assistant Secretaries had enjoyed considerable power for some time. While Roosevelt had the good fortune to step into an important administrative position, which he managed to keep important, it no longer overshadowed that of the Secretary.

Even when Daniels was absent, Roosevelt could run the Navy only in a limited way, but there was much for him to do. The outgoing Assistant Secretary, Beekman Winthrop, went over many matters with him, and he learned his new tasks rapidly.[14] Already, on March 19, 1913, when he first served as Acting Secretary, he demonstrated such marked competence that the heads of bureaus, after calling upon him, commented favorably upon his familiarity with naval affairs. He himself modestly informed his wife, "I must have signed three or four hundred papers today & am *beginning* to catch on."[15] As he wrote a friend, he was "somewhat busy trying to find out" whether he was "afloat or ashore in this Department," but even while he was doing so, the position was "in every way congenial."[16]

Customarily, Roosevelt was in charge of civilian personnel, including labor in the navy yards. Within a couple of years he handled all contracts which did not involve policy matters, and shared the task of preparing annual estimates for the budget. In practice he had more power than Assistant Secretaries in most other departments, in part because there were generally several of them in each department; there was only one in the Navy. His scope of activity was quite broad, for he took charge of whatever matters the Secretary might assign to him or whatever he succeeded in taking over for himself. Many years later, Daniels wrote that he had often been asked what part of naval activities

* Howe reported to FDR on the abolition of the wine mess: "You will doubtless be given opportunity to sustain this program, certainly by private argument with the officers you meet on the Coast and possibly at some formal occasion. I know how greatly you regret not being here at the time to share in some of the glory. As it is, of course, I can tell the newspapermen nothing except that you are away and naturally know nothing about it."[13]

Roosevelt had been most interested in. The real answer, he said, lay in a remark Roosevelt used to make, "I get my fingers into about everything and there's no law against it." [17]

At first, most of Roosevelt's work was routine, of a sort that could go through his office almost automatically. A tremendous amount of paper required his signature, and he prided himself at this time upon keeping up with it. It was a smooth-functioning office, and Roosevelt was fortunate enough to inherit a loyal and competent personal secretary, Charles H. McCarthy, who had served under several previous Assistant Secretaries. While Roosevelt was learning his new duties, McCarthy continued to handle many small matters, involving the disposition not only of paperwork, but sometimes crank visitors as well.[18]

For his other assistant, Roosevelt picked his own man. He wrote an invitation and shortly received an answering telegram: "I am game but it's going to break me . . . L. M. Howe." [19] Together, Howe and McCarthy made an excellent, although not always harmonious, team, and Roosevelt well appreciated the relative worth of each. "Howe goes to Newfoundland tomorrow and I shall try to clean up his back work for him!" Roosevelt confided to his wife in the fall of 1916. "He is so wonderful on the big things that he lets the routine slide. I need a thoroughgoing hack without brilliancy like the faithful McCarthy to keep things running!" [20]

In the Navy Department, Howe handled the multitudes of contracts that passed through the Assistant Secretary's office, and eventually many of the problems involving workmen in the yards. In some of this work, inexperience led him into difficulties, but more often than not he was competent. Paymaster General Samuel McGowan described him as "one of the hardest workers I ever saw . . . deeply interested in the Navy and its welfare." [21] In 1916, after Howe had visited the New Orleans Navy Yard, the naval constructor there wrote Roosevelt, "It is a source of wonder to me how a man not connected with the Naval Service can have obtained in three years, the detailed knowledge of the situation that is possessed by Mr. Howe." [22]

Despite his capabilities, Howe created a bad impression. Even Eleanor Roosevelt for many years disapproved of him, and did not learn really to like him until he was quite kind to her during the 1920 campaign. His uncouth appearance and unpleasant personality repelled most officers and some labor leaders.[23] They remember him as "the ugliest thing you ever saw!" and "frightfully self-conscious," an atrocious dresser, whose clothes "looked as if they were second or third hand."[24] The impeccably garbed officers, to air their resentment against taking orders from this underling, cast aspersions even upon his personal cleanliness, and laughed over scuttlebutt that upon one occasion the Assistant Secretary told a captain that he was going to send Howe to inspect a ship.

"If you do, do you know what will happen?" the captain is supposed to have asked Roosevelt. "As soon as he comes aboard they will take him upon the foc'sle, strip him and scrub him down with sand and canvas."[25]

Within the office, Howe was often hard to work with, for along with his intense loyalty to Roosevelt went a vehement jealousy of anyone who might be a rival for his favor. His office-mates and Roosevelt's friends who dropped in at the department unite in recalling both his brilliance and his bad humor. One of these, George Marvin of *World's Work* has written: "It always made Howe extremely sore when a few others, like myself, passed through his office, without any reference to him, on our way to see the Assistant Secretary. Howe was a vindictive, as well as an extremely astute, individual and he never forgot his earlier inferiority complexes."[26]

Secretary Daniels regarded Howe as one of the strangest men he had ever met and one of the smartest, but felt, "He would have sidetracked both President Wilson and me to get Franklin Roosevelt to the White House."[27]

Altogether, Roosevelt had a small but effective staff. It did not need to be large. The Navy Department which Roosevelt joined in 1913 seemed a colossal organization compared with that of a generation earlier, but was tiny compared with what was to follow. The Navy of his father's day had consisted of a few clerks and officers presiding over a small collection of floating museum pieces, mostly relics of the Civil War and even the War of 1812. The main function of these vessels had been to provide repair work for favored shipyards, or perhaps to serve as reminders of the early days of naval glory. In the attic of the Navy Department, Roosevelt took great pleasure in discovering the records of this sailing era, neatly filed in wooden chests and presided over by an elderly seaman. But downstairs in the minds of some of the high-ranking officers with which he had to deal he still encountered the age of sail. The Navy's new modern fleet of steam and armor was so recent that most, if not all, of the captains and admirals of the Wilson Administration had served on sailing vessels. And the department's haphazard organization still came close to functioning on a sailing basis. There were eight bureaus which had grown up through simple unorganized accretion; their jurisdictions overlapped so fantastically that up until very recently they had operated competing shops side by side in many of the navy yards.

To most Americans, including the Secretary of the Navy, a Navy and Marine Corps of 65,000 officers and men seemed large, and with its annual appropriation of $143,497,000 [28] (only a fraction of the cost of building a single aircraft carrier in the 1950's), astoundingly expensive. Compared with the Navy of thirty years before, this was a colossal marvel of modern technological efficiency. But compared with the formidable British fleet and the new German battleships and cruisers, it was of second-rate effectiveness, and inferior not only to Britain, as everyone took for granted, but also to Germany and France.

The problem of administering this large and partially obsolescent establishment, of balancing the overwhelming American desire for peace and economy against the pressures of expansionists and the alarms of those who feared the military upsurge of other major powers – these were among the imponderables that faced Secretary Daniels. But to a crack yachtsman with a broad and ready knowledge of nautical lore and big-navy doctrine, it seemed simple enough. Roosevelt was in his element. Far from making him feel uncomfortable, the Navy ceremonials were perquisites in which he took delight, and the public attention they received were excellent advertising both for him and for the Navy. In his new position, as he remarked, "I now find my vocation combined with my avocation in a delightful way." [29]

In addition, as a politician Roosevelt understood the necessity of dramatizing the Navy to the electorate. What was most desirable for the Navy must also be made politically acceptable if it were to become more than a wardroom dream. Much as he enjoyed the speech-making and flag-waving for their own sake, he never lost sight of their larger significance or failed to produce from them every headline possible.

Traditionally the Assistant Secretary enjoyed considerable appurtenances of office. When he visited a naval vessel he was saluted by seventeen guns and four ruffles – a step below the hero of Manila Bay, Admiral of the Navy Dewey, but still four guns ahead of rear admirals who had waited nearly a lifetime for the honor. When he stepped aboard, a full guard of sixteen men would stand at attention on the quarterdeck, and the officers in dress uniform assembled to greet him.[30] This ritual, unfamiliar to Secretary Daniels and outlandish to Secretary of State Bryan, was fun for Roosevelt. Where the trappings did not exist, Roosevelt invented them. Both the President and the Secretary of the Navy had their own flags to fly on board ships, so the Assistant Secretary designed one for himself.[31]

The Assistant Secretary's privilege of commanding the services of a yacht or destroyer from time to time appealed to Roosevelt even more than the fanfare. The dispatch boat *Dolphin*,* and a small yacht, the *Sylph*, were usually at his disposal, and he made frequent use of them, both for business and pleasure.[33] There was great excitement the first time a naval vessel appeared in the Hudson off Hyde Park and Poughkeepsie, in 1913, but it soon became a familiar occurrence.[34]

On the Fourth of July, 1913, Roosevelt startled the residents of Canadian Campobello Island by ordering one of the Navy's most powerful battleships, the *North Dakota*, to participate in the Independence Day celebration at nearby Eastport, Maine. Ensign Mahlon Street Tisdale, fresh out of Annapolis, went ashore at Campobello in full dress, sword and epaulettes, to report the arrival of the vessel. A young fellow running toward him in a comfortable open shirt and flannel slacks excited his envy. Ensign Tisdale hailed him, "Where's this guy Roosevelt?" It was the Assistant Secretary to whom he was speaking. Roosevelt asked him how he had liked coming up to Campobello for the Fourth. Tisdale said the junior officers hadn't liked it at all, since they were all married and would have much preferred celebrating the holiday at Newport with their wives. But they were entertained so cordially that thirty-five years later, when the ensign had become a rear admiral, he remembered Roosevelt as "awfully nice – as nice as he could be."

While the *North Dakota* was at Campobello, Roosevelt came aboard for inspection. He informed the commanding officer in advance that he would not dress, but would require a salute to be fired, since the residents would be expecting it.[35]

On another occasion, Roosevelt ordered a destroyer, the *Flusser*, to take him on an inspection of naval installations at Frenchman Bay, Maine. The commander, Lieutenant William F. Halsey, Jr., knew that Roosevelt had some experience with small boats, but when Roosevelt offered to guide the destroyer through the strait between Campobello

* Launched in 1884, the *Dolphin* was the first steel war vessel built in the United States. It was a "marine crazy quilt" best suited for junketing.[32]

Island and the mainland, Halsey had to stifle his misgivings. As he wrote later:

> The fact that a white-flanneled yachtsman can sail a catboat out to a buoy and back is no guarantee that he can handle a high-speed destroyer in narrow waters. A destroyer's bow may point directly down the channel, yet she is not necessarily on a safe course. She pivots around a point near her bridge structure, which means that two-thirds of her length is aft of the pivot, and that her stern will swing in twice the arc of her bow. As Mr. Roosevelt made his first turn, I saw him look aft and check the swing of our stern. My worries were over; he knew his business.[36]

Another lieutenant, Harold R. Stark, knew that the Assistant Secretary "had always been in the habit of taking command, being a darned good skipper" but he did not relish the thought of turning over his destroyer to anyone. When he was cruising with Stark, Roosevelt asked to take command, but the lieutenant refused on the grounds that it was contrary to naval regulations to permit anyone else to take over. However, he promised to pilot the destroyer wherever Roosevelt wished. Roosevelt laughed and outlined a route through "the darnedest place you ever saw." Another time, aboard Stark's destroyer, Roosevelt was delighted when the commander roared at a tug that was nestling up against the stern, "Get the hell out of there!" [37] *

Such official pleasures had their serious side; they enabled Roosevelt to measure the capacities of many an ambitious lieutenant. Thanks to his good memory, he was able to retain sharp estimates of them over the intervening years, and more than one firm friendship, begun on these cruises, grew into full confidence in later times of stress.

Although Roosevelt's previous public experience had been entirely as a legislator, he by no means received as flattering a reception among Congressmen as he did with naval officers. They controlled his fate just as he, to a certain extent, did that of the officers. To deal with legislators as a colleague and as an administrator were two quite different things, and an easy familiarity with things nautical was not necessarily the key to success with the House and Senate Naval Affairs committees. Some of their members, like Representative Lemuel Padgett of Tennessee, chairman of the House committee, knew a re-

* During the White House years, FDR again and again recalled these incidents to Admiral Stark, his Chief of Naval Operations.

markable amount about the Navy; others, like "Pitchfork Ben" Tillman of South Carolina, chairman of the Senate committee, seemed primarily interested in obtaining patronage for the navy yards in their states or districts.

The problem of selling Congress upon appropriations primarily fell upon Daniels, who handled it admirably. His flat hat and shoestring tie, his combination of honesty and affability, and his long background as a Southern Democratic leader made him as trusted and in place among the Southern Democrats who were dominant at the Capitol as he seemed anomalous among the officers aboard a battleship. He made full use of his reputation for integrity, and knew how to swing various wavering congressmen into line. On many a hot summer week end, the *Dolphin* headed down the Potomac with Daniels and a group of congressional leaders aboard.[38] He could win votes not only for naval bills, but also for much else of Wilson's program. In time he became one of the main liaison men between the President and Congress.

Roosevelt had no such burden to carry at the Capitol. He appeared occasionally to testify, and displayed a technical knowledge which impressed at least the reporters present. But day by day he carried on minor transactions with individual Congressmen, most often concerning navy yards and the civilian employees of the Navy. This sometimes led to difficult interchanges with key Representatives and Senators. Those on the Naval Affairs committees were especially formidable because, if sympathetic, they could serve as advocates of bills; if unfavorable, they could kill them. Before Roosevelt had been in office a month, the vituperative chairman of the Senate Naval Affairs Committee was urging him to raise the wages of an employee in the Senator's personal domain, the navy yard at Charleston, South Carolina. Tillman complained that the previous Administration had "suppressed and discriminated against" the Charleston yard. "This ought never to have been and I propose now to see that it is stopped." And to Roosevelt he gave firm warning, "Your predecessor, Mr. Winthrop, was always very clever and kind to me, and I hope I shall have no cause to complain of you." [39] Secretary Daniels in this instance eased the pressure on Roosevelt by assuring Tillman that he would visit the Charleston yard and work out a new policy for compensation.[40]

In many of his dealings, Roosevelt did not have Daniels as a buffer. His dealings with Tammany Congressmen were, of course, an integral part of his activity in New York State politics, and required much patience. Toward some others in Congress, like James M. Curley of

Massachusetts, he could be a trifle less patient. He privately regarded Curley as "a most horrible nuisance,"[41] and preferred to deal with gentlemen in Congress, like Senator Henry Cabot Lodge, a dear friend of his wife's Uncle Ted, and Lodge's son-in-law, Representative Augustus P. Gardner, who had Groton and Harvard connections. Lodge was always cool toward Secretary Daniels; Gardner became his most vehement critic in Congress. But both men were always on most cordial terms with Roosevelt. The Assistant Secretary secured a promotion for an officer who was a nephew of Lodge's[42] and in like fashion thoroughly ingratiated himself with Gardner. "I agree with my secretary in his opinion," Gardner wrote Roosevelt. "He tells me that you are the promptest and most efficient Assistant Secretary in any Department with whom we have dealt in our 11 years of service here."[43]

Of course, a large part of the favors for Congressmen were entirely routine matters, which Roosevelt could either delegate or brush off. Howe once in a facetious manner described the technique to Roosevelt's Harvard roommate, Representative Lathrop Brown:

> Now, about your young friend . . . who appears to be one of nature's noblemen and to have nothing against him except that he has broken most of the Ten Commandments. I am willing to admit that if we bar from the Navy every gent who has become mixed up with a beautiful female we would have to put most of our ships out of commission and I am afraid we might lose an admiral or two, but in this case the young man was unfortunately caught with the goods. You have run against one of the secretary's strongest antipathies. And while I know Mr. Roosevelt will speak to Mr. Daniels about the case again, I honestly do not think he has a chance on earth. Do you want one of those "we are doing everything on earth to get this done because of the affection for the Congressman" letters or not? Will send you a masterpiece that will convince your friends that Mr. Roosevelt is sitting on Mr. Daniels' doorstep every night waiting for a chance to make one more plea when he comes home to supper, if that will ease the strain any.[44]

Relations with President Wilson were still more delicate than with Congress; Wilson was his ultimate superior, and a rather formidable man. On trivial matters, Roosevelt customarily dealt on a cordial and informal basis with the President's secretary and political advisor, Joseph Tumulty. Certainly he should have enjoyed Tumulty's good will in return for numerous patronage favors. Tumulty was from Jersey City, and Roosevelt must have wondered at times if the Hudson Tube was not jammed every morning with Tumulty's Irish friends on their way to work at the Brooklyn Navy Yard. On large questions involving policy, Secretary Daniels himself ordinarily consulted the President. Wilson demonstrated no especial fondness for the Navy, and certainly no interest in being his own Navy Secretary, but the government was still small enough that a President took a personal interest in many details. Quite a few of these fell within the jurisdiction of Roosevelt, so that, during the first years of the Wilson Administration, he frequently visited the President's office on one or another errand. Wilson's remarks to him on these occasions, while usually involving specific matters, sometimes developed into the generalizations of a brilliant teacher of political science. Roosevelt never forgot how once, early in his administration, Wilson told him, "It is only once in a generation that a people can be lifted above material things. That is why conservative government is in the saddle two-thirds of the time."[45]

With more enthusiasm than detailed understanding, Roosevelt favored the broad program of reform, especially the lowering of the tariff and the establishment of a Federal Reserve banking system, which Wilson accomplished in his first year in office. When, in the fall of 1913, the President achieved his first major triumph by signing the Underwood Tariff Act, Roosevelt was one of about fifty men standing behind him.[46] Occasionally, Roosevelt endorsed the New Freedom in speeches, but with broad, rather meaningless generalizations. "We are in a transition period," he told the Baltimore Bar Association in December, 1913. "We are passing through a period of idealism. For the first time in the history of this country a President of the United States and the members of his administration have gone before the people with a policy of ideal humanitarianism."[47] He received considerable applause, but did not follow it with any description of just what this humanitarian policy involved.

Roosevelt was identified more closely with the men than with the measures of the New Freedom. In his transaction of government and political business, at luncheons and other social functions, he associated with many of the administrative and congressional leaders. In November, 1913, a group of twenty of them organized into a luncheon group, the Common Counsel Club, which set as its objective the "promoting of principles of progressive Democracy." They hoped to attract to the Democratic party the disillusioned members of Theodore Roosevelt's disintegrating Progressive party.[48] Some of these Progressives, like Joseph E. Davies, ultimately became leading supporters of the New Deal; others, like the Assistant Secretary of War, Henry Breckinridge, important opponents.

There were also important older personages with whom Roosevelt had social relations, some of them men with ideas. Eleanor Roosevelt thinks that he drew his later concept that the forty-eight states should serve as laboratories for social experiments from Justice Louis D. Brandeis, whom he knew and respected; Roosevelt himself attributed it to Lord Bryce, whom he had met earlier. He often attended Justice Oliver Wendell Holmes's Sunday afternoon sessions for young men, but his only written comment was that a dinner at the Holmes's was "delightful." [49] There is always the suspicion that in this period ideas made more impression upon Eleanor Roosevelt than her husband, who was often preoccupied with politics and personalities. It is she who has reminisced about brilliant, sour old Henry Adams, who demonstrated a kindlier side when he sat in his carriage outside the Roosevelt home and played with their children. There were occasional lunches or dinners at the Adams mansion, where one could look out across Lafayette Square at the White House, and on one such occasion when Roosevelt was warmly discussing some matter in which he was deeply interested, Adams with even more irony than he realized said, "Young man, I have lived in this house many years and seen the occupants of that White House across the square come and go, and nothing that you minor officials or the occupant of that house can do will affect the history of the world for long!" [50]

The warm welcome the Roosevelts received from Adams, Holmes, and Lodge was due to the friendship of these men for Theodore Roosevelt. Franklin and Eleanor also inherited Uncle Ted's embassy friends: the British Ambassador, Sir Cecil Spring-Rice, and the French, Jean Jules Jusserand. They made several warm friends among the younger staff members of both of these embassies and, all together, spent a good bit of their social life with the diplomats.[51]

Roosevelt was also on cordial social terms with several Americans closely associated with the foreign service. Joseph Grew was in Berlin, but sent his congratulations as a good Grotonian and Fly Club man;[52] Frank Polk, also a Grotonian, became counselor of the State Department in 1915. In the same year, Roosevelt wrote a letter to Secretary of State Bryan recommending for the diplomatic service a young man whom he had known since a child, Sumner Welles.[53] William Phillips, another personal friend, was Assistant Secretary of State, and had his office in the same building.

Before arriving in Washington, Roosevelt had known Phillips only slightly, but he and Eleanor had known Caroline Phillips for years. Soon, together with mutual friends, the Franklin K. Lanes and the Adolph Millers,* they formed a coterie which met for dinner every few weeks – so informally that they did not seat Secretary Lane according to his rank. These were the Roosevelts' closest friends during the Wilson era.[54]

The Phillipses caught many revealing glimpses of life in the Roosevelt family. They adored the brilliant Franklin, but regarded him as rather happy-go-lucky, and never thought of him as a potential great President. Eleanor, whom everyone admired, seemed a bit remote, rather in the background while Franklin claimed the attention. Her interests centered around her children, and of necessity she was essentially domestic; in the realm of public affairs she was concerned primarily with her husband's career. She was not yet through the ten years when, as she has written, she "was always just getting over having a baby or about to have one." [55] Caroline Phillips was particularly impressed with the self-effacing fashion in which Eleanor Roosevelt tried to avoid creating trouble between Sara Roosevelt and her son. Sara, when she was with the family, was incessantly causing difficulties through her jealousy and her interference in the upbringing of the children. Amidst this, Eleanor was tranquil and outgoing – thoughtful of other people rather than herself.[56]

For Eleanor Roosevelt, her husband's new position meant suddenly increased social duties. Theodore Roosevelt urged his niece to be "particularly nice to the naval officers' wives," since they had to keep up their position with very little money. "Everything that can properly be done to make things pleasant for them should be done." [57] But there was much more to it than this. She had to make ten to thirty calls an afternoon on the wives of various dignitaries: Mondays, those of Supreme Court Justices; Tuesdays, Representatives; Thursdays, Senators; and Fridays, diplomats. At each house she repeated the formula, "I am Mrs. Franklin D. Roosevelt. My husband has just come as Assistant Secretary of the Navy." [58] There were so many social func-

* Lane was Secretary of the Interior. Miller, formerly a University of California economics professor, was his assistant until 1914 when he became a member of the new Federal Reserve Board.

tions that in order to keep up with invitations as well as the calling list, she had to employ a social secretary three mornings a week. It was not very pleasant, but it quickly wore away much of her shyness.[59]

In addition there was the ordeal of giving large formal dinners which took up most of the time any Washington family could allot to social life. The Daniels family preferred a quiet life, entertained informally scarcely at all, and thus saw little of the Roosevelts. But the Roosevelts relaxed with their intimates, and in addition saved Sunday evenings for informal suppers at which Eleanor cooked eggs in a chafing dish and served cold foods and cocoa. Especially after the outbreak of the war, Franklin often brought guests with him for lunch. So that the men could have an opportunity to talk freely without being overheard, Eleanor began the custom of asking the servants to stay out of the dining room, except when she summoned them with a little silver bell.[60]

The house at 1733 N Street over which Eleanor Roosevelt presided in Washington, like the ones in Hyde Park and New York, bore little of the impress of her personality.* "It was a comfortable old-fashioned house that I had stayed in many years before," she has written,[61] but it was filled with the furniture of her Cowles relatives from whom they rented it and on the walls was an array of nautical pictures representative of Franklin's interests.[62]

Official life in Washington kept Franklin so busy that he had much less time than previously to spend with his family. He retained as keen an interest as always in the home at Hyde Park; year after year he continued to order saplings for his land, and in 1915 added a black guillemot and a bittern to his bird collection.[63] During the summers, he usually found some time for sports at Campobello, but the long leisurely sojourns there were pretty much of the past. As a result, he saw far less of his children, both during the hectic winter, and in the summer when most of the time they were at Campobello or Hyde Park and he in Washington.

To his children, Roosevelt was a hero. He was highly affectionate, a leader in their games and derring-do, and no disciplinarian. He organized the tobogganing in the winter down the steep slope from the Hyde Park home to the Hudson River, and in the summer, the sailing through treacherous passageways around Campobello. In Washington, he liked to take them down to the Navy Department where

* By the autumn of 1917, it was too small for the large Roosevelt family, so they moved to 2131 R Street, N. W.

they would peer at the models of ships in glass cases. "There is only one thing that interferes with their perfect enjoyment of that trip," Roosevelt once said, "and that is my inability to take the boats out of the 'windows,' as they call the glass cases, and sail them in the bath tub or the river or any other wet place."[64] At night he would go up the stairs to tousle them and kiss them good night. On occasion, he would explain to them about historic houses in Virginia they were going to visit, or otherwise add to their store of knowledge; once he even gave Anna a vivid lecture on the perils of playing with matches. But their gay unruliness was evidence of his lack of sternness: they dropped water bags out of upper windows on ladies arriving for tea, and at formal dinners hid behind furniture and lit stink bombs.[65] Franklin D. Roosevelt's relationship to his children was much what his father's had been to him, that of a wise mentor and exciting playmate.

All in all, it was a thrilling and satisfying existence for Roosevelt. He undoubtedly would have been incredulous had anyone suggested that he was taking only a peripheral part in Wilson's progressive domestic program, since the Navy so dominated his thinking and action. Yet this is the impression he gave.

Assistant Secretary Roosevelt was a big-navy, a "battleship man." He demonstrated this by his immediate friendliness toward the Navy League of the United States, and the purport of his first important speech, an address of welcome to the League convention in April, 1913. The main objective of the League was a larger navy, and its membership was studded with representatives of the steel, shipping, export and international financial interests; Roosevelt was on the best of terms with its president, Colonel Robert M. Thompson, chairman of the board of the International Nickel Corporation, and with one of its vice-presidents, Herbert Satterlee, son-in-law of J. P. Morgan.

"This is not a question of war or peace," he told the League. "I take it that there are as many advocates of arbitration and international peace in the navy as in any other profession. But we are confronted with a condition – the fact that our nation has decided in the past to have a fleet, and that war is still a possibility." Therefore the Navy must act for the national good through maintaining "a fighting force of the highest efficiency."[66]

This was the keynote for many speeches to follow. The *Army and Navy Journal* commented approvingly that it "met with hearty applause."[67] The only hint of dissatisfaction came from a Tennessee editor who concluded, "After reading his manifesto about a powerful navy, one finds no difficulty in recognizing the kinship of Franklin D. Roosevelt, assistant Secretary of the Navy, to [Theodore Roosevelt] the commander at Armageddon."[68] These two opposing reactions, like the initial speech itself, had increasing echoes during the next few years.

CHAPTER X

The Tiger Refuses To Starve

I feel in a way as if I had deserted a good many of my friends in the State, but I can assure you that I am not finished there yet and you will see me back again.

— FDR, *March, 1913.*[1]

IF Roosevelt were fortunate, he could influence New York political affairs far more effectively from the Navy Department than he had from the state senate. The immediate significance of his new position, as every Democrat knew, was that he might thrust a big thumb in the New York federal patronage pie. If he could divert to his followers the well-paying postmasterships and customs collectorships that the defeated Republicans must abandon, he could build an effective anti-Tammany organization, and in the process starve the Tiger.[2]

The requisite approval of the President was far from easy to obtain. At first Wilson was not disposed to manipulate patronage even as a means of shifting control of the Democratic party from conservatives and machine men to progressives. Without thought to political consequences, he proclaimed, "I must have the best men in the nation." [3] Of course Roosevelt could argue that his candidates for offices were the most competent and progressive, but even so he did not always exercise as much influence as he would have liked.

Roosevelt would have to battle over patronage not only with Tammany but also with several more or less allied Wilson leaders. He wished to build an organization that would serve his own as well as Wilson's ends. It must be primarily loyal to Roosevelt rather than his Democratic rivals. Of these, one of the most effective was Dudley Field Malone, the attractive son-in-law of Senator James A. O'Gorman. Malone seemed to come out ahead in the first skirmishes for the President's favor. He went riding with Wilson one afternoon soon after the inauguration, and to him the President assigned the task of evaluating the records of men in the consular service so that the best ones could be given attractive posts regardless of party affiliation.[4] In practical political terms this naturally meant the selection of men more friendly to Malone and O'Gorman than to Roosevelt.

Technically, O'Gorman was a member of Tammany, but since he had fought within the organization on behalf of Wilson, he was entitled to strong consideration in the making of New York appointments. Differences between Roosevelt and O'Gorman were more progressive versus conservative and upstate versus city rather than reform versus machine. It was primarily good political strategy that led Roosevelt to identify O'Gorman with Tammany. If need be, O'Gorman could block Roosevelt appointees by wielding the customary power of senatorial courtesy. The Senate would without question refuse to ratify an appointment in New York that did not have his approval. When McAdoo and Roosevelt persuaded Wilson to nominate a United States District Attorney whom O'Gorman opposed, the Senate rejected the appointment without a dissenting vote.[5] At times like these, Roosevelt told friends that he regretted having helped make O'Gorman a Senator, that O'Gorman was worse than "Blue-eyed" Billy Sheehan.[6]

Roosevelt's relations with Secretary of the Treasury McAdoo were even more complex, but generally far more satisfactory. A comparative newcomer to politics, McAdoo followed his success as Wilson's campaign manager with extensive efforts to build a following of his own that might ultimately bring him the Presidency.[7] Roosevelt was always an ally, but the degree of his support shifted from time to time.*

A key obstacle in the way of Roosevelt's aspirations was the patronage-wise Postmaster General, Albert Sidney Burleson of Texas, whom Wilson appropriately enough dubbed "the Cardinal." Burleson tried to convince the President that orthodoxy in the dispensation of offices was essential to pushing a reform program through Congress. As Burleson pointed out, it would mean immediate votes for Wilson's measures; he did not add that it would leave the party machinery under the continuing control of the Old Guard. Wilson on the whole came to accept this formula although it sometimes meant the sacrifice of progressive men in order to obtain progressive measures.[9]

* Despite the close political association of the two men, there was almost no correspondence. After Roosevelt's internecine battle with McAdoo at the 1924 convention, he made light of the one-time alliance. In 1931 when a political writer recalled his activities on behalf of a McAdoo anti-Tammany organization, he asserted, "I strongly opposed McAdoo's plan all through the Wilson administration."[8]

Roosevelt could control patronage only through a combination of complex maneuvering and fortuitous circumstances. The intricacies of the struggle for the collectorship of the Port of New York well illustrate this. With its opportunities to place party workers in customs jobs, it was the choicest federal prize in the state. Ironically, Wilson, while he was functioning on a basis of choosing the best-qualified men, first offered it to one of Roosevelt's strongest sponsors, George Foster Peabody, a wealthy Democrat. But Peabody, who had no interest in personally building a following, declined it.[10] Roosevelt seemed to be in a strong position to influence Wilson's next choice. The New York *Herald*, perhaps inspired by its former reporter Howe, asserted that he had "long been a favorite of the President," hence would be successful in steering appointments away from Murphy's machine. Wilson, the *Herald* declared, had no intention of fighting Tammany Hall or any other organization, but also no desire to defer to it in appointments.[11]

"The only way in which the State situation can be really improved," Roosevelt asserted, was for Wilson to accept his candidate for collector, John K. Sague, the banker mayor of Poughkeepsie. He felt certain that Sague's name was "at the top of the list," since both McAdoo and the President expressed the feeling to him that Sague was the man for the place. But already Roosevelt was too experienced to think he could win such a coup without a stiff fight. "Political exigencies of various kinds," he warned, could "arise to block all our plans."[12]

The worried Tammanyites lost no time in manufacturing political exigencies, and enlisted O'Gorman to aid them in bringing pressure upon the President. Within a day or two they neutralized Sague so completely that when Roosevelt hurried to the White House with four of his supporters, the most they could ask Wilson was that he compromise rather than capitulate. They argued that if Tammany received no patronage, within a short time they would capture the party in the state and align it with the Administration. The President listened politely, but did not commit himself.[13]

The battle was relentless; O'Gorman and Roosevelt continued to protest against each other's candidate. As the obvious way out, Secretary McAdoo proposed they compromise on Frank Polk, an old friend and Groton classmate of Roosevelt's, a progressive Wilsonian but not a member of either faction. Both O'Gorman and Roosevelt protested against Polk and stood their ground until Wilson worked out an elaborate compromise. He gave appointments to several better-grade Tammany men; most notably he made Justice James W. Gerard Ambassador to Germany. At the same time, he gave the collectorship to a progressive Democrat who was vigorous, competent, and independent of both Tammany and Roosevelt's faction, John Purroy Mitchel. The machine obtained some customhouse positions, and Roosevelt obtained an appointment as appraiser of merchandise for Sague.[14]

Roosevelt fared better in the slow task of building support through postmasterships. Under the division of spoils on Capitol Hill, Burleson's post offices were the private preserve of the Representatives—"congressional patronage." All other offices were "senatorial patronage." Of course, where congressmen were Republican, they could not share in the spoils, and this left the allocation of most of the post offices in upstate New York unsettled. Throughout his sojourn in Washington, Roosevelt devoted much energy and attention to placing those friendly to him in post offices. Often the snarls and tangles surrounding a $2000-a-year appointment filled a fat dossier, and required all the skill and tact that both Roosevelt and Howe could command to straighten out amicably.[15] They had to circumvent older and better-entrenched Democratic leaders in most districts, and they also had to get around the established system of forwarding recommendations from local and county Democratic committees to the Democratic Senator. There were strong ties of allegiance between many a small-town Democratic leader and the boss in Manhattan. Then too, for a long time Burleson was suspicious of the jaunty Assistant Secretary. He sent Roosevelt lists of post-office vacancies, but was quite cautious about accepting his recommendations. Fortunately for Roosevelt, he and Howe were able to carry on much of their negotiations over small offices with a far more amenable politician, the First Assistant Postmaster General, Daniel C. Roper.[16] Through him, Roosevelt won a few clear victories over the Tammany Tiger.*

Howe once explained the mechanics of one of these cases to the absent Roosevelt:

> I saw Mr. Roper again today. We are getting what you might call chummy. Postoffice matters are going nicely and I think Ketcham is sure to win out in Orange County after my talk. Mr. Burleson had his talk with the President and came back, accord-

* Roper became Secretary of Commerce in FDR's cabinet.

> ing to Mr. Roper, undecided. Mr. Roper says he argued with him some more and that Mr. Burleson finally concluded to put it through and that he was going to break the news to O'Gorman in a few days. If you hear of that portion of the Post Office Department roof sailing off into space accompanied by a violent explosion you will understand that the interview took place.[17]

Even from the distance of Washington, Roosevelt ran the risk of becoming caught in the sudden shifting of the party battle lines in New York. If he had been in Albany in 1913 it might have been disastrous. Even before he left the state senate, the new governor, "Plain Bill" Sulzer, had relabeled the Executive Mansion the "People's House," and proclaimed his absolute independence of Tammany. Roosevelt and his allies encouraged Sulzer in this course, but did not take him very seriously. "I sincerely hope," Roosevelt commented, "that the Governor will prove in the end to have a spine and also a brain to make it move in the right direction." [18] By May, Sulzer's fight against Tammany was clearly no sham, for he was engaged in a knockdown battle. Reformers backed Sulzer, but because of his unsavory record and theatrical manner, did so gingerly.

The Tammany answer was to start impeachment proceedings against Sulzer on the grounds that he had speculated on the stock market with campaign funds. The governor in return charged that the machine had looted millions in the repairing of the state capitol and the construction of prisons and highways. Most of his accusations were vague, but the public was ready to believe them. During the long struggle between Sulzer and Tammany, Roosevelt was an amused but cautious spectator. Like most progressives, he sided with Sulzer, but did so covertly. "There is a certain grim, ironic humor," Roosevelt commented, "in the spectacle of Tammany seeking to remove a governor . . . [for] violating the elections laws." [19] Howe carefully guided Roosevelt past various traps that lay in the way of co-operation with Sulzer, preparing for him "a nice pussy-footed answer" to one of the governor's numerous appeals.[20] When the impeachment was imminent, Sulzer wired Roosevelt to intercede with President Wilson. Apparently Roosevelt did so, but Wilson wisely decided not to interfere.[21]

On October 17, less than a month before elections, Governor Sulzer was convicted and removed from office. The result was an overwhelming repudiation at the polls of all Democrats, Tammany and independents alike. Roosevelt had worked in the state assembly elections for fusion between liberal Democrats and Progressives, especially on behalf of several young Progressives. The most notable of these was the younger Hamilton Fish, who had incurred the enmity of a Putnam County Republican machine politician. "I am a little worried about Ham Fish," Roosevelt confessed,[22] but Fish and some others who had gone into the Progressive party from the Republican, won election.* In New York City, Tammany suffered overwhelming defeat; the fusionists elected Collector Mitchel as mayor on a clean-government ticket, and newspapers predicted the speedy ouster of Murphy as leader of the organization.

At once, Roosevelt asked Wilson to commission him to move into the void and build a substantial Administration organization. The President had never liked Tammany and now that its ranks were shattered had less need to conciliate it in order to hold congressional votes. Roosevelt proposed that the President hold up patronage until upstate leaders could meet at the White House "and present their case more or less as a unit." [24] Wilson gave his approval,[25] but the conference did not materialize, probably because in the months that followed he did not want to appear publicly as favoring one New York Democratic faction over others, or to boost Roosevelt's personal political fortunes.†

Less than a month after the Tammany debacle, Roosevelt gave signs of seeking the nomination for either governor or United States Senator. A flattering article in the New York *Sun*, December 10, 1913, bore the marks of a Howe-inspired trial balloon. It claimed that unless the new governor, Martin H. Glynn, proved himself independent of Tammany, the Wilson Administration would favor Roosevelt in 1914.[27] This heralded the opening of a rather widespread movement among independent Democrats to make Roosevelt the nominee either for governor or United States Senator.[28] While touring the state, a member of the New York Conservation Commission tested out "the political weather signs" for Roosevelt. "I found all over," he reported, "that a suggestion of you for Governor next fall was practically universally well received; and your strategic position is very strong." [29] Rumors reached Roosevelt that Colonel House and other important Democratic leaders shared this feeling.[30]

* The following summer, Roosevelt tried to persuade Fish to run for the state senate, and promised if he would, "I shall violate every rule I have made and come up and stump the district for you." [23]

† Wilson appointed Malone to succeed Mitchel as collector, and won the important support of O'Gorman for the Federal Reserve bill.[26] Open aid to FDR would have jeopardized this valuable alignment.

Roosevelt's strategy was simple and timeworn. In the next few months he stated repeatedly that he was not a candidate, and could not conceivably be a candidate for governor. Thomas Mott Osborne hinted after a conversation with Governor Glynn that unless the governor fought Tammany, independents would come out for Roosevelt. With a surface casualness, Roosevelt scoffed to Glynn, "By the way, if you happen across the inspiring idiot who started the report that I might be, or under any circumstances could be, a candidate for Governor you will do me a real favor by taking him into a quiet corner and firmly convincing him that he is absolutely mistaken." [31] At the same time, Roosevelt did nothing either to conciliate Tammany, or to stifle the talk in his behalf.[32]

Prudence dictated this sort of circumspect policy. For one thing, the movement was confined to rumors rather than any ground swell; for another, Roosevelt as a member of the Wilson Administration dared not act contrary to the President's wishes. At the end of March, he queried Wilson:

> Ralph Pulitzer has sent a special man to Washington to ask me to write an article on the New York situation for the *World*.
>
> Hitherto I have steadfastly refused to be quoted about New York politics in spite of considerable pressure – I do not think it right for me to speak if it is to be misconstrued as voicing the opinion of the Administration –
>
> And yet the present situation is so critical that before I give a definite answer I would deeply appreciate a five minutes talk with you, as it occurs to me that if I do say anything it might help rather than embarrass the Administration.[33]

Wilson did not grant the interview, but replied incisively:

> The Secretary brought me your letter yesterday and I have been thinking over it very seriously.
>
> My judgment is that it would be best if members of the administration should use as much influence as possible but say as little as possible in the politics of their several states. I think that just at the present time, particularly, it is difficult to comment serviceably upon the condition of affairs in New York, because while we may think we see the way they are unfolding themselves, the plot is not yet clear.
>
> I know you wanted my frank opinion. I give it with hesitation and yet with a good deal of confidence.[34]

For some months Roosevelt dutifully followed Wilson's advice. While he continued to work among the county organizations on behalf of his own candidates for postmasters [35] he made no general statements.

In June, Roosevelt publicly was continuing his intermittent disclaimers which caused everyone to connect his name with the governorship, and privately was canvassing the possibilities of running. He had no chance of winning without aid outside the progressive Democrats, since Glynn was supporting the Wilson program and would be formidable. The only possible additional support could come from the New York Progressive party, but it hoped to run Theodore Roosevelt in order to strengthen its organization.[36] Franklin commented, "If Colonel Roosevelt is a candidate . . . I will not run against him. You know blood is thicker than water." [37] Shortly thereafter he declared that he would not become a candidate for governor, but he added this new qualification: unless he could obtain the Progressive as well as the Democratic nomination. This seemed to indicate the drift of things. At the beginning of July, Mayor Mitchel went to Oyster Bay for a "social visit" with the Colonel, but there were no tangible results. Theodore did not become a candidate, nor did he seem to regard blood as thicker than water. Although he had a high opinion of Franklin, he made no offer of support and, on the contrary, tried to work out a fusion arrangement with liberal Republicans.[38]

Altogether the situation became extremely discouraging. Roosevelt on the one hand could not count upon Progressive aid; on the other he could be sure he would feel the full fury of organization men not only in the city but upstate as well. President Wilson was agreeing to channel patronage through McAdoo, and Roosevelt was willing to assist McAdoo. This might strengthen the independents, but it would also certainly bring organization retaliation. As a first result, Roosevelt obtained the selection of one of Murphy's bitterest enemies as a customs collector,[39] and the story circulated that Wilson would next appoint forty postmasters, many in important cities such as Utica and Binghamton, and each would be an anti-Murphy man.[40] Since these appointments would come after the Senate adjourned, they would not have to run the gantlet of Senator O'Gorman until after the election.[41]

The most violent of battles over the postmastership centered in Roosevelt's own city of Poughkeepsie. Months earlier, Edward E. Perkins curtly warned, "Hope you will try to keep out of the P. O.

matter here. It will be a bitter fight and a good thing to leave alone for any one looking forward to future success in the party, not only here, but in the State." [42] Of course, he did not, and although Perkins enlisted the aid of O'Gorman, Roosevelt achieved the nomination of his own candidate.[43] This led to a vigorous roar of protest from both Perkins and Tammany. Perkins formally announced that he was planning to retire as treasurer of the Democratic state committee in protest against Roosevelt's arbitrary methods – his policy of "rule or ruin." [44] In a Poughkeepsie newspaper, he launched so savage an attack that Roosevelt warned he would hold the paper strictly accountable. "Mr. Wilson is hearkening to the young and rash Roosevelt," it proclaimed. "The Old Guard here resents this action of Roosevelt's . . . NO IRISH NEED APPLY. They claim he is animated by racial and religious prejudice in the matter, rather than by actual hostility to Tammany." [45]

On top of this, State Chairman William Church Osborn publicly spanked his former protégé. He announced upon his return from a tour of the upstate area that he found the party there in such a complete state of demoralization that he doubted if it could elect a single Congressman. Dissatisfaction over the appointments of postmasters was the main reason, said Osborn, and President Wilson was not so much to blame as several "self-interested little busy bodies who had had the President's ear and who have convinced him that many perfectly good Democrats are only Tammany heelers." [46] As if this were not damaging enough, Representative John J. Fitzgerald, chairman of the Committee of Appropriations and Tammany spokesman in the House, threatened on July 23 that he and the twenty Democratic Representatives in Congress from New York City who had supported the Wilsonian program would take decisive action. "Their success in the coming campaign may be essential to the control of the House by the Democratic party," Fitzgerald warned. "They have been pictured as the representatives of crooks, and grafters, and political buccaneers, and their slanderers profess to be the authorized spokesmen of the Administration." [47]

This finished Roosevelt. President Wilson immediately let it be known "that he had the kindliest feeling for Mr. Fitzgerald and did not indorse the characterization of Tammany Congressmen as representatives of crooks, grafters, and buccaneers." [48] He had already preceded these conciliatory hints with more important action. Several days previously, Mitchel, Polk, and Malone visited Wilson to try to get him to back Roosevelt for governor.[49] "They put it up very strongly to the President," Roosevelt reported,[50] but they found him aloof. As for Roosevelt, under fire as he was from Tammany, Osborn, and incidentally McCombs,[51] there was little he could do but put teeth into his denials that he sought the governorship, and issue a statement that would stick.* With the New York City Democrats opposed to Roosevelt in a block, and the upstate Democrats far from united behind him, this should have been the end of it. So far as the governorship was concerned, it was.

As for the senatorship, on August 13 Roosevelt wrote in routine fashion, "Personally, if I were not engaged in this work in the Navy Department, I should like nothing better than to get into the fight actively." [54] Later that same day he precipitately announced that he would be a candidate in the Democratic primary. To Howe, who was on vacation, he wired that an "important political development" compelled his candidacy. "My senses have not yet left me," he added.[55] Howe certainly must have wondered, since he would have strenuously argued against so rash a venture.†

What was the "important political development" that changed Roosevelt's mind? According to Ernest K. Lindley it was "the impression that it was Wilson's positive wish." [56] Josephus Daniels always believed that McAdoo had persuaded Roosevelt. Daniels himself was against it, and warned Roosevelt that he probably would not carry the primary; if he did, he would be likely to lose in November. Roosevelt told Daniels he would seek Wilson's advice, but apparently did not do so.[57] Roosevelt's impression of the President's wishes undoubtedly came through McAdoo. In a similarly uncertain way, he hoped for fusion with the Progressive party.[58] But above all, the new development was strong upstate pressure upon him.

Early in August, Roosevelt was in communication with a group of upstate Democrats, led by Louis Antisdale of the Rochester *Herald*, who were trying to persuade him to enter the senatorial contest as the running mate of their reform gubernatorial candidate, a flamboyant

* FDR declared: "When I said I was not a candidate and that I would not accept the nomination, I did not say it in diplomatic language, but seafaring language, which means it." [52] FDR also denied in private correspondence that he was a patronage dispenser. He informed a disappointed Saratogan, "I supposed you had more common sense than to believe in silly newspaper stories that I am the official dispenser for the State of New York." [53]

† Eleanor Roosevelt had no part in the decision, since she was at Campobello Island awaiting a baby. Four days later, Franklin D. Roosevelt, Jr. was born.

New York Irish reporter, John A. Hennessy. It was Hennessy who had conducted the investigations of Tammany during Sulzer's short regime, and he was promising to pull from a little black book the facts and figures to destroy the machine.[59] On the evening of August 12, at Antisdale's telegraphic request, Roosevelt attended a conference in New York City. It was the next day that he announced that through a "stern sense of duty" he would run for the good of the party upstate.[60]

Roosevelt had to run without open Administration support; to reporters he declared that he was announcing his candidacy without consulting Washington officials. This left him in a peculiarly vulnerable spot while Tammany cast about for a candidate. There was a flurry of liberal commendation of his candidacy [61] while regular Democrats heaped scorn upon it.[62] The Poughkeepsie *News-Press*, at the instigation of Perkins, vilified him.*

Then there was a foreboding silence as Murphy decided upon a candidate. Almost anyone but Roosevelt would do.[64] There were rumors that it would be William Randolph Hearst,[65] whose name long since had become a stench to a considerable part of the electorate. "I have been offering up prayers," Roosevelt admitted from Campobello, that the stories "may come true. It would be magnificent sport and also magnificent service to run against him." [66] Hearst's New York *American* subsequently reported that the publisher had received an offer, but declined it.[67]

Roosevelt's spirits rose as he and Howe interpreted Tammany's delay in coming forth with a candidate as an indication that no one wished to run against him. "The truth is," explained Howe overoptimistically, "that [they] haven't anything to say against you and no one is very anxious to bell the cat. Particularly when they have an idea that the President occasionally pats him on the back, calls him 'pretty pussy' and gives him a nice saucer of warm patronage milk to drink!" [68]

Roosevelt's luck for once was against him. After days of inaction,

* The Dutchess County Democratic Committee did finally endorse FDR, and delivered the vote to him in the primary. But the *News-Press* attack made him furious. "I had thought of answering," he snapped, "but for the present at least I think a dignified attitude of paying no more attention to their attack than I would do to the obscene language of a drunken man is the best policy. But *some day* I am going to come back with a right hook that will catch not only the *News Press* but also some of the crooked old fossils of poughkeepsi [*sic*] squarely between the eyes." [63]

Boss Murphy scored a coup by nominating James Gerard, a wealthy, liberal, impeccably honest member of the organization. As Ambassador to Germany, Gerard in September, 1914, was rescuing Americans stranded by the outbreak of the war. His name was in the headlines daily and his heroic reputation would make it hard for Roosevelt to defeat him. Besides, his diplomatic post identified him so closely with the Wilson Administration that the anti-Tammany men could not well attack him.[69]

It was a sad blow. At first Roosevelt whistled in the dark by predicting that Gerard would refuse to run. "I am not yet willing to believe," he declared wistfully, "that [Murphy] can drag an Ambassador away from important duties to make him a respectable figurehead for a bad ticket."[70] If the Administration quietly requested Gerard not to run, there was a fraction of a chance for Roosevelt. Gerard cabled the State Department that he would accept the nomination if the President and the Secretary of State approved, but that he might not be able to make a long campaign, or even campaign at all, since he could not leave Berlin until all Americans and their interests were cared for.[71] Bryan queried Wilson:

> Asst. Sec. Roosevelt is as you know a candidate & has, as I understand, the endorsement of Secs. McAdoo & Redfield. I have also felt that Roosevelt would be the best man – having the advantage of being actively progressive & an upstate man. Gerard could not of course leave Berlin in the near future. What do you wish said to Gerard? He will do as you wish.[72]

Wilson did not intervene.*

In consequence, Roosevelt was in the unhappy position of campaigning against Tammany, but not against Tammany's candidate. Roosevelt could not very well attack the silent Gerard, except to claim that out of the nine thousand petitions filed for Gerard, all but 140 came from Tammany sources.[74] He called upon Gerard to state publicly whether if elected Senator he would accept Murphy's control, and whether if the war continued and American interests required him to remain in Berlin, he would consider that his duty lay there or in the Senate.[75] These rhetorical questions received no answer. By the close of the campaign, Roosevelt was complaining rather

* FDR was in part the victim of conflict among Wilson's advisers. While McAdoo, Malone, and House favored FDR, Tumulty, Burleson and Attorney General James C. McReynolds were conciliatory toward Tammany.[73]

pathetically, "It is difficult to conduct campaigns against moles. Murphy's candidates under his advice, refuse to come out of their holes and declare their principles in accord with the spirit of the direct primary." [76]

Nor could Roosevelt do more than hint that he was the administration candidate. His friends circulated rather inaccurate whispers that Bryan, either at Wilson's suggestion or with his approval, had tried to persuade Gerard not to run.[77] Roosevelt strongly attacked the Tammany-dominated state convention for failing to give unqualified endorsement to the New Freedom; [78] he aired his usual charges against Murphy, and warmly praised the Wilson Administration. "There's as much difference between a Murphyized Albany and a Wilsonized Washington," he declared, as "between the lower regions and the upper regions." [79] Perhaps with a slight glance backward at the gubernatorial campaign of 1898 (when Theodore Roosevelt successfully distracted attention from embarrassing state issues with the American flag) he decorously introduced a patriotic note by describing how the Navy forces had recently taken Vera Cruz.[80] None of this could overcome the fact that Gerard was an even more prominent member of the Wilson Administration.

If Gerard was dependent upon Tammany support, so, ironically, Roosevelt would be, if he succeeded in the primaries. When Roosevelt was asked what he would do after the primary, he retorted that he would accept its results, and even if he lost, remain within the party.[81] On other occasions he fell back on his old formula that his quarrel was with Murphy; not with the honest and progressive men to be found within Tammany. Yet if Roosevelt obtained the nomination, he could not win in November without Murphy's active aid. The Washington *Star* inquired, "Why tear the hand that feeds? Why lambast Mr. Murphy before primary day, and cuddle up to him between then and election day?" [82]

One other weakness in Roosevelt's campaign was his running mate Hennessy, whose exposures of Tammany graft seemed likely to drive independent voters toward the Republicans rather than purge the party. Upstate, Hennessy and his brogue inspired more mirth than confidence. "Hennessy's a Clown," one headline proclaimed, "Good as Finley Peter Dunne's Original in Mr. Dooley." [83] Howe grumbled a year later, "He ruined us and he will sink any ship on which he is a passenger." [84]

At least, the vigorous campaigning spread Roosevelt's name within the state more widely than ever before. In directing strategy, Howe was "playing the game the same way I did in the State Senatorial campaign – letting Hennessy look after the cities while I go gunning up in the rural districts which Tammany has never thought worth looking after." [85] Dipping into his bag, Howe polished up some of the tricks that worked so magnificently later in the 1920's. He solicited endorsement from navy yard labor leaders [86] – but slipped when he let circulars go out that did not bear the union label.[87] He sent "personal" letters from Roosevelt to rural editors, asking their advertising rates; [88] later he placed a few ads, and sent out a stereotyped "news" plate. This "boiler plate" was of long-range value because it carried an attractive photograph in place of the haughty visage so widely circulated earlier. After looking at the picture, the octogenarian reformer, Dr. Mary Walker, wrote Roosevelt she wished she could campaign for him, his face showed such "*grand ideals*." [89] The accompanying printed matter incorporated an old device, a headline asserting what Howe did not dare state in the body of the story: "Wilson's Assistant Secretary of Navy has Backing of National Administration." [90]

It was only the second time that Roosevelt had campaigned actively. The three weeks speaking in September gave him additional experience, but he still had a good bit to learn, as one small-town Republican editor made clear in a thoughtful, critical appraisal:

> He is quiet and unassuming, has the demeanor and poise of the student, and with his youthful scholarly face and soft accent, he gives no indication of the stubborn attitude that his friends claim he can assume on occasion. His speech . . . did not consume more than twenty minutes. . . . While he refrained as far as possible from alluding to himself directly, some of his utterances were planned with the skill of an old campaigner, and the inference was very plain. He dealt entirely with general political conditions, and when his speech was finished, his listeners knew no more about his attitude on the great questions of the day than they did before he began.
>
> Mr. Roosevelt is not an orator, but he gives a plain offhand talk. He impresses the listener with his honesty of purpose, but there is nothing to show that he could make any impression in the United States Senate. The great personal force and magnetism necessary to push forward great national issues seem to be entirely lacking in him, and when compared to such a man as Elihu Root he cuts a sorry figure as a great statesman.[91]

Wherever he went, Roosevelt created a mildly favorable impression, but he was too young and unsure a campaigner to stir any excitement. His was a shoestring tour through overwhelmingly rural areas, where there were few Democrats save for a scattering of federal and state officeholders. In many counties, most of those few who would bother to go to the polls on primary day, had ties with the state machine rather than the Wilson Administration. Among Progressives, Roosevelt had little opportunity to demonstrate his vote-getting power, since few of them voted in the Democratic primary.

Before the election, the state headquarters predicted that Gerard would defeat Roosevelt 8 to 1 in New York City, and by a majority upstate.[92] The gamblers at Schumm's Café on Fulton Street, Brooklyn, were more impressed with Roosevelt; they would give no odds against him, although they were betting 5 to 3 on Gerard.[93] They were seriously wrong.

The outcome was as thorough a chastisement of Roosevelt as Murphy could have wished: he lost by an over-all ratio of well over 2 to 1 – in the city, almost 4 to 1; upstate, more than 2 to 1. He received a total of only 76,888 votes to 210,765 for Gerard, and 23,977 for McDonough. The only scanty satisfaction he could feel was that he did carry 22 out of the 61 counties of the state.*

These puny victories gave the ever buoyant Roosevelt an opportunity to rationalize some success out of his campaign. Returning to Washington in fine humor, he went far beyond the facts to claim that his ticket had won outside of New York City. Thus he implied that the rest of the state was autonomous – free from Tammany domination.[95] "On the whole, I think the primary fight was well worthwhile," he boasted, "as I carried a majority of the counties of the State and was beaten only through the solid lineup of New York City." [96]

A month after Roosevelt's political disaster, the entire Democratic party suffered a similar debacle in New York State; James Wadsworth snowed under Gerard to win the senatorship.† "I deeply regret the

* The only one with a large vote was Monroe, 3374 to 1360; in most of the rest, FDR won with a total of only a few hundred votes. In the Adirondacks, he carried Clinton County with 183 votes, Montgomery with 85, and Tioga with 76. He won in Dutchess County by the overwhelming majority of 461 to 93.[94]

† After the primaries, FDR cabled Gerard, "Hearty congratulations. Shall abide result primaries. In addition will make active campaign for you if you declare unalterable opposition to Murphy's leadership and all he stands for. Please answer." [97] Gerard replied days later, "Thanks for your assurance of support. Of course, I intend to represent the Democratic party and the people, and no faction or individual, if elected." [98] Roosevelt then announced his support of Gerard.

defeat of Gerard," Roosevelt announced. "I am sorry for the defeat of the Democratic ticket in New York, but I am not entirely surprised."[99] There was much in both defeats for Murphy and Roosevelt to ponder. Josephus Daniels years later gave a perceptive analysis: "That incident and others in later off year elections proved that city machines can control nominations but can rarely secure victory for their nominee in the regular election."[100] The moral for Roosevelt and Murphy was obvious; no matter how much they might detest each other, the obvious way to victory was through coalition. Roosevelt without the city machine could not even win the primary; the machine without progressive candidates could not win the election. When Theodore Roosevelt was governor he had functioned in this sort of delicate balance with the machine; Franklin D. Roosevelt in time came to do likewise.

Immediately after the election, Roosevelt continued the not entirely inconsistent policy of trying to build a sturdy upstate organization. Tammany was weak in the rural areas, as the 1914 election again demonstrated; this new machine could conceivably serve as an adjunct rather than enemy of the city group.[101]

There were several minor flare-ups of intraparty warfare, and Roosevelt made one last spectacular public appearance as a fighter of Tammany. This came in the spring of 1915 when he went to Syracuse to testify on behalf of Theodore Roosevelt, who was being sued for libel by Boss Barnes.[102] He provided strong substantiation to one of Theodore Roosevelt's statements, that there had been collusion between the Republican Barnes and the Democratic Murphy at the time of the struggle over Sheehan. While Theodore sat listening "alert and smiling," Franklin effectively linked the two bosses.[103] "Franklin Roosevelt was up here yesterday," Theodore wrote his wife, "and made the best witness we had yet, bar Davenport."[104] Later, victorious, he thanked Franklin: "You have a right to congratulate me on the verdict, because you were part of it. I shall never forget the capital way in which you gave your testimony and the impression upon the jury."[105] Franklin as well as Theodore was the victor; in the public mind he had tied himself to his idol more closely than ever before.

Of equal significance in Franklin Roosevelt's political dealings was the quiet unspectacular fashion in which he gradually demonstrated "a willingness to keep hands off" if Tammany would do likewise.

An excellent example of this was the cleanup of the Brooklyn Navy Yard. In the fall of 1914 when Roosevelt was fighting Tammany, he transferred several active political workers from the yard on the grounds that jobs there had long been under the control of Representative William M. Calder, "a Brooklyn Republican, who had a superbly arranged working agreement with the Democratic organization." Between the "Tammany Hall Republicans and 'Billy' Calder Democrats," Roosevelt explained, "no one outside of the alliance had a chance. I initiated the cleaning up of this situation by shifting some men to other yards." [106]

The following year, Roosevelt was taking a new view of the machine, and of the leading Democrat involved in this, Representative John J. Fitzgerald of Brooklyn. Although Fitzgerald in 1915 was in open revolt against Wilson over the appointment of a United States Attorney and a Marshal, Roosevelt arranged unofficially for Fitzgerald's two young sons to take part in the laying of the keel for the battleship *California*,[107] and with remarkable warmth offered to help Fitzgerald campaign. Almost daily, Fitzgerald dropped by Roosevelt's office to ask favors concerning the Brooklyn yard; sometimes he was accompanied by his Republican friend, Calder. "Usually Roosevelt would grant the requests," Fitzgerald has reminisced, "but sometimes he would say, 'The old man is against this and I can't do anything.' " Almost always, Fitzgerald remembers, Roosevelt sent them away happy, for he was "a very, very cooperative man." [108]

While speaking in Greenwich Village in the fall of 1915, Roosevelt took occasion to praise Tammany's candidate for sheriff, Al Smith. He pronounced Smith "worthy, not only of any political gift in the power of the citizens of the city but of any gift in the power of the people of the State." [109] The next year he obtained the postmastership of New York City for Robert Wagner, but Wagner, wishing to be a judge, declined it.[110] It was easy for Roosevelt to find much to say in favor of Tammany men like Smith and Wagner, active in support of progressive factory and welfare legislation.[111]

These overtures did not mean that Roosevelt was joining Tammany, but did signify a "live and let live" attitude growing out of the painful reality that neither of the two factions could carry the state without the aid of the other. Collaboration with Tammany was in line with the President's political policy. In the summer of 1916 Roosevelt came up from Washington to the state Democratic convention at Saratoga Springs, and helped work out compromises. Tammany gave in to the demand he brought from Wilson and McAdoo that Judge Samuel Seabury receive the nomination for the governorship in return for a free hand for the organization in New York City.* However, Tammany rejected the administration candidate for Senator.[114] Of course, Roosevelt's rationale for this was that the 1916 election would be critically close and the Wilson Administration would need the unreserved support of Tammany. If the Tiger could not be starved, perhaps it could be tamed.

* FDR received intimations that Tammany would like to use him to sidetrack the Seabury candidacy, but "declined to flirt." [112] Nor did he change his own personal opinion of Boss Murphy. He wrote Eleanor that he had "conferences all morning with every political potentate that you ever heard of in the State from C. F. Murphy *up*." [113]

CHAPTER XI

Learning About Labor

> For seven and one-half years I have had under me in the Navy Department from 50,000 to 100,000 civilian employees. . . . I have gone on the theory that disagreements can be settled by talking things out around a table . . . that any man or woman could come . . . direct to headquarters. . . . The result has been that the Navy has not had a single strike or a single serious disagreement during that whole period. It means further that we have had happy Navy Yards, with a wholly satisfactory output of work.
>
> — FDR, *August 18, 1920.*[1]

FEW of the lessons Roosevelt learned in Washington were of more lasting value than those that came out of his supervision of the shore establishment of the Navy with its thousands of civilian workers. It taught him relatively early in his political career the knack of getting along with the leaders of labor, and making himself popular with the rank and file. Before many months had elapsed, he learned to speak the language of the labor leaders, and mastered the sometimes intricate task of manipulating the labor vote. Here, more clearly than in any other aspect of naval administration, Howe led the way. While McCarthy advised on the relative reliability of labor representatives,[2] it was Howe who insisted that Roosevelt attend hearings in person rather than delegate labor relations to someone else. Time and again, Howe ushered labor leaders into Roosevelt's office, and persuaded him to spend hours learning their viewpoint that he might otherwise have spent golfing with friends of high social standing.[3] *

Through most of the Wilson Administration, Howe was the trou-

* Eleanor Roosevelt feels Howe performed an enormous service in impressing upon FDR the significance of labor, and in getting him to broaden his group of associates. Roosevelt was not snobbish or undemocratic in his early political career; it simply would not have occurred to him that an up-and-coming young politician should not spend too much time in social circles.

ble shooter who hastened to yards where strikes threatened. He acted swiftly, sometimes secretly, and often to the intense distaste of the officers in charge in order to head off the trouble. Always he did so in the name of Roosevelt, and almost invariably he sided with the workers. No one could have more thoroughly won the dislike of the naval officers or the support of the union leaders. If Howe did not actually say that laboring men had votes and the admirals did not, he at least acted on that premise.[4]

Although labor leaders and naval officers were often at opposite poles, Roosevelt, through Howe, achieved the nearly impossible by maintaining cordial relations with both. Many officers took out their resentment against prolabor policies on Howe; union leaders gave full credit for favors to Roosevelt. The marked difference between the acidity of the one and the affability of the other, together with their startling physical contrast, helped make this possible.

Maintenance of good labor relations in the yards meant more than promotion of better working conditions. It also meant the building of one's own political following, or, often of more importance, the weeding out of the enemy within, whether of another faction of the Democratic party or the Republican party. Of course, Roosevelt always insisted that he would not allow politics of any sort within the navy yards. He explained, "It is not good business . . . nor is it good politics." [5] The best way to make the yards produce votes for the Democratic party, he declared,[6] was to manage them efficiently.*

A snarl of administrative problems, complicated by politics and tradition, made the yards almost fantastically inefficient. They formed a Gordian knot which all the intelligence and ingenuity of Roosevelt's predecessors had failed to cut. Could Roosevelt as an aspiring politician make a strong record as a competent manager of the shore establishment without losing some of his political following? He accepted the challenge almost blithely. In retrospect some naval experts might question his complete success as an administrator, but no one would doubt his triumph as a politician.

Much of what achievement Roosevelt could claim as an administrator came because his judgment of men, while by no means infallible, was right more often than not. Caution was not part of his make-up, and

* Nevertheless, FDR engaged in a steady conferring or withholding of favors in keeping with the requests of politicians in districts including navy yards. For instance, in 1918, Howe was clearing promotions at the New York yard with a Democratic Congressman, James P. Maher.[7]

he was ready to give wholehearted support to any imaginative person who promised quick action. He demonstrated this in his first month in Washington, when Daniels assigned him to work with the Bureau of Yards and Docks to devise means to salvage and complete a huge dry dock which had collapsed while under construction at Pearl Harbor. The contractors claimed that it was impossible to build a dock on the treacherous site that the Navy had chosen. Roosevelt conferred at length with a naval civil engineer, Frederick Harris, who suggested a method of constructing a floating dock on the unstable coral foundation.* Typically, Roosevelt sided with Harris, fought to overcome numerous delays in production, and ultimately won out.[9]

When Roosevelt made inspections of navy yards, however, the achievement seemed a political as well as a technical one. His supervision of the yards provided him as well as the Secretary with the opportunity for inspection tours, not only up and down the Atlantic seaboard, but also occasionally from coast to coast. On these trips a diligent but still comparatively obscure administrator could meet Democratic leaders in distant localities, make emphatic statements that commanded local headlines, and thus lay groundwork for a national following.

On his first visit Roosevelt went no farther than to the Washington Navy Yard, and he ordered that the customary salute and military honors be omitted.[10] But a few days later, like many a producer with a new theatrical production, he went to Philadelphia for a full-scale tryout, in which he demonstrated an immediate understanding of the possibilities of inspections.

For a week before the Assistant Secretary's arrival at Philadelphia, Captain Albert Weston Grant, the commandant, and his staff, had made preparations for the big day.[11] They greeted Roosevelt impressively with a company of Marines drawn up at attention, while a brass band played a fanfare, and a battery on the pier fired a salute. Roosevelt spent an hour with Captain Grant going over plans for the yard, then set forth on the tour of inspection, accompanied by reporters, to whom he advocated, as his own, the commandant's proposals for expansion.[12] He could be sure that all this would receive a most favorable press in Philadelphia, for the previous Secretary of the Navy had wished to close the yard as being useless.[13]

* In the Second World War, FDR had Harris, at that time a civilian, build huge floating dry docks which were towed thousands of miles across the Pacific.[8]

By contrast, Roosevelt remarked to newspapermen, with a gesture toward nine battleships moored in the basin, "That's fine. One of the best features of this yard is its fresh water anchorage. Its location is ideal."

The machinery as well as the ships interested Roosevelt, and he particularly noted an experiment station for testing oil, which he said had "already paid for itself ten times over." He unequivocally endorsed Captain Grant's proposal to build a 1700-foot dry dock, which of course, would bring considerably more repair work to Philadelphia.

"What do you think of the facilities for construction?" a reporter asked.

"Oh, this is a fine place to build a battleship."

While Roosevelt intimated that the President favored liberal expenditures at the Philadelphia yard, he added that if the city wanted the government to spend money there, it must expect to contribute liberally. It must dredge the Schuylkill River channel to the proper depth, and clean up the stagnant marsh on League Island next to the yard, which he denounced as a breeder of malaria and a menace to health. He assumed the role of administrative spokesman. "It is the intention of the President to follow the policy of former administrations in maintaining the navy on a fighting basis," he declared. "New ships will be built as needed, the naval stations will be improved and the country will be at all times in readiness for emergencies. There will be no useless expenditures, however, but there will be steady improvement in strength and equipment."[14]

The inspection was an effective performance, and drew large headlines in the Philadelphia newspapers. The following day, Roosevelt repeated it in New York, and thenceforth again and again with variations in theme to meet local conditions from Kittery to Pensacola and from San Diego to Bremerton. Of course, inspections also involved a considerable amount of careful checking upon men and machines; they were not entirely play and politics.* Roosevelt handled this side with aplomb too.

*A single one of the numerous instructions the chief of the Bureau of Steam Engineering gave FDR before he visited Pacific Coast yards in the spring of 1914, well illustrates the difficult, technical side of inspections:

> Inquire why work costs so much more at Bremerton than it does at Mare Island. On some small work on which they have apparently specialized they make a very good showing . . . [but] in the manufacture of a boiler about 2 years ago, their cost was about 70% more.[15]

In the same clear-cut self-assured manner he assumed during inspections, Roosevelt from time to time outlined in interviews and in speeches a program for all personnel of the Navy, both uniformed and civilian. For the benefit of naval officers and their families, he urged that each ship be assigned a "home yard" to which it would always go for repairs. Officers would thus know where to establish their families in order to spend the maximum time with them. For enlisted men, he wished to make life aboard ship "as agreeable and interesting as possible" * and to make them feel "that the government is taking an interest in them as human beings and not simply as units of a big machine." [17] This side of the program never came to much; Roosevelt before 1917 was more concerned about labor.

The workingmen's greatest need, Roosevelt believed, was a continuous system of apportioning jobs in navy yards and on ships so that they would be steadily employed without layoffs. Before the Wilson Administration, he declared in a campaign speech years later, there had been tremendous fluctuations in employment: "The naval officers were thinking only about the needs of the military side of things. The entire Atlantic Fleet would be brought to the Navy Yard for overhauling. We would take on ten or fifteen thousand additional men during a period of a month or six weeks. Then the Fleet came out again, and ten or fifteen thousand men would be laid off." In addition, the navy yards were making little use of their manufacturing facilities. "The result was great hardship. . . .

"Well, we started investigating; and on the investigating committee we put mechanics from the yards themselves, as people who knew the most about it. The results were: first, the establishment of a system of costs that proved that over a great many years of work in the Navy Yards the Government made material more cheaply than we could buy it; and, second, an arrangement so that the schedule of employment could be maintained on a fairly even basis throughout each year." [18]

This sort of program developed only slowly, and at times involved comparatively minor matters. Roosevelt during his Philadelphia inspection called attention to the numerous safety devices on machines, and declared the government should lead the way for private corporations in a "greater safeguarding of the lives of the mechanics." [19] Again, he expressed his approval of a recreation room for employees at the New York Yard. "Nothing to my mind promotes efficiency so much," he

* In the summer of 1913, FDR donated a Roosevelt Cup to go yearly to the ship whose enlisted men made the best swimming record.[16]

wrote, "as the feeling amongst the employees that they are 'all members of the same club.'"[20]

This was good provender for newspaper readers, but what the workmen themselves most wanted was quick and adequate redress of their grievances. Roosevelt took a personal approach: "We want cooperation," he told a group of machinists. "We want to get down and talk across the table with you and to right your wrongs; to do everything in our power for you and for the service, but you must remember that in doing this we must obey the laws which are laid down by Congress. This may look to you as if I am trying to pass the buck along, but that is not the case." * He emphasized his willingness to give the workmen a voice: "I want you all to feel that you can come to me at any time in my office, and we can talk matters over. Let's get together for I need you to teach me your business and show me what is going on."[21]

This invitation was scarcely necessary, for hardly a day passed without a labor delegation visiting Roosevelt's office. Two union representatives, Albert J. Berres and N. P. Alifas, most often headed these; ultimately these men came to function as much like company union men as labor delegates, they became so wholeheartedly the partisans of the Assistant Secretary.

Roosevelt's initiation into the complications of labor relations came in the spring of 1913 with a flare-up in Boston over the so-called Taylor system of scientific management. Labor as a whole already viewed this as an acutely dangerous form of exploitation, on the grounds that it meant far more work at a lower unit rate of pay. Taylor and his engineer followers on the other hand, described it innocuously as the standardization and systematization of industrial operations through a study of the details of shop operation and the movements involved in each individual job. Engineers scientifically planned and routed these jobs by timing the most efficient workers with a stop watch, and setting their pace as the minimum allowable for each operation. This stimulated the workers to produce more in a shorter period. But it also made them unhappy, for it implied fewer jobs, and lower pay or even discharge for the less efficient.

In its earlier expositions, the Taylor system was social Darwinism applied to the steel industry, and could not have had much appeal to a

* FDR told the workers he would like to create a board made up of the heads of departments and some of the workmen themselves, and send it to Europe to study shop conditions there with the aim of bringing improvements to the navy yards.

progressive like Roosevelt. Only the fittest could or should survive. "All employees should bear in mind," Taylor wrote, "that each shop exists, first, last, and all the time for the purpose of paying dividends to its owners. They should have patience and never lose sight of this fact." [22] But by the middle of the Progressive era, Taylor was explaining his views in the more persuasive terms of the greatest good for the workingman and the consumer. Higher productivity for the general welfare was the all-important aim, and if buried beneath it was the blunt, inescapable reality that under Taylor's system only one pig-iron handler in eight could make good, there was the comforting reassurance that most of the rejected seven could find jobs somewhere.

Thus it was that Roosevelt, ambitious to set a record for efficiency in the industrial division of the Navy, planned to study Taylor's book, and to visit him to discuss the system.[23] Nor is it surprising that the navy yard workers, generally employed for somewhat less than the prevailing wage scales in nearby private industry, and sometimes faced with the problem of trying to appear busy when there were not enough tasks to go around, should look upon the system as a menace to their jobs. They were ready to echo the protests of arsenal workers. When the War Department experimented with it at the Watertown Arsenal, the unions there complained to Congress. William E. Borah conducted a Senate investigation in 1911–1912 and reported that government employees unanimously said it meant a "relentless speeding up" and those in private shops testified that it was "harsh and oppressive and altogether undesirable." [24]

Despite this willingness of Congress to listen to the complaints of speeded-up government workers, several young engineers with commissions as constructors in the Navy wished to introduce the system, if need be in disguised form, as a means of improving the output in their yards. The older officers, content to allow the yards to function as they had in the past, almost always sided with organized labor against them.[25]

When the commandant at Boston, Captain DeWitt Coffman, detected infiltration of the system in the form of job sheets, he bluntly asserted his opposition to it, and recommended punishment of the guilty subordinates. This might well have ended the matter, but a Boston Congressman, James Curley, eager to champion labor, called upon Roosevelt in Washington with a letter from the Boilermakers and Ship Metal Workers Union at the Boston yard, in which they stated that they had held a meeting and voted to walk out. Roosevelt was alarmed, and at once requested an officer in the Navy Department to telephone the commandant. Coffman in turn held a three-hour conference with the labor leaders and devised a truce; he would recommend the transfer of two assistant constructors who were to blame.[26]

This was not a final settlement of the matter; union men in other navy yards all over the United States became alarmed for fear either the Taylor system or the similar Vickers-Maxim program would be introduced. They sent a delegation headed by Alifas, president of the Washington workers' association, to call on Roosevelt and ask him to suspend the existing system of shop management until he had conducted a thorough investigation. Roosevelt listened in a friendly fashion, and promised them he would not extend it into either the Taylor or Vickers program without holding hearings first.[27] Then, in order to conciliate the unions, he made a visit of inspection to Boston on May 19.

At the Charlestown yard, Roosevelt made a careful building-by-building survey with the commandant, who made charges, not at all borne out by the evidence, that "work that should have been done in 19 hours," due to the planning system "required 11 days to perform." Roosevelt departed to lunch with Harvard friends, then returned in the afternoon to confer with the laborers. The workingmen's representatives also claimed that the planning was inefficient. Because of the nonproducers on the planning board, they said, the planning of a ten-cent labor job created $1.90 in overhead charges.[28]

Even though Roosevelt's sympathies were not entirely with the workers, he responded by echoing cautiously the commandant's indignation against planning. When the labor representatives made continued objections even to the including of job specification data on time cards, Roosevelt carefully replied, "Of course, I can readily see how there must be some records kept, some data recorded on which to base future estimates and costs of work, but it may be that this system might be refined." But Roosevelt would not promise the abolition of all systems.[29]

Once clear of these embarrassing matters, Roosevelt delivered his usual abundance of cheering news to the labor representatives and newspapermen. The yard would be equipped for building revenue cutters, supply ships, and, ultimately, larger craft; there would be more permanent employment for the men; more ships of the dreadnought class would come to the yard for repairs; and Navy enlisted men would do no more than 1 per cent of the total repair work. This compensated for the way in which Roosevelt had parried a number of labor demands by saying he would have to refer them to Secretary Daniels for decision. And, as he hurried off to catch a train for Washington, he remarked to the joy of the laborers that he was quite certain that as a result of his visit, two or three officers at the yard would soon be elsewhere.[30]

Whatever satisfaction Roosevelt might have felt over his appeasement of the Boston workers must have evaporated shortly when he received a letter from a former Harvard acquaintance, Arthur A. Ballantine of the Boston firm of Gaston, Snow and Saltonstall.* Ballantine wrote with deep concern that he had dined the night before with the two naval constructors whom Roosevelt had marked for execution. These capable men, he asserted, had cut costs in the Hull Division by about 35 per cent, and were saving the Navy Department $450,000 per year.[31] Ballantine backed his letter by sending to Roosevelt in person a brilliantly persuasive young Harvard Law School graduate who was the attorney in the Bureau of Insular Affairs of the War Department. This was Felix Frankfurter, who described to Roosevelt how successful the Taylor system had been at the Watertown Arsenal, and persuaded him to allow an expert to make an unofficial survey of the Boston yard. This done, Frankfurter drafted, and obtained Roosevelt's consent to, a telegram to Ballantine:

> Had very satisfactory talk with Roosevelt. Fear as to loss to government service of men in question entirely idle. Department anxious for efficiency and economy, as well as permanently sound labor conditions. Opposed to Taylor system as such, but experimenting in other yards with view to arriving at other adequate system.[32]

The breezes from Harvard Yard had wafted the constructors to safety, but a menacing gale still blew from the Boston Navy Yard and every other navy yard in the country. Nor could Roosevelt overlook the hostile wind from Capitol Hill. Consequently, when Frankfurter's expert made his report, Roosevelt drafted, but did not send, a firm reply:

> I find, even with my short experience, that I cannot wholly agree with some of your conclusions. . . . I have been impressed

* Ballantine, who was Under Secretary of the Treasury at the close of the Hoover Administration, remained to serve under FDR during the banking crisis in the spring of 1933.

> with certain findings and conclusions of the Congressional Committee that recently investigated the Taylor system . . . and in particular do I agree with them that "Any radical change in factory management should be gradual evolution out of that which had preceded. . . . Neither the Taylor system nor any other should be imposed from above on an unwilling working force." [33]

There, in the face of the hostility of the unions, the matter rested. Roosevelt refused to make a clear-cut choice between the two sides. He did continue to study the War Department system, but in 1915 Congress brought to an end any possibility of its introduction into the Navy Department by approving an appropriation bill rider which outlawed efficiency systems. Thereafter, the rider was attached every year.[34] This ended the buffeting of Roosevelt: he had weathered the storm.

The problem of setting wage scales for the workmen was less critical but called for equally skillful navigation over many years. Here again, Roosevelt had to steer a cautious course between the Scylla of stirring labor trouble through low wages and the Charybdis of buying labor good will at the expense of the industrial budget. He became so adroit at this that over the years he managed to take credit for many if not all of the concessions that labor gradually won, and with a shrug of his shoulders could imply that the blame, when labor did not get its demands, lay with the cautious Wage Board or the Secretary of the Navy. In retrospect, he made it all seem very simple. Not more than a week after he arrived in Washington, he said, he received a delegation from the Brooklyn Navy Yard who asked him to change the existing method of fixing the wage scale there:

> I said, "Fine. How is it done?" "Well," they said, "do it yourself." I said, "Why, hasn't it been done by the Assistant Secretary in the past?" "No, it has been done by the officers." And then they went on to tell me how unjustly the wage scales in all of the Navy Yards on both coasts and on the Gulf of Mexico had been arranged each year by a special board of officers.
>
> After I had been there I think three days longer, I got Joe Daniels to sign an order making it the duty of the Assistant Secretary to fixe the wage scale each year.[35]

Actually the process was far more complicated and drawn-out than this. In the first place, there was real need for a change in the wage system. Since 1862, a cumbersome piece of machinery had ground out the scale once a year. The law provided that it should conform "as nearly as consistent with the public interests, with those of private establishments in the immediate vicinity of the respective yards." Accordingly the commandant of each yard appointed a wage board from among his subordinate officers. This met on the first of November, sent questionnaires on wages to all the larger firms in the area employing similar types of labor, and gave the workmen at the yard the opportunity to present oral testimony at hearings. On the basis of this evidence, the board tabulated wage rates and sent its recommendation to Washington. If approved, they went into effect on the first of January.[36] Usually the reports did not reach the Navy Department much before Christmas, so that there was little or no time to examine them carefully or grant appeals. The disgruntled employees, feeling that their case was prejudiced, asked Roosevelt for more time for hearings, and for labor representatives on the wage boards. Above all, they wished the Navy Department to set wages not on the basis of prevailing rates in private industry but according to living standards and costs.[37]

In considering this request Roosevelt had, of course, to weigh its effect upon production and budget. The question came before him first as a result of the action of Congress, which granted a wage increase beginning July 1, 1913, in the Washington Navy Yard, on the basis of the high cost of living in the area. When Secretary Daniels asked him to investigate whether it could be put into effect before July 1 when the Naval Appropriation Act would take effect, he replied in the negative. The Navy Department did not have the funds for an immediate increase without cutting down its industrial output, and he did not consider a deficit advisable.[38]

Roosevelt realized that this substantial increase which Congress voted to the Washington workers on the basis of the high cost of living in the area, opened the entire question of wages at all other yards and stations. He seriously doubted if the customary wage boards could correctly decide these complex matters, and contrary to his later recollection, was not enthusiastic about adding labor members to them. "It is questionable," he advised Daniels, "whether . . . [that] would have any good results." He did, however, strongly endorse the union plea for a different basis for setting the scale. The Navy Department should request the Department of Labor to gather statistics on comparative wage scales and costs of living. Whatever the Secretary did, Roosevelt advised, should be accomplished quickly in order to get an additional appropriation from Congress. "A general increase of even five percent . . . would mean an additional cost to the Department of over a million dollars," he reminded Daniels. To pay this amount out of the current appropriation "would mean a curtailment of the work to be performed by the various Bureaus and would result in decreased efficiency in the Department." [39]

In the ensuing negotiations, Roosevelt won the support of Daniels, but the commandants of the navy yards were firmly opposed to any different basis for determining wages and to the appointment of labor representatives to the wage boards. They effectively overrode Roosevelt when they met under his chairmanship, and altogether kept the system much as it had been before.[40]

In the new wage-setting program, however, Roosevelt did achieve more prestige and somewhat greater power. The date for convening the wage boards was a month earlier, October 1, which gave ample time for hearings and review of the scales. This enabled Rosevelt to intervene. He could, and did, attend hearings at East Coast yards, examine the wage schedules, and, if he wished, hold additional hearings in Washington. While he in turn had to present his recommendations to the Secretary for final decision, he made himself the key figure in wage negotiations. This did not lead to any spectacular increases for the employees – only an average of about 6 per cent in 1914, and no change in 1915 – but it did mean that even more labor delegations went to the Assistant Secretary, where they sometimes gained their requests, and always were charmed by the Roosevelt smile.[41] In January, 1919, when Roosevelt was abroad, labor delegates negotiating with Daniels were able to win only limited concessions. Berres advised them to "take what is offered and go after the rest when Mr. Roosevelt returns." [42]

Of course, Roosevelt did not always keep the unions happy, and there were times during the war when labor negotiations involving the tremendous additional influx of shipyard workers became exceedingly complex and touchy. Strikes frequently threatened, but the only navy yard where men actually quit work seems to have been at Norfolk, where despite the efforts of both Roosevelt and Howe for several years, there was continuous friction between the workers and the industrial manager.[43] In this instance, much of the trouble was not the manager's fault, but resulted from highly unsatisfactory buildings and equipment which created unsanitary and even dangerous working conditions.

Roosevelt often did not side with the naval officers running the yards. He did recommend that the assistant chiefs of the Bureau of Construction and Repair and the Bureau of Yards and Docks, should be naval officers rather than the chief clerks.[44] But he was insistent that supervision over industrial work in the yards should be in the hands of men trained in engineering. "There is one fundamental proposition which the officers of the Navy as a whole (though there are many exceptions) have never learned," he wrote later. "That is, that just because a human being has graduated from the Naval Academy and seen the usual naval service, he is not therefore fitted to manage the whole or a part of a Navy yard."[45] In the fall of 1914, he obtained the Secretary's signature to orders dividing the duties within several of the navy yards. The commandant, who was ordinarily a line officer with a background of "usual naval service," should have charge of only "the administration of strictly military questions affecting the yard," while an industrial manager, an officer from the Construction Corps of the Navy, with engineering training and experience, would have charge of "the administration of all industrial activities in the Yard."[46] This was a clear-cut move toward greater efficiency.

It would be less easy to justify on grounds of efficiency the order, of which Roosevelt was chief sponsor, to reopen the closed Southern yards at Pensacola and New Orleans. Most naval experts regarded them as worthless, and were urging the Navy Department to proceed in the direction of closing additional yards. Roosevelt looked at the yards from a different angle. They offered a way of building enthusiasm for the Navy along the Gulf Coast, and among Southern Congressmen. Anyone who reopened the yards could win political popularity in several Southern states. In Roosevelt's agile mind, therefore, there began to revolve schemes to salvage these yards and make them serve some useful function for the fleet.

With a tentative solution already in mind, Roosevelt went South on assignment from Secretary Daniels in late November, 1913, taking with him Eleanor and his cousin Laura Delano. The official rounds of inspection and entertainment made the trip arduous as well as delightful. Mixed with memories of drinking *café brûlé* in a room illuminated only by the light of the burning brandy in the coffee, were those of being routed from bed after only a couple of hours' sleep to resume travel with no breakfast offered them except warm champagne. At a stag dinner, Roosevelt made a speech that his audience deemed too short, so he arose again and delivered another. This trip and others like it "were feats of endurance," Eleanor Roosevelt has written, "and, in the doing, they built up strength." [47]

Not much could be done with the overgrown grounds and forlorn buildings at Pensacola; the machinery could serve little practical use. Roosevelt "entered a majority of the buildings, asked numerous questions, and often soiled his hands turning oily wheels and pulling white leaded levers," a reporter wrote. "From the questions asked it was evident that he was more interested in the housing of the eight hundred marines which he said had been definitely ordered here, than in the early operation of the machinery." [48] To use Pensacola for the housing of men was a better makeshift than Roosevelt realized at the time. It apparently did not occur to him to use it for naval aviators too, but in January, 1914, they began moving into the abandoned yard, and in time built it into the greatest of the naval air training centers.[49]

The New Orleans yard with its well-equipped shops was different. Surely, Roosevelt reasoned, some worth-while use could be found for these. He argued that the yard should be reopened for repair purposes, and that while the "half a dozen gunboats and surveying ships" the Navy kept permanently stationed in the Gulf and Caribbean would not alone justify this, the government as a whole could economize through the repair and maintenance of craft kept in the Mississippi and Gulf waters by the Army, Treasury, and Department of Commerce. When he queried the War and Treasury Departments, he received favorable replies; he urged Daniels to persuade the Secretaries personally to cut the red tape. On this basis, the New Orleans yard was reopened,[50] and remained open until the Republicans again came into power and closed it.* Other departments made little or no use of its facilities, but Louisiana politicians remembered with gratitude what Roosevelt had done. In 1924, when Roosevelt was trying to round up convention votes for Al Smith, a New Orleans attorney wrote him: "Many of us from the South recall with great pleasure the interest you always displayed in legislation for the benefit of the South, recalling explicitly the fact that through your exclusive efforts New Orleans retained the naval yard." [52]

Altogether, Roosevelt's motivations and the pressures upon him in his supervision of the navy yards were so many that it is not always

* Emory Land, remembering this as one of the things in which FDR always took a dogged interest, has remarked that one of the reasons he wished to declare a partial emergency in 1941 was so he could reopen the New Orleans Navy Yard.[51]

easy to disentangle and evaluate them. Certainly a number were often present – the desire to maintain good labor relations, to do what was politically expedient, to run the industrial plant in a scientific and efficient way, and to build the nation's defenses. Considering the complexity of these, and their frequent incompatibility, his record was creditable. "There is no question that the Navy Yards exist primarily for the efficient handling of the fleet," he wrote an officer in 1921. "I am perfectly willing to admit that it is not easy to reconcile war fitness with the demands for economy and businesslike management, yet . . . I am certain that an improvement existed in 1917, let us say, over conditions in 1913." [53]

CHAPTER XII

Another Roosevelt vs. the Trusts

> The general policy of the Government ought to be to utilize to the *best* advantage the various Government plants. . . . Further than this, I still believe that it is a wise policy to award contracts for battleships and battle cruisers in sufficient numbers to private plants to keep them occupied.
>
> — FDR TO JOHN S. LAWRENCE, *August 8, 1916.*

LESS than three years before Roosevelt became Assistant Secretary of the Navy, he had been a clerk for Carter, Ledyard, and Milburn, one of the most powerful defenders of corporate monopolies. In Washington, just the reverse was the case – he was subordinate to one of the most outspoken foes of these same monopolies. Daniels through the Raleigh *News and Observer* had long battled the very tobacco trust which retained Roosevelt's former law firm as its attorneys; as Secretary of the Navy he took advantage of his formidable position to make effective his war against the vested interests. He was the right man at the right time. One observer, exaggerating somewhat, told Ernest K. Lindley:

> Daniels was one of the few living men who had the exact combination of qualities needed to grapple with the Navy as it was in 1913. He had no personal friends in the Navy, and he had the Puritan's conscience and stubbornness. He entered the department with a profound suspicion that whatever an Admiral told him was wrong and that every corporation with a capitalization of more than $100,000 was inherently evil. In nine cases out of ten his formula was correct: the Navy was packed at the top with dead wood, and with politics all the way through, and the steel, coal and other big industries were accustomed to dealing with it on their terms.[1]

It was inevitable that Daniels should soon be slashing away at privilege both within and without the Department, and it was just as inevitable that he should reap ridicule. Representatives of companies that profited from Navy contracts, joined with injured naval officers in denouncing him. Yet Roosevelt, who helped carry out some of the Secretary's antimonopoly policies, not only avoided most of the clamor against Daniels but actually gained the praise of some of the Secretary's most vindictive enemies.[2]

The approach of the two men toward the Naval purchases was as fundamentally opposed as Roosevelt's admiration of gold braid and Daniels's distrust of it. While the new Secretary's initial approach to his position was that of an agrarian hater of monopoly, the Assistant Secretary's was that of a confirmed big-navy man determined to salvage every wasted nickel in order to build a stronger fleet. Their point of agreement was a common zeal for efficiency. To Daniels this was often an end in itself; to Roosevelt it was never more than the means to a greater end.*

Over a period of time, Roosevelt without much difficulty absorbed part of his chief's viewpoints. They were characteristic of the South and the West, and Roosevelt's easy familiarity with them ultimately aided him in attracting voters from these areas. Even though his principal objective at the time was economy, his experiences in dealing with corporations also influenced somewhat his thinking during the New Deal.

To enemies of Roosevelt, the very suggestion that he could economize is an occasion for laughter, and they have delighted in pointing to his private as well as his public life to try to prove him a wastrel whose parents considered him incapable of handling money. The facts belie this. As a young man he was exceedingly careful with his own money, as indeed his mother had taught him to be. On the rare occasion when he allowed some bills in Paris to go unpaid for two years after his honeymoon, he received a sharp admonition from her, and apologized, "hereafter I shall pay cash!"[4] While as Assistant Secretary he was quite well-to-do – John Gunther estimates his and his wife's

* In these matters, FDR shared the attitude of the Navy League leaders who were strongly co-operative. Years after Colonel Thompson, the nickel magnate who was head of the League, had severed all relations with Daniels, FDR was still on friendly social terms with him. Also, the successful entrepreneur rather fascinated FDR. On June 18, 1913, he wrote: "George Westinghouse, inventor, promoter, capitalist & jack of all trades came to see me this morning about the installation of his turbines on the new battleship 39. He has extraordinary enthusiasm & forcefulness for a man of his years, but I can't make out whether I would care to make him trustee of my estate."[3]

joint income at $27,000 – the demands upon his funds were great, since he was maintaining a large household with as many as ten servants.[5] To those innumerable persons who wrote requesting contributions, he usually sent checks, but protested his precarious financial condition. Later, wartime and postwar inflation made him feel particularly hard pressed; in 1920, he warmly thanked his mother for a sizable birthday check, which he said would not go for doctor's bills they could wait – but for "paying the gas man and the butcher lest he infants starve to death." [6] Habitually he preferred to eat at home because it was cheaper, often saved taxi fares through riding streetcars, and wore the same suits for years. His automobile was secondhand. Although his passion for collecting led him to make many expenditures, these were generally both small and shrewd.[7] He was proud of the way his naval prints rapidly increased in value. In the Navy Department, as at home, though he had no fear of quite large spending, he had a keen eye for small waste, at least until the war came.

Shortly after taking office Roosevelt began to scrutinize the contracts that came over his desk, so as to make certain the Navy received full value. This literally meant "economy to the last cent": Daniels once ordered him to investigate why the Bureau of Yards and Docks awarded an oil contract to a firm that bid ninety cents a barrel rather than to another that bid eighty-nine cents.[8]

Much of the work fell to Roosevelt's assistant, Howe, who as a specialist on contracts tried to achieve newsworthy economies with which to credit Roosevelt. Howe carefully questioned every piece of paper as though he expected to find each bidder conspiring to cheat the government.

In fact, on almost every contract, large or small, the triumvirate of Daniels, Roosevelt and Howe seemed to suspect collusion to avoid competitive bidding, and often there were grounds for suspicion. Just before the end of the fiscal year 1913, a $100,000 rush order for foundry equipment came through with a request that bidding be waived in favor of one firm.[9] "Mr. Daniels raised a riot over this and ordered proposals requested from other firms, four bids were submitted, the favored son as usual being amongst the high ones, whereupon the Department again came back and requested that the low bids be not considered." So Howe reported. "Mr. Daniels replied that they must consider the low bidder, whereupon there appears to have been some fancy figuring done, and today a man who was low is haunting Mr. Daniels' office with a complaint of some kind." [10]

But the "riot" Daniels raised on this occasion was mild indeed compared with the nationwide furor he stirred up when each of three major steel companies turned in a bid of $454 per ton for armor plate for the battleship *Arizona.* He swore they were charging higher prices to the United States than to foreign countries, and he flatly rejected the bids. The steel manufacturers insisted that they had built the armor plate mills at the government's request and therefore were within their rights in submitting high bids and splitting contracts three ways, to their mutual profit. When the Secretary called for bids a second time, they again submitted identical figures. The exasperated Daniels sent Roosevelt to New York to negotiate with a British steel manufacturer who had just arrived in the United States. Roosevelt returned with a bid so much lower that it forced the American firms to reduce their price.[11]

This technique appealed to Roosevelt despite his strong nationalism; he was ready to grant contracts to low bidders outside the United States whenever he could thus save money. In June, 1913, he spent nearly a half hour with President Wilson discussing a "nice point" involving contracts with foreign firms:

> Contracts for large machines for Navy Yard use are to be let. The lowest bidder is very slightly higher than a German firm – so little that considering cost of inspection etc the American should have the award. But acceptance of the German bid would mean the payment to the U. S. Gov. of 15% duty[.] In other words the Navy w'd gain nothing, but the Treas. would gain 15% of the cost price. The President took the view that the wage earners & capital of this country would gain more by award to the Am. firm than w'd be saved to the gov. by award to the Germans. Therefore the tariff must not enter into the consideration of bids[.] I agree, but perhaps some day, pretty far off we may take a bigger view of economics than the purely nation wide one.[12]

Where the saving was great enough to justify doing so, Roosevelt did award contracts to foreign companies. In September, 1913, he ordered turbine drums for the *Arizona* from an English firm at a cost "a little more than one-third of the price offered by the lowest American bidder." [13] But this was risky. Although the American people readily became incensed over collusive bidding and monopoly tactics, American manufacturers could divert public wrath by denouncing as unpatriotic the award of government contracts to foreign concerns. When the manufacturers did so, in May, 1914, Roosevelt was quick to surrender. A Canadian firm submitted a bid of $34,349 on a flag and bunting contract, compared with an American offer of $43,095. Roosevelt announced that the American firm would receive the order.[14]

This was a minor skirmish, and the armor-plate campaign had been essentially Daniels's fight. Not so with the attempts to break up collusive bidding for coal contracts. As late as the Second World War, a sensational story was circulating around Washington: Roosevelt had misused his power as Assistant Secretary to force naval officers to purchase coal from mines in which either he or his relatives had an interest. The coal was so bad that it fused on the grates of a warship and put out the fire; the ship had to be towed back to port!

This was the story. What were the facts?

The age of oil was in its infancy, and coal was still the main fuel used by the Navy. Each year the Navy Department purchased six hundred thousand or more tons of the highest quality steaming coal directly from the mineowners or those who controlled the entire output of a mine. It would not buy from jobbers or from any mine that could not pass a rigorous test and obtain Navy approval.[15] This "accepted list" system meant, as Roosevelt later complained to the House Naval Affairs Committee, that a few mineowners maintained a tight monopoly. "The passage of a camel through the needle's eye," he declared, "was a considerably easier journey than the route of . . . independent coal on its way to the accepted list." Further, he charged, the Navy Department did not even bother to advertise publicly for bids, but merely sent letters to the owners or exclusive selling agents of the few approved mines.[16]

In this pernicious system Roosevelt discovered a naturally dramatic issue upon which to focus his energy. By a quirk of fate, this man whose father and grandfather had tried to build a soft-coal monopoly, attempted to smash a combination of the very same kind. As early as the summer of 1913, while Roosevelt was vacationing, Howe assailed Navy Paymaster General Cowie for awarding a coal contract to a firm whose bid was five cents a ton higher than another. Of course, Howe received the firm support of Secretary Daniels.[17]

When the dealers again entered identical bids, Daniels decided to award the contracts by lot, but this was a far from adequate remedy. As the time for new bidding approached, he sought a more effective weapon. One preliminary step was to relieve Paymaster General Cowie of his control over coal contracts, and place the responsibility for them in the Assistant Secretary's office. This threw the whole perplexing problem onto Howe, who was after all a reporter, not a coal expert.[18]

At the suggestion of one of the outsiders which was not receiving contracts, the coal-jobbing firm of Archibald McNeil & Sons, Howe drafted new specifications to make it possible for coal brokers to enter lower figures than the large interests closely affiliated with the railroads.[19]

When the new bids came in, ten additional companies competed, and this time the quotations varied somewhat, though not much. The lowest bidder at Hampton Roads, W. C. Atwater & Co., a regular Navy supplier, received a contract for the entire amount of its offer – 200,000 tons – at $2.80 per ton. This was a saving of ten cents a ton, a total of $20,000 for which Roosevelt could claim credit. The next highest bidder received a contract for 150,000 tons at $2.85, a saving of $7500. This second contractor was the helpful Archibald McNeil & Sons. At the same time, contracts with the Pocahontas Fuel Company, closely tied to the Norfolk & Western Railway, dropped from 170,000 tons to 12,000.[20]

Extreme dissatisfaction resulted. Senator William E. Chilton of West Virginia protested that the Navy had cut coal orders from his state at the very time when the mines were suffering from a slump in the iron and steel industry. Roosevelt sent a sharp reply Howe had written for him: "If business is so good with the West Virginia mines as to make them feel that they can afford to keep up with the combination price, even at the loss of the Navy's 600,000 tons, I do not see how they can be really suffering."[21]

Objections from within the Navy were much more serious. Ship commanders complained that the quality of much of the new coal was below Navy standards, and particularly the coal supplied by McNeil. The engineer on the *New Jersey* declared it was "of poor steaming quality, leaving a large amount of clinker and ash," and the engineer on the *Texas* reported it so inferior that consumption jumped 33.5 per cent.[22] After an investigation, the Bureau of Steam Engineering struck one of McNeil's mines from the "accepted" list. Later the Bureau banned six other McNeil mines because the coal was too volatile, and likely to cause spontaneous combustion in the bunkers.[23]

During the fall congressional hearings in 1915, Roosevelt faced the problem of explaining away before the House Naval Affairs Committee numerous stories that under the new system of contracts the Navy had purchased bad coal. At first Daniels had planned to defend the contracts in his own testimony, and Howe prepared for him an elaborate statement which painted a black picture of the machinations of the coal trust and eloquently praised the spectacular and successful fight of the Navy Department to restore free enterprise. But Howe's vigorous if imaginative report came back from the realistic new Paymaster General, Samuel McGowan, with its rhetoric so thinned down that the bare bones of unpalatable facts showed through all too plainly. Daniels decided it would be wiser to let his agile assistant handle the problem.[24]

The rumors were getting troublesome, and the House Naval Affairs Committee decided to investigate. At the hearings, Daniels briefly mentioned his part in the matter. He declared that he had rejected all the bids because they were identical to the cent – a case of "either collusion or mental telepathy,"[25] and, after further questioning, placed all responsibility on Roosevelt.[26]

The following week the Assistant Secretary came before the Committee, to talk not about coal but about defense. Big-navy Congressmen, querying him eagerly, were delighted with his promptness and candor.[27] When, finally, Representative Ernest W. Roberts managed to bring up the coal contracts, Roosevelt launched boldly into Howe's prepared statement. He sketched the monopoly conditions he had found and his efforts to smash them, but unfortunately marred his defense by quoting erroneous figures that Howe had not corrected. Roberts instantly caught these.[28]

To some of Roberts's questions Roosevelt gave effective answers. He explained, for example, that McNeil had received a Hampton Roads contract with a bid five cents per ton higher than Atwater's because the Navy required more coal than Atwater alone could furnish. But at other points he did not fare so well. He could not explain satisfactorily why McNeil received some contracts, and he wriggled out rather ungracefully when Roberts switched his attack to the bad coal that had given the fleet trouble:

> Now, the reports on the Vinton coal,* which the Willard Bros. –
>
> MR. ROOSEVELT (interposing). That was an experimental contract which has been since stricken from the list.
>
> MR. ROBERTS. The contract has been canceled?
>
> MR. ROOSEVELT. Yes, sir.

* This was the worst of the troublesome brands which FDR had ordered. Three ships reported that the ash fused badly on the grates, and the fourth that "It did not seem to burn at all, acting more like sand that had been heated."[29]

Mr. Roberts. And are you taking any coal from Willard Bros.?

Mr. Roosevelt. No sir; it was frankly an experimental contract to see whether the coal would turn out well. We only took a few hundred tons out of a contract for 5,000 tons, and we shall take no more.[30]

With this, the interchange came to an end. If Representative Roberts had hoped to stir up adverse publicity for the Assistant Secretary, he was frustrated by a coincidence. The same day that Roosevelt appeared before the committee, the British fleet suffered a humiliating setback: German cruisers slipped through their blockade and shelled three English towns. In competition with the headlines this drew, the intricacies of coal contracts had little news value. Shocked Americans were quick to interpret the thrust as a clear indication of the need for a stronger United States Navy. Many newspapers cheered Roosevelt's testimony in favor of defense, and ignored the coal inquiry.

Even the full account in the New York *Times* contained only one paragraph on coal: "When he entered the department, [Roosevelt] said. . . . There was no competition. All that had been changed. . . . In the June bids there was actual competition." [31]

Improved competitive conditions did in fact continue, although the Navy went back to some of its old practices. Unfavorable steaming reports still came in from time to time, but they received slight congressional notice. The Assistant Secretary was no longer directly responsible.[32] The new Paymaster General, McGowan, worked out more practical applications of Roosevelt's principles, and reported to him during the campaign of 1916: "Due to wider competition . . . prices for coal within the past two years have been reduced between 20 and 25 cents per ton, and during the last year on the basis of an annual consumption of 800,000 tons a saving was made of $200,000." [33]

In his own behalf Roosevelt also tried his hand at contract negotiations in 1915. He finally had begun the extensive remodeling of the house at Hyde Park, and was keeping a firm grasp of the details. "By the way *what* have H. & K. told you about the Library?" he inquired of his mother in one letter. "Do please not let any contract till I have a chance to see the offer and to go into details of construction, as I have several 'thoughts' and there is much to be decided about shelves etc." He took off a tower, gave the house a stucco front, and built on a large library-living room on the first floor. Over this new section he constructed bedrooms – one for his wife, one for his mother, and one for himself in between. It was an exciting architectural adventure. When it was done he was well pleased with its appearance, and with the work of the contractor, Elliott Brown, whom he later hired for some of the Navy's construction.[34]

While Roosevelt specialized on coal for the Navy Department, Howe operated similarly in several other fields for the glory of Roosevelt. He had tried to use jobbers as the means of breaking collusive coal bidding; in some areas, like cotton textiles, he tried to eliminate middlemen as a means of bringing down prices. With this in mind, as well as to send business to his wife's home town, he invited a Fall River textile manufacturer to bid directly on Navy contracts.[35] But Howe was not too successful when he attempted to pare the profits of commission merchants by this means. With more success he attacked pernicious block bidding.* Sailors seldom could buy any tobacco except Bull Durham until Howe changed things, and increased the number of brands of tobacco, toothpaste, and similar items sold to sailors on shipboard. But the *Army and Navy Register* charged he was misusing his power to force sailors to buy unknown brands, and was driving worthy bidders away from the Navy Department.[37] Fortunately for Roosevelt, as Howe pointed out, the attack largely concerned "the wicked performances of my wicked self," and left the Assistant Secretary unscathed.[38]

Daniels was delighted with the efforts of Roosevelt and Howe; he proclaimed in his first annual report that through "better and fuller competition" the Navy had already saved $150,000.[39] Actually, during its first year, the policy resulted in a few loudly proclaimed victories, and not a little amateurish floundering. Thereafter, the business end of the Navy ran far more efficiently than ever before, but this was less the work of Roosevelt and Howe than of the new Paymaster General, McGowan, and the excellent group of subordinates he brought in to run the Bureau of Supplies and Accounts. Chief among these was

* Block bidding was a sort of legerdemain in which agents took little profit or even lost money on some items in order to sell other merchandise at a high profit. A food merchant, for example, would offer to sell the Navy a large quantity of asparagus at a price below the market, and a small quantity of beef at a very lucrative price. The block bid might quite well be low enough to get the dealer a contract for both items. He then could count upon the Navy to take all the beef contracted for, since it used great quantities, but very little of the asparagus, for which there was little demand. Consequently his total profit would be large. Howe tried to smash the system by splitting up contracts among the lowest bidders on each item. Thus, in a bid low on asparagus and high on beef, the bidder would get a contract for asparagus – and only asparagus.[36]

Christian J. Peoples, the pay director. "McGowan and Peoples were of the same height, wore the same uniform, were inseparable," Daniels reminisced, "and when they would come . . . together into the Secretary's office, dressed in white . . . Franklin Roosevelt and I would call them the 'Gold Dust Twins,' and we would say 'Let the Gold Dust Twins do your work,' and they did it. More than four billion dollars passed through the purchasing department with never a breath of scandal or graft or paying too much for an article purchased."[40]

More often, Roosevelt called them the "Heavenly Twins," and they sometimes so styled themselves in notes to him. He was on the most cordial of terms with them, gave them whatever they wished, and in return, along with Daniels, was able to take credit for their efficiencies. At their request, Roosevelt arranged with Daniels that all matters should come from them to the Assistant Secretary personally, rather than in a cumbersome fashion through a chain of command.[41] The result was a speeding up in awards and actions on requisitions (and, of course, a freer hand for the "Heavenly Twins"). Roosevelt often expressed delight with their results. Once he congratulated McGowan upon "the magnificent way" in which he had "successfully delivered knockout drops to Congressmen and others and made them believe they were getting candy."[42] Roosevelt's reward was better than candy, for at the beginning of the 1916 campaign, McGowan prepared for him a memorandum enumerating savings which totaled over $1,300,000.[43]

Most of these were due to the initiative of McGowan, though Roosevelt had taken a strong interest in a few of them. Before the new Paymaster General arrived, Roosevelt had given verbal orders to a marine captain to investigate graft in commissaries on the Pacific Coast,[44] and had inaugurated a program for the salvage of scrap metals in the navy yards. The Navy, by selling scrap to dealers and rebuying melted-down pig metal, had been receiving only about 50 per cent of the metal value. In the year 1915 alone, under Roosevelt's program, the Navy reclaimed four million pounds of scrap at a saving of $370,000. When three thousand tons of scrap iron were about to be dumped at Bremerton, Washington, because local dealers would not buy it, Daniels ordered it transported as ballast in a collier to Philadelphia, where it sold for an average of nine dollars a ton.[45]

By sending colliers loaded with coal to the Pacific Coast and the Orient, the Navy saved $500,000 over what merchant vessels would have charged. Roosevelt saw further potentialities for saving when prices rose drastically in the United States after the outbreak of the

First World War. By buying vital materials directly at the source and transporting them home as ballast in returning colliers, he could buy more cheaply and cut transportation costs. This involved dramatic international negotiations of the sort Roosevelt liked. As a result, in February, 1916, he secured a two-year supply of tin at Singapore at three cents a pound less than the American price for the past six or seven years, 1,500,000 pounds of shellac in Calcutta for $67,000 less than the lowest bid in the United States, f.o.b. Calcutta, and 5,000,000 pounds of nitrate from Antofagasta, Chile, at a saving of $60,000.[46]

Economy was also the key to Roosevelt's attitude toward government manufacturing. A zeal for saving money led him on numerous occasions to add to the manufacturing facilities in the navy yards, but he wished to protect the Navy without harming legitimate private interests. As part of his campaign for over-all economy, he declared in 1914 that the waste due to politics, especially political appropriations, had been five million dollars in the previous year alone; a budget system would eliminate much of this.[47] "Hot-air and pork barrel patriotism," which arose over the locating of a naval manufacturing plant irritated him. After he had spent two days listening to "wild arguments by every county and every state in the Union on the site," he wrote overoptimistically to a friend: "Some day we shall get rid of the pork-barrel altogether."[48]

Roosevelt believed that the navy yards would be invaluable in case of war. "We should maintain every existing Government plant," he suggested to Daniels in 1915, "running it as economically as possible in time of peace, but in such a way that it can in the event of war be readily expanded to the utmost capacity."[49] This meant, he explained elsewhere, that "each one should be used for the purpose for which it is best suited." The Navy should build auxiliaries at Boston, submarines at Portsmouth, and so on.[50] It should expand manufacturing facilities where necessary to produce items otherwise difficult to obtain or unduly expensive. For example, the electrical fittings which went into the *New Mexico* and other battleships of its class were not normally manufactured by private industry. The cost was high and delivery slow. Consequently, Roosevelt recommended to the House Naval Affairs Committee, early in 1917, that it appropriate $50,000 for machine tools so that the Portsmouth yard could manufacture them.[51]

This did not mean that Roosevelt was ready to go as far as Daniels in advocating extensive government manufacturing. When a member of the House Naval Affairs Committee queried him in 1916, he equivocated somewhat. The Navy Department was increasing the number of different things it was making, he stated, but "I do not think that the Government should manufacture everything to the exclusion of all private plants at the present time. Possibly we may come to it." [52] Thus Roosevelt avoided antagonizing Daniels, while parrying men like Representative Frederick A. Britten, an emphatic foe of any government construction, who denounced the Navy for "its mad desire to do . . . shipbuilding." [53]

Roosevelt wished to develop a dual system of government and private manufacture for the Navy, which would be more complementary than competitive. It would promote both economy and national defense to encourage the largest possible development of both public and private munitions plants and shipyards. "We should . . ." he wrote his friend Robert R. McCormick, "in time of peace have a definite program of construction and a definite program for building up the shipbuilding, armor, and gun manufacturing and labor facilities of the country." [54] Consequently, he was quite willing if not anxious to see much business go to private establishments, and was even ready to lend the aid of the Navy in obtaining contracts for American shipyards to construct foreign naval vessels. When on January 15, 1917, he was suddenly called before the House Naval Affairs Committee to testify on shipbuilders' profits, he either did not have the opportunity or the inclination to fit his testimony to that of Secretary Daniels, who appeared the same day. As a result, an ideological difference between the two men emerged quite sharply. Daniels claimed that contracts pending with private shipbuilders would allow them excessive profits; Roosevelt did not seem to think so. Daniels made little allowance for overhead in calculating the cost of government manufacture; Roosevelt made heavy allowance for it. Daniels was far more enthusiastic over government manufacturing. He believed that if private enterprise charged reasonable prices, the government need not manufacture more than one third of what it needed, if higher, two thirds, and if exorbitant, all.[55]

Roosevelt was diplomatic enough not to take a blunt public stand to the contrary; his differing figures indicated his divergence of opinion. But he wrote confidentially to a relative, how displeased he was with a measure Daniels had finally secured from Congress to build an armor plant large enough to fill all the Navy's needs to the exclusion of private manufacturers:

I agree with you about the asininity of the project as it went through Congress. I did my best to have the eleven millions cut to five, with the idea of building only a small plant for three purposes:

(*a*) To determine actual cost of manufacture.

(*b*) To experiment in the improvement of armor.

(*c*) To use as a nucleus for great expansion in time of war.

All of these objects were entirely legitimate and would not have ruined anybody's legitimate business. I hope now to have the plant combined into an armor plate, projectile and heavy forging plant. If these other items can be added for the original amount of eleven millions it will cut down the total production of armor plate and at the same time give us testing and cost-keeping facilities which are entirely legitimate.[56]

Here, then, was the role of government manufacturing – to serve as a yardstick for the measuring of prices. In time of war, it would be an adjunct of private industry; in time of peace, a regulator. Limited government production could not destroy monopoly, but should expose and eliminate a prime evil of monopoly, exorbitant prices. There is no hint that Roosevelt wished at any point to break up huge corporations like United States Steel into smaller competing units. Rather, his concern was to keep prices at a reasonable level, and the manufacturing activities of the Navy shore establishment helped to fill this function.

CHAPTER XIII

"A Navy To Cope with Any Situation"

I look for the time that war will cease, but it is not likely to be in my age nor that of my children. Till that time, then, those connected with the Army and Navy should stand out for proper services.

— FDR, *April, 1914.*[1]

ON the afternoon of October 25, 1913, Roosevelt stood with a group of friends on top of the charthouse of the dispatch boat *Dolphin*, through his binoculars watching a line of nine battleships bound for a six weeks' cruise in the Mediterranean.[2] As they steamed past him in review, each with bluejackets lining its rails and a band playing vigorously, he sent an appropriate farewell: "In sending you as representatives of the United States Navy of today, we hope to show to the Old World that the achievements and traditions of the past are being sustained and carried to a still more splendid future. Good luck and God speed."[3]

Both the review and Roosevelt's words pleased most newspapers; the New York *Herald* regarded it as "one of the finest naval spectacles since the steaming of the fleet on its world cruise."[4] There was only an occasional tart dissent. "Hot air, by the book!"[5] the Portland *Telegram* labeled Roosevelt's words; the Galveston *News* agreed: "If these battleships symbolize anything to the rational mind, it is that we, like most other nations, have not been able to get away from the medieval notion that slaughter and destruction are still the indispensable means of settling international controversies. There is some mockery, it seems to us, in parading battleships before alien peoples as an expression of our good will."[6]

If indeed Roosevelt had voiced a paradox, neither he nor Daniels was particularly aware of it. Daniels was concentrating upon the immediate objective of creating educational opportunities for enlisted men and improving conditions in the Navy, but he hoped the day would come when large fleets would no longer be necessary. Periodically he advocated an international conference to limit naval armaments. Still, to him, the Mediterranean cruise was genuinely a friendly gesture.

To Roosevelt, fleet reviews and target practice were among the most thrilling of all spectacles, and he buoyantly enjoyed them as gala occasions.* As the wife of the Assistant Secretary, Eleanor Roosevelt felt it was her duty to participate in them, even though she still had a tendency to be seasick.† At target practice in the autumn of 1913, she was feeling particularly queasy when a young officer, Emory Land, asked her if she would like to climb a mast. She readily agreed, since "though I had very little interest in anything, I thought that to do something would be a relief." So up she went, despite the giddy height above the deck, and surprisingly got over her seasickness.[9] The officers were delighted with her enthusiasm, and contrasted it favorably with the dogged fashion in which Mrs. William Jennings Bryan sat on a chair and ignored the gunnery.[10]

Roosevelt was sufficiently sophisticated to realize that warship displays were more than sport, and that the friendship they inspired was in some part compounded of awe. With his thorough grounding in big-navy doctrines, he must have been well aware of the real significance of the world cruise of 1907 to 1909 to which the New York *Herald* referred. Theodore Roosevelt had sent the fleet just after a serious crisis with Japan; at Yokohama it was received by cheering crowds. Franklin Roosevelt never forgot either that in case of war the Navy was America's main bulwark, and he regarded war as a constant and by no means remote threat.

The Navy Department's elder exponents of a strong fleet filled Roosevelt with respect and admiration. Very soon he fell under the influence of the General Board, the advisory body of senior officers, over which Admiral George Dewey, victor at Manila Bay, presided. Year

* FDR took a select group of friends and administrators, including Assistant Secretary of War Henry Breckinridge, to attend the farewell at Hampton Roads. While there, he and Breckinridge "tried a lot of stunts": "We climbed, and vaulted, and lifted, and ran, and in every instance there was a tie. He is a bit taller than I am and weighs less. I am three years older, but there we were, in a perfectly even contest every time." [7]

† FDR patiently coached his wife upon what to do when she boarded a battleship, whom to shake hands with, and what parts of the ship not to visit. He also taught the protocol to his children; Elliott was expected, whenever he came aboard a warship, to face the stern and salute the flag. Anna, who was sensitive to noises, buried her head in her mother's lap the first time she heard a seventeen-gun salute fired for her father, and on later occasions put cotton in her ears. But Eleanor Roosevelt, who was somewhat deaf, did not mind the noise, and quickly learned nautical ways.[8]

after year the General Board had advised that America build toward a fleet of forty-eight battleships.[11] Secretary Daniels, who also respected the General Board, and regarded Admiral Dewey with hero worship, published their annual report for the first time, but in his own recommendations he halved their yearly building proposals.[12]

Time and again Roosevelt publicly took sides against his chief in favor of the strong-navy demands of these senior officers. He was particularly close to two members of the impressive but impotent Council of Aides: Rear Admiral Bradley A. Fiske, Aide for Operations, and Rear Admiral William F. Fullam, Aide for Inspection.* Both these admirals soon became targets for Secretary Daniels, because they favored a big shipbuilding program and also because they wanted a centralized officer control like the General Staff of the Imperial German Navy.[13] In spite of Daniels's opposition to them, Roosevelt deeply admired both men, gained their esteem and remained on friendly terms with them.† Their influence contributed considerably to his excitement over a new and acute crisis with Japan in the spring of 1913.

Under pressure from farmers and workers, the California legislature passed an act preventing alien Japanese from owning land in the state. Jingoistic newspapers in both Japan and the United States stirred up a tempest, and the Japanese Government sent President Wilson a peremptory note demanding that he override the legislation. Its tone so alarmed Wilson that he did not make it public for fear of generating a major war scare. With difficulty he kept the Joint Army and Navy Board within bounds when it drew up plans for fleet and troop movements in the Far East and urged the quick transfer of the Asiatic Squadron from its vulnerable anchorage in the Yangtze River off Shanghai to the Philippines. These plans leaked to the press (Daniels suspected Fiske was responsible) and created additional excitement.[15] At a Cabinet meeting, Daniels warned that any major movement of the Asiatic Squadron to protect the Philippines would be dangerous, provocative, and impotent. President Wilson agreed. He indignantly for-

* Fiske was one of the most versatile technicians the Naval Academy had ever produced. He was not only a brilliant inventor but the strongest advocate of a naval general staff – a powerful officer. Daniels had less trouble with Fullam, whom he relegated to command of the reserve fleet in Pacific waters during the First World War.

† Yet when Daniels hung on the troublesome admiral one of the most famous trade names of the period, "Fiske Tires," Roosevelt was so delighted that he remembered the joke for years, and when he was in the White House, wrote Daniels his recollection of it.[14]

bade the Army and Navy Board to hold further meetings, and ordered the Navy Department to refrain from any sudden ship movements.[16]

During the crisis Roosevelt's sympathies were entirely with the militants. Later, he complained to Admiral Mahan that the Administration had left the vessels of the Asiatic Squadron in a precarious position. "I did all in my power to have them return nearer their base," he explained, "but the President and Secretary of State felt that the chief danger to the negotiations lay in a possible explosion of the Japanese populace and that any movement on the part of our ships which might be considered as hostile might help to cause such an explosion. Orders were therefore sent against my protest to Admiral Nicholson, telling him not to move out of the Yangtze river. Of course, if hostilities had developed these ships would have been interned or overwhelmed by a superior force without difficulty."[17]

These opinions were typical of Roosevelt's private disagreements with the policies of his chief. Daniels always believed that on this occasion Admiral Fiske had been "militant and really would like to have seen war with Japan." Certainly Fiske did prepare a startling confidential memorandum at the height of the crisis. He addressed it to Daniels, and gave a copy to Roosevelt. Warning that Japan might launch an attack upon the United States to gain the fertile Hawaiian and Philippine Islands, he predicted they could easily take both groups of islands and "stand pat" for several years until the war-weary Americans were ready to sue for peace on Japanese terms.* Daniels scoffed, but Roosevelt listened and remembered.†

Had a surprise attack come, the Navy obviously would have been in no shape to meet it. The Navy lacked men, material, warships, and colliers. Even if it were to commandeer every suitable vessel flying the American flag it would fill no more than a quarter of the need for colliers alone.[20] Daniels showed no signs of disturbance; he felt that shortages were not immediately relevant because war would be avoided. Brisk preparations would on the one hand alarm Japan, and on the

* Fiske envisaged a war of siege in which the United States would cut Japan off from all other countries except Korea, but ultimately weary of the expense. "During these two years our entire fleet, practically speaking, would have to be maintained off the southern coast of Japan. To do this would be enormously expensive; and even if no actual battleship battle were fought, it is probable that many of our ships would be lost through the agency of submarines, mines, and torpedoes."[18]

† In 1934, FDR recalled to Henry L. Stimson how a Japanese student at Harvard in 1902 had unfolded to him plans for expansion – plans which, as FDR recounted them, were remarkably similar to the Tanaka Memorial.[19]

other, unduly strengthen the big-navy men in the Department.* In contrast, Roosevelt gave ready support to Fiske's demands for a comprehensive armament program covering "organization, personnel, material, guns, torpedoes, mines, and particularly aviation." Admiral Fullam once testified: "With the exception of the Assistant Secretary of the Navy and the General Board nobody gave a willing ear to the seriousness of the situation and the Navy Department proper was exclusively busied with a routine of peace, totally indifferent to the possibility of a state of war being forced upon us." [22]

Roosevelt took the scare seriously, and prepared to move swiftly if attack came. He wrote a plan which began with the hypothesis: "Word comes next Monday that hostile fleet has sailed." Then:

Send messenger to see Schwerin – at San Francisco He can get information as he is graduate of Annapolis & runs the Pacific Mail

1. Auxiliaries.–
2. Naval Militia
3. Fuel
4. Foreign Ships
5. Recruiting
6. Officers.
7. Censorship –
8. Japs in Service.
9. Olangapo

Fill vacancies in Personnel
Concentrate Asiatic Fleet at Manila.
Commission monitors
Tel. Guam to plan Supply ready –

London about Kongo

Argentine Ships.[23] †

This was all the action he could take, but for Roosevelt to remain completely inactive during such a time was unthinkable. While the

* In contrast to the pacific Daniels, Secretary of War Lindley M. Garrison made vigorous defense preparations. Representative Richmond Hobson, a jingoist, told the House Naval Affairs Committee later, "In the month of May, and for several weeks . . . our gunners at Corregidor stood at their guns night and day; provisions for a two years' siege were assembled; the harbor was mined; troops from all over the island were brought into Corregidor, and everything was prepared . . . except a transfer of the Government from Manila." [21]

† Olangapo was the American naval base in the Philippines. The monitors were

crisis continued, Secretary Daniels left Washington for a few days. Again, as in 1898, a Roosevelt was Acting Secretary, but he did not send battle orders to an admiral, or put the fleet on a fighting basis as his cousin had done. His one move was no more than a comic-opera version of such large and spectacular actions. Ignoring Wilson's instructions against moving naval vessels unnecessarily, he allowed secret orders to go to the commander of the submarine torpedo flotilla at Newport to put to sea immediately. The next day the Acting Secretary announced to the press, "Without previous warning, emergency orders were issued yesterday from Washington, directing that the submarines be sent to sea with the greatest possible speed. The rapidity with which the crews were gathered together and the boats got under way is exceedingly gratifying to the Department."[24] This was insubordination, but apparently no one criticized Roosevelt for it.

Roosevelt's greatest value to the militant admirals was not in the ordering of impetuous gestures like this, but in his role as an emissary to Daniels. At the Senate investigation in 1920, Admiral Fullam explained exactly how. In 1913, Fullam "got very much wrought up" about the danger of war, and drew up a memorandum of things that ought to be done at once:

> But I did not take that to Mr. Daniels at all. I did not feel encouraged to take it to him, because I had seen Admiral Fiske take papers like that to him, and he would not pay any attention to it. . . . I took it to Mr. Franklin D. Roosevelt . . . who usually – always – took a lively interest in the Navy and in the cooperation of the Navy with the Army; and I was encouraged to go to him frankly. . . .
>
> I said, "Mr. Roosevelt, do you approve of this," He read it over, and he said, "Yes; every bit of it." I said, "Will you take that as yours, and do not mention my name as ever having written it, and will you present it to the Secretary of the Navy this afternoon?" He said he would, and he took it in there, and I remember so well that he sat down in his chair, and he put this paper on the [floor] . . . between his feet, and he read off from time to time the items: and, coming from him as a civilian to the Secretary of the Navy, it had some effect, and some of those things were done.[25]

---

ancient and worthless harbor defense vessels, useful, however, to quell public fears. The *Kongo* was a Japanese battlecruiser being constructed by the British. Several Argentinian warships were under construction in American yards.

Admiral Fiske similarly used Roosevelt for small errands. He obtained Roosevelt's signature on a memorandum to Daniels proposing joint Army-Navy maneuvers for the summer of 1914. The mock battle – never held – would have pitted a "European" invasion force of twenty dreadnoughts against an ineffective defense force of only ten battleships, in order to impress the public with the weakness of American defense. Again, when Fiske wished to send the House Naval Affairs Committee some data on the German Navy indicating its "enormous superiority to our fleet," he obtained the signature of Roosevelt rather than Daniels on the letter.[26]

While Roosevelt shared the private alarm within the department, publicly he remained calm and circumspect. When reporters asked him in May, 1913, if the Navy was planning to mobilize against Japan, he repeatedly replied in the negative.[27] "There is no Japanese scare," he scoffed. "Japan doesn't want war and neither does this country. The trouble is not a national one. It is a California question purely."[28] But on at least two occasions he went on to pay backhanded compliments to the alarmists. Their periodic warnings that war was imminent served a useful purpose, he said, since the public often noted then for the first time how superior the United States Navy was in both tonnage and manpower to that of Japan. "Thus the jingoes unconsciously conduct a campaign of education which makes more for peace than war."[29]

For the time being Roosevelt publicly professed, in marked contrast to his private belief, that "There never was a time in our history when the sea-fighting arm of the service was in better condition than at present." Moreover, "additions to the fleets already planned assure that we will be ready for anything at any time."[30] When he was asked if he would favor building new ships, he parried, "That is something that will not come up until next January."[31] One Hearst newspaper, the Baltimore *American*, took him to task editorially for overestimating the power of the American Navy.[32]

Thereafter, Roosevelt seldom gave offense in this fashion. In the ensuing summer months, the trivial remnant of the Japanese scare gradually evaporated; by the time it had disappeared, Roosevelt had reversed his public stand, and like Hearst and Hobson was trying to educate the electorate on the gross inadequacies of the Navy.

One of the earliest and most enthusiastic volunteers to aid Roosevelt in this task was his fellow Grotonian, Robert R. McCormick of the Chicago *Tribune*. In October, McCormick requested an appointment for a conference, because, as he explained, he thought they had a good deal in common besides early training.[33] When the meeting did not take place,[34] he wrote again asking Roosevelt to provide him with thirteen pictures of battleships to run each Sunday during the coming summer in the rotogravure section of the *Tribune.* He declared that he was disturbed by the conduct of Congress in diverting money which should be spent for national defense to pork-barrel projects, and wished to bring pressure from home upon the spoilsmen. If Roosevelt gave him the material to make the campaign, he predicted, the Middle West Senators and Representatives, irrespective of party, would vote for the full Navy program.[35] To this Roosevelt replied, "I am starting the wheels to work and think I can get you some really fine photographs that are out of the ordinary run and which will make copy that your Sunday editor simply cannot refuse. It is very good of you to give us this chance, and I assure you it is much appreciated." [36]

By December, 1913, Roosevelt was ready personally to take the case for a bigger Navy to the public. In a series of addresses then and during the next few months, he moved rapidly toward an extreme position. In April, 1914, he dropped all caution, and stated in an interview, "Dreadnoughts are what we need. You can't fight Germany's and England's dreadnoughts with United States gunboats, strange as it may seem, and the policy of our congress should be to buy and build dreadnoughts until our navy is comparable to any other in the world." [37]

These were strong words, for they advocated a policy more militant than even the Navy General Board's proposals. Roosevelt was calling for a fleet not merely superior to all excepting England's – all big-navy men had long urged that – but second to none. In 1914, no other big-navy man, not even the fire-eating Richmond Hobson, publicly advocated a Navy of this size.[38] But Roosevelt made this statement at the height of excitement over a new international crisis, at the time when the Navy had just bombarded Vera Cruz.

The Mexican crisis had its roots in the period of "Dollar Diplomacy" before the Wilson era. Long years of American exploitation had come to a close in 1910 with the overthrow of the investors' benefactor, aging President Porfirio Díaz, by a middle-class leader. But in February, 1913, the new President in turn was the victim of a counterrevolution fostered by investors and landowners, which left Victoriano Huerta clinging tenuously to power. President Taft's ambassador, Henry Lane Wilson, speaking on behalf of American investors urged immediate recognition of Huerta. These investors owned over half the oil, three quarters of the mines and smelters, and two thirds of the railroads in Mexico.[39]

When Woodrow Wilson became President in March, he refused to listen to the Ambassador or his wealthy backers, and instead inaugurated a policy of nonrecognition on behalf of the Mexican masses.* Huerta's enemies quickly began a new revolt, and in the ensuing months, violence continued. Ambassador Wilson remained in Mexico, opposed to the President's policies, until July, 1913, when he was recalled to Washington. Upon his return, he "talked steadily" against nonrecognition and nonintervention, Roosevelt reported.[41] Undoubtedly this had some effect on Roosevelt himself with his love of excitement. "The Mexican situation is really the only matter to disturb our quiet existence," he wrote. "It is being regarded as a very threatening and imminent danger." [42] He rather wistfully commented on the efforts of a relative to avoid a foreign service assignment there, "Personally if I were in the Dip[lomatic] Service I would beg for Mexico, as it is the only place just now where there is real action." [43]

Indeed there was the possibility of "real action," for if Huerta did not resign and was not defeated by more acceptable revolutionaries, the United States might have to choose between recognizing him or fighting him. Force might well lead to the very imperialism that President Wilson disliked.

For the Navy, the dilemma became increasingly onerous. Secretary Daniels ordered fleet units to Mexican waters to protect American lives and property. There, as the vessels rode at anchor month after month along the stifling hot coast, crew morale degenerated and officers' tempers grew edgy. In December, 1913, Roosevelt wrote Rear Admiral Frank F. Fletcher, commander of these ships, requesting him to perform a minor errand ashore. He concluded facetiously, "You need not, however, take this personal note as an order to land marines!" [44] But Admiral Fletcher took him seriously, and felt called upon to protest, "I am afraid my dispatches have caused undue alarm in Washington." The naval forces, he said, would not be employed against the "Constitutional bandit rebels" in any manner that would embarrass the Administration.[45]

Although Admiral Fletcher obediently continued President Wilson's

* "My ideal is an orderly and righteous government in Mexico," the President explained a year later, "but my passion is for the submerged eighty-five per cent of the people of that Republic who are now struggling toward liberty." [40]

policy of "watchful waiting," tension between the Mexican and American governments gradually increased to a point where the most minor mishap might well detonate an explosion. At this point, in the spring of 1914, Roosevelt left for a tour of the Pacific Coast. It was an area he had never visited. Animosity toward both Mexico and Japan was greatest there, but the journey was supposedly planned simply as an inspection trip, which would involve much checking at each of the Navy's installations from San Diego to Puget Sound.[46] This was of minor import compared with the verbal orders Roosevelt carried with him: "Every warship on the Pacific Coast is to prepare for sailing in fighting trim on a moment's notice."[47]

Roosevelt left Washington April 3, 1914. As he crossed the Southwest he heard rumors that Americans scattered through isolated parts of northern Mexico were being murdered, and even talk that the manifest destiny of the United States dictated expansion southward. By the time he reached San Diego, the incipient crisis was unfolding. It seemed a minor incident at first: On April 9, Rear Admiral Henry T. Mayo, stationed at Tampico aboard the same dispatch boat *Dolphin* which had so often taken Roosevelt on jaunts, sent seven of his men ashore to load supplies. They were arrested by a Mexican colonel, then after a few minutes' detention were released by a superior officer who apologized for his subordinate's lack of knowledge of international law. Admiral Mayo chose not to accept the apology, and to Secretary Daniels's intense regret, did not bother to refer the matter to Washington, but resorted at once to traditional Navy quarter-deck diplomacy. He delivered an ultimatum to Huerta's general to raise and salute an American flag, and to follow this gesture with a more formal apology.[48]

"I understand the State Department is yelling blue murder because Mayo on his own initiative commanded a salute," Howe informed his absent chief. "I am afraid Mayo is not a good 'watchful waiter.' "[49] However, Bryan and President Wilson decided to back him up, and delivered a first and then a second ultimatum to Huerta. On April 14, Secretary Daniels, under orders from the White House, dispatched all available warships from Norfolk to Mexico. The next day's newspapers were filled with rumors of war, and Senator William E. Borah proclaimed, "This is the beginning of the march of the United States to the Panama Canal."[50]

As Roosevelt went up the Pacific Coast, he spread the message among

Navy men: "be ready." * But in his public statements, he remained calm [51] despite the almost hysterical dispatches flashing from Washington. On April 16, San Francisco papers carried the story that Secretary Daniels had ordered the Assistant Secretary to take personal charge of the movement of the Pacific Fleet toward a rendezvous at San Diego. In point of fact, the Secretary had wired Roosevelt to "make such suggestions to department as you think wise." [52] By the time the Assistant Secretary arrived in Portland, on April 19, President Wilson's second ultimatum to Huerta had expired, and so also some of Roosevelt's semblance of serenity. Reporters hurried aboard the train, eager for news, and he did not disappoint them. "We're not looking for trouble," he said, "but we're ready for anything." [53]

On the afternoon of April 20, President Wilson told Congress he wished to use armed force to sustain Admiral Mayo, and asked for a resolution of confidence and support. A few hours later, in Seattle, Roosevelt prefaced a set speech on Wilson's domestic program with a vigorous defense of his Mexican policy. The President, he said, had "put the ten commandments into his foreign policy," and repeatedly expressed his consideration for all the Mexican people. How could the President be expected to recognize the government of a ruffian like Huerta who had wrested power from another leader by the foul means of assassination? "Recognition would have meant a lowering of ideals in international relations just as much as if we recognized in our own private lives and relations the man whose hands were unclean."

"I know that the president and his cabinet have come to the decision [to use force in Mexico] with prayer, earnest thought and sorrow," Roosevelt continued. "In Washington, the men high up in the government are fundamentally opposed to war. They have tried their best to prevent a clash for a long time. They have done more to bring arbitration of international difficulties than any other nation has done. But the day has come when studied insults are aimed directly at the nation. You may rest assured that when the administrative patience is exhausted, and the administration has made up its mind, the thing will be seen through to the end."

Roosevelt paused dramatically to read a brief dispatch from Washington: the House had voted to uphold Wilson by a vote of 337 to 37. Two of the 37 dissenters, he pointed out, were Republican Representatives from the State of Washington. "Just thirty-seven by their

* FDR doubled the workmen on a large radio station being constructed at San Diego, and at San Francisco promised substantial expansion of Pacific Coast bases.

vote put themselves in their true character," he declared. "Party fealty was greater than national fealty. These men cannot see above party affairs. They have not put back of them the days when Republicans could oppose Democrats, and Democrats Republicans, with impunity, disregardful of the merits of a cause." [54]

While Roosevelt was calling down jeers on those opposed to intervention, the President in Washington was meeting with part of his Cabinet to decide what measures to take. His military advisers could see no alternative to war. Already Wilson had drafted plans to occupy Vera Cruz in order to prevent a German ship from landing munitions for Huerta, and before morning he issued an order to take the city. The next day, while the fighting was going on, Roosevelt at Bremerton helped arrange fleet and Marine Corps movements on the Pacific Coast. He wired to inquire the Department's plans for action on the west coast of Mexico. Daniels put a damper on Roosevelt with his reply in which he failed to answer these queries and stated only that since most of the Pacific Fleet would go to Mexico, Roosevelt could be of more aid in Washington and should return as planned. Obviously he did not wish his bellicose assistant to organize large-scale action.[55] Daniels was as aware as Franklin of Theodore Roosevelt's precedent, and left no opportunity for repetition of it.

In consequence, it was an overwrought and not too well-informed young official who entrained for Washington several days later. Vera Cruz had been occupied, but not in the bloodless way the President had anticipated. The Mexicans had suffered 126 killed and 195 wounded; the Americans, 19 killed, 71 wounded.[56] At each train stop, Roosevelt talked briefly to reporters. "We are merely engaged in the occupation of a city, it is not a war," he announced in Butte on April 24 in a last attempt to sound calm.

The following night in Minneapolis, Roosevelt could no longer conceal his excitement. The train had scarcely come to a full stop when he jumped off and hurried up the platform hunting a newspaper. When a reporter handed him one, he intimated that he had no knowledge of the Administration's plans. "I've just had my share to do following out orders and it has kept me busy," he apologized. Nevertheless, he was quite willing to state the meaning of the crisis. "War," he snapped, "and we're ready." [57]

Roosevelt was telling the literal truth when he said he had no inside knowledge of what was going on in Washington. The next morning's paper carried not only his prediction of war, but also the news that

President Wilson had accepted an offer of mediation by Argentina, Brazil, and Chile.[58] The crisis was over, but not for Roosevelt. Now that it was past, the young man who had remained publicly calm to the very height of the trouble continued for a full day or more to give out explosive interviews. It was as though he could not accept the reality of a mediated solution.

"I do not want war," Roosevelt exclaimed in Milwaukee the next morning, "but I do not see how we can avoid it. Sooner or later, it seems, the United States must go down there and clean up the Mexican political mess. I believe that the best time is right now." [59] A few hours later, he talked to Chicago reporters somewhat more cautiously, by this time ascribing the militancy to others: "The war spirit is sweeping the West like a prairie fire. The general opinion is that since the United States has finally started military activities they should be carried through to a finish with no compromise. Many persons and newspapers are openly advocating annexation as the only solution of the Mexican problem. This sentiment seems to be growing." [60] As for his own opinions, Roosevelt now refused to comment. He was ready instead to utilize the war scare as an object lesson of the need for preparedness, an argument for a large Air Force and a Navy second to none.[61]

Back in the Navy Department in Washington, under the influence of Daniels, all interviews ceased. But Roosevelt still expressed himself privately in a letter to a friend. "Of course, things at the moment look quiet and not as warlike as last week," he noted pensively, "but I am not convinced that the worst is over." [62]

Although Roosevelt was excited about Mexico when he returned from the Pacific Coast, his trip had convinced him more than ever that the Navy's most powerful potential enemy was Japan. A well-known Los Angeles physician presented him with a copy of Homer Lea's *The Day of the Saxon*, and many a leader on the Pacific Coast was ready to share Lea's fear of a "yellow peril." [63] Roosevelt had sensed an undercurrent of fear which the amicable settlement of the 1913 crisis with Japan had not entirely dissipated. The Navy could far more effectively meet a surprise Japanese attack if all its battleships formed a single powerful fleet in the Pacific. But many people would oppose this concentration since they still believed that the Navy existed for coastal defense. Hence it should be split into two fleets ready to fend off any invader of either coast.

A few American naval authorities favored two fleets for another reason. While they recognized Japan as the most likely foe, they talked of their fear of the Imperial German Navy. Germany figured in all potential war plans. "The very first thing I found when I went to the Navy Department in 1913," Roosevelt later remarked, "was that in every naval programme. . . . our criterion up to 1914 – the Power that we were building to guard against – was Germany.[64] But Germany was no menace as long as Great Britain had the largest fleet in the world. This friendly fleet formed a comfortable bulwark against that of Germany; as long as it dominated the North Sea, the United States had nothing to fear in the Atlantic. When big-navy men talked in alarmist fashion about the menace of either Germany or Great Britain, they were doing so mainly to try to frighten Congress into making larger appropriations. A London reporter once asked Roosevelt, "The idea of challenging Great Britain's position on the sea was not thought of?" He replied flatly, "No, it was not." [65]

In the Pacific, the United States could not count upon the friendly fleet of another power to overawe Japan; the Navy must maintain its own balance. It could best do this, Theodore Roosevelt solemnly admonished Franklin, by keeping the battleships together: "I do not anticipate trouble with Japan, but it may come, and if it does it will come suddenly. In that case we shall be in an unpardonable position if we permit ourselves to be caught with our fleet separated. There ought not to be a battleship or any formidable fighting craft in the Pacific unless our entire fleet is in the Pacific. Russia's fate ought to be a warning for all time as to the criminal folly of dividing the fleet if there is even the remotest chance of war." [66]

Franklin Roosevelt took these words to heart. He had seen them in action when they constituted President Theodore Roosevelt's policy during the crisis with Japan in 1907.* Since then, the battleships had remained in the Atlantic. Had they been in the Pacific, they doubtless would have been a powerful aid to American Asiatic policy – but Eastern navy yards would nearly have gone out of existence.[68]

Roosevelt had discovered during his trip to the Pacific Coast that, when the Panama Canal should open, in less than a year, people in the Far West would demand the allocation of part of the fleet to the Pacific. He was "struck by the total lack of any correct conception

* When President Theodore Roosevelt received Mahan's nervous admonition not to divide the fleet, he was indignant that Mahan could think him capable of such an act of "utter folly"; he would no more think of doing so than "going thither in a rowboat myself." [67]

of fleet operations," and undertook to educate Californians by making "several speeches outlining the military danger of dividing our battleships between the two oceans." These talks certainly owed no little of their effectiveness to his proposal that the Navy should spend more money in the West. "One impression that has gained headway here I wish you would correct," Roosevelt declared in Los Angeles. "The battleship fleet will not be divided between the Atlantic and Pacific coasts. Naval strategy will not permit this. When the fleet is on the Western coast it will be in its entirety." [69]

"The people out there," Roosevelt reported with delight, "were very quick to grasp the idea that if the whole fleet goes to the Pacific Coast the facilities on that coast for taking care of the Fleet would have to be greatly increased." After his return to Washington he interviewed several California Congressmen, who were "extremely reasonable." They grasped the military advantages of Roosevelt's program, but showed a more intense interest in the proposed additions to the yards. Roosevelt could also expect the faithful co-operation of the more progressive officers on sea duty, such as Captain William S. Sims, and he found most officers within the Navy Department favorable.[70] He proposed to the General Board, with every hope of endorsement, that it create a cruiser squadron "to be based on the Pacific Coast and to visit the Atlantic Coast during the times the main Fleet is in the Pacific." [71]

More than this, Roosevelt wished to forestall the considerable pressure, both political and sectional, to split the fleet, which he anticipated would develop when the canal opened. Who better could educate the public in advance than his idols, Theodore Roosevelt and Mahan? He begged them both to write magazine articles. These, he wrote Theodore Roosevelt, "would bring more results than if a hundred other officers and men in public life were to say the same thing." [72]

Mahan immediately inquired how he could specifically help, and a lively correspondence ensued. He not only endorsed Roosevelt's general ideas, but also the proposal for a cruiser squadron and a battleship squadron, since "It would insure the constant concentration of the main fleet, with regular practice in shifting from one coast to the other, and consequent familiarity with the passage of the Canal." [73] In compliance with Roosevelt's suggestions, he wrote an article: "The Panama Canal and the Distribution of the Fleet," in which he warned, "Halve the fleet, and it is inferior in both oceans." [74] It was the last

Mahan ever wrote. By the time it appeared, the outbreak of the European war had already injected new issues into the complex naval defense problem. The fleet remained in the Atlantic, and the question of dividing it did not become important again until five years later.

In the fall of 1914, Mahan moved to Washington, and late in November, depressed and not at all well, visited the Navy Department. He called upon Secretary Daniels, but was disappointed to find the Assistant Secretary out. The following week, Mahan became seriously ill, and a few days later the greatest exponent of sea power died without having met his greatest disciple. However, Roosevelt already had amply demonstrated his faith in Mahan's theories; a time was to come when he would put them into execution on a global scale.[75]

CHAPTER XIV

"The Greatest War in the World's History"

> I agree with you entirely that the situation in Europe is due to no person or persons and that it is the outcome of national forces. Incidentally, one cannot help feeling that these national forces are going to continue to line up against other national forces which are hostile to them for many generations to come, even in spite of all the efforts of Mr. Carnegie.
>
> — FDR, *August 12, 1914.*[1]

IN late July, 1914, came an explosion in the Balkans. Even Roosevelt, who for months had been exhorting the American public to build powerful and still more powerful naval armaments, had paid little attention to the slow sputtering of the fuse during the days and weeks after the assassination of Archduke Franz Ferdinand in Sarajevo, Bosnia, on June 28.

During July, the Assistant Secretary, like most officials in the Navy Department, was preoccupied with the continuing Mexican crisis,[2] and conferences with the State Department over the deploying of Marines where they could speedily occupy Haiti and Santo Domingo.[3] This was exactly the sort of international maneuvering Roosevelt relished, but within a few days the European detonation made it look like busywork. On the first of August, Germany declared war on Russia; and Roosevelt at once recognized the cataclysmic implications. "These are history-making days," he commented a few hours later, while riding on a train to Reading, Pennsylvania. "It will be the greatest war in the world's history." [4]

Roosevelt was on his way to Reading to dedicate an anchor from the battleship *Maine*. A Democratic member of the House Naval Affairs Committee, John H. Rothermel, had proudly secured it as a monument for the city of Reading, but his opponent in the primaries called "fraud" so loudly that it helped lead to Rothermel's defeat. Too late to salvage the election, the Congressman had Roosevelt come to authenticate the relic. Thus, as armies were mobilizing in Europe, Roosevelt was standing in a park, minutely tracing the pedigree and history of one outmoded battleship anchor. He was perfectly well aware of the ludicrous side of the episode, and wryly made the most of it. "In certain cases controversies have arisen over the distribution of these relics," he informed the citizens, "some of which are amusing, as in the case of a town in Ohio, which after making strenuous efforts to be given the captain's bathtub as a souvenir, became so sensitive to the many jests made at its expense that they asked permission to return it. Fortunately a neighboring town was not so sensitive, and the bathtub still holds an honored position in Ohio." [5] More seriously he inquired, "Do you think that the government of a country as splendid as the United States would try to send a fake anchor here?" [6]

If he mentioned the outbreak of war in his speech, the newspapers do not record it. For, as the incident shows, the nation and even the Navy Department were far more absorbed in domestic affairs and monuments than in the new market for monuments that the four years would produce.

But the news sent Roosevelt scurrying back to Washington, fully aware that there was much to be done. He believed the Navy must quickly prepare to meet any threats that might arise from a major war across the Atlantic, and was shocked to find the Navy Department still operating as always. "Mr. Daniels," he wrote sharply, was "feeling chiefly very sad that his faith in human nature and civilization and similar idealistic nonsense was receiving such a rude shock. So I started in alone to get things ready and prepare plans for what ought to be done by the Navy end of things." [7]

At this point, Roosevelt began to bring all his influence to bear to prepare for any eventuality, even a shooting war. He began a vigorous struggle with Daniels, that continued even after America entered the war in 1917. Himself high-minded, Roosevelt nevertheless regarded Daniels's idealistic devotion to peace as being dangerously anachronistic in a warring world. Looking with somewhat condescending amusement upon the old-fashioned ideas of Daniels and Bryan, he chafed at their attitude that isolated, peaceful America must as a matter of course remain aloof and unaffected by the war, and even scoffed at their lack of technical knowledge.* "These dear good people," he

* One of FDR's favorite stories, which he told innumerable times with several variations, was in purport that Bryan did not know the difference between a battleship and a gunboat. As he first told it, he disguised the identity of Bryan and

exploded to Eleanor, had as much concept of the meaning of a modern war as four-year-old Elliott had of higher mathematics. "They really believe," he marveled, "that because we are neutral we can go about our business as usual." [10]

When Daniels proposed to send the Fleet to Europe to bring back marooned Americans, Roosevelt protested in disgust:

> Aside from the fact that tourists (female etc.) couldn't sleep in hammocks and that battleships haven't got passenger accommodations, he totally fails to grasp the fact that this war between the other powers is going inevitably to give rise to a hundred different complications in which we shall have a direct interest. Questions of refugees, of neutrality, of commerce are even now appearing and we should unquestionably gather our fleet together and get it into the highest state of efficiency. We still have 12 battleships at Vera Cruz – their "materiel" has suffered somewhat, their "personnel" a great deal! The rest of the fleet is scattered to the four winds – they should be assembled and prepared. Some fine day the State Department will want the moral backing of a "fleet in being" and it *won't be there*. . . .
>
> There seems no hope now of averting the crash. Germany has invaded France according to this afternoon's report. The best that can be expected is either a sharp, complete and quick victory by one side, a most unlikely occurrence, or a speedy realization of impending bankruptcy by all, and cessation by mutual consent, but this too is I think unlikely as history shows that money in spite of what the bankers say is not an essential to the conduct of a war by a determined nation.
>
> Rather than long drawn-out struggle I hope England will join in and with France and Russia force peace *at Berlin!* [11]

The foundation for Roosevelt's impatience was the failure of Daniels to see the need for a positive program. Daniels continued to distrust those admirals who advocated redistributing the fleet to meet the new

himself, and moved the episode from July, 1914, to the "dim and distant past": Bryan excitedly informed him, "I've got to have a battleship – there is a revolution broken out in Hayti, – American property is in danger, – I've got to have a battleship there inside of twenty-four hours!" Roosevelt replied that it would be impossible to get a battleship there, "but I have got a gunboat just across the passage at Guantánamo and it will take her twelve hours to get to Hayti." Reported Roosevelt, "The Secretary of State almost wilted and said. . . . 'My dear fellow, when I say "battleship," I don't mean anything technical. All I meant was that I wanted something that would float and had guns on it.'" [8] Despite his scorn of Bryan, FDR gave a dinner for him in January, 1914.[9]

war conditions. On August 2, Roosevelt urgently recommended to Admiral Fiske that the battleships be brought back from Mexican waters; Fiske replied that the day previously the General Board had recommended the same thing. Daniels nevertheless refused to recall the battleships. Since Roosevelt and the more aggressive admirals were thinking along parallel lines, they turned to him as the one civilian who might put their proposals into effect.[12] The most famous strategist of them all, Mahan, on August 3 suggested to Roosevelt that the battleships return, and in ensuing weeks sent several additional comments. "I write to you," Mahan explained significantly, "because I know no one else in the Administration to whom I should care to write."[13]

The flattering attention from the admirals, and the fact that Roosevelt directed most of what little action took place, gave him a heady sense of his own importance. He confided to his wife, "I am *running* the real work; although Josephus is here! He is bewildered by it all, very sweet but very sad!"[14] Roosevelt represented the Navy Department on two hastily created boards – "as Mr. D. didn't seem anxious to do it himself." One was on the maintenance of neutrality, the other on the assistance of stranded Americans in Europe. Most of the other board members were of Cabinet level, but Roosevelt participated actively in the sessions, which lasted several nights until nearly three in the morning. They led to the establishment of a Navy neutrality patrol ("Most of the reports of foreign cruisers [seen] off the coast have really been of my destroyers!") and the sending of two battleships with funds for the stranded Americans ("*I* suggested Breckinridge after declining myself to take charge.")[15]

Roosevelt's secretary reported admiringly, "The Boss has been the whole Cheese in this European business and is going along great."[16] *

* Roosevelt directed a number of minor administrative matters. When Navy censorship of wireless stations began on August 7, he took personal responsibility for enforcement of President Wilson's regulation that only neutral messages could be transmitted.[17] The following year, the French Ambassador, Jean Jules Jusserand, protested directly to him concerning a German violation.[18] When the Canadian cruiser *Rainbow* put in at San Francisco to take on coal, Roosevelt announced that the captain intended to abide by the United States neutrality proclamation.[19] In October and November, 1914, he conducted delicate negotiations to bring the interned German liner *Kronprinzessin Cäcilia* from her unsafe anchorage in Bar Harbor to Boston.[20]

From the middle of August to the end of September, 1914, he gave almost all of his time to his unsuccessful campaign for the Democratic nomination for United States Senator.

Within a few weeks, Roosevelt had done as much as was humanly possible to "alert the Navy Department," and he turned his attention in the fall to the long-range project of persuading the public that the war necessitated a drastic strengthening of the Navy. First he must teach the American people the lesson to be found in the way the British Grand Fleet was keeping the Imperial German Navy bottled up in the North Sea. A spectacular fleet engagement would have pleased him more, but he took satisfaction in the way the British had cut off German shipping.[21] However, President Wilson's insistence upon strict neutrality made it difficult for him to call public attention to this and draw the big-navy moral for the United States. At the outbreak of war, the President requested Secretary Daniels to order all officers of the service "to refrain from public comment of any kind upon the military or political situation on the other side of the water." By implication, this meant Roosevelt too.[22]

By mid-October Roosevelt, in no mood to make further concessions to the President's restrictions, embarked upon the dangerous course of openly advocating a more drastic armament policy than either Daniels or Wilson thought necessary. Chafing under restraints from above, he found it hard to remember that opposition to his chief was unseemly in an Assistant Secretary.

Roosevelt's greatest ally was a growing public demand for preparedness. Previously his big-navy talk had aroused enthusiasm only among Navy Leaguers and a relatively jingoistic fringe of the public and press. Now the sweep of the gray-clad German battalions across Belgium, with the sacking of Louvain and rumors of atrocities, angered and alarmed large segments of the population. The average American was already suspicious of the Germans, and uneasy about defenses. As preparedness became more popular, Roosevelt's audience grew, and with it, his prestige.

In the autumn of 1914, Roosevelt piped to the tune of Admiral Fiske, the Aide for Operations. "The U. S. Navy is unprepared for war," Fiske announced to Daniels in an emphatic memorandum (which he also sent to Roosevelt). He predicted that five years of conflict were ahead, and the country was in danger of being drawn into it. Consequently, he advocated an increase of 20,000 in personnel, and the establishment of a general staff, without which the United States, in a war against a great European or Asiatic power, would be as helpless "as the French were before the Germans in 1870."[23]

Blasts like this were an old story to Daniels, who continued unruffled on his moderate and peaceful course, but the incessant talk within the Department which lay behind Fiske's ominous memorandum impressed Roosevelt. Theodore Roosevelt's abrupt and dramatic abandonment of his neutral attitude that fall must have further aroused him. Others whom he admired and respected were becoming similarly militant. General Leonard Wood, recently Chief of Staff, Secretary of War Lindley Garrison, and a newly formed Army League were campaigning for drastic and immediate expansion of the military forces. At the same time, Senator Henry Cabot Lodge's energetic Republican son-in-law, Augustus P. (Gussie) Gardner,* was stirring up national excitement with his violent charges that the Navy was unprepared.[25]

"For a dozen years I have sat here like a coward," Gardner proclaimed in the House of Representatives on October 16, as he opened an attack upon what he labeled as the serious deficiencies in both the Army and Navy.[26] As a beginning toward a remedy he called for the establishment of a National Security Commission to investigate national defense.[27] President Wilson laughed when reporters asked him about Gardner's charges.[28] Two days later Roosevelt, in his role of Acting Secretary of the Navy, handed the press an elaborate memorandum which on the surface appeared to support Wilson, but in actuality aided Gardner. In it Roosevelt asserted flatly that the Navy, in order to man its ships, needed eighteen thousand more enlisted men than the limit allowed by Congress. Because of the shortage of men it could not keep thirteen of its second-line battleships in commission.[29] He clearly recognized his personal risk in issuing this statement, but confided to his wife, it "is the truth and even if it gets me into trouble I am perfectly ready to stand by it. The country needs the truth about the Army and Navy instead of a lot of the soft mush about everlasting peace which so many statesmen are handing out to a gullible public." [30]

So strong a statement, coming from within the Navy Department itself and following Gardner's vehement warnings, stirred up more widespread press attention than Roosevelt had ever before received.[31]

Secretary Daniels was probably not amused – especially when a Republican newspaper began to contrast Roosevelt's assertions with his. As a result, in mid-November Roosevelt gave the press a second

* Daniels's most vehement foe in Congress was Gardner (abetted by Lodge). Yet the Lodges, and to a lesser extent the Gardners, were on cordial social terms with the Roosevelts. Mrs. Lodge, whom Eleanor Roosevelt remembers as "one of the loveliest women I have ever known," always made her "feel really at home." [24]

memorandum, more in keeping with his role as Assistant Secretary. Laying stress upon the word "recommended," he stated, "I have not recommended 18,000 more men, nor would I consider it within my province to make any recommendation on the matter one way or the other." [32]

This setback did not lead Roosevelt to change his convictions, though it did lead him to be more cautious in his tactics. He continued to debate defense vigorously, and while he did not hesitate to state his general position emphatically, he became carefully vague in his concrete recommendations.

The strategy worked admirably when, early in December, he addressed a session of the National Civic Federation, a highly influential body of leading representatives of capital and labor.[33] His speech came after that of a brilliant and distinguished pacifist, David Starr Jordan, President of Stanford University. Jordan denounced as militarists all who opposed disarmament. Roosevelt retorted that a strong military and naval establishment was the best means of preventing war, and of significance in building this was universal military training. Horrible though military training might seem to some peace advocates, it was "just plain common sense. An able-bodied boy is better from every standpoint than a wretched runt, including the standpoint of the man at war. Many of us who want to keep the peace believe that $250,000,000 a year for the Navy, which amounts to only one-half of one per cent of our national wealth, is merely good insurance." *

The audience cheered. Samuel Gompers, President of the American Federation of Labor, who spoke after Roosevelt, endorsed his line of reasoning, and the National Civic Federation unanimously adopted a resolution in favor of a Council of National Defense.[35]

When Roosevelt testified at a Gardner-inspired House Naval Affairs Committee hearing into the adequacy of naval defenses, he used

* A few weeks later, Roosevelt interpreted his verbal tilt with Jordan to another audience: "He believes that this country should be the Big Brother to Mankind; that we will never have war. Now, there is a saying which he referred to . . . that it takes two men to make a quarrel. Unfortunately, the events of the past three months have proved this is not so. These gentlemen are secure in their theories; this Brotherhood of Man idea is fine – but if any of these gentlemen will guarantee that we will never have a war, and if we could take their guarantee . . . I would not want to build a navy; but unfortunately in the present state of civilization, nobody is able to give that guarantee. . . . As a matter of fact, pensions should be charged up to the David Starr Jordans of this country. They are the result of a lack of commonsense preparation.[34]

the same tactics.[36] Only a week previously President Wilson had laid down an explicit military policy in his Annual Message to Congress, and Daniels had corroborated it. Wilson granted that the National Guard should be strengthened, but denounced proposals for compulsory military training, or for a large increase in the Army. While he wished the Navy to be strong, he implied that plans for the construction of additional ships should await a careful appraisal of the results of the European war.[37] Two days later, Daniels translated the President's position into specific terms for the House Naval Affairs Committee: a moderate building program, almost identical to that of 1913, which should include two battleships as opposed to the four which the Navy General Board recommended, and no additional enlisted men until the next session of Congress.[38]

Against the weight of authority of the President and the Secretary of the Navy, very few subordinate government officials dared give open support to big-navy views. Gardner remarked that "a most alarming case of lockjaw has come upon Army and Navy officers alike since this pestilence of mine started." [39] But Roosevelt took delight in participating in the debate. He considered himself a moderate, and predicted that he would be "grilled between the 'peace-at-any-price' sophists and the wild-eyed enthusiasts like our friend Hobson." But he thought it his role to help awaken the country to a study of defense questions "from a more intelligent point of view." [40]

Roosevelt, appearing before the Naval Affairs Committee, was thoroughly conversant with a mass of technical data, and ready to advocate a strong defense program through citation of "facts" rather than by the statement of policies of his own. In this manner, he might defend the big-navy viewpoint without openly offending his chief. Both Admiral Fiske and some of the active younger officers had primed him.* He was quick in his answers, persuasive in his approach, and exceeded his own expectations. Correspondents were unanimous about the fine appearance he had made before the Committee. Everyone "followed the testimony . . . with keen interest," the New York *Sun* reported. "He exhibited a grasp of naval affairs that seemed to astonish members of the committee who had been studying the question for years." [42]

* The most notable of the younger advisors was Emory S. Land, who as a graduate student at the Massachusetts Institute of Technology had known Roosevelt at Harvard. Land, who had assisted Roosevelt at motorboat shows, was an expert on construction problems and submarines. He conferred with Roosevelt, and sent him a detailed, cautiously phrased letter.[41]

Those who rumored that Roosevelt was at odds with Secretary Daniels were disappointed. "It would not be my place to discuss purely matters of policy," he asserted at the outset. Although Gardner (through Representative P. H. Kelley) and Hobson quizzed him sharply during his five hours before the Committee, he steadfastly refused to budge from this position,[43] and did not contradict his superior on any point. Nevertheless his testimony on details, together with the overtones and innuendos of his prudent answers, slowly added up to a position decidedly different from that of his chief. Roosevelt agreed with Daniels that the Navy was even more efficient than in the past. But, unlike Daniels, he felt that its relative efficiency compared with the fleets of warring powers was rapidly decreasing. At best it was third among the world's navies.

Roosevelt's analysis of the Navy's readiness for war was also far less optimistic than that of Daniels and other subordinates who had previously testified. Again he pointed to the large number of warships only partially manned. In case of war, he said, it would take thirty to fifty thousand additional trained men to ready them for action, and he used Naval War College figures to prove it. This was in irreconcilable contrast to the estimate of less than five thousand submitted by Daniels's chief of personnel, Admiral Victor Blue.[44]

While the Secretary of the Navy had given the impression that vessels being held in reserve could almost instantly be made ready for battle, Roosevelt implied that it would be a long and painstaking process. A reserve ship would not be in top fighting trim in less than three months. Training of additional men would be even more time-consuming: it took nine months to a year to turn out a good ordinary seaman.[45]

Roosevelt emphatically recommended the building of a strong naval reserve in order to provide basic training for those who would fill in the crews in time of war. Daniels had also recommended a reserve, to be made up of former enlisted men, and had predicted that in time of war the Navy could expect twenty-five thousand of them to return to service. Roosevelt was much less sanguine, though he did not contradict his superior outright.[46] He proposed a considerably larger reserve, and suggested equipping it with vessels so good that it would appeal to civilians. Almost the only ships which the very small state-operated Naval Militia possessed were dilapidated old yachts commandeered during the Spanish–American War. If the Navy were to recruit large numbers of reservists, it must "offer them greater facilities, to make it more attractive to the average private citizen and businessman, or anybody in the private walks of life, to spend a certain length of time away from his play hours, and do some pretty stiff work." [47]

Altogether, this testimony was not as spectacular as the statement that Roosevelt as Acting Secretary had handed to the newspapermen in October, but neither was it a repudiation of those earlier opinions. Roosevelt was well satisfied with the way he had comported himself. It was "really great fun and not so much of a strain, as the members who tried to quiz me and put me in a hole did not know much about their subject and I was able not only to parry but to come back at them with thrusts that went home. Also I was able to get in my own views without particular embarrassment to the Secretary." [48]

However carefully Roosevelt had worded his testimony so as not to jar Daniels, the fire-eating Gardner at once began to construe it in a manner derogatory to the Secretary of the Navy. Two ardent and forthright advocates of a bigger Navy, Admiral Fiske and Captain Yates Stirling, succeeded Roosevelt on the stand; on December 18, Gardner followed them. "During the last three days," he exulted, "we have been having the truth and nothing but the truth and the truth in good plain language. For this he thanked the two officers, and the Assistant Secretary. "I admire the courage of Franklin Roosevelt," he asserted, and then, with liberal references to Roosevelt's press statement and testimony,* he delivered a strong blast at Daniels and his policies.[50]

Gardner had laid bare Roosevelt's preparedness convictions from between the lines of his testimony. Far from being displeased, Roosevelt subsequently provided Gardner with further data with which to attack Daniels and argue for preparedness. In the spring of 1915, Gardner wrote Daniels asking for Naval Intelligence lists of British and German naval losses. With these, he wished to combat the widespread view that losses were so heavy that the relative strength of the United States Navy was growing rather than diminishing.[51] Roosevelt, as Acting Secretary, sent Gardner the tables, and added in a covering letter that because the belligerent powers were building warships very rapidly, he was "forced to the conclusion that our navy probably stands fourth on the list at the present time." [52]

* Gardner mentioned Roosevelt by name nine times; he cited the press statement three times, and Roosevelt's testimony four times. At the beginning of January, Gardner again used Roosevelt's "facts" as the basis for a widely quoted newspaper article.[49]

Roosevelt requested Gardner not to mention that he had officially received the information from the Navy Department; but Gardner wished to quote Roosevelt's "exceedingly interesting" letter. Consequently, he called Roosevelt by long-distance telephone to ask him "whether I was at liberty to use his name in citing the facts. He gave me permission but subsequently withdrew it on peremptory orders from the Secretary of the Navy." A few days later, Gardner pursued the matter further in a conversation. Roosevelt then suggested that Gardner have his father-in-law, Senator Lodge, whom Daniels might not dare refuse, ask the Secretary for a compilation of foreign naval losses. Gardner complied, rather than publish the latter – which he felt he had every right to do, since it was from the Acting Secretary of the Navy – because he did not wish to get Roosevelt into trouble.[53] When Lodge wrote Daniels, he received nothing useful – a table of losses, but with it a blunt statement that the Navy Department had no data on British and German naval construction.[54] Gardner bided his time, and, in January, 1916, when the Administration no longer opposed preparedness, obtained Roosevelt's permission and published the letter.[55]

Roosevelt engaged in this feeding of information to his chief's most vehement political opponent because he ardently believed in preparedness.* Perhaps the petty nature of the offense, bordering on juvenile naughtiness, is what caused Daniels to overlook it and to ignore Roosevelt's dance on the edge of insubordination as one would the pranks of a spirited child.

In his more open efforts to try to sell the country on preparedness, Roosevelt appeared more to advantage. He tried to emphasize the Mahan doctrines that the Navy must be powerful enough to meet an enemy fleet on the high seas and destroy it there. He repeatedly ridiculed the old American notion, still prevalent, that the Navy need merely be ready to defend the American shoreline. That sort of defense, he continually pointed out, would mean the immediate abandonment of Alaska, Panama, and the insular possessions, which to most Americans was unthinkable. Diplomacy was the first line of defense, he emphasized; if it failed the nation must depend upon the next

* He also privately gave Gardner information on the unsatisfactory functioning of submarines. On May 26, 1915, he read to Gardner over the telephone an intercepted fleet radio dispatch which indicated that only five out of eleven submarines were still able to operate in maneuvers. Gardner gave this to the press, but could not get the newspapers to publish it, since he could not name his source.[56]

line, the Navy, during the eighteen months or so that it would take to raise and train an army of a million men or more.[57]

How weak that defense was, Roosevelt wished to demonstrate through naval maneuvers in the spring of 1915.[58] They could, as it were, act out the sensational warning of Hudson Maxim, the inventor, in his *Defenseless America* – that if anything happened to the British Grand Fleet, the United States would be powerless before the Imperial German Navy.* The General Board wished to hold the usual sort of theoretical exercises; Roosevelt persuaded it, instead, to draw up plans for an invasion game off Narragansett Bay, and insisted to Daniels, "The maneuvers should make a definite impression on the minds of the men in the streets." [60] The Secretary agreed to the new plan; and the invading "red" fleet, not surprisingly, won the games.[61]

"I am glad for many reasons," Roosevelt privately commented, "I think the effect on the country at this time will be good." [62] Publicly, he stated that the maneuvers showed serious deficiencies in scout ships, battle cruisers, and submarines.[63]

Within the Navy Department, Roosevelt was ready, as always, to heed the counsels of admirals who warned against dividing the Fleet, or taking it at that time to Pacific waters. He relayed their admonitions in respectful but firm terms to President Wilson, even though, in so doing, he was abandoning a tremendous naval pageant of the sort for which he had a deep fondness. The Navy was planning to celebrate the opening of the Panama Canal in 1915 by assembling the Atlantic Fleet, and with a battleship at the head bearing the President, the United States Navy and warships of other nations were to parade through the Canal and up the Pacific Coast to the expositions at San Diego and Los Angeles. Since the previous June, Roosevelt had been making these plans with Wilson,[64] but by January, 1915 – with the British tightening their blockade, and the Germans intensifying their submarine warfare – the project seemed unwise. "It is absolutely essential that you should be present at the Canal if the opening is to take place," Roosevelt explained to the President. "If you are not there, the whole celebration would fall flat and could do us no good either at home or abroad." Wilson, he granted, could keep in touch with

* Roosevelt read the Navy Department copy of *Defenseless America*, and assured Maxim, "The public interest that exists now will be much sustained by your contribution." [59] Howard Brooks points out that there was a strong similarity between the Navy's "Black Plan" of defense and Maxim's book.

Washington by radio or cable, "but this could not in any way take the place of your personal hand on the wheel in the event of an emergency." Moreover, some officers felt that "the main fleet should be kept intact in the Atlantic. They do not view with any equanimity the possibility of getting a part or the whole of the fleet into the Pacific in a comparatively unprepared condition and of being unable to guarantee that it could return at a moment's notice through the Canal." [65] Ultimately, President Wilson decided not to hold any formal opening ceremonies – though purportedly because of landslides in the Culebra Cut rather than increasing difficulties in the Atlantic.[66]

In March, 1915, Roosevelt accompanied Vice President Thomas R. Marshall on an official visit to the Panama Pacific Exposition at San Francisco. Roosevelt was in charge of all the arrangements for the trip.[67] It was a pleasant interlude from the serious defense debate, and he made the most of it. As Acting Secretary he sent orders to the Flag Officer of the Pacific Fleet for the Assistant Secretary's salute.[68] He had long since designed an Assistant Secretary's flag for Fleet reviews; for this occasion he devised one – the first in the nation's history – for the Vice President.* When Marshall reviewed the Fleet off the Exposition grounds at San Francisco, the flagship broke it out from aloft.[69] Years later Roosevelt still chuckled over a memory of the Vice President going aboard, so flustered that he shook hands with the enlisted men lined up as sideboys [70] – though few besides naval officers would think this particularly funny. Roosevelt, firm in his knowledge of naval procedure, cut a fine figure [71] with his special aide, Lieutenant Husband E. Kimmel. † From morning to night, Roosevelt and William Phillips, who was chairman of the government commission, wore top hats and tailcoats as they went from one foreign pavilion to another to dedicate each. They took turns making short speeches.

The Roosevelts and Phillipses shared a hotel apartment, and Phillips noticed Eleanor Roosevelt's watchful interest in her husband's work. (She inquired over coffee one morning if he had received a certain letter. He had. Had he answered it? No. Should he not? Yes. Should he not answer it right away? He agreed that he should, and immediately wrote a reply.) [72]

* The flag is on exhibit at the Roosevelt Library.

† In 1941, Admiral Kimmel was Commander in Chief of the Pacific Fleet, in charge at Pearl Harbor.

At first Roosevelt received so little publicity that Howe jokingly recommended that he fire his press agent and "try to get at least a line in amongst the patent medicine advertisers." [73] At Los Angeles, he fared much better. One of the Navy's tragically unsatisfactory submarines, the *F-4*, submerged off Pearl Harbor, and failed to return to the surface. All the officers and crew were lost. The American public was shocked; Roosevelt expressed his own distress, but warned that it was "only one of the sad things that must be expected in any great navy." [74] His own immediate reaction was characteristic: he went aboard a submarine at Los Angeles Harbor, and, despite heavy seas, had it dive and go through its paces. He returned elated: "It was fine and for the first time since we left Washington we felt perfectly at home." Then he left aboard a destroyer for San Diego, although the swell was so extreme that "during the half hour in which . . . the destroyer remained in sight, it was seen to bury itself time and time again in the raging seas." [75]

Back once more in Washington, this lover of action chafed over the failure of the government to make a stronger protest against the repeated German sinkings of vessels, contrary to international law. In February, 1915, Germany had announced that, in retaliation against the unlawful British blockade, it would commence submarine warfare.* On May 7, to the horror of the entire nation, the huge British passenger liner, the *Lusitania*, was torpedoed, and sank in eighteen minutes. Nearly 1200 persons drowned; 124 of them were American citizens. Newspapers referred to the sinking as "wanton murder," and in the weeks that followed, the excitement grew. Suddenly, public opinion caught up with Roosevelt.

President Wilson followed a cautious, deliberate course of action.

* Roosevelt's law partner, Henry Hooker, played a leading part in a famous effort to get cotton through the blockade. In December, 1914, on behalf of a client, he negotiated the purchase of the Hamburg-America steamship *Dacia*, for $165,000, and contracted for it to carry cotton to Europe. He wired Roosevelt for aid in obtaining American registration. Roosevelt refused; he felt that his friend Breitung was "taking a very long chance and the whole transaction is fraught with many possible international complications." When the British Government hesitated to seize the vessel, because it would further stir up difficulties with the United States (cotton was not yet contraband), the American Ambassador to Great Britain, Walter Hines Page, solved the dilemma for the British by suggesting that they have the French capture the *Dacia*. Hooker subsequently became strongly pro-Allies, and after American entrance into the war served on General Leonard Wood's staff.[76]

Three days after the sinking, he remarked in a speech that "There is such a thing as a man being too proud to fight" – a statement which ardent preparedness advocates twisted and denounced. But he followed the remark with stern notes to Germany, in the second of which he asserted that he would hold Germany to "strict accountability." [77] Secretary of State Bryan, who had signed the first note reluctantly, felt that the second note might well provoke war. Rather than sign it, he submitted his resignation on June 9, 1915.[78]

Roosevelt – not privileged, of course, to sit in on the tense Cabinet sessions which preceded this – sent the President a longhand note [79] expressing his stanch approval: "I want to tell you simply that you have been in my thoughts during these days and that I realize to the full all that you have had to go through – I need not repeat to you my own entire loyalty and devotion – that I hope you know. But I feel most strongly that the Nation approves and sustains your course and that it is *American* in the highest sense." *

To a friend, Roosevelt reiterated, "We have had a somewhat disagreeable few days down here, but I think there is no question that the country as a whole is standing squarely behind the President." [81] He was quite correct; public opinion accepted Wilson's new note. As tension continued during the weeks that followed, Roosevelt seemed to feel increased respect for the President, and irritation with all those who would not engage in vigorous preparedness planning. "What d' y' think of W. Jay B?" he inquired of Eleanor, "I can only say I'm disgusted clear through." † By implication this disgust seemed to include Daniels, whose views were quite similar to Bryan's, for he added, "J.D. will *not* resign!" [84]

Roosevelt was so impatient with anyone who would not wholeheartedly back preparedness that he refused to take an honorary posi-

* President Wilson answered, June 14, 1915: "Your letter of June ninth touched me very much and I thank you for it with all my heart. Such messages make the performance of duty worth while, because, after all, the people who are nearest are those whose judgment we most value and most need to be supported by. With the warmest regard and appreciation . . ." [80]

† In the summer of 1915, FDR was so disdainful of Bryan that he commented, after attending an official dinner given by Bryan's successor, Robert Lansing: "It was a delight to see a Secretary of State who is a gentleman and knows how to treat Ambassadors and Ministers from other civilized nations." [82] By the fall of 1934, apparently impressed by the furore the Nye Committee raised against munitions makers and international bankers, who purportedly tricked the United States into the war, President Roosevelt commented to Daniels, "Would that W.J.B. had stayed on as Secretary of State – the country would have been better off." [83]

tion with the Boy Scouts until he was assured repeatedly that they would not again disseminate David Starr Jordan's pacifist statements, as they previously had done. In his criticism of the Scouts, Roosevelt was following the lead of one of the most vehement advocates of immediate preparedness, Theodore Roosevelt's intimate friend, General Leonard Wood.[85] He also followed T.R. and Wood in their respect for the Secretary of War, Lindley Garrison, who was advocating drastic defense measures. On June 23, 1915, Roosevelt gave vent to his indignation in a penciled note which he filed among his papers. It expressed the attitude he seemed to feel during those long wearing months.

He had lunched that noon, at the Shoreham Hotel, with Daniels and Secretary of Commerce William C. Redfield. . . .

> As were were walking over Mr. Daniels talked of the difficulty of our position: that Germany might not agree to give up her submarine warfare – that if she did not & refused to do so ever so politely, what could we do? He seemed worried & bewildered questioning without daring to suggest to himself any answers then he said – "you know one or two men in the Cabinet spend a lot of time working things out to an ultimate conclusion[?] For instance Garrison has kept on speculating about what we could do or should do in case Germany does not back down – of course he has that kind of a mind, the mind of a lawyer & it makes him see a whole lot of unnecessary bogies. Why as a matter of fact we couldn't do anything against Germany except to withdraw Gerard & what good would that do? If we broke off relations it would upset things terribly in this country – today the people are a unit behind the President but if we had to act, there would be all sorts of opposition & suggestions of courses to pursue & the President would become only the leader of a faction."
>
> I asked him "Do you think people would stand for raising an army?" He said "No, it would create terrible divisions of opinion."
>
> ---
>
> This reminds me that Garrison told me yesterday that Daniels had said to him "I hope I shall never live to see the day when the schools of this country are used to give any form of military training – If that happens it will be proof positive that the American form of government is a failure."
>
> ---
>
> And then he went on to me "You know it was just that that made Bryan resign – the fear of the next step if Germany does

not give in. It is a mistake to look too far ahead, to cross the bridges before we get to them; it is sufficient to take up each step as it comes up."

This line of talk & thought is of course entirely typical – My one regret is that the Cabinet has not more Garrisons – the President is not getting real information because the Daniels & Bryans prevent discussion of the future steps because it is a disagreeable subject. I know for a fact that the President has not had the advice of a single officer of the Army or of the Navy on the question of what we could do to carry out our declared policy. Daniels is right that to break off diplomatic relations merely would accomplish nothing – the German submarine warfare would be conducted in the same way in violation of law & humanity. But we must consider what else we could do. Things can be done which would possibl[y] make Germany realize our determination. They are military and economic steps. We shall be forced to think of them, to choose which will best serve our purpose, unless we go on negotiating by notes & more notes – But of this there is a limit – witness the War of 1812."[86]

CHAPTER XV

"We've Got To Get into This War"

> The broad idea of national defense is to protect not merely the continental interests of this nation, but all of its interests, wherever they may be, to keep our territory over the sea, to preserve our international policies and trade.
>
> — FDR, *December 18, 1915.*[1]

THE alarms and pressures of the summer of 1915 finally led President Wilson to advocate preparedness. In addition to the drawn-out and unsatisfactory exchange of notes with Germany over the *Lusitania*, there were growing fears of Japanese aggression, particularly if Germany and Japan were to ally themselves against the United States. The organized clamor for armament from without the Administration, coupled with the insistence of Colonel House and others from within, was irresistible. On July 21, 1915, Wilson ordered Daniels to put the best minds in the Navy Department to work drawing up an adequate naval program to submit to the next Congress. Daniels immediately enlisted the aid of Roosevelt.* [3]

* Roosevelt was at Campobello, convalescing from an appendicitis operation. He had a sudden attack at 6 o'clock on the morning of July 1, and was operated upon at 2 o'clock in the afternoon. He made a rapid recovery. Daniels demonstrated his strong affection for FDR by arranging his schedule so that Roosevelt could go to Campobello for the rest of July to recuperate, and sent his "love and happiness that you are coming on so finely." Theodore Roosevelt wired his concern, and the Naval Attaché at the Japanese Embassy, Commander Kichisaburo Nomura, expressed his "best wishes that your convalescence will be as quick as possible." Nomura at the time of Pearl Harbor was Japanese Ambassador to the United States. Louis Howe prepared an elaborate illustrated booklet: *Ye Sad Ballade of ye Navies' Pride* . . . An attached card explained:

> This is all bound
> Round and
> Round and
> Round with red tape
> BECAUSE
> Everything in the Navy
> Department is done
> That Way.[2]

After the many months during which Roosevelt had risked Administration wrath because of his preparedness agitation, he now took particular satisfaction in Wilson's new instructions. He hoped that the Administration, by drawing up a strong program, could forestall the Republicans and Progressives from capitalizing upon preparedness sentiment in the 1915 and 1916 political campaigns.[4] After hastily sending to several subordinates in the Navy Department for information upon which to base plans,* he waited impatiently until it was time to return to the Navy Department. He would serve as Acting Secretary for several weeks while Daniels vacationed. "That means," he prophesied, "that things will hum."[7]

Washington was in a state of nervousness when Roosevelt arrived in mid-August. The long-threatened Marine intervention in Haiti had finally begun, and on August 19 the simmering crisis with Germany flared up again with the sinking of the *Arabic*. At first this threatened serious trouble. "I have seen Lansing today," Roosevelt reported on August 21, ". . . and I think the President will really act as soon as we can get the facts. But it seems very hard to wait until Germany tells us her version and I personally doubt if I should be quite so polite."[8] However, the German Ambassador, Count Johann H. von Bernstorff, alarmed by the mounting war fever in America, went beyond his instructions from the German Foreign Office to assure Lansing that the incident was contrary to orders, and would not be repeated.[9]

This pacific turn of events hindered Roosevelt in one of his main projects: to try to persuade President Wilson to create a Council of National Defense. While Daniels had assigned him a relatively minor segment of the naval planning, Roosevelt was ready for his part to push an over-all scheme for supervision of industrial mobilization. A University of Wisconsin history professor with a flair for selling his ideas in high places, Alfred L. P. Dennis, had a conversation with Roosevelt at the end of August, and convinced him of the desirability of establishing a Council of National Policy, or Defense, to co-

* Daniels assigned to Roosevelt, as his particular undertaking, the development of a sound scheme for developing and utilizing the navy yards, "A hard nut to crack."[5] Roosevelt from Campobello immediately sent to the Paymaster General for data, and many schemes revolved through his mind. He explained facetiously, "It is an awful mistake to go away and have absolutely nothing to do except to make toy boats for the children, because one's mind unconsciously tries to invent all sorts of things for the true workers to do."[6]

ordinate the entire preparedness effort.[10] The warring European nations had already created similar bodies. Roosevelt at once took the plan to Wilson. His approach indicated some concession on his part toward Wilson's moderation, for he decried to the President the talk of some of those with whom he had earlier seemed so much in sympathy – "the paid propaganda organized by the extremists, which is hurting those who are soberly and rationally considering National Defense." Emphasizing the "rational," that is to say "moderate," position, he assured Wilson that the people were deeply interested in "rational preparation." [11] After his talk he reported that he had interested Wilson, and hoped to get the Council "*in time*," [12] but could "accomplish little just now as the President does not want to 'rattle the sword' while Germany seems anxious to meet us more than half way." [13]

The project remained dormant throughout the winter of 1915–1916, although Roosevelt, in response to the prodding of Dennis, continued to agitate it in Washington.[14]

"I wish I could write the Democratic platform this year," he confided to Dennis in May. "It would make history if I could, but you can count on me to do everything possible to get some reference included. This will, of course, depend a good deal on whether the President allows a suggestion of this kind to stand and I am gunning for this approval now." [15] He was rather irritated at the slowness of the Administration in creating a permanent organization to plan war production. "I think there is an excellent chance at least of improving things," he explained, "and without intending to throw bouquets at myself, I think I am the only person in Washington in the Administration who realizes the perfectly wonderful opportunities, nationally and politically, to accomplish something of lasting construction." [16]

The Assistant Secretary was undoubtedly overestimating his own value. The authorization for a Council of National Defense went through Congress in August, 1916, as a rider on the Army appropriation bill, and Roosevelt was no more zealous than several others on its behalf.[17] He was correct, however, in thinking it could be of lasting significance – in May, 1940, as France was about to collapse, he reconstituted the Advisory Commission of the Council as the first important defense agency of the Second World War.[18]

But in the summer of 1915, while Roosevelt was making little progress in pushing this basic defense proposal, he had to take out his craving for action in very minor ways. Early in the year he had predicted: "I just *know* I shall do some awful unneutral thing before

I get through!"[19] Quite the contrary was the case in actuality. He comported himself with a high degree of circumspection during those tempting days when he was Acting Secretary, coming nearest to actual policy making when, in September, 1915, he finally announced a plan for the creation and training of a naval reserve. He was impressed with General Wood's civilian camp for the training of army officers at Plattsburg, New York, and would have visited it if he could have found the time. He hoped to develop something similar for the Navy the following summer.[20] Ever since he had come into the department, he had been agitating for a comprehensive reserve program, and by this time he had reached the point where his impatience exceeded his caution. For here was a singular counterpart to his occasional bold statements and his covert delivery of information to Gardner; it was with some anxiety that he wrote his wife on September 2, "Today I sprang an announcement . . . and trust J.D. will like it! It is of the utmost importance and I have failed for a year to get him to take any action, though he has never objected to it. Now I have gone ahead and pulled the trigger myself. I suppose the bullet may bounce back on me, but it is not revolutionary nor alarmist and is just common sense."[21] Roosevelt's apprehension was needless, since this was no more than a proposal and his insubordination, if any, was of the mildest sort. The following summer his plan went into effect.[22] It provided for a reserve of 50,000 men, made up both of former officers and enlisted men and of volunteer civilians, especially those who were familiar with ships, engines, or radio, or who could man auxiliary patrol boats.[23]

As a lifelong lover of small boats, Roosevelt spoke frequently at boat shows and encouraged the development of powerboat squadrons which in time of war could maintain harbor or coastal patrols.[24] The following spring, when several private powerboats built to government specification were in operation,* he donned oilskins and rode across Boston Harbor in a volunteer submarine chaser. The boats were in the naval reserve, which meant they were to be inspected at regular intervals and kept ready for immediate service as patrol boats, scouts, or dispatch carriers.[25]

In organizing a reserve, Roosevelt was preoccupied with these

*These boats, in which Roosevelt took so much interest, were the forerunners of the subchasers of the First World War, and the PT Boats of the Second World War. They were 40 feet long and had a speed of 21 knots. Roosevelt had the Navy Department set standards for reserve powerboats of three sizes: 45, 55, and 75 feet in length. By comparison, PT boats were 70 feet in length and had a speed of over 60 miles per hour.

wealthy men's speedboats. This interest was a means of luring a number of influential yachtsmen into supporting the Navy, but was even more a reflection of his own background. Even after the United States entered the war, he rode his small-boat hobby to the limit.

Out of Roosevelt's reserve scheme there did, as he hoped, emerge a naval counterpart of Wood's Plattsburg program, which enabled civilians to go at their own expense on a training cruise which would prepare them for service in case of war. In 1915, he said he had been trying for two and a half years to get a cruise. "I have not been able to make much headway . . ." he confessed, "though I have been pushing it constantly."[26] The success of the Plattsburg camp, and the changed attitude of President Wilson, enabled him to convince Daniels by the next spring.[27] But Daniels was slow to put Roosevelt's plans into operation.[28] This irked Roosevelt, who feared his chief was delaying because the program did not have congressional authorization and would appeal primarily to the elite.* Roosevelt tried to disabuse him on both points. He assured him that the cruise would appeal to more than just "college boys, rich young men, well-to-do yachtsmen, etc." He emphasized, "I want to remind you of the fact that I have twice been elected to office in a fairly large and cosmopolitan kind of district and that I can rightly claim to be in touch with every element in the community. You may, therefore . . . accept my word for it that the proposed naval training cruise would be carried out on absolutely democratic lines."[30]

Daniels finally agreed, and tried to put the emphasis upon enrolling skilled craftsmen who would be of use to the Navy in time of war. Roosevelt still hoped to include also "the large class of yachtsmen and pleasure boat owners who are pretty well at home on the water," but even he was ready to bar college students who merely wanted an interesting experience.[31]

Actually, enrollments came in very slowly.[32] And despite all Daniels's efforts, the background of these trainees was almost identical – except for a leaning toward yachts – to that of many well-to-do young men in the Plattsburg program.

* Roosevelt clearly indicated his desire to gain the support of influential people, in a comment in October, 1916, on distribution of seats for the Army-Navy game. He pointed out: "During the last two years practically all of the spare seats of the Army were distributed from the Harvard Club and I think it did real good, because it was appreciated by the kind of people who can be of more service to the Army and Navy than the average complete outsider who goes to the Polo Grounds to see the game merely as a spectacle."[29]

Roosevelt took a strong proprietary interest in what he took to calling "my cruise," and was irked when the Secretary baptized it the "John Paul Jones Cruise." [33] The reservists embarked from several ports aboard nine battleships of the reserve force of the Atlantic Fleet, which participated with thirty or forty other vessels in war games off Block Island and target practice in Tangier Sound.[34] Although not everything went smoothly, most participants were enthusiastic, and Roosevelt himself was "elated at the real success of what even I had to regard as an experiment during its first year." [35]

Despite his satisfaction, Roosevelt continued to feel that this single cruise was no more than a tiny earnest of what ought to be done. Both the officers of the regular Navy and those in the naval militia continued to stand in his way.[36] As a result he concluded in the fall of 1916 that either in the Army or the Navy it was next to impossible to give militia proper training. "The day of the militia has come to an end," he declared, "and . . . we must organize something very radically different." [37] Conversations with British and French naval officers stationed in Washington confirmed him in his belief that "we *must* create a large and effective naval reserve of personnel and material." [38]

This led Roosevelt to reiterate, even more strongly, his old faith in universal military training.[39] He felt that "people all over this country are coming to realize more and more that they owe a personal obligation to the Government . . . to assist . . . in time of war." [40] In November, 1916, he recommended in a speech that the nation undertake a census of both machinery and manpower: "It will include both men and women, some for the trenches, some for the machine shops, some for the offices, some for the railroads and some for the sewing machines. National mobilization will not make us militaristic any more than it will make us Chinafied." [41]

The nation undertook nothing so drastic as a labor draft; indeed, even the draft of soldiers did not come until after American entrance into the war. In the limited field of the naval reserve itself, Roosevelt achieved relatively little. "I worked from 1913 down to 1917, mostly in vain," he once admitted, "in an effort to get something better than the old and wholly inadequate Naval militia. The war then proved that while we did pretty well with the raw officer material, nearly 25,000 of them, we could have done vastly better if we had been able to pick, choose and train before the war began. After the war was over, I again tried in vain to get the Navy Department really interested in continuing an adequate Reserve, especially of officer material, but again the interest on the part of the Service was so slight that I got nowhere."[42]

At the same time, Daniels was achieving remarkable success in enlisting the aid of scientists on behalf of the Navy. In the autumn of 1915, he helped establish a Naval Consulting Board, which provided the Navy with valuable technical advice, and at the same time drew quantities of favorable publicity. This was a committee of inventors to sift over suggestions and develop worth-while devices. Roosevelt was intrigued with the possibilities, and especially liked Daniels's plan to appoint Thomas A. Edison chairman of the Board.[43] In common with the American public, he had great respect for Edison, and knew that the inventor was already at work on devices to improve submarines.[44] But concerning the Board as a whole, he wavered between being enthusiastic and accepting the cynical view of naval officers that it was impractical. On the one hand, "Most of these worthies are like Henry Ford, who until he saw a chance for publicity free of charge, thought a submarine was something to eat!"[45] On the other, "There is one thing certain . . . and that is that all the scientific men of this country are going to cooperate."[46]

Roosevelt could achieve little within the Navy Department in preparing for war, so he concentrated upon selling preparedness to the public; both in private and public he frequently expressed his dissatisfaction over the relative inaction of the government. In the spring of 1916 he spoke before the annual meeting of the Navy League, even though Daniels boycotted it; on another occasion he spoke from the same platform with two of the most caustic critics of the Administration, Leonard Wood and Theodore Roosevelt.[47] When Secretary of War Garrison resigned in February, 1916, purportedly because of his advocacy of compulsory military training,[48] newspapers frequently mentioned Franklin D. Roosevelt as a possible successor. The Washington *Herald* even claimed that he and General Goethals were the two strong contenders, and that "no appointments would be welcomed with greater joy on the part of War Department officials."[49] Several labor leaders wrote to the President on his behalf, and "all the newspaper boys are pulling for him," McCarthy reported – but these were no more than evidences of his popularity with newspapermen as well as with jingoists.[50] Wilson picked Newton D. Baker, who was far from being a rabid advocate of preparedness.[51]

Roosevelt considered his mission largely one of educating the people to the needs of the nation. When hecklers challenged him, he demonstrated something of the patience of a schoolmaster facing rather dull pupils.[52] A good deal of what he wrote and said was simplified military and naval doctrine – a sort of Mahan for the masses. A theme of economic nationalism was at the root of much of it. Unilateral disarmament, as some pacifists advocated, could lead only to the overrunning of this country by those envious of its abundance. "National jealousies and national ambitions do exist," he warned, "and . . . a great many nations and peoples are jealous of us. . . . The question comes down to this: if you believe there is any possibility of an attack upon our country, whether upon our shores or our island possessions or our trade with foreign lands, then you become at once a believer in adequate national defense." [53] This was an enlarged view, since in it Roosevelt would include any interest anywhere in the world: "Americans have always been ready and willing to protect Americans wherever they are, by force of arms if necessary." [54] Over a long period of time, prosperity depended upon foreign trade and overseas possessions. "If you cut off the United States from all trade and intercourse with the rest of the world you would have economic death in this country before long." Moreover, it would end the humanitarian work of the United States in its possessions and Latin America.[55]

In private, Roosevelt even more bluntly followed this line of reasoning, which was, interestingly, close to that of the Navy League. When a retired admiral warned him against British greed, he retorted, "What you say about the British attitude towards their own trade is, of course, proved by history. Is it not, however, equally true that any other nation that gets control of the seas in the same kind of way and obtains trade supremacy would act in very much the same way towards other nations? In other words, the European attitude, whether it be German, or British, or Russian or French, is essentially one of national selfishness. I am not at all sure that we are free from this ourselves. And after all . . . the answer is . . . 'build the ships.' " [56]

In the selfish age of competing nations, armament rather than world government was for the time being the only solution. "We may hope some day that there will be one nation," Roosevelt granted, "but the fact is that today there are a great many nations and a great many peoples with different ideals and different thoughts, some that seem hopelessly irreconcilable." [57] Consequently, although "Extremists, sincere, perhaps, say it would be better for the whole world to abolish war. . . . That millennium will come some day, but you and I will not be there." [58] If one accepted that view, there was no alternative to supporting thoroughgoing armament – no middle road: "Either we want adequate preparedness, or we want none. Half a navy is worthless. Unless we have an adequate navy it would be cheaper, it would save more lives, it would be better for us all to have no preparation at all and to let anybody that wishes come right along and take from us whatever they choose. . . . But I do not believe we are going to do that." [59] To put it nationalistically, "An adequate navy is notice served by the United States upon the nations of the world that war shall never again be fought upon American soil." [60]

The price of an adequate Navy would not be exorbitant. Roosevelt granted to his audiences, at the end of 1915, that it sounded big in dollars and cents: $500,000,000 in five years.[61] "If it cost a billion extra each year we might come close to giving this country the adequate defense it needs." But in terms of national income this was not much. "Why, we spend more money per year for chewing gum . . . than we do to keep our Army, and more money is spent for automobile tires than it costs to run the Navy." [62] The only financial difficulty was the American desire to keep taxes low. While in England the income tax was from 10 to 30 per cent, Americans would balk at paying more than 2 per cent.[63]

Roosevelt devoted the greater part of his speaking and writing to an analysis of what adequate defense entailed. If it could fend off a surprise attack, the Fleet would give the United States an opportunity to build an Army. But there was a serious possibility that the Navy, by itself, would not be sufficient protection, and must have behind it an Army large enough to withstand the first shock of invasion. There was always the chance that several of the world's largest naval powers might suddenly form a coalition powerful enough to destroy the United States Fleet no matter how large it might be. Without mentioning nations, Roosevelt was hinting at the eventuality that a victorious Germany might ally itself with Japan. "This war has shown us," he warned, with direct allusion to Italy, "with what facility nations change partners." [64] Consequently, the nation should develop a much larger army immediately – a standing force of a hundred thousand men and a reserve of a million.[65] Lack of adequate preparedness would be "a crime against mankind. It would mean the loss of lives, of national ideals and perhaps of nationality itself." [66]

In keeping with 1915 concepts of an attacking force, he emphasized the need for battleships and cruisers, and tried to refute a growing heresy that quantities of submarines would be sufficient to protect the American shoreline. The submarine had not replaced the battleship, he asserted in the *North American Review*, and at its existing stage of development it was "not sea-going or sea-keeping; it is not fast; and it is extremely vulnerable. Already devices for its destruction are multiplying." [67]

When Roosevelt testified before the House Naval Affairs Committee on March 28–29, 1916, he was bold enough to advocate a larger building program than Secretary Daniels had recommended.[68] This was safe enough, for by then public opinion clearly supported large-scale preparedness, however unready it might be to consider entering the war against Germany. Roosevelt was near the forefront of the movement. On June 14, Flag Day, when President Wilson marched in a "preparedness parade" in Washington, and then occupied a reviewing stand, Roosevelt stood nearby.[69] Four days later, President Wilson called out the entire National Guard to serve on the Mexican border, where Pancho Villa several months before had raided a New Mexican town. Ostensibly the purpose of the expedition was to police the border; actually it served to train the troops and bring the preparedness excitement to a high pitch.[70] A few days after Villa's attack, Roosevelt had confided, "I am, frankly, in hope that this Mexican business will amount to enough to make the people really understand." [71] A few days after the President ordered the National Guard to the border, Roosevelt, in an address before the New York naval reservists, asserted that the naval reserve might be called out too. Just what use they could be along the Rio Grande, he did not explain. When the toastmaster remarked, "I know it would not hurt your feelings if the word 'Assistant' were crossed out of this man's title," the reservists cheered uproariously.[72]

If this remark were part of the political onslaught upon Secretary Daniels and President Wilson, Roosevelt would have none of it. He did not forget that 1916 was an election year. Though in preparedness matters he might side with some of the sharpest foes of the Administration, he was quick to defend both the President and the Secretary from Republican attack. As early as the end of March, Republicans at the congressional hearing asked him why work on the *New Mexico*, being built in the Brooklyn Navy Yard, was going so slowly. He asserted that the constructors were working two shifts – "fast enough to incorporate material into the ship as fast as that material is delivered." If construction went on twenty-four hours a day, it could not go any faster.[73] Quick to perceive that this could be a vulnerable point of attack in the campaign ahead, he recalled from sea duty Emory S. Land, a highly capable young constructor, and assigned him along with Howe to the task of running down materials. They speeded up construction considerably on the *New Mexico* and two sister ships building in private yards. Though Roosevelt suggested a premature launching, they were not able to get them down the ways before the election.[74] At least, thanks to their efforts, Roosevelt was able to claim, in response to Republican charges, that in ship construction the Navy had "gone faster than ever before," and in its total program would "absolutely fill up the building facilities of the country." [75]

Another most effective way of answering Republican criticism was to label it as unpatriotic, as likely to slow up the preparedness effort. In denouncing political attacks, Roosevelt hit upon a happy metaphor, one of those not really applicable but thoroughly understandable allusions to simple neighborhood things. It was of the sort that he used with effect throughout his public career: *

"Every minute of time taken up in perfectly futile and useless argument about mistakes in the past slows up construction that much. Worse than that it blinds and befogs the public as to the real situation and the imperative necessity for prompt action. How would you expect the public to be convinced that a dangerous fire was in progress, requiring every citizen's aid for its extinguishment, if they saw the members of the volunteer fire department stop in their headlong rush toward the conflagration and indulge in a slanging match as to who was responsible for the rotten hose or the lack of water at the fire a week ago?" [77]

Of course, taking refuge in patriotism did not prevent Roosevelt from counterattacking with charges that the Navy under Wilson was far more efficient than under his two predecessors. This, curiously, led Roosevelt to cast aspersions upon the globe-circling cruise of which Theodore Roosevelt was so proud: "When the fleet went around the world it was necessary, in order to commission all of the sixteen battleships and the few auxiliaries which went with them, to strip many other vessels of their officers and men, to borrow here, there and the other place . . . with the result that, while the main fleet was in full

* On December 17, 1940, FDR made use of a similar analogy in explaining his proposal for Lend-Lease: "Suppose my neighbor's home catches fire, and I have a length of garden hose four or five hundred feet away. If he can take my garden hose and connect it up with his hydrant, I may help him to put out his fire." [76]

commission, the naval establishment as a whole was seriously weakened." [78]

A few weeks later, Franklin received a gentle communication from Theodore, who commented that after hearing this charge, he had asked a naval officer for confirmation, "because my memory was not in accordance with the statement as you made it." He quoted the officer's letter, which refuted Franklin's rash comment.[79] The younger Roosevelt immediately checked personnel figures within the department, found that he was completely wrong, and sent profuse apologies. "I have tried right along to give only correct facts about the Navy and not to gloss over mistakes," he declared. "And I will myself take the first opportunity to say something about the correct figures of the cruise." [80]

Franklin Roosevelt was on safer ground in attacking the Taft Administration. This he made stick. When President Taft reviewed the Fleet at a "great mobilization" in New York Harbor in 1912, Roosevelt charged, the ships were not only seriously undermanned, but some were in such bad shape that they had to be towed to their anchorage, while others could be kept afloat only by working pumps day and night.[81] Franklin explained to Theodore that he was basing this assertion in part on personal observation. "It was ridiculous to call that assemblage of ships 'a mobilization.' " [82] Theodore, long since hostile toward Taft, not only did not dispute this, but corroborated the accusation that the Navy had been short of men at the time.[83] In the fall, Franklin Roosevelt repeated the charge during the political campaign and added accusations that naval gunnery had slumped badly during the Taft Administration. This drew vehement denials from Taft's Secretary of the Navy, George von Lengerke Meyer.[84]

Secretary Daniels was a major Republican target during the campaign of 1916. While he spent much of the summer and autumn on the hustings answering charges that he had allowed the Navy to deteriorate, Roosevelt remained in the Navy Department as Acting Secretary, and authorized as drastic preparedness measures as he dared. In addition, he spent part of his time on Capitol Hill, helping nurse through the naval appropriations bill, by this stage so large that it frightened some of the Congressmen.

One of the phenomena of the approaching 1916 election had been a general Administration appeasement of Tammany, and Roosevelt continued to be particularly conciliatory toward his old political foe, John J. Fitzgerald, chairman of the key House Appropriations Committee, long one of the most vehement opponents of a big Navy. He handled Fitzgerald so adroitly that the Congressman became a strong backer of the bill.[85]

In the summer, Roosevelt did his usual political stint in Maine, since it was close to Campobello, and extolled the great achievements of the naval yard at Kittery (across the state line in New Hampshire it was always referred to as the Portsmouth yard).[86] And as usual, Maine went solidly Republican.* In October, he campaigned in upstate New York, on Long Island, and in Rhode Island, and continued to concentrate upon the issue of naval efficiency. When the Republican candidate for President, Charles Evans Hughes, made a sneering reference to Secretary Daniels's efforts to school the sailors, and said, "We must pay less attention to punctuation and more to targets," it was Roosevelt who delivered the retort.[88] In terms which would have sounded indecorous even coming from Daniels, he charged Hughes with insulting the officers and men of the Navy:

"Does Mr. Hughes not know what the navy knew, that the navy in March, 1913, was a hollow shell, and that complete reorganization was imperative? . . . I can show him millions of dollars, item by item, saved through common sense business organization. I can show him an organization that would not break down in case of war. I can show him long-range shooting with big guns that has surprised and delighted every officer in the fleet. . . . The navy is growing; it must grow more. It is using the appropriations wisely and honestly. All it needs now is boosting and not knocking."[89]

At Providence, Roosevelt followed this up with a blanket reference to the unfair attacks upon Wilson and his advisers:

"Misquotations and misrepresentations – yea, lies – have been used by the President's opponents. I say lies because this is a good 'Roosevelt' word to use."[90]

The careful manner in which Roosevelt avoided much reference to other aspects of Wilson's Administration indicated no more than a

* During the hot early weeks of the 1916 campaign, Roosevelt's greatest personal concern was that his children should not become victims of the serious infantile paralysis epidemic then at its height. Carefully following medical advice, he kept them isolated at Campobello through September. Because he was afraid they might be exposed on a train, he wished to use the *Dolphin* to return them to Hyde Park. Secretary Daniels at first opposed this, for fear it would have political repercussions, but gave permission after the Maine election. At the beginning of October, the *Dolphin* brought the children home, apparently to their pleasure, but not to that of the commander, William D. Leahy, who recalled thirty years later how they roamed all over the ship.[87]

division of labor in the campaigning. He shared the general belief that Hughes was decidedly in the lead – every state where Roosevelt spoke went Republican [91] – but he wished to see Wilson take the offensive on the basis of the New Freedom. He wrote:

"The Democratic campaign ought not to be one of answering individual issues selected by the Republicans. We ought to go out and make the fight on the really great accomplishments of the past four years. It is true, of course, that in four years we have made mistakes – some of the legislation is experimental and may not work well in practice – but there is enough legislation which has proved its wisdom and enough situations that have been proved to have been well handled that they give us enough ammunition to last for many months.* Personally I look for the pendulum to swing back to the President in the course of a very few weeks. We must depend, of course, largely upon his own speeches between now and election day and I only wish that he would enter very vigorously into a short campaign which would sweep Mr. Hughes off his feet during the last two weeks." [93]

This Wilson did, and delivered speeches forceful in comparison with the rather uninspired ones of Hughes. His cautious preparedness policy seemed the most important issue. He was arming the country and taking a strong stand in dealing with the warring nations, but was by no means militant. As for Secretary Daniels, he might have brought down upon his own head the scorn of the Navy League and the jingoists, but in theaters, motion pictures of Daniels and the Navy brought the loudest cheers. A large percentage of Americans wanted adequate armaments, but not war. From Martin H. Glynn's keynote speech until election day, the Democrats took advantage of this sentiment with their slogan, "He Kept Us Out of the War." The President never echoed this, but his deliberate policies were in marked contrast to Theodore Roosevelt's bombastic demands for drastic action; even the careful Hughes granted in October that had he been President at the time the *Lusitania* was

* FDR's adherence to the progressive Wilson domestic policy by no means pleased his conservative mother and aunts. In August, 1915, when he had dinner with his mother and his Aunt Doe (Mrs. Paul R. Forbes), he wrote Eleanor that his aunt "gave the usual line of talk 'agin the government' and I delivered eulogy per contra. Think it did Aunt Doe good at least." After another of these discussions, in October, 1917, his mother sent him a querulous letter extolling *noblesse oblige:* "With the *trend* to 'shirt sleeves,' and the ideas of what men should do in always being all things to all men and striving to give up the old-fashioned traditions of family life, simple home pleasures and refinements . . . of what use is it to *keep up* things, to hold on to dignity and all I stood up for this evening." [92]

sunk, he would have been firmer with Germany than Wilson.[94] Consequently, Wilson seemed somewhat more committed than Hughes to a peaceful course of action.

How the voters would react was far from certain, although Wall Street betting odds favored the Republicans. On the evening of the election, Roosevelt along with a number of Administration leaders attended the elder Henry Morgenthau's dinner party at the Biltmore.[95] The early returns were so strongly Republican that they quelled the gaiety like the handwriting at Belshazzar's feast,[96] but the irrepressible Roosevelt jokingly proceeded to lay plans to enter into a law partnership with Frank Polk, Counselor of the State Department.[97] At midnight, when he left the gloomy Democratic headquarters at the Biltmore with his friend Secretary of the Interior Lane,[98] he was convinced that Hughes had been elected. He entrained for Washington, but upon his arrival the next morning, found that all the later returns pointed to the re-election of Wilson.[99]

"The most extraordinary day of my life," Roosevelt informed Eleanor on Wednesday. "After last night, Wilson may be elected after all." [100] But the election was in doubt even the following day — "Another . . . of the most wild uncertainty."

Finally, California went to Wilson by less than four thousand votes, and the President carried the election. "It is rumored," cracked Roosevelt in a speech the following week, "that a certain distinguished cousin of mine is now engaged in revising an edition of his most noted historical work, *The Winning of the West*." [101] As he mulled over the campaign, he added to Eleanor, "I hope to God I don't grow reactionary with advancing years." [102]

It is not surprising that Roosevelt thus chose to interpret the election as a triumph of Wilson's liberal domestic issues. So far as the contest involved foreign policy, while Roosevelt publicly supported Wilson he must have privately preferred Hughes. He had already come to the conclusion, just when is uncertain, that the United States must fight Germany. Daniels in after years set the time about six months before the American entrance, sometime in the fall of 1916. More than once Roosevelt came into the Secretary's office and exclaimed, "We've got to get into this war." * Each time Daniels fervently replied, "I hope not." [104]

* During these years, the Roosevelts continued to see much of the British and French ambassadors, and could not have failed to absorb a good bit of their viewpoint. Mrs. Charles Hamlin noted in her diary that at a dinner in December,

In public, Roosevelt whenever necessary came to the defense of Wilson's foreign policy. In October, 1915, he declared that the Administration in its first two years had faced more dangers and difficulties than any other Administration since the Civil War, but without acting in a spectacular manner and without fireworks, had succeeded in keeping peace with honor.[105] In the campaign, Roosevelt, with marked success, called upon Clio, the muse of history, to serve as the handmaiden of politics. He had, of course, invoked her many times on behalf of a big Navy, but now she must serve to defend Wilson's middle-of-the-road foreign policies. It was a successful tactic, and in time became one of his favorite devices, even though in 1916 he used it on behalf of a cause to which he had not given his heart: He read to his audiences a stinging attack upon W—— for refusing to enter a European war. Then he explained that W—— in this instance stood for Washington, not Wilson; that the author was Tom Paine; and the occasion, the first President's insistence upon neutrality during the war between England and France.[106]

If an appeal to history could thus serve on the hustings, could it not also help convince a President who was also a scholar of history that his course of action was too slow, that the time for neutrality might well be past? Wilson was inactive at the end of 1916 while his final efforts to bring about a negotiated peace were pending, and friends complained to Colonel House that the President lacked punch, and seemed to favor "peace at almost any price" while things were drifting in "an aimless sort of way." [107] At this precise psychological moment, while Wilson was working upon an appeal to the people of the warring nations for a "peace without victory," a peace to be maintained through a world system of collective security, Roosevelt sent this historian-President an original memorandum in the hand of James Monroe, written in 1814, after the United States had given up her long struggle for neutrality and entered the Napoleonic wars. He suggested Wilson might like to have it because "it is in many ways so interestingly parallel to events of the day." * In this manner he was able

---

1916, she seated the Roosevelts on either side of the Spring-Rices, "so everyone was happy as they were great friends." The conversation centered on the war: "The Ambassador was a bit impatient about our seeming slowness to get into the fight." [103]

* In a covering note, Roosevelt remarked, "I came across the enclosed memorandum while going over some papers I acquired many years ago." President Wilson replied, "It was certainly most generous of you to send me the Monroe manuscript. It is unusually interesting and I shall value it highly." [108]

to advocate to the President a policy he would never have dared express in his own words, for in part Monroe's memorandum read:

> A war in Europe, to which Great Britain with her floating thunder, and other maritime powers, are always parties, has long been found to spread its calamities into their remotest regions. Even the U. S., just and pacific as their policy is, have not been able to avoid the alternative of either submitting to the most destructive and ignominious wrongs from European Belligerents, or of resisting them by an appeal to the sword: or to speak more properly, no other choice has been left to them but the time of making the appeal; it being evident that a submission too long protracted, would have no other effect than to encourage and accumulate aggressions, untill they should become altogether intolerable; and untill the loss of honor being added to the other losses, redress by the sword itself would be rendered more slow and difficult.[109]

CHAPTER XVI

Progressivism by the Sword

One of my jobs was to look after a couple little republics that our navy is running.

— FDR, *cited in Helena, Montana,* Independent, *August 19, 1920.*

I think it was a certain Queen of England who said that after her death "Calais" would be found written on her heart. When I die, I think that "Haiti" is going to be written on my heart, because for all these years I have had the most intense interest in the Republic of Haiti, and the development of its people in a way that will never mean exploitation by any other nation.

— FDR, *October 14, 1943.*

PRESIDENT Wilson, in January, 1917, was trying to face up to a progressive dilemma: should he resort to the frightfulness of war in a gamble to try to bring great and lasting benefits to mankind? Would the idealistic end justify the martial means? That was the question. Upon the principle itself – that overseas armed intervention could logically go hand in hand with progressivism – he had long since come to act in conformity with that warrior at Armageddon, Theodore Roosevelt. Repeatedly President Wilson and Secretaries Bryan and Daniels had accepted in practice the concept of the "white man's burden": that the United States should use force to bring the benefits of progressivism to backward countries to the south. Of course this, unlike the beckoning European crusade, involved limited, fairly bloodless interventions.

As for Franklin D. Roosevelt, he had repeatedly demonstrated his enthusiasm for this dramatic employment of violence to achieve presumably democratic aims. Although he did little to mold the basic policies, he gave impatient shoves here and there, and was quick to follow when Wilson, in his scholarly, idealistic fashion, cast aside the discredited materialism of "Dollar Diplomacy," to proclaim as his objective "the development of constitutional liberty in the world." When Wilson at the end of 1913 emphasized that "the United States will never again seek one additional foot of territory by conquest," he by no means heralded a new isolationism. In order to be democratic, these areas must be prosperous; American investment could promote prosperity. While Wilson opposed the extortion of unfair concessions and high interest rates, he wished American businessmen to be active abroad in a gentlemanly fashion.[1] Of course, in order to support either safe investments or democracy, areas also must be stable; Wilson's actions as well as his speeches seemed to aim at bringing law and order to turbulent small nations to the south, if necessary at bayonet point. Apparently he felt that, once dictators and outlaws were put down, then American policing, sanitation, and education would cause orderly democratic processes to develop. As a tacit corollary, American opportunities for honorable trade and investment would expand in this orderly atmosphere. But the basic aim, whether for the benefit of investments or for defense, was to develop greater stability in the Caribbean.[2]

Roosevelt as a young progressive wholeheartedly accepted this viewpoint. To him the American exploits in Panama and the Philippines had meant the bringing of modern technology and medicine to dark corners of the earth. Whether the agent was the government or a businessman, Roosevelt was equally ready to applaud. Goethals, the Army engineer in Panama, was a hero of his, but he also looked with favor upon Doheny,* the oil magnate in Mexico.[4] His fondness for martial display made him less sensitive to the unsavory side of armed intervention than was his conscientious chief, Daniels. "You know that the things we were forced to do in Haiti were a bitter pill to me," Daniels once reminded Roosevelt, "for I have always hated any foreign policy that even hinted of imperialistic control." Roosevelt's friend, Franklin Lane, knowing Daniels's queasiness, would rise at Cabinet meetings, and with mock seriousness proclaim, "Hail the King of Haiti." [5] Roosevelt would have liked to be the butt of this gibe.

Through his broad background, Roosevelt from the beginning of his sojourn in Washington was keenly interested in international affairs. His friendships in diplomatic and State Department circles continued to flourish. Out of them came frequent suggestions across

*One of the largest American investors in Mexico, Edward L. Doheny, later of Teapot Dome notoriety, was the second largest contributor to the Democratic campaign fund in 1916, and did much to help swing the critical state of California to Wilson.[3]

the dinner table, or in correspondence. Roosevelt's dealings with the State Department were usually in this manner, rather than through regular channels, and he received his impressions directly and forcefully.*

He took over with pleasure whatever minor diplomatic tasks came his way, whether it were sending the body of a Venezuelan Minister back to La Guayra on a battleship,[8] or greeting a statesman from Brazil. "I remember very well," he recounted to Daniels, "your sending me on the *Mayflower* to Hampton Roads with Mr. Bryan and Elihu Root to meet Senhor Lauro Muller, the Foreign Secretary of Brazil, and how I spent one horrible evening translating Doctor Muller's French and German with great difficulty to Mr. Bryan and Senator Root." [9]

In 1915 when a dispute arose between the Argentine Naval Commission and the Fore River Shipbuilding Corporation, which was just finishing the battleship *Moreno*, it was Roosevelt who conducted delicate negotiations to iron things out. The American shipyard had received the contract to build the *Moreno* only after vigorous competition with European firms; it had won out largely through the active assistance of the State and Navy Departments.[10] Subsequently it sublet the construction to the New York Shipyard, which by the beginning of 1915 had finished the vessel.[11] The Argentine Navy sent two transports of sailors to Philadelphia to take over the ship, but because of a dispute over charges for alterations, could not obtain delivery.[12] Roosevelt conferred with the Argentine naval officers, the ambassador, and the shipbuilders. He was determined to cut the red tape in a hurry, and came quickly to the conclusion that whatever the sum

* For example, FDR discussed Latin American and Haitian affairs with Boaz W. Long, Minister to Salvador. Long "used to run across from Mr. Bryan's department of State to Mr. Daniels' department of the Navy to have little conferences" with FDR.[6] From the Secretary of the Legation at Santo Domingo, John Campbell White, Harvard '07, he received a rather typical communication in September, 1914:

> MY DEAR FRANKLIN:
>
> I am writing this line . . . in the hopes of persuading you to use your influence in Cabinet Councils in favor of landing troops here, & keeping them for a while. There are too many people who want to hold office in this country & live off the country. When they do not get what they want they start a revolution. American intervention is always in the offing, but they have never yet had a dose of it on shore & think it is never coming. Now is a fine opportunity. The northern portion of the country is in a state of anarchy, & the front page of the home papers is taken up with war news.[7]

which Argentina should pay for the vessel, the contract called for expeditious delivery and subsequent settlement through arbitration.[13] The main dispute holding up delivery seemed to be between the two shipyards. Behind the New York yard was its owner, Bethlehem Steel; therefore Roosevelt concentrated upon Charles Schwab of Bethlehem Steel, and tried unsuccessfully to bring Andrew Mellon into the conferences.[14]

Within a few days, Roosevelt brought about an amicable settlement. The Argentine Navy took possession of the *Moreno*, and President Wilson dined aboard it before it headed south to Buenos Aires.[15] In urging a policy of moderation upon Schwab, Roosevelt bluntly stated his own and the Navy's policy in the realm of foreign trade:

"You will, of course, recognize the interest that this Government has in the building of both the *Rivadavia* and the *Moreno*, not only because this Government took such an active part in obtaining the contracts, but also because of its desire to see that the Argentine Government shall receive the ships. . . . It is probably no secret to you that the Argentine Government has been thoroughly dissatisfied over the seizure of a number of its ships and munitions of war being constructed in Europe at the time of the outbreak of war last Summer, and if the Argentine Government can be made to feel secure in this country I have no doubt that there will be many opportunities given us for increased business." [16]

Battleship diplomacy of this sort was of minor interest to Roosevelt. Like his "Uncle Ted," he was more concerned over the threat to United States defense implicit in the weak Caribbean republics. They would be easy for Europe to dominate; unfriendly nations might use them as bases against the United States. Part of the answer lay in acquiring territory in the area, and then building strong bases. When Admiral Fiske wrote a memorandum in December, 1913, recommending that the Navy obtain Central American bases on the Gulf of Fonseca and the Corn Islands, Roosevelt as Acting Secretary endorsed the memorandum over to the General Board for comment. Admiral Dewey and the Board added their approval, and put into motion the machinery to obtain the areas.* Roosevelt kept the document as a souvenir.[18]

* In the fall of 1919, FDR as Acting Secretary sent a formal letter to the Secretary of State, suggesting that the United States take possession of another small bit of land in the Caribbean, Swan Island off the coast of Honduras, which had been continuously occupied by American citizens since its discovery in the

Roosevelt wished the United States to build one or more powerful bases in the Caribbean. He warned the House Naval Affairs Committee in 1916 that in case of war an enemy would try to strike in the area; therefore it must be protected. He abandoned his early advocacy of Guantánamo, Cuba, because it would be difficult to defend from land. St. Thomas in the Danish West Indies would be advantageous because it was almost hurricane-proof, and Samaná Bay on the east coast of Santo Domingo was also excellent, but he particularly favored a small island off the coast of Puerto Rico, Culebra, which he envisaged as a potential Helgoland.[19]

A little later, the United States acquired the Danish West Indies, which it renamed the Virgin Islands. Roosevelt was pleased; he was planning a Caribbean trip at the time, and hoped he could be in St. Thomas on the day of transfer so that he could be the first to raise the United States flag over the new possession.[20] He commented to Stephen Bonsal, author of *The American Mediterranean*, "Incidentally, we have simply got to control those islands as a whole – the sooner the better – The next step is to purchase the Dutch interests!"[21]

In his attitude toward subject peoples, Roosevelt's feelings were more progressive than materialistic. He believed in paternalistic imperialism, and wished to provide the colonials with the best possible care. He first demonstrated this in 1914, when problems concerning Samoa came to his attention. The question arose whether the Navy Department could properly establish dispensaries for the medical care of Samoans. Roosevelt answered emphatically, "Yes" – since the Navy controlled all governmental functions there, "the responsibility for the welfare of the inhabitants necessarily rests primarily on this Department. If Hookworm and Tuberculosis are prevalent and the establishment of dispensaries would improve conditions . . . it is the duty of the Department to take favorable action."[22]

In 1915 when a dispute arose concerning private business in Samoa,

---

1840's. It might be of value as the location for a radio station. He added an informal covering letter suggesting that this be done quietly in order not to stir up controversy: "I have wondered whether it would not be possible to have a Naval vessel go in there, hoist the flag formally, put a few stores or other material ashore and appoint the radio man of the United Fruit Company as Naval Custodian. Then, at some future date several years hence, we could mention the Islands in some way in a Naval Appropriation Bill in the usual course of things. In other words, I fear that although no other nation has apparently claimed the sovereignty over the Islands, still our formal assumption of such sovereignty at this time might be criticized, and might stir up protests from Central American countries or a discussion in Congress."[17]

Roosevelt declared that the territory was so small and could support so little beyond the native population that it could "never become a field for American colonization or business enterprise." The reason for annexing it was to acquire a naval base, and defense matters were paramount. The government should endeavor to make the living conditions of the Samoans as good as possible, and to "prevent the natives from being robbed by traders of any nationality." In addition the Navy Department must [23] "see that the Governor is at all times a man of discretion and common sense." *

From the argument that the United States must acquire possessions for its own national defense, Roosevelt moved with questionable logic to the stand that the United States must arm to defend its possessions. This was essential, he asserted, to prevent an aggressor from interfering with "the great humanitarian work almost completed at Panama, done with our money for the benefit of all mankind." This also applied to "Hawaii and Porto Rico and . . . the countries of Central and South America which we have regarded as cherishing the same ideals of liberty as we." [25]

It was this sort of thinking that led Roosevelt to follow with pride and enthusiasm the American occupation of Haiti: for here was a classic example of a mismanaged little nation, where armed intervention, in theory, should have brought democracy and prosperity. As he stated in 1922, in a vigorous defense of the intervention: "The story of Hayti prior to the landing of American Marines in 1915 is a story of almost unbelievable butchery and barbarism, which, if told in its entirety, would shock every person in the civilized world. . . . Presidents and Emperors succeeded each other in rapid succession. Their going was usually accomplished by murder and the slaughter of thousands. The result was that when 1915 came the inhabitants of Hayti, taken as a mass, were little more than primitive savages, living in mud and wattle huts, skillfully concealed in the underbrush. This was true of over 95% of the population. . . . Hayti was no more a Republic in our accepted sense of the term, than were the principalities of India, before the advent of the British." [26]

* Sometimes the Navy officers in command at Samoa had to deal with problems for which their Annapolis training had given them little or no preparation. A classic example was Regulation No. 6 of Commander C. B. T. Moore USN, Governor of Samoa, July 17, 1907, abolishing a "heathen and barbarous" marriage custom, "commonly known as 'Faamasei'au,'" or breaking of the hymen by other than the groom. The fathers of the brides, who had auctioned off the privilege, were furious that the Navy interfered.[24]

As revolution succeeded revolution with scarcely a letup, the State and Navy Departments watched events carefully. No American lives were in jeopardy, for the Haitians scrupulously avoided injuring whites; American property and investments were insignificant in value. If there had been any threat of German intervention, that ended with the outbreak of the First World War, when the British kept the German Fleet corralled in the North Sea. Nevertheless, the strategic reason was doubtless paramount. The European war might end at any time and leave the Germans free to take over Môle-Saint-Nicolas,[27] the potential area for a base.*

At the request of Secretary of State Bryan, Roosevelt, as Acting Secretary in July, 1914, had sent seven hundred Marines to Guantánamo, only a day's sail from Haiti. He publicly announced that they were there in order to be available "in case any emergency should arise which would make it advisable for them to be on hand for the protection of life and property." [29] The commanders prepared plans for the occupation of Port-au-Prince and Cap Haitien,[30] but intervention did not take place until a particularly barbarous revolutionary outbreak in July, 1915. Roosevelt was at Campobello at the time, and subsequently lamented, "It is certainly a curious coincidence that as soon as I go away we seem to land marines somewhere." [31]

Roosevelt took an intense interest in the Marine occupation. At first it was limited, and the State Department policy not clear,[32] but soon Marines took over the entire country. The educated Haitian mulattoes who formed the elite at Port-au-Prince seemed at first to favor the landings. But they became hostile when "friendly officials," subservient to the United States, ratified a treaty reducing Haiti to the status of a protectorate.

Serious problems arose concerning the governing of the country. Technically, it was under a Haitian president and assembly; actually, the Marines ran a Garde d'Haïti or Gendarmerie which maintained order, and began to take over the building of roads and other public works.

Since delicate policy matters were not easy to decide from Washington, Daniels decided to send Roosevelt on a visit of inspection. The Assistant Secretary was delighted to go, and made the trip serve in-

* Daniels commented to FDR in 1933: "The danger of that pivotal country, so near our shores, falling into the control of some European nation, added to the business of assassinating presidents, made it imperative for us to take the course followed." [28]

cidentally as a midwinter vacation. He had General Littleton W. T. Waller map for him the most scenic route through Haiti and Santo Domingo,[33] and invited several friends to accompany him on his tour of what he called the "Darkest Africa of the West Indies." [34] He left Washington on January 21, 1917, in a driving snowstorm, accompanied by Major General George Barnett of the Marine Corps, John A. McIlhenny, Chairman of the Civil Service Commission, and his Harvard chum, Livingston Davis. They traversed Cuba en route, and at Havana George Marvin, a former Groton master, and an editor of *World's Work*, joined them.[35]

In Cuba, Roosevelt observed the functioning of an American protectorate of much longer standing than Haiti, and became convinced that excellent improvement was possible under the tutelage of the United States. "Silk hatted, frock coated, etc.," he called upon President Mario García Menocal, and came away an enthusiast for "orderly progress": "I had a good talk with him & like him. He is distinctly the gentleman, – business man, – orderly progress type & no opponent has questioned his honesty. . . . Cuba it seems to me needs a continuation of 'orderly progress' & not of radicalism for some time to come. There is no doubt that in the essentials which the U. S. insists on – sanitation, order, finance –, Cuba has lived up to her agreement." [36]

Ironically, it was only a few days later that a smoldering revolution flared up. The Wilson Administration blamed the revolt on German agents and sent troops which, though they did not establish military government, remained in Cuba until 1922.

From Havana, the party went by rail to Santiago * and boarded a destroyer. The next morning, January 26, they awoke in the Bay of Port-au-Prince.[38] "I have never been in Naples," Roosevelt later commented, "but this Bay with its wonderful setting must be the equal of anything in Italy." [39]

"Presently the whole Atlantic fleet came into view," wrote Davis, "silhouetted against a little white town nestling on the shores of the bay with huge bowl-shaped mountains rising behind it." [40] The

* "I thought again of the gallant dash to sea of Cervera's Fleet in 1898 and I felt again in view of the hopeless right turn which he made along the Coast, he would have been far better off if his four cruisers and two torpedo boats had headed directly out to sea and into the middle of the American Fleet. He might easily have caused such confusion among ships which had held the same position for many weeks that he might have seriously wounded several of our ships before he lost his own." [37]

fifty vessels were decked out with admirals' flags and gay bunting. As Roosevelt's destroyer passed through the lanes of ships, he stood on the bridge, graceful and dignified, taking the salutes. After Admiral Mayo, the commander in chief, came aboard to pay his ceremonial call, Roosevelt and his party went ashore in the admiral's barge – dressed in cutaways and tall hats, although the heat was already stifling.[41] Roosevelt inimitably recorded what ensued:

> When we landed at the end of the long pier, we were met by a number of gentlemen in frock coats and silk hats. I assumed, erroneously, that they were the Mayor of Port au Prince and representatives of President D'Artignave. As they stepped forward, with a scroll, I bowed and delivered the speech I had intended as my official address as Assistant Secretary of the Navy. . . . I had translated [it], with a good deal of difficulty, into French and delivered it thus.
>
> We all entered automobiles and to the shore end of the wharf we drove, where we were met by another delegation. This time it was the Mayor and as I had but one speech, I redelivered it again, explaining to the amusement of all, that I had prepared only one speech in French and was therefore repeating it.
>
> Then to the Palace of the President, where we were ushered upstairs into a red plush and gold drawing room where we met the President and his Cabinet, and I made the same speech for the third time.

The speech was conventional enough, and ended with a piece of verbal sleight-of-hand that attempted to make forceful occupation compatible with sovereignty:

> I am particularly glad that I can be here when the American fleet is paying you a visit of courtesy. . . . They greatly appreciate your expressions of goodwill and will carry home many of the most delightful feelings toward the sovereign people of Haiti.[42]

Through his use of French, his strict observance of protocol, and his obliviousness to the color line, Roosevelt made himself decidedly popular with the Haitian elite.* He ignored the blunt force represented

* George Marvin served Roosevelt in a particularly useful capacity because he had been in Haiti twice before. He helped Roosevelt prepare talks, both formal and informal, in French, for the many occasions when he spoke, and "supplied him with information which prevented any possible *faux pas* with extremely sensitive colored 'Democrats,' as well as with anecdotes which implied

by the Atlantic Fleet and the Marine Corps, which underscored the actuality that while he was present, he was the real master of Haiti. Roosevelt gravely maintained the fiction that President Dartiguenave was his superior. When the President of Haiti started to climb into his official limousine ahead of the United States Assistant Secretary of the Navy, Smedley Butler, Major General and Commandant of the Haitian Gendarmerie, seized President Dartiguenave's coat collar and started to pull him back, but Roosevelt stepped aside and insisted that the Haitian should take precedence.[44]

Much as Roosevelt relished the parties and protocol of the Haitian capital, he enjoyed still more what followed. After three or four days, he started at the head of a large group on an inspection trip through the mountains toward Cap Haitien to the north. It was in fact a small military expedition, for there was some possibility of attack by Haitians of the sort who had always participated in revolutions – the *cacos*, or bandits, who sporadically fought the Marines. The group included not only General Cole, Commandant of the Marines in Haiti, and General Butler, but also about one hundred and fifty Marines, fifty Gendarmes, and fifty pack animals. On the first day they followed a solidly built old French road, not suitable for automobiles, but in good enough shape for Roosevelt to order Butler to repair it before he began construction of a new modern highway. They spent the first night on the Plaine d'Artibonite: "On looking down at it from the top of the mountain, somebody said that it contained half a million people. There was no sign of habitations or highways or cultivated land – only an occasional curl of smoke rising from the jungle. Our road had become a trail and the 200 men in the party had to proceed single file. . . . The night was comfortable, though we heard rifle shots from the hills and an occasional bullet going by overhead." [45]

The next day the party covered forty miles. Roosevelt ordered it to start at six in the morning, and called a halt for a rest after each two-hour interval. By night they were at Hinche, in the heart of the *caco* area, and again had to take precautions. The slight element of danger (Hinche was to be the center of subsequent *caco* uprisings) lent a pleasurable excitement to the trip.

On the final day, Roosevelt climbed to the top of a hill to inspect

---

a familiarity with Haitian customs and Haitian history." [43] This was one of the early occasions when Roosevelt made deft use of a technique which helped give him the reputation, while he was President, for being something of a wizard – his knowledge was so amazing.

Fort Rivière, which Smedley Butler and twenty-four Marines had captured from the *cacos* a few months before. Butler and about eighteen Marines had crawled up through a drain into the courtyard of the Fort, where they surprised about three hundred *cacos*. Roosevelt proudly recorded the details, which bore a strong resemblance to Theodore Roosevelt's war reminiscences, or the reporting of Winston Churchill. Butler was about to crawl into the drain when an old sergeant said to him:

> "Sorry, Sir, I was in the Marines before you were and this is my privilege." Butler recognized his right and the Sergeant crawled through first.
>
> On coming to the end within the courtyard, he saw the shadows of the legs of two cacos armed with machettes guarding the hole. He took off his hat, put it on the end of his revolver, pushed it through, felt the two machettes descend on it, and jumped forward into daylight. With a right and a left he got both cacos, stood up and dropped two or three others while his companions, headed by Smedley Butler, got through and onto their feet. Then ensued a killing, the news of which put down all insurrections we hope for all time to come. There were about 300 cacos within the wall and Butler and his 18 companions killed over 200 of them, others jumping over the wall and falling prisoners to the rest of the force of Marines which encircled the mountain.
>
> I was so much impressed by personal inspection of the scene of the exploit that I awarded the Medal of Honor to the Marine Sergeant and to Butler.[46]

With his inspection of the bloody scene, Roosevelt combined much good-natured camaraderie and more conventional sight-seeing. He shot a dove, had himself photographed with it, and upon his return to Washington passed off the picture as one of the "Great Haitian Shrink Bird," which when shot would shrink away to nothing unless immersed immediately in boiling water. Roosevelt claimed that the one he shot was three or four feet from wing to wing, but was down to pigeon-size before he could douse it. He also made his friend Livingston Davis * the butt of several mild jokes. One night "we all went for a swim in the creek, just outside the town. We were having a wonderful swim in a state of nature when, on looking up, we found

* After their return, Davis presented FDR with a wrist watch. FDR commented, "Two years ago I should have considered [it] impossible unless I put on petticoats, but customs change and as long as he men like you and the officers in Haiti can wear them I guess I can too."[47]

that the entire female population was lining the banks. They had never seen a white man in this condition before and seemed to take it quite calmly. We came out, dried off, and dressed – all except Davis, who insisted on sending for his bathing suit before coming out." [48]

By the time the party reached the coast, most of its members were exhausted. "It was a tough ride," Marvin recalled, "tropic heat, rough trails. . . . We forded rivers, climbed elevations, slept *al fresco.*" But Roosevelt, who was "the life of the pilgrimage" was always gay and animated, enormously interested in all he saw ". . . and he never got tired." [49] Few in the party were enthusiastic when he announced his intention of climbing a four-thousand foot peak to see the citadel of King Christophe, and he was merciful enough to call for volunteers. "Two thirds of the party had sense enough to refuse," Henry Latrobe Roosevelt once said. "I was one of the dumbbell third, and while Frank came down as fresh as he started, the rest of us staggered to bed." [50] To Roosevelt it was a climax of romantic adventure.* He gathered legends about Christophe from several old Haitians – how Christophe had once marched a company of troops over the side of a precipice, and in the end shot his wife with a silver bullet and himself with a gold one.

In this area of fascinating ruins and striking scenery, Roosevelt envisaged possibilities for commercial development. "On our descent, we stopped at Sans Souci and I made up my mind that here was the spot for a lovely resort, gardens, trails and a beach not far away. Most of the old Palace could easily be put back and the guests would use Fort Rivière with its cool nights for living purposes." [52]

Throughout his stay in Haiti, Roosevelt conversed earnestly and long with the Marine officials, the American minister, Arthur Bailly Blanchard, President Dartiguenave, and several members of his government. On his trip to Cap Haitien, he talked with local officials, some of whom opposed Dartiguenave, and with parish priests.[53] He even came into some slight contact with the common people: it was a favorite remark of his that a Haitian woman using an old sock brewed him the best coffee he ever tasted.[54]

From all these people, "we heard no complaints," General Barnett stated in 1920, "but on the contrary heard many reports which indicated that conditions in Haiti were better than they had been for a

* On his way back from Casablanca in 1943, FDR ate a birthday luncheon while his airplane was over Haiti. He had the pilot circle low so he could point out the route he had followed in 1917.[51]

very great many years." [55] Considering the nature of the Marine occupation, this was not surprising. All the Americans in Haiti to whom Roosevelt talked were wholeheartedly in favor of continued and greater intervention; [56] most of the Haitians were of the segment of the elite who were benefiting from it. In addition, Roosevelt could see the immediate economic and sanitary improvement. "In riding across the Island . . . through Mirebalais, Hinche, Pignon, St. Raphael, Dondou, and Milot, we found every one of these towns apparently possessed by the clean-up, paint-up idea," Marvin declared in a magazine article which Roosevelt read and approved before publication.[57]

Since Roosevelt saw in Haiti what the Marines wished him to see, his preconceptions were almost completely borne out. He traversed the island in a holiday mood, and apparently ignored the seamy side of the occupation: the mutterings of discontent which flared up, before the end of 1918, into the large and dangerous Charlemagne Peralte rebellion. This revolt came about largely as a result of Butler's road-building program, which Roosevelt so heartily endorsed. Butler built many miles of highway in a very short time at remarkably little cost, since the Haitian government applied the ancient French custom of the *corvée*, or forced road work. The local authorities assembled gangs of Haitians, took them miles from their families, and worked them for long periods of time for little or no money. Roosevelt's party encountered at least one such gang on their way across the mountains. Roosevelt made no note of it, but Davis wrote, "During the wait for lunch, we encountered some one hundred natives working out their taxes on the trail who gave a dance and song in our honor." [58] At Christmas time when word came that a road was open to Cap Haitien, Roosevelt radioed,[59] "Well done." *

In Cap Haitien, where Roosevelt reviewed the Marines and Gendarmerie,[61] he received four petitions asking for amelioration of Marine justice. Several of these asked for the release from prison of the mistress of a local barkeeper. The man had killed an American in a brawl and fled to the interior; since September, his mistress had

* Butler, delighted, replied, "Now, we realize that our work is really attracting some attention and are consequently much happier. The Gendarmerie built 21 miles of roads in five weeks and five days, through the worst tropical wilderness I have ever seen; a road over which I ran my heavy Stutz touring car, in the rainy season, without exterior help. . . . This road to date has cost not over $250.00 a mile. . . . It would not do to ask too many questions as to how we accomplished this work, it is enough to say, that the people of Haiti are satisfied and pleased, everyone from the President down." [60]

been imprisoned without interrogation or charge, as a hostage for his return.[62] Roosevelt preserved the petitions, but there is no evidence that he took any action upon them, or even took them seriously.[63]

Roosevelt's unqualified endorsement of the work of the Marines in Haiti gave no hint that there was sufficient discontent to cause an uprising. He asserted that professional bandits, of necessity, had turned to less productive but more honorable occupations; and for the first time in Haitian history, planters were able to harvest and market their crops without molestation. A President was "elected" without a shot being fired, and a start was made toward reorganizing the financial system. He was reported as saying "that after going through the country he felt sure that ninety-nine per cent of the inhabitants were not only satisfied with what has been done for them by the United States but that they would look with terror on an abandonment by this country of its interest in their welfare."

The government in Washington was gratified by the success of the occupation, though it continued to fear that German agents might yet stir up trouble.[64]

In Washington, Roosevelt worked during the next two years to further the Marine policies. He informally kept in communication with his cousin Colonel Henry Roosevelt, with Butler, and with McIlhenny, who left the Civil Service Commission to take charge of Haitian finances. When Butler complained indirectly about an administrative snarl, Roosevelt declared that he favored abolishing the complicated "threefold form of government" which left Haitians the fiction of self-government, and replacing it with an open occupation like that of Santo Domingo, with a Marine officer as military governor. This policy ultimately went into effect, but not until the Harding Administration, and obviously through no influence of Roosevelt's.[65]

Much the same was true of the drafting of the highly controversial American-inspired Constitution of Haiti, which some critics have called the "Roosevelt Constitution." The main difference between this and numerous earlier constitutions was a provision that foreigners could own land.[66] This alarmed Haitians, who feared a return to a system of large plantations and landless laborers; it seemed important to the Administration as a means of encouraging capital investment in Haiti and thus bringing economic stability.* Roosevelt, years later,

* Part of the furor over the highly unpopular Constitution grew out of its artistic Marine-sponsored ratification, 69,377 to 355. Even the Commandant of

denied the charge that he had been persuaded by Roger L. Farnham, in charge of Haitian interests of the National City Bank, to draft or approve this provision. On the occasions when he saw Farnham he did not discuss the Haitian Constitution, he asserted. "I do not think that I ever saw the Constitution until somebody came around to see me from the State Department to ask my opinion about some wholly minor questions." [68] In truth, Roosevelt was not the father of the Haitian Constitution; but then, no one would ever have said he was if he had not expansively given himself the credit for it during the 1920 campaign.

After the adoption of the Haitian Constitution, Roosevelt continued to toy with schemes for investments in Haiti which would involve development of the Île de la Gonâve,[69] or the establishment of variety stores.[70] In addition, he was happy to do small favors for friends. In 1919, on behalf of a friend in Lee, Higginson and Company, he radioed the military governor to inquire the rate of issue and market price of Dominican Republic bonds,[71] and he gave letters of introduction to Hamilton Fish, Jr., who visited Haiti. Fish returned to urge further encouragement of American investors and the sending of additional Marines to wipe out bandits.[72]

In the spring of 1919, Peralte's *caco* bands became so bold that they raided even into the area near Port-au-Prince. When the Haitian Minister in Washington complained to the State Department that the fault lay in large part with the Gendarmerie,[73] the sympathetic State Department forwarded the complaint to Roosevelt, with the suggestion that the seventy-four Marines in the Gendarmerie were insufficient; the number should be markedly increased.[74] Roosevelt as Acting Secretary had already complied with a State Department request to order four hundred additional Marines to Haiti,[75] but he resented insinuations that improper Marine management of the Gendarmerie was responsible for the revolt. He cabled to McIlhenny a confidential request for information; McIlhenny confirmed State Department charges that there had been serious friction and bad feeling between the Gendarmerie and other American officials, but declared that the current Commandant of the Gendarmerie had brought the trouble to an end. Further, the Marines had smashed the largest of the bandit bands, and

---

the Gendarmerie, General John H. Russell, felt that this result warranted some explanation, and he sent a nine-point memorandum to Washington, explaining how this could occur without the Marines influencing the result! [67]

were engaged in the tedious but sure process of eliminating the remnants.[76]

McIlhenny's reassuring report pleased Roosevelt, since it gave him the opportunity to disparage the State Department complaints: "The State Department people seemed to be raising a good deal of Cain generally about the situation in Haiti and Santo Domingo, and seemed to have the impression that things were going badly under the Navy and Marine Corps in both republics. I do not know what was back of all the smoke, but my own guess has been that some people are causing trouble for purely personal reasons, and that other people are trying to change the present status into a purely military or purely civil government."[77] Of course, Roosevelt himself only two years before had favored a purely military government.

In May, 1919, Roosevelt answered criticism of the Dominican administration by sending his friend Polk, the Acting Secretary of State, excerpts from the Military Governor's quarterly report which emphasized that order was being maintained and the Guardia Nacional (comparable to the Gendarmerie) was efficient. Polk was so impressed that he asked Roosevelt if the Navy Department could not withdraw the Marines and leave the policing of Santo Domingo entirely to the Guardia, in order to remove "as much as possible a seeming show of force in our administration of Dominican affairs." Roosevelt sent the query through channels to the Military Governor; the reply was favorable, and in 1924 the Marines left.[78]

Here was a hint of the future – of the Good Neighbor method of stabilization. Ultimately – but in the case of Haiti not until 1934 – the United States built in each country a constabulary so strong and efficient that without Marine aid it could maintain order and put down revolutions. Unfortunately, whoever controlled the police force thus controlled the country. Sometimes, as in the case of Trujillo in the Dominican Republic, this did not lead to democracy.

CHAPTER XVII

On the Brink of War

> [I] really [have] no more idea than an outsider as to whether the situation is going to end in hostilities soon, in the future, or not at all. . . . Personally I believe things are very ominous — or shall I say hopeful?
>
> — FDR TO WILLIAM GORHAM RICE, *March 7, 1917.*

THE war in Europe must have seemed very remote to Roosevelt on the evening of February 3, 1917. He was dining in the flower-filled courtyard of a beautiful old palace in Santiago, Santo Domingo, as the guest of the Marine Commandant and his wife. It was a gala occasion. Near the end of the dinner, Roosevelt's orderly brought him a code message from Secretary Daniels; Roosevelt stepped outside and read, "Because of political situation please return to Washington at once. Am sending ship to meet you and party at Puerto Plata tomorrow evening."

"When I went back to the table," Roosevelt recalled,[1] "my face must have been rather long because Mrs. Kane [the Commandant's wife] asked me if I had had bad news. I told her that we would have to leave immediately . . . and I added that I did not know what had happened, but that the Secretary had said the recall was based on political conditions." *

Roosevelt's cryptic reply led everyone to assume that he had secret information, and that war was imminent.[3] The others knew that a crisis with Germany was in the making. On the afternoon of February 2, they had received news by radio that Germany had announced its intention to begin unrestricted submarine warfare.[4] Consequently,

* FDR wrote, undoubtedly facetiously, that when he said he was returning because of political conditions . . .

> Mrs. Kane looked at me in horror and said, "What can political conditions mean: It must be that Charles E. Hughes has led a revolution against President Wilson."
>
> I replied, "My dear lady, you have been in the tropics too long!" [2]

it was in a state of considerable excitement that he started back to the United States aboard the collier *Neptune*.* Later he vividly remembered the tension:

> No one knew anything for certain except that the German Ambassador in Washington, Count von Bernstorff, had been given his passports and it seemed probable that the United States and Germany were already at war.
>
> As we headed north through Caicos Island passage on our way to Hampton Roads no lights were showing, the guns were manned and there was complete air silence.
>
> Still without any definite knowledge of what had actually happened, we landed at Fortress Monroe on the morning of February 8th. The Colonel in command seemed utterly surprised, insisted that there was no war, that no special preparations were going on and that he had no orders from Washington to stand by.
>
> Late that afternoon we were back in Washington. I dashed to the Navy Department and found the same thing – no diplomatic relations with Germany broken off, no excitement, no preparations, no orders to the Fleet at Guantanamo to return to their home yards on the East Coast.[5]

In the weeks of inaction that followed, Roosevelt felt sadly let down. Early in March he commented to one of his traveling companions, "Does it not seem more or less of a joke that we made that wild dash north just one month ago?"[6]

The reason for the delay and inaction was easy to find, for the debate over whether or not the United States should declare war on Germany was not yet resolved. President Wilson, like his young subordinate Roosevelt, had come to feel that war was inevitable, and even desirable. Unlike Roosevelt, the President hesitated to take the fearful responsibility of starting it. When Wilson learned of the German declaration of unrestricted submarine activity, he exclaimed, "This means war,"[7] and a few weeks later explained, "From the very beginning I saw the end of this horrible thing; but I could not move faster than the great mass of our people would permit."[8]

Roosevelt, only thirty-five, impatient and far from reflective, came to appreciate the President's attitude only in retrospect, when he him-

* FDR was not in too much of a hurry to sort through a pile of confiscated arms and knives, in which he found a sword later identified by the Metropolitan Museum as a Spanish cavalier's sword of about 1510. It is now at the Roosevelt Library.

self carried heavy responsibility. Then one incident stuck in his mind so vividly that as late as 1939 he recounted it accurately. It may have served as a guide to his action during the autumn months of 1941, when the United States again was on the brink of war with Germany, and the mature Roosevelt, to the irritation of many of his advisers, would lead the country no further:[9]

"I was Acting Secretary of the Navy and it was the first week in March. . . . I went to see the President and I said, 'President Wilson, may I request your permission to bring the Fleet back from Guantanamo, to send it to the Navy Yards and have it cleaned and fitted out for war and be ready to take part in the War if we get in?' And the President said, 'I am very sorry, Mr. Roosevelt, I cannot allow it.' But I pleaded and he gave me no reason and said, 'No, I do not wish it brought north.' So, belonging to the Navy, I said, 'Aye, aye, sir,' and started to leave the room. He stopped me at the door and said, 'Come back.' He said, 'I am going to tell you something I cannot tell to the public.* I owe you an explanation. I don't want to do anything . . . by way of war preparations, that would allow the definitive historian in later days to say that the United States had committed an unfriendly act against the Central Powers.' "[11]

While Roosevelt was anxious to act, this was still a period of painful indecision for Wilson. He was of a more reflective temperament than the younger man,[12] and against his desire to destroy the German Empire and take a position of leadership in drawing up a just and lasting peace, he balanced the heavy price. He told Daniels, and at various times several others, what he feared that would be. Twenty years later, at the outbreak of the Second World War, Daniels cited this to Roosevelt, obviously not in Wilson's exact words but in keeping with his ideas.[13] The President had said:

> There are two reasons why I am determined to keep out if possible.
>
> The first is that I cannot bring myself to send into the terrible struggle the sons of anxious mothers, many of whom would never return home.
>
> The second is that if we enter this war, the great interests

* FDR did not embellish the anecdote in the two decades since he first told it. In 1919 he quoted Wilson as having said, "I want history to show not only that we have tried every diplomatic means to keep out of the war; to show that war has been forced upon us deliberately by Germany; but also that we have come into the court of history with clean hands." [10]

which control steel, oil, shipping, munition factories, mines, will of necessity become dominant factors, and when the war is over our government will be in their hands. We have been trying, and succeeding to a large extent, to unhorse government by privilege. If we go into this great war all we have gained will be lost and neither you nor I will live long enough to see our country wrested from the control of monopoly.[14]

There is no indication that Roosevelt either at the time or later reckoned the drastic cost of war or expected extreme reaction to ensue. During most of his career he felt that tides of public policy inevitably ebbed and flowed, and that after a few years of liberal reform, reaction followed, war or no war.

For Secretary Daniels the price, both in these matters and in lives, was horrible to contemplate. Wilson doubtless pointed this out to him because he was the member of the Cabinet most strongly opposed to entrance; with the growing group who were recommending war, Wilson discussed the positive gains. Throughout March, 1917, Wilson continued to weigh the two sides while the necessity of coming to a decision weighed heavily upon his mind. Roosevelt once acquired the diary of a White House supernumerary which portrays Wilson during these weeks as a profoundly troubled man, ill part of the time, personally irascible, keeping to himself and avoiding his routine duties, while vital papers piled high on his desk.[15] He was a soul-stricken Calvinistic Hamlet.*

Meanwhile, the conflict between the advocates of war and those of peace rent the entire nation, and extended into both the Cabinet and the Navy Department. In the Navy, Secretary Daniels was eager to apply Wilson's yardstick, and make no move which the Germans (or historians) could conceivably interpret as an act of aggression. His Chief of Naval Operations, Admiral Benson, a cautious, deliberate Georgian, loyally carried out his superior's wishes. Throughout the crisis, Daniels was still hoping against hope that war could be avoided. "If any man in official life ever faced the agony of a Gethsemane, I was the man in the first four months of 1917," he once wrote. "From the beginning of the war in Europe, I had resisted every influence that was at work to carry the United States into the war." [17] The Secretary

* There is a hint of the extent to which Wilson viewed this as a moral question in his retort to Burleson who asserted in the cabinet meeting of March 20 that unless the President called Congress the people would force action: "I do not care for popular demand. I want to do right, whether popular or not." [16]

seems never to have rid himself of the feeling that vigorous armament preparations would lead in the direction of war, and during February and March predicated his policies on the assumption that, somehow, the United States would be able to remain at peace. While he continued to press long-range naval building, which would make the fleet more powerful three or six years hence, he blocked as far as possible any moves dictated by the likelihood of immediate American entrance into the war.

Intense criticism of Daniels, both at this time and shortly after the war, came from Roosevelt and those naval officers who, whether or not they favored war, considered it inevitable. They felt that the Navy should put itself into fighting shape, both in men and ships, before the declaration of war, so that when it came America could immediately strike a decisive blow on the seas. Although Daniels throughout the neutrality period was the butt of the militants, a majority of Democrats wanted to keep out of war, and as late as November, 1916, the American voters by a slender margin seemed to prefer Wilson for that reason. It would have been difficult to prove to them, then, that Daniels's dogged refusal to put the Navy on a war footing was not the best means to maintain peace. Had the nation not entered the war, he might well have been hailed as a wise and farseeing statesman.

The fact that the United States did enter the war vindicated Roosevelt and the militants in the eyes of the public, and appreciably raised Roosevelt's political stock. Once again he was on the winning side.

Those who favored war took the offensive during the crisis, and redoubled their aggressive, vociferous tactics. It was logical for them to heap praise upon Roosevelt as a means of deprecating Daniels and Wilson. Within the Republican ranks in the East, the Old Guard was dominant and the Progressives either inconsequential, or, like Theodore Roosevelt, safely back in the fold. These conservatives were clamoring for war, castigating Wilson and, when it occurred to them, lauding Franklin D. Roosevelt. He was popular with large numbers of well-educated, well-to-do Easterners to whom both the Secretary of the Navy and the President were anathema. He was the darling of Colonel Robert M. Thompson of the Navy League, was engaged in cordial correspondence with J. Pierpont Morgan, and was on warm terms with Leonard Wood. His admiration for Theodore Roosevelt had not dimmed in the least, although T.R. was daily devising new and more picturesque epithets to heap upon Wilson. And, of course, naval officers who found him useful continued to lavish flattery upon him; leaders of navy yard labor looked to him for salary increases; and newspaper reporters appreciated his camaraderie and colorfulness. Whatever their motives, his following was influential and enthusiastic.

"Secretary Daniels has been criticized for four years, but there has been little, if any, criticism of his assistant, for the simple reason that there has been little to criticize," an admiring Washington correspondent wrote typically,[18] and an editorial proclaimed, "Mr. Daniels has one, only one, virile-minded, hardfisted, civilian assistant. Uncuriously enough his name is Roosevelt."[19]

At times the support of Roosevelt's followers was warmer than it was discreet. Thus, they nominated him for Secretary of the Navy, on the foolish assumption that Wilson would repudiate Daniels. Immediately after the 1916 election, Colonel Thompson inquired if Roosevelt would object to a Navy League campaign to make him Secretary. "You have mastered the details of administration," Thompson flatteringly remarked; "you have shown a wide and strong grasp of the principles which must be employed in carrying on the Navy and . . . it will be impossible for President Wilson to find anyone else who can in the next four years do as much for the Navy and for the Country as you can.[20] He might have added that no other Democrat would do as much for the Navy League program. Of course, Roosevelt made no reply.*

Within the next few weeks, President Wilson received letters, similar or identical, from union leaders at yards as remote as Charleston, South Carolina, and Vallejo, California – all praising Roosevelt for his excellent work as Assistant Secretary, and suggesting that if Daniels did not remain in the Cabinet, Roosevelt be made Secretary.[21]

"I am having a perfectly good time with many important things to do and my heart is entirely in my work," Roosevelt informed a friend who wrote him in similar vein. "Personally I have no use for a man who, serving in a subordinate position, is continually contriving ways to step into his boss's shoes and I detest nothing so much as that kind of disloyalty. I have worked very gladly under Mr. Daniels and I wish the public could realize how much he has done for the Navy. I would feel very badly indeed if friends of mine should unwittingly give the impression that I was for a minute thinking of taking his place at the head of the Navy."[22]

Actually, Roosevelt himself was in a precarious position. Had

* The humor magazine *Life*, March 9, 1916, made the most ludicrous proposal: make FDR Secretary of the Navy, and T.R., Assistant Secretary!

Daniels resigned, he too might have had to leave the department; had Daniels displayed other than a remarkable forbearance, he could have requested Roosevelt's resignation. Roosevelt was well aware of this uncertainty, and as late as March 1, 1917, confessed, "I do not know definitely where I shall be next winter." [23]

Daniels, in point of fact, enjoyed the confidence of Wilson. His recollection long afterward was that at the time he had been sure of this, and that those around him did not realize how close he was to the President.[24] In any event, he continued on as Secretary, and retained his headstrong, impulsive subordinate.

As for Roosevelt, encouraged as he was by every opponent of the Administration, he believed in the rightness of his own views as contrasted with those of Wilson and Daniels. His private irritation coursed over a wide area: "I have any amount of work to do," he had exploded to his wife in November, 1916, "and J.D. is too damned slow for words – his failure to decide the few big things holds me up all down the line." [25]

Among those who were normally enemies of the Administration, he could most unreservedly give vent to his pent-up emotions. To his Groton friend, Bert McCormick, he confided that when he, Medill McCormick, and Gussie Gardner spoke at an Alpha Delta Phi banquet, no reporters were present so "we talked with the lid off much to our mutual satisfaction." [26] However, Roosevelt, when he was with Daniels, was perfectly open about his feelings. When Daniels complained about the "spectacle of General Wood . . . saying America could be taken, had no army and no navy to defend itself," the Assistant Secretary frankly "defended Wood's propaganda." Daniels felt Wood "ought to retire from the army and take the stump or observe military orders." [27] Daniels did not force conformity of this sort upon his own assistant.

At the time, Roosevelt did little to disguise his disgust at the government's inaction, and after the war he became an outspoken public critic. Yet a comparison of Roosevelt's proposals in February, 1917, with his criticisms in 1920, demonstrates that even he was more gifted with hindsight than with foresight. This is apparent in his reply to McCormick's request for his expert opinion on what sort of naval preparedness the Chicago *Tribune* should advocate: [28] "In the event of sudden war," Roosevelt postulated, "the hasty passage of a universal training bill and the hasty passage of an appropriation for additional battleships and battle cruisers would probably be of no value to the

Navy during the course of that particular war. These things must be provided beforehand." * Subsequently, appropriations for new ships, as Roosevelt predicted, were of little worth, but hundreds of thousands of new men were trained, contrary to his expectation. He predicted the addition of only "about 40,000 additional men for the regular Navy, and at least the same number for . . . secondary defense." In point of fact, the Navy grew from 54,000 enlisted men in 1916 to 497,000 by the end of the war.[30] Roosevelt seemed to think largely in terms of a naval war to be fought with existing fleets, plus an extensive coastal defense system centering around commandeered yachts and volunteer crews.

In the light of this, Roosevelt subsequently implied too much foresight for himself, and gave too little credit for the work of others. He asserted in 1925 that before the dismissal of Bernstorff, the Navy "had worked out *no plans* looking to the United States entry into war." [31] He thus overlooked the rather extensive planning that followed the sinking of the *Lusitania* in 1915.[32] Roosevelt granted that after February 1, 1917, "much general discussion took place," but "no general plan was adopted, partly because of lack of information from Europe, partly because of wide divergence of opinion among officers, and partly because the Administration did not encourage discussion until war became certain." [33] Actually, on February 3, the day the United States severed diplomatic relations with Germany, the Navy Department ordered all naval vessels to report on their preparedness for war,[34] and the next day the General Board proposed a comprehensive war program: mobilize and refurbish the fleet, hasten construction, increase personnel, seize German vessels, arm merchantmen, begin patrolling, and plan with the Allies for offensive operations. Their planning suffered from the same miscalculation as Roosevelt's; they underestimated the extent to which the Navy would grow. Otherwise it seemed unexceptionable.[35] And finally, on February 5, Captain Thomas P. Magruder, chief of the Division of Naval Affairs, sent Roosevelt a confidential memorandum outlining the probable na-

* In a cordial interchange of letters in which they addressed each other as "Frank" and "Bert," McCormick offered, and Roosevelt accepted for the Navy, a 75-foot motor yacht, the *Arval*. McCormick assured Roosevelt that the *Tribune* had forgotten the past, would know no partisanship, and would be the most forceful newspaper in the country in supporting the Navy Department in any steps it adopted to bring the Navy to fighting efficiency and to increase its strength. McCormick said he would like nothing better than to keep in touch with Roosevelt if this could be done without embarrassment to him.[29]

ture of the war, and making a number of suggestions. Magruder envisaged exactly what developed for the Navy, a limited war against Germany in which the United States would not need its battleships, but would undertake complete maritime co-operation with the allies.[36] It was ridiculous, therefore, to say the Navy had done no planning.[37] There was no lack of plans; there was a deliberate refusal to execute them because of instructions from the White House. Newton D. Baker ran the War Department with a similar loyalty to Wilson.

Roosevelt also gave the impression in several speeches in 1920 that against considerable opposition, emanating even from the White House, he had boldly slashed red tape and made war preparations. "From Feb. 6 to March 4," he said, "we in the navy committed acts for which we could be, and may be yet sent to jail for 999 years. We spent millions of dollars, which we did not have – forty millions on one contract for guns alone to be placed on ships to fight the subs. We had only 100 ships and 1,000 were needed. The work came on fast. We went to those whom we had seen in advance and told them to enlarge their plants and send us the bills."[38]

Secretary Daniels resented these later attacks and the inference that all these activities had gone on behind his back. "I sent for Earle," the chief of the Bureau of Ordnance, he recorded in his diary in 1920, "who said . . . all orders had been made after conference by me."[39]

Similarly, Daniels was ready the rest of his life to brand as nonsense Navy yarns about how various officers conspired with Roosevelt's approval to expand tremendously the naval training stations, especially at Great Lakes. Captain William Moffett, who was Commandant at Great Lakes, obtained funds from the Bureau of Navigation for temporary expansion, and when that Bureau ran short, obtained more money from the Bureau of Yards and Docks. The chiefs of both bureaus, Admirals Leigh Palmer and Frederic Harris, had persuaded Roosevelt to approve some of the allotments. Finally, Admiral Harris had to ask Daniels for additional money. The Secretary, who thought the Great Lakes station was expanding too rapidly, sent for the admirals and told them to prepare to go to Chicago immediately with him. Roosevelt laughed, and told the admirals to prepare to be court-martialed when Daniels discovered what they had done. But when Daniels arrived, he attended a big review, inspected the tremendously expanded buildings, and made a speech in which, according to Admiral Harris, he took all the credit.[40] "So, until this day," Ernest K. Lindley once wrote, "none of the officers behind the scenes knows whether they slipped anything over on Daniels." [41] Daniels years later tersely commented that they did not; he had been well aware all along of what had been going on.[42] *

Whatever the simple fabric of truth in this story, Admiral Harris had embroidered it in the telling, and it is significant primarily because it was typical of what was told. Daniels was deliberate and sometimes dilatory. Roosevelt, in contrast, was quick to make decisions, and enjoyed abetting the officers. Nevertheless, Daniels kept policy reins in his own hands and was, as his own day-to-day diary account proves, aware of major activities in the Navy Department. Roosevelt primarily authorized minor matters; the orders that he ferreted out of the Secretary's desk and signed as Acting Secretary, were ones that Daniels would not miss.[44]

In the rush of wartime business, Roosevelt was entitled to authorize matters as "Acting Secretary" even when Daniels was in the next office, but again these did not involve policy. When General Charles McCawley of the Marine Corps, who had feuded with the Secretary early in his administration, wished a truck at Philadelphia, he addressed a personal note to his friend Franklin, "I hope you can see your way to write 'Acting' underneath your signature and return the papers to me." [45] There were even stories that some officers arranged occasions to call Daniels out of Washington so that Roosevelt could sign authorizations. On the other hand, huge quantities of paper normally went through Roosevelt's office. Emory S. Land ordinarily took his requisitions there, not to try to bypass Daniels, but because that was where they were supposed to go.[46]

Yet Roosevelt dearly loved a semblance of insubordination. John M. Hancock, who was in charge of Navy purchasing during the war, states that officers would frequently report to Roosevelt that they were running into difficulties with Daniels. Roosevelt would wink and remark that he would be Acting Secretary the following Tuesday.[47] A Marine colonel recalled being with the Paymaster General when Roosevelt called up, reported that the Secretary was out of town, and asked if there were anything he wanted done.[48] All this certainly helped create the impression that Roosevelt was really running the Navy Department and added to his personal reputation. One

* The Great Lakes Station would accommodate 2000 men before the war, 6000 by 1916, and 40,000 by 1918.[43] Daniels, for other reasons, held the teller of this story, Admiral Harris, in low esteem.

officer thinks that Roosevelt survived the debacle of the Wilson Administration partly because of the way he signed things.[49]

There were chores enough to keep Roosevelt occupied during the crisis weeks. He devoted an unwarranted amount of his attention to his old love, small boats,* but did also negotiate important contracts.[50] In his desire for economy, he was at complete harmony with his chief; in his zeal for speed, he frequently ran into a stone wall. He tried to hurry up delivery of brass tubing, castings, and other materials essential to complete ships under way, and to a limited extent, was still trying to beat down prices, which had risen spectacularly through 1916.

At the end of 1916, when steel corporations and their shipbuilding subsidiaries made outrageously high bids for naval construction, Roosevelt and Howe at the direction of Daniels pressured them into substantial reductions. Carnegie Steel, for example, agreed to reduce its prices approximately seven or eight dollars a ton.[51] Roosevelt tried to obtain similar discounts in the price of copper from Daniel Guggenheim, president of the American Smelting and Refining Company. He sent Howe to negotiate,[52] and himself wrote persuasively:

"You know, of course, of the arguments used by many of the opponents of the creation of an adequate defense – especially by people in the central portion of the country – that most of the demand for an increase in the Army and Navy is fostered by those business interests which would derive the greatest financial benefit therefrom. It is needless for me to tell you that I feel sure that nine-tenths of these allegations are entirely false, but I should, frankly, like to have as many examples as possible to prove that the business interests of the country as a whole are unselfish in their attitude . . . the more substantial the foregoing of obtainable profits the more will the public recognize the unselfish and truly patriotic motives behind the act." [53]

Guggenheim responded by agreeing to the equivalent of a 25 per cent rebate on copper.[54] This was before the German declaration of unrestricted submarine warfare, and it applied only to a limited few naval orders. In the subsequent months of crisis, the important task of beating down prices for all war supplies was mainly in the hands of Bernard Baruch. Roosevelt congratulated him upon obtaining a gen-

* FDR's friend, Vincent Astor, who worked with him to organize owners of powerboats, promised in time of war to donate the yacht *Noma*, and J. P. Morgan promised the magnificent *Corsair*. Both were large enough to be of real service.

eral reduction in the price of copper, "a real service, not only to us, but to the whole country." [55]

There were many other sorts of negotiations in which Roosevelt participated. He tried to obtain from the British the plans for their seaplanes, and even one of the planes itself. But the Admiralty refused to supply them until the United States entered the war,[56] then turned around and tried to obtain from Roosevelt information on the Navy's new submarine detector.[57]

There was a flood of trivia too: incessant inquiries from friends and strangers alike as to how they could enter the service, preferably into sinecures at high rank. And there were all sorts of defense schemes. The most remarkable of these was an elaborate plan Hiram Maxim submitted for a sort of private home guard to thwart German invasion and rapine.[58]

The country seemed at a standstill. Yet through these weeks, it actually moved as steadily toward war as Roosevelt could have wished.

Early in February, 1917, those in favor of a war policy were strongly advocating the arming of merchant vessels. This would make it possible for the ships to defend themselves against surfaced submarines; it also made the visit and search demanded by international law hazardous for the submarine commander, and consequently was a virtual guarantee that the ships would be torpedoed without warning. In other words, while it seemed a logical means of protecting American rights on the high seas, it was also an almost sure method to provoke sinkings which would involve the United States in war.

President Wilson was ready to provide arms for merchant ships, but felt he should not supply Navy guns and crews without authorization from Congress. P. A. S. Franklin, president of the American Lines, on February 9 and 10 urged Roosevelt to provide guns; without them his line could not (or would not) sail its steamships. He would send the *Mongolia* to London, provided "she could be fitted with one good six inch gun on her stern and supplied with a proper crew." [59] Roosevelt investigated, found the Navy possessed six 6-inch guns, and after exploring legal questions, concluded that the Navy under an old statute could lawfully loan them to the steamship companies provided it obtained suitable bond. He strongly argued that the Navy should do this in order that the major steamships might sail. "I believe that the position of the American Line is well taken," he declared, "—that they cannot square it with their consciences to let their passenger ships leave New York without some protection, either convoyed or armed." He urged Daniels so to inform Wilson in order that the President might arm the ships without asking Congress for authority.[60]

The Secretary forwarded Roosevelt's memorandum to the President,[61] but Wilson steadfastly refused to take advantage of this loophole, even though several of his cabinet members hotly urged him to do so. Instead, on February 26 he asked Congress to enact a measure enabling the government to arm the ships. A few days later, on March 2, a group of antiwar Senators filibustered the bill to death – one of them was O'Gorman of New York. Wilson roundly denounced them as "a little group of willful men, representing no opinion but their own," and began to consider arming the ships anyway.[62]

Roosevelt reflected his impatience over this deliberate course in one of his sporadic attempts at a diary. He attended the inaugural on March 5, at which Wilson proclaimed that Americans were no longer provincials, and had turned to "armed neutrality" to protect their rights.[63] Roosevelt's only comments were, "Too far away to hear Address – Little enthusiasm in crowd." That evening: "Saw Colonel House at White House at 6 & gave him some guarded views about condition of Navy & opposed strongly sending fleet through Canal in event war. Looks like running away. Bad for morale of fleet & country & too far to bring home if Canal blocked or German submarines in Caribbean[.]" [64]

The following day, Wilson called at the Navy Department and discussed with Daniels whether or not the ships should be armed. On March 8, he decided to do so, but gave no orders.[65] Roosevelt complained on March 9: "White House statement that W[ilson] has power to arm & *inference* that he will use it. J[osephus] D[aniels] says he will by Monday. Why doesn't the President say so without equivocation[?]"

On Sunday, March 11, Roosevelt was in New York, and once again aired his dissatisfaction:

> Saw Col. House 10–11. Outlined principal weaknesses of Navy – J.D.'s procrastination – Benson's dislike of England – failure to make plans with France & England & study their methods – necessity if war comes of going into it with all force – money, troops etc. He was sympathetic & agreed to main points.
>
> Navy Yard 11–2 – Little accomplished on work of District Defense – No head to run things. They start arming ships tomorrow. Confusion as to guns etc.

Dined Met[ropolitan Club] – Neil Bliss, T.R., Gen. Wood, J. P. Morgan, Elihu Root, Mayor Mitchell, Gov. Edge of N. J. etc. Tradition of army & navy outlined. Discussion of 1 how to make Administration steer clear course to uphold rights 2 how to get active increase army & navy. Decided to use Governors' Conference to demand this. Root inclined to praise Administration's present course – T.R. wanted more vigorous demand about future course – less indorsement of past. I backed T.R.'s theory – left for Wash[ington]. Told J.D. things not satisfactory Boston & worse N. Y. He said nothing." [66]

On Monday, March 12, President Wilson, without congressional action, gave orders to place guns and crews – the armed guard – on merchantmen. Daniels the next day conferred with Roosevelt and Admiral Benson on the instructions to officers who would command the armed guard. "It was a rather solemn time," Daniels wrote, "for I felt I might be signing what would prove the death warrant of young Americans and the arming of ships may bring us into war." [67] Roosevelt's only comment was, "Lansing's suggestion that they be allowed [in the zone] to fire on ships [submarines] showing no colors was eliminated at Benson's objection.

"Asked Sec'y in presence Benson that matters pertaining to naval district defense be put under me. To be discussed tomorrow. Something *must* be done soon to organize & expedite work." [68]

Obviously, Wilson was becoming strongly disposed toward a declaration of war. Long convinced of the unrighteousness of the German cause, he was infuriated by the Zimmerman note, in which Germany invited Mexico in the event of war to join her as an ally and regain her lost provinces. At about the same time, the Russian revolution eliminated a moral problem in his mind by replacing an autocracy with a constitutional monarchy.* There was no longer a despot among the democracies fighting the Central Powers. Finally he gave thought to the great possibilities for a just and lasting peace if America sat at the conference table. On March 18 came the report that German submarines had torpedoed three American ships, and two days later, the Cabinet, even including Daniels, advised Wilson to ask Congress for a declaration of war. The President on March 21 issued a call for Congress to meet April 2.[69]

Even the decision to fight did not mean that Daniels was as yet ready

* Subsequently, in November, 1917, Lenin and the Communists overthrew Kerensky's constitutional monarchy.

to advocate throwing the total manpower and resources of the United States into the war; he favored a limited war. Out of Daniels's reluctance grew a delightful but obviously inaccurate tale, still circulating around the Navy Department a generation later, that when Ambassador Walter Hines Page requested the Navy to send a high-ranking officer to conduct liaison work in London, Daniels buried the request in a file basket. President Wilson unexpectedly dropped in, and while he was chatting in the office with the Secretary and Assistant Secretary, Roosevelt deftly fished the request out of the basket, suggested Admiral William S. Sims, got the President's approval, and left Daniels with no other course of action.*

When the evening of April 2 arrived, Franklin and Eleanor Roosevelt went through the rain to the Capitol to hear President Wilson deliver his war message to Congress. Placing a strong emphasis upon right and justice, he elaborated upon highly idealistic war aims. "The world must be made safe for democracy," he asserted.

Eleanor Roosevelt "listened breathlessly and returned home still half dazed by the sense of impending change." [71] As for her husband, he prepared a comment for the press:

"No statement about American national honor and high purpose more clear or more definite . . . could be made. It will be an inspiration to every true citizen no matter what his political faith, no matter what his creed, no matter what the country of his origin." [72]

This was as close as Roosevelt came to a public expression of Wilsonian idealism then, or during the seventeen months of fighting that followed. His time, effort, and thought all poured into the more immediate task of winning the war.

* The source of this story in somewhat less colored form was FDR himself, who told it to reporters on April, 1919, when Sims returned from London. What had happened was that Daniels consulted with President Wilson on March 25, and decided to send Henry Braid Wilson. When Admiral Wilson expressed a preference for sea duty, Daniels discussed with Roosevelt who the second choice should be, and both agreed that Admiral Sims, president of the War College, would be ideal. He was the most pro-British of the American flag officers, had close friends in the Admiralty and in case of war would have quick access to essential information. Daniels sent for Sims the next day, and sent him incognito to England.[70]

CHAPTER XVIII

The First Battle of the Atlantic

The elimination of all submarines from the waters between the United States and Europe must of necessity be a vital factor in winning the war.

— FDR TO WOODROW WILSON, *October 29, 1917.*[1]

WHEN, on April 6, 1917, the United States declared war upon the German Empire, Roosevelt came into his own. Here at last was the excitement, derring-do, and grand-scale conflict for which he had longed. Momentous decisions faced the Navy, and he eagerly helped resolve them. While older, more conservative men flinched from the enlisting of several hundreds of thousands of sailors and the spending of several billions of dollars, he found such staggering numbers and unheard-of enterprises stimulating. He met them with aplomb. Here was the most serious crisis which had yet confronted America, and in measuring up to it Roosevelt was at his best. Here also, although he could not know it, was a dress rehearsal for his greatest future role.

Though he would have preferred to do otherwise, Roosevelt had to go through the war as a civilian administrator. From the beginning he worried over not being in active service. Theodore Roosevelt came to Washington in April, 1917, vainly seeking permission to lead a brigade to France. His overwhelming enthusiasm must have come close to luring Franklin into uniform.* "Uncle Ted was always urging Franklin to resign," Eleanor Roosevelt remembers; T.R.'s sons were all in uniform and he felt Franklin should be too. But both friends and foes of the Administration so emphatically told Roosevelt the Navy Department seriously needed his services that they counterbalanced Theodore Roosevelt's advice.[3] "Franklin Roosevelt should under no circumstances, think of leaving the Navy Department," Leonard Wood wrote

* FDR arranged an interview for T.R. with Secretary of War Baker, and did his best to try to get T.R. permission to go overseas. T.R. was so excited when he saw FDR that he could talk about little but the war.[2]

in July, 1917. "It would be a public calamity to have him leave at this time." [4] Secretary Daniels was just as emphatic.*

Through chance, a bellicose article of Roosevelt's, which he had written months earlier, appeared in the April *Scribner's* at the psychological moment to make him seem a man of action. Just as the schoolboy should be trained for inevitable fisticuffs, he argued in it, so the nation must train for inevitable war: "We know that every boy who goes to school is bound sooner or later, no matter how peaceful his nature, to come to blows with some schoolmate. A great people, a hundred million strong, has gone to school." [6] The chairman of the Packard Company, Henry B. Joy, was so impressed that he advertised in twenty large Middle Western newspapers, "You American open your eyes and read the first published statement by a high government *civilian* official Franklin D. Roosevelt Ass't Sec'y of the Navy about unprepared America and placing the blame on *you* where it belongs!" [7]

No doubt this sort of acclaim helped contribute to the high estimate Roosevelt placed on his own views when he clashed with Daniels. While the two men continued to have a high personal regard for each other,[8] the conflict between them heightened. The difference was that now, with the country committed to war, it degenerated from a schism over policy to one concerning method. The new gigantic scale of armament which challenged Roosevelt seemed to alarm Daniels. The Secretary still thought in terms of economy, the Assistant Secretary, results; Roosevelt was a gambler, Daniels was not. If previously Roosevelt was reprehensible because of his impatient wish to push ahead of the President's deliberate policies, now Daniels was at fault through his failure to act fast enough in throwing the Navy into the war. In the final analysis, Daniels, not Roosevelt, was Secretary of the Navy, and while the Assistant might claim credit for achievements, Daniels must take full responsibility for errors.

On the day President Wilson signed the declaration of war, a reporter, Richard Boeckel, asked Roosevelt, "Has the fleet been mobilized?"

"I can't tell you," Roosevelt replied, "but you have a right to know. Come along and we'll find out." He took Boeckel into the next office, and said to Daniels:

* Of course, there is some possibility that Daniels and Wilson, in addition to placing a high estimate on the value of FDR's services, had no interest in helping him build a martial reputation. Daniels in retrospect commented on FDR's anxiety to get into uniform, "I always thought he had this in mind: Theodore Roosevelt had gone up that way." [5]

"Here is a newspaperman. He wants to know and all the rest want to know whether the fleet has been ordered mobilized."

"Tell the young man," Daniels said quietly, "that an announcement will be made in due course."

When they had left the room, Roosevelt said:

"You see. . . . It was the best I could do."

Boeckel commented later, "He did not on that occasion, except by implication of his tone, criticize his superior. There were other occasions, however, when he was less tactful."[9]

Nor did Roosevelt try in the least to conceal his impatience from his chief. At about this time, he wrote a longhand note:

> DEAR MR. DANIELS –
>
> *Do please* get through two vital things *today*.
>
> 1. Get that Interior Building or give it to War Dept. & let us take latter's space here
>
> 2. Authorize calling out Naval Militia *& Reserve*. It is essential to get them if we are to go ahead
>
> FDR.*

On the top of this someone penciled, "Do you always follow his advice?"[11]

Roosevelt tried to gain as large a voice as possible in both administration and operation of the Navy. On April 7, he tried to bring into the department as his personal assistant, one of his adherents, Rear Admiral Herbert Winslow, a retired officer who was a big-navy man. Admiral Benson, the Chief of Naval Operations, thinking this was aimed at him, was agitated, and that night had a long talk with the Secretary. Daniels tersely decided, "No division of power as to operations – " and declined to sign the order.[12]

Of course, Roosevelt could justify his attempts to speed things up on the grounds that the Navy was by no means ready for full-scale combat when war was declared. Nevertheless in some areas, such as the purchasing of supplies, the Navy had moved even more rapidly than

* The Secretary was inured to outbursts like this. The previous year, Roosevelt, when he wished to obtain quick authority to improve some firetraps at the Norfolk Navy Yard, dashed off a memorandum which reached Daniels's desk:

> The *actual present* danger of this situation should be explained to the Secretary and he must understand that *immediate* legislation is necessary – If it is delayed we can & should be indicted for murder first degree, if one of these places goes up in smoke
>
> FDR[10]

the Army. Roosevelt afterwards liked to tell how Paymaster General Samuel McGowan and his assistant in charge of purchasing, John M. Hancock, had placed such large supply orders that a few days after the United States entered the war Roosevelt was ordered to the White House. There both President Wilson and the Chief of Staff of the Army, Major General Hugh Scott, confronted him. The President said, "Mr. Secretary, I'm very sorry, but you have cornered the market for supplies. You'll have to divide up with the Army." [13]

Roosevelt's evaluation of the wartime achievements of the Navy varied sharply through the years. During the war he was harshly critical, and especially aimed his barbs at Daniels. By 1925 he had shifted ground and, although still critical at points, heaped most of the blame upon conservative officers, like Admiral Benson. Still later, he praised the entire Daniels administration of the Navy as a phenomenal success: perhaps because he had mellowed, perhaps also because his close association with it meant that the greater its achievements, the greater his glory.

Roosevelt seriously feared that, unless the United States armed hastily, the Allies would lose the war on the Atlantic. The Germans, in resorting to unrestricted submarine warfare, had been well aware that they would thereby bring America into the conflict, but were confident that despite this, they could starve England out of the war before the United States could mobilize its strength. In the spring of 1917, Germany was coming close to making good on her gamble. Admiral Sims was horrified when Admiral Jellicoe told him in April that the German sinkings were at the rate of 900,000 tons per month. Jellicoe added, "They will win, unless we can stop these losses — and stop them soon." [14]

The younger officers in the United States Navy, together with Roosevelt, saw clearly that the greatest task of the Navy during the war would be to bring the submarines under control. They felt that the British were far too conservative and unimaginative in their antisubmarine campaign, since they were keeping many of their smaller vessels with the Grand Fleet in its vigil to prevent the Imperial German Navy from emerging, and were engaging in no more than fairly limited patrolling against the submarines. Conservatives on the Board of Admiralty continued to block convoying proposals. The younger men in the Navy Department in their impatience with the British had the sympathy of both Daniels and Wilson. As late as July 2, 1917, the President wrote the Secretary, "As you and I agreed the other day, the

British Admiralty had done absolutely nothing constructive in the use of their navy and I think it is time we were making and insisting upon plans of our own, even if we render some of the more conservative of our own naval advisers uncomfortable." [15]

In the two months before the United States entered the war, Roosevelt had persuaded the Chief of Naval Operations and the General Board to plan comprehensive antisubmarine defenses.[16] He attended several meetings of the General Board between March 15 and April 5, at which, as he remembered, they concentrated upon this problem, since as yet "the sending of American troops (except possibly on a very small scale) to France was practically unthought of." Backed by a few younger officers, Roosevelt "was working for a plan to send *all* our destroyers to European waters at our entry into the war. This move was, before April 6, stepped on by all the higher officers in the Navy Department, for the very good reason that they still visualized the U. S. Atlantic Fleet as a fleet entity, and could not imagine stripping that fleet." Upon American entrance into the war, the British and French commanding officers in the western Atlantic arrived and demanded the destroyers. Within twenty-four hours they won out, although, as Roosevelt pointed out, it involved breaking up the fleet.[17] * Yet even after this, he declared, the Navy did not for some time face up to sending battleships to the North Sea, or organizing a complex convoy system.† "There was still no adequate conception of the tremendous part the Navy would later play in the war."

Many Americans continued to think that the United States should participate only in a limited way. When the Selective Service Act was being debated in Congress, Speaker Champ Clark asserted, "in the estimation of Missourians there is precious little difference between a conscript and a convict." On the contrary, Roosevelt insisted, it was impracticable "to wage a sort of separate war against Germany," and the United States should co-operate to the fullest extent with the Allies.[19]

Not until the arrival of the main British and French missions late

* On April 21, 1917, Daniels wrote in his diary, "R— proposed we should send destroyers to England & tell her we would expect her to furnish in return some of her best dreadnaughts. . . . L[ansing] had made the same suggestion to Cabinet & President had not approved."

† The Admiralty had not yet sanctioned convoying; the United States Navy, especially through Sims in London and William V. Pratt in the Navy Department, strongly insisted upon it, and by early summer it began. FDR later claimed Pratt was more responsible for it than Sims. In any event, it was the most effective of all antisubmarine measures.[18]

in April did Americans learn how desperate the plight of the Allies was. Then it appeared that the blank check which the United States had tendered in declaring war, could not be filled in with a limited sum. A French mission came to the United States, not at all sure how much it could get, and first learned from Roosevelt that it could demand a good deal. The head of the mission was a rather touchy former premier, René Viviani; the naval representative was Vice Admiral Chocheprat, but Marshal Joffre, renowned in America as the hero of the first Battle of the Marne, attracted most of the attention.[20] Roosevelt was assigned to meet the French at Hampton Roads, and bring them up the Potomac on the presidential yacht, *Mayflower*. In consequence, he had "twenty-four hours of quite intimate conversation" with them [21] before they reached Washington or saw anyone else. "My outstanding impression was that none of them had any real idea of what America was really going to do to help in the war," he recalled. "The situation which they had left at home was a desperate one, and while of course they anticipated all kinds of financial and manufacturing and foodstuff assistance from us, they had no information as to the amount of military or naval assistance they could expect. When I told Viviani and Joffre that we expected to go into the military and naval operations on the largest possible scale they seemed impressed and intensely gratified. As a matter of fact that was the primary object of their visit – to bring word back to France as to the exact military and naval help they could count on." [22]

While the French and British missions were in Washington, Roosevelt "saw a good deal of all of them." Later he intimated that he abetted the French in obtaining from the White House a definite guarantee that the first American troops would embark for France before the end of June.

While Roosevelt coined no magic phrase like "blood, toil, tears, and sweat," he clearly outlined their equivalents to the public. "We are in for something pretty bad," he warned early in June. "Before this time next year every man, woman, and child will know that we are at war. Unless haste is made we stand a chance of losing the war. The clear blue sky isn't yet in sight." [23] When the first American troops reached France a month later, he declared at Chautauqua that it was "mere luck" they arrived safely, that a German torpedo missed one of the transports by only a few feet. At best the country must expect to lose troops, munitions, and foodstuffs in the perilous Atlantic crossing.[24] These predictions turned out to be so excessively grim that in August, some time after he had given the National Security League permission to publish his speech, he revoked it, because since then "a great deal of water" had "gone over the dam." [25]

Through the summer of 1917, he was extremely upset by what he regarded as the dilatory behavior of both the Secretary of the Navy and the Chief of Naval Operations. When a British officer reminded him that the famous diarist Pepys had reorganized the Royal Navy in the Restoration period, and added that the business methods had not changed since, Roosevelt retorted that those of the United States Navy had not changed since Christopher Columbus.[26] "The old machine is creaking horribly under the additional burden," he pointed out, "and, unless scissors are applied to the red tape and better organization started pretty soon, I fear there will be a great deal of justifiable criticism before we get through." [27]

On July 12, Roosevelt sent to the Secretary a memorandum, heavily underscored, in which he called for an immediate estimate of the number of destroyers and submarine chasers to be constructed. Unless he let contracts for the subchasers by September 1, the private organizations building them would disintegrate through lack of work.[28]

Again, on July 26:

> Assistant Secretary of State Phillips came to my office, showed me a telegram to Lansing from Ambassador Page, dated July 20th, in which Page quotes suggestion made to him by First Lord of Admiralty and others that Admiralty would be very glad to have five or six of our naval officers detailed to the Admiralty itself. . . . Phillips said he had taken this telegram to Daniels on July 20th and wanted to be able to reply to Page. I sent for Benson and Benson, after some hesitation said he *thought* Secretary Daniels had told him that the President had directed that the matter be held in abeyance. Personally I do not believe for one moment that the President has ever heard of this telegram or request. It is slumbering somewhere between the Secretary and Benson.* . . .
>
> July 27th: I happened into the Secretary's office this afternoon and found him signing a big batch of Bureau of Navigation mail. The letters were dated July 5th." [29]

* In an earlier memorandum, FDR included subordinates from Admiral Benson on down in his bill of particulars:

> The Chief of Operations, Admiral Benson, proceeds cautiously and slowly from day to day with little questions of despatching gunboats around the West Indies, with pleasant chats with American and foreign officers, . . . and every matter of real moment is delayed from 24 hours to 24 weeks.

Some of this criticism leaked to the press – whether through Roosevelt, it is hard to say. At least one correspondent interpreted the Assistant Secretary's remarks at the Navy League reception for the British admirals as strong censure of Daniels. It was "the first criticism that has been made by a man who is on the inside," this correspondent pointed out, and added that under an order Lansing had promulgated, if an Assistant Secretary of State should be so critical, he would be subject to dismissal.[30] The *Wall Street Journal* called the next day for the dismissal, not of Roosevelt, but of Daniels. It cited a businessman as remarking, "If we had a Secretary of the Navy who could merely sign his name we should be better off than we are now," and added as was inevitable, "Who is the man . . . who is pushing things along? That's easy: Franklin D. Roosevelt."[31]

While editorials may have been inspired, Roosevelt's major tactic was to try to get his complaints before President Wilson. He could not, of course, go directly to the President without being guilty of the sort of insubordination that could only result in dismissal. This would have been a disaster for Roosevelt and would have created a furor among critics of the Administration. Nor did he, as Theodore Roosevelt unquestionably would have done, resign in bombastic protest and enter the armed forces. Instead, he encouraged a third person to present the case against Daniels to Wilson without his own name being involved. The person was one of the most famous of American historical novelists, Winston Churchill, who was already renowned in the United States before the British Winston Spencer Churchill became known.*

The American Churchill, although a Progressive Republican, was a friend and admirer of President Wilson, to whom he had in the past rented his New Hampshire summer home. Over twenty years before,

---

. . . [Those below him] do not grasp the broad situation, they fail to come to decisions and spend their time magnifying ridiculous details. Further down the line among the various Bureaus and in the general business organization of the Department and the navy yards there exists an exceedingly bad esprit de corps. The morale is slack and the result is shown in every transaction the Navy Department makes at the present time.

* FDR mentioned in a letter, July 26, 1917, that he was "just back from lunch with Winston Churchill," which caused the editor of his personal letters to fall into the natural error that the British statesman had first met FDR in Washington in the summer of 1917, rather than in London the following summer. FDR himself, when he came upon an old letter at Christmas time, 1943, was not sure whether it was from the novelist or prime minister, and did not even remember the 1917 episode to which it related.[32]

he had graduated from the Naval Academy, and for this reason volunteered his writing services to Roosevelt.[33] The Assistant Secretary readily accepted; he felt Churchill could do more than "turn out mere 'write-ups' or recruiting posters of Navy life." [34]

When Churchill in May, 1917, began to explore the Navy Department as an "interviewer and correspondent," he turned out a series of syndicated newspaper articles, but found the role "a little bit strange." [35] As he interviewed various naval officers, he became more and more upset over the poor morale and the criticisms of the Secretary. Although the article on the naval administration which he wrote for the August *Atlantic Monthly* was "critical only by implication," he confessed to Roosevelt: "As I dig into this situation, it grows more complicated and serious. Our Navy Department. . . . is suffering from the hookworm – certainly not through any fault of yours." He asked for a conference with Roosevelt, to obtain more information, which he would hold confidential. Just what he would do with it he was not yet certain, but he did not feel it should be aired in a sensational way.[36]

In July, Churchill decided to present the matter directly to President Wilson. He prepared a careful statement, complete with concrete citation of delays. Obviously he tried to be fair, paying tribute to the attractive personality of Daniels, and granting that in the last few weeks the Secretary had shown signs of being less obstructionist. Though eminently reasonable, Churchill did warn that various newspapermen and Congressmen were anxious to expose the impasse in the Navy.

While Churchill was drafting his critique, he made a luncheon engagement to see Roosevelt, "away from the Department, in order that you may check up the information you have given me." [37] Next he took his memorandum to the President. Apparently Churchill impressed upon Wilson the need to circumvent Daniels, Benson, and a few of the conservatives, for he subsequently reported to Roosevelt that the talk with the President went pretty well.[38] Wilson wrote Churchill that he had taken up the matters with Daniels, and thought he had "things in course to carry out the essential purpose you had in mind." [39] He sent Daniels a memorandum written on his own personal typewriter, which recommended that younger men receive authority in both purchasing and operations.[40]

Roosevelt was pleased and felt that the protest was bearing fruit when the President told Daniels and several top admirals that the Navy must embark upon an aggressive program against submarines.[41]

After this, or on a similar occasion at about the same time, Roosevelt commented, "I am encouraged to think that he [Wilson] has *begun* to catch on, but then it will take lots more of the Churchill type of attack."[42] Daniels himself was rather relieved by Churchill's mild recommendations: "I had heard he was going to criticize me rather severely, but I think not."[43] Daniels left Admiral Benson and other of the older officers in power, but apparently speeded up his own decisions. In the autumn, the Navy was functioning very actively on a large scale, and Roosevelt's criticisms subsided.[44]

Quite possibly Daniels did delay some decisions early in the war, but Roosevelt also still had some things to learn. The quick results he so cherished were not always achievements. His skirmishes with his chief repeatedly illustrated a major strength and weakness stemming from the same characteristics: his rather uncritical willingness to listen to almost any novel ideas, his strong support of the proponents of these whether they were worthy or not, and his optimistic confidence that through slashing red tape he could achieve the impossible and in record time. In total, his wartime record was magnificent, because his measure of success spectacularly outweighed his failures.

One of Roosevelt's major controversies with Daniels from February of 1917 through the spring of 1918, revolved around the establishment of a coastal patrol and the construction in quantity of various types of small boats for the purpose. He knew a good deal about such craft, and had always loved them. According to one of the most eminent naval constructors, Emory S. Land, Roosevelt at all periods of his life had definite views about ship design, some of them worthless, and some sound. "He was a great trial and error guy," Land points out, "but he did have some good ideas." He would present numerous proposals of his own, but "ultimately he nearly always went along with the advice of the professionals." When, however, he had an idea that was rejected, he would often take it from one man to another until he found someone who liked it. Then, armed with the approval of that one person, he would take it back and use the approval to beat down one after another of those who had disagreed. In that way, he would usually win a compromise.[45]

While Roosevelt was irked over the slowness with which the Navy obtained and subsequently made use of legislation to take over craft for patrol purposes, he was even more upset over the failure to construct patrol boats with the rapidity he would have liked. He was one of those who, as he himself later said, overestimated the need for protection against submarines along the American shoreline. He took seriously the estimate of the Division of Operations that the Navy should have 4200 scouting, mine-laying, mine-sweeping, and patrol vessels along both coasts of the United States. Subsequently Operations cut the figure to 1200 for the Atlantic Coast alone, but the Navy obtained nowhere near that number of vessels.[46]

Roosevelt's fear of German submarines, combined with his love for yachts, led him in the weeks before the declaration of war to expand his earlier plans for a voluntary patrol into a program for the building of quantities of small boats. In February, 1917, he called a conference of naval experts who decided to use all the steel shipbuilding facilities for the construction of destroyers, the most effective vessels for hunting down submarines. Remaining shipyards should produce the largest possible type of wooden, gasoline-propelled submarine chasers, which might be of some auxiliary value.[47] By the end of February, the Bureau of Construction and Repair was drawing up plans for a seaworthy 110-foot patrol boat. As Roosevelt later boasted, the "110′ wooden submarine chasers with 3 gasoline engines [were] an extraordinarily successful boat; i.e., large enough to be sea-keeping and to cross the ocean under their own power, and to stay out for long periods." [48]

The slowness with which the Navy constructed the boats caused Roosevelt to fulminate, but in 1925 he pointed out that the plans were drawn up in March and the first boats delivered in June – "a very wonderful record." Contrary to Roosevelt's expectations, they were particularly useful in European waters.[49]

Although Roosevelt was able subsequently to take credit for helping promote the 110-foot submarine chasers, after the war he never referred to their counterpart, which he had promoted with equal energy – small 50-foot harbor-patrol launches. He tried to justify these to the General Board and ship-construction officers on the ground that shipbuilders could turn them out rapidly, and they would serve a useful function while the larger subchasers were still on the ways. To motorboat lovers, he declared that these smaller craft could serve to carry on naval police work in harbors, inlets, and sounds on both coasts. They could run down rumors of secret enemy wireless stations, gun-running depots, submarine fuel or repair bases, or even submarines taking shelter in secluded waters.[50]

Secretary Daniels and officers in the Bureau failed to share Roosevelt's rather romantic view of the usefulness of these boats. By dint of arguing before the admirals on the General Board on March 24, that constructors could turn out no more than 200 to 250 of the 110-foot boats by January 1, 1918, he obtained their verbal agreement in his presence that it would be wise to build smaller boats as a stopgap if they could be turned out for use during the summer and autumn of 1917.[51] The next day, representatives of the Bureaus told the General Board that 500 of the larger boats could be turned out by January 1. So the Board members reversed themselves, and Roosevelt protested.[52]

The 50-foot boats obviously would be of little use outside of harbors except in smooth weather, and so the officers continued to oppose their construction. Some suspected that Roosevelt was being influenced by Arthur P. Homer, a representative of Sterling Motors, in whom he had great faith. Homer, he asserted, was "a thoroughly live person," whose prowess had caused the Navy Department to modify "its first view that he was somewhat of a tall talker." Roosevelt had twice sent Homer to England for aircraft data. Next he became a prime mover in the fight for 50-foot boats; they would be powered with Sterling engines.[53]

Several times Daniels wrote in his diary remarks such as, "Roosevelt urged more motor boats to be used for patrol. Will order many, but are they valuable? How much of that sort of junk shall we buy?"[54] When Daniels failed to order the boats, Roosevelt on his own authority either authorized or tentatively arranged for the construction of a number of them. The officers in the Bureaus recommended that the contract be not approved, and Roosevelt jokingly threatened to send one of them to Guam.[55] When Captain Hugh Rodman angrily opposed building the 50-foot boats because 110-foot boats were obtainable,[56] Howe approached Rodman, who was waiting to go to sea, and hinted that it would be to his advantage to favor the boats. Rodman cursed him roundly.[57] Through sheer persistence, Roosevelt had his way, although the Secretary continued to think that the small boats were worthless. "If worst had come to worst," he once wrote, "they might have been some good, but my recollection is that we never did find much use for them."[58]

These same characteristics – this willingness to accept almost any novel idea, and to fight for it doggedly until he could achieve success – led to Roosevelt's most notable achievement during the war, the laying of the North Sea mine barrage. It was not of Roosevelt's conception; at least he was not alone in thinking of it, but he was so vigorous in promoting it that Admiral Harris once remarked, "If it hadn't been for him, there would have been no Scotch mine barrage."[59]

The purpose of the mine barrage, as of the patrol boats and the convoy system, was to cut down losses from submarines. The concept, a comparatively simple one, had long since occurred to President Wilson. More than once, even before the United States entered the war, he remarked to Daniels, "Why don't we shut the hornets up in their nest?" [60] Consequently, when Roosevelt began promoting a mine project, he had no difficulty in obtaining the support of the President. Roosevelt himself explained in 1921 how he became interested.

> The first week we were in the war I had been studying a map of European waters, had measured the distances across the English Channel, across the North Sea from Scotland to Norway and across the Strait of Otranto at the mouth of the Adriatic. I had examined the depths of the waters in those places, and had come to the conclusion that some kind of a barrier, if it could be worked out on the technical side, offered the proper strategical solution of keeping German submarines out of the Atlantic and out of the Mediterranean. I talked to several officers in Operations at that time and also to several people in the Bureau of Ordnance and all of them turned it down or paid very little attention to it with the single exception of Commander [Simon T.] Fullinwider who told me he thought we ought to work on a new type of deep sea mine as a possible solution of the problem, and he agreed with me on the strategic wisdom of the suggestion.
>
> Within two or three days of this two other men came to me with practically the same idea in mind. The first of them was Colonel E. Lester Jones of the Coast and Geodetic Survey. . . . His suggestion was for a line of nets with bombs attached. [Rear Admiral Frederic R.] Harris, of Yards and Docks, also brought up a plan which as I remember it called for a combination of mines and nets. These plans were discussed with a number of officers in Operations and were turned down as being too cumbersome and not practical, but their value lay in the studies . . . of the ocean bottom, currents, etc. . . .
>
> About the first week in May . . . Admiral de Chair turned up with the Balfour Mission and I spent a long time going over the possibility of closing off the North Sea and the Adriatic with him. He did not enthuse over the subject, and I talked also with Mr. Balfour who pointed out the diplomatic effect of closing up the three-mile stretch of water along the North Coast." [61]

Daniels wired Admiral Sims, who was conducting liaison in London, to propose a mine barrage to the Admiralty. Sims replied that their consensus after a full conference with him was that "all barrages whether of mines or nets or both are not an absolute solution for the fundamental reason that nets do not stop submarines and mine barriers cannot wholly be effective unless they can be maintained by patrol at all points." * Therefore, the Admiralty and Sims strongly recommended instead an increase in the number of patrol craft.[63]

Undaunted, Roosevelt prepared an elaborate memorandum proposal for Admiral De Chair to present to the Admiralty upon his return to England. He told the Admiral that submarine losses were approximating the original German estimate of a million tons a month, and that continuation of them "means inevitable disaster within a comparatively short period." All methods then being used combined were not successful, because the number of submarines thus destroyed probably did not equal the German production of new ones.

British efforts to close the English Channel were largely successful, Roosevelt pointed out; therefore, all that remained was to close the passage between Scotland and Norway to prevent submarines from going to their hunting grounds. True enough, the British had tried to mine the area around the powerful German base at Helgoland, but it was easy for the Germans to sweep mines from that area. The North Sea line would be close to British bases, and therefore comparatively easy to patrol. As for the diplomatic question which Lord Balfour had raised, concerning the closing of the waters of neutral Norway, Roosevelt declared: "The use of territorial waters of neutrals by belligerent warships is carefully guarded by definite restrictions in international law, and if Norway fails to carry out her direct obligation to prevent the use of a narrow line along her coast as a means of . . . [passage] by German submarines it would seem perfectly fair to carry out this duty for her." He proposed the construction of a barrier of nets, and of mines, according to what types proved most satisfactory at various depths and in various currents. It might involve the laying of a thousand miles of nets and a half million mines at a cost of from $200,000,000 to $500,000,000. This was still a staggering sum in 1917, but Roosevelt felt it well worth expending in comparison with the value of merchant tonnage being sunk.[64]

Roosevelt submitted this memorandum both to the British and to the Secretary and various officials within the Navy Department. At first there was considerable skepticism. Even Admiral Harris, who

* The British also feared the barrage would seriously interfere with the free movement of the Grand Fleet. Admiral Beatty told FDR in the summer of 1918 that he was opposed to any mine barrier.[62]

later took much credit for sponsoring the plan, felt the operation would be so stupendous, difficult, and uncertain in effectiveness as to be hardly worth while. However, both the British Admiral De Chair, and the American Chief of Naval Operations, Admiral Benson, displayed a willingness to investigate the proposal.[65]

In July, Roosevelt received unfavorable responses to his recommendation from both the Admiralty and the French Ministry of Marine.[66] By that time, however, he was well on his way toward a solution of the practical problems. On June 4, he had seen President Wilson, and obtained his support for the establishment of a commission to report on the advisability of carrying out his plan on a large scale.[67] It consisted of representatives of the Navy Department and the Coast and Geodetic Survey of the Department of Commerce. There was some friction between the two groups, since the Navy representatives wished to concentrate upon mining experiments, and the Coast Survey upon nets. Roosevelt continued to favor a combination of two or three types of nets and mine barriers [68] but was receptive to almost any idea, no matter how farfetched. One suggestion which appealed to him for a while was to run across the Atlantic two lanes guarded by a series of nets on each side of each lane. Each section was to have a submerged buoy with a radio attachment. If the net were penetrated or disturbed, the buoy would rise and signal, and a destroyer would rush to the spot. Commander R. R. Belknap, commander of the Navy mining force, pointed out to Roosevelt the colossal tonnage of net that would be required, and the difficulty of getting a destroyer to the danger spot in time. Actually, considerable difficulties were involved in any use of nets. The Coast Survey experiments in the relatively calm waters of Long Island Sound turned out badly.[69] The net guarding New York Harbor was of such poor quality that someone remarked, "The only way the Germans would be killed or injured by coming in contact with the net is that they would die laughing." [70] The Admiralty based much of their opposition to Roosevelt's proposals upon the failure of antisubmarine nets in the English Channel.[71]

The net controversy, and the objections to the barrage on this account, dissolved when a talented inventor, Ralph C. Browne, brought to the Navy Department an antenna firing device.* Long antenna

* At the end of 1928, FDR was reported as saying: "I was sitting in my office one day when this typical inventor wandered in while my office people were away for a few moments. He had a beard and the regular inventor's black bag . . . We had what we called a 'crank' department in the navy. . . . But he insisted on showing me his model. . . . I called down Admiral Earle and showed him what

wires attached to the mines made an electrical contact and set off the mine if a submarine touched them. Thus Browne provided the Navy with the key to a successful antisubmarine barrier. Even without Browne's device, according to Roosevelt's later judgment, a barrage "could and would have been laid – perhaps with not as great effectiveness and probably at greater cost." [73] But, as soon as Commander Fullinwider adapted the device for use with a Navy mine, Roosevelt had a lever with which he successfully obtained approval for the project. He had had the continued interest of Wilson and Daniels; now the officers in the Division of Operations fell into line.[74] Daniels took strong measures; he again directed Sims to place the proposal before the Admiralty. Sims, still not approving personally, did so, and the Admiralty again rejected it.[75] The Secretary next sent the Commander-in-Chief of the Atlantic Fleet, Admiral Mayo, to London to work for the project in person. Mayo finally wore down the skepticism of the British naval officers, so that, as Roosevelt once put it, "Admiral Sims and the British Admiralty said to the Navy Department, in effect: 'We think the plan is a bit wild-eyed but go ahead if you want.' " [76]

This was late in October. "I told you so in May," Roosevelt remarked to Daniels, and handed him "a very stinging memorandum," in which he asserted that if the mine barrier were to be constructed at all, it must be "with a different spirit from any of the operations up to now. It will require prompt decision all along the line." [77]

The President and Secretary put the project into execution with as much speed and energy as Roosevelt could wish. The day after Roosevelt wrote his memorandum, Wilson and the Cabinet approved the barrage – though on the basis of other recommendations besides his * – and manufacture of the mines and assembly of a mine-laying fleet began.[78] At the time of the Armistice, the barrage was not yet complete, but already contained 70,000 mines, laid at a cost of $80,000,000.

---

the man had. At first he was skeptical, but . . . this man who looked like a crank had what we had been looking for." When Browne, who in fact had arrived at the Navy Department in the company of a manufacturer and a distinguished scientist-member of the Council of National Defense, protested this description, FDR apologetically wrote him, "I was just as horrified as you were when I read the stories which were subsequently printed." [72]

* When the time for decision came, Daniels accepted the barrage proposal only with reluctance, and not on the basis of FDR's advice, but that of officers in the Navy Department. "A stupendous undertaking," he noted. "Perhaps not impossible but to my mind of doubtful practicability. North Sea too rough and will necessitate withdrawing all our ships from other work and then can we destroy the hornet's nest or keep the hornets in?"

It came too late to be a really decisive factor; the convoy system, and the use of patrols equipped with detection devices and ash-can depth charges, had cut submarine sinkings to a less dangerous total. Yet Roosevelt from the perspective of the White House liked to think that the barrage contributed very materially to the winning of the war:

> German submarines began to run foul of the mine barrage by August 1918. During the next few weeks at least two submarines were sunk at the barrage. Several others were seriously injured. Word spread among all the German submarines that this devilish new barrier made it far more difficult and dangerous to get out into the Atlantic and to get back home. There is no doubt in my judgment that the morale of the German submarine officers and men was badly shaken by the mere fact of the existence of the barrage. . . .
>
> It seems also to be a fact that discontent in the German submarine force became vocal by the early part of October 1918; that these mutterings spread from the submarine force to the German battleships and cruisers and that it had great influence in what turned out, shortly thereafter, to be definite mutiny in the whole of the German navy.
>
> It may not be too far-fetched, therefore, to say that the North Sea mine barrage initiated by the American Navy and literally forced on the British Navy had something definite to do with the German naval mutiny, the subsequent Army mutiny, and the ending of the World War.[79]

It was less farfetched to ascribe the German naval mutiny to all the antisubmarine activities combined, as indeed, Roosevelt did in March, 1919. "The ceaseless vigil of the aerial patrol, the subchasers, destroyers and other craft was getting on the nerves of the Germans," he pointed out then. The barrage came as one final hazard.[80] But whatever the relative weight of the factors, Roosevelt had played some part in all of them, and could take satisfaction in having contributed to the winning of the first Battle of the Atlantic.

CHAPTER XIX

War Administrator

> Franklin D. Roosevelt . . . isn't hidden nor inconspicuous. But he is a man whose obvious powers are such as to make you wonder how a democracy of opportunity can afford to leave him subordinated now, when the need is not so much for measures – of which there have been, Heaven knows enough – but for men.
>
> — RALPH BLOCK, *July 4, 1918.*

> "See young Roosevelt about it" . . . [was] a by-word in Washington.
>
> — TIME, *May 28, 1923.*

THE pressure of war work matured Roosevelt as an administrator and as it added to his stature, it molded his mind. It not only increased the likelihood that he would someday achieve a position of power, but to some extent predetermined how he would then meet crises. Politicians and businessmen, both Democrats and Republicans, agreed that he was one of the most capable as well as most likeable young men in Washington. He demonstrated an ability to get things done when the nation placed an almost hysterical premium upon that trait, and the wartime secrecy in the "silent service," as the Navy was called, led many to credit him with brilliant achievements yet to be announced. "The hats of all are off to you for the way you've handled things in the navy," Kermit Roosevelt wrote, "& we all realize that the amount you've really done compared to what we know is in ratio with the surface to the submerged part of an iceberg! & equally as efficient!" [1]

Roosevelt stored away many impressions for the future, for Wilson's leadership in time of war impressed him even more than had the peacetime achievements. In 1925, when he felt that a writer was ascribing the united wartime effort of Americans to the people themselves rather than to the President, he chided, "This was the result – not the cause. If Wilson and his cabinet ever get historical praise for anything it should be for the very remarkable leadership and direction of public opinion which resulted in the grand effort. It was carefully thought out, the right men — Baruch, Daniel Willard, Hoover, Garfield, etc. — were called in, and, in other words, the American organization for war was created *from the top down,* NOT *from the bottom up.* This is most important." [2]

Although Roosevelt was one of the secondary figures in this organization, he represented the Navy in so many diverse activities throughout the war agencies that he became familiar with much of their workings. He presided, for example, over a conference on war-risk insurance,[3] and headed a committee to report measures for the postwar rehabilitation and vocational education of wounded men.[4] However, he wisely declined an invitation to become a member of the Aircraft Production Board, which might have involved him in some responsibility for the most deplorably snarled of the war programs.[5] Through his alter ego, Howe, he was familiar with other areas of administration, for in addition to assuming new duties as Assistant to the Assistant Secretary, Howe became a member of the Munitions Board, a special committee on transportation in the Council of National Defense, and a precedent committee to determine priorities for manufacturers. Howe remarked, "I rarely have any complaint of a lack of things to do." [6]

Neither did Roosevelt. Even before the war he had worked and played with a spectacular verve, but the new pace called for greater efforts, and left him worn, tense, and irritable at times. He showed these strains very seldom, but there were signs of them in the self-righteousness with which he worried about delays in the Navy Department during the summer months of 1917. And in his personal life, there were serious changes. There was not much heroic about remaining a civilian in the government when one's contemporaries were training for service on the Western Front, or for antisubmarine warfare. Admiral Sims, in the spirit of the times, described the patrols to Roosevelt as "the greatest hunting game whatever," in which any "red-blooded young American would want to take a hand." [7] Roosevelt in Washington was ready to agree. About all he could do, though, was to take some solace in the thought that he was a potential target of German agents. In the fall of 1944 when he came upon an old revolver he reminisced:

> In the spring of 1917, just before or after we declared war, the Secret Service found in the safe of the German Consul in New York, a document headed: "To be eliminated." The first name on

the list was that of Frank Polk; mine was the second, followed by about eight or ten others.

As a result, the Secret Service asked us both to carry revolvers as we both habitually walked to and from our offices. I was given the revolver and the shoulder holster. I wore them under my arm for three or four days. Although a fair shot with a revolver, I realized that it would take me about 30 seconds before I could reach inside my overcoat and coat, haul out, cock, aim and fire. By that time I would normally be dead with the assassin half a mile away!

I put the revolver in the top table drawer where it remained for 25 years.[8]

This or another gun figured in a trivial episode in the summer of 1917 which illustrated his nervousness. After he had sent Eleanor and the children to Campobello, he remained behind, alone in the house, ill with a cold. "Last night," he confessed to Eleanor, "I thought I heard a burglar and sat at the head of the stairs with the gun for half an hour, but it turned out to be the cat."[9]

In a rare mood of despondency, he wrote his wife: "I really can't stand that house all alone without you, and you were a goosy girl to think or even pretend to think that I don't want you here *all* the summer, because you know I do! But honestly *you* ought to have six weeks straight at Campo, just as *I* ought to, only you can and I can't! I *know* what a whole summer here does to people's nerves and at the end of this summer I will be like a bear with a sore head until I get a change or some other cold weather – in fact as you know I am unreasonable and touchy now – but I shall try to improve."[10] *

Eleanor evidently told his mother that he had a cold, for he received a telegram and letter[12] from Sara Roosevelt, to whom he replied in a firm and cheerful manner:

"My cold is gone & you mustn't worry one second – if I get another or a tummy ache I will wire you to come, but I really feel that you would not get any satisfaction in a visit unless I am laid up, as I leave the house at 7:15 A.M. for physical exercises, breakfast with the other

* There were rumors, apparently emanating from a prominent society figure who had the sharpest tongue in Washington, that FDR during this period was enamored of another woman, who, being a Catholic, would not marry him even if he got a divorce. In view of the consistently endearing fashion in which he always wrote Eleanor, and the lighthearted way in which she has described how he dazzled the "lovely ladies" during the campaign of 1920, these rumors seem preposterous. They reflect more on the teller than on FDR.[11]

exercisers & get to the Dept. at 9. I rarely am able to leave for lunch & don't get home till just in time for dinner." [13]

Except for his all too frequent illnesses, Roosevelt took much satisfaction in the physical exercises. In May, 1917, Walter Camp, the famous Yale coach, expressed to Frank Polk and to Roosevelt the fear that Washington leaders would break down under the strain of their additional labors, unless they took adequate workouts.[14] Roosevelt, already concerned over the failure of most executives to keep in physical condition, urged Camp to come to Washington and help him work out "some kind of a definite plan" for everyone in the Navy Department to keep physically fit.[15] Camp quickly agreed to come and, with Roosevelt's backing, tried to introduce twice-daily setting-up exercises for everyone in the Navy.[16] It took many months to sell the Navy on this, but very shortly a group of cabinet officers and subordinates, with Roosevelt a prime mover, began exercising under Camp's supervision four mornings a week.[17] Camp wrote admiringly: [18]

> Mr. Roosevelt is a beautifully built man, with the long muscles of the athlete. Even his hard and confining work has not caused much deterioration as yet, but his heart and lungs cry for more exercise already. His color has improved even in a week and his muscular control has gained. His spirit is resilient, and his effect upon others is, like Secretary McAdoo's, salutary in that he imparts some of his own vitality. His chief progress is coming in a restoration of that vitality upon which he has been drawing lately.*

Camp was not alone in regarding Roosevelt as a magnificent physical specimen. Government girls used to watch with admiration as he strode past on his way to work. A reporter wrote that he had a bearing that a matinee idol might envy. "His face is long, firmly shaped and set with marks of confidence. There are faint wrinkles on a high straight forehead. Intensely blue eyes rest in light shadow. A firm, thin mouth breaks quickly to laugh, openly and freely. His voice is pitched well, goes forward without tripping. He doesn't disdain shedding his coat on a hot afternoon; shows an active quality in the way he jumps from his chair to reach the cigarettes in his coat. He is a young man, a young man with energy and definite ideas." [20]

Despite his recurring throat ailment in the summer of 1917, his spirits

* Yet the irony was that Secretary Daniels, who doggedly refused to exercise with Camp, remained in perfect health during the war, while FDR was repeatedly ill.[19]

were normally high. Anna Roosevelt Cowles saw a good bit of him at that time, and appreciated his buoyancy and kindness. "She speaks of you as her debonair young cousin, so brave and so charming," Admiral Cowles wrote, "but the girls will spoil you soon enough, Franklin, and I leave you to them." [21] In writing his wife, Roosevelt was highly gleeful when she received her first – and thoroughly garbled – newspaper publicity as a saver of food. He wrote her how proud he was to be "the Husband of the Originator, Discoverer and Inventor of the New Household Economy for Millionaires." She replied, "I never will be caught again that's sure and I'd like to crawl away for shame." [22]

Nevertheless, the episode was the forerunner of a drastic shift in Eleanor Roosevelt's way of life. Until this time she was largely engrossed in her children and her social duties. Increasingly she began to engage in war work: she knitted, visited the naval hospital, and through the summer heat of 1918, worked sixteen hours a day in the corrugated iron cook shack of a Red Cross canteen, preparing food for soldiers bound overseas. As a result of her new experiences, she felt she was becoming more tolerant, and more sure of her ability to run things; it was a "liberal education." [23] For her, as for her husband, the war was an important period of training for tasks ahead. Both the Roosevelts led especially hectic existences.

As the work increased drastically at the Navy Department, Roosevelt and Howe assumed numerous new duties, but for a long time they had no additional assistants. "I have tried to get something done," Roosevelt complained, "but the Secretary seems entirely unwilling to add to our badly overworked staff." [24] Nor did Daniels follow the practice of other departments and hire additional Assistant Secretaries.[25] Finally, toward the close of 1917, Roosevelt obtained his friend, Livingston Davis, as a special assistant to handle problems concerning the civilian employees, Naval Reserve, and Militia.[26] Davis, though he provided Roosevelt with delightful companionship and was well liked by the officers, proved to be devoid of independent ideas and did little to lighten the Assistant Secretary's load.[27] At about the same time, Roosevelt lost his reliable and experienced secretary, Charles H. McCarthy, to the Emergency Fleet Corporation. McCarthy at the time that he left paid tribute to one of Roosevelt's finest attributes as an administrator: "It is only a big man and real executive who can distinguish between the minor details of such an office, which you have properly left to those in whom you have had confidence, and the bigger problems which you have so ably handled yourself." [28]

Roosevelt hired a former teacher of shorthand, Renah H. Camalier, who was deeply impressed by Roosevelt's perfectly phrased, rapid-fire dictation. Together with Chester Grey, an assistant, Camalier handled large volumes of correspondence, and throughout the day kept letters flowing in to Roosevelt's desk for signature. Despite the pressure, Camalier remembers, Roosevelt was so congenial that it was a pleasure to work for him. "If it was after office hours he wouldn't hesitate to play cards or smoke cigarettes with you." [29]

An enlisted man, who subsequently became a successful radio writer, had similar impressions. After the Armistice, this man was one of three sailors stationed at the Naval Observatory, where Roosevelt had one of his offices. They were not supposed to carry cigarettes in their blouse pocket, and certainly not filched ones, but whenever they ran short, one or another would think up a pretext for duty in Roosevelt's office, and fill up his pocket from the lead-lined boxes of fine cigarettes bearing the New York Yacht Club insignia. Roosevelt delighted in trying to catch them.

One night when this enlisted man was on guard duty, he sat at Roosevelt's desk and admired the stationery. On the spur of the moment he put a piece of it into a typewriter and wrote a letter to his wife, so fantastic that he thought it would give her a laugh, extravagantly claiming that her husband had barehanded rounded up a ring of spies that were trying to steal secret documents at the Observatory, and that for his heroism he was to be awarded the Congressional Medal of Honor. He signed Roosevelt's name to it and mailed it off. But his wife took it seriously, and got in touch with the editor of the local newspaper, who wired the Navy for details. The next day, the sailor was called into the Assistant Secretary's office, and Roosevelt handed him the telegram from the editor. The sailor confessed the truth, and Roosevelt with a straight face proceeded to enumerate all the heinous offences he had thus committed: forgery, impersonation of the Assistant Secretary, and so many others that the sailor expected to be sent to Portsmouth for life. At this point, Roosevelt could no longer contain himself, and burst into hearty laughter. He told the sailor that if he would promise never to do anything of the sort again, he would drop the charges. This zest for a good joke made it easier for Roosevelt to carry his heavy work schedules.*

* Another means of relaxation – although undoubtedly a very minor one – was to invent names for ships. There was ample room for this, the Navy was ex-

In the afternoons when Roosevelt came to the Observatory he had a customary method of departure. Typically he called a cab in advance, but worked long after five o'clock. From time to time his wife called up, and finally he departed precipitately. He came rushing out of the door, half into his coat, and dashed down the Observatory steps two or three at a time, bobbing up and down like a man jumping rope.[31]

Newspapermen normally saw Roosevelt at 11 in the morning and 4 in the afternoon,[32] and because of his affability he was a favorite of theirs. They came to his main office in the building next to the White House where, like most visitors, they saw him in an official setting: "He works in one of the thousand square, high ceilinged rooms . . . with maps of Europe and ocean routes around him, a bronze bust of John Paul Jones on the inevitable mantelpiece and his commission from President Wilson framed on the wall. His desk is considerably neater than most Washington desks.* At one corner is a vase with fresh flowers." [33]

In this setting, Roosevelt appeared the epitome of the vigorous, efficient, and successful executive. Almost inevitably, he came to re-

panding so rapidly. FDR was afraid the Navy would run out of names of officers for destroyers, and prepared a long list of Indian names, beginning "Absecon, Accomac, Acushnet, Agamenticus, Agawam, Algoma," and so on. Secretary Daniels vetoed this suggestion. He wished to hold the destroyers for persons, since he feared the Navy might lose many before the war was over. Consequently FDR, as Acting Secretary, prepared an order decreeing that new destroyers should continue to be named after distinguished officers of the service, mine sweepers were to be named after birds, and tugs should continue to receive Indian names—and he attached his list—so that at least if they did not get onto destroyers they would appear on something afloat. He also prepared a list of bird names for mine sweepers, no difficult problem for an amateur ornithologist: "lapwing, owl, robin, swallow, tanager," and so on. For scout cruisers, he jotted down city names: "Spokane, Springfield, Omaha, Albuquerque, and Mobile." He tentatively assigned Rochester to one, then changed his mind in favor of Syracuse; Atlanta superseded Baton Rouge, which he assigned to Gunboat No. 21, which he had previously dubbed the "Beaufort." He worked up a list of admirals for battle cruisers: "de Grasse, d'Etaing, Porter, Farragut, Dewey," and John Paul Jones, and a list of historic ship names, beginning "Active, Advance, Adventure," and proceeding through "Yankee." Ultimately, when he could not apply these to anything else, he suggested them for the 200-foot Ford Boats. He even let the public into the fun of thinking up a name for this class of boats, and listed the replies he particularly liked. They ranged from K.K. (Kaiser Killer) to F.D. (Ford—For Democracy—Franklin D.) to O.C. (Ocean Cooties) which last name in view of the subsequent performance of the boats might have been most appropriate. They were called "Eagle Boats," a name not on FDR's list.[30]

* This changed with time. When FDR was president, his desk looked like the display counter in a curio shop.

ceive credit for all manner of war achievements; it is difficult to determine how much of this he earned. That is particularly true in the highly important field of contracts. The Navy was justly proud of its excellent record in procuring war supplies, a record for which not only Roosevelt but also Secretary Daniels, Paymaster General McGowan, and the efficient Supply Corps could claim achievement. Howe, too, played an important part in this, but turned all credit Roosevelt's way. While the supply officers admired and appreciated Roosevelt's zeal for speed and his personal attractiveness, they felt that both he and Howe at times tended to award contracts on a political or personal basis. One officer felt that Howe used to steer them in the right political direction,[34] and another that Roosevelt in making awards "was a sucker for anyone who was a classmate or a member of the Newport crowd. Riches or social position gave a man great validity." [35] One particular promoter, Homer, although not of this background, was so thoroughly in the good graces of Roosevelt and Howe that the supply officers thought they saw many signs of his influence. When the Bureau of Engineering recommended that a contract for engines go to a certain manufacturer, the proposal came back from Howe with Homer's firm, Sterling Motors, substituted. Since the first manufacturer had known of the Bureau of Engineering decision in his favor, this caused considerable embarrassment. Again, John M. Hancock, who was in charge of purchasing, saw Roosevelt in the absence of Howe, and got approval for a large contract for the production of a naval device; it was later changed. Roosevelt had a tendency to vacillate, and say "yes" to the last man.*

In self-defense, the supply officers worked out a device to end this. When papers went to Roosevelt after that, Hancock or one of the others would first prepare a telegram in his own office, and have copies of the contract ready to mail out. As soon as Roosevelt gave his approval, he would rush out the telegram and contract. The first time this new procedure was tried, Roosevelt managed to make capital of the fact that he could not switch the contract. He called up the politician concerned and explained that while he would have liked to help him out, the Navy was on a war footing, and was handling these matters so rapidly that it had already awarded the contract.[36]

* Daniels wrote in his diary, June 26, 1918, "Clerk . . . grilled to find out who was concerned with him in giving out information about bids . . . said he had to use a great deal of bull on F.D.R. to get him to give contract to his favorite who was not the lowest bidder."

Roosevelt and Howe seem to have developed a particular flair for speeding up procurement. Howe had gained experience in his special assignment to hurry up construction on the battleship *New Mexico* during the campaign of 1916. By April, 1917, he was quite adept. The Navy could obtain no bidder for steel castings for the turbines of the *North Dakota*, except one firm which wished to waive all specifications, substitute inferior material, and charge not the customary six to eight cents per pound, but fifty cents per pound for twenty tons of castings. Roosevelt put Howe to work on the problem, and Howe quickly succeeded in inducing the American Steel Foundries Company to undertake the work in keeping with specifications at nine cents per pound. Again, when the Portsmouth yard, after three advertisements, was unable to obtain a bidder for submarine castings, Howe, after a half hour of telephoning, obtained a foundry and within twenty-four hours the work was under way.[37]

If cajoling would not work, Roosevelt was ready to resort to commandeering. He considered doing so before finally recommending the award of a large torpedo contract,[38] and in lesser matters frequently did commandeer needed materials. The instance which Howe liked most frequently to relate concerned a generator needed to complete a plant to produce vital fittings for destroyers. Without the generator, the construction of destroyers might lag, but General Electric could not start building it for three months. Howe obtained a blank commandeering order from Secretary Daniels, and on a tip located a generator on its way to New York. The plant began operation on time, but the opening of the Hotel Pennsylvania was delayed three months.[39]

Roosevelt's most general use of commandeering was to obtain merchant and patrol vessels for naval use. Paymaster General McGowan set up plans, which went into effect upon the declaration of war, for a Committee on Merchant Naval Auxiliaries, with Roosevelt as chairman, to purchase or charter merchant ships.[40] Roosevelt augmented it with a Special Board for Patrol Vessels.[41] Both boards had slow going. Many owners of yachts and ships offered them to the government for nominal fees; J. P. Morgan and Ralph Pulitzer were ready to charter their yachts for a dollar a year.[42] But many others held out for exorbitant evaluations. Roosevelt cited as examples one yacht costing less than two hundred thousand dollars for which the owner asked four hundred thousand, and tugs or fishing boats costing fifty or sixty thousand dollars for which commercial interests asked two hundred thousand dollars. "As a rule," he granted, "the yachting public have come forward in a most patriotic manner, and given not only their boats but their services to the Navy." [43] As for the remainder, he felt the country should have the services of their vessels without being robbed or forced to haggle over the price.[44] Congress granted the authority.

In the realm of construction of camps, Roosevelt was equally impatient with delay. The Navy Department was so slow at first, that there was fear that recruiting would have to stop until new facilities could be built.[45]

As a stopgap measure, the Navy League and the New York Mayor's Committee on National Defense even began to raise funds for construction of a temporary cantonment, and sent Roosevelt a check for $25,000. But the total estimated cost would run between a quarter and a half million dollars, and the need was only temporary, so the project was abandoned.[46] Roosevelt obtained an officer's commission for a New York contractor, Elliott C. Brown, who had recently remodeled the Roosevelt home at Hyde Park, and set him to work building training camps.[47] By the early summer, the Navy was building a big base in a park in Brooklyn under a cost-plus-10-per-cent contract. Roosevelt was indignant when he came upon "a definite plot to rob the government" through a "combination of plumbers and contractors," and called upon the United States District Attorney for the New York City area to crush it.[48] In the spring of 1918, Brown erected a camp at Pelham Bay in New York City, in a way that Roosevelt most warmly admired.* "Everything is booming," Brown wrote. "In the meantime, holy murder is being committed hourly." Again Brown reported, "Things are underway in great shape. You will have some beautiful requisitions to sign someday, but I'm getting everything bought before sending them in! So it makes no difference what anyone does with them." Roosevelt replied happily, "I will sign the requisitions with my eyes closed." [50]

Roosevelt was less proud in future years of his role in erecting temporary buildings in Potomac Park, along Constitution Avenue in Washington. They were so solidly constructed that they were still in use through the Second World War and after – still a long row of

* According to Lindley, Brown finished the Brooklyn receiving ship cantonment two months before contracts were let, and finished the Pelham Bay station two months ahead of schedule at a saving of one third less than the cost elsewhere.[49]

ugliness between the Lincoln Memorial and the Washington Monument. When Roosevelt began to develop plans for the temporary Navy building, Representative Swagar Sherley warned him he could not legally put it in a public park. Roosevelt obtained a ruling to the contrary from the Solicitor of the Navy Department, but informed Sherley: "In order to relieve your mind in regard to my going to Atlanta [Penitentiary], I want to assure you solemnly and finally that before we erect so much as a temporary toilet in a public park, we shall ask permission of the Honorable, the Congress of the United States."[51] Secretary Daniels obtained four million dollars for construction,[52] and by the Armistice the new Navy Building was in use. Roosevelt subsequently disclaimed responsibility for its site and that of its neighbor, the Munitions Building: "My plan was to put them in the oval just below and almost touching the White House gardens, and to make them of such superlative ugliness that their replacement would have been insisted on even before now! However, as on some other occasions, my well laid plan fell through!"[53]

As Roosevelt realized, there was an intimate relationship between contracts, construction, and labor. As wages shot upward, he participated in almost daily conferences for the renegotiation of fixed-price contracts, and sought to stabilize rates of pay in order to keep cost-plus contracts from soaring in total. "There were many contracts on a fixed price basis in existence at the beginning of the war," he once explained. "The bidders, at the time of making their estimates, had every reason to assume a normal labor market during the period of the contract. The demand for war material by foreign countries, and the later demand for materials for our own use was, of course, something which could not be predicted. Reckless bidding for labor at any price by holders of cost-plus contracts for munitions, particularly in what are known as the Metal Trades, threatened to strip the Navy Yards of workmen."[54]

At the beginning of the war Roosevelt had sent telegrams to key naval contractors exhorting their employees to do their "real patriotic duty" and stay by their jobs rather than enlist in the armed forces.[55] Later he met the new threat through the most widely used device of the war administration: the establishment of a board to set wage standards high enough to hold the workers. The Secretaries of War, Navy, and Labor appointed an Arsenals and Navy Yard Wage Adjustment Committee, with Roosevelt representing the Navy Department, and Walter Lippmann, the War Department.[56] It immediately collected wage recommendations from both wage boards and employees of government plants,[57] and within a few weeks reported a scale of wages below what the employees requested, but an average of 10 per cent above earlier rates.[58] On this basis, Roosevelt and the committee reached a one-year agreement with the presidents of the unions. The unions protested because the scale was not higher, but it was so attractive that the railroad workers demanded that their pay be raised to comparable rates. McAdoo, who had added administration of the railroads to his other duties, was incensed and protested to the President, according to Daniels, that "the Army and the Navy had gone hay-wire on increases." [59]

What was more important, Roosevelt subsequently explained, was that the new schedule came to affect almost all of the many industries filling cost-plus contracts. The Navy refused to authorize higher wages than this in payment of workers in factories producing for the Navy on a cost-plus basis. As a result, "This standard almost immediately became universal in most trades throughout the country. The Navy made no objection to any Contractor paying lower wages in case he could reach an agreement to that effect with his workers, but, of course, the practical result of this action was to establish an entirely new and higher scale throughout the country, as no firm could keep its employees at a lower rate when they could obtain the standard scale almost anywhere they applied." [60]

Roosevelt's only fear was that labor might be able to demand a revision in less than a year on the plea that living costs had increased substantially. He wished, therefore, to have the Department of Labor and the Department of Agriculture establish a living standard index, based on the expenditures of a man with an average-sized family who was earning $1500 a year. "If this could show how much his butcher's bill, grocery bill, clothing bill, amusement bill, etc. is at the present time, together with the present prices of the commodities he buys, we would be in a position later on to make a comparison." [61]

Through similar agreements, Roosevelt co-operated to bring about standard wage scales for laborers constructing both Army and Navy camps, and workers building ships for either the Navy or the United States Shipping Board.[62]

While these and similar boards did manage on a piecemeal basis to maintain wage standards and prevent strikes, Roosevelt became strongly convinced of the need for an over-all war labor board or labor administration. Felix Frankfurter, a War Department expert, was the main proponent of the plan.[63] Morris L. Cooke, who subsequently held various New Deal positions, at about the same time proposed a labor council or "national service on industrial relations." [64] Roosevelt prepared a memorandum in which he warned that the current haphazard method by which each department was independently handling labor problems as they arose was a drag on war output. Therefore, he suggested a Labor Administrator, to which existing agencies would delegate some of their authority.[65]

Roosevelt went before the Council of National Defense and argued in behalf of these proposals, but the Council rejected them on the grounds that they were the function of the Department of Labor.[66] Later, the Council recommended that Secretary of Labor Wilson should reorganize his department and enlarge its activities to simulate a War Labor Administration. This led to the establishment of the National War Labor Board and the War Labor Policies Board, forerunners of the labor boards of the New Deal period.[67]

In his own dealings with organized labor during the war, Roosevelt depended heavily upon his ability to win friends when he met leaders face to face. During wage controversies, he personally conferred with the union presidents.[68] When a submarine manufacturer had labor troubles, Roosevelt admonished him, "I have always believed that a perfectly frank talk over matters of this kind will in nearly all cases obviate difficulties." [69] He stood ready to mediate informally between disaffected workers and their employers, as in the case of difficulties at the Lake Torpedo Boat Company and the Sperry Gyroscope Company.[70] In negotiations, he insisted that companies carry out their contracts with the unions, and demanded that they reinstate employees allegedly dismissed for union activities.[71]

On the other hand, Roosevelt fended off union encroachments. Samuel Gompers, president of the American Federation of Labor, had pledged maintenance of open-shop working conditions during the war. He and seventeen presidents of important unions – all except the carpenters – entered into an agreement with the Navy and the Shipping Board. When carpenters who were working for a subcontractor insisted upon a closed shop, Roosevelt warned that although the contract was not directly with the government, nevertheless the government would step in and complete construction, "using, of course, Civil Service employees who are taken on without reference to whether they belong to a union or not." [72] In February, 1918, when carpenters went on strike in New York and Baltimore, and demanded that the

Shipping Board pay them two dollars a day more than they had agreed to accept the preceding November, Roosevelt strongly urged President Wilson to hold the line against them. He pointed to the fact that navy yard carpenters, and all other trades outside of the navy yard, were abiding by their agreements with the Shipbuilding Labor Adjustment Board. "I feel very strongly," he warned the President, "that if negotiations are opened by any other government agency looking to a settlement with a *single trade* along lines different from the regular agreement with the Federation of Labor, the whole situation will become very much involved and it may lead to a total disruption of the existing satisfactory agreements." [73] Roosevelt was determined that labor should receive what he considered fair but not preferential treatment, and should abide by its agreements. To a cousin he wrote: "You are quite right in thinking that the organized labor people are out for all they can get. It is human nature and I do not blame them. Nevertheless, there must be an end to giving in to one hundred per cent of their demands, and I see already a tendency to stiffen up on the part of the government." [74]

Roosevelt's personal preference would have been for universal service. "I have all along taken the position in this greatest of wars," he informed an editor, "that national service should apply to all men and women and not only to the actual men in the Army and Navy. The quicker this principle is understood the better it will be for the country." [75] Yet had Congress passed such a measure, the Navy would have been hard pressed to find employment for many of the types of workers. Arthur Train, a leading lawyer, and inventor of the shrewd fictional lawyer, Mr. Tutt, asked what business and professional men between the ages of 45 and 55 could do to help the country. Roosevelt granted the question was a difficult one: "For instance, in my own Department I need the services of ten thousand shipfitters, plumbers, carpenters, etc., but would be put to it to find any proper work for the President of the Bar Association." [76]

In the absence of any opportunity to press for universal service, Roosevelt did at least work for a limited measure for which he could marshal strong arguments. In convoys crossing through the war zone, captains of merchant ships at times dangerously disobeyed orders; on other occasions they allowed discipline to become seriously lax among the crews. Only 30 to 40 per cent of the seamen were American citizens.[77] Roosevelt tried in vain for many months to sell the Shipping Board upon the Navy position that it was "essential that all ships crossing the war zone should be officered and manned by men who are subject to discipline." He proposed a scheme to bring the merchant officers and crews into the Naval Reserve, and to provide the officers with Navy training in maintenance of discipline.[78] The Shipping Board preferred to give its own training to officers, and Roosevelt countered that it was "preposterous to suppose that adequate merchant officers can be turned out in a four or five weeks' course of instruction, no matter how good the school." Rather than place a penalty upon the merchant marine captains for disobedience, he wished "indoctrination in the art of maintaining discipline and obeying orders. In other words, it is better to maintain efficiency for the sake of efficiency rather than by fear of punishment." [79]

The Shipping Board had entered into an agreement with the Seamen's Union concerning wages, but Roosevelt felt that would not prevent the Board from turning ships over to the Navy to man as long as the number manned by the union members was not decreased. Many of the union seamen, he suggested, could become members of the Naval Reserve.[80]

None of these arguments for the time being seemed to have any effect upon the Shipping Board, and Roosevelt complained that it was apparently "afraid of the Navy and wants to start a little Navy of its own." [81] But the final victory was his. Six months later, the Shipping Board capitulated and agreed to man with naval personnel all commercial vessels engaged exclusively in the trade to ports within the war zone. As far as possible, they would place Navy men upon those occasionally going into war ports. [82]

In almost all of these activities, Roosevelt functioned without seeking publicity.* Indeed, when he was engaged in negotiations with the Shipping Board, he was embarrassed when one newspaperman aired the controversy in a fashion which threatened to impede its settlement.[85] He was, of course, keenly interested in the molding of public opinion. In most respects he accepted the Committee on Public In-

* A notable exception was the drive in his name to obtain public donations of binoculars, the "Eyes for the Navy" campaign. Altogether the Navy received over 50,000 pairs of glasses. All but four or five pairs out of each hundred were usable for lookouts on vessels. After the war, the Navy sent the glasses back to their owners, accompanied by handsomely engraved certificates with a facsimile signature of FDR.[83] Occasionally, too, FDR participated in Liberty Bond Rallies. At one in Washington, he appeared with Mary Pickford and Marie Dressler, and carefully preserved Miss Pickford's autograph in a scrapbook. She remembered many years later her alarm when a railing collapsed, and Marie Dressler, who was far from sylphlike, crashed down on Roosevelt.[84]

formation interpretation of the war, which in private and in his few public appearances, he sought to promulgate.

Roosevelt's view of the Germans as a monstrous nation grew increasingly grimmer. In April, 1917, he co-operated with J. Franklin Jameson, Executive Secretary of the American Historical Association, to search naval records for supposedly suppressed dispatches from Dewey which would indicate that the Germans demonstrated sinister designs during the siege of Manila Bay. The records could not be located; indeed, they did not exist.[86] Roosevelt told an audience at Chautauqua in the summer of 1917 that he had seen numerous signs of ominous German penetration into the Caribbean during his three visits to the area, and warned that Germany had thus been laying a rope around the neck of the American people. "And friends," he added, "if this war had not come, or having come will end in favor of that government, that noose will be drawn tighter and choke us." [87] By September, 1917, he was recommending to Secretary of State Lansing the immediate translation of a book on German atrocities. Roosevelt had been told the account could be relied upon, and was sure its publication "would have an excellent effect at the present time." [88]

During the war Roosevelt showed a full willingness to curtail freedom of speech and the press. In this he was going no further than the rest of official Washington: Postmaster General Burleson was closely watching the staid Kansas City *Star*, which was printing Theodore Roosevelt's anti-Administration bombasts, and avowed he was quite ready to bar it from the mails if it went too far.[89]

Roosevelt demonstrated startling wrath when the April, 1917, number of the *Fra*, published by the followers of Elbert Hubbard, sarcastically attacked the line of reasoning that he strongly advanced that same month in *Scribner's*. The writer seemed to have Roosevelt specifically in mind. "When I read," the *Fra* editor began, "that the purblind and contentious Mr. So & So, with patriotic hyperbole, advocates *Enforced* Military Service for American boys, I see red and exhale profanity! What a splendid test it would be, I think to let Mr. So & So and his five sons climb into dongerees, and incog. shuffle up the dingy stairs of some Recruiting Office . . . and enlist. After one year in 'the Service' in the ranks, let them come out, and vote on the *benefits* they derived." [90] Although obviously the article was written before the declaration of war or enactment of selective service legislation, Roosevelt sent it to one of the Assistant Attorney Generals with the comment that he did not know if any law covered the case, but he wished "you would send the writer and his whole plant to Atlanta for the rest of their natural lives." [91] The Department of Justice replied that there was no statute which prohibited publication of such articles.[92]

When subsequent legislation and prosecutions cut off antiwar agitation, Roosevelt expressed his satisfaction.* The United States Attorney for the Northern District of New York obtained the conviction of four persons for distributing a socialist pamphlet against the war, and sent a copy to Roosevelt, with the explanation that he thought it might "increase the already widespread desire of eligible young men to secure exemption from service," and inspire contempt for the government and its officers.[94] Roosevelt replied that he was glad the attorney was conducting the prosecutions: "I know how difficult it is to make absolutely clear to the public the distinction between prosecution and persecution. Pamphlets of this kind are undoubtedly attacks not on the individuals who make up the Government but on duly constituted government itself, and I cannot help feeling that in certain parts of the country especially every effort should be made to stamp them out." [95]

Perhaps because of his personally warm relations with newspapermen, Roosevelt was ready to take a fairly moderate position on censorship. Before American entrance into the war, he had supervised censoring of outgoing radio messages; in April, 1917, he participated in devising a program for voluntary press censorship.[96] He was mild in his attitude toward the *Scientific American*, whose editor expressed irritation over visits from Navy representatives who wished to know the source of information which the magazine was doing no more than reprint.[97] When the New York *Sun* published an article about an aerial torpedo which the Navy was developing (a prototype of the Nazi V–1 buzz bomb), he asked the newspaper to make no further mention of it.[98] He sent a popular picture of a similar rocket to the officer in charge of experimentation, and learned that it bore not the slightest resemblance to the experimental device.[99] Roosevelt's personal concern was to prevent vital information from leaking to the enemy and he

* FDR wished to limit the civil liberties only of those who opposed the war. He was ready at the same time to urge greater opportunities for Negroes. He wrote a strong letter to Major General William C. Gorgas, the Surgeon General, on behalf of a Negro doctor who wished to enter the Army Medical Reserve Corps.[93]

favored a stricter censorship, "not on incoming news, but on outgoing mail, cables, and telegrams." [100]

On the positive side, in May and June of 1918, Roosevelt delivered a series of speeches in which he sought to interpret the meaning of the war. They were a logical continuation of those of 1915 and 1916, only somewhat tempered with Wilsonian idealism. In approved Administration fashion, he distinguished between the German Government and its people by pointing to the co-operation of German-Americans in the Liberty Loan drives.[101] Those who thought they could win an easy victory through starving the Germans or waiting for a revolution in Austria were deluding themselves.[102] Nor should they take the war posters too literally: "There is one of them that says, 'Food will win the War.' It isn't so, and we know it." The same went for Liberty Bond posters.* "We can't buy victory with gold . . . right deep down there is only one thing that will win this war . . . and that is the biggest thing of all – it is the men in khaki and blue on the other side." [104] Everyone must do everything possible to back up these fighting men. "National slackers are the biggest factor that we have to contend with in this country; men who will not buy bonds, or stamps, or help in any way, but they will soon learn the fundamental principle of liberty. It will be taught them. The war is teaching them every day." Roosevelt did not suggest how. Certainly he could not have condoned the vigilante spirit with which citizens' committees were forcing conformity, but he said nothing whatever against it.[105]

For the future, despite the popularity of the slogan that this was the "war to end wars," Roosevelt wished to see continued armament. He told a Drexel Institute graduating class that universal military training had come to stay. In this war, the United States was protected by the troops of France and Britain during the first year. "That will not always happen if future wars come," he warned. "War is after all but a passing crisis in the life of a nation. War is a culmination of evils, a sudden attack on the very existence of the body politic. But

* In the summer of 1917, FDR explained to his mother the function of Liberty Bonds: "It is too dear of you to put each of the children into the Liberty Loan Bonds & I am glad too that you have been able to subscribe for $10,000 – for I couldn't even take $10 worth as I am trying still to pay off a subscription to the Farmers Loan & Trust Co new stock! I do *not* think it wise to sell out anything you now have in order to take more – In the first place you would get a low price & secondly if others did this it would upset things. The loan is intended primarily for uninvested or liquid assets – not to take the place of existing permanent investments." [103]

the national life can never be called free from danger even in the most unruffled periods of peace. The fight is constant and will be never ending so long as the nation endures. People have talked much of internationalism . . . of the day when nation will no longer rise against nation. But until that day is here, we must recognize existing conditions." [106]

Roosevelt's pessimistic view proved all too correct, and he was to have further opportunity to serve as a war administrator. Already during the First World War he was displaying many of the characteristics that typified him as Chief Executive – though notably he did not have the opportunity as later to create a considerable number of organizations. He had serious weaknesses but despite these his total achievements were impressive. Admiral Land once summed up Roosevelt's work in the period succinctly: "I'd give him a hell of a strong plus mark." [107] Already in the summer of 1918, Roosevelt was in a position to collect a political reward for that grade – if he felt ready to do so.

CHAPTER XX

Mission to Europe

> Though I did not wear a uniform, I believe that my name should go in the first division of those who were "in the service," especially as I saw service on the other side, was missed by torpedoes and shell, and had actual command over "materiel" navy matters in Europe while I was there.
>
> — FDR TO H. H. RICHARDS OF GROTON SCHOOL, *June 28, 1921.*
>
> I have loved every minute of it.
>
> — FDR, *July 19, 1918.*

IN the early months of 1918, three intriguing possibilities faced Roosevelt. Since the Navy Department by this time was well organized for war, he need no longer feel he was indispensable in Washington, and instead might venture along one of several courses which promised adventure, and perhaps greater fame. In May, 1918, a Philadelphia *Public Ledger* photographer took a striking picture of him standing beside Daniels and grinning self-confidently down at President Wilson's offices next door.* Roosevelt joked that the photographer had caught "my chief and myself in the act of casting longing glances at the White House." [2] But it was something more than a joke that numerous New York politicians, from the city as well as upstate, at that very time were dangling under his eyes a possible key to the White House – the governorship of New York. Or would a period of service in the armed forces be a better key? He had the example of Theodore Roosevelt in the Spanish-American War, but

* In his memoirs, Daniels recalls he asked FDR why the Assistant Secretary's grin so completely surpassed his own:

> He said he did not know of any particular reason, only that he was trying to look his best.
>
> "I will tell you," I answered. "We are both looking down on the White House and you are saying to yourself, being a New Yorker, 'Someday I will be living in that house' – while I, being from the South, know I must be satisfied with no such ambition." [1]

also the more immediate example in the World War of both Theodore Roosevelt and Leonard Wood blocked from the fighting in France. He would need an administrative blessing not only to enter the service, but also to get to the front. Otherwise he might end up obscurely in some camp in the United States.* The final possibility, long in the back of his mind, was that he might persuade the Secretary and President to let him go to Europe in his official capacity, which would guarantee that he would at least have an opportunity to see some of the fighting. Only a few months after the outbreak of war in 1914, he vainly sought to head a mission to study the war organization of the British and French navies. The Admiralty coldly declared it would be "very inconvenient," and the French were even more definite in their refusal.[4] After America entered into the war, he reacted to the exasperating "delays and red tape of office work" with the frequent refrain, "I wish they would send me over to the other side." [5] He ultimately succeeded in making the trip, and although it was a dubious political asset, he always considered it one of the greatest adventures of his life.

In order to go abroad, he gave up whatever opportunity he may have had to run for governor in 1918. The fact that he even received consideration was an important outcome of the most momentous political switch in his career. For on the Fourth of July, 1917, six years after he had led the fight to keep "Blue-eyed Billy" Sheehan out of the Senate, Roosevelt consummated his peace with Boss Murphy. He was the main speaker at the 128th annual Independence Day celebration of the Society of Tammany, and was photographed side by side with Sachem Murphy garbed in ceremonial regalia. This picture, even more clearly than the better-known one with Daniels, indicated the direction of Roosevelt's gaze.[6] The sudden friendliness between Franklin and the men he had so long been denouncing was confusing to Sara Roosevelt, who had not been brought up in a political atmosphere. "Don't let the July 4th speech worry you," her son reassured her, " — anybody in the State of N. Y. will tell you where I stand, & you must remember that the meeting was a purely patriotic one & that it was addressed by a Democratic Senator from Colorado, a Republican Congressman from California, a N. Y. Progressive, and an up state Democrat myself." [7]

This may have convinced his mother, but it did not fool many newspapermen. The Republican New York *Tribune* later declared that the Tammany leaders had invited him "to give the 'long talk' in the Wig-

* FDR's brother-in-law, Hall Roosevelt, a flight instructor, was never able to get overseas although he frequently beseeched FDR to work on his behalf.[3]

wam" in order "to give him 'the once over'" and that he made a favorable impression upon the large audience. In consequence, before many months had passed, numerous Tammany leaders were suggesting him for governor. It was not that Murphy had developed a sudden fondness for the young man he previously detested, but that upstate farmers, saddled with heavy taxes, seemed to be restless under the regime of the Republican Governor Whitman, who was expected to run for a third term.[8] If Roosevelt could capitalize sufficiently upon his state senate record as a friend of the farmer, and upon the lure of the Roosevelt name to former Progressive voters, he might be able to cut seriously into the rural majority of the Republicans. Tammany could take care of New York City.

Of course, Roosevelt labeled the *Tribune* talk as "utterly wild," but nevertheless listened intently to much more of the same. As was already customary, he received a flurry of letters from upstate supporters urging him to run for governor. He could take their aid for granted; the serious question would be whether Tammany was behind him. Murphy, whatever show he might make of noninterference, would control a majority of the delegates at the nominating convention. It was more significant, therefore, when he began to receive overtures, if not from Murphy, at least from substantial underlings. The dapper Jimmy Walker, beloved of Tammany, remarked cagily,[9] "Your name is frequently used around New York, looking a little to the future, and it is always a pleasure to hear it." * At the end of May, a prominent Tammany man, John M. Riehle, president of the National Democratic Club, publicly came out for him. At the same time, a supporter in the customs house quoted to Roosevelt from a canvass of several district leaders:[10]

> Hon. Wm. E. Kelly, County Clerk Kings County: – "Franklin Roosevelt has the opportunity of his lifetime. . . . He can win, and I hope he makes the run. I am strong for him. . . ."
>
> Hon. Thomas J. McManus: – "A corking good man. I am for him. . . ." His district will give you 5,000 majority.
>
> Daniel E. Finn, leader 1st Assembly District, would not commit himself, – a little too early yet.

And so forth.

Roosevelt replied, "I note with some amusement that Cagey Dan

* It was no pleasure for Walker in 1932 when, after hearings before Governor Roosevelt, he resigned as mayor of New York City.

Finn is sitting on the fence as usual." He hedged by remarking that the situation was extremely difficult, and went into his customary exposition of the patriotic importance of his work in Washington which it would not be right for him to leave, even for so desirable a position as the governorship. He was gratified to have so many supporters, and admitted he had been "greatly surprised to find many of these friends in somewhat unexpected quarters." But he continued to be noncommittal.[11]

That was Roosevelt's consistent position during the many months that various New York politicians tried to persuade him to run. Through April, he insisted that for the duration of the war, he was entirely out of politics, which meant not only that he would not run for governor while the war lasted, but also that he would not, as in the past, back one New York faction against another. When one of the 1911 insurgents tried to enlist his support for a fight in Buffalo, he replied, "You flatter me very much when you say that I know the political situation in Erie County. I don't know the political situation in Erie County. I never did know the political situation in Erie County, and I doubt if any human being ever could know the political situation in Erie County. It is too intricate for any one brain to grasp more than a slight portion of its devious windings. . . . As you know, I have really paid no attention to politics since the war began."[12]

Roosevelt left open a slight loophole which might lead to his candidacy: while he would not run while the war lasted, "It would be foolish and idle for any man to say what he would or would not do in the future, particularly when the entire situation, international and political, may change overnight."[13] Therefore, for a long time, he admonished politicians to avoid naming possible candidates, and concentrate upon principles.[14] While the war lasted, Roosevelt's very importance in Washington could be a political liability since his opponent could smear him for leaving war work;[15] should the fighting end suddenly, he would be a strong candidate in a "khaki election." Could Roosevelt have foreseen that the war would be over by election time, he might well have been a candidate, and he would surely have won. But Tammany may have been using Roosevelt only as a stalking-horse for its own Al Smith,* preferring to gamble on win-

* A former state chairman confided, "I am not so sure that the New York City people are decided upon an upstate candidate. From things I have heard, I am inclined to think that they would like to have a sentiment develop up the state for Al Smith."[16]

ning with a reliable candidate rather than to obtain more certain victory with a former insurgent.

In June, the devastating German drive, which for a second time brought the enemy frighteningly close to Paris, had not entirely spent its force; the Allied counteroffensive had not yet begun. Peace seemed quite distant. Roosevelt again suggested to Daniels that one of them should go to Europe and see the war in progress with his own eyes. Otherwise they were chess players moving their pieces in the dark.[17] Since the President wished Daniels to remain in Washington for frequent conferences, the Secretary decided to send Roosevelt. The President approved the mission, but according to Daniels also said: "Tell Roosevelt he ought not to decline to run for Governor if it is tendered to him." This pleased Roosevelt, but he told Daniels he did not expect to get the nomination. "We agreed," Daniels noted in his diary, "that going to the war zone in the early summer would not affect the question."[18]

Nevertheless, Roosevelt five days later conclusively eliminated himself as a candidate. Dutchess County Democrats were poised ready to start a movement for him, but he emphatically implored John E. Mack to do his best, without quoting Roosevelt in any way, to prevent the nomination.[19] He enclosed for publication a predated letter in which he recommended for governor an upstate man, William Church Osborn, his long-time benefactor.[20] Osborn was a man whose nomination Tammany would obviously block, and beyond this single letter, Roosevelt gave him no support whatever.[21] "Frankly, what I fear," Roosevelt explained to Mack, "is that they will try to draft me and put it up to the President, and in such case I fear that the President will ask me to run." If "this damned thing" met with Wilson's approval, "it would be might[y] hard to refuse to run."[22]

Just before he sailed, Roosevelt conferred with the President. The day previously, his pronouncement for Osborn appeared in the newspaper, yet later he repeatedly asserted that both in the interview at the White House and in New York he had worked not for Osborn but for Al Smith. Indeed he went so far as to declare that although he himself had the support of even Murphy, he sold both Tammany and upstate leaders on Smith.* "President Wilson asked me whether I would ac-

* While he was President, FDR asserted:

. . . about the middle of June the political situation in the State of New York suddenly flared to the front. Governor Whitman was selected to run for a third term but we believed that a well-known Democrat could decede to the request . . . to be the candidate for the Governorship." When Roosevelt again declined, "the President discussed with me the names of other candidates," and finally brought up and endorsed that of Smith.[24]

The day after this interview with Wilson, Roosevelt wrote the President a letter which does not bear out his later account:

> I entirely forgot on Sunday Evening to speak to you of a personal matter which might come up during my absence – the question of my being nominated for the Governorship of New York – I have tried in every way to stop it, but some of your friends & mine have talked of the possibility of forcing it while I am away & of asking you to encourage me to accept it –
>
> I sincerely hope the matter will not come up – I have made my position entirely clear that my duty lies in my present work – not only my duty to you and to the country but my duty to myself – If I were at any time to leave the Assistant Secretaryship it could only be for active service – Furthermore may I say that I am very certain that it would be a great mistake for either you or any member of the Administration to ask that I give up war work for what is frankly very much of a political job in these times. I cannot accept such a nomination at this time either with

---

feat him. The old question between up-state and New York City was raised. Charles F. Murphy, who had the final say in the whole of the City, and sufficient support in several large up-state cities to give him control of the Convention, had come to realize that a New York City candidate would stand little chance of election if forced through by the City Organization. The secretary of Tammany Hall, Mr. Thomas Smith came to Washington to see me with the message from Mr. Murphy that he would be very glad to support me for the governorship as there seemed no other up-state candidate who was well-known in every part of the state and who, at the same time, had a definite connection with War service. I told Mr. Smith I was extremely sorry but that I could not even consider accepting. . . . Mr. Smith went to New York and returned a few days later to ask me to give Mr. Murphy some recommendations on up-state candidates. A careful check of the field convinced me that the best-known Democrat in the State was Alfred E. Smith. . . . It was pointed out by Mr. Smith and Mr. Murphy that Alfred E. Smith was not only a Tammany man but a Catholic. My reply was that the demand for his nomination for Governor could well originate with the up-state delegates and that in war-time, the church to which he belonged would not be raised as an issue in any community.

Before I sailed, therefore, I communicated with many of my friends among the Democratic leaders up-state suggesting to them that they should start an organized movement for the nomination of Alfred E. Smith. When I sailed on July ninth this part of the political program was well under way and I left the balance of it in charge of Louis Howe.[23]

honesty or honor to myself — I think I have put off all danger of it but in case you are appealed to I want you to know frankly what I feel & I know too that you will understand and that you will not listen to the appeal.[25]

The evidence shows either that Roosevelt's memory was faulty, or that he privately knifed Osborn at the very time he was publicly endorsing him. Osborn, after Tammany had rejected him, angrily decided to oppose Smith in the primaries. When Osborn then asked Roosevelt for support, Howe was happily able to tell him that Roosevelt could do nothing because he would be away for a long time.[26] At the same time, Howe asked Mrs. Roosevelt to "suggest confidentially" when she next wrote her husband, that both the President and Daniels would like him to delay his return until after the New York primaries, "to avoid Mr. Roosevelt's being placed in the awkward position of either having to repudiate Mr. Osborn or to come out against the man who will undoubtedly receive the majority of votes. . . . After they have had a few days to cool down, Mr. Roosevelt can unequivocally come out for the man selected by the voters of the primaries, and no one will feel hurt."[27] This strategy worked to perfection.

Roosevelt undoubtedly had missed an important opportunity to become governor, but the timing would have been bad, since he could not conceivably have gone from Albany to the White House in 1920. The flurry on his behalf had been excellent publicity; his refusal to run, still better. What was more important, he was now of such stature that he could obviously choose the opportune moment after the war to run for either governor * or United States Senator.[29]

Thoughts of either position quickly vanished from Roosevelt's mind on July 9, when he boarded a new destroyer, the U.S.S. *Dyer*, bound for the war zone. His assignment was to check into a number of troublesome matters. Dozens of bases were being established in Europe without definite or final contracts with either private owners or the British or French governments. Roosevelt feared that after the war this might lead to chaotically complicated claims. In addition he wished to inform Admirals Sims and Wilson of the exact state of affairs at home, and to make inspections so that he could give a comprehensive

* He expected Smith to lose, which would have left FDR free to run in 1920. As for 1918, he once wrote, "That was a Republican year, and most of us expected the defeat of . . . [the] candidate for Governor."[28]

report to Secretary Daniels and President Wilson on conditions overseas.[30] He took a technical staff with him.

Although Roosevelt could have gone overseas on a relatively stable and comfortable transport, he chose to make the trip aboard a hastily completed, newly commissioned destroyer. He embarked on this, his twenty-first crossing of the Atlantic,[31] in a high spirit of adventure. This topped all his countless yachting trips, and he made the most of it. It was a shakedown cruise through the war zone, in which Commander Fred H. Poteet had to work out flaws in the ship and the green crew, keep on guard against submarines, and entertain the effervescent Assistant Secretary. All this must have been of considerably more satisfaction to Roosevelt than to Poteet. Roosevelt, as his position entitled him to do, dominated life on shipboard. He took over the commander's cabin, and on the two occasions when there was an alarm at night, dashed to the bridge in his pajamas.[32] In the daytime, he wore a uniform of his own design, "khaki riding trousers, golf stockings, flannel shirt & leather coat – very comfy & warm, does not soil or catch in things."[33]

The *Dyer* stood by the Ambrose Light Ship until after dark when a troop convoy came down the channel. The destroyer swung into place on the starboard beam and accompanied it to sea. "A wonderful sight," Roosevelt rhapsodized, " – five monsters – in the half light – weirdly painted – too dark to see the men on board, but it thrills [me] to think that right there another division is on the way to the front . . . Sea smooth & a lovely night for submarines."[34]

Submarines continued to have a grim fascination for Roosevelt. Two nights later, in a rare mood, he wrote:

> At dusk the five great transports were silhouetted in the West astern of us – clear cut black shapes, no motion, no life, yet peopled like a city and moving on. And later they are just dim looms in the darkness abeam of us – moving on.
>
> And tomorrow morning they will re-appear in all their details of camouflage and bow wave and wake and a thousand khaki points along the rail & on the forecastle – that is if a submarine doesn't run amuck at the critical period of dawn[.]
>
> That gives one a round turn once in a while – the good old Ocean is so absolutely normal – just as it always has been – sometimes tumbling about and throwing spray like this morning – sometimes gently lolling about with occasional points of white like tonight – but always something known – something like an

Photo by Paul Thompson

Charles F. Murphy and John A. Voorhis with FDR at Tammany Hall, July 4, 1917

In May, 1918, the photographer caught "my chief and myself in the act of casting longing glances at the White House"

old friend of moods and power – And the little ships of 20,000 or 30,000 tons, manned by the friends of the old Ocean have held their course in high faith. . . .

But now though the Ocean looks unchanged, the doubled number on lookout shows that even here the hands of the Hun False God is reaching out to defy nature; that ten miles ahead of this floating City of Souls a torpedo may be waiting to start on its quick run; that we can never get our good Old Ocean back again until that God and the people who have set him up are utterly cut down and purged.[35]

Fortunately as they zigzagged across the Atlantic, they encountered nothing worse than rough seas. Roosevelt almost seemed to welcome these as an opportunity to demonstrate his resilience. "I hope I won't lose more than all my insides – I still hope to retain my self-respect," he commented before he left,[36] and he did even better than he hoped. The *Dyer* bounced around so badly one night that he could sleep only in a crack between the mattress and the back of the bunk; crockery went flying across the wardroom, and Roosevelt "ate snatches sitting braced on the transom." But he was able to eat, and although he became weary from holding on with his arms and legs all day, unlike several of the officers he did not become seasick.[37]

When a little excitement took place on Saturday, July 13, Roosevelt heralded it, "A great day – all sorts of things popping." At 5:30 in the morning a whistle blew an "alert," and Roosevelt dashed to the bridge where he found "A huge convoy of merchantmen – twenty-eight in all ambling along." They were badly out of formation, and an easy mark for a submarine – proof, Roosevelt noted, of how wrong the Shipping Board was to "insist that merchant crews & officers are just as good in war time & that they don't need naval discipline." It was a serious mistake to route them so that they saw the troop convoy at all, and had the two convoys passed through each other in the dark an hour or two earlier, the result might have been tragic collisions.[38]

At ten o'clock during gun drill, one of the crew members accidentally shot off a 4-inch gun, and the shell went whistling by, within a few feet of the heads of Roosevelt and his party on the bridge. "The Assistant Secretary was not far from it," Captain McCauley recalled, "but his only reaction was amusement at Poteet's somewhat choleric investigations." [39]

At 10:30 the *Dyer* left the France-bound convoy in order to head directly east for the Azores to refuel. Roosevelt thereupon hoisted his Assistant Secretary's "flag at the main for the first time – not having wished to interfere in any way with the command of the convoy by Capt. Day on the America . . . & stood off to the right – alone."

After lunch, when Roosevelt and Poteet were smoking in the chart-house directly under the bridge, "A voice suddenly came down the tube – It said very quietly: 'We think we see a periscope on the star-board bow.' In 1½ seconds we were on the bridge, though it seemed ages. The skipper blew the 'Alert' & about that time I picked up the object through my binoculars about 1,000 yards away – We swung sharp right at full speed & headed directly for it; word being passed to the men at the depth charges aft to stand-by." They fired three shots at it, and then, when they drew closer, saw that it was "only a keg with a little flag on it." [40]

The final thrill came on July 15, when within sight of the Island of Fayal in the Azores, "both engines went wrong – & we lay an easy mark for passing submarines for an hour." [41] Soon the engines were repaired, and the *Dyer* stopped at Horta, and subsequently at the American base, Ponta Delgada. He met officers and officials, at an official dinner gave a speech in response to a toast,[42] and inspected the base. The *Dyer* refueled, and took Roosevelt on to England. In the next few weeks, Roosevelt twice crossed the Irish Sea and the English Channel by destroyer. These trips too were relatively eventless, but travel by destroyer was far more exciting than travel aboard a transport, and Roosevelt exulted at the time, "I am very very glad I chose this way of crossing the ocean." [43]

Out of his excitement and spirit of adventure, and out of his yearning to be a participant in actual armed conflict, his recollections of these routine voyages began shortly to grow in content and color. It was natural for his imagination to elaborate upon reality.

The facts formed no more than a scanty outline: the delay outside Horta harbor, and a report at Ponta Delgada the next day that a German submarine within *fifty* miles of there was chasing a Portuguese merchant vessel. At the time, Roosevelt mentioned this report to Secretary Daniels, but only as proof that the Azores base needed anti-submarine vessels.[44] Writing to Eleanor during the same period he managed, by implication at least, to bring the submarine much closer than he did in his official letter: "A German submarine was off this port yesterday but did not dare attack!" [45] By the autumn of 1918, when he dictated additional details to his wife, the submarine had come closer still. This report described the events off Ponta Delgada:

"Both engines again heated up when we were six miles fr[om] the Breakwater. We lay motionless for ½ hour keeping of course a careful lookout but absolutely unable to move. When we got in to harbour we heard that at the particular moment we were lying to a submarine was seen following a Portuguese ship off the breakwater. Of course we would have been an easy mark but if the sub did see us she undoubtedly decided to avoid destroyers as all wise subs now do." [46]

As time passed, Roosevelt's narrative had the submarine sneaking up closer and closer to the *Dyer*. Aided by an inaccurate newspaperman, the story reached its near-ultimate form in the Salt Lake City *Tribune*, July 8, 1920. Roosevelt who was passing through recounted the adventure to his former Marine orderly. A listening reporter transformed the *Dyer* into a battleship; while it was being repaired, "a German submarine came up on one side of the battleship and then disappeared. Shortly afterward it was seen on the other side, and then it again disappeared and was not seen again.

" 'We didn't know of our danger until later,' said Secretary Roosevelt. 'The submarine was not seen from our ship, but from the cliff about two miles away, and we received the report later. The Germans evidently thought that we were on the lookout for them and did not realize our helpless condition.' " The story was news to the orderly.[47]

The trip so impressed Roosevelt that he commissioned an artist to paint a scene which he ultimately hung behind his desk in the study of the Roosevelt Library at Hyde Park, and titled "U.S.S. Dyer, Flagship of Assistant Secretary of the Navy in Harbor Ponta del Gada, Azores, July, 1918." *

While Roosevelt was President, the sea stories about the destroyer trips grew still more wonderful. In 1938, he had his naval aide, Dan Callaghan, write A. W. Johnson (who had been in command) for the full account of the remarkable happenings on the *Kimberley* when it carried Roosevelt and the First Lord of the Admiralty from Milford Haven, Wales, to Queenstown, Ireland. Johnson meticulously replied that the *Kimberley* had sunk no submarines; † on the return voyage

* The artist, whom he had befriended, was C. E. Ruttan. Roosevelt gave a romantic account of how he assigned Ruttan to accompany the fleet and paint war pictures – a story quite out of keeping with Ruttan's more prosaic official record.[48]

† Johnson did recall that the *Kimberley* had an empty larder, and he was able to borrow only four apples and half a leg of lamb. He instructed his officers to

when Roosevelt was not aboard, it had, apparently, sighted a periscope which promptly disappeared.[49]

The destroyer trip was of little significance except as an indication of Roosevelt's thirst for excitement. His weeks in England and on the continent not only gave him the opportunity to analyze the operation of overseas bases, but gave him considerable practice in the arts of diplomacy. The long round of protocol began on July 21 when the *Dyer* zigzagged into Portsmouth, with Roosevelt on deck snapping pictures of the harbor, and Nelson's flagship, H.M.S. *Victory*. A large group of officers were waiting and immediately came aboard: not only the American Vice Admiral Sims and his staff, but also Rear Admiral Sir Allan Frederick Everett, the Naval Secretary to the First Lord of the Admiralty. "I am told that it is a very great honour to have had Everett sent down to greet me," Roosevelt commented. "Personally I think it is because they want him to report as to whether I am housebroken or not." He took Roosevelt directly to the Ritz Hotel in London where the Admiralty provided him with "a magnificent Suite." [50]

Roosevelt was delighted to find that despite the tremendous losses suffered from the German onslaught toward Paris from March through June, there was an "absolute unanimity among all the Government people here to see this thing through to more than what they call a 'patched-up peace.' " [51] He wrote Eleanor: "In spite of all that people say one feels a lot closer to the actual fighting here[.] The counter attack in the Rheims salient has heartened every body enormously – Our men have undoubtedly done well – One of my Marine regiments has lost 1200 & another 800[.]" [52]

With thoughts like these in the forefront of his mind, Roosevelt did not utilize his sojourn in England as just another outing. Austerity and inflation were a constant reminder of the war. Prices were up, and many commodities scarce: his favorite silk pajamas had gone up from 30 to 61 shillings a pair, so he bought only three pairs rather than six. When he visited people, he was meticulously careful not to eat his host's scarce rationed sugar, and explained that his wife had warned him not to do so before he left home. But to his surprise, at one home he was served a large platter of bacon for breakfast – a commodity almost unobtainable in Washington. He never forgot this, and deter-

eat nothing, and hoped Roosevelt and the distinguished guests would feel too seasick to eat lunch. But they felt fine, and "the lamb and apples were completely devoured."

mined in the Second World War that recipients of Lend-Lease should receive only fair allocations of scarce American foods. He did relax one week end at Cliveden with Lady Astor, "the same, enthusiastic, amusing, talkative soul as always," [53] and held an "old fashioned reunion of 1904" at a London club with Ned Bell and Livingston Davis.[54] Even most of his recreation was of martial nature. He went to a big entertainment for overseas servicemen his first evening in London. "Theatre packed with khaki & a few of my Navy men." [55]

Roosevelt's conferences with the British officials began immediately. On his first morning in London, he went with Sims and McCauley to call on Sir Eric Geddes, the First Lord of the Admiralty, who held the cabinet position comparable to the American Secretary of the Navy. Geddes, who had spent years in the New World, was a large man, aggressively cordial – "he had awfully nice eyes & a smile," Roosevelt recalled, "but is more like a successful Am[erican] business man than any Br[itish] Cabinet officer one is accustomed to picture." The presence of the officers made Roosevelt feel so uneasy that he resolved next time he would leave them in the anteroom or turn his back on them, as "This form of interview is not calculated to get anybody anywhere either officially unofficially or personally." [56] But McCauley felt otherwise. It seemed to him that Roosevelt and Geddes were "on good terms immediately," and that the First Lord "talked freely of the activities of the British." Geddes rapidly outlined to Roosevelt the progress that the British were making in prosecution of the war, and even showed him some sketches of antisubmarine towers and nets they were planning to erect as a barrier across the English Channel. Sims had known nothing of these. He also told Roosevelt of plans, which must have seemed even more fantastic at the time, but which held enormous significance for the future: the H.M.S. *Furious* was being fitted as an airplane ship, with a clear deck aft upon which airplanes could take off and land. The new H.M.S. *Vindictive* was to have all its guns, smoke pipes, and hatches at one side to provide a clear deck space upon which airplanes could land.[57]

Geddes particularly impressed Roosevelt with the magnitude of the British effort compared with that of the Americans. British airplane production was going along at the rate of 550 a week, but in the past week the United States had produced only two seaplanes and 200 motors. British escort vessels were convoying about six million tons per month, compared with only a quarter million for all other allies, including the United States.[58]

The war was going well. During the great German offensive against Paris which had just come to a close, the German plane losses had been double those of the British. The Germans were building submarines at a rate of twelve a month, but England was commissioning eight destroyers a month. In operations against the German base at Helgoland, their policy was "to sting them all the time."

The readiness with which the First Lord of the Admiralty gave Roosevelt secret information was well calculated to win his confidence, and lead to significant discussions. In the next few days Geddes and Admiral of the Fleet Sir Rosslyn Wemyss, the First Sea Lord, took up several important questions with the Assistant Secretary. They wished to negotiate toward a dovetailing of the British and American construction programs to meet the needs of 1919 operations. For example, Geddes suggested that the two navies between them possessed sufficient submarine chasers and should stop building them. The British also inquired if the Americans could assign destroyers to the North Sea patrol when larger numbers arrived a few months hence. Roosevelt did not make commitments, but dutifully reported these matters to Daniels.[59]

Already at the first interview, Geddes turned to the topic of greatest importance to the British. They were dissatisfied, not only with the disastrous defeats of the Italian Army, but also with the inactivity of the Italian Navy. It would scarcely venture from its bases, and the Italian Government would not agree to put it under the unified command of a British Admiral. Here, the vigorous young man might be of service, and Geddes asked if when he visited Rome he would not intercede to try to get more activity and co-operation.* After the interview with Geddes, Roosevelt had lunched with the Foreign Secretary, Lord Balfour, and again discussed the Italian Navy. Balfour said he would take up the subject with Prime Minister Lloyd George, and talk to Roosevelt about it again before he left for the continent. Subsequently Balfour told Roosevelt he had discussed it with the Cabinet and that they all heartily approved.[60]

Geddes further prodded Roosevelt by informing him that Sir James Rennell Rodd, the Ambassador to Italy, was of the opinion that if Geddes and Roosevelt went to Rome for a quiet conference, they could persuade the Italians to accept Admiral Sir John Jellicoe as the Admiral-

* Roosevelt's reminiscences do not mention the discussion of Italy with Geddes, and give the impression that Roosevelt initiated the project through his conversation with Balfour.

issimo of the Mediterranean. The French would be quite in accord, and at a later stage Clemenceau could be told what was being done. Geddes was quite anxious that a French envoy should not accompany Roosevelt and himself to Rome.[61]

Here Roosevelt found himself at the center of a significant mission, involved in a heady diplomatic intrigue. From the time Geddes first broached the subject, Roosevelt was ready to revise his plans and visit Italy if he could be certain it would help.[62] The unanimity of British feeling convinced him he should go, but he reassured his chief, who was no lover of the English, that he was well aware of the British aims, and was bent on furthering the war effort rather than serving as their cat's-paw. "The trouble seems to be chiefly with the Italians themselves," he explained, "and a certain amount of jealousy of the French in regard to the Adriatic, and of the British in regard to their rather condescending attitude about things in general. I think that Geddes rather wanted to go to Italy with me, but it would be a great mistake for us to go together, and I think I have succeded in heading him off. The Italians may not love us, but at least they know that we have no ulterior designs in the Mediterranean. The trouble is that their Navy people at the top are thinking more about keeping their fleet intact at the end of the war than of winning the war itself."[63] Even before he received this letter, Daniels cabled: "Glad you are going to Rome."[64]

In addition to carrying on discussions with the Admiralty, Roosevelt spent much of his time inspecting both American and British installations. Shortly after his arrival in England he left with Geddes on a three-day inspection trip to Queenstown, where an American naval force of twenty-four destroyers was providing escorts for convoys, and where the Navy was constructing an air station for patrol planes.[65] Roosevelt was completely charmed by the British commanding officer, Admiral Sir Lewis Bayly, "curt, dry, exacting . . . essentially a just man . . . but also underneath a certain shyness a very human man with a twinkle in his eye." Roosevelt strongly recommended to Geddes that he be retained in command even though his normal tour of duty had expired, and was delighted when Geddes agreed to do so.[66] With Bayly, he had a long talk "about the need for an Officer's Club, the liquor question, the moral question, the Irish Question & about U. S. Destroyers in general." The area was a touchy one in which to maintain an Anglo-American base, since the Irish were chafing for independence, and were not only anti-British but somewhat anti-American. Admiral

Bayly avoided trouble by refusing to allow sailors shore leave in the Irish city of Cork.[67] *

Roosevelt also spent considerable time at his desk at the United States Navy headquarters in London, 30 Grosvenor Gardens. He was pleased with the functioning of staff there, and reported to Secretary Daniels that Admiral Sims held the "entire confidence of the Admiralty people, besides their personal friendship; and yet it is very comforting to find that he is just as good an American as he ever was, and he keeps his sense of humor through a whole lot of stuff that would turn some people's heads." [69]

Roosevelt learned much of value to the Navy Department from these inspections and conferences. For example, the laying of the North Sea mine barrage was proceeding well; but while the Admiralty was committed to it, "Admiral Sir David Beatty, Commanding the Grand Fleet south of the barrage line, has from the beginning shown little enthusiasm, and has in fact insisted on various modifications of channels through the barrage." Admiral Sims was insisting that the barrage run from land to land without gaps, and Roosevelt recommended that the Navy Department back Sims to the limit.

From a study of the intelligence methods of the Admiralty, Roosevelt concluded that the Navy Department should emulate the British and speed plans to co-ordinate the Office of Naval Intelligence more closely with the Division of Operations.

Above all, Roosevelt strongly disapproved of the unsound way in

* FDR reminisced about his Queenstown inspection in a talk to the crew of the U.S.S. *Houston*, July 21, 1934. (This talk is not in his *Public Papers*):

> They tried the experiment of sending about two hundred of our people to Cork . . . and the young ladies invariably preferred the American boys and, of course, the young gentlemen of Cork didn't like that with the result that they staged a raid on our seamen. There being about a thousand civilians, they drove our men back to the train and they came back with a good many broken heads. Liberty from that time was suspended until the Mayor of Cork gave assurance that the town people would behave better the next time.
>
> However, when I went on this inspection, as I remember on the U.S.S. MELVILLE, a machine ship, we came to one of the machine bays about amidships, and Captain Pringle looked over in a corner and found a large canvas covering something and turned to a chief petty officer, a very large-red-headed man by the name of Flanigan and said, "What's under that?" Flanigan saluted and said, "I'll look, sir." He went over and lifted up the canvas and there was the finest assortment of brass knuckles and pieces of lead pipe that you ever saw. Captain Pringle said to Flanigan, "What's that for?" Flanigan with a grin said: "Captain, sir, that's for the next liberty trip to Cork, damn these Irish." [68]

which the Navy was conducting business with its allies. There was no over-all authority like that within the Navy Department at home, nor was there any general business policy. The officers overseas thought first in terms of operations, and in their concentration upon getting things done, postponed decisions as to who should pay for the work, how, when and under what policy. He cited an instance in which the Navy took over under a verbal agreement an airfield and buildings at Eastleigh which the Admiralty was constructing under a $900,000 contract. Although the contract was completed the previous spring, and the Navy occupied the field, "nobody in London knows whether the United States or Great Britain will pay for the contract or whether the cost will be shared." Again, American destroyers were being repaired under an Admiralty contract with Cammell-Laird of Liverpool. The repair yard was sending itemized bills to the Admiralty, whose accountants passed on their accuracy, and forwarded them to Admiral Sims. He authorized payments without question. Roosevelt granted that personally he had no more doubt than Admiral Sims that the charges were correct, but was concerned because the Navy neither inspected nor checked the figures. "You and I are, after all, responsible to the President and the Congress," he warned Daniels. Later, in France, Roosevelt found similar slack conditions.

Roosevelt was careful not to blame Admiral Sims for this state of affairs; he felt it was physically impossible for Sims to supervise more than operations. The remedy, he thought, would be to appoint another civilian as Assistant Secretary of the Navy, then himself return to Europe to handle financial problems during the war and demobilization at its end.[70]

Certainly in operations, business affairs, and liaison, Roosevelt gained an invaluable firsthand view of the problems that faced the United States in conducting a war in Europe. But, at the time, the thrill of conversing with war leaders overshadowed these more technical matters.

One notable day, July 29, was packed with exciting experiences for Roosevelt. In the morning, he had a forty-minute audience with King George V, who deeply impressed him with stories of "wanton destruction of property by the Germans," and of deeds too horrible to include even in the Bryce Report. "The King has a nice smile and a very open, quick and cordial way of greeting one," Roosevelt remembered. "He is not as short as I had expected, and I think his face is stronger than photographs make it appear. This is perhaps because his way of speaking is incisive, and later on when he got talking about German atrocities in Belgium his jaws almost snapped." Roosevelt and King George got along so well that at times they were both talking at once.[71] That noon, Roosevelt and Geddes were guests of the Anglo-American Luncheon Club. Each spoke, and McCauley proudly recorded that "Roosevelt was easily the center of popular attention. He spoke easily and well, as always." [72] The talk should have been popular, for Roosevelt gave full credit to the Royal Navy for its work in transporting and escorting American troops to France. He pointed out that in June, over 60 per cent of the Americans came over in British transports and under British escort.[73]

In the evening, as the climax of the day, Roosevelt attended a dinner at Gray's Inn in honor of the war Ministers.[74] Afterwards, he wrote Eleanor about Lord Curzon's speech, and the response of General Smuts for South Africa, but failed to mention what many years later seemed the most important event of the day: at that dinner he met Winston Churchill for the first time.[75] Obviously these two men made little impression upon each other at the time, since several months later Roosevelt did not record the meeting in his detailed recollections, and Churchill entirely forgot the episode.[76] *

On the day after his encounter with the Prime Minister of the future, Roosevelt had lunch at the American Embassy with the Prime Minister of the First World War, David Lloyd George. He impressed Roosevelt as being thickset, just like his pictures, but of tremendous vitality. They talked of the strikes threatening British ship and munitions production, and Roosevelt assured Lloyd George that if strikes developed, "the Br[itish] unions w[ou]ld obtain no sympathy fr[om] our [American] Federation of Labour . . . & that on the contrary a firmer attitude by the Br[itish] govt w[ou]ld receive hearty applause fr[om] the U. S. He seemed greatly pleased & intimated that he had decided on a firmer hand in the future." [78]

In total, Roosevelt's interviews with the British leaders had relatively small effect upon the war effort – though had it gone into 1919, the integration of British and American naval construction would have become significant. Rather, again, Roosevelt was gaining experience

* Churchill's lapse of memory irritated Roosevelt in 1941. Subsequently the Prime Minister made up for it by mentioning in his memoirs that he had met Roosevelt at Gray's Inn, and was "struck by his magnificent presence in all his youth and strength." [77]

and storing up impressions upon which he was to draw two decades later in the second world crisis. At the time, and later, he was far more excited over his visit to the Western front. On the day after his talk with Lloyd George, he embarked at Dover for military adventure in France and diplomatic negotiations in Italy.

CHAPTER XXI

"I Have Seen War"

> I have seen war. I have seen war on land and sea. I have seen blood running from the wounded. I have seen men coughing out their gassed lungs. I have seen the dead in the mud. I have seen cities destroyed. I have seen two hundred limping, exhausted men come out of line – the survivors of a regiment of one thousand that went forward forty-eight hours before. I have seen children starving. I have seen the agony of mothers and wives. I hate war.
>
> – FDR, *August 14, 1936.*

ON July 31, 1918, a British destroyer flying the flag of the Assistant Secretary of the Navy carried Roosevelt and his party from Dover to Dunkirk. It was only a two-hour trip, but it took him from the relative security of England almost to the front lines. Suddenly, for the first time, he saw the frightful devastation of the battle area. "As we were running into the narrow mouth of Dunkirk Harbor," Roosevelt wrote, "it became perfectly clear why our first Navy Aviation Squadron has had such a bad time. There is not a whole house left in this place. It has been bombed more than any other two towns put together in fact. It may be truthfully said it has been bombed every night that flying was possible for three years."[1] Yet the houses gave only a hint of the damage that rapidly improving technology of war had already made possible. Roosevelt did not see a pane of glass in town nor a building not pock-marked by shell fragments, yet he marveled that, considering the incessant attacks, the destruction was so small. The answer, he found in Calais, was that until recently the bombs had ranged in size from fifty to three hundred pounds – comparatively light. More recently the Germans had begun dropping some that weighed eight hundred to twelve hundred pounds. But, Roosevelt learned, the United States Navy was more than keeping up with this advance in armaments: the following week it would start sending night bombers over German territory carrying bombs weighing

1750 pounds. Of course, they were intended solely for military objectives.[2]

Some of the American seaplanes, Roosevelt found, were no match for those of the Germans. The small, slow planes in the Navy squadron at Dunkirk were useful only to search for submarines fairly close to the harbor; they had to retreat hastily whenever German seaplanes appeared. Since larger planes could not use Dunkirk harbor, Roosevelt recommended that the Navy should not expand the station.[3]

From the coast, he drove inland to Saint Inglebert, where he hoped that evening to see the Navy night bombing squadron leave on its mission. He waited nearly two hours, but the slight ground mist did not lift and the planes could not take off. While waiting, he chatted with the young junior lieutenant in command, Robert A. Lovett,* who "seems like an awfully nice boy." [4] During the night, which he spent at a nearby château, he watched a German air attack upon Calais. He observed dryly, "Evidently the Boche did not think the ground mist too heavy." [5]

En route to Paris, Roosevelt had to cut southward along a still uncomfortably narrow strip of land through Boulogne to Abbeville so as to avoid the menacing German lines. On the way he stopped at the British General Headquarters, where he was pleased to find that the American liaison officer was his old friend Major Robert Bacon – a Morgan partner, who had been one of the most ardent advocates of American intervention. Major Bacon went over the military maps with Roosevelt and showed him the latest position of the British troops.[6]

During the afternoon, Roosevelt and his party continued to pass freshly dug trenches and barbed-wire entanglements, but in the evening were magnificently housed as the guests of the French Government in the Hotel Crillon in Paris.[7] Again, as in London, Roosevelt plunged into a succession of official interviews and conferences. In his "full regalia and accompanied by staff," he met the admirals, the Minister of Marine, and the Minister for Foreign Affairs.[8] He attended a lunch given by President and Mme. Poincaré at the Élysée Palace, a lunch not in his own honor but in honor of Food Administrator Herbert Hoover, who had recently arrived in Paris. Though the guests wore cutaway coats, the occasion was so informal that Roosevelt even had to introduce himself to the Poincarés.[9] He was far more impressed later that afternoon when he met Premier Georges Clemenceau:

* Lovett became Secretary of Defense in 1951.

"I knew at once that I was in the presence of the greatest civilian in France. . . . He almost ran forward to meet me and shook hands as if he meant it; grabbed me by the arm and walked me over to his desk and sat me down about two inches away. He is only 77 years old and people say he is getting younger every day. He started off with no polite remarks because they were unnecessary." He showed Roosevelt on a map the latest advances around Château-Thierry, and then like George V, "launched into a hair-raising description of the horrors left by the Boche in his retreat."

"Then still standing he said – 'Do not think that the Germans have stopped fighting or that they are not fighting well. We are driving them back because we are fighting better and every Frenchman and every American is fighting better because he knows he is fighting for the Right and that *it* can prevail only by breaking the German Army by force of arms.' He spoke of an episode he had seen while following just behind the advance – A Poilu and a Boche still standing partly buried in a shell hole, clinched in each other's arms, their rifles abandoned, and . . . in the act of trying to bite each other to death when a shell had killed both, and as he told me this he grabbed me by both shoulders and shook me with a grip of steel to illustrate his words, thrusting his teeth forward towards my neck." [10]

When Roosevelt called on Joffre, he came closer to getting kissed. But he successfully dodged "this charming little ceremony" or "accolade." He felt more at ease when he visited Theodore Roosevelt, Jr., and Archie Roosevelt, although he envied them their uniforms. At least he was in no danger of being bussed. They were "wonderfully interesting and they can't say enough for the American troops. They both have really splendid records." [11]

A few days later, Franklin also had the experience of being under enemy fire. When he left on August 4 for the battle area, his only worry was that he might not actually get to the front lines. Both at the time and in subsequent months he vented his full wrath upon the unfortunate American naval attaché who tried unsuccessfully to arrange a safe and soft trip for him through villages captured many days previously.* He thwarted the attaché and embarked upon a strenu-

* According to McCauley, this disturbed FDR's "remarkable equanimity" for the "first and only time on the trip." "He said emphatically that he had not come as a sightseer and wanted to be familiar with what was going on at the front [and] . . . soon proved . . . he was going to run his own show himself." FDR was so wrathful that he not only obtained removal of the offending attaché

ous and dangerous regimen which was as near as he could make it to an approximation of actual participation in the fighting. After several days of it he wrote with relish, "The members of my staff have begun to realize what campaigning, or rather sight-seeing, with the Assistant Secretary means." [13]

Roosevelt lunched with the French commanding general, who, to Roosevelt's delight, praised the valiant fighting of the Marine regiments in Belleau Wood. After lunch they went through the Wood, so recently the scene of bitter fighting: "In order to enter the wood itself we had to thread our way past water-filled shell holes and thence up the steep slope over outcropping rocks, overturned boulders, down trees, hastily improvised shelter pits, rusty bayonets, broken guns, emergency ration tins, hand grenades, discarded overcoats, rain-stained love letters, crawling lines of ants and many little mounds, some wholly unmarked, some with a rifle stuck bayonet down in the earth, some with a helmet, and some, too, with a whittled cross with a tag of wood or wrapping paper hung over it and in a pencil scrawl an American name.

"Over the top of this first rise [one] would look but a short distance for the ground was so cut up with ridges, ravines, boulders, tree trunks and the remains of what had once been underbrush." Roosevelt could well envisage how difficult and bitter the fighting had been through terrain like this, where "the ground was broken up, tumbled, irregular ridges and gas-filled ravines." He wrote: [14] "There is no use going into the details of those two weeks, of the days when food and ammunition could not be brought up, of the wounded who could not be brought out, of the detachments which could not maintain contact, and of the darkness and constant fighting without rest or sleep. It is enough to know that not one day passed without some advance, until an enemy defending force, first and last three times our number, had been wholly cleared from every foot of the Bois de la Brigade de Marine." *

Finally, that afternoon, Roosevelt realized his keen wish; at Mareuil en Dole, which the Americans had just captured, he was able to witness heavy fighting. The Sixth United States Gun Battery was shelling the German lines seven kilometers away; French and German airplanes

---

from his Paris post, but the following spring tried to oust him from his next station.[12]

* The French commanding officer told FDR that he had so renamed Bois de Belleau in honor of the heroic Marines; subsequently through "a mean piece of hokus pokus by some narrow-minded army officer," it became Bois des Américains.

were having a dogfight overhead; and antiaircraft guns were sending up a barrage.[15] "Just as we descended from the motors a loud explosion went off very close by. Some of the party jumped perceptibly, realizing that we were within easy range of the Hun artillery. It was, however, only one of our own 155's so cleverly camouflaged in a tree just off the road that we had not noticed its presence. . . . We visited the other guns of the battery of 155's, fired one of the guns, and then returned all the way to Château Thierry.[16] *

The next day, outside of Nancy, Roosevelt found the Marines of the Second Division about to return to the front, although they had sustained 40 per cent casualties at Belleau Wood, another 20 per cent loss at Soissons, and had had no rest period. They had been given "more hard and continuous fighting than any other two American Divisions put together." When he inspected one of the battalions of the Fifth Regiment, "drawn up the length of the narrow village street," the majority were in Army khaki, since they had worn out their own uniforms months earlier, but the large number of replacements in olive drab made it easy to visualize the heavy casualties. They "looked wonderfully well" despite the two months of constant fighting, and did not complain about having to go back into action. Major General John A. Lejeune pointed out that his khaki-clad troops were hardly distinguishable from Army men, and he wished they could wear the Marine Corps button on the point of their collars. Roosevelt immediately assumed responsibility and "issued an order that this device be worn in recognition of [their] splendid work." [18]

At Verdun, Roosevelt again was under enemy fire. The titanic battle, which had so tragically bled the French, was over. They had heroically held the great barrier fortress, which long symbolized their will to resist the Germans, but only at a cost of 300,000 casualties; the enemy in failing had lost an equal number. Roosevelt visited the citadel,

* This adventure was always fresh in FDR's mind. In 1931, without asking directions he took his son Elliott to Mareuil. "We found the roads, the slope, the bushes, the wall and the broken roof [of a barn], exactly as I had described them, after 13 years. There was a new section of wall, and too, the new tile just where the hole had been." As for the episode when the American gun crew had startled the visitors, on December 11, 1944 (only four months before his death), FDR dictated a sequel: "after we had accepted the laughter of their gun crews we went into the thicket and the C.O. trained them [the French 155's] on a German-held railway junction about 12 miles north. I pulled the lanyards, and a spotting plane reported that one shell fell just short of, and the other directly on, the junction and seemed to create much confusion. I will never know how many, if any, Huns, I killed!" [17]

still garrisoned with four thousand troops, and read the famous sign on a board near the entrance, "*Ils ne passeront pas*" – "They shall not pass." The Commandant provided the Americans with French helmets and gas masks, and took them onto the battlefield. The damage down to the Meuse River was great enough, but beyond they entered a far worse area where the fighting had been heaviest.

The Commandant pointed where the village of Fleury had been, but "not a brick on the tumbled earth would verify his statement." They stopped to take a picture, but the French officer hurried them on, since they had undoubtedly been seen from a German observation balloon, and the Germans would start shelling the sharp turn in the road they were traversing – a turn ominously called "Dead Man's Corner." "We passed on to the south slopes of Fort Douamont, a quarter of a mile beyond, and sure enough the long whining whistle of a shell was followed by the dull boom and puff of smoke of the explosion at the Dead Man's Corner we had just left." The shelling continued at six-minute intervals.[19] They climbed to the fort in single file, spread out at a distance of forty paces. As each shell came whining over their heads, the Colonel held up his arm; if he dropped it, they were to dive into the nearest shell hole. The fort was indistinguishable from the surrounding terrain and they entered it by crawling through a small tunnel on their hands and knees. Within they could periodically feel the muffled shock of shells bursting outside,[20] but when Roosevelt gazed out on German trenches, about a mile away on the side of the opposite ridge, "there was literally no sign of life."[21]

These glimpses of warfare impressed themselves deeply upon Roosevelt: the devastated terrain, the German destruction of civilian property and even a hospital, the scattered gray-clad German dead not yet buried, the stench of decaying horseflesh, the fetid air within the forts, the incredible hardships the troops were undergoing, and their bone-deep fatigue. Yet he was fascinated rather than repelled, thrilled by the patriotism and heroism of the American and Allied troops, and oppressed by a sense of guilt and deprivation because he was not sharing their vicissitudes.

He departed from Verdun on August 7, and two days later was in Rome to participate in a quite different sort of adventure. While the excitements of international negotiation could not compare with those of armed combat, they also were stimulating. En route, Roosevelt passed through Turin where he met various Italian officials, the American consul, and an acquaintance who was serving as a captain in the

United States Army Air Corps, Fiorello La Guardia. The consul and La Guardia complained of the difficulty in getting supplies across the Italian-French border and asked for more men to handle them and keep the traffic open. Later Roosevelt arranged this with the head of the American Red Cross in Italy.[22]

In Rome among both the cabinet ministers and the populace as a whole, Roosevelt tried to strengthen the will to fight. He emphasized how much aid the United States was planning to give Italy, and inquired how much Italy intended to do in return. But he found, "They are more anxious to know what we are doing and going to do than to speak of their own work." [23]

Roosevelt also tried to bolster pro-American feeling among newspapermen. Both the French and British were spending more money in Italy than the Americans, and Captain Charles E. Merriam, Commissioner to Italy of the Committee on Public Information, was concerned over the headway Italian socialists were making with their charges that the United States was an imperialist nation with interests contrary to those of Italy.[24] Merriam arranged for Roosevelt to talk to the editors and correspondents. Roosevelt spoke for about forty-five minutes, while the Italian undersecretary for the press and propaganda, Romeo Stuart Gallenga, translated. (He was so frank in some of his remarks that Gallenga refused to translate them,* and at points the press reports of the speech carried blanks with the explanation: *censura.*[26]) "I can tell you," Roosevelt said, "that fresh American troops will be sent to Italy, for henceforward the unity of our single front is as it should be, recognized as complete, solid, and indivisible." [27] Merriam reported home that Roosevelt had provided "our best news story of the week." [28]

Though Roosevelt made good copy, he did not succeed in winning over the Italian Cabinet to a militant naval policy. Austria was so obviously tottering that a vigorous sea and land offensive might well knock her out of the war; the combined Allied naval strength in the Mediterranean was more than adequate to destroy the Austrian fleet and support military operations on the Dalmatian coast. The younger Italian officers wished action, but the Marine Minister and the Commander in Chief of the Navy were determined to keep the capital ships

* A Harvard alumnus in charge of oral propaganda for the United States remembered that before the conference Gallenga was worried for fear FDR might be indiscreet. Merriam suggested that he might omit questionable remarks from his translation. Furthermore, Merriam arranged to tug at his coat if he, Merriam, wished a deletion. During the speech, Merriam pulled at Gallenga's coat twice.[25]

intact, and refused to take risks. "I insisted on keeping to the main point, the enormous superiority of the combined French, Italian, British, Japanese and American naval strength in these waters over Austria," Roosevelt reported.[29] But the Italians were adamant. Captain McCauley reported one remarkable interchange between Roosevelt and one of the Italians. Inquired Roosevelt: "Do you think it wise to keep the Italian Battle Fleet at all times in harbour, rather than sending them out for exercises, drills and target practice?" The Italian retorted: "The Austrians do not dare bring their Battle Fleet out and so have no more opportunity for drill and exercises than we have. We feel sufficiently superior to defeat them if they should decide at any time to come out of harbour to meet us."[30] Roosevelt commented afterward, "This is a naval classic which is hard to beat, but which perhaps should not be publicly repeated for a generation or two."[31]

Prime Minister Orlando was more receptive to Roosevelt's suggestions. After a long talk with him, Roosevelt concluded: "Things have worked out all right. I have proposed a plan for the creation of a General Naval Staff in Mediterranean, Adriatic and Aegean waters, to be composed of a Britisher, probably Jellicoe, as senior member or chairman, and one member each from the French, Italian, American and Japanese Navies. This obviates the Italian and French objections to a British Commander-in-Chief, and while it does not give complete unity of command it would be a distinct step towards unity of action and a policy directed more along the lines of an offensive."[32]

Oddly enough, Roosevelt then reported to Daniels that the Italians had "finally agreed to the proposition of a commander-in-chief for the naval forces in the Mediterranean," which, of course, was quite a different thing from a chairman of a joint naval staff. They insisted upon one reservation, that they continue to hold complete command over conduct of operations in the Adriatic. Roosevelt agreed to this, trusting that the Italian commander in chief would co-operate with the Allied chief.[33]

In a similar vein, Roosevelt suggested to the First Lord of the Admiralty a compromise solution which would please the British, French, and Italians. All three would get something: the British Admiral Jellicoe could serve as senior officer of the joint staff; the Italians could enjoy continued inactive autonomy in the Adriatic; the French, having the most capital ships in the Mediterranean, could have command of all the ships outside of the Adriatic, with the fine title, "Mediterranean Grand Fleet," and a French admiral in command.[34]

This may have been satisfactory to both the British (who gained a command) and the Italians (who lost nothing), but it displeased the French, whose commander would be subordinate in title if not in authority to the British. In Washington, Ambassador Jusserand complained to Secretary of State Lansing that Roosevelt had asserted in Rome that the United States wished an English commander in the Mediterranean.[35] This was precisely what Roosevelt had done on the assumption that he had Daniels's blessing in doing so,* but Daniels reacted to Jusserand's report as though it were news to him, and wrote in his diary: "Lansing asked if FDR was authorized to tell Italy we favored the British plan. . . . I said no; on the contrary I had written him our country favored allied command but declined to say who should command." [36]

Although it is by no means clear whether or not Roosevelt overstepped himself, the minor tempest apparently irritated the President. On September 10, Wilson asked Daniels henceforth to inform him of the names and mission of any civilians going abroad before he designated them, because "too many men go over assuming to speak for the Government." [37] The armistice came too soon for Roosevelt's mission to bear much fruit. The negotiations did serve one purpose: they provided a bit of education for Roosevelt.

In contrast, Roosevelt's inspection of naval air stations after his return to France led to the most meritorious achievement of his entire trip. His visit to the main base and assembly center at Pauillac, near the mouth of the Gironde, superficially was like innumerable others. The air stations were another remarkable example of American enterprise. "In nearly every case," he reported, they "have been built up from nothing. Their erection has been done by Navy personnel from the digging of the foundation to the putting on of the last coat of paint." [38] Roosevelt dined with the three thousand enlisted men in their new mess hall, and tried to raise their morale by praising them for persisting at such uninteresting, though important, work.[39] Afterwards he flew along the Gironde in one of the seaplanes.[40] But in addition, he thoroughly checked upon the incredibly bad conditions in which airplanes were arriving from the United States for assembly,[41] and cabled an indignant report to Daniels:

* On August 13 FDR wrote his chief: "Sir Eric Geddes and the British have wanted to put in Jellicoe as Commander-in-Chief, and I found from cables that you, through the State Department, had directed that we back up the British in this effort." This letter may not have arrived at the Navy Department by September 3 and 5, when Lansing complained to Daniels.

"During the past three months, seaplanes have been shipped to France in such numbers as to congest the ports greatly, yet not a single one of these planes today is equipped to fly in service, and only eight can fly at all." Due to lack of proper inspection, "Liberty motors required over 200 man hours of overhauling before they were in proper shape for use." One motor had two pounds of sand in the cylinders; many others were short of parts or improperly assembled. Gasoline pumps were defective, and only 8 starters were received for 145 motors. Not a single bombsight or spare part was sent. "Wings had to be completely rebuilt on account of the fabric joining being imperfect. Over 50% of the propellers received abroad were found unsafe due to glaring imperfections." Cable queries to the Navy Department seldom brought an answer within ten days, and then frequently only after being repeated. Roosevelt urged Daniels to order drastic action in all the bureaus concerned "as present conditions are scandalous."[42]

Navy officials in Washington answered these criticisms by claiming that planes being assembled at a coast station in the United States flew without difficulty after only twenty to thirty hours of work; sabotage of engines was taking place after inspection, but resultant damage was so negligible that it could easily be remedied. Missing parts were in subsequent shipments long overdue, and gasoline pumps would function properly if the pitch of the propellers were changed. Nevertheless, the Bureaus would send representatives abroad to follow up matériel.[43]

Roosevelt was not interested in these explanations of minor matters. He felt that basically the fault went far beyond the present difficulties.* The most serious flaw in naval operations in Europe lay in aviation. This was not the fault of Captain Hutch I. Cone, who had "surmounted obstacles and cut red tape in a masterly fashion." Nor was it the fault of the Office of Naval Aviation in Washington. Rather, the troubles grew out of the basically impotent organization of the air arm. The fault, Roosevelt formally reported to the Secretary, "lies primarily in a thoroughly unsound system within the Navy Department, a system which I have verbally and in writing protested against to you on

* To deal with immediate problems, FDR recommended placing a man of marked business ability in charge of naval aviation and giving him sufficient authority to demand and receive information and action from the various bureaus. He also wished: "(a) coordination of the various Bureau work, (b) a complete and active follow up system, (c) complete open order reports being sent abroad every ten days; (d) effective departmental routing system; (e) Bureau of Distribution; (f) an Inspection Department which will function; (g) assembly of all planes including test flights before shipment abroad."[44]

many occasions. Just as long as the present indistinct and indefinite relationship exists between the Office of Aviation and the different bureaus concerned, the same trouble will continue. The Office of Aviation has practically no authority or means of following up the work of the bureaus. The result is that aviation as a whole might be said to be the child of a half dozen parents, each of these parents having and exercising equally great and equally little authority over the child. The result is that the child is being badly brought up. . . . If Aviation is going to be under the control of the Office of Aviation, that Office should have the power to follow up the work which the different bureaus are doing for it. If the Office of Aviation is given that power, *and exercises that power*, it will be possible to tell who is to blame for any trouble in the future. I commend this to your very special attention, because I am not a believer in an air ministry, but unless we do something in the Navy Department, the present situation will strengthen the hands of those who would take Naval Aviation away from the Navy Department."[45] For the time being, Roosevelt's demand for the establishment of real authority in the Office of Naval Aviation was ignored.* Agitation for a separate air force grew, as he had prophesied, but ironically it was the efforts of General Billy Mitchell to strip the Navy of its air bases that led in 1921 to an Act of Congress establishing a powerful Bureau of Aeronautics in the Navy Department.[47]

As Roosevelt traveled along the coast of France, he gloried in his role of "trouble shooter." After several days more he hastily wrote Eleanor from Brest, "It has been a frightfully busy week – on the road each day from 6 A.M. to midnight – & we have done all manner of interesting things all the way from South of Bordeaux to here – all by auto – flying stations, ports, patrols, army stores, receptions, swims at French watering places etc. etc."[48]

On the way, they went down the Loire to St. Nazaire, where Rear Admiral Charles P. Plunkett was mounting huge 14-inch, fifty-caliber naval guns on railroad carriages for use along the Western front. These guns, originally designed for battle cruisers, had a maximum range of twenty-five miles, and could counter the heaviest German artillery. While in Washington, Roosevelt had helped foster the proposal for a

* FDR had no success in arguing his viewpoint on aviation after he returned to Washington. When he presented his criticisms before the weekly meeting of the Council in the Navy Department, three bureau chiefs disagreed with him. They argued that the Navy by then had airplanes to spare, and that the situation had improved since Roosevelt inspected Pauillac.[46]

naval battery, and now upon meeting Admiral Plunkett garbed in Army uniform,[49] he got the idea that this battery contained the answer to his problems. If he could serve with it, he could fulfill two of his dearest dreams: he could be a naval officer, and at the same time participate in front line fighting.*

Only two days previously Roosevelt had commented to the enlisted men at Pauillac, "It is hard for me to go back to a dull office job at Washington after having visited the lines where our boys are making history." [51] When Roosevelt inquired if he could join the battery, the Admiral "asked me if I could swear well enough in French to swear a French train onto a siding and let his big guns through. Thereupon, with certain inventive genius, I handed him a line of French swear words, real and imaginary, which impressed him greatly, and he said that he would take me on . . . with the rank of Lieutenant Commander." [52] Subsequently, Roosevelt hinted to Eleanor that he did not think he would be in Washington for long, and even penciled, but did not send, a cable to Secretary Daniels announcing his plan to enter the service.†

Again, Roosevelt visited Paris. The representative of the Committee on Public Information, James F. Kerney, felt that the psychological moment had come to bolster French morale and damage that of the Germans by announcing the Allied triumphs in antisubmarine warfare. Kerney chose Roosevelt as the man to hold a press conference, because of his success in Italy. Roosevelt did so on August 21,[54] and, as he recalled many years later, made the story "just as big as I possibly could":

"I received the French press at 11:00 A.M. in the hotel . . . and they were all in full dress suits, with white ties . . . nearly all of them were the *rédacteurs* – the editors – of the papers. They were having the

* Almost at the same time in New York State, Eleanor Roosevelt encountered her Uncle Theodore at the funeral of a relative. Theodore reproached her because Franklin was not in the armed forces, and urged her to use her influence to get him to enlist. She became quite angry because she felt it was her husband's own business, and was well aware how anxious he was to get into the Navy.[50]

† PRIVATE FOR THE SECRETARY – *London, September 4.*

For your own information only I have long thought of my proper duty in this war and now after organization work is nearly completed I am certain I should be in active service in some capacity. Army has asked me to consider work in France but in view of long associations I naturally prefer Navy if possible and therefore will ask you about October first for a commission in Navy or Marines that will insure service at front. I do not need to tell you how hard it will be for me to end our work together, but know you will understand[.]

ROOSEVELT.[53]

privilege of being received by '*Monsieur le Ministre.*' Apparently it created the most awful furor."[55] He dispensed with an interpreter, sat on the edge of a table, and told the newspapermen he would address them in an idiom made famous by his Uncle Ted, "Roosevelt French," which he subsequently described as "perfectly awful."* They responded by describing him glowingly, and carrying at length his encouraging statement that the war effort was "over the hump."[57]

From Paris, Roosevelt returned to the front. The British were not very cordial in their invitation, so he left his staff behind, and visited General Haig only briefly.[58] He traveled just back of the lines through St. Pol and St. Omer to LaPanne, one of the few Belgian towns in the Allied-held sliver of only 235 square miles. There he witnessed a battle just off the beach between destroyers and German submarines. He was under continual bombardment by German long-range guns, and underwent two air raids during the night. The next day he lunched with King Albert, who warned him that the Germans were making propaganda use of the American naval bombing of German-held Belgian towns, and the resultant killing of Belgian women and children. At King Albert's request, Roosevelt sent orders to confine bombers to strictly military targets.[59]

Through all this, the Assistant Secretary continued at his usual phenomenal pace.[60] But, as so frequently happened, Roosevelt was beginning to pay the price of his strenuousness. As he and his party drove through the night with no headlights to Paris, 240 miles away, he was running a fever of 102.[61] This he ignored (Eleanor Roosevelt learned of it only indirectly). In Paris he received the American commander, General Pershing,[62] and he called upon the Allied commander, Marshal Foch, to confer for an hour over the co-operation of Admiral Plunkett's batteries with the French land forces.[63] He was much impressed with the simplicity of Foch's headquarters, and the manner in which Foch obtained freedom to ponder major decisions by refusing to wear himself down with masses of detail.[64]

* FDR never tired of telling how at the end of the interview he told the editors that American cabinet members not only received the press (which French ministers refused to do), but did so twice a day:

"Next morning I went around to breakfast with old man Clemenceau, and as I went into the room, Clemenceau came at me, just like a tiger, with his claws out. . . . He said, 'Ah, you overthrow my Government. . . . You lose the war.' Well, I was horrified. I said, 'Oh my, what have I done?' He said, 'The French news men, they come – they want to see me – they want to see me and my Cabinet once a day, and some of them say twice a day. . . . I will resign first!' . . . So I darn near overthrew the Government and lost the war."[56]

The party recrossed the Channel to England on a destroyer, and was twice bombed en route. Roosevelt went on with conferences and inspections. He drove to the Firth of Forth to visit the American battleship squadron which, under the British Grand Fleet, was helping guard against the Imperial German Navy. He visited the American Admiral Rodman and lunched with the British Admiral Beatty. In the afternoon he watched a practice attack of small British airplanes upon the United States flagship *New York*. In the north of Scotland, he thoroughly inspected the North Sea mine barrage, and was so pleased with its success that he recommended laying a similar barrage across the Straits of Otranto to block Austrian submarines from the Mediterranean. His proposal was approved, but came too late to be put in effect.[65]

After completing his work in London, Roosevelt returned to France for the trip home. The crossing this time was so rough that the heavy waves swept a man overboard, and the trip took over fifteen hours instead of the customary four and a half. For three days more, Roosevelt worked at top speed, then collapsed in his bunk on the *Leviathan*. He was dangerously ill, not only with a type of influenza so virulent that it was killing many people, but also with double pneumonia. When the ship reached New York on September 19, he had to be taken ashore on a stretcher, and he could not return to the Navy Department until the middle of October.[66] *

During his convalescence, Roosevelt drafted a clear and perceptive report for Daniels in which he not only enumerated his adventures, but also made valuable suggestions for improvements in overseas naval administration.[67] The Secretary was well pleased, and in his own annual report to the President praised the thorough inspection, the important conferences, and the "clear, concise, and illuminating report" of the "clear-headed and able Assistant Secretary of the Navy."[68]

But Roosevelt was still far from ready to confine himself to naval administration. Even before he returned to Washington he planted the rumor that he was planning to enter the service – one newspaper even

* T.R. wrote from Sagamore Hill on September 23:

DEAR FRANKLIN,

We are deeply concerned about your sickness, and trust you will soon be well. We are *very* proud of you.

With love,
Aff. yours
THEODORE ROOSEVELT

Later, Eleanor will tell you of our talk about your plans.

asserted he would become an ordinary seaman.[69] He had no intention of doing this, and did check carefully to find out if he could get a commission from the Bureau of Navigation.[70] Finally he approached the Secretary; Daniels said he could no longer conscientiously ask him to stay, and let him carry his request to Wilson. The result was an anti-climax:

"I went to see the President and the President told me that in his judgment I was too late – that he had received the first suggestions of an armistice from Prince Max of Baden, and that he hoped the war would be over very soon." [71]

For Roosevelt, the excitement of having a finger in the drafting of armistice terms was some slight compensation. Discussions over them went on simultaneously with a national political campaign at the end of October, 1918. Probably because Roosevelt was still too weak from pneumonia to take an active part in the canvass, he remained at the Navy Department while Secretary Daniels stumped for the party.* This meant that as Acting Secretary of the Navy he voiced to the President his views on policies toward Germany. "This international situation," he wrote on November 1, "has meant an immense number of important telegrams and operations, including conferences with the President." [74]

While Roosevelt's role was not of critical importance, he did, to the limit of his authority, back the Navy demands for the surrender or internment of substantially all of the German fleet. This was a proposal sponsored by the British Admiralty and opposed by Marshal Foch. To the Navy, any armistice would seem comparatively worthless unless it meant the immobilization of the German fleet – in essence its unconditional surrender – since otherwise the North Sea vigil would have to continue. On October 29, Admiral Benson cabled from Paris the drastic proposals of the Inter-Allied Naval Council. Captain William V. Pratt, Acting Chief of Naval Operations, wrote a memorandum criticizing the terms as going beyond President Wilson's specifications, and as being so harsh that they might drive Germany to play "her last naval card." There was some basis for these misgivings; had the German admirals retained control of their fleet they would have sent it forth for a last desperate battle. But Acting Secretary Roosevelt disagreed.

* Politically, FDR did little more in 1918 than to endorse Al Smith for the New York governorship,[72] and to express some hint of private skepticism over President Wilson's plea to the electorate to endorse the war administration by returning a Democratic Congress.[73]

He sent Benson's cable and Pratt's memorandum to President Wilson, adding to them his own opinion that naval terms should be as severe as army terms.[75] In the end Roosevelt's view prevailed.

Once again, he was taking the popular position. Public opinion in the United States, aroused to a high pitch of war hatred, wanted something similar to unconditional surrender on land as well as on the sea. "On to Berlin" was a popular rallying cry among those most bellicose Americans thousands of miles from the muddy front line trenches. Theodore Roosevelt proclaimed, "Let us dictate peace by the hammering of guns and not chat about peace to the accompaniment of the clicking of typewriters."[76] Franklin Roosevelt did not make any such public statements, but he did suspect – or because of his dogged ambition to get into uniform, hope – that more fighting might be necessary. As late as November 9, when the armistice proposals had gone to the Germans, he confided to a close friend, "Naturally we are all waiting impatiently for the definite news here today. The consensus of opinion seems to be that the Boche is in a bad way and will take anything, but I personally am not so dead sure as some others."[77]

But two days later the Armistice came. For once Roosevelt's remarkably good fortune had not been with him, and while he had truly seen war, to his lasting regret he had not been a member of the armed forces.* He may well have been thinking of himself when he sent condolences to an admiral who had spent the duration shepherding a fleet of tied-up warships:

"Some day, I suppose, the country will recognize that all this work in the inactive areas had to be performed, and also that it was well done. . . . I have about come to the conclusion that there is an awful lot of luck in this game, anyway. The officers of distinct mediocrity may, by good fortune, happen to be at the exact point where something big is happening at the psychological moment, and it sometimes makes Field Marshals or Presidents out of them. We have all had our share of that kind of luck."[79]

Despite his disappointment, at the end of the war Roosevelt could take pride in achievements remarkable for a man not yet thirty-seven years old. He had served spectacularly as a key progressive legislator

* FDR wrote in 1922: "While my position was civilian in the sense that I did not wear a uniform, it was in all other respects just as much military as if I had been an Admiral. This is because of the fact that under the Constitution and laws, the President is Commander-in-Chief of the Army and Navy. Next in rank is the Secretary of the Navy, next the Assistant Secretary, next the Senior Admiral, etc. all down the line."[78]

in New York State and as a dynamic subordinate in the Wilson Administration. He had stored up political, administrative, and diplomatic knowledge far beyond his years. For Roosevelt personally, as for the nation as a whole, the Armistice was bringing an era to a close. He had served his apprenticeship, and in the new age ahead would be ready for bigger roles.

Bibliographical Note

No career in American history could be more amply documented than that of Franklin D. Roosevelt, the number of memoirs concerning him is so large, and the body of manuscripts he left so enormous and full. Several diligent scholars have prepared volumes chronicling Lincoln day by day; for much of Roosevelt's career they might record his activities hour by hour. There are an estimated forty tons of papers.

Roosevelt himself in 1939 described how his papers had grown through "what my family has called the bad habit of acquisitiveness." When Roosevelt was librarian of the Hasty Pudding Club at Harvard, an elderly book dealer advised him to save everything. "Well," Roosevelt declared, "that has been thrown in my teeth by all the members of my family almost every week that has passed since that time. I have destroyed practically nothing. As a result, we have a mine for which future historians will curse as well as praise me. It is a mine which will need to have the dross sifted from the gold. I would like to do it but I am informed by the professors that I am not capable of doing it. They even admit that they are not capable of doing it."

There is much gold amidst the dross, and, thanks to the excellent arrangement of the papers by the Roosevelt Library staff, it is easy to extract. The extent and variety of the papers bearing upon the period this volume covers are remarkable. Because of the generous spirit of the Roosevelt family and the trustees of the Roosevelt Library, almost all (excepting those relating to personal finances) are open to qualified researchers. They vary from boyhood essays to drafts of 1914 campaign speeches, and include official letters and memoranda, personal correspondence (except family letters), newspaper clippings and photographs, and even such mementos as autographed menus, and French ration coupons of the First World War. A large number of the thousands of books bear Roosevelt's signature; a very few also contain notations. In addition, the Louis McHenry Howe papers at the Roosevelt Library are useful for the naval period. There are detailed descriptions of these collections in the annual reports of the Roosevelt Library.

Official papers of the Secretary of the Navy (including countless numbers with Roosevelt's signature) are in the National Archives. There is also a small but significant collection of "personal papers of the Assistant Secretary." Footnote references to official papers include file numbers by which they may be located in the Archives. Excerpts from ships' logs covering cruises when Roosevelt was aboard are in the Navy Department's Office of Naval Records and History.

The Josephus Daniels papers in the Library of Congress contain considerable material of importance, especially the often cryptic but occasionally revealing references to Roosevelt in the Daniels diaries. There is other manuscript material in the Woodrow Wilson papers at the Library of Congress, and in the Henry Cabot Lodge papers.

A copy of the manuscript of Mrs. Charles Hamlin's recollections and diary entries on Roosevelt is in the Roosevelt Library; it appeared in part in the *New Republic* (April 15, 1946, 114:528–531).

Despite all the riches of the manuscript and printed materials, they fail to answer certain questions. Several persons most generously helped to fill these gaps through interviews or correspondence. Among them were: Reginald R. Belknap, Renah H. Camalier, Josephus Daniels, Michael Francis Doyle, John J. Fitzgerald, John M. Hancock, Frederick Harris, Herbert Hoover, Dudley Knox, Emory S. Land, William D. Leahy, Charles H. McCarthy, John E. Mack, George Marvin, James O. Richardson, Eleanor Roosevelt, Harold R. Stark, Margaret Suckley, Joseph K. Taussig, Mahlon S. Tisdale, Archibald D. Turnbull, and Henry Braid Wilson. Several others whose names are not listed here provided confidential information.

The National Park Service, under the supervision of George A. Palmer and the historians at the Roosevelt home, has made tape recordings of the reminiscences of Hyde Park persons who knew Roosevelt. Other interviews containing information on Roosevelt (and some manuscripts) are among the extensive materials being gathered by the Oral History Project at Columbia University under the direction of Allan Nevins.

Roosevelt's family letters, voluminous for the years he was at Groton, and rapidly diminishing thereafter in quantity but not importance, are in Elliott Roosevelt, editor, *F.D.R., His Personal Letters* (3 vols., New York, 1947–1950). I am grateful to Duell, Sloan and Pearce for permission to quote from them. Many of Roosevelt's own reminiscences are in *The Public Papers and Addresses of Franklin D. Roosevelt*, edited by Samuel I. Rosenman (13 vols., New York, 1938–1950).

Of the innumerable books dealing in part or in entirety with Roosevelt, I have found the following most helpful: Eleanor Roosevelt's candid and illuminating memoirs, *This Is My Story* (New York, 1937), and *This I Remember* (New York, 1949), from which I have quoted with the permission of Harper & Brothers; John Gunther, *Roosevelt in Retrospect* (New York, 1950), a perceptive piece of reporting on Roosevelt's personality and career; Ernest K. Lindley, *Franklin D. Roosevelt, A Career in Progressive Democracy* (New York, 1931), a most useful account of Roosevelt's career from the perspective of 1931, despite the normal inflation of a campaign biography; Donald Day, *Franklin D. Roosevelt's Own Story* (Boston, 1951), a selection from his writings; James Rosenau, *Roosevelt Treasury* (New York, 1951), a well-edited anthology; Noel Busch, *What Manner of Man?* (New York, 1944), an interesting psychological study, unfortunately based on inadequate secondary evidence; Richard Hofstadter, *The American Political Tradition* (New York, 1948), which contains a diamond-sharp vignette.

Roosevelt's patrician ancestry made him an especially alluring subject for genealogists. Alvin Page Johnson, *Franklin D. Roosevelt's Colonial Ancestors* (Boston, 1933), is a standard study; Karl Schriftgiesser, *The Amazing Roosevelt Family, 1613–1942* (New York, 1942), is a sprightly popular account. Rita Halle Kleeman, *Gracious Lady: The Life of Sara Delano Roosevelt* (New York, 1935) from which I have quoted excerpts of letters and diaries with the permission of Appleton-Century-Crofts, Inc., contains vivid descriptions of the more immediate Delano ancestors, and is an invaluable portrait of Sara Delano Roosevelt and her young son. The more widely known *My Boy Franklin* (New York, 1933) by Sara Delano Roosevelt, as told to Isabelle Leighton and Gabrielle Forbush, contains delightful anecdotes and comments. I have quoted Roosevelt's remarks on his ancestors from Theodore H. White, editor, *The Stilwell Papers* (New York, 1948) with the permission of William Sloane Associates, Inc.; and from Clifford W. Ashley, *Whaleships of New Bedford* (Boston, 1929), with the permission of Houghton Mifflin Company. Two graphic and sympathetic accounts re-create Roosevelt's Hyde Park background: Olin Dows, *Franklin Roosevelt at Hyde Park* (New York, 1949), and Clara and Hardy Steeholm, *The House at Hyde Park* (New York, 1950).

Frank D. Ashburn's brilliant and definitive *Peabody of Groton* (New York, 1944), from which I have quoted with the permission of Coward-McCann, Inc., provides invaluable background on Roosevelt's education. Frances Perkins, *The Roosevelt I Knew* (New York, 1946), gives a glimpse of him as a state senator; George Mowry, *Theodore Roosevelt and the Progressive Movement* (Madison, Wisconsin, 1946), contains a clear exposition of complicated New York politics; Arthur S. Link, *Woodrow Wilson: The Road to the White House* (Princeton, 1947) is definitive on Wilson's nomination and the campaign of 1912; John M. Blum, *Joe Tumulty and the Wilson Era* (Boston, 1951) is indispensable on Wilsonian politics, and briefly mentions Roosevelt's role; Ray Stannard Baker, *Woodrow Wilson, Life and Letters* (7 vols., Garden City, New York, 1927–1939), is highly useful.

Josephus Daniels has lengthy, affectionate accounts of Roosevelt as Assistant Secretary in *The Wilson Era* (2 vols., Chapel Hill, North

Carolina, 1944–1946). In addition there is much useful background information on the Navy Department in: Donald Mitchell, *History of the Modern Navy* (New York, 1945); George T. Davis, *A Navy Second to None* (New York, 1940); Harold and Margaret Sprout, *The Rise of American Naval Power, 1776–1918* (Princeton, 1939); and Henry P. Beers, "The Development of the Office of the Chief of Naval Operations," *Military Affairs* (Spring, 1946–Winter, 1947, volumes 10 and 11). Robert G. Albion's forthcoming *Makers of Naval Policy*, parts of which I saw in manuscript, was most important of all. It is a superb history of the Navy Department. William Phillips generously permitted me to see pages bearing on Roosevelt in his unpublished memoirs. Lela Stiles kindly let me see parts of her forthcoming biography of Louis M. Howe. Not available in time for me to use, Carroll Kilpatrick, editor, *Roosevelt and Daniels: A Friendship in Politics* (Chapel Hill, North Carolina, 1952), contains the published correspondence of the two men.

I have cited other books and articles in the footnotes.

Acknowledgments

The generosity of a number of persons who have given freely of their time, information, and criticism, has made this book possible. I owe much to them.

Spencer Brodney first suggested in 1944 that I do a study of Roosevelt's naval years; he has continued to be helpful and encouraging as the project has progressed and expanded since. Robert G. Albion aided me immeasurably with his wealth of knowledge and material on the Navy Department. Jonathan Daniels gave me full access to his father's papers and aided me in many ways.

Richard N. Current perceptively read the entire manuscript in its final draft and made many helpful suggestions on both style and content; Arthur E. Bestor, Jr., similarly criticized large parts of it. I have benefited greatly from the careful reading and excellent suggestions of: Spencer Brodney, Jonathan Daniels, Herman Kahn, Arthur M. Schlesinger, Jr., and Rexford G. Tugwell. Beatrice Kevitt Hofstadter critically read parts of an early draft, and did much to set the later style. The following also read the manuscript in part: Robert G. Albion, Allen Drury, Charles C. Griffin, Fred Harrington, William B. Hesseltine, Richard Hofstadter, Charles Nowell, and James G. Randall.

At all stages, the manuscript and proofs have benefited from the skillful editing of Stanley Salmen, Ned Bradford, and the staff of Little, Brown and Company.

I have also received material aid from: Catherine Atwood, Howard K. Beale, Frederick C. Dietz, John Garraty, Robert Lunny, Horace Samuel Merrill, Fred Albert Shannon, and Kenneth M. Stampp.

The staffs of libraries have been uniformly of extraordinary help. My debt to those at the Roosevelt Library is very great, especially to: Herman Kahn, the present director, Fred Shipman, the former director, Edgar Nixon, George Roach, Margaret Suckley, Raymond Corry, William J. Nichols, Carl Spicer and Robert Jacoby. I also wish to thank George A. Palmer of the National Park Service, Katherine Brand of the Library of Congress, Carl Lokke of the National Archives, Icko Iben and Nelle M. Signor of the University of Illinois Library, and Eileen Thornton of the Vassar College Library. I am grateful also to Admiral John B. Heffernan, Director of Naval History, and his staff.

I wish to make grateful acknowledgment to the Roosevelt Library for permission to quote from manuscripts and to reproduce the photographs in this volume, and to the Daniels family, Lodge family, and Mrs. Woodrow Wilson for permission to quote from manuscripts. I have listed in the Bibliographical Note those who have given me permission to quote from books, and who have provided me with information.

Liberal research grants from the University of Illinois and Pennsylvania State College did much to ease the financial burden of preparing this book. I also appreciate the offer of a grant from the Salmon Fund at Vassar College. For research assistance I am especially grateful to Gertrude Thayer Almy, who has faithfully attended to a multitude of onerous details, and to George Lobdell, William Glickman, and Warren Slaughter; for typing, to Norma Tedford, Ruth Ridler, and Margaret Mulligan. Finally, to mention the greatest debt the last, I owe an inestimable amount to my wife, Elisabeth Margo Freidel.

Notes

Abbreviations

FDR: Franklin D. Roosevelt
ER: Eleanor Roosevelt
FDR mss.: Franklin D. Roosevelt manuscripts, Franklin D. Roosevelt Library, Hyde Park, New York. Unless otherwise attributed, all manuscripts cited are from this collection.
PPA: Samuel I. Rosenman, editor, *The Public Papers and Addresses of Franklin D. Roosevelt* (13 vols., New York, 1938–1950). These are cited by year covered by volume; i.e., PPA, 1936, etc.
PL: Elliott Roosevelt, editor, *F.D.R., His Personal Letters* (3 vols., New York, 1947–1950)

CHAPTER I

The Roosevelts and the Delanos

1. Anne Wintermute Lane and Louise Herrick Wall, eds., *The Letters of Franklin K. Lane, Personal and Political* (Boston, 1922), 352.
2. San Diego *Union*, April 14, 1914.
3. Sara Delano Roosevelt, as told to Isabelle Leighton and Gabrielle Forbush, *My Boy Franklin* (New York, 1933), 4.
4. Rita Halle Kleeman, *Gracious Lady: The Life of Sara Delano Roosevelt* (New York, 1935), 122, 132; Clara and Hardy Steeholm, *The House at Hyde Park* (New York, 1950), 65.
5. Interview with ER, May 1, 1948.
6. PL, 1:443, 464–465; Kleeman, *Gracious Lady*, 5.
7. FDR, "The Roosevelt Family in New Amsterdam before the Revolution," December, 1901, ms. in Roosevelt Library.
8. FDR to Philip Slomovitz, March 7, 1935.
9. PL, 3:942.
10. Karl Schriftgiesser, *The Amazing Roosevelt family, 1613–1942* (New York, 1942), 108–121; Alvin Page Johnson, *Franklin D. Roosevelt's Colonial Ancestors: Their Part in the Making of American History* (Boston, 1933), 18–21; Carl Lotus Becker, *The History of Political Parties in the Province of New York, 1760–1776* (Madison, Wisconsin, 1909), 185, 209, 272.
11. Schriftgiesser, *The Amazing Roosevelt Family*, 121; PPA: 1938, 525.
12. Schriftgiesser, *The Amazing Roosevelt Family*, 119, 177–180.
13. *Ibid.*, 180, 181–182, 186–187.

14. *Ibid.*, 188.
15. PL, 3:1224.
16. Confidential source.
17. Charles E. Beachley, *History of the Consolidation Coal Company, 1864–1934* (New York, 1934); *National Cyclopedia of American Biography*, 24:11, 12; Henry V. Poor, *Manual of the Railroads of the United States for 1868–69 . . .* (New York, 1868), 306; Walter Sanderlin, *The Great National Project: A History of the Chesapeake and Ohio Canal* (Baltimore, 1946), 237, 271; *Railroad Gazette*, May 26, 1876, 8:232.
18. George H. Burgess and Miles C. Kennedy, *Centennial History of the Pennsylvania Railroad Company 1846–1946* (Philadelphia, 1949), 279, 280, 347; Stuart Daggett, *Railroad Reorganization* (Cambridge, 1908), 145–148; Frederick A. Cleveland and Fred W. Powell, *Railroad Finance* (New York, 1912), 308; *Railroad Gazette* (December 2, 1871), 3:369; (December 14, 1872) 4:535; (November 22, 1873) 5:475; (May 9, 1874) 6:178; (December 8, 1876) 8:540.
19. PL, 1:68.
20. PL, 1:254–255.
21. Dwight Carroll Miner, *The Fight for the Panama Route: The Story of the Spooner Act and the Hay-Herran Treaty* (New York, 1940), 25–30; Nicaragua Canal Construction Company, *The Inter-Oceanic Canal of Nicaragua; Its History, Physical Condition, Plans and Prospects* (New York, 1891); Maritime Canal Company of Nicaragua, *The Nicaragua Canal* (Atlanta, 1895); Henry F. Pringle, *Theodore Roosevelt; A Biography* (New York, 1931), 330.
22. *Railroad Gazette* (January 25, 1884), 16:75; (February 22, 1884) 16:153; (June 6, 1884), 16:435; Frank F. Hargrave, *A Pioneer Indiana Railroad, The Origin and Development of the Monon* (Indianapolis, 1932).
23. FDR to Robert K. Mackey, October 27, 1924.
24. PL, 1:133, 135.
25. A. Merriman Smith, *Thank You Mr. President* (New York, 1946), 37–38.
26. Delaware and Hudson Canal Company, *Annual Reports*, 1868–1900; Delaware and Hudson, *A Century of Progress: History of the Delaware and Hudson Company, 1823–1923* (Albany, 1925); Chester Lloyd Jones, *The Economic History of the Anthracite-Tidewater Canals* (Philadelphia, 1908), 91–103.
27. PL, 1:481.
28. New York *Tribune*, December 9, 1900, 5:1.
29. Raymond Moley, *After Seven Years* (New York, 1939), 95.
30. PL, 3:942–943.
31. Joseph W. Stilwell, *The Stilwell Papers*, edited by Theodore H. White (New York, 1948), 251. The passage is copied from a photograph of the manuscript page among the illustrations. Quoted with the permission of William Sloane Associates, Inc. Copyright, 1948, by Winifred A. Stilwell.
32. Kleeman, *Gracious Lady*, 34–36; Schriftgiesser, *The Amazing Roosevelt Family*, 197, 198, 201.

33. Schriftgiesser, *The Amazing Roosevelt Family*, 315; Ward McAllister, *Society as I Have Found It* (New York, 1890), 224.

34. Richard Hofstadter, *The American Political Tradition and the Men Who Made It* (New York, 1948), 314.

35. [Genieve Lamson, ed.,] *Dutchess County* (*American Guide Series*, Philadelphia, 1937), 89.

36. *Ibid.*, 17.

37. Schriftgiesser, *The Amazing Roosevelt Family*, 191–195; "American Carriage Horses," *Harper's Weekly* (April 15, 1893), 37:363.

38. PPA, 1944–1945: 45–46; FDR to Theodore G. Jervey, August 15, 1928; Charles C. Tansill to the writer, November 21, 1949.

39. Kleeman, *Gracious Lady*, 316.

40. *Ibid.*, 25.

41. *Ibid.*, 24.

42. *Ibid.*, 36.

43. *Ibid.*, 41.

44. Ernest K. Lindley, *Franklin D. Roosevelt: A Career in Progressive Democracy* (New York, 1931), 46.

45. *Ibid.*, 43–60; Sara Roosevelt, *My Boy Franklin*, 9; FDR to Harold Hartshorne, August 2, 1922.

46. Kleeman, *Gracious Lady*, 61–62, 63.

47. *Ibid.*, 64–73.

48. *Ibid.*, 92.

49. *Ibid.*, 82–83.

50. *Ibid.*, 100–102.

51. *Ibid.*, 102–110, 111, 120.

52. *Ibid.*, 114.

53. *Ibid.*, 120.

54. *Ibid.*, 122.

55. *Ibid.*, 147.

CHAPTER II

Boyhood

1. Kleeman, *Gracious Lady*, 129.

2. *Ibid.*, 125.

3. Sara Roosevelt, *My Boy Franklin*, 12.

4. Kleeman, *Gracious Lady*, 128.

5. ER, ed., *Hunting Big Game in the Eighties: The Letters of Elliott Roosevelt, Sportsman* (New York, 1933), 34.

6. Kleeman, *Gracious Lady*, 138–139.

7. *Ibid.*, 137.

8. *Ibid.*, 136–137.

9. *Ibid.*, 152–153; Lindley, *Roosevelt*, 47.

10. Sara Roosevelt, *My Boy Franklin*, 6.

11. Kleeman, *Gracious Lady*, 169–170; Sara Roosevelt, *My Boy Franklin*, 19.

12. Kleeman, *Gracious Lady*, 150–152.
13. Sara Roosevelt, *My Boy Franklin*, 21.
14. Kleeman, *Gracious Lady*, 139, 173.
15. PL, 1:8.
16. Lindley, *Roosevelt*, 45; PL, 1:156–157. For the fullest account of Gloster see PL, 3:784–785.
17. Kleeman, *Gracious Lady*, 170–171.
18. Sara Roosevelt, *My Boy Franklin*, 19.
19. *Ibid.*, 26.
20. *Ibid.*, 33.
21. *Ibid.*, 9.
22. *Ibid.*, 31; Kleeman, *Gracious Lady*, 175–176; Lindley, *Roosevelt*, 47.
23. Sara Roosevelt, *My Boy Franklin*, 18, 33.
24. *Ibid.*, 30–31; Kleeman, *Gracious Lady*, 172.
25. Kleeman, *Gracious Lady*, 155.
26. PL, 1:16.
27. Kleeman, *Gracious Lady*, 171.
28. PL, 1:21–22.
29. Kleeman, *Gracious Lady*, 134.
30. FDR to Jeanne Rosat-Sandoz, February 4, 1935.
31. Kleeman, *Gracious Lady*, 178.
32. *Ibid.*, 191.
33. Sara Roosevelt, *My Boy Franklin*, 32–33.
34. PL, 1:11, 12.
35. Kleeman, *Gracious Lady*, 172–173; ER, *This Is My Story* (New York, 1937), 104.
36. Sara Roosevelt, *My Boy Franklin*, 26.
37. PL, 1:15.
38. PL, 1:23.
39. Sara Roosevelt, *My Boy Franklin*, 13.
40. Kleeman, *Gracious Lady*, 153–154.
41. *Ibid.*, 162, 164.
42. Interview with Josephus Daniels, May 29, 1947.
43. PPA, 1936:323.
44. PL, 1:249–250, 257.
45. Kleeman, *Gracious Lady*, 174.
46. PL, 1:18.
47. Kleeman, *Gracious Lady*, 176.
48. *Ibid.*, 156; PL, 1:198–199.
49 Kleeman, *Gracious Lady*, 181–182; Sara Roosevelt, *My Boy Franklin*, 27–28.
50. New York *Times*, November 25, 1949; Olin Dows, *Franklin Roosevelt at Hyde Park* (New York, 1949), 165.
51. PL, 1:370.
52. *Ibid.*, 1:18, 19.
53. Kleeman, *Gracious Lady*, 185.
54. *Ibid.*, 188.
55. PL, 1:184, 195, 213.

56. Sara Roosevelt, *My Boy Franklin*, 49, 50; Kleeman, *Gracious Lady*, 198.

57. See PL, 1:485.

58. FDR, Introduction to Clifford W. Ashley, *Whaleships of New Bedford* (Boston, 1929), iv, v. This passage follows the ms. in the FDR papers, dated Albany, 1929. Quoted with permission of Houghton Mifflin Company.

59. PPA, 1928–1932: 887.

60. Philadelphia *Record*, April 6, 1913.

61. Lindley, *Roosevelt*, 51.

62. PL, 1:6.

63. *Ibid.*, 1:13. In 1890–1891 FDR was tutored by a Miss Riensberg. "Franklin's marks – 1890–91 with Miss Riensberg – Hyde Park," FDR mss.

64. Mademoiselle Sandoz began tutoring FDR September 28, 1891. Grade books, copy books, and exercises are in the Roosevelt mss. Sandoz to FDR, January 30, 1933.

65. Kleeman, *Gracious Lady*, 183.

66. *Ibid.*, 183.

67. See *ibid.*, 185.

68. FDR to Sandoz, March 31, 1933; February 4, 1935.

69. PPA, 1944–1945: 70–72 (although the note fails to mention the delivery in French); see also PPA, 1943:369.

70. For an excellent detailed account of Mademoiselle Sandoz, see Constance Drexel, "Unpublished Letters of F.D.R. to His French Governess," *Parents' Magazine* (September, 1951), 26:30–31, 80–84.

71. Kleeman, *Gracious Lady*, 154.

72. *Ibid.*, 189–190; PL, 1:17, 18, 207, 208, 251; interview with ER, May 1, 1948.

73. Interview with ER, May 1, 1948.

74. Kleeman, *Gracious Lady*, 189.

75. *Ibid.*, 144.

76. PPA, 1944–1945:413–414.

77. FDR, address at Chicago, October 2, 1932, Governor's Press Release File.

78. Sara Roosevelt, *My Boy Franklin*, 22.

79. PPA, 1936:597.

80. PL, 1:19.

81. Kleeman, *Gracious Lady*, 161–162.

82. New York *Times*, February 4, 1933.

83. *Ibid.*, January 17, 1933. See also Christian Bommersheim to Roosevelt family, July 1, 1891. FDR attended only from May 23 to July 1, 1891.

84. PL, 1:20.

85. PL, 3:943.

86. PPA, 1944–1945:560.

87. Lindley, *Roosevelt*, 50; Interview with ER, May 1, 1948.

88. Kleeman, *Gracious Lady*, 165; Lindley, *Roosevelt*, 50–51.

89. Kleeman, *Gracious Lady*, 165. See also PPA, 1944–1945:162.

90. Kleeman, *Gracious Lady*, 166.

91. Interview with ER, May 1, 1948.

CHAPTER III

Groton

1. New York *Times*, June 3, 1934.
2. Kleeman, *Gracious Lady*, 193.
3. Cleveland Amory, "Goodbye, Mr. Peabs," *Saturday Evening Post* (September 14, 1940), 213:69.
4. PL, 1:37.
5. *Ibid.*, 1:45.
6. Amory, "Goodbye, Mr. Peabs," 73.
7. George Biddle, "As I Remember Groton School," *Harper's* (August, 1939), 179:300.
8. Frank D. Ashburn, *Peabody of Groton* (New York, 1944), 296, 358. Copyright, 1944, by Frank D. Ashburn. Reprinted by permission of Coward-McCann, Inc.
9. *Ibid.*, 377.
10. *Ibid.*, 322.
11. *Ibid.*, 347.
12. PPA, 2:419.
13. Ashburn, *Peabody*, 38.
14. *Ibid.*, 67.
15. PL, 1:315.
16. "Twelve of the Best American Schools," *Fortune* (January, 1936), 13:48–49.
17. Ashburn, *Peabody*, 112–113.
18. *Ibid.*, 317–325.
19. Biddle, "As I Remember Groton School," 296.
20. Ashburn, *Peabody*, 43, 177.
21. ER, *This I Remember*, 69–70, quoted from the slightly variant version in *McCall's Magazine.*
22. PL, 1:61.
23. Ellery Sedgwick, *The Happy Profession* (Boston, 1946), 60–61.
24. PL, 1:130.
25. Kleeman, *Gracious Lady*, 204–205; for FDR's Groton courses, see PL:1, *passim.* The curriculum is in *Groton School, 1899–1900* (Ayer Mass. [1899]).
26. Biddle, "As I Remember Groton School," 295.
27. Ashburn, *Peabody*, 97; Biddle, "As I Remember Groton School," 295.
28. PL, 1:104.
29. *Ibid.*, 40, 207.
30. *Ibid.*, 1:97.
31. *Ibid.*, 1:40.
32. Earnest Brandenburg and Waldo W. Braden, "Franklin D. Roosevelt's Voice and Pronunciation," *Quarterly Journal of Speech* (February, 1952), 38:27. See also Laura Crowell, "Roosevelt the Grotonian," *Ibid.* (February), 1952), 38:31–36.
33. ER, *This I Remember*, 43.

34. Biddle, "As I Remember Groton School," 296.
35. Sara Roosevelt, *My Boy Franklin*, 40.
36. PL, 1:283.
37. Kleeman, *Gracious Lady*, 194.
38. PL, 1:35.
39. *Ibid.*, 1:35, 36, 38; Ashburn, *Peabody*, 257.
40. PL, 1:40.
41. *Ibid.*, 1:47, 228, 337, 339, 347.
42. *Ibid.*, 1:51.
43. *Ibid.*, 1:60, 247.
44. *Ibid.*, 1:47, 55, 61, 64, 66, 67.
45. *Ibid.*, 1:61, 62.
46. *Ibid.*, 1:61, 63.
47. *Ibid.*, 1:72, 78–79.
48. *Ibid.*, 1:78.
49. *Ibid.*, 1:105.
50. *Ibid.*, 1:110.
51. *Ibid.*, 1:112, 115.
52. *Ibid.*, 1:119.
53. *Ibid.*, 1:128.
54. *Ibid.*, 1:120–121.
55. *Ibid.*, 1:130.
56. *Ibid.*, 1:155, 156, 184.
57. New York *Globe*, June 2, 1911.
58. Both inscribed copies in FDR Library.
59. PL, 1:160–164.
60. *Ibid.*, 1:178.
61. *Ibid.*, 1:194.
62. Kleeman, *Gracious Lady*, 196.
63. PL, 1:192.
64. *Ibid.*, 1:197–198.
65. *Ibid.*, 1:200–202.
66. Lindley, *Roosevelt*, 52.
67. PL, 1:205; Sara Roosevelt, *My Boy Franklin*, 42–45.
68. PL, 1:207.
69. Kleeman, *Gracious Lady*, 203; PL, 1:230; Mrs. Charles Hamlin, "Some Memories of Franklin Delano Roosevelt," ms. at FDR Library.
70. PL, 1:227.
71. *Ibid.*, 1:245, 366, 437.
72. *Ibid.*, 1:240.
73. *Ibid.*, 1:242.
74. *Ibid.*, 1:244.
75. *Ibid.*, 1:187, 240, 241, 251. While at Harvard FDR frequently participated in the Boys' Club Program; see Chapter IV; PL, 1:451 ff.
76. PL, 1:389–391, 409, 411; Kleeman, *Gracious Lady*, 198.
77. PL, 1:212.
78. *Ibid.*, 395–396.
79. George Marvin, "Notes on Franklin D. Roosevelt as Assistant Secre-

tary of the Navy, 1913–1920," unpublished ms. in possession of the present writer.

80. PL, 1:332, 334.

81. Marvin, "Notes on Franklin D. Roosevelt as Assistant Secretary of the Navy."

82. Biddle, "As I Remember Groton School," 296.

83. PL, 1:34.

84. *Ibid.*, 1:393.

85. *Ibid.*, 394–395.

86. *Ibid.*, 1:401; see 399.

87. PL, 1:413.

88. Ashburn, *Peabody*, 341.

89. *Ibid.*, 344.

CHAPTER IV

Harvard

1. PL, 1:503.

2. William James, "The True Harvard," *Harvard Graduates Magazine* (September, 1903), 12:7.

3. Rollo Walter Brown, *Harvard Yard in the Golden Age* (New York, 1948), 13–15.

4. A. Lawrence Lowell, "Dormitories and College Life," *Harvard Graduates Magazine* (June, 1904), 12:525.

5. W. R. Thayer, in *Harvard Graduates Magazine* (June, 1901), 9:487–491.

6. PL, 1:370–372, 423, 425; Kleeman, *Gracious Lady*, 207.

7. *Harvard Alumni Bulletin* (April 28, 1945), 47:443.

8. PL, 1:423–424.

9. *Ibid.*, 1:445, 446.

10. P[hilip] G[reenleaf] C[arleton], in *Harvard Alumni Bulletin* (May 26, 1945), 47:516.

11. *Ibid.*, 47:516; FDR, diary. See also L. LeRoy Cowperthwaite, "Franklin D. Roosevelt at Harvard," *Quarterly Journal of Speech* (February, 1952), 38:37–41.

12. PL, 1:428.

13. *Harvard Crimson*, September 29, October 9, 12, 1900.

14. Lindley, *Roosevelt*, 54.

15. PL, 1:430.

16. *Ibid.*, 1:465.

17. *Ibid.*, 1:427, 428, 451, 452.

18. *Ibid.*, 1:428.

19. *Ibid.*, 1:456; *Harvard Crimson*, October 16, 1900.

20. New York *Telegraph*, November 30, 1913; FDR to Michael E. Hennessy, October 22, 1931.

21. PL, 1:431; FDR membership card in the Harvard Republican Club, undated.

22. New York *Telegraph*, November 30, 1913; *Harvard Crimson*, April 30, 1901.

23. *Harvard Crimson*, June 15, 1901.

24. PL, 1:408.

25. New York *Herald*, October 19, 20, 1900.

26. PL, 1:430, part of comment deleted by editors.

27. Interview with ER, May 1, 1948; the source of the quotation from a Harvard friend is confidential.

28. PL, 1:429.

29. Kleeman, *Gracious Lady*, 207–209.

30. *Ibid.*, 213.

31. *Ibid.*, 214–215.

32. *Ibid.*, 221.

33. Sara Roosevelt, *My Boy Franklin*, 55–56.

34. Kleeman, *Gracious Lady*, 221.

35. PL, 1:456–458.

36. Kleeman, *Gracious Lady*, 215–216; PL, 1:458; FDR diary, July 28, 1901.

37. Kleeman, *Gracious Lady*, 217–218.

38. PL, 1:460–461.

39. *Ibid.*, 1:463–464.

40. *Ibid.*, 462–463; a copy of the seating plan on the platform at Yale is in the FDR mss.

41. PL, 1:466.

42. *Ibid.*, 1:467–468; FDR diary, January 3, 1902.

43. PL, 1:469; FDR diary, January 9, 1902.

44. PL, 1:470.

45. *Ibid.*, 1:487.

46. S. A. Welldon, in *Harvard Graduates Magazine* (June, 1903), 11:569; *Harvard Crimson*, April 3, 1903; PPA, 1939:116.

47. Lindley, *Roosevelt*, 56, 57.

48. PL, 1:474, 486, 487.

49. *Harvard Crimson*, January 23, 1902.

50. *Ibid.*, March 17, April 2, May 24, 1902; FDR diary, May 14, 1902.

51. Kleeman, *Gracious Lady*, 226–227.

52. PL, 1:477.

53. PL, 1:479–480.

54. FDR diary, October 1, 1903.

55. PL, 1:505–506.

56. FDR mss.

57. PL, 1:504–505; FDR to Burke Boyce, September 25, 1922.

58. PL, 1:507.

59. *Harvard Crimson*, September 30, 1903, cited in PL, 1:500.

60. PL, 1:507.

61. Portland *Oregonian*, April 20, 1914.

62. Editorial in *Harvard Alumni Bulletin* (April 28, 1945), 47:444.

63. *Harvard Crimson*, October 15, 1903.

64. PL, 1:510.

65. *Harvard Crimson*, November 2, 1903, cited in PL, 1:512–513.
66. *Ibid.*, November 4, 1903.
67. *Ibid.*, December 5, 1903; January 4, 1904.
68. *Ibid.*, December 15, 1903.
69. *Ibid.*, December 14, 1903.
70. Washington *Herald*, April 1, 1914.
71. *Harvard Crimson*, December 17, 1903.
72. *Ibid.*, December 19, 1903.
73. *Ibid.*, December 3, 1903; January 15, 1904.
74. *Ibid.*, January 5, 1904.
75. *Ibid.*, January 22, 1904.
76. *Ibid.*, December 17, 1903.
77. *Ibid.*, January 30; May 19, 1904.
78. PL, 1:516.
79. FDR to Sidney Gunn, August 23, 1928.
80. FDR to Robert M. Washburn, August 18, 1928.
81. Lindley, *Roosevelt*, 64; PL, 1:483.
82. *Harvard Alumni Bulletin* (April 28, 1945), 47:444.
83. PL, 1:531.
84. Kleeman, *Gracious Lady*, 233.
85. PL, 1:518.
86. Kleeman, *Gracious Lady*, 235.
87. PL, 1:517.
88. ER, ed., *Letters of Elliott Roosevelt*, viii.
89. ER, *This Is My Story*, 24.
90. *Ibid.*, 51; Kleeman, *Gracious Lady*, 234.
91. ER, *This Is My Story*, 89, 97–99, 101–102.
92. PL, 1:531.
93. ER, *This Is My Story*, 99, 120–121.
94. *Ibid.*, 107–109.
95. Kleeman, *Gracious Lady*, 241.
96. Sara Roosevelt, *My Boy Franklin*, 63; FDR diary, *passim;* quotation from a Harvard friend, confidential source.
97. Endicott Peabody to FDR, November 30, 1904.
98. New York *World*, cited in Mark Sullivan, *The Turn of the Century*, Vol. 1 of "Our Times: The United States 1900–1925" (New York, 1926), 195.
99. ER, *This Is My Story*, 120.
100. Kleeman, *Gracious Lady*, 235.
101. PL, 1:523.
102. PPA, 1944–1945:46–47.
103. Kleeman, *Gracious Lady*, 235–240.
104. *Ibid.*, 241.
105. S. A. Welldon, in *Harvard Graduates Magazine* (September, 1904), 13:130.
106. Kleeman, *Gracious Lady*, 222.
107. Ashburn, *Peabody*, 176–177.
108. PPA, 1941:460.

109. PL, 1:505.

110. FDR to Jerome D. Greene, July 10, 1922; Moley, *After Seven Years*, 173–174.

111. Earle Looker, *This Man Roosevelt* (New York, 1932), 32.

CHAPTER V

Beginnings

1. Sedgwick, *The Happy Profession*, 74–75.

2. Horace Coon, *Columbia Colossus on the Hudson* (New York, 1947), 231.

3. Looker, *This Man Roosevelt*, 48.

4. Ashburn, *Peabody*, 121.

5. PPA, 1941:457–458.

6. FDR's notes on Burgess's Constitutional Law, 1904–1905. FDR mss.

7. Columbia University, *Bulletin of Information, School of Law Announcement*, 1906–1907:17–18; Coon, *Columbia*, 228; PL, 2:73.

8. Rudolf Tumbo, Jr., Registrar, Columbia University Law School, Result of Examination of F. D. Roosevelt, August 24, 1906.

9. PL, 2:73.

10. PL, 2:85.

11. FDR to Hollis Godfrey, December 13, 1927.

12. Coon, *Columbia*, 99.

13. Esca C. Rodger, "Want To Be a Lawyer? Talk It Over with Franklin D. Roosevelt," *American Boy* (June, 1927) 28:3.

14. FDR diary, October 7, 1904.

15. FDR, speech at Jackson Day Dinner, January 8, 1938; PPA, 1938:38.

16. ER, *This Is My Story*, 123. There is a boxful of inauguration mementos at the Roosevelt Library.

17. New York *Herald*, March 18, 1905.

18. Kleeman, *Gracious Lady*, 244; Lindley, *Roosevelt*, 68.

19. ER, *This Is My Story*, 126.

20. ER, *This Is My Story*, 126.

21. PL, 2:30.

22. *Ibid.*, 2:73.

23. *Ibid.*, 2:100.

24. *Ibid.*, 2:66.

25. *Ibid.*, 2:84.

26. *Ibid.*, 2:80.

27. ER, *This Is My Story*, 163.

28. *Ibid.*, 139–165, tells with remarkable candor and some poignancy of her adjustment to marriage and particularly to her mother-in-law.

29. ER, *This I Remember*, 14–15, discusses finances.

30. ER, *This Is My Story*, 138; PL, 1:58–59, 65, 68–69.

31. ER, *This Is My Story*, 162.

32. *Ibid.*, 149–150.

33. Kleeman, *Gracious Lady*, 246.

34. Jane F. Tuckerman to FDR, undated; Daniel R. Lucas to Eleanor Blodgett, June 8, 1909; Eleanor Blodgett to Hudson-Fulton Committee on Public Health and Convenience, June 9, 1909; John R. Eustis to Eleanor Blodgett, August 10, 1909; FDR to Eleanor Blodgett, August 27, 1909.

35. FDR, autobiographical sketch, prepared for Edgar L. Murlin, ed., *The New York Red Book* (Albany, 1911).

36. John Hopkins to FDR, February 10, 1908.

37. A. T. Ashton to FDR, April 23, 1906; Lindley, *Roosevelt*, 69; ER, *This Is My Story*, 150.

38. FDR mss.

39. Edmund L. Baylies to FDR, June 10, 1907.

40. FDR to Louisa Baylies, August 8, 1932.

41. PPA, 1941:457–458.

42. Looker, *This Man Roosevelt*, 49–52. This story may be exaggerated.

43. Edwin DeT. Bechtel to FDR, November 1, 1932, enclosing Photostats of his "clear and systematic entries" on the progress of the case of *George O. Lord* v. *United States Transportation Company*, ultimately an important case in the state. There are papers concerning the legal affairs of relatives in the FDR mss.

44. Rodger, "Want To Be a Lawyer?" 3. Roosevelt was referring to his work among Italians through the St. Andrew's Club; he did not spend a whole summer at it.

45. Noel F. Busch, *What Manner of Man?* (New York, 1944), 74–75.

46. ER, *This Is My Story*, 142; FDR diary, January 1, 1903.

47. ER, *This Is My Story*, 166.

48. FDR to Robert M. Washburn, August 18, 1928. See also PPA, 1936 214–215.

49. Grenville Clark, in *Harvard Alumni Bulletin*, April 28, 1945, 47:452.

50. Bechtel to FDR, November 1, 1932.

51. Lindley, *Roosevelt*, 70.

52. John E. Mack interviewed by George A. Palmer, February 1, 1949. Transcript in FDR mss.

53. PPA, 1933:338.

54. L. J. Magenis to FDR, August 10, 1928.

55. FDR to L. J. Magenis, August 15, 1928.

56. Campaign expenditures account in FDR mss.

57. Kleeman, *Gracious Lady*, 252–253.

58. *Ibid*., 252.

59. Alden Hatch, *Franklin D. Roosevelt* (New York, 1947).

60. Poughkeepsie *Eagle*, September 30, 1910.

61. Theodore Roosevelt to A. R. Cowles, August 10, 1910, in Theodore Roosevelt, *Letters to Anna Roosevelt Cowles . . .* (New York, 1924), 289.

62. George Mowry, *Theodore Roosevelt and the Progressive Movement* (Madison, Wisconsin, 1946), 134–155.

63. Lindley, *Roosevelt*, 71–72. For an interesting and useful reminiscence of Roosevelt's nomination and campaign, see Morgan H. Hoyt, "Roosevelt Enters Politics," *The Franklin D. Roosevelt Collector* (May, 1949), 3–9.

64. Interview with John J. Fitzgerald, June 17, 1948.

65. Enclosure in FDR to Edward Hayden, September 12, 1928.
66. Poughkeepsie *Eagle*, October 7, 1910.
67. Poughkeepsie *Eagle*, October 27, 1910.
68. PPA, 1933:339.
69. New York *Times*, September 5, 1932; interview with Margaret Suckley, September 26, 1947.
70. ER, *This Is My Story*, 167.
71. Poughkeepsie *News-Press*, October 27, 1910.
72. *Ibid.*, October 27, 1910.
73. Warren Moscow, *Politics in the Empire State* (New York, 1948), 81, 82.
74. Poughkeepsie *News-Press*, October 27, 1910.
75. *Ibid.*, October 27, 1910.
76. FDR, address at Hyde Park, November 5, 1910, longhand ms.
77. Edgar M. Wilcox to FDR, January 18, 1911.
78. Clipping from Poughkeepsie paper, November 1, 1910.
79. Poughkeepsie *Eagle*, October 28, 1910.
80. FDR, address at Hyde Park, November 5, 1910.
81. Poughkeepsie *Eagle*, November 11, 1910; *The New York Red Book*, 631, 644.
82. Frances Perkins, *The Roosevelt I Knew* (New York, 1946), 9.
83. PPA, 1933:385.
84. Chalmers Wood to FDR, January 18, 1911.
85. FDR to Chalmers Wood, February 1, 1911.
86. FDR memorandum to Earle Looker [1931].

CHAPTER VI

Roosevelt or the Tiger?

1. Louis McHenry Howe, "The Winner," *Saturday Evening Post* (February 25, 1935), 205:6.
2. Sherrard Billings to FDR, January 31, 1911; FDR to Billings, February 27, 1911.
3. FDR diary, January 1, 1911.
4. Allan Nevins, *Grover Cleveland: A Study in Courage* (New York, 1932), 399, 494–498.
5. William F. Sheehan to FDR, October 25, 1910.
6. FDR diary, January 1, 1911.
7. *Ibid.*, January 2, 1911.
8. *Ibid.*, January 3, 1911.
9. *Ibid.*, January 3, 1911.
10. New York *Times*, January 22, 1911; Lindley, *Roosevelt*, 86–88.
11. Lindley, *Roosevelt*, 81; FDR, *The Happy Warrior, Alfred E. Smith: A Study of a Public Servant* (New York, 1928), 4.
12. New York *Post*, January 14, 1911.
13. Draft statement, January 16, 1911, FDR mss.
14. Edmund R. Terry, "The Insurgents at Albany," *The Independent* (September 7, 1911), 71:536–537.

15. New York *Times*, January 18, 1911.
16. New York *Times*, January 18, 1911.
17. Albany *Knickerbocker Press*, January 18, 1911; New York *Times*, January 18, 1911.
18. New York *Tribune*, May 5, 1915.
19. William Grosvenor to FDR, January 19, 1911.
20. New York *Globe*, February 6, 1911.
21. Frank M. Patterson to FDR, January 18, 1911.
22. New York *Post*, January 17, 1911.
23. New York *American*, January 18, 1911.
24. New York *World*, January 17, 1911, cited in PL., 2:162.
25. Virginia Tyler Hudson, in New York *Globe*, February 6, 1911.
26. New York *Herald*, April 1, 1911.
27. New York *Sun*, January 20, 1911.
28. Terry, "Insurgents," 538.
29. New York *Times*, January 22, 1911.
30. ER, *This Is My Story*, 173–174 Lindley, *Roosevelt*, 90–91.
31. FDR, memorandum, January 18, 1911.
32. Sara Roosevelt, *My Boy Franklin*, 78–79.
33. New York *Times*, January 18, 1911.
34. New York *Sun*, January 20, 1911.
35. Buffalo *Enquirer*, January 30, 1911; Lindley, *Roosevelt*, 85.
36. Albany *Knickerbocker Press*, January 18, 1911.
37. Albany *Times Union*, January 23, 1911.
38. New York *World*, January 26, 1911.
39. Rome *Sentinel*, January 27, 1911.
40. Terry, "Insurgents," 538.
41. J. Rhinelander Dillon to FDR, January 24, 1911.
42. New York *Times*, January 22, 1911; Lindley, *Roosevelt*, 88–89.
43. New York *Post*, February 8, 1911.
44. Theodore Roosevelt to FDR, January 29, 1911.
45. Lindley, *Roosevelt*, 92. The petition is not in the FDR mss., but there is one from the Poughkeepsie Trade and Labor Council, Henry Prinz, President, February 27, 1911.
46. FDR to Raymond G. Guerney, February 3, 1911.
47. FDR to James F. Baldwin, February 9, 1911.
48. FDR to Guerney, February 3, 1911; Edmund Platt to FDR, April 26, 1911; FDR to Platt, May 1, 1911.
49. Thomas Newbold to FDR, January 18, 1911.
50. Baldwin to FDR, January 25, 1911.
51. Lindley, *Roosevelt*, 84.
52. New York *World*, January 26, 1911; *The New York Red Book*, 120.
53. Lindley, *Roosevelt*, 92.
54. FDR to Paul Fuller, February 23, 1911.
55. New York *American*, February 5, 1911.
56. According to Terry, this happened in early February (Terry, "Insurgents," 538). In mid-March, Murphy was still ready to back Cohalan (FDR to Montgomery Hare, March 22, 1911).

57. FDR to Walter F. Taylor, February 17, 1911.
58. Terry, "Insurgents," 539.
59. New York *Tribune*, May 5, 1915.
60. For Stetson's viewpoint on trusts, see Francis Lynde Stetson, "Government and the Corporations," *The Atlantic Monthly* (July, 1912), 110: 27–41.
61. Hare to FDR, March 9, 14, 1911.
62. New York *Tribune*, May 31, 1911.
63. New York *Times*, May 31, 1911.
64. New York *Tribune*, March 28, 1911; Edgar T. Brackett to FDR, August 6, 1921, enclosing memorandum.
65. Terry, "Insurgents," 539; New York *Tribune*, March 29, 1911.
66. FDR to Fuller, April 14, 1911.
67. New York *Tribune*, April 1, 1911.
68. Albany *Globe & Commercial Advertiser*, May 31, 1911.
69. New York *Tribune*, April 1, 1911.
70. FDR to J. B. Murray, April 3, 1911.
71. New York *Post*, April 1, 1911.
72. Terry, "Insurgents," 539.
73. James A. O'Gorman to Robert Wagner, March 31, 1911, in FDR mss.
74. FDR to Murray, April 3, 1911.
75. New York *Tribune*, April 1, 1911.
76. New York *Herald*, April 1, 1911.
77. Saratoga *Sun*, April 1, 1911.
78. New York *Post*, April 1, 1911; *The Nation* (April 6, 1911), 92:334–335; FDR to Henry H. Wells, April 6, 1911.
79. FDR to Ferdinand Hoyt, April 12, 1911.
80. FDR to James Barkley, April 4, 1911.
81. FDR to Murray, April 3, 1911.
82. FDR to H. W. Lunger, January 30, 1928. Italics mine.

CHAPTER VII

Progressive State Senator

1. FDR, address before Saturn Club, Buffalo, New York, December 23, 1911.
2. ER, *This Is My Story*, 176.
3. For analyses of the Progressive movement, see particularly Hofstadter, *The American Political Tradition;* Mowry, *Theodore Roosevelt and the Progressive Movement;* William Diamond, *The Economic Thought of Woodrow Wilson* (Baltimore, 1943); and Mowry, "The California Progressive and His Rationale: A Study in Middle Class Politics," *Mississippi Valley Historical Review* (September, 1949), 36:239–250.
4. Perkins, *The Roosevelt I Knew*, 10–11.
5. FDR to William C. Rodgers, May 24, 1911.
6. New York *Telegram*, February 7, 1911.
7. FDR to T. A. Malloy, March 1, 1911.

8. Watertown newspaper, about May 30, 1913, FDR scrapbook; FDR to Thomas J. Comerford, August 26, 1914.
9. Perkins, *The Roosevelt I Knew*, 11.
10. New York *World*, June 8, 1911.
11. Clipping, FDR mss.
12. New York *Globe*, June 2, 1911.
13. Newspaper clipping, June 28, 1911, FDR mss.
14. Perkins, *The Roosevelt I Knew*, 24–25.
15. FDR, *Happy Warrior*, 6.
16. New York *Tribune*, March 26, 27; April 6, 1911.
17. FDR to Rev. Richard Russell Upjohn, March 24, 1911.
18. FDR to George Haven Putnam, March 17, 1911.
19. FDR to Raymond B. Fosdick, February 25, 1915.
20. Crystal Eastman Benedict to FDR, May 12, 1911.
21. File 35, FDR mss.
22. Paul Kennaday to FDR, March 8, 1912, and much correspondence; Ernest Bohm, Central Federated Union of Greater New York, to FDR, February 5, 1913.
23. Howe, "The Winner," 7, 48.
24. Alburtis Nooney to FDR, January 12, 1912, and subsequent correspondence.
25. Thomas D. Fitzgerald to FDR, November 1, 1912.
26. Abram I. Elkus to FDR, February 6, 1913; FDR to Abram I. Elkus, February 13, 1913.
27. New York *Post*, May 22, 24, 1911.
28. FDR to Richard E. Connell, April 24, 1911.
29. New York *Mail*, April 27, 1911.
30. FDR to William Pierrepont White, June 2, 1911.
31. New York *Mail*, April 27, 1911.
32. FDR to C. R. Miller, May 2, 1911.
33. FDR, speech in File 31, FDR mss.
34. New York *Times*, June 7, 1911; see also New York *Post*, May 29; June 1, 1911.
35. FDR to Silas Wodell, May 9, 1911.
36. FDR to W. M. Simonson, March 22, 1912.
37. FDR to Charles S. Berry, February 8, 1911.
38. FDR, speech April, 1911. FDR mss.
39. FDR, speech before convention of the Intercollegiate Civic League, April 11, 1912.
40. FDR to J. DeLancey Verplanck, July 13, 1911.
41. PL, 2:167.
42. New York *Sun*, October 5, 1911.
43. Poughkeepsie *Enterprise*, January 12, 1912; FDR to Hamilton Fish, Jr., March 27, 1912.
44. FDR to Anna G. W. Dayley, February 1, 1911.
45. FDR to Frances C. Barlow, May 24, 1911.
46. Poughkeepsie *Eagle*, May 30, 1911.
47. FDR to Caroline E. Furness, March 20, 1912; FDR to Martha E.

Beckwith, March 19, 1912; ER, *This Is My Story*, 180. Several petitions and letters signed by Vassar faculty members are in the FDR papers.

48. New York *Herald*, September 8, 1911.

49. Elizabeth B. Grannis to FDR, September 9, 1911.

50. FDR to John C. Richberg, September 28, 1911.

51. New York, *Legislative Record*, 1911, 346; PL, 2:172.

52. FDR to C. L. Boothby, March 24, 1911.

53. FDR to James Albert Patterson, State Superintendent, Anti-Saloon League [1913].

54. Patterson to FDR, March 24, 1913, enclosing editorial entitled. "An Advocate of Christian Patriotism," from the *American Issue*, March, 1913.

55. [Ray Thomas Tucker,] *Mirrors of 1932* (New York, 1931), 85; FDR memorandum to Earle Looker [1931].

56. FDR to Rev. Charles G. Mallery, February 17, 1911; FDR to Rev. Augustus F. Walker, April 14, 1911. On prize fighting, see FDR to O. G. Villard, September 28, 1911.

57. FDR to Rev. J. J. Cowles and Rev. W. L. Hughes, June 20, 1911; see also FDR to Edwin R. Pease, April 26, 1911.

58. FDR to John K. Sague, May 8, 1911.

59. Poughkeepsie *News-Press*, March 7, 1913.

60. Rev. Lyman Abbott to FDR, June 1, 1911; FDR to Abbott, June 2, 1911.

61. FDR to Edward A. Conger, June 27, 1911. However, in the autumn he stated he was "heartily in favor" of the clause, but must vote on the basis of the charter as a whole (FDR to Mary M. McGuire, September 28, 1911).

62. Albert de Roode to FDR, August 17, 1911.

63. PL, 2:170–171; Brooklyn *Citizen*, September 8, 1911.

64. New York *American*, September 18, 1911.

65. PL, 2:172–174.

66. Henry F. Pringle, *Alfred E. Smith: A Critical Study* (New York, 1927), 160.

67. Pringle, *Smith*, 161.

68. FDR, address before Saturn Club, Buffalo, New York, December 23, 1911.

69. New York *Times*, December 25, 1911.

70. Poughkeepsie *News-Press*, March 5, 1912.

CHAPTER VIII

The Roosevelt Wagon and the Wilson Star

1. FDR, statement on the death of Woodrow Wilson, February, 1924.

2. Arthur S. Link, *Wilson: The Road to the White House* (Princeton, 1947).

3. Lindley, *Roosevelt*, 120.

4. PL, 3:467.

5. FDR to T. M. Osborne, March 19, 1912.

6. Andrew D. Meloy to FDR, February 25, 1911.
7. FDR to John H. Prentice, March 17, 1911.
8. FDR to Ira Crane, March 27, 1911.
9. FDR to Gerald L. Hoyt, March 17, 1911.
10. Poughkeepsie *Enterprise*, January 12, 1912.
11. John G. Jones to FDR, April 19, 1912.
12. FDR to Jones, May 15, 1912.
13. FDR planned to plant 8000 in 1912 (PL, 2:179).
14. Poughkeepsie *News-Press*, March 5, 1912.
15. FDR to S. D. Stockton, February 22, 1912.
16. FDR to Dexter Blagden, February 21, 1912.
17. FDR to Joseph P. Chamberlain, October 29, 1912.
18. Clipping, Albany paper, April 1, 1912; New York *Tribune*, March 1, 15, 1912.
19. New York *Post*, April 13, 1912.
20. William Gorham Rice to FDR, December 23, 1911.
21. FDR to J. P. McGarrahan, June 5, 1912.
22. FDR to Osborne, March 19, 1912.
23. FDR to Henry Markoe, Jr., March 20, 1912.
24. Osborne to FDR, April 6, 1912; Edward M. Bassett to FDR, April 8, 1912.
25. New York *Post*, April 11, 1912; New York *Herald*, April 12, 1912; New York *Tribune*, April 12, 1912. FDR was nominated as an alternate, but "the Orange delegation concluded to get out from under and withdrew your name." J. J. Bippus to FDR, April 12, 1912.
26. New York *Post*, April 13, 1912; Osborne to ER, April 17, 1912.
27. FDR to Theodore Roosevelt, April 5, 1912.
28. PPA, 1938:504.
29. PL, 2:187.
30. *Ibid.*, 2:185.
31. *Ibid.*, 2:189.
32. *Ibid.*, 2:187.
33. FDR to Rice, May 15, 1912.
34. FDR to Thomas M. Upp, May 22, 1912.
35. Julian B. Beaty to FDR, September 10, 1912.
36. FDR to Upp, May 22, 1912.
37. [L. M. Howe] to FDR, June 5, 1912.
38. FDR to Otis L. Beach [1912].
39. New York *Tribune*, June 24, 1912.
40. Hare to FDR, July 4, 1912.
41. New York *Tribune*, June 25, 1912; New York *Post*, June 25, 1912.
42. New York *Post*, June 25, 1912; Beaty to FDR, June 20, 1912.
43. "To the delegates . . ." June 25, 1912.
44. New York *Tribune*, June 4, 1912.
45. FDR to O'Gorman, June 10, 1912; O'Gorman to FDR, June 15, 1912; Lindley, *Roosevelt*, 103.
46. New York *Tribune*, June 28, 1912.
47. FDR to Markoe, March 20, 1912.

48. Lindley, *Roosevelt*, 103–104, PL, 2:191.
49. Link, *Wilson*, 446.
50. New York *Post*, June 29, 1912.
51. *Ibid.*, June 28, 1912.
52. *Ibid.*, June 25, 1912.
53. New York *Tribune*, June 28, 1912; New York *Times*, April 1, 1931.
54. Hare to FDR, July 4, 1912.
55. Link, *Wilson*, 448–465; see also unsigned article, "How Bryan Hurt Wilson," New York *Post*, July 1, 1912.
56. PL, 2:192.
57. Hare to FDR, July 4, 1912.
58. Hare to FDR, July 4, 1912.
59. New York *Post*, July 18, 1912.
60. New York *Tribune*, July 4, 1912; New York *Post*, July 3, 1912.
61. New York *Tribune*, July 18, 1912.
62. New York *Tribune*, July 18, 1912.
63. New York *Herald*, July 30, 1912.
64. New York *Tribune*, July 18, 1912.
65. Poughkeepsie *News-Press*, June 1, 1912.
66. Copies of resolutions in FDR mss.
67. New York *Tribune*, September 30, 1912.
68. New York *Tribune*, October 4, 1912; New York *Post*, October 7, 1912.
69. New York *Post*, October 5, 1912.
70. FDR to Thomas Pendell, January 24, 1912.
71. FDR senatorial mss., Box 9, File 19.
72. FDR to McGarrahan, June 5, 1912; Charles W. Cosad to FDR, June 15, 1912.
73. FDR to Sague, February 14, 1912.
74. FDR to Pendell, January 24, 1912.
75. PL, 2:193.
76. PL, 2:196; Poughkeepsie *News-Press*, August 26, 1912.
77. John Keller and Joe Boldt, "Franklin's on His Own Now; Last Days of Louis McHenry Howe," *Saturday Evening Post* (October, 1940), 213:42.
78. Howe to FDR, undated [*c.* August 1, 1912].
79. Howe was on another payroll part of the time.
80. Interview with ER, May 1, 1948.
81. Rice to FDR, October 30, 1912.
82. W. C. Osborn to FDR, October 14, 1932; FDR to — October 26, 1912. This apparently went to every member of the Grange in the area. Howe to FDR, undated.
83. FDR to Albert E. Hoyt, November 19, 1912; Philbrick to FDR, November 7, 1912; FDR to Philbrick, November 19, 1912.
84. New York State, *Legislative Record and Index*, 1913; FDR to Stephen J. Clum, November 18, 1912. Ellen Kemble Lente to FDR, October 14; November 10, 1912.
85. Howe to FDR, undated.

86. FDR to — November 1, 1912.

87. George W. Phillips to FDR, October 26, 1912; FDR to Phillips, November 19, 1912.

88. FDR to Mack, October 29, 1912; Osborn to FDR, October 27, 1912.

89. George E. Schryver to FDR, October 26, 1912.

90. FDR to James McShane, November 19, 1912.

91. James G. Meyer to FDR, February 3, 1912; FDR to Meyer, February 8, 1912.

92. FDR to Eugene Wells, November 19, 1912.

93. Confidential source.

94. *The New York Red Book* (Albany, 1913), 677.

95. Walker to FDR, November 7, 1912.

96. Osborn to FDR, November 6, 1912; candidate's statement of election expenses, incompletely filled out, copy in FDR's hand. Cf. Pendell to FDR, November 18, 1912; Comerford to FDR, November 6, 1912.

97. FDR to Amasa Parker, Jr., November 19, 1912.

98. See Liberty Hyde Bailey to FDR, January 31, 1913; FDR to Bailey, February 4, 1913.

99. FDR to Sextus E. Landon, February 7, 1913.

100. Arthur H. Ham, Director, to FDR, February 18, 1913; FDR to Ham, February 19, 1912; FDR to Pierre Jay, February 28, 1913.

101. FDR to Landon, February 7, 1913.

102. "To the members . . ." January 31, 1911; Publicity Committee, Fruit and Produce Association and National League of Commission Merchants (New York Branch), February 5, 1913, February 7, 1913 – printed statements. One of these began, "Loss to the farmers of millions of dollars every year . . ." Another stated that the bill would require 2500 inspectors or more at a cost of $5,000,000 in New York City or more than $10,000,000 for the state.

103. Osborn to FDR, February 13, 1913.

104. T. Harvey Ferris, in "Minutes of Hearing before Joint Committee on Agriculture of the Senate and Assembly held February 10, 1913 . . . in re Senate Bill No. 377." There were earlier hearings on January 28 and 29.

105. New York *Telegraph*, November 30, 1913.

106. Osborn to FDR, February 5, 1913; FDR to Albert Knapp [March, 1913].

107. FDR to Horace V. Bruce, March 10, 1913.

108. See, as examples, FDR to T. E. Bullard, February 18, 1913; W. H. Vary and W. N. Niles, Legislative Committee of the Grange to — March 1, 1913 (multigraphed).

109. Bruce to FDR, March 21, 26, 1903; Lindley, *Roosevelt*, 109–110.

110. FDR to Joseph Tumulty, January 13, 1913.

111. FDR to Lawrence B. Dunham, January 22, 1913; FDR to George B. Burd, January 22, 1913.

112. Interview with Michael Francis Doyle, October 27, 1947. Doyle had been treasurer of the Woodrow Wilson League in Pennsylvania.

113. Interview with ER, May 1, 1948.

114. Lindley, *Roosevelt*, 110.

115. Josephus Daniels, *The Wilson Era, Years of Peace, 1910–1917* (Chapel Hill, 1944), 124.

116. *Ibid*.. 126. See also Daniels's diary, March 6, 9, 1913, Daniels mss.

117. *Ibid*., 124–127. See also Daniels to Woodrow Wilson, March 11, 1913, Daniels mss.

118. John M. Stiles to FDR, March 1, 1913.

119. Seth Low to FDR, March 10, 1913.

120. Osborn to FDR, April 11, 1913.

CHAPTER IX

At T.R.'s Desk

1. FDR to Sara Roosevelt, March 17, 1913.

2. Arthur W. Macmahon and John D. Millett, *Federal Administrators*, (New York, 1939), 247.

3. Robert G. Albion, interview with Frederick Hale, September 9, 1946.

4. New York *Telegraph*, November 30, 1913.

5. Villard to FDR, March 14, 1913.

6. New York *Sun*, March 19, 1913.

7. Washington *Post*, April 30, 1913.

8. [Elting Morison,] *Naval Administration. Selected Documents on Navy Department Organization 1915–1940*, 5.

9. *Army and Navy Journal*, March 18, 1913.

10. Daniels, *Wilson Era*, 1:122–123.

11. *Army and Navy Register*, April 11, 1914, citing New York *Tribune*.

12. Interview with Daniels, May 29, 1947.

13. Howe to FDR, April 4, 1914.

14. *Army and Navy Journal*, March 18, 1913.

15. PL, 2:200.

16. FDR to Aymor Johnson, March 28, 1913.

17. Daniels, *Wilson Era*, 2:253.

18. Interview with Charles H. McCarthy, June 8, 1948.

19. Howe to FDR, March 23, 1913.

20. PL, 2:330.

21. Samuel McGowan to John D. Donald, February 1, 1916, Howe mss.

22. H. Wright to FDR, March 7, 1916, Howe mss.

23. Interview with Doyle, October 24, 1947.

24. Interview with Frederick R. Harris, April 7, 1948.

25. Interview with Joseph K. Taussig, June 7, 1947.

26. Marvin, "Notes on Franklin D. Roosevelt as Assistant Secretary of the Navy," [1946], in author's possession.

27. Interview with Daniels, May 29, 1947.

28. U. S. Secretary of the Navy, *Annual Report, 1913* (Washington, 1913), 5.

29. FDR to Charles A. Munn, March 26, 1913.

30. Yates Stirling, *Fundamentals of Naval Service* (Philadelphia, 1917), 80–83.

31. These flags are in the museum of the Roosevelt Library.

32. New York *World*, December 18, 1921.

33. Concerning FDR's use of the yachts, see PL, 2:210, 212–213. He also had some supervision of the Presidential yacht, *Mayflower* (the wheel of which now decorates the sun porch at Hyde Park). See FDR to Wilson, August 1, 1913; August 24, 25, 27, 28, 1915; FDR to Joseph Tumulty, April 29; October 23, 1919, Wilson mss.

34. FDR to Sara Roosevelt, May 27, 1913; Edmund Pendleton Rogers to FDR, June 9, 1913; clipping, FDR scrapbook; Daniels to FDR, August 7, 1913.

35. Interview with Mahlon Street Tisdale, May 24, 1948; Henry B. Wilson to FDR, July 7 [1913].

36. William F. Halsey and J. Bryan, III, *Admiral Halsey's Story* (New York, 1947), 18.

37. Interview with Harold R. Stark, May 26, 1948.

38. USS *Dolphin*, Logbook, Office of Naval History, Department of the Navy.

39. Benjamin R. Tillman to FDR, April 12, 1913; Assistant Secretary of the Navy, Private Papers, Box 67, Office of the Secretary of the Navy records, National Archives. Hereafter this collection is referred to as Naval Archives.

40. Daniels to Tillman, April 15, 1913, Naval Archives.

41. FDR to Andrew J. Peters, December 19, 1917.

42. Henry Cabot Lodge to FDR, August 1, 1913; FDR to Lodge, August 2, September 15, 1913.

43. Augustus P. Gardner to FDR, June 25, 1913.

44. Howe to Lathrop Brown, September 21, 1915.

45. PL, 3:219.

46. New York *Times*, October 5, 1913.

47. Baltimore *Sun*, December 3, 1913.

48. Joseph E. Davies to FDR, November 26, 1913; Washington *Herald*, December 1, 1913.

49. PL, 2:217; ER, *This I Remember*, 53–54.

50. ER, *This Is My Story*, 236–237; ER, *This I Remember*, 53–54.

51. ER, *This Is My Story*, 234–237, 305–306.

52. Joseph C. Grew to FDR, March 31, 1913.

53. Sumner Welles to FDR, March 1, 1915; FDR to Welles, March 15, 1915; FDR to William Jennings Bryan, March 15, 1915.

54. ER, *This Is My Story*, 198–199, 233.

55. *Ibid.*, 163.

56. William Phillips, "Memoirs," unpublished ms.

57. Theodore Roosevelt to FDR, March 18, 1913.

58. ER, *This Is My Story*, 196, 208–209.

59. *Ibid.*, 199.

60. *Ibid.*, 199, 209–210.

61. *Ibid.*, 196.

62. New York *Telegraph*, November 30, 1913.

63. M. Abbott Frazar Co. to FDR, September 20, 1915.

64. New York *Telegraph*, November 30, 1913.

65. Anna Roosevelt, "My Life with F.D.R.," *The Woman* (June, 1949), 22:58–60, 106–109; Kleeman, *Gracious Lady*, 262–265; John Gunther, *Roosevelt in Retrospect* (New York, 1950), 197–199.

66. Clipping, April 10, 1913, FDR scrapbook.

67. *Army and Navy Journal*, April 12, 1913.

68. Clipping, Knoxville, Tennessee paper, April 13, 1913, FDR scrapbook.

CHAPTER X

The Tiger Refuses To Starve

1. FDR to George S. Bixby, March 24, 1913.

2. Rochester *Herald*, March 17, 1913; Villard to FDR, March 14, 1913.

3. Burton J. Hendrick, *Life and Letters of Walter Hines Page* (New York, 1925), 1:113.

4. D. F. Malone to Ray Stannard Baker, in Baker, *Wilson*, 4:42f. FDR's career-diplomat friends, Edward Bell and Joseph Grew, were not injured by the change in administration.

5. New York *Times*, December 15, 1914.

6. Interview with Daniels, May 29, 1947.

7. John M. Blum, *Joe Tumulty and the Wilson Era* (Boston, 1951), 79.

8. [Tucker], *Mirrors of 1932*, 91; FDR memorandum for Looker, undated.

9. Baker, *Wilson*, 4:45–46.

10. *Ibid.*, 4:32.

11. New York *Herald*, March 28, 1913.

12. FDR to Sague, April 3, 1913.

13. New York *Times*, April 11, 12, 1913.

14. *Ibid.*, March 23, 1914.

15. There are thirteen boxes of post-office patronage correspondence in FDR's Assistant Secretary of the Navy file.

16. Daniel C. Roper to FDR, April 13, 1913.

17. Howe to FDR, April 7, 1914, Howe mss.

18. FDR to Frederick Northrup, March 28, 1913.

19. FDR, statement, September 19, 1913.

20. Howe to FDR, June 28, 1913; FDR to William Sulzer, June 30, 1913; Sulzer to FDR, June 17, 1913.

21. New York *Times*, November 2, 1913.

22. FDR to T. Douglas Robinson, October 14, 1913; Robinson to FDR, October 8, 1914.

23. FDR to Fish, July 20, 1914.

24. FDR to Henry F. Burgard, November 11, 1913; not sent.

25. Howe to Sague, November 19, 1913.

26. Blum, *Tumulty*, 78.

27. New York *Sun*, December 10, 1913.

28. Stuart G. Gibboney to FDR, December 11, 1913.

29. Robert Rosenbluth to FDR, February 1, 1914.
30. E. T. Larkin to FDR, February 6, 1914.
31. FDR to Martin H. Glynn, January 24, 1914.
32. New York *Post*, January 15, 1914; New York *Herald*, February 10, 15, 1914; New York *Times*, February 10, 1914; St. Louis *Globe-Democrat*, February 10, 1914 FDR to Gibboney, February 13, 1914.
33. FDR to Wilson, handwritten note, *c.* March 31, 1914, Wilson mss.
34. Wilson to FDR, April 1, 1914, Wilson mss.
35. Howe to FDR, April 4, 7, 1914.
36. Mowry, *Theodore Roosevelt*, 300.
37. Lindley, *Roosevelt*, 131.
38. Clipping, FDR scrapbook; Mowry, *Theodore Roosevelt*, 300–301; Lindley, *Roosevelt*, 131–132.
39. New York *Times*, July 14, 1914.
40. *Ibid.*, July 19, 1914.
41. FDR to G. F. Peabody, July 1, 1914. In this letter FDR speaks of seventy postmasterships.
42. Edward E. Perkins to FDR, December 29, 1913.
43. New York *Times*, July 21, 1914. At about the same time, FDR was credited with selection of anti-Tammany postmasters at St. Johnsville (Utica *Press*, July 16, 1914) and several other places.
44. New York *Times*, July 21, 1914.
45. Poughkeepsie *Star*, July 20, 1914; FDR to Mack, undated telegram.
46. New York *Times*, July 22, 1914.
47. *Ibid.*, July 23, 1914.
48. *Ibid.*, July 24, 1914.
49. New York *Post*, July 22, 1914.
50. FDR to Howe, July 23, 1914.
51. FDR to Howe, July 23, 1914.
52. New York *Times*, July 24, 1914.
53. FDR to William M. Martin, July 23, 1914.
54. FDR to Rosenbluth, August 13, 1914.
55. FDR to Howe, August 13, 1914, Howe mss.
56. Lindley, *Roosevelt*, 132.
57. Daniels, *Wilson Era*, 1:131.
58. FDR to Osborn, August 4, 1914.
59. Louis Antisdale to FDR, telegram, August 4, 1914; New York *Tribune*, August 14, 1914.
60. FDR to Charles F. Rattigan, August 14, 1914; FDR to Randall M. Saunders, August 14, 1914; see also FDR to Rosenbluth, August 14, 1914; FDR, memorandum for the press, August 13, 1914.
61. For example, Utica *Observer*, August 15, 1914.
62. New York *Sun*, September 6, 1914.
63. FDR to Pendell, September 2, 1914.
64. New York *Tribune*, August 18, 1914.
65. Albany *Knickerbocker Press*, August 21, 1914.
66. FDR to Howe, August 22, 1914, Howe mss.
67. New York *American*, August 27, 1914.

68. Howe to FDR [August 24, 1914], Howe mss.
69. Tarrytown *News,* October 27, 1914.
70. New York *Times,* September 8, 1914.
71. James W. Gerard to Bryan, September 10, 1914, Wilson mss.
72. Bryan to Wilson [before September 19, 1914], Wilson mss.
73. Blum, *Tumulty,* 79, 80.
74. New York *Herald,* September 12, 1914.
75. Binghamton *Republican Herald,* September 28, 1914.
76. Albany *Knickerbocker Press,* September 27, 1914.
77. *Ibid.,* September 21, 1914.
78. Port Jervis *Gazette,* September 5, 1914; Auburn *Citizen,* September 5, 1914.
79. Batavia *News,* September 26, 1914.
80. Cooperstown *Freeman's Journal,* September 23, 1914.
81. New York *Record and Times,* September 26, 1914.
82. Washington *Star,* September 21, 1914.
83. Amsterdam *Sentinel,* September 16, 1914.
84. Howe to Lathrop Brown, September 21, 1915, Howe mss.
85. Howe to FDR, August 29, 1914, Howe mss.
86. Charles H. McCarthy to Howe, September 22, 1914.
87. A. J. Berres to FDR, August 3, 1932, California Box 33, Democratic National Committee mss.
88. FDR to Howe, August 24, 1914, Howe mss.
89. Mary Walker to FDR, September 28, 1914.
90. Babylon *Leader,* September 25, 1914, and numerous other newspapers.
91. Walton *Chronicle,* September 23, 1914.
92. Poughkeepsie *News-Press,* September 24, 1914.
93. Brooklyn *Times,* September 28, 1914.
94. New York *Times,* September 30, 1914.
95. Albany *Knickerbocker Press,* October 4, 1914.
96. FDR to Langdon P. Marvin, October 19, 1914.
97. New York *World,* September 30, 1914.
98. New York *Tribune,* October 26, 1914.
99. Poughkeepsie *Enterprise,* November 5, 1914.
100. Daniels, autobiography, draft, Daniels mss.
101. FDR, memorandum, December 19, 1914.
102. Theodore Roosevelt to FDR, March 18, 1915; William H. Van Benschoten to FDR, April 15, 1915.
103. Washington *Herald,* May 5, 1915; New York *Tribune,* May 5, 1915.
104. Clipping from a handwritten letter from Theodore Roosevelt to Edith Roosevelt, enclosed in Edith K. Roosevelt to ER, October 31, 1921.
105. Theodore Roosevelt to FDR, May 29, 1915.
106. New York *Tribune,* February 2, 1915; for an attack on FDR, see New York *Tribune,* February 1, 1914. See also Howe to FDR, August 18, 1914; FDR to Howe, August 22, 1915 [?], Howe mss.
107. FDR to Burd, September, 1915; FDR to John J. Fitzgerald, September 3, 1915; Fitzgerald to FDR, September 8, 1915.

108. FDR to Fitzgerald, September 3, 1915; interview with Fitzgerald, June 17, 1948; interview with McCarthy, June 8, 1949.
109 New York *World*, October 30, 1915.
110. Lindley, *Roosevelt*, 133–134.
111. *Ibid.*, 133.
112. PL, 2:319.
113. PL, 2:321. Italics mine.
114. PL, 2:316–317, 319, 321; clippings, FDR mss.

CHAPTER XI

Learning About Labor

1. FDR, address at Butte, Montana, August 18, 1920.
2. Interview with McCarthy, June 8, 1948.
3. Interview with ER, May 1, 1948.
4. Interview with Doyle, October 24, 1947.
5. New York *Sun*, September 26, 1915.
6. FDR, address at Kittery, Maine, August 26, 1916.
7. Howe to James P. Maher, January 25, 1918, Howe mss.
8. New York *Times*, July 21, 1949.
9. Interview with Harris, April 7, 1948; Daniels, *Wilson Era*, 2:576–581; Harris to FDR, March 24, 1913; H. R. Stanford to Daniels, March 21, 1913; H. R. Stanford, "Pearl Harbor Dry Dock" (reprinted from American Society of Civil Engineers, *Transactions*, 1916, 80:223–337).
10. *Army and Navy Journal*, March 22, 1913; Washington *Post*, March 21, 1913.
11. Philadelphia *Record*, March 22, 1913.
12. A. W. Grant to FDR, April 5, 1913, enclosing memo of FDR visit to yard, March 29, 1913; Philadelphia *Public Ledger*, March 30, 1913.
13. Mitchell, *History of the Modern Navy*, 158. Meyer tried to close useless bases, including Philadelphia.
14. Philadelphia *Public Ledger*, March 30, 1913.
15. Robert S. Griffin to FDR, April 2, 1914.
16. New York *Times*, August 5, 1913; FDR to Charles J. Badger, January 14, 1914; Badger to FDR, April 14, 1914, FDR mss.; Daniels to FDR, February 23, 1938, Daniels mss.
17. Newburgh *News*, April 8, 1913 [?], clipping in FDR scrapbook; New York *Times*, August 5, 1913.
18. PPA, 1928–1932:61–62.
19. Philadelphia *Record*, April 6, 1913.
20. FDR to N. R. Usher [1916?].
21. Washington *Post*, April 30, 1913.
22. Frederick W. Taylor, "Shop Management," Society of Mechanical Engineers, *Transactions*, 1884, vol. 24, in *Congressional Record*, May 15, 1945, 4674.
23. FDR, memorandum of engagements, June 23, 1913.
24. U. S. 62nd Cong., 2nd Sess., Senate, *Report No. 930*, cited in *Congres-*

sional Record, May 15, 1945, 4674. See also *Investigation of the Taylor System of Shop Management*, Hearing before the Committee on Labor of the House of Representatives, U. S. 62nd Cong., 1st Sess. (Washington, 1911); and *Taylor and Other Systems of Shop Management*, Hearing before the Committee on Labor of the House of Representatives, U. S. 62nd Cong., 2nd Sess., House of Representatives, *Report No. 403*. Both of these latter are in the FDR papers, Naval Archives.

25. John R. Edwards, "The Fetishism of Scientific Management," *Journal of the American Society of Naval Engineers* (May 1912), 24:355–416. A marked copy is in FDR papers, Naval Archives.

26. Memorandum of telephone conversation between D. W. Coffman and A. G. Winterhalter, April 23, 1913; Coffman to Daniels, April 23, 1913, telegram, FDR papers, Naval Archives; clipping, Boston newspaper, April 25, 1913.

27. N. P. Alifas *et al.* to FDR, May 7, 1913; Alifas to FDR, May 24, 1913, FDR papers, Naval Archives; Springfield, Massachusetts, *Republican*, May 9, 1913.

28. FDR to Daniels, April 14, 1913, FDR papers, Naval Archives. Howe dictated this letter. Coffman to FDR, May 22, 1913; Boston *Post*, May 20, 1913; Boston *Globe*, May 20, 1913.

29. "Hearings before Assistant Secretary Roosevelt at Commandant's Office, May 19, 1913," stenographic report, FDR papers, Naval Archives, Box 67.

30. Boston *Globe*, May 20, 1913.

31. Authur A. Ballantine to FDR, May 22, 1913, FDR papers, Naval Archives.

32. Felix Frankfurter to FDR, May 26, 1913; Frankfurter to Ballantine, May 24, 1913, telegram, FDR papers, Naval Archives. Frankfurter sent FDR a copy of Secretary of War Henry L. Stimson's report for 1911.

33. FDR to Robert G. Valentine, July 31, 1913 (marked in FDR's hand: *Proposed letter Not Sent*).

34. Secretary of War Lindley M. Garrison to FDR, October 13, 1913; FDR to Garrison, October 14, 1913; FDR to Frank P. Walsh, Chairman, Commission on Industrial Relations, March 11, 1914, FDR papers, Naval Archives; *Congressional Record*, May 15, 1945, 4669–4677.

35. PPA, 1928–1932:60–61.

36. Director of Navy Yards to Secretary of the Navy, March, 1913, Naval Archives.

37. "Navy Yard Wages, 1913–1915," memorandum, December 30, 1914, Director of Navy Yards, correspondence, Naval Archives, Box 68; Alifas *et al.* to FDR, May 7, 1915, FDR papers, Naval Archives.

38. FDR to Daniels, April 14, 1913, FDR papers, Naval Archives. Howe dictated this letter.

39. FDR to Daniels, June 25, 1913, FDR papers, Naval Archives.

40. Howe to FDR, June 28, 1913; Washington *Herald*, June 12, 1913; New York *Herald*, July 9, 1913.

41. "Navy Yard Wages, 1913–1915," FDR mss.

42. Circular letter issued to all locals by the International Wage Ad-

justment Committee appointed at special convention of the International Federation of Draftsmen's Union held in Washington, D. C., January 20–23, 1919.

43. E. E. Holland to FDR, September 18, 1815; FDR to Richard Morgan Watt, September 28, 1915; Louis Y. Post to FDR, July 5, 1917; Watt to FDR, June 29, 1917, FDR mss.; FDR to Daniels, March 7, 1918, Wilson mss.

44. FDR to Daniels, March 4, 1916.

45. FDR to H. T. Wright, July 6, 1921.

46. Navy Yard, New York Order No. 2, October 22, 1914, and similar orders for other yards, in Director of Navy Yards, correspondence, Naval Archives. Daniels signed this order, but FDR promulgated it as Acting Secretary. Secretary of the Navy, *Annual Report . . . 1914*, 11–12.

47. ER, *This Is My Story*, 199–203.

48. Clipping, Pensacola paper, November 17, 1913, FDR scrapbook.

49. William F. Fullam, Report of remarks in a hearing before the General Board [about 1914] in FDR mss; Archibald D. Turnbull and Clifford L. Lord, *History of United States Naval Aviation* (New Haven, 1949), 38; Secretary of the Navy, *Annual Report . . . 1914*, 8–9.

50. Leonard Wood to FDR, November 15, 1913, enclosing Wood to Chief of Quartermaster Corps, November 14, 1913; Daniels to FDR, August 26, 1914; FDR to Daniels, August 29, 1914, enclosing memorandum for Secretary of the Navy in the Matter of the Utilization of the New Orleans Navy Yard, FDR papers, Naval Archives; New Orleans *Picayune*, November 15, 1913; U. S. 63rd Cong., 2nd Sess., *Congressional Record*, 51:8179, Joint House Resolution 253, passed and signed.

51. Interview with Land, May 27, 1948.

52. Louis Goldman to FDR, June 2, 1924.

53. FDR to H. T. Wright, July 6, 1921.

CHAPTER XII

Another Roosevelt vs. the Trusts

1. Lindley, *Roosevelt*, 117–118.
2. Interview with Daniels, May 29, 1947.
3. Memo in FDR mss.
4. PL, 2:127.
5. John Gunther, *Roosevelt in Retrospect*, 76.
6. PL, 2:486.
7. ER, *This Is My Story*, 203–204.
8. FDR to Daniels, July 29, 1913.
9. Howe to FDR, June 30, 1913.
10. Howe to FDR, June 30, 1913.
11. Lindley, *Roosevelt*, 129–130.
12. FDR, June 18, 1913.
13. Clipping, FDR scrapbook.
14. Boston *Post*, May 18, 1914.
15. Interview with John M. Hancock, April 14, 1948; interview with

James O. Richardson, June 6, 1947. For detailed testimony concerning naval coal policy see House Naval Affairs Committee, *Hearings, 1915, passim; Hearings, 1916*, 778.

16. *Hearings, 1915*, 958–959. Howe prepared FDR's statement.
17. Howe to FDR, June 30, 1913.
18. Howe to Allerton D. Hitch, April 7, 1914; *Hearings, 1915*, 804.
19. Willis G. Townes to Howe, May 17, 1914; the Department to Bureau of Supplies and Accounts, May 18, 1914 (memorandum dictated by Howe). Concerning the McNeil Company, see New York *Herald*, November 24, 1914.
20. Townes to Howe, May 25, 1914; *Hearings, 1915*, 337–345 *et passim.*
21. FDR to William E. Chilton, July 13, 1914.
22. *Hearings, 1915*, 337–347.
23. *Hearings, 1915*, 175, 346–348; McGowan to FDR, November 27, 1914; McGowan to Daniels, undated, *c.* November 1914, analyzing Howe's draft of proposed coal statement.
24. McGowan to Daniels *c.* November 1914. For the statement see *Hearings, 1915*, 957–964.
25. *Hearings, 1915*, 804.
26. *Ibid.*, 805.
27. New York *Herald*, December 16, 1914.
28. *Hearings, 1915*, 957–958.
29. *Ibid.*, 346–348.
30. *Ibid.*, 974, 976–977.
31. New York *Times*, December 17, 1914.
32. *Hearings, 1916*, 491–492, 2351–2352.
33. McGowan to FDR, August 7, 1916.
34. PL, 2:295, 297; Clara and Hardy Steeholm, *The House at Hyde Park*, 122–125.
35. Howe to George H. Hawes & Co., August 22, 1914.
36. Interview with Hancock, April 14, 1948.
37. *Army and Navy Register*, April 4, 1914.
38. Howe to FDR, April 4, 1914.
39. Secretary of the Navy, *Annual Report, 1913.*
40. Daniels, autobiography, draft, Daniels mss.
41. Christian J. Peoples to FDR, September 11, 1915; FDR to Daniels, November 19, 1914.
42. FDR to McGowan and Peoples, August 4, 1915.
43. McGowan to FDR, August 7, 1916.
44. A. T. Marix to FDR, January 5, 8, 1914, with attached papers.
45. Thomas F. Durning to FDR, January 5, 1916. Quantities of Durning correspondence, most of it with Howe, are in the FDR papers.
46. McGowan to FDR, August 7, 1916; FDR to Cecil Arthur Spring Rice, June 21, 1916; FDR to Eduardo Suarez Mujica, January 10, 28, 1916; [FDR?] to Voetter, January 13, 1916; Suarez Mujica to FDR [January 19, 1916].
47. New York *Times*, December 6, 1914.
48. FDR to Roger A. Derby, September 20, 1916.

49. FDR to Daniels, August 3, 1915, Daniels mss.
50. FDR to John S. Lawrence, August 8, 1916.
51. FDR to Lemuel P. Padgett, January 6, 1917.
52. U. S. 64th Cong., 1st Sess., House of Representatives, Naval Affairs Committee, *Hearings*, March 29, 1916, 3:3484.
53. *Ibid.*, 3451.
54. FDR to Robert R. McCormick, March 9, 1917.
55. U. S., *Hearings before the Committee on Naval Affairs of the House of Representatives . . . 1917*, 931, 946–974, *et passim.*
56. FDR to Warren Delano, January 5, 1917.

CHAPTER XIII

"A Navy To Cope with Any Situation"

1. San Francisco *Chronicle*, April 16, 1914.
2. New York *Herald*, October 26, 1913; FDR to George W. Laws, October 24, 1913.
3. FDR to Badger, October 25, 1913.
4. New York *Herald*, October 26, 1913.
5. Portland, Oregon, *Telegram*, November 4, 1913.
6. Galveston, Texas, *News*, October 28, 1913.
7. New York *Telegraph*, November 30, 1913.
8. ER, *This Is My Story*, 211–212; Elliott Roosevelt, *As He Saw It* (New York, 1946), 17.
9. ER, *This Is My Story*, 207.
10. Yates Stirling, *Sea Duty; The Memoirs of a Fighting Admiral* (New York, 1939), 142.
11. Secretary of the Navy, *Annual Report, 1913*, 25–26.
12. *Ibid.*, 6, 25–26; Daniels, *Wilson Era*, 1:501–512.
13. Bradley A. Fiske, *From Midshipman to Rear Admiral* (New York, 1919), 329; Daniels, *Wilson Era*, 1:239, 273; interview with Daniels, May 29, 1947.
14. Daniels, *Wilson Era*, 1:242–243; interview with Daniels, May 29, 1947.
15. Thomas A. Bailey, "California, Japan, and the Alien Land Legislation of 1913," *Pacific Historical Review* (March, 1932), 1:36–59; Bailey, *Theodore Roosevelt and the Japanese-American Crises* (Palo Alto, California, 1934); Outten J. Clinard, *Japan's Influence on American Naval Power 1897–1917* (Berkeley, California, 1947), 102–114.
16. Daniels, *Wilson Era*, 1:161–168; interview with Daniels, May 29, 1947.
17. FDR to Alfred Thayer Mahan, June 16, 1914.
18. Fiske to Daniels, May 13, 1913, copy in Roosevelt papers.
19. Henry L. Stimson and McGeorge Bundy, *On Active Service in Peace and War* (New York, 1948), 301–302.
20. Paymaster Higgins to the Department, April 28, 1913.
21. House Naval Affairs Committee, *Hearings . . . 1915*, 822–823.
22. Senate Naval Affairs Subcommittee, *Naval Investigations, 1920*, 1:758.

23. FDR memorandum [spring, 1913].
24. New York *World*, May 10, 1913.
25. Naval Investigation, 1:808–809. A memorandum in the Roosevelt papers probably is the one to which Admiral Fullam referred.
26. Fiske, *From Midshipman to Rear Admiral*, 540. See also 577–578. FDR, "Tentative Suggestions for Holding Joint Army and Navy Maneuvers during Summer of 1914," October, 1913.
27. Boston *Herald*, May 20, 1913.
28. Watertown *Standard*, May 29, 1913.
29. Los Angeles *Examiner*, May 26, 1913.
30. *Ibid.*, May 26, 1913.
31. Watertown *Standard*, May 29, 1913.
32. Baltimore *American*, May 27, 1913.
33. McCormick to FDR, October 24, 1913.
34. FDR to McCormick, November 20, 1913.
35. McCormick to FDR, December 31, 1913.
36. FDR to McCormick, January 10, 1914.
37. Milwaukee *Sentinel*, April 27, 1914.
38. George T. Davis, *A Navy Second to None: The Development of Modern American Naval Policy* (New York, 1940).
39. Baker, *Wilson*, 4:236–352; Harley Notter, *The Origins of the Foreign Policy of Woodrow Wilson* (Baltimore, 1937), 222–231; Daniels, *Wilson Era*, 1:180–207.
40. Baker, *Wilson*, 4:236.
41. FDR to Daniels, July 29, 1913.
42. FDR to Daniels, July 29, 1913.
43. FDR to Sara Roosevelt, July 29, 1913.
44. FDR to Frank F. Fletcher, December 5, 1913.
45. Fletcher to FDR, December 21, 1913.
46. Griffin to FDR, December 21, 1913.
47. Minneapolis *Tribune*, April 26, 1914.
48. Baker, *Wilson*, 4:313–316; Daniels, *Wilson Era*, 1:191.
49. Howe to FDR, April 11, 1914.
50. Baker, *Wilson*, 4:319–320.
51. San Francisco *Chronicle*, April 16, 1914; San Francisco *Examiner*, April 16, 1914.
52. San Francisco *Bulletin*, April 16, 1914; Daniels to FDR, April 16, 1914.
53. Portland *Oregonian*, April 20, 1914.
54. Seattle *Post-Intelligencer*, April 21, 1914. The speech was printed in part in the Seattle *Washington Democracy*, April 24, 1914. On April 27, Representative Johnson sharply retorted to Roosevelt's attack. *Congressional Record*, August 1, 1914, 14304.
55. The FDR mss. contain draft telegrams in FDR's hand, sent from Bremerton. FDR to Howe, April 21[?], 1914; Howe to FDR, April 22, 1914.
56. Baker, *Wilson*, 4:229–234; Daniels, *Wilson Era*, 1:197–198.
57. Butte, Montana, *Anaconda Standard*, April 24, 1914; Butte *Post*,

April 24, 1914; Butte *Miner*, April 25, 1914; Minneapolis *Tribune*, April 26, 1914.

58. Baker, *Wilson*, 4:334–335.

59. Milwaukee *Sentinel*, April 27, 1914.

60. Chicago *Examiner*, April 27, 1914. For similar statements, see Chicago *Record Herald*, April 27, 1914.

61. *Ibid.*, April 27, 1914.

62. FDR to Meredith Blagden, April 30, 1914.

63. Homer Lea, *The Day of the Saxon* (New York, 1912), inscribed: *Franklin D. Roosevelt from Alfred James Scott, Los Angeles, April 11th 1914.* FDR mss.

64. London *Telegraph*, January 30, 1919.

65. *Ibid.*, April 27, 1914.

66. Theodore Roosevelt to FDR, May 10, 1913.

67. Bailey, *Theodore Roosevelt and the Japanese-American Crises*, 212.

68. Harold and Margaret Sprout, *The Rise of American Naval Power 1776–1918* (Princeton, 1939), 295.

69. Clipping, Los Angeles paper, April, 1914, FDR scrapbook; FDR to Mahan, May 28, June 16, 1914; FDR to Theodore Roosevelt, July 17, 1914.

70. William S. Sims to FDR, September 21, 1914; FDR to Mahan, May 28, June 16, 1914; FDR to Theodore Roosevelt, July 17, 1914.

71. FDR to Mahan, June 16, 1914.

72. FDR to Mahan, May 28, 1914; FDR to Theodore Roosevelt, July 17, 1914. TR did not reply. FDR wrote him less than two weeks before the outbreak of the European war, which quite possibly accounts for this.

73. Mahan to FDR, June 2, 26, 1914.

74. Mahan, "The Panama Canal and the Distribution of the Fleet," *North American Review* (September 1914), 200:406–417. For an analysis of this article, see W. D. Puleston, *Mahan* (New Haven, 1939), 348–349.

75. Ellen Lyle Mahan to FDR, January 9, 1915; New York *Times*, December 2, 1914.

CHAPTER XIV

"The Greatest War in the World's History"

1. FDR to O. J. Merkel, August 12, 1914.

2. PL, 2:223.

3. *Ibid.*, 223–236.

4. New York *Times*, July 18, 1914.

5. Reading, Pennsylvania, *Eagle*, August 1, 1914. For lengthy excerpts from the speech, see PL, 2:234–236.

6. Clipping from Reading paper, August 1, 1914, FDR scrapbook.

7. PL, 2:238.

8. FDR, speech before the Republican Club, January 30, 1915.

9. New York *Herald*, January 25, 1914.

10. PL, 2:238.

11. *Ibid.*, 2:238–240.

12. Fiske to FDR, August 4, 1914.
13. Mahan to FDR, August 3, 4, 18, 1914.
14. PL, 2:243.
15. *Ibid.*, 2:245; William Gibbs McAdoo to Garrison, August 5, 1914; McAdoo to Daniels, August 5, 1914, with note from Daniels to FDR on bottom; New York *Times*, August 5, 6, 1914.
16. Charles H. McCarthy to Howe, August 8, 1914.
17. New York *Times*, August 7, 1914.
18. J. J. Jusserand to FDR, September 6, 1915.
19. New York *Times*, August 8, 1914.
20. FDR also received a number of inquiries about different people abroad. See list of 37 in FDR mss. (Fall, 1914). FDR to Alexander Julian Hemphill, October 5, 1914; FDR to Joseph D. Bedle, October 13, 1914; Bedle to FDR, October 31, November 9, 1914; C. von Helmolt to FDR, November 6, 1914.
21. FDR to ER, August 10, 1914.
22. Wilson to Daniels, August 6, 1914, Wilson mss.
23. Bradley A. Fiske to the Secretary of the Navy, memorandum, November 9, 1914.
24. ER, *This Is My Story*, 237.
25. Mowry, *Theodore Roosevelt*, 310–315; Frederic L. Paxson, *American Democracy and the World War; Pre-war Years, 1913–1917* (Boston and New York, 1936), 199–201; Mark Sullivan, *Over Here, 1914–1918* (vol. 5 of *Our Times: The United States, 1900–1925* (6 vols., New York, 1933), 5:209–212.
26. U. S. 63rd Cong., 2nd Sess., *Congressional Record*, 51: pt. 15, 16745; New York *Times*, October 17, 1914.
27. New York *Times*, October 16, 17, 1914.
28. *Ibid.*, October 20, 1914.
29. *Ibid.*, October 22, 1914. The *Times* printed the statement in full.
30. PL, 2:256–257.
31. New York *Tribune*, October 23, 1914; New York *World*, October 23, 1914; New York *American*, October 23, 1914. See also New York *Sun*, October 23, 1914; New York *Post*, October 22, 1914; FDR, speech before the Republican Club, New York City, January 30, 1915.
32. FDR, memorandum for the press, November 18, 1914.
33. "Our National Defense," National Civic Federation, program, Fifteenth Annual Meeting, Hotel Astor, December 4 and 5, 1914.
34. FDR, speech before the Republican Club, New York City, January 30, 1915. See also New York *Sun*, January 30, 1915.
35. New York *Times*, December 6, 1914.
36. Augustus P. Gardner to FDR, November 17, 1914; FDR to Gardner, November 25, 1914, with FDR notation on bottom that it was not sent; *Hearings . . . 1915*, 1059.
37. Baker, *Wilson*, 6:5; Woodrow Wilson, *The New Democracy* (New York, 1926), 1:226–227.
38. *Hearings . . . 1915*, 571–572, 586.
39. *Ibid.*, 1062.

40. FDR to William S. Cowles, December 15, 1914.

41. Land to FDR, December 1, 1914; interview with Land, May 27, 1948.

42. New York *Sun*, December 17, 1914. For a similar opinion see New York *Herald*, December 16, 1914. The lengthy New York *Times* report, December 17, 1914, is reprinted in full in PL, 2:261–265.

43. New York *Sun*, December 17, 1914; *Hearings . . . 1915*, 921–995. For an analysis of the testimony dealing with coal see Chapter XI.

44. *Hearings . . . 1915*, 932. Roosevelt's figure did not include an estimated seven thousand to enlist from the Naval Militia.

45. *Ibid.*, 936–939.

46. *Ibid.*, 934–936.

47. *Ibid.*, 928–929.

48. PL, 2:260–261.

49. U. S. 63rd Cong., 3rd Sess., *Congressional Record*, 52: pt. 6, 164–165.

50. *Hearings . . . 1915*, 1059.

51. Gardner to Daniels, April 17, 1915; see also Daniels to Gardner, April 12, 1915.

52. FDR to Gardner, April 20, 1915.

53. Gardner to Lodge, May 18, 1915, Lodge mss.; see also Gardner to FDR, May 3, 1915; and FDR to Gardner, May 5, 1915, requesting Gardner not to use his name at all.

54. Lodge to Gardner, May 27, 1915, Lodge mss.

55. Gardner to FDR, November 30, 1915, January 6, 1916. New York *Times* (January 18, 1916) published the letter.

56. Gardner to Lodge, May 26, 1915, Lodge mss. See also Gardner to FDR, April 28, 1915; Schaefer to FDR, April 30, 1915 – with FDR note, May 1, 1915, on bottom; Gardner to FDR, November 30, 1915.

57. Scranton, Pennsylvania, *Tribune-Republican*, February 5, 1915.

58. Fiske took credit for the idea. Fiske, *From Midshipman to Rear Admiral*, 577–578.

59. FDR to Hudson Maxim, October 15, 1915.

60. FDR to Daniels, March 16, 1915.

61. New York *Times*, May 26, 1915.

62. FDR to Caspar F. Goodrich, May [?] 1915.

63. New York *American*, May 28, 1915.

64. Wilson to FDR, June 2, 1914; FDR to Daniels, August 14, 1914; Robert Lansing to FDR, August 1, 1914.

65. FDR to Wilson, January 18, 1915.

66. New York *Times*, April 20, May 18, June 2, 1915.

67. FDR to Thomas R. Marshall, March 10, 1915, telegram.

68. FDR, Acting Secretary of the Navy, to Flag Officer, U.S.S. *Colorado*, March 15, 1915, Naval Archives, file number 3768–455½.

69. San Francisco *Chronicle*, March 23, 1915.

70. FDR to Daniels, July 26, 1932, Daniels mss.

71. San Jose *Mercury Herald*, March 28, 1915.

72. Memoirs of William Phillips, unpublished ms.

73. Howe to FDR, March 24, 1915, Howe mss.

74. San Diego *Sun*, March 29, 1915.

75. Los Angeles *Tribune*, March 29, 1915.

76. Henry Hooker to FDR, September 10, 1914; FDR to Hooker, December 28, 1914; FDR to Langdon Marvin, December 31, 1914.

77. Baker, *Wilson*, 5:351–353.

78. *Ibid.*, 5:354–359.

79. FDR to Wilson, June 9, 1915, Wilson mss.

80. Wilson to FDR, June 14, 1915, Wilson mss.; Baker, *Wilson*, 5:359.

81. FDR to Langdon P. Marvin, June 10, 1915.

82. PL, 2:285.

83. FDR to Daniels, October 3, 1934, Daniels mss.

84. PL, 2:270.

85. Leonard Wood to James E. West, November 6, 9, 1914; West to Wood, November 7, 20, 1914; Theodore Roosevelt to West, November 12, 1914; West to FDR, May 15, 27, 1915; FDR to West, June 23, 1915; FDR to Wood, May 28, June 23, 1915; Wood to FDR, May 29, 1915; Washington *Star*, June 11, 1915.

86. FDR, memorandum, June 23, 1915.

CHAPTER XV

"We've Got To Get Into This War"

1. Flushing *Times*, December 22, 1915.

2. New York *Herald*, July 2, 1915; Daniels to FDR, July 1, 1915; Theodore and Edith Roosevelt to ER, telegram, July 3, 1915; Kichisaburo Nomura to FDR, July 15, 1915. On July 18, FDR was able to leave for Campobello, New York *Mail*, July 17, 1915.

3. Baker, *Wilson*, 6:8–16; Davis, *A Navy Second to None*, 206–213; Wilson to Daniels, July 21, 1915.

4. FDR to Daniels, August 3, 1915.

5. Daniels to FDR, July 23, 1915.

6. FDR to McGowan and Peoples, August 4, 1915.

7. FDR to Howe, August 6, 1915.

8. PL, 2:283.

9. Paxson, *Pre-War Years*, 259.

10. Alfred L. P. Dennis to FDR, [Nov. ?] 11, 1915.

11. FDR to Wilson, September 3, 1915, Wilson mss., enclosing and commending Martin J. Gillen to FDR, August 27, 1915, in which Gillen suggested a board of businessmen to co-ordinate defense production.

12. PL, 2:288, 290.

13. *Ibid.*, 2:288.

14. For Dennis's ideas, see his letter in New York *Times*, April 24, 1916.

15. FDR to Dennis, May 11, 1916. Roosevelt failed to get it, and, as was politically expedient, the Democratic plank on preparedness was a compilation of patriotic generalities. New York *Tribune*, June 17, 1916.

16. FDR to Dennis, June 9, 1916.

17. Paxson, *Pre-War Years*, 304–305.

18. PPA, 1940:205, 243.

19. PL, 2:267.

20. Leonard Wood to FDR, August 14, 1915; FDR to Wood, August 16, 1915. FDR was too busy in Washington to visit the camp.

21. PL, 2:291.

22. FDR, memorandum for the press, September 2, 1915.

23. PL, 2:292–293, for the complete plan as published in New York *Times*, September 3, 1915.

24. FDR to editor, *Motorboat*, September 3, 1915.

25. Boston *Herald*, April 29, 1916; Boston *Transcript*, April 28, 1916.

26. John L. Saltonstall to FDR, July 29, 1915; FDR to Saltonstall, August 7, 1915.

27. FDR to Robert W. Emmons, October 22, 1915; Saltonstall to FDR, February 9, 1916; A. Lawrence Lowell to FDR, February 5, 1916; FDR to Lowell, February 9, 1916.

28. Daniels to FDR, February 17, 1916.

29. FDR to C. E. Smith, October 24, 1916.

30. FDR to Daniels, February 16, 1916.

31. FDR to Joseph E. Raycroft, March 8, 1916.

32. Boston *Post*, April 30, 1916; FDR to Kenneth F. Simpson, May 17, 1916; Saltonstall to FDR, May 5, 9, 15, 1916; FDR to Saltonstall, May 17, 1916; FDR to F. Taylor Evans, May 10, June 21, 1916; Evans to FDR, June 17, 1916; FDR, form letter, May 16, 1916; FDR to Thomas Newhall, July 22, 1916; FDR, "The Naval Plattsburg," *Outlook*, June 28, 1916, 495–501.

33. PL, 2:317; FDR to Henry H. Van Cleaf, August 17, 1916.

34. Navy Department press release, after September 12, 1916.

35. FDR to E. Sohier Welch, September 23, 1916; see also Welch to FDR, September 18, 1916; FDR to Newhall, September 20, 1916; William D. Cutter to FDR, October 5, 1916.

36. FDR to W. R. Van Auken, July 13, 1928.

37. FDR to William M. Ingraham, November 21, 1916.

38. FDR to F. E. Chadwick, October 25, 1916.

39. FDR to Ingraham, November 21, 1916.

40. FDR to Roger Upton, November 18, 1916.

41. Chicago *Herald*, November 13, 1916; clippings in FDR mss.

42. FDR to Van Auken, July 13, 1928.

43. Interview with Daniels, May 29, 1947.

44. Thomas A. Edison to FDR, September 10, 1915.

45. PL, 2:296; Mitchell, *History of the Modern Navy*, 200.

46. New York *Sun*, November 20, 1915.

47. New York *American*, June 10, 1916; see also Brooklyn *Eagle*, April 15, 1916.

48. Baker, *Wilson*, 6:31–37.

49. Washington *Herald*, February 12, 1916; see also Kansas City *Post*, February 11, 1916, Washington *Post*, February 13, 1916, Washington *Star*, February 13, 1916.

50. C. M. McCarthy to Howe, February 16, 1916, Howe mss.

51. Baker, *Wilson*, 6:37–39.

52. FDR to Eckford C. DeKay, May 24, 1916.

53. Flushing *Times*, December 22, 1915.
54. Washington *Post*, January 15, 1916.
55. Flushing *Times*, December 22, 1915.
56. FDR to Chadwick, October 25, 1916.
57. Flushing *Times*, December 22, 1915.
58. Cleveland *Leader*, May 16, 1916.
59. FDR, speech before first Women's National Conference of Women's Section, Navy League, November 15, 1915.
60. Binghamton *Press*, January 24, 1916.
61. Cincinnati *Commercial Tribune*, December 19, 1915.
62. Brooklyn *Eagle*, December 22, 1915.
63. Poughkeepsie *Eagle*, January 5, 1916.
64. Cincinnati *Commercial Tribune*, December 19, 1915.
65. *Ibid.*, December 19, 1915.
66. Baltimore *Sun*, May 27, 1916.
67. FDR, "The Future of the Submarine," *North American Review* (October, 1915), 202:507.
68. *Hearings . . . 1915*, 3441, 3548.
69. Washington *Star*, June 15, 1916; New York *Sun*, rotogravure, June 25, 1916.
70. Paxson, *Pre-War Years*, 300–301.
71. FDR to John K. Roosevelt, March 16, 1916.
72. New York *American*, June 24, 1916.
73. *Hearings . . . 1915*, 3432–3433.
74. Interview with Land, May 27, 1948; Land to FDR, June 12, 1916; FDR to Land, June 15, 1916; Land to FDR, July 14, 1916. By mid-July the *New Mexico* had gained 7 per cent on the *Idaho* and 6 per cent on the *Mississippi.*
75. FDR to Charles H. Derby, October 11, 1916.
76. PPA, 1940:606–615.
77. Navy League Convention, April 13, 1916.
78. PPA, 1940:606–615.
79. Theodore Roosevelt to FDR, May 26, 1916.
80. Bureau of Navigation to FDR, June 6, 1916; FDR to Theodore Roosevelt, June 7, 1916.
81. *Hearings . . . 1916*, 3:3429.
82. FDR to Theodore Roosevelt, June 7, 1916.
83. Theodore Roosevelt to FDR, May 26, 1916.
84. New York *Sun*, October 28, 1916; Washington *Star*, October 28, 1916; Albany *Argus*, October 28, 1916.
85. Interview with Fitzgerald, June 17, 1948.
86. FDR, speech at Kittery, Maine, August 26, 1916, press release; Bangor *News*, August 30, 1916.
87. Peters to FDR, August 21, 1916, encloses a pamphlet on infantile paralysis; interview with William D. Leahy, May 24, 1948; PL, 2:325–338.
88. New York *Sun*, October 28, 1916.
89. Albany *Argus*, October 28, 1916.
90. Washington *Star*, October 28, 1916.

91. FDR to Reginald K. Shober, January 2, 1917.
92. PL, 2:275, 313.
93. FDR to Townes, September 22, 1916.
94. Baker, *Wilson*, 6:248–301.
95. Henry Morgenthau to FDR, November 4, 1918.
96. Baker, *Wilson*, 6:298.
97. New York *Herald*, November 8, 1916.
98. Washington *Times*, November 8, 1916.
99. Clipping, November 8, 1916, FDR mss.
100. PL, 2:338.
101. Clipping, FDR mss.
102. PL, 2:339.
103. Mrs. Charles Hamlin, "Some Memories of Franklin D. Roosevelt," ms. in FDR Library.
104. Interview with Daniels, May 29, 1947.
105. New York *World*, October 30, 1915.
106. See Thomas Paine, "Letter to George Washington, dated Paris, July 30, 1796," *The Life and Works of Thomas Paine*, William M. Van der Weyde, ed. (10 vols., New Rochelle, N. Y., 1925), 5:139–201.
107. Edward M. House, *The Intimate Papers of Colonel House*, Charles Seymour, ed. (4 vols., Boston and New York, 1926–1928), 2:413.
108. Baker, *Wilson*, 6:415; Wilson to FDR, January 3, 1917, Wilson mss.
109. Baker, *Wilson*, 6:415.

CHAPTER XVI

Progressivism by the Sword

1. Woodrow Wilson, *Selected Addresses and Public Papers*, Albert Bushnell Hart, ed. (New York, 1918), 16–21.
2. Frank Freidel, "The Haitian Pilot-Plant," *Politics* (March, 1944), 1:43–45, compares this with the Good Neighbor Policy; see also Ludwig L. Montague, *Haiti and the United States, 1714–1938* (Durham, North Carolina, 1940), 210–211.
3. Morgenthau to FDR, May 10, 1917.
4. There are several commendatory notes from FDR to Edward L. Doheny in the FDR mss.
5. Daniels to FDR, July 15, 1933, Daniels mss.
6. Boaz W. Long to FDR, July 7, 1916; Long to FDR, November 12, 1930.
7. John Campbell White to FDR, September 9, 1914.
8. PL, 2:221.
9. FDR to Daniels, July 26, 1932, Daniels mss.
10. Seward W. Livermore, "Battleship Diplomacy in South America; 1905–1925," *Journal of Modern History* (March, 1944), 16:31–48.
11. New York *Times*, February 18, 1915.
12. I. Galindez, Argentine Naval Commission to Fore River Co., February 8, 1915.

13. FDR to C. M. Schwab, February 11, 1915.

14. Schwab to FDR, February 13, 1915; FDR to Andrew W. Mellon, February 15, 1915, telegram; Mellon to FDR, February 15, 1915, telegram.

15. New York *Times*, March 30, 1915.

16. FDR to Schwab, February 11, 1915. Initials on this letter indicate FDR personally dictated it; it is not one prepared elsewhere in the Navy Department for his signature.

17. FDR to Secretary of State, August 28, 1919; FDR to Alvey A. Adee, Second Assistant Secretary of State, September 6, 1919.

18. Aid for Operations to Secretary of the Navy, December 3, 1913, with endorsements; original in FDR mss.

19. *Hearings . . . 1916*, 3:3488–3492.

20. FDR to Goodrich, January 9, 1917.

21. FDR to Stephen Bonsal, January 18, 1917, Photostat in FDR mss.

22. Navy Department to Bureau of Medicine and Surgery, 6th endorsement, May 18, 1914.

23. FDR, memorandum, December 17, 1915.

24. Naval Archives, file number 3931:656–761.

25. Flushing *Times*, December 22, 1915.

26. FDR, "Memorandum in Regard to Hayti" – called forth by bulletin dated April 8, 1922, of National Council for Reduction of Armaments.

27. Montague, *Haiti and the United States*, 210–211.

28. Daniels to FDR, July 15, 1933.

29. Clipping, FDR mss.

30. Robert L. Russell to John J. Knapp, July 30, 1914.

31. FDR to Daniels, August 7, 1915.

32. William S. Benson to FDR, August 4, 1915.

33. FDR to John A. McIlhenny, December 20, 1916.

34. FDR to John Purroy Mitchel, December 20, 1916.

35. FDR diary, January 21–25, 1917; Marvin, "Notes on Franklin D. Roosevelt as Assistant Secretary of the Navy."

36. FDR diary, January 24, 1917. The Havana *Heraldo de Cuba* (January 24, 1917) carried a remarkably garbled account of Roosevelt's visit.

37. FDR, "Trip to Haiti and Santo Domingo 1917."

38. Livingston Davis, "Haitian Log," FDR mss. U.S.S. *Wainwright*, U.S.S. *Pennsylvania*, Logs, January 25, 26, 1917. Office of Naval Records and Library.

39. FDR, "Trip to Haiti and Santo Domingo."

40. Livingston Davis, "Haitian Log."

41. *Ibid.;* Marvin, "Notes on FDR"; George Marvin, "Healthy Haiti," *World's Work* (May, 1917), 34:33–34.

42. FDR, "Trip to Haiti and Santo Domingo." A copy of the speech is in the FDR mss.

43. Marvin, "Notes on FDR."

44. Interview with George Marvin, spring, 1946.

45. FDR, "Trip to Haiti and Santo Domingo."

46. FDR, "Trip to Haiti and Santo Domingo"; FDR to Livingston Davis, March 3, 1917.

47. FDR, "Trip to Haiti and Santo Domingo." The bathing episode took place at St. Raphael. Davis, "Haitian Log."

48. FDR, "Trip to Haiti and Santo Domingo."

49. Marvin, "Notes on FDR."

50. Ross T. McIntire, *White House Physician* (New York, 1946), 7.

51. *Ibid.*, 157.

52. FDR, "Trip to Haiti and Santo Domingo."

53. Marvin, "Notes on FDR"; George Barnett to Secretary of the Navy, memorandum, Naval Archives, file number 5526–321:½ [1920].

54. Interview with Margaret Suckley.

55. George Barnett, Brigadier General USMC, to Secretary of Navy, "Memorandum *re* Affairs in Haiti," Naval Archives, file number 5526–321:½ [1920].

56. Marvin to FDR, April 23, 1917.

57. Marvin, "Healthy Haiti," 44–49.

58. Davis, "Haitian Log," January 29 [1917].

59. FDR to Smedley Butler, December 21, 1917.

60. Butler to FDR, December 28, 1917.

61. FDR, "Trip to Haiti and Santo Domingo."

62. Angel Maria Medrano to FDR, February 1, 1917; Dr. Ambrois de Hally [?] to FDR, February 2, 1917; J. B. Colcanap, *prêtre*, to FDR, February 2, 1917.

63. De Hally to FDR, February 2, 1917.

64. Boston *Transcript*, February 17, 1917. Writing in 1933, Daniels commented to FDR, "Your trip of inspection . . . gave to the President and the Navy Department actual knowledge of the situation." Daniels to FDR, July 15, 1933, Daniels mss.

65. FDR to McIlhenny, July 14, 1917; Montague, *Haiti and the United States*, 239–240.

66. Haiti, Constitution of 12 June, 1918, Title II, Section 1, Article 5; Montague, *Haiti and the United States*, 229.

67. John H. Russell to CNO, memorandum, June 17, 1918, Naval Archives file no. 5526–141. For charges of Marine manipulation, see U. S. 67th Cong., 1st Sess., Senate, Select Committee on Haiti and Santo Domingo, *Inquiry . . . Hearing . . . 1921*, 76 ff.

68. FDR to Horace G. Knowles, February 12, 1930; Knowles to FDR, February 9, 1930.

69. Henry Latrobe Roosevelt to FDR, February 17, March 24, 1917.

70. FDR to McIlhenny, October 14, 1922; McIlhenny to FDR, July 13, October 18, 1922; Howe to McIlhenny, August 11, 1922; McIlhenny to Howe, August 11, 1922. See also A. P. Homer to FDR, June 3, 1920, regarding another Haitian scheme.

71. William McCormick Blair to FDR, May 8, 19, 1919; FDR to Flag Santo Domingo, May 5, 1919; Flag Santo Domingo to Secretary of the Navy, May 10, 1919.

72. Hamilton Fish, Jr., to FDR, October 22, 1919.

73. The commandant had ordered the *corvée* discontinued in October, 1918. Montague, *Haiti and the United States*, 233.

74. Haitian Minister to Secretary of State, April 5, 1919; William Phillips to Hallett Johnson, April 5, 1919; J. C. Dunn to Johnson, April 7, 1919; A. W. Catlin, Daily Diary Report, Headquarters, First Provisional Brigade USMC, March 23, 1919; all in FDR mss.

75. FDR to Secretary of State, March 25, 1919, Naval Archives, file number 5526–179.

76. McIlhenny to FDR, May 2, 1919.

77. FDR to McIlhenny, May 23, 1919.

78. FDR to Frank L. Polk, personal, May 7, 1919; Polk to FDR, May 23, 1919; FDR to Josiah S. McKean, May 29, 1919; McKean to FDR, May 26, 1919; FDR to Polk, May 31, 1919.

CHAPTER XVII

On the Brink of War

1. FDR, "Trip to Haiti and Santo Domingo, 1917"; Davis, "Haitian Log"; Marvin, "Notes on FDR." The commandant was Colonel T. P. Kane.

2. FDR, "Trip to Haiti and Santo Domingo, 1917." See ER, *This Is My Story*, 243.

3. Marvin, "Notes on FDR."

4. FDR, "Trip to Haiti and Santo Domingo, 1917."

5. *Ibid.* FDR was being accurate in describing the lack of preparation for war, but improved the story of his lack of information en route from Haiti. There is a news bulletin, "Press from Arlington," received by the USS *Neptune* on February 7 [1917] in the FDR mss.

6. FDR to Preston Davie, March 6, 1917.

7. Joseph P. Tumulty, *Woodrow Wilson as I Know Him* (Garden City, 1925), 255.

8. *Ibid.*, 257.

9. Robert E. Sherwood, *Roosevelt and Hopkins* (New York, 1948), 382; Stimson and Bundy, *On Active Service*, 366–376.

10. Harrison J. Thornton, "The Two Roosevelts at Chautauqua," *New York History* (January, 1947), 28:55.

11. PPA, 1939:117.

12. Interview with ER, May 1, 1948.

13. Wilson, cited in Daniels to FDR, September 4, 1939, Daniels mss. In 1929 Daniels quoted the Wilson conversation in similar words to Ray Stannard Baker. Baker, *Wilson*, 6:506. Wilson talked in the same vein to Frank Walsh and W. C. Adamson.

14. Daniels to FDR, September 4, 1939, Daniels mss.

15. In FDR mss.

16. Daniels diary, March 20, 1917, Daniels mss.

17. Daniels, autobiography, Daniels mss. See also Daniels, *Wilson Era*, 2:23.

18. Theodore G. Joslin, clipping, *c.* March, 1917, FDR mss.

19. Chicago *Post*, March 20, 1917.

20. Robert M. Thompson to FDR, November 16, 1916.

21. W. W. Britton, International President, Metal Polishers, Buffers, Platers, Brass and Silver Workers Union of North America, to Wilson, December 13, 1916; J. J. Calir, Secretary, Atlantic Lodge No. 50, International Brotherhood of Boiler Makers and Iron Ship Builders and Helpers of America, Charleston, South Carolina, to Wilson, December 23, 1916; C. W. Bradley, Secretary, Metal Trades Department, A.F.L. Metal Trades Council, Vallejo, California, to Wilson, January 10, 1917, all in Wilson mss., File VI, Box 41.

22. FDR to Edwyn Johnstone, November 22, 1916.

23. FDR to Thomas W. Lamont, March 1, 1917.

24. Interview with Daniels, May 29, 1947; Wilson to Daniels, May 27, 1922, Daniels mss.

25. PL, 2:339.

26. FDR to McCormick, March 1, 1917. This was at the 85th Convention, Alpha Delta Phi, Baltimore, February 22–24, 1917. Program in FDR mss.

27. Daniels diary, March 23, 1917, Daniels mss.

28. McCormick to FDR, March 6, 1917.

29. McCormick to FDR, February 3, March 6, 1917; FDR to McCormick, March 1, 1917.

30. FDR to McCormick, March 9, 1917; Mitchell, *History of the Modern Navy*, 199, 200; Secretary of the Navy, *Annual Report, 1918* (Washington, 1919), 71–72.

31. FDR, memorandum for Captain Thomas G. Frothingham, September 1, 1925.

32. See, for example, McGowan, Busanda to Navy Department (Op), June 24, 1915, in reply to Operations and General Board requests for plans which included twenty-six pages on supply planning alone.

33. FDR, memorandum for Frothingham, September 1, 1915.

34. Baker, *Wilson*, 6:460.

35. Mitchell, *History of the Modern Navy*, 199.

36. Thomas P. Magruder to FDR, February 5, 1917.

37. Newburgh *Journal*, January 14, 1920.

38. Boston *Globe*, March, 1919, clipping in FDR mss. Note FDR explanation to the press, February 2, 1920.

39. Daniels, diary, February 2, 1920, Daniels mss.

40. Interview with Harris, April 7, 1948.

41. Lindley, *Roosevelt*, 143.

42. Interview with Daniels, May 29, 1947.

43. Secretary of the Navy, *Annual Report, 1918*, 117.

44. R. G. Albion, interview with Ezra Allen.

45. Charles McCawley to FDR, February 13, 1917.

46. Interview with Land, May 27, 1948.

47. Interview with Hancock, April 14, 1948.

48. R. G. Albion, interview with Colonel Butler, June 18, 1946.

49. Interview with A. D. Turnbull, May 28, 1948.

50. New York *Times*, February 26, 27, 1917; New York *Herald*, March 1, 1917; New York *World*, February 24, 1917. See also extensive correspondence in FDR mss.

51. FDR to Daniel Guggenheim, November 29, 1916; McGowan to FDR, memorandum on battle cruisers, January 15, 1917; New York *Times*, January 7, 1917; clippings, FDR scrapbook; *Hearings . . . 1917*, 931–937, 946–971, contains detailed testimony by Daniels and FDR on the reductions.

52. Howe to FDR, December 21, 1916.

53. FDR to Guggenheim, November 29, 1916.

54. Howe to FDR, December 21, 1916; Edward Bush to Howe, December 27, 1916; Guggenheim to FDR, December 13, 1916; FDR to Murry Guggenheim, March 9, 1917.

55. FDR to Bernard Baruch, March 22, 1917.

56. W. C. MacDougall to FDR, February 23, 1917.

57. Guy Gaunt to FDR, February 28, 1917.

58. FDR mss., February–April, 1917.

59. P. A. S. Franklin to FDR, February 9, 10, 1917.

60. FDR to Josephus Daniels, memorandum, February 10, 1917; Ralph Earle to FDR, February 10, 1917.

61. See Daniels to Wilson, February 10, 1917, Wilson mss.

62. Baker, *Wilson*, 6:471–472, 475.

63. *Ibid.*, 6:482–483.

64. FDR diary, March 5, 1917.

65. Daniels, *Wilson Era*, 2:28; Daniels diary, March 6, 8, 9, 1917, Daniels mss.

66. FDR diary, March 9, 11, 1917.

67. Daniels diary, March 13, 1917, Daniels mss.

68. FDR diary, March 13, 1917.

69. Daniels diary, March 18–20, 1917, Daniels mss.

70. New York *Tribune*, April 10, 1919, interview with Daniels, May 29, 1947. For a careful, step-by-step account of this, in which Daniels closely followed his diary and documents, see Daniels, *Wilson Era*, 2:65–67. See also Wilson to Daniels, March 24, 1917, written on Wilson's own typewriter, Daniels mss., cited in Daniels, *Wilson Era*, 2:66. Daniels diary, March 26, 1917, Daniels mss.

71. ER, *This Is My Story*, 245.

72. FDR, press statement, April 3, 1917.

CHAPTER XVIII

The First Battle of the Atlantic

1. PL, 2:367.

2. ER, *This Is My Story*, 249–250; interview with ER, May 1, 1948; Pringle, *Theodore Roosevelt*, 594–595.

3. Interview with ER, May 1, 1948.

4. Cited in Langdon Marvin to FDR, July 17, 1917.

5. Interview with Daniels, May 29, 1947.

6. FDR, "On Your Own Heads," *Scribner's* (April, 1917), 61:413.

7. Henry B. Joy to FDR, April 2, 1917; Robert Bridges to FDR, April 9, 1917.

8. Interview with ER, May 1, 1948.

9. Richard Boeckel, "All the World Likes a Roosevelt," *Independent* (July 17, 1920), 91–92.

10. Undated, handwritten memo in Daniels mss.

11. In Daniels mss.

12. Daniels diary, April 7, 1917, Daniels mss.

13. Lindley, *Roosevelt*, 140.

14. William S. Sims, *The Victory at Sea* (Garden City, 1920), 9.

15. Wilson to Daniels, July 2, 1917, Daniels mss.

16. Thomas G. Frothingham, *The Naval History of the World War* (3 vols., Cambridge, 1924–1926), 3:33–36; FDR, memorandum on submarine situation in May, 1917, President's personal file, FDR mss.

17. FDR, memorandum to Frothingham, September 1, 1925. For an account placing Daniels in an unfavorable light, see Tracy Barrett Kittredge, *Naval Lessons of the Great War* (Garden City, 1921), 195–197.

18. FDR to Frothingham, October 16, 1925.

19. FDR to Harold C. Hansen, April 18, 1917.

20. Daniels diary, April 9, 1917, Daniels mss.

21. FDR to Livingston Davis, April 28, 1917.

22. FDR to Daniels, February 25, 1921.

23. Clipping, Washington paper, June 2, 1917, FDR scrapbook.

24. FDR, Chautauqua speech of July 7, 1917, cited in New York *Herald*, clipping in FDR scrapbook. See also Thornton, "The Two Roosevelts at Chautauqua."

25. E. L. Harvey to FDR, July 16, August 1, 6, 15, 17, 1917; FDR to Harvey, August 16, 18, 1917.

26. FDR to Charles C. Burlingham, May 22, 1917.

27. FDR to Osborn, June 6, 1917.

28. FDR, memorandum to Daniels, July 12, 1917.

29. FDR, memorandum, July 26, 1917, original not signed; FDR, memorandum [May 10, 1917].

30. Brooklyn *Eagle*, May 10, 1917.

31. *Wall Street Journal*, May 11, 1917.

32. PL, 2:354–357; Margaret L. Suckley to Winston Churchill, January 3, 1944; Churchill to Suckley, January 9, 1944.

33. Churchill to FDR, April 7, 1917; FDR to Churchill, April 18, 1917; Henry Hollis to FDR, April 17, 1917; Richard and Beatrice Hofstadter, "Winston Churchill: A Study in the Popular Novel," *American Quarterly* (spring, 1950), 2:12–28.

34. FDR to Churchill, April 18, 1917.

35. Churchill to FDR, May 25, 1917.

36. Churchill to FDR, June 30, 1917.

37. Churchill to FDR, July 22, 1917.

38. PL, 2:354.

39. Cited in Churchill to FDR, August 3, 1917.

40. Wilson to Daniels, August 2, 1917, enclosing a memorandum of July 29, 1917, Daniels mss.

41. Daniels diary, August 16, 1917, Daniels mss.

42. PL, 2:356–357.

43. Daniels diary, August 2, 1917.

44. FDR did continue to heap criticism upon Admiral Benson, as for example in a memorandum of October 16, 1917, but ceased the onslaught on his chief.

45. Interview with Land, May 27, 1948.

46. FDR, memorandum [May 10, 1917].

47. FDR to Frothingham, October 21, 1925.

48. *Ibid.*

49. *Ibid.*

50. FDR, cited in interview with T. Orchard Lisle, March 28, 1917, *Motorship* (April, 1917), 17.

51. FDR to Naval Operations, memorandum, March 3, 1917; Benson to FDR, March 8, 1917.

52. FDR memorandum to Daniels, April 4, 1917.

53. Homer to FDR, April 6, 7, 1917; FDR to Eugene C. Tobey, December 29, 1916.

54. Daniels diary, March 21, 1917, Daniels mss.; Daniels, *Wilson Era,* 2:254. He expanded this entry from memory.

55. Interview with Richardson, June 6, 1947.

56. Daniels, diary, March 26, 1917, Daniels mss.

57. Interview with Richardson, June 6, 1947. On the controversy as a whole see Daniels, *Wilson Era,* 2:254. In a draft section of his autobiography, Daniels asserted that FDR almost made a contract for the boats; in an interview, May 29, 1947, he declared that FDR had actually made the commitment, Daniels mss.

58. Daniels, draft of autobiography, Daniels mss.

59. Interview with Harris, April 7, 1948. Lindley, *Roosevelt,* 160. For an excellent treatment of FDR's role in obtaining the barrage, see Lindley, *Roosevelt,* 149–161.

60. Interview with Daniels, May 29, 1947; Daniels, *Wilson Era,* 2:47. There is no evidence in the FDR mss. of correspondence between FDR and Wilson in October, 1916, as Daniels states, in *Wilson Era,* 2:83. FDR receives full credit for his role in promoting the barrage in Navy Department, Office of Naval Records and Library, Historical Section, Publication No. 2, *The Northern Barrage and Other Mining Activities* (Washington, 1920), 17. He appears less important in the account in Daniels, *Wilson Era,* 2:83–91.

61. FDR to Daniels, February 25, 1921, Daniels mss. FDR misspelled Fullinwider as "Fullenwider."

62. FDR, memorandum to Frothingham, "The Inception of the North Sea Barrage" [*c.* 1925].

63. Sims to Daniels [*c.* May 17, 1917], ONI paraphrased.

64. FDR, memorandum on the submarine situation, May 24, 1917. President's personal file, FDR mss.

65. Harris to Daniels [*c.* May 26, 1917], Daniels mss.

66. D. R. De Chair to FDR, July 12, 1917; ONI translation, July 27, 1917, of Minister of Marine to French Naval Attaché at Washington, June 22, 1917.

67. FDR to Wilson, June 5, 1917.

68. FDR to J. Bernard Walker, July 24, 1917; FDR to McCormick, June 9, 1917.

69. Confidential source.

70. E. Lester Jones to Wilson, June 28, 1917, Daniels mss.

71. Reginald R. Belknap to FDR, August 2, 1917; De Chair to FDR, July 12, 1917. For arguments on behalf of nets, see E. Lester Jones to Wilson, June 28, 1917; Wilson to Daniels, July 3, 1917, Daniels mss.; Thomas Robins to Walker, August 17, 1917, copies[?]; Jones to FDR, August 9, 1917.

72. New York *Times*, December 27, 1928. For a similar account, see Lindley, *Roosevelt*, 155–156; Ralph C. Browne to FDR, December 31, 1928; Ralph Earle, statement in Salem, Massachusetts, *News*, December 29, 1928; FDR to Browne, January 28, 1929.

73. FDR, memorandum on submarine situation in May, 1917, President's personal file, FDR mss.

74. FDR to Daniels, February 25, 1921, Daniels mss.

75. FDR, memorandum to Frothingham, "The Inception of the North Sea Barrage" [*c.* 1925].

76. FDR, memorandum on submarine situation in May, 1917, President's personal file, FDR mss.

77. PL, 2:363; Daniels diary, October 29, 1917, Daniels mss.

78. Daniels diary, October 29, 30, 1917, Daniels mss.

79. FDR, memorandum on submarine situation in May, 1917, President's personal file, FDR mss.

80. New York *World*, March 16, 1919.

CHAPTER XIX

War Administrator

1. Kermit Roosevelt to FDR, June 6, 1917. Kermit, son of Theodore, was a first cousin of Eleanor Roosevelt.

2. FDR to Frothingham, October 16, 1917.

3. L. S. Rowe, Acting Secretary of the Treasury, to FDR, October 15, 1917.

4. Daniels diary, February 25, 1918, Daniels mss.; Prosser to William B. Wilson, March 25, 1918.

5. Daniels diary, October 1, 1917, Daniels mss.

6. Howe to Howard Moody, June 1, 1917, Howe mss.

7. Sims to FDR, May 31, 1917.

8. FDR, memorandum, September 18, 1944, in Roosevelt Library Museum Catalogue, 45–21–10.

9. PL, 2:348.

10. *Ibid.*, 2:347.

11. Olive Clapper, *Washington Tapestry* (New York, 1946), 238; Gunther, *Roosevelt*, 73; ER, *This Is My Story*, 318–319.
12. *Ibid.*, 2:348.
13. FDR to Sara Roosevelt, undated [July, 1917].
14. Walter Camp to FDR, May 16, 1917.
15. FDR to Camp, June 2, 1917.
16. Camp to FDR, October 9, December 22, 1917.
17. William Kent to FDR, July 6, August 14, 1917; Roper to FDR, August 22, 1917.
18. Camp to FDR, July 25, 1917.
19. Interview with Daniels, May 29, 1947.
20. New York *Tribune*, July 4, 1918.
21. Cowles to FDR, August 17, 1917.
22. PL, 2:349–350.
23. ER, *This Is My Story*, 250, 253–260, 266–267.
24. FDR to Joseph M. Price, April 19, 1917; FDR to Herbert L. Satterlee, July 5, 1917.
25. Daniels, *Wilson Era*, 2:255.
26. FDR to Daniels, October 20, 1917.
27. Interview with Hancock, April 14, 1948.
28. McCarthy to FDR, December 9, 1917.
29. Interview with Renah H. Camalier, May 28, 1948.
30. Memoranda, mostly undated, in FDR papers. There are further lists in the Naval Archives. FDR, Acting Secretary, to Bunav via C & R, undated; FDR, Acting Secretary, General Order No. 345, November 17, 1917; FDR to C & R, February 26, 1918; FDR, names suggested for Ford submarine destroyers, February 25, 1918, FDR mss.; Daniels diary, November 6, 1917, Daniels mss.
31. Confidential source.
32. Interview with McCarthy, June 8, 1948.
33. New York *Tribune*, July 4, 1918.
34. R. G. Albion, interview with Ezra Allen, October 4, 1947.
35. Interview with Hancock, April 14, 1948.
36. Interview with Hancock, April 14, 1948.
37. Howe to Daniels, memorandum, April 7, 1917, Daniels mss.
38. FDR to Daniels, December 21, 1917.
39. Lindley, *Roosevelt*, 144–145.
40. McGowan to Daniels, March 9, 1917, approved April 5, 1917; McGowan to Benson, April 6, 1917.
41. FDR to Frederick N. Freeman, April 18, 1917.
42. McCarthy to Leigh C. Palmer, April 24, 1917; J. P. Morgan to FDR, April 23, 1917; Ralph Pulitzer to FDR, April 25, 1917.
43. FDR to William B. Rogers, Jr., June 11, 1917.
44. New York *Globe*, May 14, 1917.
45. FDR, memorandum [May 10, 1917].
46. Lewis L. Clarke to FDR, May 5, 11, 1917; FDR to Clarke, May 10, 1917; Robert M. Thompson to FDR, May 5, 1917; FDR to Thompson, May 8, 1917.

47. Elliott C. Brown to FDR, April 4, 1917.
48. FDR to Francis G. Caffey, July 14, 1917.
49. Lindley, *Roosevelt*, 141–142 gives a slightly different version of Brown's activities.
50. Brown to FDR, March 1, 1918; FDR to Brown, March 5, 1918; FDR mss.; FDR to Daniels, July 26, 1932, Daniels mss.
51. FDR to Swagar Sherley, May 7, 1917.
52. Daniels to Wilson, April 25, 1917, Daniels mss.
53. FDR to Charles Moore, December 15, 1923.
54. FDR to H. J. Galloway, October 24, 1925.
55. FDR to Terry Steam Turbine Co., April 4, 1917; Wellman-Seaver-Morgan Co., April 4, 1917.
56. Memorandum of first meeting . . . August 6, 1917.
57. [FDR?], memorandum for the press, August 24, 1917.
58. Daniels diary, September 14, 1917, Daniels mss.; Alifas to Wilson, September 25, 1917, copy in FDR mss. Tumulty to Daniels, September 25, 1917.
59. Daniels, draft of autobiography, Daniels mss.; see also Daniels, *Wilson Era*, 2:253.
60. FDR to Galloway, October 24, 1925; see FDR to J. W. Powell, November 3, 1917, urging the Fore River Shipbuilding Corporation to accept the navy yard scale.
61. FDR to Daniels, October 5, 1917.
62. The Cantonment Adjustment Board was primarily an Army device. Louis B. Wehle, Counsel, Adjustment Commission, Council of National Defense to FDR, August 11, 1917; Wehle to Newton D. Baker, August 9, 1917, Photostat in FDR mss.; Baker and Gompers, correspondence relative to adjustment and control of wages and hours, and conditions of labor in the construction of cantonments, June 19, 1917. On the other hand, Roosevelt was active in establishing the Shipbuilding Labor Adjustment Board, and successfully suggested V. Everit Macy, President of the National Civic Federation, as chairman. FDR to Daniels [undated, 1917] suggesting Macy, in Daniels mss.; Macy to FDR, November 28, 1917.
63. A lengthy, unsigned memorandum, December 4, 1917, FDR mss., proposes an organization and gives reasons for it.
64. Morris L. Cooke to FDR, December 14, 1917.
65. [FDR?] memorandum, undated [*c.* December 15, 1917].
66. Daniels diary, December 19, 1917, Daniels mss.
67. Frederick L. Paxson, *America at War* (Boston, 1939), 261–262.
68. Daniels, press conference transcript, October 3, 1917, Daniels mss.
69. FDR to R. H. M. Robinson, October 13, 1917.
70. FDR to Robinson, October 13, 1917; Brooklyn *Eagle*, May 3, 1918.
71. Brooklyn *Eagle*, May 3, 1918.
72. FDR to Henry B. Endicott, October 15, 1917.
73. FDR to Wilson, February 16, 1918, Wilson mss.
74. FDR to Lyman Delano, March 16, 1918.
75. FDR to Herbert Myrick, November 27, 1917.
76. Arthur Train to FDR, November 20, 1917; FDR to Train, Novem-

ber 23, 1917. When Train wished to publish this statement FDR toned it down. Train to FDR, November 26, 1917; FDR to Train, November 23, 1917; Train to FDR, December 20, 1917; FDR to Train, December 22, 1917.

77. FDR to Raymond B. Stevens, December 12, 1917, with attached quite startling accounts of disobedience on the part of the ships' captains, and of bad crews. FDR to Daniels, December 18, 1917.

78. FDR, draft letter to Edward N. Hurley, undated [*c.* November, 1917].

79. FDR to Stevens, December 12, 1917.

80. FDR to Daniels, December 18, 1917.

81. FDR to J. W. Miller, December 19, 1917.

82. Charles R. Page, Commissioner, U. S. Shipping Board, to Daniels, July 5, 1918, carbon copy in FDR mss.

83. Lindley, *Roosevelt*, 145; A. Robert Elmore to FDR, November 9, 1917; Thomas A. Kearney to FDR, November 10, 1917; Washington *Star*, February 18, 1918; *Sea Power* (January, 1918), 4:32; (April, 1918), 4:276.

84. Letter from Mary Pickford in the possession of Raymond Corry; Washington *Star*, April 7, 1918.

85. FDR to Henry Howard, December 12, 1917.

86. J. Franklin Jameson to FDR, April 24, 1917; FDR to Palmer, April 26, 1917; FDR to Badger, May 5, 1917; Badger to FDR, May 7, 1917. Daniels failed to gain permission from Mrs. Dewey to print a suppressed chapter from Dewey's reminiscences of the siege, in which he described the way he had dressed down a German officer who came aboard the *Olympia*. Daniels, *Wilson Era*, 2:621–622.

87. Thornton, "The Two Roosevelts at Chautauqua," 53. For further developments of this theme, see FDR, "What the Navy Can Do for Your Boy," *Ladies' Home Journal* (June, 1917), 34:25.

88. FDR to Lansing, September 20, 1917. The book was by a Dr. Stuermer.

89. Daniels diary, October 5, 1917, Daniels mss.

90. Felix Shay, "The Only Sane Test," the *Fra* (April, 1917), 19:3–4.

91. FDR to Samuel J. Graham, April 17, 1914.

92. Charles Warner, Assistant Attorney General, to FDR [April, 1917].

93. FDR to William C. Gorgas, August 7, 1917.

94. D. B. Lucey to FDR, November 19, 1917.

95. FDR to Lucey, November 23, 1917.

96. Bonsal to FDR, April 22, 1917.

97. J. Bernard Walker to FDR, July 26, 1917. See also James R. Mock, *Censorship 1917* (Princeton, New Jersey, 1941), 106–107.

98. Mock, *Censorship*, 105.

99. FDR to W. S. Smith, July 3, 1917; Smith to FDR, July 10, 1917.

100. FDR to Elbert F. Baldwin, July 14, 1917.

101. Bridgeport, Connecticut, *Telegram*, May 21, 1918.

102. New York *Telegram*, May 4, 1918.

103. FDR to Sara Roosevelt, undated, in envelope postmarked June 6, 1917.

104. Springfield, Massachusetts, *Union*, May 20, 1918.
105. New York *Telegram*, May 4, 1918.
106. FDR, commencement speech, Drexel Institute, Philadelphia, May 1, 1918.
107. Land added he would give FDR the mark on the basis of what he did in Daniels's absence. Interview with Land, May 27, 1948.

CHAPTER XX

Mission to Europe

1. Daniels, *Wilson Era*, 1:129.
2. FDR to Randolph Marshall, May 25, 1918.
3. ER, *This Is My Story*, 261–262.
4. Powers Symington to FDR, December 23 [1914]; W. Graham Greene to Symington, December 19, 1914; FDR to William F. Bricker, December 3, 1914; Bricker to FDR, December 24, 31, 1914.
5. FDR to Caspar Benton, August 7, 1917. See also Daniels diary, August 13, 1917; FDR to Edward Bell, December 4, 1917, not sent; FDR to Harris, March 25, 1918; PL, 2:372.
6. Clippings, FDR scrapbook; Washington *Post*, July 5, 1917; program, Annual Celebration, Society of Tammany or Columbian Order, at Tammany Hall, 14th Street near Third Avenue, Wednesday, July 4, 1917.
7. FDR to Sara Roosevelt, undated [*c.* July, 1917], in envelope postmarked June 6, 1917. This letter has been misdated in pencil at the top: June 5, 1917.
8. New York *Tribune*, February 11, 1918.
9. James J. Walker to FDR, November 30, 1917.
10. New York *Tribune*, May 28, 1918; William E. Malone to FDR, May 28, 1918; see also Malone to FDR, June 17, 1918.
11. FDR to Malone, June 10, 1918.
12. FDR to George B. Burd, May 6, 1918. FDR did offer to support Burd if he became an active candidate.
13. FDR to Fred J. Sisson, May 7, 1918, unsent.
14. FDR to George A. Blauvelt, April 18, 1918.
15. New York *Sun*, July 21, 1918.
16. Winfield A. Huppuch to FDR, June 17, 1918.
17. Daniels, *Wilson Era*, 2:263.
18. Daniels, draft of autobiography. Slightly different wording appears in Daniels diary, June 17, 18, 1918.
19. FDR to Mack, June 22, 1918.
20. FDR to Mack, June 18, July 3, 1918; New York *Times*, July 6, 1918.
21. Osborn to FDR, July 6, 1918, marked "File No answer!"
22. FDR to Mack, June 22, 1918.
23. FDR, memoranda of trip to Europe, 1918, undated in President's personal file, FDR mss.; see also FDR to Ray Stannard Baker, October 24, 1938, copy in Baker mss., Library of Congress.

24. FDR, *Happy Warrior*, 8–10.
25. FDR to Wilson, July 8, 1918, longhand copy in FDR mss.
26. Howe to FDR, July 17, 1918; Osborn to Howe, August 22, 1918; Howe to Osborn, August 26, 1918.
27. Howe to ER, August 17, 1918, Howe mss.
28. FDR, *Happy Warrior*, 8–10.
29. See, for example, Antisdale to FDR, May 25, 1918.
30. Daniels wrote in his diary, June 6, 1918, "FDR . . . wishes to go abroad." FDR's orders were sweeping in scope. See Daniels to FDR, travel orders. At the bottom of these is the notation that FDR received traveling expenses totaling $240; official entertaining, $600.31; obtaining information, $115.00.
31. FDR to ER, July 17, 1918. The accounts of the trip are remarkably complete. He kept a diary at the time, and wrote letters to his wife, his mother, and Secretary Daniels. After his return he dictated (apparently in part when he was recovering from pneumonia in October, 1918, and partly while he was recovering from infantile paralysis in the fall of 1921) additional recollections to ER which he wove in with the letters to her and parts of the diary account to form a consecutive narrative. This covers the period through August 16, 1918. It appears in PL, 2:375–439. Parts of it were first published in Lindley, *Roosevelt*, 166–178. In subsequent years, FDR added bits to his reminiscences – the last he dictated in December, 1944. The FDR mss. also include the reminiscences of Captain Edward McCauley, Jr., and the diary of Livingston Davis. FDR to Robert Bridges, December 24, 1918; interview with ER, May 1, 1948.
32. Edward McCauley, Jr., reminiscences; PL, 2:383.
33. FDR to ER, July 19, 1918; PL, 2:383.
34. FDR diary, July 9, 1918.
35. *Ibid.*, July 11, 1918.
36. FDR to Howe, July 8, 1918.
37. FDR diary, July 11, 1918; PL, 2:379.
38. FDR diary, July 13, 1918.
39. McCauley, reminiscences; FDR diary, July 13, 1918.
40. FDR diary, July 13, 1918.
41. *Ibid.*, July 15, 1918.
42. Translation from *Diario dos Açores*, July 19, 1918, enclosed in Herbert O. Dunn to FDR, September 2, 1918.
43. FDR to ER, July 17, 1918.
44. FDR to Daniels, July 18, 1918. "While we were at Ponta Delgada, a German submarine was reported attacking a Portuguese steamer 50 miles away. Admiral Dunn had literally nothing which could go out."
45. FDR to ER, July 17, 1918.
46. Note 3 (in ER's hand) in FDR, account of trip. See PL, 2:380, which does not indicate FDR subsequently dictated this passage. Captain McCauley in his detailed reminiscences fails to mention this episode.
47. Salt Lake City *Tribune*, July 8, 1920.
48. Roosevelt Library, data on painting, Acc #42–237–1; C. E. Ruttan, official record, and obituary 1939, also in Roosevelt Library.

49. A. W. Johnson to Dan Callaghan, June 23, 1938. See also Busch, *What Manner of Man?*, 90–91.

50. ER's penciled notes and typed copy; PL, 2:384–385; London *Times*, July 23, 1918.

51. FDR to Daniels, August 2, 1918.

52. FDR to ER, July 26, 1918; PL, 2:388.

53. Nancy Astor to FDR, undated; Lewis Bayly to FDR, November 14, 1930; FDR to ER, July 28, 1918; PL, 2:388.

54. FDR diary, July 26, 1918.

55. FDR to Sara Roosevelt, July 22, 1918; PL, 2:385.

56. ER's penciled notes; FDR diary, July 22, 1918; PL, 2:385.

57. [Edward McCauley, Jr.?], typed notes, taken at conference with Sir Eric Geddes, July 21, 1918.

58. PL, 2:385; McCauley, reminiscences, based upon notes he took at the conference.

59. FDR to Daniels, July 27, 1918.

60. ER, penciled notes; PL, 2:385, 394.

61. Geddes to FDR, August 2, 1918.

62. FDR to Daniels, July 22, 1918.

63. FDR to Daniels, August 2, 1918.

64. Daniels to FDR, August 5, 1918.

65. McCauley, reminiscences; London *Times*, July 27, 1918.

66. FDR diary, July 23, 1918; FDR to Daniels, July 27, 1918; PL, 2:387. See also FDR on Bayly, London *Times*, June 17, 1919.

67. FDR diary, July 23, 1918; FDR to Daniels, July 27, 1918.

68. Undated mimeographed copy of speech, Office of Public Information, Navy Department.

69. FDR to Daniels, July 27, 1918.

70. FDR to Daniels, draft report, October 16, 1918; report, October 21, 1918.

71. ER, penciled notes, fall, 1918; PL, 2:389–391; "Court Circular," London *Times*, July 30, 1918.

72. McCauley, reminiscences.

73. ER, penciled notes; PL, 2:392; London *Times*, July 30, 1918.

74. London *Telegraph*, July 30, 1918.

75. FDR to ER, July 30, 1918; PL, 2:392; London *Telegraph*, July 30, 1918, lists Winston Churchill.

76. Sherwood, *Roosevelt and Hopkins*, 350–351.

77. Winston Churchill, *The Gathering Storm* (Boston, 1948), 440.

78. ER, penciled notes; PL, 2:392–393.

CHAPTER XXI

"I Have Seen War"

1. FDR diary, typed copy. Parts of this and the following are on Rome stationery, which may indicate that FDR dictated them to Camalier while in Europe. See also PL, 2:395–396.

2. FDR diary; PL, 2:396–399.
3. FDR to Daniels, August 2, 1918.
4. PL, 2:400.
5. *Ibid.*, 2:401.
6. *Ibid.*, 401–403.
7. *Ibid.*, 2:404–405.
8. *Ibid.*, 2:407–408.
9. PL, 2:408.
10. FDR diary; PL, 2:409–410.
11. PL, 2:411–412.
12. McCauley, reminiscences; McCauley to Director of Naval Intelligence, September 30, 1918; FDR to Daniels, April 3, August 28, 1919.
13. PL, 2:416, 421.
14. *Ibid.*, 2:407–418. At one point I have followed the slightly different wording in the ms. in the FDR mss.
15. McCauley, reminiscences.
16. FDR diary; PL, 2:420, 421.
17. FDR, memorandum dictated at Warm Springs, Georgia, December 11, 1944, and initialed by him in pencil.
18. FDR diary; PL, 2:425–426.
19. FDR diary; PL, 2:429, 430.
20. Livingston Davis, memoirs, August 6, 1918; McCauley, reminiscences.
21. PL, 2:431.
22. McCauley, reminiscences.
23. PL, 2:432–433.
24. James R. Mock and Cedric Larson, *Words That Won the War; The Story of the Committee on Public Information, 1917–1919* (Princeton, 1939), 287, 289.
25. Rudolph Altrochi in *Harvard Alumni Bulletin* (September 22, 1945), 48:31.
26. Charles E. Merriam to FDR, January 4, 1938.
27. Reuters dispatch in London *Times*, August 12, 1918. For Italian accounts of the speech, see Rome, *La Tribuna*, August 11, 1918, and Rome, *Giornale d'Italia*, August 11, 1918.
28. Merriam report, August 13, 1918, cited in Mock and Larson, *Words That Won the War*, 291.
29. PL, 2:433.
30. McCauley, reminiscences, attributes this to Minister Del Bono, and FDR to the Commander, Admiral Thaon di Revel; PL, 2:433–434.
31. FDR diary, August 10, 1918; PL, 2:434.
32. FDR diary, August 11, 1918; PL, 2:434.
33. FDR to Daniels, August 13, 1918.
34. FDR to Geddes, August 28, 1918 (two letters of this date).
35. Daniels diary, September 3, 5, 1918.
36. Daniels diary, September 3, 1918. There is no record of the letter to which Daniels refers in the FDR papers.
37. *Ibid.*, September 10, 1918.
38. FDR, draft report, October 16, 1918.

39. Pauillac *Pilot,* August 27, 1918.
40. FDR diary, August 14, 1918.
41. PL, 2:436.
42. FDR to Daniels, August 17, 1918, cablegram; FDR to Daniels, memorandum regarding the difficulties in foreign aviation work, August 10, [*sic*], 1918, Daniels mss. The latter is misdated. FDR diary, August 15, 1918; PL, 2:436–437.
43. Lieutenant Commander Walter A. Edwards, Junior Aid for Navigation, USN Forces Operating in European Waters, memorandum for the Chief of Staff, September 5, 1918, copy in FDR mss.
44. FDR to Daniels, August 10 [*sic*], 1918, Daniels mss.
45. FDR to Daniels, draft report, October 16, 1918.
46. Daniels diary, October 24, 1918.
47. For an excellent account of this, and an appreciation of the Navy's air role in the First World War, see Turnbull and Lord, *History of United States Naval Aviation,* 81–193.
48. FDR to ER, August 20, 1918; PL, 2:439.
49. McCauley, reminiscences.
50. Interview with ER, May 1, 1948.
51. Pauillac *Pilot,* August 27, 1918.
52. FDR to Daniels, February 14, 1941, Daniels mss.
53. FDR's request in a letter to Livingston Davis, October 11, 1918, not to mention the matter of a commission to Daniels, seems to indicate that he did not send this cable.
54. James F. Kerney to FDR, August 19, 1918.
55. PPA, 1941:432; Charles O. Maas, "A History of the Office of the United States Naval Attaché, American Embassy, Paris . . . 1914–1918."
56. PPA, 1941:432–433. For a variation, see Lindley, *Roosevelt,* 179.
57. Albert G. de Gobart, "Un Entretien avec Le Ministre de la Marine Américaine," and numerous clippings from French newspapers; PPA, 1941: 432.
58. H. C. Roberts to FDR, August 20, 1918; memo for Maas or McCauley [August 21, 1918].
59. Livingston Davis diary; McCauley, reminiscences; FDR, draft report, October 21, 1918; FDR to Hutch I. Cone, August 28, 1918.
60. McCauley, reminiscences.
61. Davis diary, August 23, 1918.
62. John J. Pershing to FDR [August 9–11, 1918].
63. Davis diary; ER to Howe, September 10, 1918, Howe mss.
64. PPA, 1935:250–251.
65. McCauley, reminiscences.
66. *Ibid.;* Davis diary; Charles Belknap to ER [September, 1918]; ER to Howe, September 22, 1918, Howe mss.
67. FDR, draft reports, October 16, 21, 1918.
68. Secretary of the Navy, *Annual Report,* 1919, 12.
69. New York *Sun,* October 31, 1918.
70. FDR to Davis, October 11, 1918.
71. FDR to Daniels, February 14, 1941, Daniels mss. FDR did not see

Wilson until some time after October 29, 1918. By then, armistice negotiations were well under way – FDR to Wilson, October 29, 1918.

72. FDR to Al Smith, October 14, 1918, two letters; Smith to FDR, October 19, 1918; New York *World*, October 21, 1918; FDR to A. J. Elkus, November 1, 1918.

73. FDR to Robert A. Widenmann, October 28, 1918.

74. FDR to Edward Staats Luther, November 1, 1918.

75. FDR to Wilson, enclosing Benson to Secretary of Navy (CNO), and William V. Pratt to FDR [all three *c.* October 29, 1918], Wilson mss.

76. Thomas A. Bailey, *Woodrow Wilson and the Lost Peace* (New York, 1944), 40.

77. FDR to Lathrop Brown, November 9, 1918. For an analysis of the debate over naval armistice terms, see Harry R. Rudin, *Armistice, 1918* (New Haven, 1944), 285–319.

78. FDR to J. Sterling Bird, July 7, 1922.

79. FDR to William P. Fullam, December 28, 1918.

Index